Taking passage: Is there any vacation experience more romantic? The sea, the stars, strolling the deck with your significant other—what a package! In this photo, Norwegian Cruise Line's *Norway,* one of the classiest (and most classic) ships sailing today, makes its way into New York Harbor. *(Photo courtesy Norwegian Cruise Line.)*

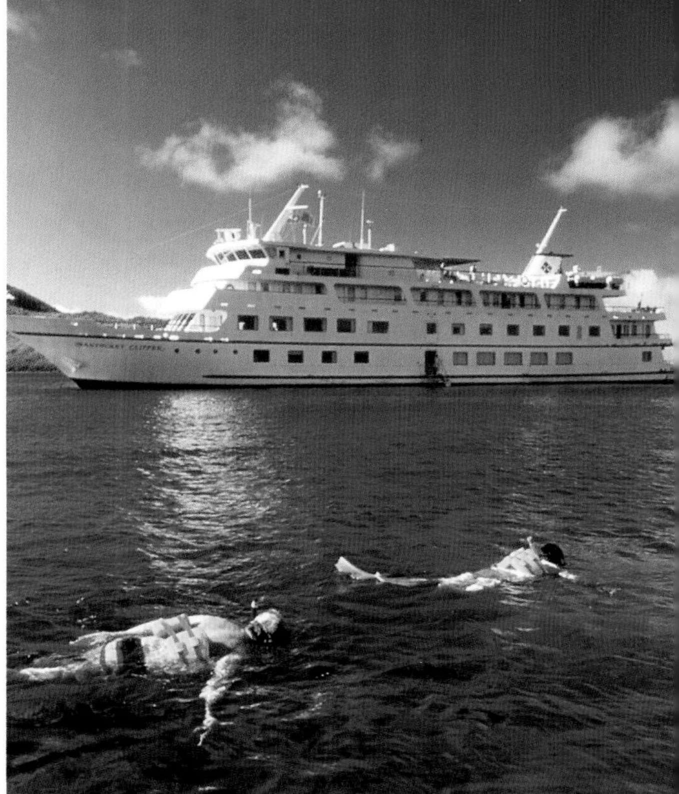

What are the Caribbean's blue waters for if not snorkeling? Every cruise line offers snorkeling excursions, and on some ships—such as Clipper's *Nantucket Clipper,* shown here—you can jump in right from the ship, either via a doorway or from a platform that's lowered into the water. *(Photo courtesy Clipper Cruise Line.)*

Ever had visions of yourself as Erroll Flynn, sailing a tall ship on a straight course for adventure? You may not be able to pilot the boat yourself, but aboard the Caribbean's sailing ships you can at least pretend, and have a heckuva good time doing it. Besides Windjammer Barefoot Cruises' ships (such as the *Yankee Clipper,* pictured here), Star Clippers, Club Med, Tall Ship Adventures, and Windstar all offer various levels of wind-driven good times, at varying levels of luxury. *(Photo courtesy Windjammer Barefoot Cruises.)*

Alaska aboard a small ship: Because of the smaller number of passengers, you can get a more intimate and active vacation that might include hiking, kayaking, and some up-close-and-personal whale watching, but don't expect luxury cabins or waiters in tuxedos. *(Photo courtesy Alaska's Glacier Bay Tours & Cruises.)*

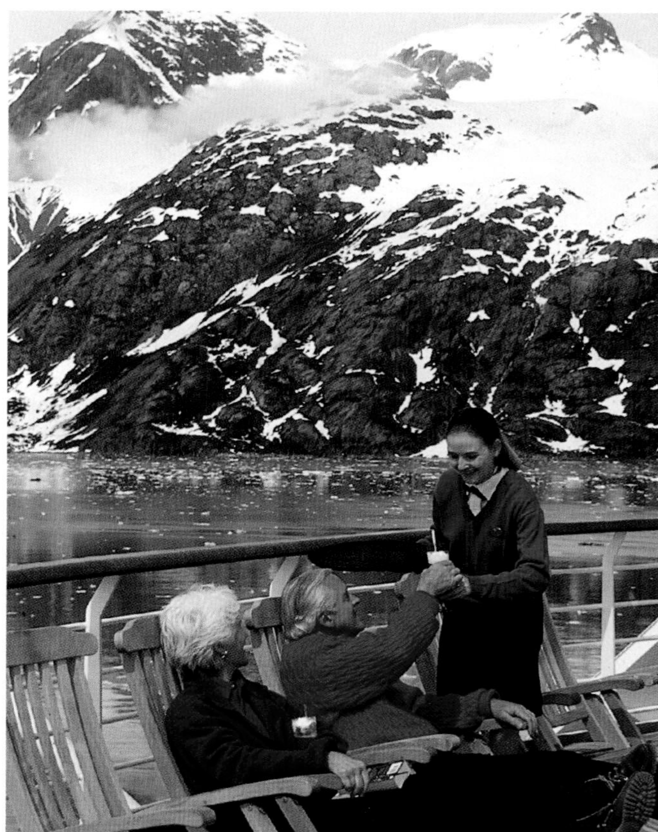

Alaska aboard a big ship: If you want to see the glaciers, visit the port towns, and get an eyeful of Alaska's remarkable scenery, but you also want pampering and a range of activities options to keep you busy, the large-ship experience might be more your thing. *(Photo courtesy Princess Cruises.)*

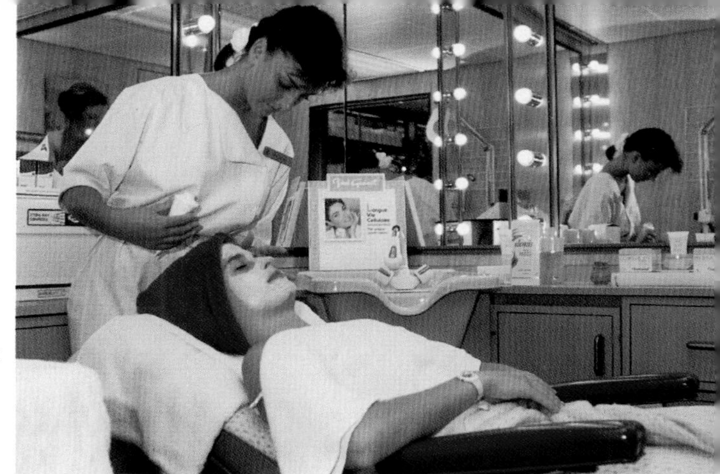

I speak from personal experience: There's nothing like getting pampered at an on-board spa to make you feel like you're really on vacation. *(Photo courtesy Holland America Line.)*

Mesmerizing, isn't it? The Dutch Chocolate Dessert Extravaganza is a fixture aboard Holland America's ships. Grown people turn into little kids at the candy store window just thinking about it. *(Photo courtesy Holland America Line.)*

When the aerobic juices start flowing (or when you just feel *really* guilty about all the food you ate the night before), it's time to hit the gym. Many of the gyms aboard newer ships—like this one aboard the *Sun Princess*—are set on upper decks, so you'll have a nice view while you work out. *(Photo courtesy Princess Cruises.)*

Passengers go for broke aboard Commodore Cruise Line's *Enchanted Isle.* Feeling lucky? *(Photo courtesy Commodore Cruise Line.)*

The Roman Bacchanal Toga Night aboard Costa Cruises. Hail the conquering waiters and bring me another goblet of wine! Do you see yourself getting into the occasion or hanging back, flabbergasted? More reserved types might take advantage of room service on nights like these. *(Photo courtesy Costa Cruises.)*

Who says cruise ships are no place for real men? The sports bar aboard Norwegian Cruise Line's *Norwegian Dream* provides a place for the guys to keep themselves centered and catch up on the action. *(Photo courtesy Norwegian Cruise Line.)*

An inside double aboard Princess Cruises' *Dawn Princess.* If you're not planning on doing more than sleeping and showering in your cabin, an inside stateroom can be a real money-saver. *(Photo courtesy Princess Cruises.)*

For comparison, an outside veranda double aboard the *Dawn Princess.* If you're planning to spend a lot of time in your cabin; love the idea of sunning, dining, and dancing on a private veranda; or just can't imagine waking up without the sun streaming in, one of these might be for you. *(Photo courtesy Princess Cruises.)*

For even more comparison, an outside double with picture window and sitting area aboard a Radisson Seven Seas vessel. Radisson is serious understated luxury—a kind of floating European hotel—and the accommodations go up from here to include spacious suites that executive types would feel right at home in. *(Photo courtesy Radisson Seven Seas Cruises.)*

Does this sum up the Carnival experience, or what? A 114-foot waterslide, a Jacuzzi, and tanned folks taking the sun while waiters bring them drinks—all while their ship carries them to yet more fun in the sun. It's orgiastic technicolor whoopie in a nutshell. *(Photo courtesy Carnival Cruise Line.)*

The Grand Plaza atrium aboard Princess Cruises' *Sun Princess*. Such multi-deck atriums are a central feature of most modern cruise ships, and serve as a focal point around which customer-service, reception, and shore-excursion desks—as well as shops, lounges, and bars—are often arranged. *(Photo courtesy Princess Cruises.)*

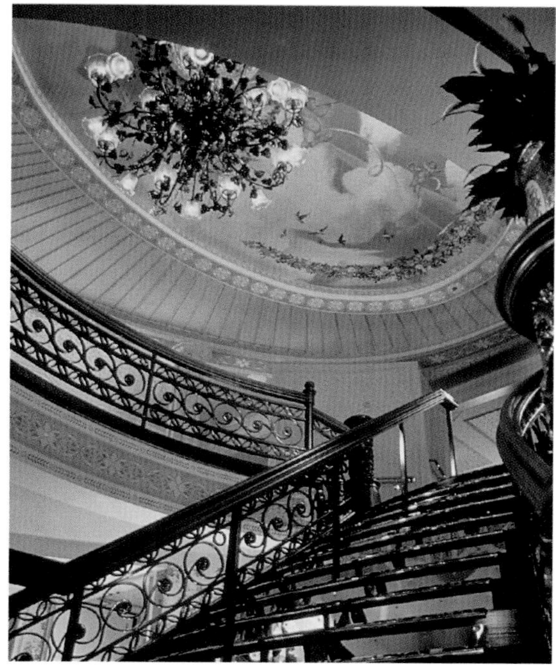

The Grand Staircase aboard Delta Queen Steamboat Company's *American Queen*. The period details pretty well sum up the kind of authentic 19th century vibe of these paddlewheel vessels. Can't you just imagine Leonardo DiCaprio waiting at the top of those stairs? *(Photo courtesy Delta Queen Steamboat Company.)*

A show lounge aboard Radisson Seven Seas Cruises. Imagine yourself slipping into something nice after a day touring one of the ports, then heading for a fine dinner and, afterwards, taking in a jazz set while sipping a cocktail. Life can be so nice. *(Photo courtesy Radisson Seven Seas Cruises.)*

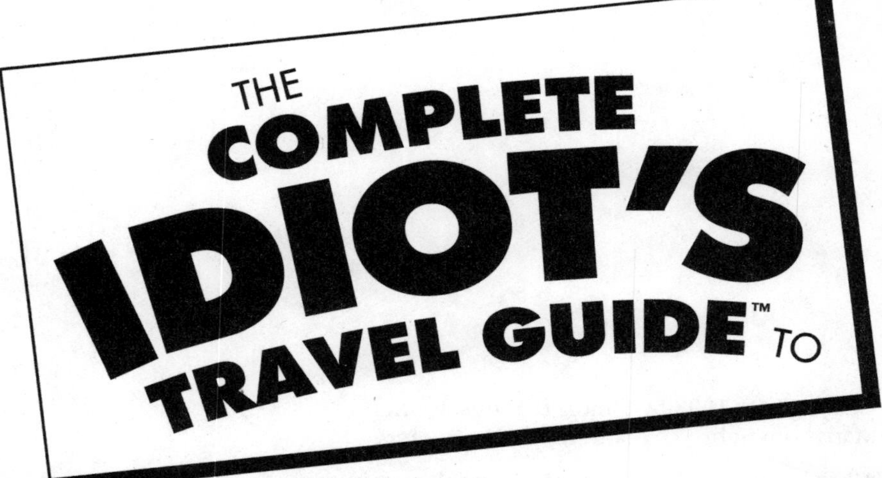

Cruise Vacations

by Fran Wenograd Golden

Macmillan Travel Alpha Books
Divisions of Macmillan Reference USA
A Simon & Schuster Macmillan Company
1633 Broadway, New York, NY 10019-6785

ISBN 0-02-862302-9
ISSN 1096-7648

Editor: Matt Hannafin
Production Editor: Carol Sheehan
Photo Editor: Richard Fox
Design by designLab and Holly Wittenberg
Digital Cartography by Raffaele DeGennaro
Illustrations by Kevin Spear
Whale illustrations in chapter 24 by Giselle Simons
Page layout: Lissa Auciello and Toi Davis
Proofreader: David Faust

Special Sales
Bulk purchases (10+ copies) of Frommer's and selected Macmillan travel guides are available to corporations, organizations, mail-order catalogs, institutions, and charities at special discounts, and can be customized to suit individual needs. For more information write to: Special Sales, Macmillan General Reference, 1633 Broadway, New York, NY 10019.

Manufactured in the United States of America

Contents

Maps

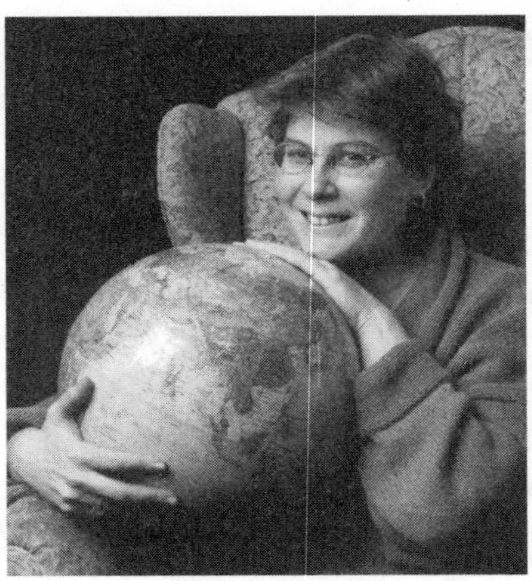

Photo: *Elin Spring*

About the Author

Fran Wenograd Golden cruises the world as cruise editor for *Travel Weekly,* the travel trade newspaper, where she's been on staff since 1984. Earlier, her work appeared in publications as diverse as the *New York Times* and *Popular Mechanics*. Also a former radio and TV reporter, Fran has more recently talked travel on Public Radio and cable TV. She is also the author of *TVacations: A Fun Guide to the Sites, the Stars, and the Inside Stories Behind Your Favorite TV Shows* (Pocket Books, 1996). She lives north of Boston with her husband, Ed, and their two kids.

An Invitation to the Reader

In researching this book, we discovered many wonderful ships, restaurants, hotels, shops, and more. We're sure you'll find others. Please tell us about them, so we can share the information with your fellow travelers in upcoming editions. If you were disappointed with a recommendation, we'd love to know that, too. Please write to:

The Complete Idiot's Travel Guide to Cruise Vacations
Macmillan Travel
1633 Broadway
New York, NY 10019

An Additional Note

Please be advised that travel information is subject to change at any time—and this is especially true of prices. We therefore suggest that you write or call ahead for confirmation when making your travel plans. The authors, editors, and publisher cannot be held responsible for the experiences of readers while traveling. Your safety is important to us, however, so we encourage you to stay alert and be aware of your surroundings. Keep a close eye on cameras, purses, and wallets, all favorite targets of thieves and pickpockets.

Introduction

Okay, I admit it: I used to cringe at the whole idea of taking a cruise, and the first time I took one, it was not without a lot of hesitation. To be honest, I just couldn't imagine myself spending a week of my life on a cruise ship. Yuk!

I feared being seasick. I feared feeling bored and trapped.

Neither turned out to be true, and after one week on the ship during my first cruise experience I cursed myself for not booking a longer trip.

Why?

Because while I had envisioned myself alone in a dark, dank cabin, head-over-toilet with seasickness, in reality I found being on a cruise to be the most relaxing, stress-free, and even luxurious vacation experience I'd ever had.

And yes, it was fun, too.

Part of it had to do with the incredible and unmatched sense of freedom you get from just being on the open seas. *The blue sky meeting the blue-green sea with only mild ripples distinguishing the horizon…* Okay, so I'm no poet, but trust me, it's great!

But more important, from the moment I boarded the vessel I felt pampered and taken care of. The friendly crew ushered me onboard and made it very clear they'd be available at my beck and call; just a wave of my hand or a quick phone call would bring me whatever I needed, including a cold beer or a dry towel. I would be forced to concentrate solely on things that gave me pleasure.

My big choices each day were whether to sit on the deck and chat with new-found friends, go to the gym and work out, or find a quiet place to read a book—or have a massage, or take a nap in my cabin, or participate in a raucous group activity, or go for a swim, or on days when we stopped at a port, to go on an organized tour or just go off exploring on my own.

There was so much to do, I couldn't possibly do it all. But if I wanted, I could even choose to stare off into the sea and do absolutely nothing, and no one would think twice about it.

No one demanded any more of me.

Add to that the sheer value of a cruise (your cabin, food, entertainment, onboard activities, and such are all included in the price) and the fact that on a cruise you only have to unpack once, and you have one heck of an attractive vacation offering.

That's why when I hear the word "cruise" now, instead of thinking, "No way!", I'm saying loud and clear, "I'm there!"

How to Use This Book

This book could just as easily be called *Everything You Always Wanted to Know About Cruises in North America* or *The First-Timers Complete Guide to Cruise Vacations.*

I've tried to anticipate your every question about the cruise experience and to provide the answers, making this what I believe to be the most comprehensive book on the cruise experience available. I'll walk you through the whole process, from looking at your first cruise brochure to stepping confidently onto your ship's teakwood deck—and beyond. Besides just being practical, though, I've also written with the idea that the whole subject of cruising should be just plain fun, so don't expect any dry lectures.

So What's Included?

This book is divided into seven parts.

Part 1, Making the Decision, tells you about the cruise industry and knocks down some common misconceptions about cruising—that it's too expensive or that you'll get bored, for example. It also tells you how to book your cruise at the best price and helps you decide what kind of ship and cruise experience will be best for you.

Part 2, The Cruise Lines & Their Ships, discusses all the major cruise lines and their vessels and offers honest reviews to help you target the ship that's right for you.

Part 3, From Booking to Boarding: Cruise Planning Practicalities, takes you through the process of booking a cruise, including how to find a good travel agent, and covers what you need to know before you get on the ship, from packing tips to passports and how much cash you'll need.

Part 4, Taking Passage: The Ports of Embarkation, offers you information on the ports of embarkation, with advice on how to make the most of your time if you arrive early or plan to stay a few days in the port city after your cruise.

Part 5, The Cruise Experience: What to Expect, covers just about everything you can expect to experience shipboard during your cruise vacation, starting with the moment you arrive on the ship. Special chapters are dedicated to families with children and single travelers, and there's even a chapter with tips on how not to embarrass yourself.

Part 6, Land! I See Land!: Visiting the Ports of Call, offers insights on what to do at the ports of call, highlighting the top attractions and best shore excursions.

Part 7, All Good Things Must Come to an End: Wrapping up Your Cruise, helps you finish up your cruise vacation in a carefree manner, including advice on tipping and packing.

Extras

This book has several special features that you won't find in other guidebooks—features that will help you make better use of the information, and find it faster.

For your reading pleasure, cruising edification, and (sometimes) sense of humor, I've also sectioned off little tidbits of useful information in **sidebars,** which come in four types:

Sea Stories

Here's where you go for fun facts, oddball anecdotes, and random musing from the wide world of cruising.

Smooth Sailing

Here, you'll find ways to save time, save money, avoid lines and hassles, and streamline the business of arranging your cruise and taking your trip.

Life Preservers

These boxes steer you away from rip-offs, activities that aren't worth it, shady dealings, and other pitfalls.

Ahoy, Mateys!

These boxes contain handy facts, words of wisdom, hints, and insider advice.

Sometimes, the best way to fix something in your mind is to write it down, and with that in mind, I've provided **worksheets, quizzes,** and **checklists** to help you get it all straight in your head and make your decisions. (Underlining or highlighting as you read along isn't a bad idea, either.)

Lastly, the **appendixes** in the back of this book list phone numbers, addresses, and web sites for all the cruise lines and provide other practical information in an easy-to-access form.

Acknowledgments

No book of this scope could be completed, especially on a tight deadline, without more than a little help from my friends.

I'd like to send a special thank you to the following:

Contributors Mark Chapman, Laura Dennis, Felicity Long, and Ed Golden.

My coworkers at *Travel Weekly,* especially Jerry Brown, Ernie Blum, Mary Kane, and Bill Poling; and my bosses, Nadine Godwin and Donna Tunney.

The cruise line public relations departments, and Bernadette Suski Harding, formerly of Diana Orban Associates.

My editor and fellow cruise enthusiast Matt Hannafin (this book was his idea), who has a great sick sense of humor.

Erin and Eli Golden, for understanding when Mommy is busy and for not complaining about all that fast food.

Part 1

Making the Decision

You probably have a million and one excuses why you haven't been on a cruise vacation yet. In chapter 1, it's my goal to show you why those excuses are baloney, and why a cruise is the right vacation choice for you. I'll present some common misconceptions about cruising and seek to dispel them.

Included is a brief history of the cruise industry, from the days of Charles Dickens to "The Fun Ship" and The Love Boat *and beyond, designed to show you not only how the times but the cruise ships themselves have changed.*

In chapter 2, I'll show you why you shouldn't be concerned about whether you can afford to take a cruise. You'll see why, bottom line, cruising is a great vacation value, and I'll show you how to be sure you get your cruise vacation at the best price.

Choosing the right ship is the number one factor in ensuring that you get the cruise vacation of your dreams, and in chapter 3, I'll help you figure out what your vacation goals are—determining where you want to go, when you want to go, what you want to see and do, and what type of ship you want to sail on—and I'll give you a quiz to help you target the cruise vacation that's right for you. I'll also offer special advice for singles, travelers with disabilities, families, and honeymooners.

Chapter 1

Be the First One on Your Block

In This Chapter

- A history lesson: The cruise industry as we know it
- A rundown of who's cruising today
- All the assumptions people make about cruising, and why they're wrong

So you think you might want to take a cruise vacation? You are not alone. According to the Cruise Lines International Association (CLIA), the industry's marketing group, some 63% of American adults surveyed say they dream of taking a cruise sometime in their lives. That's 74 million people!

The CLIA marketing folks have jumped on this statistic with a vengeance, producing an $8 million advertising campaign called "You Haven't Lived Until You've Cruised," which includes ads that note, "A resort just sits there. A cruise will move you..." Apparently, though, not all of us have been so moved yet, since only about 10% of the U.S. population, or somewhat more than 30 million people, has ever taken a cruise. But that number is up from 4% only 10 years ago.

What does that mean? It means that you still might have a chance to be the first one on your block to try it.

Reasons people give for not choosing a cruise vacation are varied: *I'll get sick. I'll get fat. I'll be bored. I'll be referred to by the rest of the passengers as "the kid."* As I'll show later in this chapter, these are all largely untrue. But before we get to specifics, let's take a brief look at where the cruise industry has been and where it is today.

A Brief History Lesson

What we today think of as the leisure-cruise industry has its roots in the early 1840s.

Among the earliest cruise passengers was Charles Dickens, who booked passage in 1842, along with 86 fellow travelers, on a mail ship called *Britannia,* operated by Canadian Samuel Cunard, founder of the Cunard line.

Writing in *American Notes* about his journey from Liverpool to Halifax, Nova Scotia, and Boston, Dickens described cramped quarters (the lounge, he says, was "not unlike a gigantic hearse with windows in the sides"), coffin-like cabins, and passengers, including himself, getting seasick (although he claims that he just got woozy).

Things had improved by the time Mark Twain took a transatlantic voyage on the steamship *Quaker City* in 1867. At least he didn't get sick. In *The Innocents Abroad,* Twain wrote, "If there is one thing in the world that will make a man peculiarly and insufferably self-conceited, it is to have his stomach behave himself, the first day at sea, when nearly all his comrades are seasick."

But at least the shipboard accommodations had improved. Twain described his cabin as having "room to turn around in, but not to swing a cat in, at least with entire security to the cat."

Okay, so Dickens and Twain probably weren't quoted much in early cruise advertisements. But despite the bad press, passenger cruise ships became increasingly popular.

Sea Stories

Author William Makepeace Thackeray was the first to write of taking a leisure cruise when he traveled in 1844 on a series of P&O ships (the parent company of today's Princess Cruises) to Malta, Greece, Constantinople, the Holy Land, and Egypt. In his *From Cornhill to Grand Cairo,* he describes his "delightful Mediterranean cruise." But, like the other early cruise writers, he also writes of people getting seasick.

Modern Cruising

As late as about 30 years ago, cruising was considered mostly a form of transportation. Getting on a ship, no matter how luxurious, was designed to get you from point A to point B, and sometimes also to points C and D.

In 1958, however, a sea change occurred. Cruise transportation was rendered somewhat obsolete when Pan Am flew the first nonstop jet flight from New York to Paris. People now had a viable and quicker transportation option.

But as the Jet Age emerged, so did a new concept in the cruise industry: cruises marketed not just as transportation but as moving vacations—a sort of hotel that floats.

In 1966, Ted Arison, who would later form Carnival Cruise Lines, and Knut Kloster, who would later form Norwegian Cruise Line, introduced the *Sunward,* a converted car/passenger ferry that debuted as a Caribbean cruise ship. The *Sunward* began offering 3- and 4-day cruises that traveled from Florida to the Caribbean and back again, and the success of the venture quickly drew other competitors and laid the foundation for what would become an unprecedented cruise marketplace.

In the years that followed, Carnival (the industry's biggest success story with its "fun ship" theme) would do much to further the idea of the cruise ship as a vacation destination, and the Caribbean would become and remain—even to this day—cruising's top destination.

The Love Boat

In the 1970s, the cruise industry was able to shed what had been mostly a white-gloved-old-lady reputation and become a truly mass-market phenomenon.

The industry got a big boost in 1977 with the introduction of the TV series *The Love Boat*. Using the real Princess Cruises ship *Island Princess* and its twin, *Pacific Princess*, as floating sets, *The Love Boat*—produced by Aaron Spelling (*Beverly Hills 90210* and *Melrose Place*) and Douglas Cramer (*Love, American Style*)—was virtually a weekly 1-hour prime-time commercial for the cruise industry.

The Love Boat's weekly vignettes about love and romance nearly always had a happy ending. And that didn't hurt the image of the cruise industry one bit, either. Neither did the fact that some of the show's interior scenes were shot on a Hollywood set, including shots of pretend cabins that were much larger than those on the actual ships.

The Love Boat ran on ABC from September 1977 to September 1986 and was broadcast in 29 languages to 93 countries. Suddenly, everybody wanted to cruise, including major stars who signed on for guest shots on the show, attracted by the on-ship filming schedule.

Sea Stories

Fred Grandy, who played Gopher on *The Love Boat,* went on to serve four terms in the U.S. House of Representatives as a Republican congressman from Iowa (1986–94) and later served as president of Goodwill Industries International.

Princess Cruises made the most of the exposure by signing on actor Gavin MacLeod (Capt. Merrill Stubing) as its pitchman and adapting "The Love Boat" as its nickname. Even today, if you sail on a Princess ship, you'll hear a lounge-lizard rendering of *The Love Boat* theme song ("...the Luuuuuve Boat...") blaring out of speakers as the ship embarks.

The Love Boat: Favorite Episodes

Six original cast members of *The Love Boat* were on hand to christen the ship *Dawn Princess* in 1997—their first reunion in more than a decade. The former cast members were asked to describe some of their personal favorite episodes:

Gavin MacLeod (Capt. Merrill Stubing): The "Love Boat Follies" episode, which starred Ethel Merman, Carol Channing, Della Reese, Ann Miller, Van Johnson, and Cab Calloway; the two-part episode in which Vicki finds out that Captain Stubing is her father; and the episode in which the captain gets married.

Fred Grandy (Gopher, the purser): The episode in which Gopher and Isaac are offered jobs managing a resort hotel in the South Pacific. Gopher takes the job (it's his last episode), but Isaac doesn't.

Ted Lange (Isaac Washington, the bartender): The episode in which Isaac and Gopher are detectives in Hong Kong and work with Gene Kelly.

Bernie Kopell (Dr. Adam Bricker, the ship doctor): The episode in which Juliet Prowse plays Doc's ex-wife, and the episode in which Loretta Switt plays a severe Russian commander.

Lauren Tewes (Julie McCoy, cruise director): The Alaskan show with Tony Roberts, and the Halloween episode with Vincent Price.

Jill Whelan (Vicki Stubing, resident kid): The episode in which Vicki discovers she's the captain's daughter, and the episode in which Vicki does a soft-shoe dance with Ginger Rogers.

Cruising Today

The cruise industry in 1970 catered to only a half million passengers. But that was then and this is now: The industry has increased something like fourfold since the 80s; more than 5 million of us took a cruise in 1997, and that number is expected to rise to 7 million by the year 2000.

It's not just a matter of numbers, though: The cruise product has changed radically in the last 30 years. In fact, since cruise ships typically have a life span of only 25 to 30 years, much of the North American fleet is new. It seems like a new and often gargantuan vessel is being launched every other month, and the biggest ones carry upwards of 2,600 passengers. For example, Royal Caribbean's Eagle Project, with ships slated for launch at the end of 1999 and in 2000 and 2002, will add three 136,000-ton vessels that will each

carry more than 3,000 passengers. That makes these ships about double the size of the 1969-built *QE2*.

At the same time that cruise ships have been growing, the cruise experience in general has been going up the evolutionary ladder and, in the process, getting more diverse.

A lot of the change has come as a result of cruise companies realizing that they're not just competing against other cruise companies but against land-based vacations. The lines have taken steps accordingly, and you can now find on cruise ships most offerings you would find at land-based resorts—even including golf, sometimes via high-tech simulated machines, other times on real shipboard greens, and still other times as shore-excursion options.

Extensive market research of the wants and needs of consumers has resulted in new destinations, new ship designs (including a proliferation of rooms with balconies), new activities on and off the ships, new themes, and new cruise lengths that better reflect real peoples' preferred vacation patterns. (Hey, not everyone can get 2 weeks off at one time.)

Cruise lines have also made it easier to book cruise vacations by adding airfare options and offering transfers, making one-stop shopping available for those who want it. And the best news for consumers is that increased capacity in the form of new ships has led to increased competition and lower prices.

Cruise lines have also discovered that once people cruise, they'll likely be back for more. In fact, some 84% of cruise passengers become repeat guests. And because of this, the number one goal of the cruise lines is to get people to try a cruise and to make sure those first-timers have a good experience and will want more.

It's Back!!!

Love is truly in the air in the cruise industry. In the spring of 1998 the Love Boat returned, under the title *Love Boat: The Next Wave,* airing on UPN, filmed aboard Princess Cruises' *Sun Princess,* and starring veteran TV actor Robert Urich as the captain. Yes, it's another Aaron Spelling production, and yes, it sticks pretty close to the format established by the original. On one show, for instance, the characters included a divorced couple, each on board with their younger lovers, who realize they're still in love; a pair of virginal anthropologists who come aboard to pursue mating research before tying the knot; and a chief purser, who has an encounter with a music star. Hoping for a *Titanic*-sized hit, UPN promoted the show as a mathematical equation: "Romance + Ship - Iceberg = Love Boat: The Next Wave."

As one cruise executive recently put it, the goal of the cruise folks is to send passengers home saying "That was the best vacation," and "I didn't know you could do that on a cruise."

Of course, they'd also like you to tell that to a friend, who will tell it to a friend, who will tell it to a friend...

Obviously, the cruise lines are accomplishing their task of making people happy, since, according to CLIA (the cruise lines marketing group), cruising is the top-rated vacation category, with 36% of first-time cruisers reporting they were "extremely satisfied" with their cruise experience. That compares to 26% who reported they were "extremely satisfied" after resort vacations, and 24% who said they'd give the big thumbs up to vacations that they'd put together themselves.

What all this statistical gobbledegook means is that if you take a cruise, chances are you'll like it! And, as Martha Stewart would say, "That's a good thing."

Interestingly, I've found that people generally want to take another cruise even if they weren't on a ship they particularly liked the first time around. It's the *concept* of cruising that everyone finds so attractive.

Why? Here's the top reasons first-time cruisers gave CLIA for liking their cruise vacation:

- ☺ The all-inclusive price
- ☺ The pampering
- ☺ The fact that it's hassle-free (you only have to unpack once)
- ☺ The fine dining
- ☺ The possibility of real relaxation and "getting away from it all"
- ☺ Having "everything planned for you"
- ☺ The ability to visit several destinations
- ☺ The fact that it's a good value for the money
- ☺ Simply, that it's fun

Who Cruises?

There is no longer such a thing as a typical cruise passenger. While demographics vary from ship to ship and cruise line to cruise line, the reality is that when it comes to cruise vacations, there's something for everyone, from young kids to seniors and including singles, couples, honeymooners, and families.

And because there are so many bargains out there, nearly everyone can afford to cruise. Cruising can, in fact, be a bargain when compared to most land-based vacations.

You don't have to be rich to do it! And you don't have to be old, either.

Ahoy, Mateys!

The average cruise passenger is 49, but 34% of cruisers are under age 40, and the fastest-growing sector of the cruise population is in the 25–39 age group. Some 73% of cruise passengers are married, with the median household income being about $50,000 a year (although almost one-third of cruisers has an annual household income of less than $40,000).

—Cruise Lines International Association

So What's Stopping You from Cruising?

Everybody's got an excuse, but most of them are just a bunch of hooey when it comes right down to it. Here's some common misconceptions.

It's Too Expensive!

Since this is a big sticking point for a lot of people, I've devoted the second part of this chapter to this topic, but to state it briefly, don't get sticker shock. First of all, buying a cruise is kind of like buying a car: You never really pay the list price. And second, when you consider everything that's included in your cruise price—cabin, meals, activities, parties, entertainment, and the option of airfare and transfers—you'll see that it's actually a cost-conscious vacation choice.

Cruises Aren't for Kids!

Big wrong here. Cruise companies know that their demographic target includes people with kids (some 32% of cruise vacations are booked by families with children) and have adapted their activities programs accordingly. Most cruise lines offer supervised activities for kids, especially during school holiday periods, and also offer baby-sitting at an additional charge. It's hard, in fact, to imagine a land-based resort that can match all the kids activities offered on board some ships.

I'll Get Seasick!

No promises here, but most ships are well-stabilized, and popular cruising areas tend to be in calmer waters, particularly in the Caribbean (although the Atlantic can sometimes be rough) and in Alaska's Inside Passage.

Unless you're particularly prone to seasickness, you probably don't need to worry much. But if you are, there are medications that can help, including Dramamine and Bonine (although it's recommended that if you use either medication, you not drink alcohol; Dramamine, in particular, can make you drowsy). Both can be bought over the counter, and most ships have supplies available on board—the purser's office may even give them out free. Another option is the Transderm patch, available by prescription only, which goes

behind your ear and time-releases medication. The patch can be worn for up to 3 days, but comes with a slew of side-effect warnings. Some people have also had success in curbing seasickness by using ginger capsules available at health-food stores. I like to use the acupressure wristbands available at most pharmacies. When set in the proper spot on your wrist, they effectively ease seasickness, although I've found in particularly rough-weather situations that I need to supplement my band with medication.

There's No Medical Attention on the Ship!

Actually, nearly every ship (and certainly every large ship) has a fully-equipped medical facility and staff (usually, one doctor and two nurses) on board to handle any emergency. The medical center on a ship typically has set office hours but is open on an emergency basis 24 hours a day. A fee is charged.

A doctor I talked to on a Norwegian Cruise Line ship once (while my son was being treated for strep throat) said he could do anything up to and including an appendectomy on the ship. If you have a major medical emergency at sea, however, you will most likely be air-lifted by helicopter to a nearby hospital.

If you have a chronic health problem, it's best to check with your doctor before booking the cruise and, if you have any specific needs, to notify the cruise line in advance. This will insure the medical team is properly prepared to offer assistance.

You can purchase commonly used medications at the onboard medical center or in the ship's gift shop or general store.

I'll Feel Stuck!

Ships are big these days, and the newest ones are bigger than big. It can take days to explore all the diverse spaces they offer, which include tiered atriums and rooms with lots of windows, as well as plenty of open deck space. You won't feel claustrophobic or trapped on a big ship any more than you would at a resort hotel.

Some people, however, fear the words "day at sea"—meaning days when a ship does not visit a port, depriving you of the chance to put your feet on dry land. If you're one of those people, consider this: It's hard when you're on a ship not to experience the sense of calmness and freedom that comes from being in the middle of the ocean. That's why experienced cruisers purposely seek itineraries with days at sea.

That said, if this is a bugaboo issue for you, you might want to choose a ship that makes lots of port stops for your first cruise.

I'll Be Bored!

Not likely. As one cruise-line executive recently put it, activities offered on cruise ships vary from the sublime to the ridiculous, and they really do

include something for everyone. Intellectuals can attend a lecture. Sports nuts can shoot hoops. Intellectuals who are also sports nuts might even be able to find a sporting lecture.

There are gyms to work out in, spas to relax in, pools to swim in, stores to shop in, contests to play, games to win, movies to watch, and musicians to hear. You can do everything on a cruise ship, from playing bingo to getting your scuba-diving certification. And shuffleboard players can even do whatever it is they do, too.

And as if that's not enough, you can always sit in a deck chair and do nothing. It's your vacation!

There's No Sightseeing!

Big wrong again. Cruise ships visit some 1,800 ports around the world. You can literally take a boat to Casablanca or a slow boat to China, if you so choose. And ships even go places you can't get to any other way, like the private islands some cruise lines operate in the Bahamas.

Depending on the port of call, you can explore ancient ruins, bicycle down a 10,000-foot volcano, visit museums, take a helicopter or small-plane flightseeing tour, explore miles of beaches, eat native foods, or look for shopping bargains.

And you have a choice of doing your exploring in a group—the cruise lines offer packaged shore excursions for an extra charge—or on your own.

The cruise lines are very aware that one reason people cruise is to visit new destinations. And they carefully put together itineraries that allow enough time in port to see the particular region's highlights.

There Are Too Many People!

There are a lot of people on big ships and a lot of things to do, but no one will force you to mingle or participate. If you want to sit and read a book in a quiet deck chair or watch a movie in your cabin, you can feel totally comfortable in doing so.

That said, realize that cruising is by nature a group travel experience, and if you really don't like to be around people, it might not be exactly the right vacation choice for you. While some ships have introduced casual dining areas where you can, in fact, sit alone at meals, meals are social events in the majority of ship dining rooms, and cruise passengers are seated with other guests. Even if you do choose to seclude yourself, though, chances are a friendly crew member will still be nearby, ready to cater to your every whim. Avoiding human contact totally on a cruise ship is difficult.

Most ships take great care in trying to avoid having passengers deal with crowds and wait in line, but the reality is that sometimes, especially on the big vessels, you have to. If you can't tolerate crowds or lines at all, you might want to consider choosing a smaller ship.

There Aren't Enough Food Choices!

Food is a big part of the cruise experience, and no matter what ship you choose, there's bound to be plenty of it, although it might not always be of gourmet quality. (If you're a real foodie, be sure to choose a line known for fine cuisine.)

Realizing changes in the way people eat, most lines have adapted their menus to include low-fat and vegetarian choices. On some ships, you can even find sushi. And realizing that people might not want to eat a five-course meal in a formal setting every night, some lines are also creating more casual dining options, such as alternative cafes and pizzerias.

While some ships still offer midnight buffets, a new trend is to have a least one eating venue on board open on a 24-hour basis. And most lines also offer room service, although selections on the room service menu might be limited.

The lines can handle special diets, but they advise clients with dietary concerns to contact the ship in advance. Kosher meals are not always available.

But I'll Get Fat!

Okay, they (the ominous naysayers) say the average person gains an average of 5 pounds on a 1-week cruise, but I say that you don't unless you really want to. In fact, if you try hard, you might even be able to lose a pound or two. How?

First of all, many dining-room menus on ships offer spa cuisine options, and my experience has been that it's often really good. Also, fresh fruit abounds on buffets, especially in the Caribbean, and makes a good breakfast or lunch option, and buffets also tend to offer salads galore.

And then there's exercise. Ships pretty much all have gyms, and on newer ships especially, they tend to be spacious and popular places, often with ocean views and featuring treadmills, stair-climbers, bikes, and weights. And ships generally also offer an extensive menu of enticing exercise and dance classes (all included in your cruise fare), from beginner to advanced, run by instructors I've usually found to be lively and entertaining.

Organized deck walks are usually offered, and if group exercising is not your thing, cruise ships have designated walking and jogging areas where you can do it on your own. And I tend to try to burn a few extra calories by taking stairs instead of elevators (climbing 12 stories works wonders for your calf muscles).

Of course, you can also walk when the ship docks, and shore excursions often include active and thus calorie-burning options, such as kayaking and mountain biking.

It Might Not Be Safe!

Hey, the *Titanic* happened a long time ago, and a gazillion things have changed since then as far as safety is concerned. Ships today have plenty of

lifeboats for everyone (crew included), they have radar to help spot those pesky icebergs, and they follow so many safety regulations that it sets your head spinning to contemplate them all.

The reality is, there have been very few deaths on North American–based cruise ships in the last 30 years.

Still, prior to sailing, everyone on a cruise ship is required to participate in a safety drill that includes trying on a nifty orange life jacket and locating your assigned lifeboat. These drills are conducted in accordance with the International Convention of Safety of Life at Sea, signed in London in 1948, which set standards for the operation of passenger ships.

Life Preservers

Signs seen recently on a ship's bridge:

"Eternal Vigilance Is the Price of Safety"

"Schedule Is Less Than Safety"

Heard in conversation with a megaship captain, explaining why his ship had four engines:

"More engines, more safety!"

Rather than icebergs, the biggest safety concern even on the newest ships today is fire. In 1994, the International Maritime Organization updated its *Safety of Life at Sea* (SOLAS) standards for fire safety, and cruise ships are required to have both alarm and sprinkler systems. Because of grandfather clauses in the rules, though, some lines have until the year 2005 to fully comply. Consequently, you might want to inquire in advance whether a ship is fully equipped with smoke detectors and alarms as well as low-level emergency lighting for escape pathways.

Cruise ships in the U.S. undergo rigorous quarterly inspections by the U.S. Coast Guard, which looks for compliance with its requirements, including those on conducting lifeboat and firefighting drills. It is standard for all crew members of cruise ships to receive fire-prevention and firefighting training, as well as extensive instruction on emergency debarkation procedures and lifeboat handling.

In addition, ships have comprehensive health and safety programs that include biannual inspections by the Centers for Disease Control. Each ship receives a score from these rigorous inspections, and the scores are publicly available from the CDC—by mail, published in *Consumer Reports Travel Letter*, and via the CDC web site at ftp://ftp.cdc.gov//pub/ship_inspections/shipscore.txt.

Security is also a concern of the cruise lines, and guests and crew are required to provide ID when boarding and reboarding a vessel (passengers are issued special boarding cards). Visitors are not generally allowed on a ship unless on a prearranged basis.

When you board a ship, hand-carried luggage generally is x-rayed, and passengers walk through an airport-type security screening system.

There's Nothing to Do at Night!

Au contraire. Nighttime is one of the liveliest times on a cruise ship. There's that five-course meal to look forward to, for one thing. And then, depending on the ship, you can head off to a lounge to dance to your old-time favorites, pulse to the beat in the disco, try your luck in a glitzy casino, sip drinks at a piano bar, check out the stogies at a cigar bar, hear lounge-lizard or comedy acts, see a Las Vegas–style review, enjoy a Broadway-type play, see a feature film, or just plain walk on the deck and stare at the stars until sunrise. And don't forget the midnight buffet.

Best of all, it's all included in your cruise fare. There are no admission charges to any of the entertainment events. You only have to pay for your drinks.

And if you're in a port at night, you can also partake of the local evening attractions.

I Don't Have Anything to Wear!

Yes you do. Most ships have only 2 formal nights during a 1-week sailing. On these nights, men can wear a suit (preferably dark) or tux (most lines will rent you one if you don't own your own). Women can wear anything from a simple cocktail dress to a glitzy ballgown and feel totally appropriate. If you don't want to dress up at all, some ships also offer casual dining options.

Some lines also will have 2 semiformal nights during a 1-week sailing, meaning that men should wear jackets and women should wear any sort of dress or pants suit.

Casual attire is the norm during the day. On casual nights in the dining room, most people still tend to shed their shorts and T-shirts for something a tad dressier. The only real rule is that most formal dining rooms on ships discourage people from wearing shorts at dinnertime.

I Won't Be Able to Play Sports!

Okay, you can't—but only if basketball, racquetball, tennis, trapshooting, and golf don't count as sports. And then, of course, if you're not looking for a heavy workout, there's shuffleboard and bocci ball.

And that's not to mention watersports, including scuba and snorkeling classes and activities such as jet skiing and water skiing offered from special launches off some ships' sterns.

Of course, the activities offered vary according to the ship, but nearly every vessel offers something for the sports-minded.

Thanks to satellite technology, you might even be able to watch sporting events, with some ships introducing sports bars. And you can participate in activities such as skiing—at least on a virtual-reality basis—in state-of-the-art video arcades.

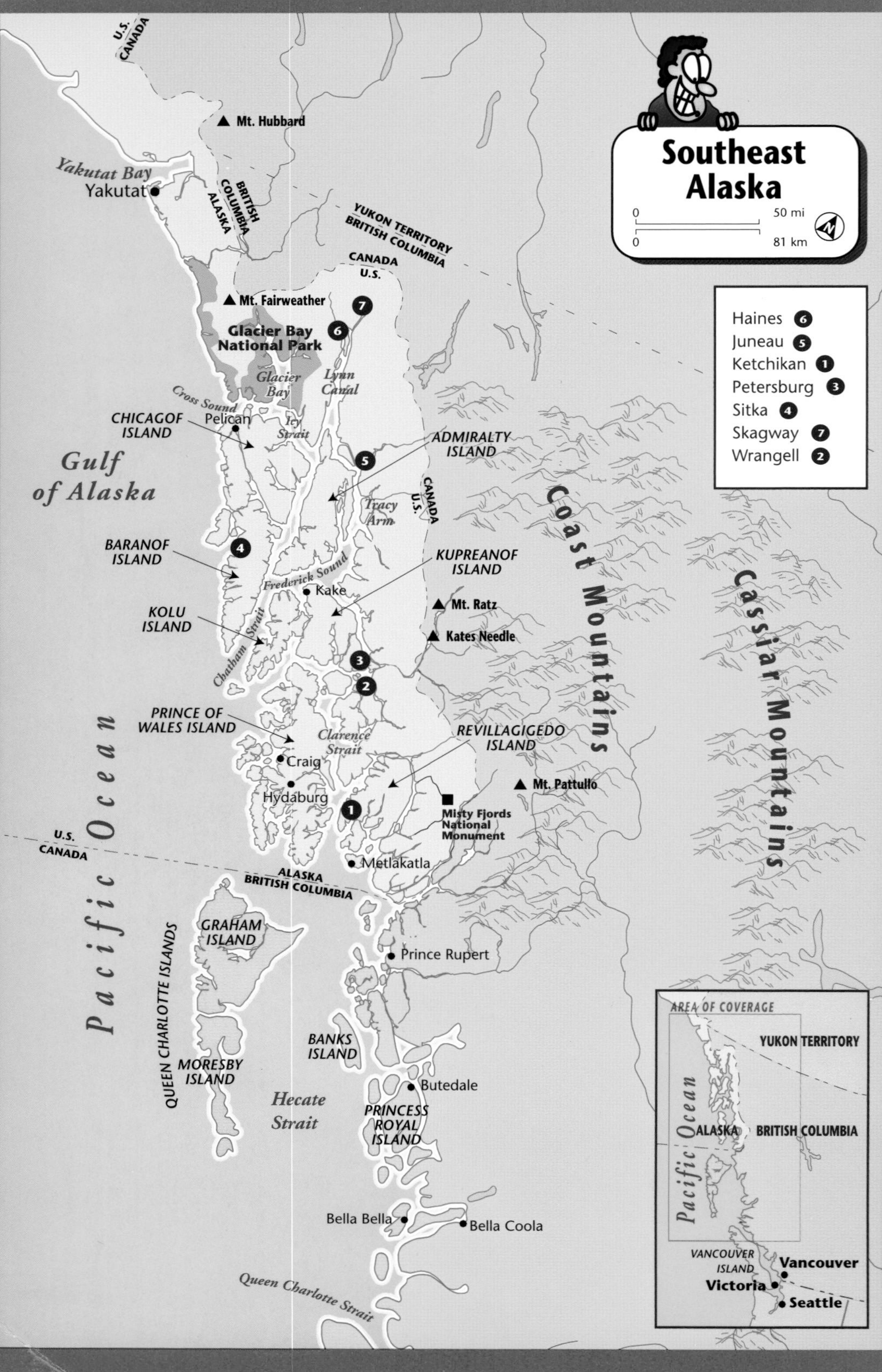
Southeast Alaska
0
50 mi
0
81 km
Haines 6
Juneau 5
Ketchikan 1
Petersburg 3
Sitka 4
Skagway 7
Wrangell 2
U.S.
CANADA
Mt. Hubbard
Yakutat Bay
Yakutat
BRITISH COLUMBIA
ALASKA
YUKON TERRITORY
BRITISH COLUMBIA
CANADA
U.S.
Mt. Fairweather
Glacier Bay National Park
Glacier Bay
Lynn Canal
Cross Sound
Pelican
Icy Strait
CHICAGOF ISLAND
Gulf of Alaska
ADMIRALTY ISLAND
CANADA
U.S.
Tracy Arm
BARANOF ISLAND
Frederick Sound
KUPREANOF ISLAND
Kake
Mt. Ratz
Kates Needle
KOLU ISLAND
Chatham Strait
Coast Mountains
Cassiar Mountains
PRINCE OF WALES ISLAND
Clarence Strait
REVILLAGIGEDO ISLAND
Craig
Hydaburg
Mt. Pattullo
Misty Fjords National Monument
Pacific Ocean
U.S.
CANADA
Metlakatla
ALASKA
BRITISH COLUMBIA
GRAHAM ISLAND
QUEEN CHARLOTTE ISLANDS
Prince Rupert
BANKS ISLAND
MORESBY ISLAND
Hecate Strait
Butedale
PRINCESS ROYAL ISLAND
Bella Bella
Bella Coola
Queen Charlotte Strait
AREA OF COVERAGE
YUKON TERRITORY
Pacific Ocean
ALASKA
BRITISH COLUMBIA
VANCOUVER ISLAND
Vancouver
Victoria
Seattle

The Caribbean Islands
0
200 mi
0
320 km
N
Atlantic Ocean
Cape Canaveral
Tampa
FLORIDA
Freeport
Fort Lauderdale
Miami
Key West
Straits of Florida
THE BAHAMAS
Nassau
Havana
Cuba
Yucatan Channel
TURKS AND CAICOS ISLANDS
Little Cayman
Grand Cayman
Cayman Brac
CAYMAN ISLANDS
Montego Bay
Ocho Rios
Jamaica
Kingston
Haiti
Dominican Republic
Port-au-Prince
Santo Domingo
GREATER ANTILLES
Puerto Rico
San Juan
VIRGIN ISLANDS
Tortola
Anegada
Virgin Gorda
St. John
St. Thomas
St. Croix
Anguilla
St. Maarten/ St. Martin
Barbuda
Saba
St. Kitts
Antigua
St. Barthélemy
St. Eustatius
Nevis
Montserrat
LEEWARD ISLA
WINDWARD ISLANDS
LESSER ANTILLES
Guadeloupe
Dominica
Martinique
St. Lucia
St. Vincent
THE GRENADINES
Grenada
Tobago
Port of Spain
Trinidad
Caribbean Sea
DUTCH LEEWARD ISLANDS
Aruba
Curaçao
Bonaire
COLOMBIA
VENEZUELA
Caracas
Ports Covered in This Book:
Antigua
Aruba
Barbados
Cozumel & Playa del Carmen
Curaçao
Freeport/Lucaya
Grand Cayman
Grenada
Guadaloupe
Jamaica
Key West
Martinique
Nassau
St. Barts
St. Croix
St. Kitts
St. Lucia
St. Maarten & St. Martin
St. Thomas & St. John
San Juan
Tortola & Virgin Gorda

I Won't Be Able to Stay in Touch!

But you won't be entirely isolated from the outside world, either. Most ships have a daily newspaper that features news headlines from the wire services, and many now offer CNN on in-room TVs.

Most staterooms have telephones that offer direct-dial-access phone calls from sea, but making calls from the ship is pricey (the cheapest I've seen is about $6.95 per minute). You can also call someone on shore, for a fee, from the ship's radio. It's better and generally cheaper, however, to make your phone calls when your ship stops at a port.

Your friends and family can also usually call you for an even larger fee via satellite communications.

Many ships also offer fax service (again, for a large fee), and some are experimenting with offering e-mail.

It's standard on ships to offer stamps for sale and to have a mailbox that's emptied by the crew at port calls—just remember that you have to use the stamp of the country from which the letter is being mailed.

I'm Single!

Before the movie *Titanic* hit the screen, about 27% of cruise passengers traveled solo, with that number pretty equally divided between men and women. Since the movie pushed the idea of shipboard romance into the public's collective head, however, that number might rise. My bet is we'll see more women looking for Leonardo types than we'll see actual Leonardo types. (And ditto for men and Kate Winsletts.)

A Sinking Ship Gathers Bookings

Before the movie *Titanic* premiered, cruise lines, unsure what another movie about the world's biggest ship disaster would do to their bookings, braced for a storm. When the movie finally hit the silver screen, however, it became clear nearly immediately that rather than an iceberg-sized cold shoulder, the lines could instead expect a wave of new business.

It seems romance rules over tragedy. What most of us took away from the mega-hit flick was an image of romance at sea. And who wouldn't want a piece of that?

The increased interest in a cruise vacation inspired by the movie included a lot of younger folks, women in particular. I figure it's just a matter of time before Leonardo is doing cruise line ads. Wonder if he can sing as good as Kathie Lee?

Cruise lines were quick to remind that today's modern ships have more than enough lifeboats to accommodate all passengers and crew, and they have radar and other gizmos to spot icebergs, which haven't really been a problem recently in the number one cruising area—the Caribbean.

Cruise ships offer a friendly ambiance that is well-suited for mingling. And most ships offer parties for singles early on, so you'll know who you are.

Many ships also offer single cabins as well as single rates for double staterooms. And if you want a roommate to share a double room, most cruise lines will help you find one.

Cruising's Not for Honeymooners!

Oh, it absolutely is. Cruising is by nature romantic. You can cuddle in a deck chair, stroll on the deck at sunset, gaze at the stars, dance the night away, and have breakfast in bed (double, queen, and king sizes are offered on most ships).

Many lines offer honeymooners extras that include such treats as a bottle of champagne, and some even have special honeymoon suites.

Also, some ships offer packages that include a marriage ceremony or, for those looking to go it a second time, a vow-renewal ceremony.

Chapter 2

Can I Afford a Cruise?: Tips on Discounts & Deals

In This Chapter

- Why you shouldn't go by the brochure price
- The benefits of booking early
- The best times to book and the best times to cruise
- Cost-cutting strategies and special deals
- What's included in your cruise fare, and what isn't

If you can afford to take a vacation, you can afford to take a cruise. An all-inclusive Caribbean cruise vacation costs on average about $200 a day or $1,400 a week, based on double occupancy (two people sharing a room). There are plenty of lower priced offerings as well, starting at less than $100 a day. And remember, that includes accommodations; as many as eight meals a day (for those who can eat that much); a plethora of onboard activities, including sports; resort-style amenities, such as swimming pools and gyms; admission to Las Vegas–style shows, piano bars, discos, and other nighttime entertainment; and stops at interesting ports of call. And, in many cases, the cruise price also includes airfare and transfers from the airport to the ship.

All in all, it adds up to a good vacation value.

The following chart gives you an idea of how the price of a cruise vacation compares with that of a land-based vacation. I've tried to come up with realistic estimates (obviously, you can cut land-based costs by staying at a cheap motel and eating fast-food burgers).

	Caribbean Cruise (7 nights)	**Bahamas Resort (7 nights)**
Cruise fare	$1,400	N/A
Room	Included	$700
Airfare	Included	$400
Ground transfers	Included	Included
Meals and snacks	Included	$350
Beverages	$100	$150
Sports activities	Included	Additional
Entertainment	Included	$55 or more
Tips (in total)	$60	$85
TOTAL	$1,560	$1,740 or more

Brochure Baloney

Don't let the rates in cruise brochures scare you off from looking at a cruise vacation. Cruise brochures feature the highest rate for the cruise, and as a general rule, you should **never pay retail** (or the brochure price).

Most cruise brochure rates, in fact, have nothing to do with the real and typically discounted prices in the market. In fact, one Holland America Line official recently told me the most frequent discussion he has with his marketing department is to ask "What do you *really* mean?"

As a recent example, let's look at Holland America Line's rates for the *Noordam's* Western Caribbean sailings in mid- to late January. The brochure rate for the 7-night cruise started at $1,648, or $235 a day, with an early-booking fare (also listed in the brochure) of $989, or $141 a day. In reality, those booking the cruise on a last-minute basis were offered rates starting at $764, or $109 a day.

Similarly, when I asked Rick Sasso, president of Celebrity Cruises, the average price his line gets for a 7-night Caribbean cruise, he said $1,400, with the lowest rate being $880. That compares to a low-end brochure rate of $1,700.

Brochure rates generally apply only if you're traveling at a very peak period, such as Christmas or New Year's or mid-winter in the Caribbean—and even then, the early-booking discounts may apply. A cruise line may also go to its brochure rate if it sees by early-booking patterns that a particular sailing is likely to sell out, even if that sailing does not fall in a traditionally busy travel period. If the cruise line bets wrong in going to the higher rate, it can always offer last-minute discounts to fill any empty cabins.

So why do cruise lines have such high brochure rates to begin with? It's not to discourage you from taking a cruise or to give you, the potential buyer, a case of sticker shock. Rather, cruise rates at any given time are directly related to how full or empty a particular sailing is.

Discounts and deals are calculated off the brochure rates and depend on the itinerary, ship, season, and other factors.

The Early Bird Catches the Worm!

The biggest lesson to learn in looking for a cruise deal is that you can usually get a good and sometimes a great deal on a cruise vacation, with savings that can reach 50% and average around 20% to 25%, by booking in advance. These rates are also referred to as **early-bird discounts.**

Why does booking early pay off?

Cruise lines need to be as close to 100% full as possible to make a profit. The prices in their brochures represent the maximum they will charge, but to ensure that they get to a full load, the lines start out in the marketplace at much lower rates, raising prices more and more as a ship fills up.

Carnival Cruise Lines' president, Bob Dickinson, in his book *Selling the Sea: An Inside Look at the Cruise Industry* (written with consultant Andy Vladimir), describes the system this way: "In a sort of reverse striptease, the dancer starts off scantily clad and, as the performance goes on, dresses until she is, hopefully, fully clothed."

According to cruise-booking expert Bob Falcone, president of Syracuse, New York–based Cruises Inc., 99% of cruisers can get their best deal by booking in advance. Booking early also ensures that you'll have your first choice of cabin (the best cabins and cheapest cabins both tend to sell out first).

Most cruise lines announce their itineraries 10 to 14 months in advance. Some popular dates fill up fast, but generally, you can have a good choice of accommodation and still have a stab at the best rates by booking 6 to 9 months in advance.

The Late Bird May Go Wormless!

When a ship is approaching its sailing date and is still not full, lines cut rates, offering **last-minute deals.** These tend to be highly discounted, a reflection of the cruise line's panic, and generally appear in the marketplace 6 to 8 weeks before a sailing. A downside of these deals is that there are limited choices of cabins available by that time and, given the last-minute nature of the offers, you might have a hard time getting a good deal on airfare.

That's why some last-minute deals are geared more toward people who are within driving distance of a port city.

To Every Thing There Is a Season

Another surefire way to cut the cost of your cruise is to book the cruise slightly off-season, in what's known as the *shoulder season* (shouldering a high season) or in a low season.

The best times to book cruises to take advantage of seasonal savings follow:

Caribbean	September to Christmas, first and second week in January, April to June
Alaska	May and September
Bermuda	May and September
Europe	April, May, September, and October

The best bargains are usually offered for fall cruises, because September to mid-December (with the exception of Thanksgiving week) are traditionally the cruise lines' slowest months.

The Best Time to Book May Be Now

While the 1990s have mostly been a buyer's market for cruises, with all kinds of new capacities coming on, Bob Falcone of Cruises Inc. says the cruise lines are now starting to feel very secure about their future, and may turn it into a seller's market. He says that if 1998 proves to be the banner year for the industry it's expected to be, we could see fare increases of up to 20% by 1999. That might seem exorbitantly high, but consider that some lines up until now have held their fares in line with 1980s levels.

Falcone says the good news for consumers is that cruise companies tell him if they do raise their rates, they'll use the extra cash to upgrade the product, throwing a little more into areas such as food, entertainment, and other onboard offerings.

More Ways to Cut Costs

Early and last-minute discounts and seasonality impact pricing, but they aren't the only cost factors to consider when figuring the fair price to pay for your cruise vacation. You also need to look at how you'll get to the ship, whether you want to extend your vacation with a hotel stay, and what other special discounts may apply.

Booking Air through the Cruise Line

Your cruise package might already include airfare, but if not, you will be offered an air add-on. As a general rule, if you are offered air transportation from the cruise line, it's almost always best to take it. Why? First of all, as big customers of the airlines, the cruise lines tend to get very good (if not the best) discounted airfare rates, which they pass on to their customers.

Second, booking airfares with the cruise line also allows the line to keep track of you. If your plane is late, for example, they might even hold the boat. And most cruise lines include transfers from the airport to the ship, saving you the hassle of getting a cab. (If you do book on your own, you might still be able to get the transfers separately. Inquire about this with your travel agent or with the cruise line.)

Also, according to Bob Falcone of Cruises Inc., when customers try to piece airfare and transfers together themselves, they frequently make mistakes. Falcone says he has seen people even miscalculate the day the ship leaves. They arrive only to find they've missed the boat—literally.

While airlines might offer attractive fare sales in the newspapers, keep in mind that cruises tend to depart on the peak travel days of Friday or Saturday, so the discounted airfares you read about might not even apply.

The only time it might pay to book your own airfare is if you are using frequent-flyer miles and can get the flight for free, or if you are fussy about which carrier you fly or route you take (you're more or less at the mercy of the cruise line to make these choices if you take its airfare offers, and you might even end up on a chartered aircraft).

Some lines offer special deviation programs, which allow you to request specific airlines and routing for an extra fee. These requests should be made at the time of your initial deposit. Don't wait until you get your tickets to make the changes, as you'll run into hassles.

Remember: Once the ticket is issued by the cruise line, you usually aren't allowed to make changes.

If airfare is included in the cruise deal you pick, yet you choose not to use that airfare and instead book on your own, you are refunded the air portion, usually about $200 to $250.

Pre- and Post-Cruise Hotel Stays

Just as with air add-ons, the cruise lines negotiate special deals with hotels at port cities, so you might want to come in a day ahead of time and take advantage of the reduced rates. That way, you don't have to sweat it if your flight is running late. And you can take time to visit the local attractions to boot.

Repositioning Cruises & Introductory Cruises

When a cruise line moves one of its ships from one market to another, say from New England to Florida or from Florida to Alaska, it typically offers repositioning cruises at a value price. Experienced cruisers love these cruises, not only for the deals they represent, but because they tend to include more days at sea than typical itineraries.

Likewise, the lines tend to offer cut rates when they are introducing a new ship or moving into a new market. So it pays to keep track of what's happening in the industry when you're looking for a deal.

Back-to-Backs

Some lines vary cruises week to week between the Eastern Caribbean and Western Caribbean. And if you stay on the ship and take both cruises, one right after the other, you can extend your vacation, visit different ports, and get a discount of up to 50%. Some lines offer a third week free. You can also do back-to-backs on shorter cruises. On a Carnival ship, for example, you can combine a 4-day cruise to Cozumel and Key West with a 3-day cruise on the same ship to the Bahamas.

Two-for-One Deals

These offers sound good but usually don't represent the biggest cost savings available on a ship. That's because they typically are *cruise-only*, meaning that they do not include airfare. The savings in reality amount to only 25% per person on the cruise portion of your trip.

Twofer deals are almost always available in the marketplace, but before booking one, be sure to compare it to offers that combine your cruise fare with your airfare—these might offer better savings.

Discounts for Third & Fourth Passengers / Kids Fares

These discounts are designed for families and others who don't mind the closeness sharing a cabin brings. Generally, the first two in a cabin are booked at a "regular fare," with the third and fourth passengers booked at a highly discounted rate, but one that might not include airfare. You can add the four rates together and then divide by four to get your per-person, per-day fare. Some lines offer special rates for kids, usually on a seasonal or select-sailings basis, that might include free airfare. Those under age 2 generally cruise free.

Group Bookings

One of the best ways to get a cruise deal is to book as a group, so you might want to gather family together for a family reunion or convince your friends or colleagues that they need a vacation, too.

A group is generally a minimum of 16 people in 8 cabins. The savings include not only a discounted rate, but at least the cruise portion of the 16th ticket is free (on some upscale ships, you can negotiate one free ticket for groups of eight or more).

The gang can split the proceeds from the free ticket, or, just for the fun of it, hold a drawing for the ticket—say, at a cocktail party on the first night. If your group is large enough, you might be able to get that cocktail party for free, too, as well as additional onboard amenities.

Buying on Time

Worried about how you're going to pay for your trip? How about taking out a cruise loan?

Princess Cruises, Royal Caribbean International, and Royal Caribbean's sister company, **Celebrity Cruises,** all offer their customers special loan programs. Carnival Cruise Lines has also looked into starting one of its own programs.

The loans, which are repayable in 24, 36, or 48 months, are approved on an instant basis after you review your credit information on the phone with a participating bank.

Princess's loan program is aptly called the *Love Boat Loan,* and it offers rates that can vary from 14.99% to 26.99%, depending on your credit history. To apply, call ☎ **800/PRINCESS.** The program offered by Royal Caribbean and Celebrity is called *CruiseLoan,* and it offers a rate of 14.5%, with a special rate of 12.5% available for qualifying members of the lines' repeat passenger programs. To apply, call ☎ **800/321-CITI** and select option 1, "CruiseLoan."

Gay & Lesbian Travelers

Several travel agencies specialize in the gay and lesbian market, and some offer special group rates and group activities. Among the larger firms that charter ships for gay groups are **RSVP Cruises** (☎ **800/328-7787**) and **Atlantis Events** (☎ **800/628-5268**), and for lesbian groups there's **Olivia** (☎ **800/631-6277**). The ships that are chartered range from capacities of less than 200 to more than 1,500 passengers, and the rates are attractive.

Single Shares

It's not that cruise lines don't like single guests, it's just that they like to get the optimum price for each room—and that means two in a room, since all rates are based on double occupancy. That's why some lines require singles to pay supplements, ranging from 110% of the per-person double-occupancy rate to an outrageous 200%, if they choose to room by themselves.

As a single, you have two choices: Find a line with a reasonable single supplement (and there are a few out there), or let the line you choose match you up with a roommate (of the same sex). Most lines offer shared rooms on a guaranteed basis. And it's a little-known fact that if the line can't find you a roommate, under the guarantee plan, you still get the room to yourself at the shared price.

On some ships, singles looking for real savings also have the option of cramming into a shared quad (a room for four). On Carnival, you can book a guaranteed quad rate, which means that if only one or two other people book the room, you might be lucky and get a double or triple at the quad rate.

A few older ships have special cabins designed for singles, but they tend to sell out fast and aren't necessarily offered at bargain prices.

Senior-Citizen Discounts

Some lines will take 5% off the top for those who are 55 and older, and the senior rate applies even if the second person in the cabin is younger. Membership in groups such as AARP is not required, but such memberships might bring additional savings.

Repeat-Passenger or Alumni Discounts

This one's not for the first-timer, but it will be good to remember if you get hooked: Cruise lines strive for repeat business, and if you're sailing on a line you've been with before, you might be eligible for special savings or at least special onboard amenities. Now wouldn't a free bottle of champagne or an upgraded cabin be nice?

Let the cruise line or your agent know if you are a repeat guest. (And yes, it counts if you went on a cruise with your parents when you were a kid!)

Booking On Board

Another one to think about for later: Cruise lines have gotten savvy about the fact that when you're on a ship, you're a captive audience, so you might be pitched to make your future vacation plans on board. Pricewise, you'd be smart to listen up, but make sure the on-the-spot discount can be combined with other offers you might find later. Keep in mind if you do choose to book on board that you can still do the reconfirmation and ticketing through your travel agent by giving the line his or her name.

Paying in Advance

Several of the more upscale lines reward customers who are willing to pay their full fare in advance (thus giving the cruise line cash in hand). The discounts are significant enough, as much as 10%, that savvy investors might choose to go this route rather than put their money in a CD.

Free Days

This is basically a come-on offering. A line calculates its discount based on its per diems. Instead of saying it is offering a deal that can save you $200, it quotes the discount as a savings of 1 free day.

Value-Added Deals

Some lines are experimenting with all-inclusive offerings that might include precruise tours and upgrades, and occasionally, lines will offer money to spend on board the ship (in the form of a credit) instead of a discount. These deals add value to the cruise package rather than cutting the upfront price.

"From $495 . . . "

Watch out for very low prices that start with the word "from." What that means is that only very specific dates and very specific cabins (those that are least desirable) are actually priced at that rate.

What a Deal!

As you try to determine what your cruise vacation will cost, you might want to look at the ads offering deals in Sunday newspaper travel sections and on the World Wide Web. But keep in mind that with all the variables involved, a deal might not be as good a deal as it seems.

That's why I recommend you look through the newspapers and on the net for ideas, but call an experienced travel agent for your actual booking.

Travel Agents Can Save You Cash

If the system for getting the best deal for your cruise seems complicated, that's because it is (and I haven't even talked about factors such as multiple categories of cabins and different pricing by deck yet—I'll get into that later, in chapter 8, "Booking Your Cruise").

That's why more than 95% of cruise passengers turn to a travel agent, as a cruise expert, for help in choosing the best cruise at the best price. (You'll see much more about working with an agent in chapter 4, "Cruise Choosing 101.")

In a Nutshell

To recap, to get your best cruise deal, you'll want to keep these suggestions in mind:

- Book early or book late.
- Book a shoulder-season or low-season cruise.
- Book as part of a group.
- Book fall cruises.
- Use newspaper ads and the Internet to get information.
- Book through a travel agent.

What's *Not* Included in Your Cruise Fare

Now that you've looked at the best ways to save on the cruise fare, take a look at what's *not* included in that fare.

These items can add substantially to your overall vacation bill, so this is an important area.

To help figure out how much extra you'll need, consider these typical onboard costs:

Baby-sitting (per hour, for two kids)	
Private	$10
Group	$6
Bar drinks	
Soda	$1
Mixed drinks	$2.95 & up
Beauty services (shampoo and haircut)	$18 & up
Cruise line logo souvenirs	$3 & up
Dry cleaning (per item)	$3 & up
Massage (per half-hour session)	$35 & up
Phone calls (per minute)	$7 to $15
Photos	$6 to $12
Wine at dinner (per bottle)	$14 to $200

Tipping the Crew

Unless you're on a ship with a no-tipping policy (and there aren't many), add tipping to your list of extra costs. Of course, tipping is at your discretion, but with the cruise lines being so forthcoming with their tipping advice (they even have special envelopes and cheat sheets prepared to help you out), you'll feel like a crumb for not obliging.

Tips are paid at the end of the cruise (except for extra services, such as massages—these are usually given on the spot), and each passenger should reserve at least $8 per day ($56 for the week) for tips for the room steward, waiter, and busperson. Additional tips to other personnel, such as the head waiter or maitre d', are at your discretion. (See chapter 7, "A Tall Ship and a Star to Steer By: Ships with Sails," for specifics.) Most lines automatically add 15% to bar bills, so you don't have to worry about tipping your bartender (unless he or she was *really* extraordinary).

Shore-Excursion Costs

And then there are the shore excursions. These sightseeing tours are designed to help cruise passengers make the most of their time at the ports their ship visits, but they can add a hefty sum to your vacation costs.

These group tours can be pricey, ranging from about $15 for an hour-long walking tour to more than $250 per person for an elaborate offering such as helicopter sightseeing. Often, you'll be in port long enough to take more than one option, but the money can quickly add up.

Some tours are worth the money. This is particularly true, I've found, with active tours, such as those involving kayaking or mountain biking, or for tours that take you far beyond the port city (you might be better off taking the prearranged transportation than a cab).

Some shore excursions are just not worth the money. A tour might consist, for example, of just a bus trip past the main sights, with hokey commentary and the obligatory stop at a souvenir stand. If you don't like sightseeing in large groups or touring on buses, or if the main sights you want to see are close to where your ship docks, you might be better off exploring on your own.

The best way to decide is to do some research on a particular port city in advance of your trip. Decide what you want to see, calculate admission and transportation costs, and compare those to what the cruise line is offering in its shore-excursions brochure (which you should receive in advance of your trip). I've included some port information in chapters 22–25 to get you going.

Shore excursions are generally booked on board, not in advance, so before you make your decision, you have time to ask questions of the ship's tour staff, who even offer lectures on the subject. Keep in mind that this is a money-making area for the cruise line, and the role of the onboard tour folks is to get you to buy. (See part 6, "Land! I See Land!: Visiting the Ports of Call," for more information.)

Onboard Costs

Cruise lines make a substantial amount of their revenue on board. Sometimes when you get on a ship, particularly a big mass-market ship, it seems like everyone is trying to sell you something, from the bar staff with the enticing umbrella drinks to the roving photographer to the shopping opportunities that have grown to even include art auctions. The message is *buy, buy, buy.* Or, more aptly, *spend, spend spend.*

Carnival Cruise Lines president Bob Dickinson says in his book that the reason for this is that all passengers have prepaid, so the only variable left in terms of the cruise line's profit for the trip is how much those passengers spend on board.

"Successful lines can add 10% to 20% or more to the bottom line with their onboard and shore [excursion] activities," Dickinson explains.

Sea Stories

Have a guess on what the biggest source of onboard revenue is for cruise lines? Some might guess the casino, but according to Carnival's Bob Dickinson, only about 30% of passengers even visit the casino. Perhaps that's because they're too far gone to do so: The number one expenditure is on booze.

Port Charges

Port charges, taxes, and other fees are sometimes included in your cruise fare but not always, and these charges can add as much as $125 to the price of, say, a 7-day Caribbean cruise. Make sure you know what's included when you are comparing rates and calculating your overall expenditure.

Travel Insurance

You can buy *trip-cancellation insurance* (TCI) to protect yourself if, for some reason, you're not able to take your cruise, or in case your trip is interrupted. You can also buy coverage to handle the expense of any medical emergencies not handled by your regular health insurance.

Travel insurance is not a bargain, however (some would say it's downright overpriced), and you should be wary of buying too much.

Still, if peace of mind demands that you go the insurance route, expect to pay from $5 to $15 for every $100 worth of coverage, depending on what kind of coverage you choose. Several firms offer coverage that combines TCI with medical insurance, and some cruise companies (and a few large travel agencies) offer their own insurance plans.

You can consult a travel agent for more details.

Chapter 3

Choosing the Cruise That's Right for You

In This Chapter

- Separating fact from fiction in the cruise line brochures
- Choosing a cruise to suit your lifestyle
- Choosing an itinerary to suit your taste
- The lowdown on ship sizes—How big is big?
- The skinny on theme cruises
- Tips on picking a cruise for singles, honeymooners, families, and people with disabilities
- A quiz to choose the cruise for youse

Okay, now you've established that you can afford a cruise. But just like you would with any other vacation, when you're choosing a cruise, you also need to think about what you like to do and where you want to go. In this chapter, I'll run through your options, and at the end of the chapter I'll give you a quiz to help you make the big decision.

Trapped in the Land of the Look-Alike Brochures

Choosing the particular cruise that's right for you ensures that you'll have the cruise vacation experience of your dreams.

Making the right choice on the cruise line, ship, and itinerary is even more important than price. What kind of a bargain is it, for example, if you're looking for a quiet time and find yourself on a rowdy party cruise? Your fantasy vacation might be another person's nightmare (and vice versa).

Looking at cruise brochures, no matter how flashy they are (and the cruise lines put a lot of money into this particular marketing vehicle), is probably not going to help you ultimately in making the right cruise choice. All the brochures—every one—show beautiful ships and beautiful places and beautiful people. In general, the ships really do look the way they're portrayed in the full-color glossies (although low-end staterooms are rarely featured), and the places might be as beautiful—as long as you don't wander off the beaten path or look under any rocks. And the people? Well, be assured that not everyone on your cruise will look like the people in the brochures—like they've come right from central casting. (However, you might be able to pick up a few hints from the photos as to the age of the line's clientele.)

So How Do I Decide?

To help you think about what type of cruise experience you really want, consider some of the possibilities. (See chapters 4 to 7 for specific ships that cater to these categories.)

FAMILY-ORIENTED CRUISES Some lines particularly cater to families, and if you're planning to cruise with rug rats in tow, you'll want to find a ship in this category. (See more on family cruising later in this chapter and in chapter 21, "But What's the Kid Gonna Do?: Activities for Children & Teens.")

GOURMET CRUISES If food is your passion, you'll want to keep in mind that while some ships have restaurants that without any question can match anything on dry land, not all ship cuisine is as startlingly good. If you have discriminating gourmet tastes, you might want to choose a ship that makes a point of catering to foodies.

LUXURY CRUISES If you can afford a top-of-the-line ship, you'll find impeccable service, luxurious accommodations, first-class cuisine, and a sophisticated ambiance. You'll also be sailing with other well-heeled and usually well-traveled passengers who will no doubt impress you with their stimulating conversation.

PARTY CRUISES On the other end of the spectrum are party cruises, where the passengers tend to party hearty, definitely at night (the disco will be hopping until dawn) and sometimes during the day, too. People will groove on the Caribbean steel-band tunes on the pool deck (even if the ship isn't in the Caribbean), bar areas will be crowded, and everyone will be really digging those frozen drinks with the little umbrellas.

RESORT CRUISES Resort cruises are the most popular and are for people who want a vacation experience that includes the pool, the spa, the aerobics classes, the state-of-the-art gym, the sports offerings, and the constant activities, which might include scuba diving, snorkeling, watersports, and golf.

ROMANTIC CRUISES There's a reason cruising is popular with couples seeking romance: There's a romantic ambiance on cruise ships that's only slightly related to the rolling seas. Some lines have really gotten into the business of selling romance, offering packages that let you renew your wedding vows, honeymoon, or even get married on board. Some of the bigger ships feature offerings such as togetherness spa sessions, where you can schmeer your loved one with mud. But if your idea of romance is time alone, you might want to look at a ship where quiet time is easy to come by.

ADVENTURE & EDUCATIONAL CRUISES Adventure and educational cruises cater to those who want destination first, ahead of onboard luxury or activity offerings.

Where Do You Fit into the Mix?

Most ships offer at least a taste in all these areas. But knowing what your priorities are will help you when it comes to finding the cruise that's right for you.

But let's take this one step further.

Here's some traveler profiles adapted from a test prepared by the Cruise Lines International Association (most of it at least; I added the Party Vacationer category).

Where do you fit in?

The Active Traveler

On vacation, I like to be able to choose from a wide range of activities. I like playing sports such as basketball, volleyball, and racquetball. I plan to keep up with my jogging on vacation. I want access to a treadmill or stair-climber during my vacation. I'm interested in scuba diving and snorkeling.

The Adventurer

I've always wanted to visit the world's capitals and to see the sights. I like to visit places off the beaten track and see unusual things. I think it would be exciting to walk on a glacier, climb a mountain, or explore a volcano. I like to meet new people and learn about different cultures. I enjoy getting close to nature and wildlife.

The Romantic

I like romantic dinners and dancing under the stars. I like doing new things with a "special someone." I like making friends on vacation. A breathtaking view, a full moon, and a quiet place to talk sounds absolutely sublime. I want our vacation together to be something special.

The Family Vacationer

My spouse and I both work and never seem to spend enough time with our children. Even with different interests, our family enjoys vacationing together. With kids of different ages, our family needs a bunch of vacation experiences rolled into one. We need a restaurant that will satisfy all family members—burgers to continental. We are planning a family reunion and want a setting everyone can enjoy.

The Sophisticated Vacationer

When I go on vacation, I demand the very best. I've traveled the world on business, and now I'm looking for a special way to revisit my favorite places. I usually stay in a suite or a five-star hotel when I travel. World-class cuisine and impeccable service are important to me. The more exotic the destination, the more I'll like it.

The Party Vacationer

I only have a few days to get away, but I want to make the most of them. I love dancing and staying up late. The more people, the merrier. I definitely want to check out the midnight buffet. I love those frozen drinks with the little umbrellas. Bring on the activities, the nightlife, and the fun!

Hotel Preference

A simplified way to determine which cruise is right for you is to look at what kind of hotel you generally stay at.

If you're a bed-and-breakfast kind of person, you may be most comfortable on a smaller, more relaxed cruise ship; if Motel 6 is your thing, look for a budget cruise; if you're a Ritz-Carlton kind of person, mass-market ships, which tend to be more like Hyatts, might not be right for you—you'll want something more luxurious.

Where Do I Want to Go?

Almost as important as deciding what kind of cruise experience you're looking for is deciding where you want to go—if anywhere ("cruises to nowhere" are exactly that).

The most popular cruising region in the world is the Caribbean, followed by Europe and Alaska. Most first-time cruisers choose the Caribbean, with an itinerary that might include a port of call in Mexico. (See chapters 22 to 25 for specifics on what you'll find at each port-of-call destination.)

The Big Get Bigger

When it makes its debut in 1999, Royal Caribbean International's Eagle Project ship (the ship has yet to be named), will top the scales at 130,000 gross registered tons, making it the largest cruise ship afloat.

The Caribbean

For the cruise passenger, the Caribbean offers palm trees, rain forests, interesting cultures, and great shopping. But the biggest draw is the climate—so temperate that cruises are offered here on a year-round basis, although it can get downright hot in the summer.

Cruises in the Caribbean generally range from 3 to 7 nights (longer offerings are also available) and include stops at several islands, where activities such as beach-hopping, watersports, shopping, hiking through flora and fauna, and tours of local history and culture are offered.

Caribbean cruises are popular with families, travelers under age 50, and, in general, people who are active and energetic. On the ships, people tend to spend time at the pool and on the open decks, and participate in the various onboard activity offerings.

Itineraries

Most ships on Caribbean itineraries leave from Miami, Fort Lauderdale, or Port Canaveral, Florida, although itineraries also depart from Tampa, Florida; San Juan, Puerto Rico; New Orleans, Louisiana; and elsewhere. Some smaller ships leave from Caribbean islands, such as St. Maarten, St. Thomas, and Aruba.

The most popular itineraries for a 7-night Caribbean cruise follow:

- **Eastern Caribbean:** Florida to St. Thomas, St. Maarten, and either a private island (which may be owned by the cruise line) or The Bahamas.
- **Western Caribbean:** Florida to Grand Cayman Island or Jamaica (or both); Cozumel, Mexico; and Key West, Florida, or a private island.

Itineraries are also offered from San Juan, Puerto Rico, that cover a Southern Caribbean route that might include stops at Grenada, Antigua, St. Thomas, and St. Barts. And Norwegian Cruise Line offers Texaribbean itineraries from Houston, Texas, that include ports of call at Cancén; Cozumel; and Roatan, Bay Islands.

When to Go

High season in the Caribbean is from the third week in January to the Easter/spring-break period. The most popular sailings (and those most likely to sell out) are at Christmas, New Year's, Thanksgiving, and during school vacation periods—including the summer (when families flock to the region). As I discussed in chapter 2, you can find bargains in the low and shoulder seasons.

Hurricane Season

Hurricane season in the Caribbean is June 1 through November 1. But with modern satellite warning systems, you really have little to fear from these storms—ships generally have enough warning to steer clear. What a storm could mean to your cruise, however, is a slightly bumpier ride. In an extreme situation, it could mean a deviation from course that could prevent you from stopping at an island you really wanted to see, or it could put the kibosh on your shore excursion plans (for example, an acquaintance recently went snorkeling and couldn't see a thing because storms had stirred up the sand and mud).

Alaska

The Alaska cruise experience is much more destination-oriented than the Caribbean. You go for the sights more than the weather. In fact, even in

August, it might be too cold or rainy on your cruise to spend much time by the pool. You won't care, though, so gorgeous is the scenery: mountains, glaciers, fjords, islands, and forests, as well as easily spotted wildlife.

Shore excursions offer a chance to explore these sights close up—you might even get to walk on a glacier—and to take in the history and culture of the region.

While passengers on Alaska cruises tend to be older (generally, age 55 and up) and less active travelers than those in the Caribbean, you'd never know it from the activities the cruise lines offer here, which include kayaking, mountain biking, salmon fishing, flightseeing, and dogsledding. Some family cruisers are also starting to realize the educational virtues of a cruise in the region.

Itineraries

Most Alaska cruises depart from Seward, Alaska, or Vancouver, Canada. There are also a few departures from Seattle, Washington.

The most popular 7-night itinerary focuses on the southern part of the state and a stretch known as the *Inside Passage*. A typical itinerary includes stops at several port towns and islands, which might include Skagway and Juneau and/or Haines, Sitka, Ketchikan, and Valdez.

An extensive array of land tours is also offered in this region to complement the cruise itineraries.

When to Go

Alaska is a seasonal destination, with the season May to September. Lower rates are offered in the shoulder seasons (May and September).

Ahoy, Mateys!

In general, when trying to decide between the Caribbean and Alaska, you can think:

Caribbean = younger, active, sunworshiper

Alaska = older, active (or not), nature lover

Cruises Off the Beaten Path

Of course, the cruise scene in North America is not limited to the Caribbean and Alaska. First-time cruisers might want to look at the following as additional options.

Bermuda

The cruising season to Bermuda is May to September, with the best rates in May and September. The itineraries tend to be 6 or 7 nights, with 3 days actually in Bermuda and the rest of the time at sea. Like the Caribbean, cruises to Bermuda tend to attract a more active traveler and are popular with families. The Britishness of Bermuda is a particular attraction, along with the pink beaches. Most departures are from New York or Boston, with occasional departures from other East Coast cities.

Hawaii

Only one cruise line, American Hawaii, operates full-time in this market, but several other lines also visit Hawaii on a part-time basis. The season is year-round, and both the scenery and the weather are the big attractions. The cruise traveler here represents a mixed demographic, with the line making a big push to attract families.

New England & Canada

The season is May to October, with popular sailings including those during the fall leaf-peeping season. The market tends to attract older clients, except on the shorter-budget cruises from New York (which might attract families and partiers). History and scenery are the emphasis rather than the weather. On weeklong cruises, ports of call are likely to include Boston, Montreal, and/or Quebec; Nova Scotia and New Brunswick, Canada; as well as Maine and sometimes Cape Cod in Massachusetts or Newport, Rhode Island. Departures are usually from New York, Montreal, or Boston.

The Mexican Riviera & Baja

This market is most akin to the Caribbean but might be more accessible to West Coast travelers both pricewise and geography-wise. Cruises are offered here year-round, with winter being the high season. Three- to seven-day itineraries are offered from Los Angeles, and the week-long itineraries might include ports of call at Puerto Vallarta, Mazatlán, and Cabo San Lucas, as well as days at sea. The cruises tend to attract a younger crowd and are popular with families.

River & Lake Cruising

Looking for something different than an ocean cruise on a big cruise ship? You might want to consider a river cruise down the Mississippi (or the Ohio, Tennessee, and other rivers) on an authentic paddlewheel steamer. Itineraries offered by The Delta Queen Steamboat Company vary in length from 3 nights to 2 weeks, with departures from cities such as New Orleans, Memphis, and St. Louis. Cruises are also offered by other lines on these rivers, too, and on such tributaries as the Columbia and Snake rivers in the Pacific Northwest and the Erie Canal. Other cruise alternatives include low-key sailing cruises off the coast of Maine. Some of these offerings are year-round, while others are on a seasonal basis.

How Long Do I Want to Go For?

To get the most out of a cruise vacation, I suggest a 7-night itinerary. Usually, ships leave on a Saturday or Sunday afternoon and return early the following Saturday or Sunday, giving you plenty of time to do everything on the ship and still get home in time to go back to work on Monday.

But if you're a little wary of booking a full-week cruise your first time out, a 3-, 4-, or 5-night getaway cruise can still give you a nice taste of the cruise experience. These shorter cruise lengths also allow you to combine a week's vacation with land-based options—say, a visit to Disney or time on the beaches in Miami. Of course, the cruise lines have thought of this and offer an array of pre- and post-cruise land packages. And Disney packages *all* its cruises this way, combining a few days on a ship with a few days at the resort.

Remember, however, the shorter the cruise length, the more party-hearty the passengers tend to be (an exception here might be Disney Cruise Line, but it's too soon to tell).

I would not recommend that novice cruisers book a cruise longer than a week the first time out.

Size Matters

There's a big difference between the experience of being on a megaliner, which might have anywhere from 1,750 to nearly 3,000 passengers, and being on a small ship with 400 passengers or less.

To help with your choice, consider the following facts.

Megaliners & Superliners

At 70,000 gross registered tons and up, these ships tend to be glitzier, offer tons of activities, attract more of an under-50 crowd, attract more families, offer larger public rooms (including fancier casinos and larger gyms), and offer a great variety of meal options and entertainment. They tend to visit ports where shopping and beach activities are among the big attractions.

Ahoy, Mateys!

The size of ships is often described not in length but in **gross registered tons** (GRTs), which is a way to determine size that takes into account interior space used to produce revenue on a vessel. One GRT = 100 cubic feet of enclosed, revenue-generating space.

Traditional & Classic Ships

Traditional and classic ships tend to attract an older clientele but also might attract families. Service tends to be a big area of focus, and on classic ships—a category that includes some surviving vintage ocean liners—appreciation for seafaring history is a big focus as well. Entertainment and food vary. The ships may not only be older, but they also might be more elegant than their bigger and more modern peers. The ambiance might be more low-key. These ships also tend to offer a broader range of itineraries than the bigger ships.

Small Ships

Small ships tend to offer more of a relaxed pace and may offer itineraries that focus on alternative ports with shallow waters (which they can get into because of their smaller size). They might offer more of an "adventure" cruise experience. There tend to be fewer kids on board. There may be more interaction with fellow passengers than on larger ships. There will be less entertainment and less public space. The environment on the ships might be more luxurious than on larger vessels, or it might be downright rustic.

Sailing Ships

If you're a purist about oceangoing, or if you've always imagined yourself as a buccaneer Errol Flynn–type, a sailing ship might be just your thing.

The lines running sailing ships today offer as broad a spectrum of experience as is available in the industry as a whole, from the bare bones (Tall Ship Adventures) to the extravagant (Windstar), with the others (Windjammer and Star Clippers) falling somewhere in between. The unifying factor among passengers, though, is an appreciation for getting up close and personal with the elements and a willingness to be relatively loose with their itineraries—the ability to sail to certain destinations being governed to a greater or lesser extent by the prevailing winds.

More than with any other type of cruising, if this is the type of cruise for you, you'll know it. No one is wishy-washy about a sailing ship. You either love it or you don't.

Theme Cruises

In seeking a cruise that's sure to please, you might want to consider one that's tailor-made to your specific interests, whether those interests involve golf, fine wine, or Elvis.

Cruise lines have become quite creative in the theme-cruise regard, gearing specific sailings toward music lovers, sports fans, history buffs, gourmets, and so on. Princess Cruises, the *Love Boat* folks, offers cruises every year themed around Valentine's Day. In 1997, Windstar Cruises offered a cruise on the topic of ice cream, featuring the real Ben & Jerry.

Some leaders of the pack in the theme regard are:

- **Norwegian Cruise Line.** NCL offers a full roster of music cruises (country music, blues, Dixieland, Big Band, jazz) and also offers Sports Afloat cruises, featuring professional baseball, hockey, football, and basketball stars in the lineup. The line also debuted an Olympic Sports Afloat cruise in 1997.
- **The Delta Queen Steamboat Company.** Delta Queen offers themed cruises on topics such as the Civil War, the Kentucky Derby, Elvis, gardening, Mark Twain, and Big Band music. In 1997, the line also launched a series of Cajun Culture cruises.
- **Holland America Line.** HAL has been increasing its themed offerings, with an emphasis on music (including the 50s, country, 60s rock, and Big Band). The line also offers comedy cruises and sailings with film and shopping themes.

- **Crystal Cruises.** This line features culinary legends such as Jacques Pepin in its Crystal Wine & Food Festival, offered on 23 sailings in 1998. Wine experts are also on board during the sailings to share their secrets.

Special Situations

If you are single, a traveler with disabilities, honeymooners, or a family traveling together, you have additional areas to consider before booking your cruise.

Singles

If you are single and plan to travel alone, you needn't worry about dining alone; you'll be seated with other guests. (If this is a problem, you might seek a ship with alternative dining options.) You also needn't worry very much about finding people to talk to, since the general atmosphere on nearly all ships allows you to easily find conversation, especially during group activities.

Before you book, consider the following:

- Will there be other singles my age on the ship?
- Does the line offer a fair single supplement rate (see chapter 2), or can I be matched with an appropriate roommate?
- Does the line employ social hosts as dance partners?
- Are there special parties held for singles so we can meet each other?
- Does the line offer special sailings for singles (Windjammer and Commodore are among those who do).

Travelers with Disabilities

If you are a traveler with disabilities, it's important that you let the cruise line know your special needs when you make your booking.

Some lines require that travelers with disabilities be accompanied by an able-bodied person.

If you have a chronic illness, you will likely be asked to have a form completed by your doctor saying that it is okay for you to travel.

Smooth Sailing

Once on board, travelers with disabilities will want to seek the advice of the tour staff before choosing shore excursions (not all are wheelchair-accessible).

Before you book, consider these questions:

- Are there cabins that are wheelchair-accessible? How are they equipped?

- Are there elevators?
- Are all public rooms wheelchair-accessible?
- At the ports of call, will the ship pull into dock or use *tenders* (small boats) to go ashore? Can the tenders handle wheelchairs?
- Are there any special procedures for boarding and disembarking from the ship? Will you be required to line up with hundreds of other passengers (which can be quite tiring), or is there a separate special-needs desk?

Smooth Sailing

The newer ships tend to offer the largest number of handicapped-accessible cabins, with doors wide enough for wheelchairs and other special features. The *Grand Princess* and Carnival's *Destiny* top the list with 26 and 25, respectively. Holland America Line's *Rotterdam VI* offers 23 such cabins.

Families

If you're traveling with the rug rats, you'll want to make sure you know in advance what programs will be offered on your sailing, and for what ages. Some lines offer kids activities only on a seasonal basis. See chapter 21 for more info on kids activities.

Before you book, consider these questions:

- Does the line have a reduced rate for kids? (See chapter 2.) Does the rate include airfare? What is the line's cutoff age for a kid to be considered a kid?
- What does the kids' program include—arts and crafts, parties, special shore excursions, tours of the bridge, and educational activities?
- Are there likely to be other kids aboard who are my kids' age?
- How big is the ship's kids' center? Is there a special area for teens? Is there a video/game room?
- Does the line offer baby-sitting for babies/toddlers? Is it very expensive?
- Does the line have cribs available? Highchairs? Child- and infant-sized life jackets?
- Do the cabins have TVs and VCRs?

Note: Most lines do not encourage people to bring infants, some do not even allow babies, and some discourage women in the late stages of pregnancy from coming on board.

Honeymooners

Most 1-week cruises depart on either Saturday or Sunday, although there are some exceptions. You'll want to look carefully at sailing times as you plan your wedding weekend.

Smooth Sailing

Note that all children traveling without both parents must have a letter from both parents saying it is okay for them to leave the country. This is true even in cases in which the parents are divorced. If you don't have a letter, you may be denied boarding.

Before you book, consider these questions:

- Are double-, queen-, or king-sized beds available?
- Will the stateroom have a bathtub? (Most don't.) A Jacuzzi? A TV and VCR?
- Are there rooms with verandas? Is there room on the veranda for a couple of lounge chairs? A table?
- Can I book a table just for two in the dining room?
- Are there likely to be other couples your age on the ship?
- Does the line have room service? Is there a full menu, or just breakfast and sandwiches?
- Does the line have a specific honeymoon package available? Special honeymoon suites?
- Does the line offer special perks like champagne for honeymooning couples?

Quiz: What's the Cruise for You?

Now let's put it all together. Referring to this chapter and chapter 2, complete this quiz before proceeding to the ship reviews in part 2 and chapter 8, "Booking Your Cruise."

1. **What type of traveler are you?**

   a. The Active Traveler

   b. The Adventurer

   c. The Romantic

   d. The Family Vacationer

   e. The Sophisticated Vacationer

   f. The Party Vacationer

2. **What type of cruise experience do you want?**

   a. Family-Oriented Cruise

   b. Gourmet Cruise

   c. Luxury Cruise

   d. Party Cruise

   e. Resort Cruise

   f. Romantic Cruise

   g. Adventure & Educational Cruise

3. **Where do you want to travel?**

   a. The Eastern Caribbean

   b. The Western Caribbean

   c. Alaska

   d. Bermuda

   e. Hawaii

   f. New England & Canada

   g. The Mexican Riviera & Baja

   h. River & Lake Cruising

4. **Are you a big ship person or small ship person?**

   a. Big Ship

   b. Small Ship

5. **What type of hotel do you usually stay at?**

   a. Bed-and-Breakfast

   b. Budget Motel

   c. Mass-Market Hotel

   d. Luxury Hotel

6. **Approximately when do you want to travel?**

   a. Summer

   b. Fall

   c. Winter

   d. Spring

7. **Are you looking for a family, singles, honeymoon, or theme experience?** ____

   ____

8. **Do you have any special needs?** ____________________________

9. **How much do you want to spend?** ___________________________

Part 2

The Cruise Lines & Their Ships

Now that you've established what type of cruise traveler you are and what you're looking for in a cruise vacation, let's see how your wants and desires match up with what the cruise lines offer.

Once you've found a match or two (or three, or . . .), you can turn to chapter 8 for specifics on how to book your trip. I've included a worksheet at the end of chapter 4 where you can organize your choices and compare their pluses and minuses, but to make matters easier for yourself, I suggest you put a little red check mark next to the ones you like as you go through the reviews. (Remember how your teachers used to tell you not to write in your books? Now's the time to rebel. Scrawl away.) Then, when you're done, write 'em in the worksheet, and bring this book, with quiz and worksheet filled out, to a professional travel agent for additional assistance in targeting the cruise offering that's best for you.

Chapter 4

Cruise Choosing 101

In This Chapter

- An explanation of our ship ratings
- A key to the ship-specifications charts and itinerary destinations
- A word on rates
- A worksheet for keeping track of your faves

In this section, I hope to point you toward the cruise ship that's right for you by giving you quick reviews of all the major cruise lines. Let me reiterate that I suggest you seek the advice of a professional travel agent in making your final decision (see chapter 8, "Booking Your Cruise," for tips on the booking process).

You'll notice that I focus on lines sailing in and around North America. Why North America? Because you're probably a first-time cruiser, and you're unlikely to want to spend the big bucks your first time out to cruise in, say, China and the Far East. You might want to do that later, however, after you (ahem) get your feet wet. And many of the lines featured here also offer cruises in other parts of the world, most commonly in Europe.

The ship reviews are divided into three parts: cruise ships, alternative cruise ships, and tall ships, with an explanation of what each of these categories means at the beginning of their respective chapters. The reviews will give you a feel for the cruise line, the ambiance on their ships, the amenities and activities, the types of passengers you're likely to encounter, and the general type of cruise vacation experience you can expect.

Special features of each line and special deals offered by the line (that is, the discounts) are also noted.

Ship Size Comparisons

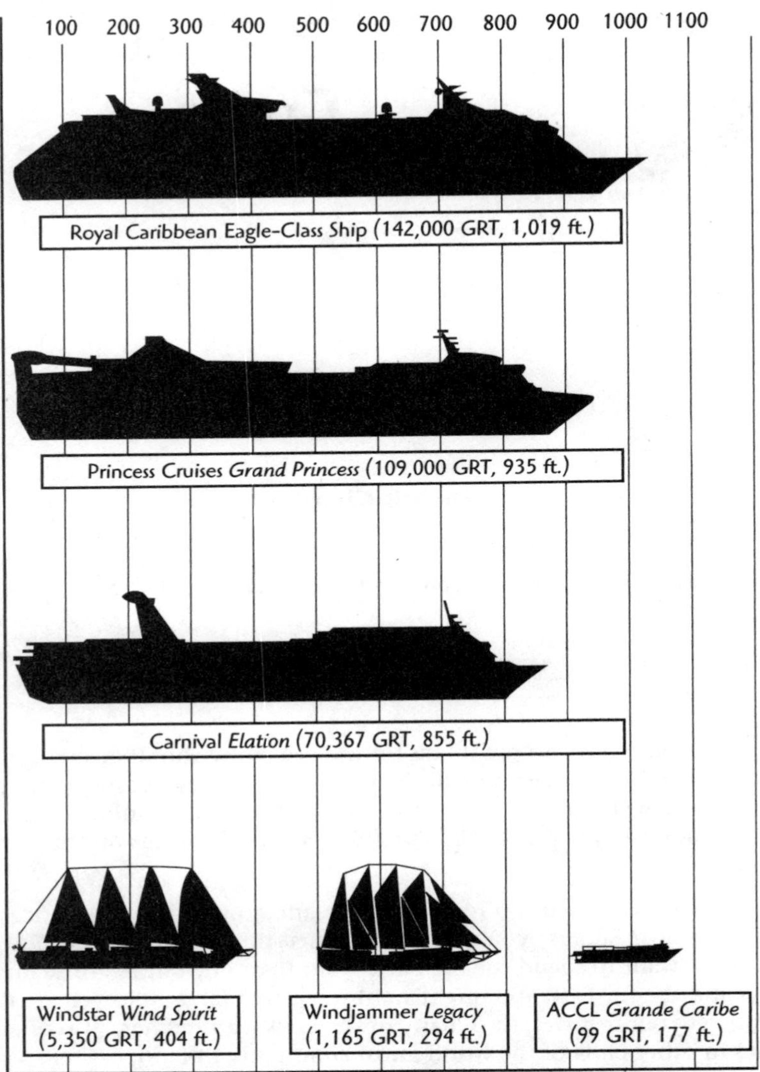

Ships selected for this chart are representative of the various size vessels sailing in the cruise market today. See the specifications tables accompanying every ship review in chapters 5, 6, and 7 to see the approximate comparative size of all the ships not shown here. (**GRT** = gross register tons, a measure that takes into account interior space used to produce revenue on a vessel. One GRT = 100 cubic feet of enclosed, revenue-generating space.)

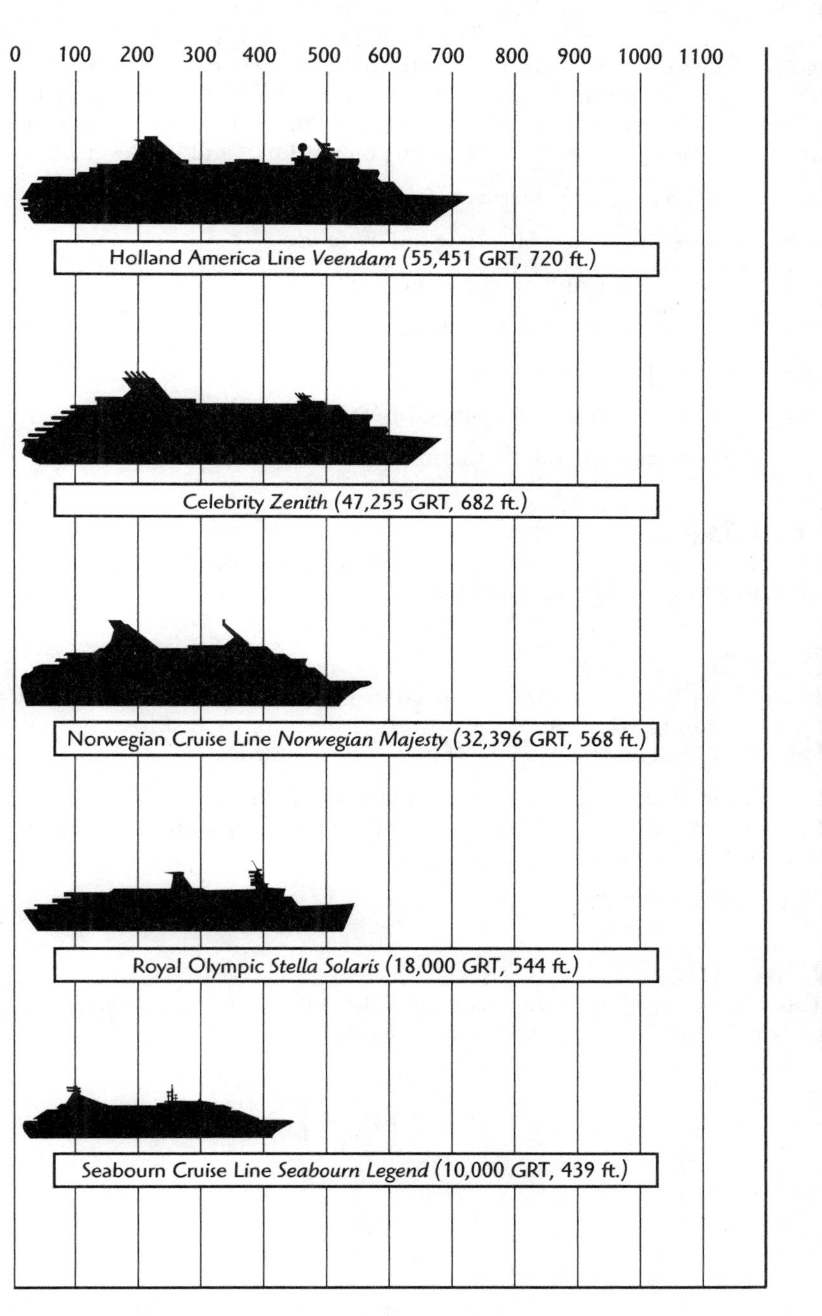
0
100
200
300
400
500
600
700
800
900
1000
1100
Holland America Line Veendam (55,451 GRT, 720 ft.)
Celebrity Zenith (47,255 GRT, 682 ft.)
Norwegian Cruise Line Norwegian Majesty (32,396 GRT, 568 ft.)
Royal Olympic Stella Solaris (18,000 GRT, 544 ft.)
Seabourn Cruise Line Seabourn Legend (10,000 GRT, 439 ft.)

The Ratings

Each review begins with "type of cruise," which is my way of saying "rating." To make the rating system really simple, I borrowed (with its creator's gracious permission) a unique and pretty well self-explanatory system developed by industry veteran and pundit Rod McLeod, now senior vice president of marketing for Carnival Corporation. McLeod calls his system "The Drinking Man's (Woman's) Guide to Cruising Segmentation," and it goes like this:

- Champagne and caviar (*very* fancy)
- Imported wine and cheese (good 'n' fancy)
- Domestic wine and cheese (fancy enough)
- Beer and pretzels (fun for everyone)
- Bread and water (bare bones)
- Evian and granola (specialty cruises)
- Prune juice and granola (mature people's specialty cruises)

Fran Says

Also at the top of each cruise review, you'll see my own quick summation of what to expect from each particular cruise line.

Details, Details

Included with each review is also a chart indicating the major cruising areas for each ship in North America, as well as specs for each ship, to give you an idea of its size and the number of passengers it carries.

Size on the charts is expressed not in tons but in *gross registered tons* (GRT), a figure that takes into account interior space used to produce revenue on each vessel (see chapter 3 for more on this).

Ship length is expressed in good old normal feet.

Itineraries

The itinerary section of the charts uses the following on somewhat of a loose basis. For specific dates, check with the cruise lines.

sp	spring
s	summer
f	fall
w	winter
yr	year-round

Also in the itinerary section, I use the following by way of geographic reference:

E. Car.	Eastern Caribbean (the cruising area from Florida to Dominica)
W. Car.	Western Caribbean (the cruising area from Florida to Cancún or Cozumel, Mexico)
E./W. Car.	Eastern and Western Caribbean (in most cases, ships designated this way alternate itineraries weekly)
S. Car.	Southern Caribbean (the cruising area from San Juan to Trinidad)
Car.	Caribbean (itineraries that don't fit into any one of the above categories)
Mex. Riviera	Mexican Riviera (California down to Baja and Mexico's west coast, cruising the Pacific)
Panama	Panama Canal (including Caribbean stops)
Central Am.	Central America (including Caribbean stops)
U.S. South	Southern U.S. states (Florida, Georgia, the Carolinas, Virginia, and Maryland), usually via the Intracoastal Waterway
NE/Canada	New England and Canada (the U.S. East Coast, cruising in the Atlantic)

Other terms used in the itinerary section of the charts should be self-explanatory.

Rates

Also included in each line's chart is an idea of the cruise prices for each ship. These are presented on a per-person, per-day basis. Multiply that number by 7, and you have the cost of a 1-week cruise; multiply it by 10, and you have the cost of a 10-day cruise, and so on.

The rates listed are for peak (high season) Caribbean travel, unless the particular ship does not sail in the Caribbean (in which case, the rates are listed on the basis of the main route the ship does sail). Since these rates are right out of the cruise lines' brochures and do not reflect standard discounts, they will tend to be on the high side. In some cases, however, cruise lines provided me with their more accurate average rate, and those cases are noted with an asterisk (*).

Ship Preferences Worksheet

Ship	Itinerary	Price per Day

Advantages	Disadvantages	Your Ranking (1–10)

Chapter 5

The Cruise Ships

In This Chapter

- All the large cruise ships in the North American market, rated and reviewed
- Notes on the big-ship cruising experience
- Previews of what's on tap from all the cruise lines

The ships featured in this chapter vary pretty greatly in size and scope and include everything from private, yacht-type vessels to classic ocean liners to really, really big and really, really new megaships—some so big, I think they should have their own category. How about whopper-ships?

Anyway, most have all the facilities you can imagine on a cruise ship and more. There are swimming pools and health clubs and spas (of various sizes), nightclubs, movie theaters, shops, casinos, bars, special kids' playrooms, and open decks where you can take the sun. In some cases you'll also find sports decks, virtual golf, computer rooms, and cigar clubs, as well as quiet spaces where you can get away from it all. There are so many rooms you won't likely feel claustrophobic.

These ships have big dining rooms and buffet areas serving more food with more variety and at more times (including midnight) than you can possibly think about or eat. And most of these ships offer formal nights when you can dine in your tux or gown.

There might also be additional eating venues, such as pizzerias; hamburger grills; ice cream parlors; alternative restaurants; patisseries; and wine, champagne, and caviar bars.

In most cases, these ships have lots and lots of onboard activities, including games and contests, classes and lectures, and a variety of entertainment options that might even include celebrity headline acts and usually include show productions, some of which are very sophisticated.

Most of the ships in this chapter offer modern comforts such as TVs and telephones in the cabins, and in some cases, even safes and minibars. The cabins themselves might be cubbyholes or large suites, depending on the ship and the type of cabin you book, and an increasingly popular option available with most lines is a private veranda.

These ships carry a lot of people, so you might have to wait in line occasionally or feel crowded at times. On the other hand, you aren't stuck with the same old faces for a week (on a bigger ship, it's easier to avoid people you don't like), and there are usually less-frequented places where you can sneak off for some quiet time.

The ships offer a comfortable cruising experience, with your well-being overseen by virtual armies of service employees. Ship stabilizers usually ensure that it's a pretty smooth sailing experience, too.

The itineraries of the biggest ships in this chapter tend to be the tried-and-true ports where your ship might be one of several visiting that day (and where duty-free shopping might be a main attraction). But the smaller ships in this category might visit alternative ports, away from the typical tourist crowds.

Shore excursions—some of them quite extravagant—are offered by all the lines.

American Hawaii Cruises

1380 Port of New Orleans Place, Robin St. Wharf, New Orleans, LA 70130-1890. ☎ ***800/543-7637.***

Type of cruise: *Domestic wine and cheese.*

Fran says: *A classic ocean liner that offers one of the best ways to see the islands, but it's not fancy.*

THE EXPERIENCE The only cruise line home-ported in Hawaii, American Hawaii operates the classic twin-funneled ocean liner *Independence*. The ship's twin sister, the *Constitution,* which was retired by American Hawaii in 1995 (and sank to the bottom of the Pacific Ocean on its way to the scrap heap

Independence *(Photo: American Hawaii Cruises)*

in 1997), was the cruise ship featured in the Cary Grant movie *An Affair to Remember.*

The *Independence,* which was renovated in 1994 to the tune of $50 million, attracts a good share of retirees, but also younger couples and families. Most are making their first trip to Hawaii.

The vessel has a strong Hawaiian theme in its decor, furnishings, and collection of artifacts, as well as in its entertainment offerings. But there's also an old ocean-liner ambiance that, while in some ways pleasing, includes a confusing layout and a rough wooden plank here and there.

The staff is all-American and both friendly and professional. The ship does not have a casino or a disco, and there are no fruit drinks in souvenir glasses. Dress is casual except for one semiformal night.

A big plus is the opportunity the *Independence* provides for touring the islands (Honolulu, Kauai, Maui, and Hawaii), and the line makes the most of an outstanding program of 55 shore excursions—among them, half-day bus trips; a day at the beach; flights on six-seater helicopters; and flights in a two-seater, open-cockpit biplane.

SPECIAL FEATURES A *kumu* (traditional Hawaiian teacher and storyteller) sails with the ship, offering lectures about Hawaiian traditions and history. Local Hawaiian music and dance troupes—including small children, teenagers, and adults—come aboard at several ports for performances.

SPECIAL DEALS Children ages 2 to 17 sharing a room with 2 full-fare passengers pay a daily rate of $40. Children under age 2 cruise free. Third or fourth guests sharing a cabin with two full-fare passengers pay $111 per day.

Hawaiian Growth Plans

American Hawaii may soon be getting bigger. The line was recently awarded a monopoly in the market by the U.S. government. In return, the line agreed to help revive the U.S. shipbuilding industry by committing to build two megaships to be introduced in 2005 and 2008. The ships, which will also be based in Hawaii, are expected to carry a combined price tag of $800 million. The line is also expected to lease or charter a vessel to expand its fleet by 1999.

American Hawaii Fleet Specifications

Ship	Itinerary	Year Built	Passengers	Crew	Size	Length
Independence	Hawaii (yr)	1951	818	315	30,090	682

American Hawaii Cabins & Rates

Ship	Outside Cabins	w/Veranda	Rates	Inside Cabins	Rates
Independence	203	none	$204–$340	218	$175–$297

FLEET NOTES The *Independence* was built as a three-class vessel, and the cabins today come in various configurations and angles—much different than newer ships with their modular design. There are 25 cabins that are specifically for singles.

Cape Canaveral Cruise Line

101 George King Blvd., Suite 6, Cape Canaveral, FL 32920. ☎ ***800/910-SHIP.***

Type of cruise: *Bread and water.*

Fran says: *For people looking for good times on a short cruise and who don't care about anything else.*

THE EXPERIENCE The *Dolphin IV,* the line's only ship, is one of the oldest cruise ships afloat and makes 2-night quickie cruises from Florida to the Bahamas and 4-night cruises that include an overnight in Key West (it's the only ship in the biz that does this). *Budget* is the word here, and to its credit, Cape Canaveral knows what it is and doesn't try to be more.

Dolphin IV *(Photo: Cape Canaveral Cruise Line)*

Passengers tend to be exuberant first-timers, ranging in ages from late 20s to late 50s, taking the quick trip to test out the cruise experience or because they have a little (but *only* a little) time on their hands. The onboard atmosphere is casual, upbeat, and friendly, although the crew sometimes acts hurried.

The ship has one dining room, which serves American fare that is not at all gourmet. Special children's menus are offered.

The focus during the day is fun-in-the-sun activities, with the small swimming pool the most popular venue. To its credit, the ship offers a good children's program, giving parents a chance to relax. At night, people crowd into the small casino and tiny disco or enjoy the various dance floors and comedy performances.

SPECIAL FEATURES The ship does not have a gym or exercise equipment, but joggers can use the boat deck, and skeet shooting is usually available. The library doubles as a movie theater.

SPECIAL DEALS Third/fourth passenger fares, early-booking discounts.

Cape Canaveral Fleet Specifications

Ship	Itinerary	Year Built	Passengers	Crew	Size	Length
Dolphin IV	Bahamas, Key West (yr)	1956	692	290	13,007	501

Cape Canaveral Cabins & Rates

Ship	Outside Cabins	w/Veranda	Rates	Inside Cabins	Rates
Dolphin IV	217	none	$100–$120	77	$70–$95

FLEET NOTES Old maritime-type teakwood decks and authentic wood trim are pleasant aspects of the *Dolphin IV,* but the ship's cabins are not so pleasant. They're small and cramped and would be inadequate were it not for the fact that most people don't bring much luggage on the ship's quick jaunts. The cabin decor is classic roadside motel, and the tiny showers require strategic maneuvering.

Carnival Cruise Lines

3655 NW 87th Ave., Miami, FL 33178-2428. ☎ ***800/CARNIVAL.***

Type of cruise: *Beer and pretzels.*

Fran says: *"Ain't we got fun?" Yeah, you got it, in big, bold, beautiful, neon splendor.*

Elation *(Photo: Carnival Cruise Lines)*

THE EXPERIENCE Carnival is the Big Kahuna of the industry, its modern fleet boasting big ships that are the boldest, most innovative, and most successful cruise ships on the seas.

A lot of the success is due to the fact that the experience of being on the ships is "fun," like the line's now famous ad campaign says. Like

How Carnival Became Carnival

In 1971, Ted Arison, with the help of investors, bought the old *Empress of Canada,* once an Atlantic ocean liner, but at the time laid up and out of work.

With a fresh coat of paint and other improvements, Arison launched it as Carnival Cruise Lines' *Mardi Gras* in March 1972. The cruise line's beginning was anything but auspicious. On her maiden voyage, the *Mardi Gras* made headlines around the world by running aground within sight of Miami Beach. The fashionable drink of the day became "Mardi Gras on the rocks," according to one observer at the time.

Arison persevered, however, and what resulted is the greatest success story in the history of the ocean-liner business. In addition to Carnival itself, the line's parent company, Carnival Corporation (of which Arison is now chairman emeritus), also owns all or a big chunk of Holland America, Seabourn, Windstar, and Costa, and in March 1998 announced plans to buy Cunard. Officials have announced plans to add to the fleets of the various brands to the initial tune of $2 billion by the start of the new century.

Kathie Lee Gifford sings, "In the morning, in the evening . . ." you'll find fun on Carnival ships, and parties, and party-hearty fellow passengers, too.

In a good week, the line carries more than 30,000 passengers (the Carnival *Destiny* alone carried 156,000 passengers in 1997), and it has among the youngest passenger demographics in the industry—mostly under age 50, including couples, singles, and a good share of families (the line carries some 160,000 kids a year). It's the same middle-American crowd found in Las Vegas and Atlantic City and at Florida's megaresorts.

The decor on these mass-market ships, with public rooms designed by the now legendary Joe Farcus, is eclectic and definitely glitzy, with a liberal use of neon and bold, bright colors. And it's playful: A piano bar outfitted like King Tut's tomb here, a room with gilded representations of ancient Greek deities there—you get the idea.

The ambiance is akin to a theme park on water, and since there's so much to do on the ships, the ports of call tend to take a back seat (but that's not to say there aren't plenty of shore-excursion offerings). Carnival's ships spend more time at sea than their peers, giving people a chance to totally enjoy the Carnival floating-resort experience, with its professionally delivered fun presented amidst glitter and glitz. (Of course, this tactic also allows more time for passengers to increase the line's onboard revenue, as well.)

Food is well-prepared and bountiful, geared toward a middle-American audience, and entertainment is splendiferous, with each ship boasting a dozen dancers, a 12-piece orchestra, comedians, jugglers, and numerous live bands, as well as big (and in some cases, giant) casinos.

Service is not as refined as on smaller and/or fancier ships, but then that's not the point here. All the Carnival ships are well-run and well-maintained, with minor annoyances like lines and frequent loud public announcements being factors that come with the mass-market experience.

Drinking and off-color jokes are part of the scene, as are contests where, for example, men can bare their chests to determine who has the hairiest. Even so, in 1997 the line tried to calm things down just a bit by banning the spring-break crowd. Under the new rules, no one under age 21 can sail alone unless sharing a room with an adult over 25 years old. (Exceptions are made for young married couples, who, presumably, can be counted on to act responsibly.)

For kids, the line offers Camp Carnival, an expertly run children's program with a plethora of kid-pleasing activities that keep the kids occupied so parents can enjoy some downtime.

SPECIAL FEATURES Carnival offers a **Vacation Guarantee** program. Any guests that are dissatisfied with their cruise can disembark at the first non-U.S. port of call and receive a refund for the unused portion of their fare, plus reimbursement for air transportation back to the ship's home port. Carnival enforces a tough no-smoking policy, banning smoking in all dining rooms and main showrooms. The *Paradise* is the world's first smoke-free cruise ship (shipyard workers weren't even allowed to smoke while building her).

Sea Stories

Carnival is the only cruise line that can boast its own **Barbie doll,** which comes complete with a Carnival beach bag and is on sale in the line's onboard gift shops. Carnival also has its own perfume line.

SPECIAL DEALS Carnival has joined forces with Amtrak to create 13 packages that combine a cruise with a rail trip. You can make reservations through your travel agent or **Amtrak Vacations (☎ 800/321-8684)**. The line also offers packages with Universal Studios Florida that combine a 3- or 4-day cruise to The Bahamas aboard the *Fantasy* with a hotel stay in Orlando and tickets to various theme parks.

The *Destiny* includes a special category of rooms called **Night Owl.** These 11 rooms are offered at a really low price but come with a caveat: They're located above the disco and consequently are not very conducive to sleeping until the disco shuts down in the very wee hours. It's a perfect deal if you don't plan to shut down till then, either.

Carnival Fleet Specifications

Ship	Itinerary	Year Built	Passengers	Crew	Size	Length
Celebration	W. Car. (yr)	1987	1,486	670	47,262	733
Destiny	E./W. Car. (yr)	1996	2,642	1,050	101,000	892
Ecstasy	Bahamas and W. Car. (yr)	1991	2,040	920	70,367	855
Elation	Mex. Riviera (yr)	1998	2,040	920	70,367	855
Fantasy	Bahamas (yr)	1990	2,040	920	70,367	855
Fascination	S. Car. (yr)	1994	2,040	920	70,367	855
Holiday	Mex. Riviera (yr)	1985	1,452	669	46,052	727
Imagination	E./W. Car. (yr)	1995	2,040	920	70,367	855
Inspiration	S. Car. (yr)	1996	2,040	920	70,367	855
Jubilee	Alaska (s) Hawaii (sp/f) S. Car., Panama (w)	1986	1,486	670	47,262	733
Paradise	E./W. Car. (yr)	1998	2,040	920	70,367	855
Sensation	E. Car. (until Dec. '98) W. Car. (yr)	1993	2,040	920	70,367	855
Tropicale	W. Car. (yr)	1981	1,022	550	36,674	660

Carnival Cabins & Rates

Ship	Outside Cabins	w/Veranda	Rates	Inside Cabins	Rates
Celebration	443	none	$194*	290	$181*
Destiny	806	480	$238*	515	$211*
Ecstasy	620	54	$214*	400	$196*
Elation	618	54	$199–$224*	402	$180–$210*
Fantasy	620	54	$214*	400	$196*
Fascination	620	54	$199*	400	$180*
Holiday	447	10	$155–$215*	279	$146–$202*
Imagination	620	54	$199*	400	$180*
Inspiration	620	54	$199*	400	$180*
Jubilee	453	10	$156–$252*	290	$155–$230*
Paradise	618	54	$199–$224*	402	$180–$210*
Sensation	620	54	$199*	400	$180*
Tropicale	324	12	$166–$200*	187	$178*

**Average rates provided by the cruise line*

FLEET NOTES The *Celebration, Holiday, Tropicale,* and *Jubilee* are the older ships in the Carnival fleet. They aren't megaships, but they are roomy, with good-sized cabins. The *Holiday* and *Tropicale,* in particular, were trendsetters of their time.

The *Destiny* was, at least in her first year, the biggest ship in the world (Princess's *Grand Princess* of 1998 is even bigger), and she offers lots of the "wows" you would expect of a ship her size. She has two sibling *Destiny*-class vessels coming soon.

Carnival's *Fantasy*-class ships—the *Ecstasy, Fantasy, Fascination, Imagination, Inspiration,* and *Sensation* (and, new for 1998/99, the *Paradise* and *Elation*)—differ in their decor but not their size, use of space, or acres of teak decking or extravagance. (The exception is their cabins, which, while neat and tidy, are really nothing to write home about.) The best way to tell the ships apart is to consider their names, which more or less reflect their interior design.

A Date with *Destiny*

The *Carnival Destiny* was the first ship to reach the 100,000-ton mark, and it made the *Guinness Book of World Records* both as the largest cruise ship and as the ship that carried the most passengers on a single voyage—3,315 on the cruise that departed April 6, 1997.

The ship is taller than the Statue of Liberty, rising 207 feet above the water at its highest point, and stretches nearly 3 football fields from bow to stern. It cost $400 million to build.

Other cruise lines, including Royal Caribbean and Princess, were so awed by the *Destiny's* size—it's really more a whopper ship than mere megaliner—that they started building their own giant vessels.

Carnival, in turn, ordered up 2 more whoppers from the Fincantieri shipyard in Italy: *Destiny's* 100,000-ton sister ships *Triumph* and *Victory,* to be delivered in 1999 and 2000, respectively.

Lest you think that Carnival is going whole-hog into gigantism, the line also has a 2,100-passenger, 82,000-GRT vessel under construction for delivery in 2000. The vessel represents a new class for the line, and Carnival has options for 2 more vessels, to be delivered in 2001 and 2002.

Celebrity Cruises

5201 Blue Lagoon Dr., Miami, FL 33125. ☎ ***800/437-3111.***

Type of cruise: *Imported wine and cheese.*

Fran says: *Definitely the best in the mid-priced category; the Century-class ships especially are works of art.*

THE EXPERIENCE Celebrity has an impressive sense of style, pays careful attention to detail, and offers service that's really exceptional—formal yet friendly. Passengers, who range in age from twenty-something honeymooners to retirees, are downright pampered.

The Celebrity fleet is among the newest in the industry, and all the ships cut sleek figures. Painted in white and blue, each features a huge X on its smokestack, which is the Greek symbol for *ch,* as in *Chandris,* the shipping family who launched the line in 1990 (and who sold it to Royal Caribbean in 1997). Though at press time the line's sailings are restricted to the North American region, Celebrity expects to enter the European market in mid-1999 with one of its newer ships, most likely the *Century.*

Mercury *(Photo: Matt Hannafin)*

Renowned designers from both Europe and the U.S. worked on the interiors of the vessels, and it shows. The result is just the right amount of drama, without resorting to glitz. And the designers also managed to make the most of traditional nautical touches, like etched glass and lots of woodwork.

The ships offer plenty of cushy lounges, open decks, and windows (particularly valuable for sightseeing in Alaska). The newer ships also feature an impressive array of intimate public rooms that include cigar bars, champagne bars, and coffee bars (and, on the *Mercury,* a martini bar as well).

The *Century, Galaxy, and Mercury* each feature the AquaSpa, a water-centered spa that tops anything else offered in the industry in terms of both size and scope. Each has a large thalassotherapy pool where water jets hit different parts of your body as you relax in Japanese (on the *Century* and *Galaxy*) or Moorish (on the *Mercury*) splendor. In addition, a plethora of exotic spa treatments is available.

The cabins on Celebrity ships are all good-sized and well-organized—there's really no bad cabin—and provide plenty of storage space.

Entertainment is usually good and in some cases is extraordinary (like pianist Naki Ataman, who was featured recently aboard *Mercury* sailings). The ships' stage productions try to be more Broadway than Las Vegas.

The cuisine is extra-special and is meticulously guided by Michel Roux, Celebrity's famous culinary consultant and one of the top French chefs in Britain. Roux, who is on board to check things out several times a year, recently told a press group visiting the *Mercury* that "no frozen rotten pastry comes on board." *Fresh* is the word. In keeping with French tradition, the cuisine generally is not low-fat, although healthy alternatives are always available. The food offerings are plentiful and served with style.

SPECIAL FEATURES Complimentary butler service is offered to suite passengers. The penthouse suites on the *Century, Galaxy,* and *Mercury* are among the largest at sea. Prearranged spa packages are available. Celebrity has a special relationship with Sony that provides for a lot of whiz-bang, high-tech features.

SPECIAL DEALS Early-bird discounts, third/fourth passenger savings, children's fares, and single-parent discounts on some sailings.

Celebrity Fleet Specifications

Ship	Itinerary	Year Built	Passengers	Crew	Size	Length
Century	E./W. Car. (yr)	1995	1,750	853	70,606	807
Galaxy	Alaska (s) Car. (f/w/sp)	1996	1,870	909	77,713	858
Horizon	Bermuda (sp/s) Car. (f/w)	1990	1,354	645	46,811	682
Mercury	Alaska (s) W. Car. (f/w/sp)	1997	1,870	907	77,713	860
Zenith	Bermuda (s/f) Mexico (w/sp)	1992	1,374	645	47,225	682

Celebrity Cabins & Rates

Ship	Outside Cabins	w/Veranda	Rates	Inside Cabins	Rates
Century	569	61	$303–$389	304	$242–$282
Galaxy	639	220	$303–$389	296	$242–$282
Horizon	533	none	$278–$348	144	$234–$268
Mercury	639	220	$303–$417	296	$242–$282
Zenith	540	none	$327–$435	146	$270–$320

FLEET NOTES The *Horizon* and *Zenith* are great ships, but when Celebrity moved into the megaliner business it topped itself with the even more impressive *Century,* then topped itself again with the *Galaxy* and again with the *Mercury.* Plans have just been announced for the line's new millennium-class ships to be built in France, with two vessels slated for launch in 2000 and 2001. If the line's track record holds up, they should be lovely ships, indeed.

Celebrity: Cruise Ship or Art Gallery?

Art is an important aspect of the Celebrity experience. And each time the line has introduced a new ship, it has increased its art-acquisition budget. The collection on the *Mercury,* for example, cost a whopping $4 million and is ultra contemporary, including not only paintings by Sol LeWitt, Jasper Johns, and Robert Rauschenberg (to drop a few of the most recognizable names) but other objects d' art, such as video installations and works in silver.

Commodore Cruise Line

4000 Hollywood Blvd., South Tower, Suite 385, Hollywood, FL 33021.
☎ ***800/237-5361.***

Type of cruise: *Bread and water.*

Fran says: *For people who like to bargain hunt, this is a cruise line of choice.*

THE EXPERIENCE The line's only ship, the *Enchanted Isle,* offers low rates and a casual cruise experience, which are attractive to first-time cruisers and to loyal repeat customers as well.

Enchanted Isle *(Photo: Commodore Cruise Line)*

The vessel itself is old, a classic ocean liner that, despite frequent renovations, shows some signs of wear and lacks a lot of modern-ship amenities. But it's the staff's approach to service that makes sailing on the *Enchanted Isle* a warm and endearing experience. These people really want you to be happy, and they offer first-class service to make sure you are.

The line was one of the first to offer Caribbean cruises back in 1966, and the *Enchanted Isle* pioneered the concept of theme cruises, which the ship continues today with relish.

Activities on the *Enchanted Isle* include the ever-popular bingo and crazy pool games that involve finding out how many Ping-Pong balls your bathing suit will hold, or participating in a wet T-shirt shirt relay. Game shows like Liar's Club, Passenger Feud, and the Newlywed / Not-so-Newlywed Game are popular diversions.

The lively entertainment offerings include musical acts, Broadway-style revues, cabaret performers, and members of the Ray Kennedy dance troupe. Gentlemen dance hosts are available to dance with single women in the disco, which features Top 40 dance music and sometimes karaoke.

Food on the *Enchanted Isle* is American-style and has been uneven in the past, although it has recently been upgraded by a German-trained head chef who features lobster, fish, and steaks, as well as luscious desserts, in the ship's somewhat noisy restaurant.

A large majority of the line's passengers come from the South, and a good share are retirees, but there are younger folks as well. School vacations, in particular, draw lots of family business.

SPECIAL FEATURES Theme cruises for 1998 include Big Band, Irish, Singles, Ski (featuring celebrity downhill skiers), and Healthy Lifestyles. The line's mascot, a fuzzy bear known as Commodore Cudley, offers tuck-in service, and there are plans to offer Commodore Cudley logo items, including stuffed animals and T-shirts.

SPECIAL DEALS Early-booking deal of half off the second fare if the first person pays full fare. Third or fourth passengers pay $199 per cruise on selected trips. Some promotions include a complimentary overnight stay in New Orleans.

Commodore Fleet Specifications

Ship	Itinerary	Year	Passengers	Crew	Size	Length
Enchanted Isle	W. Car., Central Am. (yr)	1958	725	350	23,395	617

Commodore Cabins & Rates

Ship	Outside Cabins	w/Veranda	Rates	Inside Cabins	Rates
Enchanted Isle	289	2	$174–$251	72	$165–$235

FLEET NOTES Some of the *Enchanted Isle's* cabins are quite large and well suited to families, although the ship's smallest cabins are cramped and are only really suitable for those on very tight budgets. Nine suites were added in 1997, including two that are handicapped-accessible and two that offer private balconies.

Note: Just as this book was going to press, Commodore announced an addition to its fleet. From a home port in New Orleans, the *Enchanted Capri* offers 2- and 5-night cruises in the Caribbean, visiting Cancun and Cozumel on the latter itinerary.

Costa Cruise Lines

World Trade Center, 80 SW 8th St., Miami, FL 33130-3097. ☎ ***800/462-6782.***

Type of cruise: *Domestic to imported wine and cheese.*

Fran says: *Buongiorno to "Cruising Italian Style."*

THE EXPERIENCE The origins of this line (which date back to 1860 and the olive-oil business) are in Italy, and it shows in nearly everything Costa offers, from the great food, sleek Italian design, and Italian-speaking crew (although they're not all from Italy) to the mostly Italian entertainers and the onboard activities, which include festive Roman toga parties.

The line boasts one of the most modern and beautiful fleets in the Caribbean, its ships easily identifiable by their blue and yellow smokestacks emblazoned with a huge letter C. These are not ships designed strictly for an American audience, and therein lies the charm.

CostaVictoria *(Photo: Costa Cruise Lines)*

On a Costa ship, your room steward will likely greet you with *"Buongiorno!,"* and your waiter will encourage you to *"Mangia, mangia!"* If you don't know what these words mean, never fear: The line offers Italian language lessons along with lectures on Italian art and culture.

The Italian experience here is presented in casual elegance, with warm and humorous continental flair. Naturally, this means that Italian-Americans are heavily represented among the line's clientele, which represent a good age mix, averaging somewhere in the 45-to-50 range. Even if you're not of Italian heritage, though, after a short time on board, you'll feel like you're part of one big Italian family.

The food is flavorful and as plentiful as one would expect, and it's presented with theatrical flare. Each night has a theme, such as one night when staff members dress as gondoliers and present red roses to all the women. Alternative venues include pizza cafes and patisseries serving espresso, chocolates, and pastries.

There are well-developed activities programs for both kids and teens, and at least one full-time youth counselor is available aboard each ship, year-round.

SPECIAL FEATURES An onboard priest conducts masses most days in a chapel. Entertainment includes puppet and marionette shows, mimes, and acrobatics, presented in showrooms designed to be reminiscent of 18th-century opera houses. "Proud to be an Italian" key rings are for sale in the gift shops.

SPECIAL DEALS Third and fourth passengers sharing a cabin during the "value season" pay $195 to $295 for a 7-night cruise. Passengers 65 years or older who book 90 days before a sailing get a 5% discount. Special fares for children and single parents are offered on select sailings.

Costa Fleet Specifications

Ship	Itinerary	Year Built	Passengers	Crew	Size	Length
CostaRomantica	W./E. Car. (w)	1993	1,350	650	76,000	723
CostaVictoria	W./E. Car. (w)	1996	1,928	800	54,000	817

Costa Cabins & Rates

Ship	Outside Cabins	w/Veranda	Rates	Inside Cabins	Rates
CostaRomantica	446	10	$191**	208	$161**
CostaVictoria	573	0	$194**	391	$170**

***Includes port charges*

FLEET NOTES The *CostaRomantica* is a new upper-middleweight ship that emphasizes comfort. It has a contemporary look, complemented by traditional Italian arts and crafts. The *CostaVictoria* brought Costa into the megaship era. She is technologically advanced, sleek, and stylish, with spacious and dramatic interiors.

The line's *CostaClassica* and *CostaAllegra* sail in the Caribbean, too, but are marketed to Europeans. Costa plans to introduce a new 82,000-ton megaship in the year 2000, which is being built for $390 million by Kvaerner Masa-Yards in Finland. The ship is 6,000 GRTs larger than the *CostaVictoria* (the first megaship in the fleet) and will hold 2,100 passengers.

Crystal Cruises

2121 Ave. of the Stars, Suite 200, Los Angeles, CA. ☎ ***310/785-9300.***

Type of cruise: *Champagne and caviar.*

Fran says: *And the tony award goes to . . .*

THE EXPERIENCE With two ocean-liner–size luxury ships, the *Crystal Harmony* and *Crystal Symphony,* this line is redefining luxury cruising. The state-of-the-art ships were created for a discerning clientele, and every facet of their operation follows that same philosophy. Everything is first-class, and attention is paid to every detail.

Passengers, who tend to be middle-aged or older, pay a pretty steep price for the experience, but in return, they are treated to elegant and attentive service, outstanding gourmet food, luxurious accommodations, and the facilities of a large ship without the crowds of fellow passengers. The top-quality entertainment varies from classical recitals to Broadway-style revues actually worthy of Broadway, and the ships have among the best casinos afloat (they're operated by Caesars

Crystal Harmony *(Photo: Crystal Cruises)*

Palace), enhanced by the fact that gamblers are offered drinks for free. Fitness centers are spacious.

Many of the ships' plush cabins and enormous penthouse suites come with verandas, and they are all equipped with the latest and greatest in amenities, white-gloved butler service, and Jacuzzi tubs. Concierge service is available to all passengers, and there's a business center for vacationers who need to stay in touch with the outside world.

Public rooms feature a glamorous, modern design, and no expense is spared on the accouterments, such as fresh flowers, the very best linens, china, crystal, and silver.

The food is expertly prepared from the best ingredients, and in addition to the elegant dining room, there are two specialty restaurants for alternative dining (Japanese and Italian on the *Harmony,* Chinese and Italian on the *Symphony*). The wine cellar stocks some 25,000 bottles.

Onboard activities include golf and bridge clinics; wine tastings; and classes in needlepoint, calligraphy, computers, and ballroom dancing. And there's a fabulous lecture series that has featured such notables as Wolfgang Puck, Jacques Pepin, Pierre Salinger, Judith Krantz, and Casper Weinberger. Destination experts are also brought on board to talk about specific ports of call.

SPECIAL FEATURES Gentlemen hosts are available to entertain female passengers. Extensive business services. Martini bars. Specialty restaurants. Close-captioned TV for the hearing impaired.

SPECIAL DEALS Third passenger in cabin pays minimum fare for the cruise. Children under 12 pay half-price when traveling with 2 full-fare adults. Early booking and repeat-passenger discounts are available.

Crystal Fleet Specifications

Ship	Itinerary	Year Built	Passengers	Crew	Size	Length
Crystal Harmony	Alaska (s)	1990	940	545	49,400	791
Crystal Symphony	Mex. Riviera (f)	1995	940	545	51,000	791

Crystal Cabins & Rates

Ship	Outside Cabins	w/Veranda	Rates	Inside Cabins	Rates
Crystal Harmony	461	260	$438–$572*	19	$360*
Crystal Symphony	480	342	$496–$572*	none	N/A

**Average rates provided by the cruise line*

FLEET NOTES The two ships are virtual twins, with the primary difference being that the newer *Symphony* has no inside cabins. Public areas are slightly different as well, with a bit more interior public space on the *Harmony* and more exterior deck space on the *Symphony.*

Cunard

6100 Blue Lagoon Dr., Suite 400, Miami, FL 33126. ☎ ***800/5CUNARD.***

Type of cruise: *Imported wine and cheese to champagne and caviar.*

Fran says: Upstairs, Downstairs *meets the high seas. A spot of tea over here, please, Jeeves.*

THE EXPERIENCE Cunard, the grande dame of the cruise industry, comes with an impressive pedigree (the *Mauritania, Queen Mary, Queen Elizabeth,* etc.) and today has a fleet that runs the gamut from small, yacht-like ships to large, classic superliners operating at various levels of the luxury category. The atmosphere aboard the ships is both formal and traditional (royals have walked these decks). These are definitely not glitzy party ships.

QE2 *(Photo: Cunard Line)*

The line's flagship, the *QE2,* is the most famous ship in the world and the only ship today continuing the tradition of scheduled transatlantic service. She does so with an old-fashioned class system (in this case, four classes), meaning that you sleep and dine in decks assigned to your class. She's a venerable old ship, but thanks to several major facelifts (the biggest being a $45 million redo in 1995), she has a new, contemporary design.

Her siblings include the elegant *Royal Viking Sun* and the classic *Vistafjord.* These ships sail around the world, occasionally visiting North America, though usually as part of much longer voyages.

And then there are the *Sea Goddess I* and *Sea Goddess II.* These twin ships offer some of the most luxurious cruise experiences afloat, and clients pay big bucks for the experience. The *Sea Goddess I* spends several months a year in the Caribbean. The *Sea Goddess II* used to be in the Caribbean but has been moved to Asia for the winter season.

For their part, Cunard passengers can expect ever-so-polite service, delivered by very attentive white-gloved staff in a very tasteful if not dramatic setting. Passengers tend to be experienced travelers, older and cultured, and a lot have sailed with Cunard before. The British among them (and there are many) take high tea quite seriously (pinkies out, please). Among the line's other attributes, it is particularly "gay friendly" and often hosts large groups of gay travelers.

Food is high quality and in some cases excellent, presented with flawless service at single seatings. According to the *Sea Goddess* brochure, waiters will wade "through the shallows off a tropical beach to hand you a glass of champagne."

Guest lecturers—including noted chefs, wine connoisseurs, economic advisors, professors, authors, and local port authorities—are part of the activities offerings. Entertainment varies by ship: The *QE2* features big-name performers like Bill Cosby and Tommy Tune, but the tiny *Sea Goddesses* offer only very minimal nighttime activities.

In 1998, Cunard was able to turn a not-so-great financial situation around, and it's owner, Kvaerner, promptly agreed to sell the firm to Carnival Corporation for $500 million.

SPECIAL FEATURES The *Sea Goddess I* offers all-inclusive pricing, including tips and alcoholic drinks. Tipping is included on the *QE2*. The *QE2* offers an interesting array of theme cruises and is the only cruise ship with a full-time professional librarian.

SPECIAL DEALS Frequent-traveler program, like the airlines. Early-booking discounts of 20%.

Cunard Fleet Specifications

Ship	Itinerary	Year Built	Passengers	Crew	Size	Length
QE2	Transatlantic (sp/s/f)	1969	1,500	1,015	70,327	963
Sea Goddess I	Car. (w/sp)	1984	116	89	4,250	344

Cunard Cabins & Rates

Ship	Outside Cabins	w/Veranda	Rates	Inside Cabins	Rates
QE2	659	32	$580–$1,396**	251	$465–$521**
Sea Goddess I	58	none	$657–$985	none	N/A

** *Includes airfare*

FLEET NOTES The *Sea Goddess I* is a "Lifestyles of the Rich and Famous" ship, tops in service, cuisine, and amenities. She offers a small-ship experience that is probably not for those who get claustrophobic. The cabins are all outside suites but are not particularly large. The ship is not suitable for kids.

The *QE2* is a legendary ocean liner with a vast array of services and amenities. She calls herself a "City at Sea" for good reason.

Disney Cruise Line

210 Celebration Place, Suite 400, Celebration, FL 34747-1000.
☎ ***800/951-3232.***

Type of cruise: *Time will tell. (The ships weren't launched yet at press time.)*

Fran says: *A cruise even a mouse could love.*

THE EXPERIENCE While the first of the Disney ships, the *Disney Magic,* is not set to be launched until July 1998 (the twin ship *Disney Wonder* is due out soon thereafter), we've seen the plans and toured the *Magic* during its construction and expect both ships to be lavish and spectacular, delivered in that special Disney way.

Disney Magic *(Photo: Disney Cruise Line)*

Guests will experience the Disney touch from the moment they arrive at the line's private $24 million cruise terminal in Port Canaveral and will be sprinkled with pixie dust from a giant Sorcerer Mickey wand when they board the vessels.

The line will be family-oriented for sure, but there will also be places—including an adults-only restaurant, an adults-only pool area, and a lavish spa—where couples, including honeymooners, can get away from the crowds and experience romance.

The ships will not have casinos. They *will* have extraordinary entertainment offerings, including first-run films, an ESPN Skybox featuring nonstop sports action, and three all-new Disney musical productions complete with state-of-the-art staging, lighting, and special effects. An area of the ship known as *Beat Street* will offer adults a "nighttime entertainment district" with a rock club, an improvisational comedy club, and a piano lounge.

As with Disney's entertainment, the children's facilities are likely to be among the best afloat.

Disney is promoting the 3- or 4-day cruises as part of its 7-day vacation packages, combining them with a Walt Disney World land experience; the pricing is comparable to a week's vacation at the resort alone. The cruises can also be booked separately from the theme parks, but only as space allows (passengers booking packages get first dibs).

SPECIAL FEATURES Passengers dine in a different restaurant each night of their cruise, their waiter moving with them. All cruises spend a day at the beach at Castaway Cay, Disney's new private Bahamas island, which features its own pier for easy accessibility. Entertainment is provided in the special motor coaches used for ground transfers to and from Walt Disney World, Port Canaveral, and the airport. There's a single check-in for both land and sea accommodations.

SPECIAL DEALS Early-booking discounts range from $400 to $700 per cabin for a 7-day cruise-land vacation.

Disney Fleet Specifications

Ship	Itinerary	Year Built	Passengers	Crew	Size	Length
Disney Magic	Bahamas (yr)	1997/98	1,760	964	85,000	964
Disney Wonder	Bahamas (yr)	1997/98	1,760	964	85,000	964

Disney Cabins & Rates

Ship	Outside Cabins	w/Veranda	Rates	Inside Cabins	Rates
Disney Magic	638	384	$320*	237	$224*
Disney Wonder	638	384	$320*	237	$224*

**Average rates provided by the cruise line*

FLEET NOTES The two Disney ships are nearly identical. Both pay tribute to the classic ocean liners with their deep blue hulls and twin smokestacks, while their inside decor is modern and, well, Disneyesque.

Cabins are bigger than standard, 82 suites are specifically designed for families, and 14 cabins are wheelchair accessible.

Holland America Line–Westours

300 Elliot Ave. W., Seattle, WA 98119. ☎ ***800/426-0327.***

Type of cruise: *Domestic wine and cheese.*

Fran says: *Holland America Line marked 125 years in the business in 1998, and the experience shows, although on some sailings the clientele looks like it might have been around since the early days.*

THE EXPERIENCE HAL's fleet is made up of modern ships with neither nautical history nor the line's Dutch heritage forgotten. In the public rooms, you'll find nautical memorabilia, remembering the earlier HAL ships that carried the name *Rotterdam,* for example, or the earlier *Statendam,* which was sunk by a German U-boat. History is still being created by the line, with Princess Margaret of the Netherlands herself flying to Miami in 1998 to launch the *Rotterdam VI.*

The Holland America ships are clean and lean, not overly glitzy, and impeccably maintained. Cruising on HAL ships is a fairly low-key experience, restful rather than boisterous, with not much late-night carousing. The crowds

Ryndam *(Photo: Holland America Line)*

tend to be more mature—the kind who would appreciate an old-fashioned cruising experience, friendly service, and a consistent and well-priced product.

The line has made an effort of late to attract families, creating a well-planned kids' program known as Club Hal, and additions such as sports bars and more adventure-type shore excursions are geared toward attracting a younger, more active set.

In 1998, HAL introduced its own Bahamas island, the 2,400-acre Half Moon Cay (formerly, Little San Salvador), where it has spent $16 million (including $6 million to purchase the uninhabited island) to create a facility with a white-sand beach, a Spanish fort–style welcome center, a coral reef for snorkeling, a food pavilion, a watersports center, and various shopping venues.

Food on HAL ships is international, with the dining room offering traditional favorites as well as light and healthy cuisine and pasta selections, and a children's menu. The Dutch influence shines in the special Chocolate Extravaganza Late Show midnight buffet. Room service is offered on a 24-hour basis.

The cabaret shows feature lasers and fancy costumes. Activities are plentiful and on a given sailing might include seminars, dance lessons, food demonstrations, bingo, deck games, and galley tours, as well as nighttime Country Western and Fabulous '50s parties.

SPECIAL FEATURES The line has a no-tipping policy, meaning that tips aren't required, but they are graciously accepted. All HAL ships have self-service Laundromats. Each passenger gets a free logo tote bag. Gentlemen hosts are brought on sailings of 14 days or more. The line's Passport to Fitness program offers prizes to passengers who participate in sports and fitness activities. The line was one of the pioneers of Alaska cruising and has developed the state's most extensive land-tour operation (Westours).

SPECIAL DEALS Early-booking discounts of up to 40%, low third- or fourth-passenger fares, flat-rate children's fares, special past-passenger offers, and last-minute deals are available.

Holland America Fleet Specifications

Ship	Itinerary	Year Built	Passengers	Crew	Size	Length
Maasdam	Alaska (s) Panama (f/w/sp)	1993	1,266	602	55,000	720
Nieuw Amsterdam	Alaska (s) Car. (w) Panama (sp)	1984	1,214	566	33,930	704
Noordam	Alaska (s) Panama (f/w/sp)	1983	1,214	566	33,930	704
Rotterdam VI	S. Car. (w)	1997	1,316	658	62,000	780
Ryndam	Alaska (s) S. Car. (f/w) Panama (sp)	1994	1,266	602	55,000	720
Statendam	Alaska (s) Hawaii (f) E. Car., Panama (w)	1993	1,266	602	55,000	720
Veendam	NE/Canada (s/f) Car. (f/w/sp)	1996	1,266	602	55,000	720
Westerdam	Alaska (s) E. Car. (f/w/sp)	1986	1,494	615	53,872	798

Holland America Cabins & Rates

Ship	Outside Cabins	w/Veranda	Rates	Inside Cabins	Rates
Maasdam	485	149	$349–$497	148	$321–$402
Nieuw Amsterdam	411	none	$179–$297	194	$149–$224
Noordam	411	none	$206–$311	194	$178–$242
Rotterdam VI	541	160	$238–$373	117	$203–$262
Ryndam	485	149	$245–$380	148	$210–$269
Statendam	485	149	$265–$400	148	$230–$289
Veendam	485	149	$221–$352	148	$192–$257
Westerdam	495	none	$178–$289	252	$149–$212

FLEET NOTES The *Noordam* and *Nieuw Amsterdam* are older, French-built vessels that offer a classic ocean-liner experience, complete with extra-wide halls and large teak promenades. The German-built *Westerdam* has a similar layout but is longer and not as tall (at nine decks) as her counterparts and carries more passengers.

The *Statendam, Maasdam, Ryndam,* and *Veendam* are all of the same design, built by the Fincantieri shipyard in Italy. These newer ships feature soaring atriums and wonderful viewing lounges. The *Rotterdam VI,* also built at Fincantieri, adds to the fleet a bigger vessel that sets new standards for ship design (see the sidebar), but the basic layout of its public rooms is similar to that on the *Statendam* and its sister series of ships.

Two additional ships, the *Volendam* and the *Zaandam,* are under construction in Italy and scheduled for delivery in 1999. Also, a $300 million, 1,380-passenger sister ship for the new *Rotterdam VI* has been ordered and is due to appear in the fall of 2000.

The *Rotterdam VI*

The new flagship of the HAL fleet is as trend-setting as was its predecessor, the *Rotterdam V,* back in 1959. The cruise ship made its debut in late 1997 as the fastest cruise ship afloat, with a cruising speed of 25 knots—important because it will permit the ship to make more and longer port calls on its Grand World Voyages, rather than spending all its time just getting from place to place.

The *Rotterdam VI* has several features that set it apart from the pack, including a first-of-its-kind floor of suites with private concierge service. Guests on the Navigation Deck can settle accounts, book shore excursions, and make other requests at the special concierge desk, and also relax in a private lounge.

Norwegian Cruise Line

7665 Corporate Center Dr., Miami, FL 33126. ☎ ***800/327-7030.***

Type of cruise: *Beer and pretzels/domestic wine and cheese.*

Fran says: *You'll always have something to do on an NCL ship.*

Norway *(Photo: Norwegian Cruise Line)*

THE EXPERIENCE The NCL fleet is varied, ranging from small ships (20,000 tons) to the flagship *Norway,* a classic ocean liner that's basically a floating city.

Norwegian Cruise Line excels at activities and theme cruises, and entertainment is first-rate, including full-scale Broadway musical productions and name-brand performers like Tanya Tucker. Recreational and fitness programs are among the best in the industry (the *Norway,* for one, has some 75 daily activities), as are the kids' programs, which include a Circus at Sea, where kids learn circus acts for a performance for their parents.

The onboard atmosphere is informal and upbeat, with passengers tending to be in the 25-to-49 age range and including a good share of families.

Food is generous in portions but not one of the line's strong points. In addition to the dining room, all the ships have a Le Bistro alternative venue serving Italian food. Most of the ships have ice cream parlors, and some offer chocoholic bars.

SPECIAL FEATURES At least half the cabins are nonsmoking. Scuba programs are offered. Major weekend sports games are broadcast into passengers' cabins and at the sports bars. Theme cruises are frequent and varied, including a good number of music and sports offerings. The line has its own Bahamas island, Great Stirrup Cay.

SPECIAL DEALS NCL reduces rates as needed to fill cabins. The line offers value-season rates and also sometimes offers two-for-one rates and reduced rates for third and fourth passengers in a cabin.

Norwegian Past, Norwegian Future

Norwegian is definitely a cruise company in transition. More financially healthy than in the past, the company, which has been around more or less since 1966, is in the process of growing and radically updating its fleet. Growing pains have included the fact that NCL was the only cruise line I know of to make *Hard Copy* in 1997, after passengers sued, claiming that there were air-conditioning problems on the *Norwegian Star.*

The fleet was increased by 3½ ships in 1997 (one is a partially completed hull). Two ships, the *Norwegian Dream* and *Norwegian Wind,* were stretched by sawing them in half and inserting a new 130-foot midsection into each, adding more public space and passenger capacity. And NCL officials recently unveiled plans to build 4 new 76,000-GRT ships early in the next century.

NCL has recently begun marketing its personal service, its Norwegian heritage (adding the Norwegian name to nearly all its ships), and the fact that its ships are not megaships. And the line has been diversifying its itinerary offerings to include Europe, Hawaii, and South America.

FLEET NOTES The *Norwegian Dream* and *Norwegian Wind* are twin ships that will show off their new midsections in 1998. The *Leeward* is a small ship with contemporary appeal, but it can seem rather crowded. The *Norway,* at the other end of the spectrum, is a floating city, stretching the length of 3½ football fields.

The *Norwegian Crown* offers style and grace, with its art deco features, and is the glamour-puss of the fleet. The *Norwegian Majesty* is a stylish, contemporary, midsized ship; and the *Norwegian Dynasty* is a stylish, contemporary, small ship. Both were acquired last year from Majesty Cruise Line.

Norwegian Fleet Specifications

Ship	Itinerary	Year Built	Passengers	Crew	Size	Length
Leeward	Bahamas, W. Car. (yr)	1992	950	400	25,000	524
Norway	E. Car. (f/w)	1962	2,032	920	76,049	1,035
Norwegian Crown	Bermuda (sp/s) NE/Canada (f)	1988	1,050	470	34,250	614
Norwegian Dream	S. Car. (w)	1992	1,726	863	46,000	754
Norwegian Dynasty	Hawaii (sp, f) Alaska (s)	1993	800	320	20,000	537
Norwegian Majesty	Bermuda (sp/s) Bahamas & W. Car. (f/w)	1992	1,056	438	32,400	568
Norwegian Sea	S. Car. (until 10/98) W. Car. (after 10/98)	1988	1,504	630	42,000	700
Norwegian Star	W. Car. (until 10/98)	1973	800	424	28,000	676
Norwegian Wind	Alaska (s) Car. (f/w)	1993	1,726	863	46,000	754

Norwegian Cabins & Rates

Ship	Outside Cabins	w/Veranda	Rates	Inside Cabins	Rates
Leeward	217	8	$147*	258	$130*
Norway	656	none	$147*	360	$121*
Norwegian Crown	342	16	$176*	184	$148*
Norwegian Dream	693	48	$166*	170	$142*
Norwegian Dynasty	276	10	$182*	124	$132*
Norwegian Majesty	343	none	$124*	185	$104*
Norwegian Sea	486	none	$168*	281	$140*
Norwegian Star	361	9	$157*	63	$125*
Norwegian Wind	693	48	$166*	170	$142*

**Average rates provided by the cruise line*

The *Norwegian Star* is the oldest ship in the fleet, and will only be remaining on its Caribbean routes out of Houston until October 1998, after which is sails for Australia to be used in the new Norwegian Capricorn Line, a joint venture between NCL and Australian partners, running cruises around Australia and New Zealand. Taking over its itineraries after October will be the *Norwegian Sea,* which carries twice as many passengers and, while not a glitzy ship, has its loyal followers. The *Norwegian Sea's* Southern Caribbean itineraries may be picked up in 1999 with another NCL ship, but nothing had been decided at press time.

Also in 1997, Norwegian acquired the 1,200-passenger *Aida,* a ship that will operate initially on a charter basis but might eventually end up in the Caribbean. The company has also announced plans for the *Norwegian Sky,* a new 2,000-passenger ship to be launched in August 1999. It's being built using a partially completed hull originally constructed for Costa.

Premier Cruises

901 S. America Way, Miami, FL 33132. ☎ ***800/373-2654.***

Type of cruise: *Beer and pretzels (but might be upgrading).*

Fran says: *New line, old ships.*

THE EXPERIENCE Premier Cruises is a brand-new cruise line, formed in 1997 to combine the Dolphin, Seawind, and Premier brands. The latter is famous for the *Oceanic,* known as (and now officially called) *The Big Red Boat,* which pioneered cruises from Port Canaveral combined with visits to Orlando's theme parks.

All six ships in the fleet are classic vessels that have gone through numerous renovations and now sport modern, comfortable interiors. In the past, Premier has offered budget cruises, but its intention is to move up a notch into the value-pricing category.

IslandBreeze *(Photo: Premier Cruises)*

The ships have all been painted in new colors, sporting classic nautical dark blue and white and a Premier Cruises logo. *The Big Red Boat* was left red, however, though its redness is now of a slightly darker and more dignified shade.

Premier is stressing the fact that its ships are not megaships. While some call them "old," Premier likes to call them "nostalgic," saying they should catch on in popularity for their classic nautical appeal. One benefit of the ships' age, for example, is that they all feature wide, teakwood decks. On the other hand, a downside is that the cabins tend to be on the small side.

The cruise line wants its ships to be recognized as elegant and intimate. In the past, they've been more run-of-the-mill and crowded, so it remains to be seen whether the line can accomplish the change.

As part of its upgrading efforts, the line is focusing new attention in two major areas—food and entertainment—and also on personalized service, as exemplified by its marketing-campaign slogan, "You've got our attention."

Premier tends to attract a more international crowd than some other lines, with passengers ranging in age from twenty-somethings to retirees, and including a good number of families.

In 1997, the line purchased the classic *Rotterdam V* from Holland America (not to be confused with that line's new flagship *Rotterdam VI*). She was renamed *Rembrandt* and, at least in her first year with Premier, will sail on South American charters in the winter and in the Mediterranean in the summer.

SPECIAL FEATURES Looney Tune characters like Bugs Bunny and Porky Pig appear on *The Big Red Boat, OceanBreeze,* and *SeaBreeze*. Fleet-wide, a scuba diving program run by the Professional Association of Diving Instructors (PADI) is offered. Cruise and land vacations are offered, pairing sailings with Orlando-area theme parks and island hotels.

Premier Fleet Specifications

Ship	Itinerary	Year Built	Passengers	Crew	Size	Length
The Big Red Boat (Oceanic)	Bahamas (yr)	1965	1,132	565	38,772	782
IslandBreeze	Car. (w/sp)	1961	1,146	612	31,793	760
OceanBreeze	Panama, Car., Central Am.	1955	776	310	21,486	603
SeaBreeze	Car. (w/sp) NE/Canada (s/f)	1958	846	400	21,900	606
Seawind Crown	Car. (yr)	1961	768	362	24,000	641

Premier Cabins & Rates

Ship	Outside Cabins	w/Veranda	Rates	Inside Cabins	Rates
The Big Red Boat (Oceanic)	246	8	$236–$249	358	$142–$216
IslandBreeze	272	10	$214–$242	236	$171–$199
OceanBreeze	241	none	$214–$242	150	$171–$199
SeaBreeze	247	none	$185–$242	174	$171–$199
Seawind Crown	266	2	$214–$242	101	$171–$199

SPECIAL DEALS Premier offers some free shore excursions and other free amenities (such as Champagne) in certain suites when those suites are booked at the brochure rates. Other offers include "Kids Vacation Free" promotions and standard third- and fourth-passenger rates.

FLEET NOTES The *OceanBreeze* used to be *The Southern Cross* and was christened by Her Majesty Queen Elizabeth II. The ship has an innovative design that includes the placement of her funnel and engines near the stern. It also has one of the best kids' program at sea, and consequently, she's a ship on which kids are commonly both seen and heard.

The *SeaBreeze* was built in 1958 as the *Federico C.* by Costa and has the classic lines of an ocean liner. The *IslandBreeze* is the largest ship in the fleet at 38,000 tons. She once operated as the *Festivale* for Carnival.

The *Seawind Crown* was formerly a popular cruise ship in Portugal. Her special attributes include a 208-seat movie theater that shows European and American films, and suites that offer a whopping 500 square feet of space.

Princess Cruises

10100 Santa Monica Blvd., Suite 1800, Los Angeles, CA 90067.
☎ ***800/421-0522.***

Type of cruise: *Domestic wine and cheese.*

Fran says: *The Love Boat might not provide love, but it will provide lovely times.*

THE EXPERIENCE Captain Stubing might not be working for this line in real life, but chances are if you're on a Princess ship, you'll find a charming captain. And though the bartender might not jump over the bar like Issac, he or she probably will be able to produce whatever concoction you fancy. And you'll no doubt find a smiling and charming cruise director, too, although her name won't necessarily be Julie McCoy (and, in fact, she might be a he).

Sun Princess *(Photo: Princess Cruises)*

The real-life cruise line that introduced many of us to the romantic side of life at sea by serving as a floating set for *The Love Boat* TV series is, in reality, one of the largest and best-run cruise lines in the world. Both dynamic and diverse, the company is able to please a wide variety of passengers. And, with its collection of new grand-class megaships introduced with the *Sun Princess* in 1995, Princess has moved to the top of the industry in terms of offering passengers choices and options in accommodations, dining, and entertainment.

The *Grand Princess,* which debuts this spring as the largest ship afloat, offers 710 cabins with verandas—more than any other vessel. The giant ship also offers three show lounges with different after-dinner entertainment, three dining rooms, an alternative Mexican restaurant, and other dining venues, such as bistros and pizzerias.

Even though its megaships offer megaresort facilities, Princess still also manages to offer on the vessels the kind of intimate spaces, including plush, quiet bars, that you can find on smaller vessels. To get the intimate feel in the dining rooms on the *Dawn Princess, Sun Princess,* and soon-to-be-introduced *Sea Princess* and *Ocean Princess* (due in 1999), the line created two separate dining rooms, identical in every way, thus avoiding the giant spaces found on some other ships.

The decor on Princess ships tends to be stylish and moderately upscale, but presented in a conservative way (without the glitz).

Entertainment has been given increasing attention, with the line's elaborate stage shows including amazing circus and mime performers from Asia and Eastern Europe. Casinos and discos are popular venues on Princess ships.

Food has been upgraded, and while it does not match the level offered by Celebrity, it's still above mass-market lines such as Royal Caribbean and Carnival. The pizza served at the ships' pizzerias is exceptionally good. Dollops of caviar appear at the captains' parties, and the wine cellar on each ship stocks at least 10,000 bottles.

Service on Princess ships is gracious and relaxed. Cabins are spacious, especially on the newer ships, and offer niceties that include terry cloth bathrobes, fruit baskets, and chocolates on the pillow at night.

Activities on Princess ships include sports contests, paddle tennis, virtual-reality golf, bingo, horseracing (though with real horses, of course—see chapter 17 for an explanation), dance classes, cooking classes, lectures, bridge tournaments, and audience-participation shows and contests, and all the ships have good libraries.

Passengers are a varied group and include couples, honeymooners, and singles. Singles should note, however, that despite the Love Boat image, these are hardly swingers' cruises. Passengers tend to average around age 50 but might be younger on Caribbean sailings than on, say, Alaska sailings. Some of the line's ships, and particularly those on Caribbean itineraries, attract more kids than others (several have special facilities for both kids and teens). Babies under 12 months old are not allowed on board.

Princess ships are showcases for impressive art collections that include works by David Hockney, Helen Frankenthaler, Frank Stella, Andy Warhol, and Robert Motherwell. And the ships tend to be decorated with lots of foliage.

Princess's well-organized shore excursions are among the best in the industry and offer great variety. The line is a major player in the Alaska market, offering cruise-tours that combine land tours with a cruise in the Inside Passage. The line owns its own sightseeing train and Alaska hotels, including the Mt. McKinley Princess Lodge.

On its Caribbean cruises, the line stops at its own private island, Princess Cay, off the southwestern coast of Eleuthera in The Bahamas, where passengers can enjoy fun in the sun, beach picnics, and watersports activities.

SPECIAL FEATURES Princess helps passengers pay for their cruise through its own Love Boat Loan program (see the "Buying on Time" feature in chapter 2). Spa packages are available, and a PADI scuba-certification program is offered on several of the megaships. The line has an incentive fitness program that offers freebies for participants. The newer ships have business centers with computers and fax machines (although they're open during limited hours only). Smoking is banned in the main dining and show areas of all ships.

SPECIAL DEALS Children pay 50% of the minimum rate if they share a room with two parents or guardians. Discounts of 25% to 50% are offered for early bookings.

Princess Fleet Specifications

Ship	Itinerary	Year Built	Passengers	Crew	Size	Length
Crown Princess	Alaska (s) Mex. Riviera (f/w)	1990	1,590	696	70,000	811
Dawn Princess	Alaska (s) S. Car. (w)	1997	1,950	900	77,000	856
Grand Princess	E. Car. (f/w)	1998	2,600	1,150	109,000	935
Island Princess	Alaska (s)	1971	640	350	20,000	550
Regal Princess	Alaska (s)	1991	1,590	696	70,000	811
Royal Princess	Alaska (s) Panama (f/w)	1984	1,200	520	45,000	757
Sea Princess	W. Car. (f/w)	1998	1,950	900	77,000	856
Sky Princess	Alaska (s)	1984	1,200	535	46,000	789
Sun Princess	Alaska (s) Mex. Riviera (f/w)	1995	1,950	900	77,000	856

Princess Cabins & Rates

Ship	Outside Cabins	w/Veranda	Rates	Inside Cabins	Rates
Crown Princess	614	184	$219*	181	$153*
Dawn Princess	603	411	$206*	372	$143*
Grand Princess	928	710	$215*	372	$165*
Island Princess	238	none	$266*	67	$156*
Regal Princess	614	184	$290*	181	$146*
Royal Princess	600	151	$336*	none	$261*
Sea Princess	630	411	$198*	372	$140*
Sky Princess	383	10	$243*	217	$164*
Sun Princess	603	411	$204*	372	$133*

**Average rates provided by the cruise line*

FLEET NOTES The *Sun Princess, Dawn Princess, Grand Princess,* and *Sea Princess* and *Ocean Princess* (due in 1999) are all grand-class megaships, cutting-edge vessels that provide the latest and greatest. The *Grand Princess* is the biggest grand-class ship. And Princess has announced that it will build two more of the whopper ships for debut in 2001.

The *Crown Princess* and *Regal Princess* are modern and dramatic ships, both designed by Renzo Piano, the same architect who did the Pompidou Center in Paris.

The *Royal Princess,* christened by Princess Diana, was the most expensive cruise ship ever built when she was launched (she cost $200 million) and introduced innovations like the fact that all her cabins are outside, offering views either from picture windows or verandas.

The *Sky Princess* is an older ship, with a comfortable, contemporary feel, while the smaller *Island Princess* and *Pacific Princess* (which sails in Europe and Africa) are the real vessels seen in *The Love Boat* TV show. The *Island* and *Pacific* are both classic-looking ships with the traditional wood and brass you'd expect. Cabins are on the small side, though, and none have verandas.

First *The Love Boat,* Now This . . .

The hit TV show *Baywatch* made the *Dawn Princess* its floating set for its special 200th episode, "Baywatch: White Thunder at Glacier Bay," filming the show on board an Inside Passage sailing in Alaska.

Princess provided the following facts about the filming:

- Gena Lee Nolin's (Neeley) real-life baby boy, Spencer, had a role as her on-screen baby girl, Ashley, in the show's wedding scene. For other scenes, a "stunt doll" baby was used as a double.
- For the shoot, *Baywatch* brought aboard 106 cast and crew members, 40 boxes of wardrobe (including clothes, wigs, and makeup), and about 7,091 pounds of equipment.
- The episode was originally going to be 2 hours, but *Baywatch* got so much "great" footage on board the ship and in Alaska that it was extended to 3 hours.
- While on board, star David Hasselhoff (Mitch) also filmed a couple of sequences for upcoming music videos.
- The original script was completely rewritten during the cruise.
- Each year, *Baywatch* goes through 306 pounds of body makeup and one 50-gallon drum of sunscreen.
- Several of the ship's staff had cameo roles, and cruise director Billy Hygate had a speaking part, performing the marriage ceremony for Mitch and Neeley.

Radisson Seven Seas Cruises

600 Corporate Dr., Suite 410, Fort Lauderdale, FL 33334. ☎ ***800/477-7500.***

Type of cruise: *Champagne and caviar.*

Fran says: *The kind of ships on which an executive can kick back and enjoy the best in food and service.*

THE EXPERIENCE Radisson Hotels Worldwide decided to translate its hospitality experience to the cruise industry in 1992, offering to manage and market upscale ships for its international owners. Today, the Radisson fleet includes the *Song of Flower, Hanseatic, Radisson Diamond,* and *Paul Gauguin.* A new, 490-passenger vessel (unnamed at press time) will be introduced in 1999, and will initially sail in the Mediterranean.

Radisson Diamond *(Photo: Radisson Seven Seas)*

All the ships offer itineraries geared toward affluent travelers to locations such as Europe, South America, Antarctica, and Tahiti. Only the *Radisson Diamond* visits the shores of North America.

The *Radisson Diamond* is to the cruise industry what the DeLorean was to the car industry, sporting one seriously unusual design concept: Essentially, the $125 million vessel is a giant catamaran, sporting twin hulls atop which sit the passenger areas, a design that makes for a very wide ship and, consequently, for extraordinary stability. Only 420 feet long, she is nonetheless only 2 feet thinner (at 102 feet) than the *QE2* (which is 963 feet long). From the shore, people look at the *Radisson Diamond* and scratch their heads in wonder.

Inside, thanks to her design, the *Diamond* is roomy and probably the most stable ship afloat (she's a good choice for those fearing seasickness). One downside of the design, however, is that she's very slow (usually not exceeding 12.5 knots). Another is that she has no wraparound promenade.

But these are minor details. What's more important to her passengers, many of whom are repeat guests, is that the *Radisson Diamond* offers the very finest in service, amenities, and cuisine. She's at the top of the list for the industry in all three.

The ship is popular with the country-club set, and most of her passengers are over age 50. She is also popular with corporate groups and sometimes is chartered in her entirety for company-meeting and incentive trips.

The *Diamond's* first-class cuisine would gain the highest marks even if it were on land, and it is served by professional waiters in the ship's Grand Dining Room and in the smaller alternative restaurant, The Grill. Seating in the dining rooms is on an open basis, so you choose who you want to dine with, instead of sitting according to a prearranged plan.

The line assumes most of its passengers want to entertain themselves, so organized activities are limited, but they do include lectures by well-known authors, movie producers, and oceanographers, among others. There are also card and board games, shuffleboard, and dance lessons.

The ship has a small pool, a jogging track, and a health club and spa. Daily yoga and aerobics classes and steam rooms and massages are among the offerings. A floating marina is lowered from the hull at various ports of call, offering a platform for watersports including sailing, windsurfing, and water-skiing.

SPECIAL FEATURES The line has a no-tipping policy. A headliner entertainer (usually a soloist or comedian) is brought aboard for each sailing; there are also dancers, a five-piece band, and a resident quartet. Shore excursions tend to be more creative than usual and might include a chance to race on an America's Cup sailboat. Price quotes for the line always include airfares.

SPECIAL DEALS The line offers value-added perks, such as half-off companion fares or free nights at a deluxe hotel.

Radisson Seven Seas Fleet Specifications

Ship	Itinerary	Year Built	Passengers	Crew	Size	Length
Radisson Diamond	Car. & Central Am. (w)	1992	354	192	20,295	420

Radisson Seven Seas Cabins & Rates

Ship	Outside Cabins	w/Veranda	Rates	Inside Cabins	Rates
Radisson Diamond	177	123	$400–$550*/**	none	N/A

* *Average rates provided by the cruise line*

** *Includes airfare from East Coast*

FLEET NOTES The *Radisson Diamond's* cabins are all large and luxurious suites, and there are two VIP master suites that are even bigger and more luxurious. All the suites are outside, 121 offering balconies and 53 offering bay windows.

Regal Cruises

4199 34th St. S., St. Petersburg, FL 33711. ☎ ***800/270-SAIL.***

Type of cruise: *Bread and water.*

Fran says: *Attention Kmart shoppers!*

THE EXPERIENCE Price is what attracts passengers to Regal Cruises' only ship, the *Regal Empress,* which represents the bargain basement of the cruise industry and is a classic example of the adage "You get what you pay for." Passengers who come with lower expectations, and realize that her pricing is realistic, will be the most happy.

The line is owned by investors, including Fred Kassner, president of Gogo Worldwide Vacation, who bought the former *Caribe I* from Commodore Cruise Line in 1993. After a few start-up problems, including a fire and failure to pass a couple of sanitation inspections, the line seemed to have put its problems behind it, but in 1997 the *Regal Empress* was in the news again when it had a minor confrontation with a pier in St. Andrews, New Brunswick, Canada. The incident left the ship with a big gash in her bow, bruised but still seaworthy.

Regal Empress *(Photo: Regal Cruises)*

At the end of 1997, the *Regal Empress* underwent a much-needed $6 million overhaul, which included the creation of a casual buffet setup, the addition of suites with verandas, and updates to meet *Safety of Life at Sea* (SOLAS) standards. (See chapter 1, "Be the First One on Your Block," for a discussion of SOLAS.)

The *Regal Empress's* itineraries are ambitious and unusual, ranging from 2-day party cruises from New York to 2-month cruises to South America. In 1997, the ship visited 18 countries and 41 ports of call.

The *Regal Empress* is a small old ship, without a lot of glamour, but she was built during a Golden Age of shipbuilding, and to the delight of nautical buffs still retains vestiges of that time, including etched-glass mirrors in the Caribbean Dining Room and Mermaid Lounge, sunken seating areas in the Commodore Club, art deco light fixtures, and other flourishes here and there. Her wood-paneled library is one of the prettiest at sea. All that aside, though, her standard cabins are small and dull (her suites are a decent size), and there's not much that's luxurious about her public rooms, either.

The ship has a good number of loyal followers and attracts passengers of various ages, with party-hearty types tending to fill her shorter cruises and older passengers signing on for her longer voyages.

The staff tries hard, but they don't always get things right, and they will openly tell passengers they are underpaid (a big no-no for most lines).

Food is better than might be expected, with dinners including pasta, vegetarian options, and healthy selections. Deviations from the menu, such as a request to leave off a sauce, are discouraged. Passengers dress up only slightly for dinner, with party attire (as opposed to black tie) appropriate for formal nights.

Daytime activities tend toward bingo, games, and movies, and there are special children's offerings. The quality of the show productions varies, but some are quite good. The dancers double as the ship's fitness instructors.

SPECIAL FEATURES Enclosed Promenade Deck, Ping-Pong table, video games, and Coke and candy machines. The *Regal Empress* is the only cruise ship sailing out of Port Manatee, Florida.

Regal Cruises Fleet Specifications

Ship	Itinerary	Year Built	Passengers	Crew	Size	Length
Regal Empress	Car. (w/sp) NE/Canada, Bermuda (s/f)	1953	925	396	21,909	612

Regal Cruises Cabins & Rates

Ship	Outside Cabins	w/Veranda	Rates	Inside Cabins	Rates
Regal Empress	234	6	$119–$249	221	$109–$169

SPECIAL DEALS Special rates are available for third-, fourth-, and fifth-passengers sharing a cabin with two full-fare passengers. Special standby rates and upgrades for passengers booking early are also offered.

FLEET NOTES The *Regal Empress's* mini-suites are much less cramped than her standard cabins. She also offers six larger suites with private verandas and two suites with private Jacuzzis.

Royal Caribbean International

1050 Caribbean Way, Miami, FL 33132. ☎ ***800/ALL-HERE.***

Type of cruise: *Domestic wine and cheese.*

Fran says: *Proof that big can be beautiful.*

THE EXPERIENCE What kind of cruise line would put a skating rink (complete with Zamboni machine) on a cruise ship? Royal Caribbean, that's who. This mega–cruise line (it's number 2 only to Carnival) is currently building what will become the 3 largest ships afloat, each weighing in at 136,000 GRTs and carrying more than 3,000 passengers. The temporarily named *Eagle I, Eagle II,* and *Eagle III* (to be named soon and launched in 1999, 2000, and 2002, respectively) will offer more bells, whistles, and innovations than some cruise lines have in their entire fleet (see the feature box for some details).

Despite their enormous size, the ships will no doubt be packed—after all, Royal Caribbean has made few missteps in its rise to the top of the industry. But just to make sure, parent company Royal Caribbean Cruises Ltd. spent a whopping $5 million to sponsor the half-time show of Super Bowl XXXII, which had some 1 billion viewers (or, as the line sees it, potential customers). Ads touted, among other things, the fact that Royal Caribbean and Celebrity

Cruises are now sister brands. (RCCL acquired Celebrity in 1997 in a deal worth $1.3 billion.)

The introduction of the Eagle skating rinks is not the first time Royal Caribbean has proved itself an industry trendsetter. The line introduced the generation of megaships with its *Sovereign of the Seas* in 1988. The ship was the largest passenger vessel built in the previous 50 years, but size aside, *Sovereign of the Seas* had design features that have become industry standards, including a multistory center atrium.

Rhapsody of the Seas *(Photo: RCCL)*

Royal Caribbean sells a cruise experience that's reasonably priced, mass-market oriented, and set mostly aboard megaships. There are enough activities to please almost everyone, except maybe those who hate crowds. The ships are all well-run and the product consistent, with a veritable army of service employees paying close attention to day-to-day details.

The contemporary decor on Royal Caribbean vessels doesn't bang you on the head with glitz like, say, top competitor Carnival. Rather, it's more subdued, with lots of glass, greenery, and art throughout, creating an image that's classy and witty. Its ships have outstanding public rooms and areas, including elaborate health clubs, spas, large swimming pools, and open sundeck areas. Each also features the line's trademark Viking Crown Lounge, an observation area located in a circular glass structure on the upper deck (in some cases, encircling the smokestack) that looks somewhat like an airport control tower. One downside of the older ships (those built before 1995) is their small cabins (created with the idea that cruisers won't spend much time in their cabins anyway). It's something Royal Caribbean has sought to improve with its newer builds.

The crowd on Royal Caribbean ships, like the decor, tends to be somewhat more subdued than on Carnival, although some short cruises attract their share of partiers. These ships tend to attract more of a karaoke crowd than a wet T-shirt crowd. Passengers represent an age mix from 30 to 60, and a good number of families are attracted by the line's well-established and fine-tuned kids' programs. Like Carnival, Royal Caribbean placed a ban on student groups in 1997, with those under 21 required to share a room with an adult over 25 (with exceptions made for married couples or for those whose parents are in the next room).

Food on Royal Caribbean hasn't really impressed in the past, but the line has recently begun taking steps to improve in this area. The fact that sister company Celebrity is known for its exceptional cuisine will no doubt spur Royal Caribbean further in these efforts.

In 1997, Royal Caribbean banned smoking in the dining rooms on all its vessels.

Typical activities on the Royal Caribbean ships include horse racing, bingo, shuffleboard, deck games, line-dancing lessons, and art auctions, and the line has several special offerings, including Golf Ahoy!, an elaborate golf-training program that includes play at the best local golf courses in any of 16 ports of call, as well as on pre- and post-cruise tours. The ships all also offer an extensive fitness program called ShipShape.

Royal Caribbean spends big bucks on entertainment and you can see it in the line's savvy, high-tech show productions. Headliners are often featured on the megaships, with shows having starred the likes of Lou Rawls, Phyllis Diller, David Brenner, Diahann Carroll, Connie Stevens, Ben Vereen, Vic Damone, and Jerry Lewis.

The line owns a private island, CocoCay (Little Stirrup Cay) in The Bahamas and an isolated beach in Haiti called Labadee. Both give cruisers a venue for fun in the sun, complete with watersports and all the trimmings.

Unlike most lines that work with outside vendors to provide onboard shopping, Royal Caribbean does its own, and it does so in a big way. The bigger ships feature a dozen shops, offering a wide range of shopping opportunities.

Big, Bigger, Biggest

In its massive **Project Eagle** newbuilds, Royal Caribbean is really throwing on the extras. In addition to an onboard ice-skating rink, the three Eagle-class ships, due out in 1999, 2000, and 2002 and slated to sail the Caribbean year-round, will also feature novelties such as rock-climbing walls, a roller-blading track, and a wedding chapel. And the ships will have more cabins with verandas than any ship afloat and the largest children's facilities at sea. They'll also have meeting and conference space to rival most land-based conference facilities.

How big are these suckers? Try twice the weight of the *QE2*, longer than 3 football fields, twice as wide as Broadway in New York, and taller (from the waterline) than a 20-story building.

Meanwhile, Royal Caribbean has also announced plans for its new 85,000-ton, 2,000-passenger **Voyager-class** ships, which will be built at the Meyer Werft shipyards in Papenburg, Germany, and introduced in 2001. I can hear what you're saying, visions of Eagles dancing in your head. You're saying "Only 85,000 tons? Tiny!" Think about it this way, though: That's approximately twice the tonnage of the *Titanic*.

SPECIAL FEATURES Royal Caribbean offers a wedding and vow-renewal service called Royal Romance, offering five wedding packages and one vow-renewal package. The cruise line has its own loan program, CruiseLoans, to help people pay for their vacation. (See the "Buying on Time" feature in chapter 2 for details.)

SPECIAL DEALS The Breakthrough Rate program allows for savings on most staterooms on most sailings. Special savings (of 30% or more) are available on select cruises.

Royal Caribbean Fleet Specifications

Ship	Itinerary	Year Built	Passengers	Crew	Size	Length
Enchantment of the Seas	E./W. Car. (yr)	1997	1,950	760	73,817	916
Grandeur of the Seas	E. Car. (yr)	1996	1,950	760	73,817	916
Legend of the Seas	Alaska (s) Hawaii (f)	1995	1,804	720	69,130	867
Majesty of the Seas	W. Car. (yr)	1992	2,354	822	73,941	880
Monarch of the Seas	S. Car. (yr)	1991	2,354	822	73,941	880
Nordic Empress	Virgin Islands, Bahamas (yr)	1990	1,600	671	48,563	692
Rhapsody of the Seas	Alaska (s) Hawaii (f) S. Car. (w)	1997	2,000	765	78,491	915
Song of America	Bermuda (sp/s/f) Mex. Riviera (w)	1982	1,402	535	37,584	705
Sovereign of the Seas	Bahamas (yr)	1988	2,278	840	73,192	880
Splendour of the Seas	Car. (f/w/sp)	1996	1,804	720	69,130	867
Viking Serenade	Mexico (yr)	1982	1,512	612	40,132	623
Vision of the Seas	NE/Canada (f) Car., Panama (f)	1998	2,000	660	78,491	915

Royal Caribbean Cabins & Rates

Ship	Outside Cabins	w/Veranda	Rates	Inside Cabins	Rates
Enchantment of the Seas	576	212	$228–$299	399	$171–$214
Grandeur of the Seas	576	212	$228–$299	399	$171–$214
Legend of the Seas	575	231	$321–$392	327	$242–$307
Majesty of the Seas	732	62	$214–$342	445	$157–$199
Monarch of the Seas	732	62	$214–$342	445	$157–$199
Nordic Empress	471	69	$233–$399	329	$199–$263
Rhapsody of the Seas	593	229	$228–$299	407	$171–$221
Song of America	406	none	$249–$292	295	$185–$242
Sovereign of the Seas	722	none	$249–$333	416	$166–$229
Splendour of the Seas	575	231	$239–$309	327	$189–$224
Viking Serenade	478	5	$216–$266	278	$133–$196
Vision of the Seas	593	229	$309–$379	407	$219–$289

FLEET NOTES The *Grandeur, Legend, Enchantment, Rhapsody, Splendour,* and *Vision* are all part of Royal Caribbean's Vision series. They're sister ships and are nearly identical, aside from weight and interior design variations. They are all floating cities, with the *Legend* and the *Splendour* including in their offerings 18-hole miniature golf courses.

The *Majesty* and *Monarch* are twin ships. Their forerunner, the *Sovereign of the Seas,* is similar but weighs a bit less.

The *Nordic Empress, Song of America,* and *Viking Serenade* make up the line's smaller, non-megaship fleet. (Note that *Song of America* has been sold and will sail for the U.K. firm Airtours starting in March 1999.) The line's smallest ship, the *Sun Viking,* does not sail in North America.

Royal Olympic Cruises

1 Rockefeller Plaza, Suite 315, New York, NY 10020. ☎ ***800/872-6400.***

Type of cruise: *Imported wine and cheese.*

Fran says: *Zorba the Greek in the Caribbean.*

THE EXPERIENCE In 1995, Royal Olympic was formed by combining Sun Line Cruises and Epirotiki Cruises, both well-established Greek cruise lines. Most Royal Olympic ships operate year-round in Europe, but the *Stella Solaris* makes regular runs through the Caribbean. The ship offers a traditional cruise experience with warm Greek hospitality, delivered by a team of professional Greek marine personnel.

Stella Solaris *(Photo: Royal Olympic Cruises)*

In addition to its exceptional service, Royal Olympic offers well-done lectures and entertainment and sails unique itineraries (most of the 12- to 16-day variety) that set it apart from the pack.

Passengers on the line's ships tend to be mature and affluent, and many are repeat passengers.

The *Stella Solaris* is an old ship, but it is well maintained. There aren't a lot of bells and whistles, but there are first-class amenities. Passengers feel well cared for and well fed, and they have more than a passing chance to sample Greek specialties.

And yes, there are also opportunities to dance like Zorba, with lessons given for those who don't know how. Other activities include fitness classes, bridge tournaments, arts and crafts demonstrations, backgammon, and films.

SPECIAL FEATURES On Greek Night, the crew entertains. Kids' programs are offered at holiday time. The Bloody Marys served in the Bar Grill Room are supposed to be the best on the high seas. Two gentlemen hosts serve as dance partners and otherwise socialize.

SPECIAL DEALS Early booking brings discounts of 10% to 50%, and special discounts are available for repeat passengers. Children 2 to 14 years old who share a room with 2 full-fare adults can travel for half the lowest fare, and babies under age 2 travel free.

Royal Olympic Fleet Specifications

Ship	Itinerary	Year Built	Passengers	Crew	Size	Length
Stella Solaris	Car. (w/sp)	1953 (rebuilt 1973)	620	310	17,832	544

Royal Olympic Cabins & Rates

Ship	Outside Cabins	w/Veranda	Rates	Inside Cabins	Rates
Stella Solaris	250	none	$326–$376	79	$251–$316

FLEET NOTES The *Stella Solaris* was originally constructed as a cargo ship, but she was radically configured in 1973 into a comfortable and unpretentious cruise ship. Most cabins are generous in size and include fantasy suites, which come in a variety of styles. The public rooms offer European-style elegance. One of the ship's most popular features is the figure-eight swimming pool.

Seabourn Cruise Line

55 Francisco St., Suite 710, San Francisco, CA 94133. ☎ ***800/929-9595.***

Type of cruise: *Champagne and caviar.*

Fran says: *For people who expect the best and can afford to pay for it.*

THE EXPERIENCE Okay, right up front, this is the best cruise line in the world in terms of food, service, design, itineraries, and refined environment. That said, Seabourn is not for everyone, nor does it try to be.

The customers of this line are discriminating, even about who they choose to chat with on the cruise. Don't come here looking for flashy "new rich" showoffs, 'cause you won't find any. (If you did, they'd stand out like Rodney Dangerfield in *Caddyshack*—like a sore thumb.) The *Seabourn Spirit, Seabourn Legend,* and *Seabourn Pride* are ships for the old-monied, and the discreet decor and environment prove it.

The atmosphere on board these small, ultramodern, private, yacht-like ships is hushed and ever so polite. Passengers and staff alike are well-mannered and respect each other's privacy. By design, the vessels offer plenty of space for passengers—after all, most of these people live in really big houses and are used to being able to stretch out.

The line's ships sail around the world, the *Legend* and *Pride* including North America in their carefully chosen itineraries. (Alaska was dropped as an itinerary in 1998, because the line felt its ports had become too crowded.) Shore excursions are creative and suitably upscale (no motor coach rides here).

Seabourn Legend *(Photo: Seabourn Cruise Line)*

Service is flawless, with staff members recruited from the finest hotels in Europe. Tipping is not expected.

Most passengers have household incomes that exceed $200,000 a year. Many are retired, and their net worth might top $4 million. Sometimes families come on board, but there are no organized activities for kids.

The cuisine is innovative, with French influences, and is prepared and presented in a manner you'd expect to find at Europe's top resorts. The dining room is open seating, allowing passengers to create their own private dinner parties. Men wear jackets at dinner and have tuxes for the formal nights.

During days at sea, passengers occupy themselves reading or maybe playing a game of Scrabble. Sometimes guest celebrities—including, in 1998, Walter Cronkite, Art Linkletter, and *Jeopardy* host Alex Trebek—are invited on board, but usually not on the North America sailings.

Nighttime entertainment is very low key, with the ship's soloist doubling as social host or hostess.

SPECIAL FEATURES The ships have marinas hidden in their hulls that, when lowered, provide a platform for watersports, with Sunfish, kayaks, snorkeling gear, high-speed banana boats, and water skis available for passenger use. There's also a metal mesh net that becomes a seawater swimming pool.

SPECIAL DEALS Seabourn has an early-payment program offering a 10% savings for those booking and paying for their cruise 12 months in advance. For bookings 6 months in advance, the savings is 5%. A third passenger in a suite pays 25% to 50% of the double occupancy, per-person rate. The line also has a generous repeat-passenger program. (And it must work: The line's repeat-passenger rate—some 50%—is among the highest in the industry.)

Seabourn Fleet Specifications

Ship	Itinerary	Year Built	Passengers	Crew	Size	Length
Seabourn Legend	Car. (f/w)	1992	204	145	10,000	439
Seabourn Pride	NE/Canada (f) Car. (f/w)	1989	204	145	10,000	439

Seabourn Cabins & Rates

Ship	Outside Cabins	w/Veranda	Rates	Inside Cabins	Rates
Seabourn Legend	106	2	$439–$855	none	N/A
Seabourn Pride	100	2	$439–$855	none	N/A

FLEET NOTES All the cabins are suites, and each has a 5-foot-wide picture window, a complimentary, fully-stocked bar (and we're not talking mini-bottles here), a luxurious bathroom, and a walk-in closet, among many other amenities. A couple of owner's suites on each ship are very large indeed and offer private verandas.

Silversea Cruises

110 E. Broward Blvd., Fort Lauderdale, FL 33301. ☎ ***800/722-9055.***

Type of cruise: *Champagne and caviar.*

Fran says: *We're talking ultra luxury, and these ships do it to perfection.*

THE EXPERIENCE The luxurious sister ships *Silver Cloud* and *Silver Wind* carry just 296 guests each, in true splendor. All the accommodations on the ships are in outside suites, and more space is allotted to each passenger on the *Silver Cloud* and *Silver Wind* than aboard most other ships at sea. There's also more crew, with the large staff at your service, ready to cater to your every desire, on a 24-hour basis.

Silver Cloud *(Photo: Silversea Cruises)*

The fine accouterments that complement the luxurious accommodations include Limoges china, Christofle silverware, Frette bed linens, and soft down pillows. If you don't know the brands, you probably don't belong on a Silversea cruise.

The passengers on the ships are generally experienced cruisers, not necessarily American, and certainly well-traveled. Most are in the over-50 age group. These ships are not for kids.

The atmosphere on these ships is elegant, but in a low-key way, and sociable rather than stuffy. Activity offerings include bridge and other games, aerobics, dance lessons, wine tastings, lectures, and yes, even bingo and quiz shows. Nighttime entertainment includes shows, dancing, a piano bar, a small casino, and productions featuring resident and local talent.

Both ships offer five-star cuisine served in a single seating, with guests able to dine when, where, and with whom they choose.

Silversea's pricing is all-inclusive, including wines, spirits, and champagne; tips; a shore-side event; airfare; hotel accommodations; port charges; transfers; and more.

Both the *Silver Cloud* and *Silver Wind* are designed with a mere 18-foot draught (meaning only 18 feet of ship is below the water), allowing the ships to dock in intimate harbors that are off-limits to large vessels. The ships sail around the world, with itineraries including the Mediterranean, Northern Europe and the Baltic, Africa, the Far East, and the South Pacific, as well as South America. The *Silver Cloud* even cruises the coast of the good old U.S. of A.

SPECIAL FEATURES Silversea offers a *National Geographic* Traveler series, a Golf series, and special Cordon Bleu Culinary cruises. A gentleman host program is offered on select sailings.

SPECIAL DEALS Silversea's advance-payment bonus rewards guests with a 15% savings for paying in full 6 months prior to sailing. The early-booking incentive offers 5% to 10% savings for guests booking and leaving a deposit 3 and 4 months in advance of sailing, respectively. Members of the line's Venetian Society Repeat Guest program also save 5% to 10% on selected cruises.

Silversea Fleet Specifications

Ship	Itinerary	Year Built	Passengers	Crew	Size	Length
Silver Cloud	NE/Canada (f) Car. (f) Mexico & Hawaii (w)	1994	296	210	16,800	514

Silversea Cabins & Rates

Ship	Outside Cabins	w/Veranda	Rates	Inside Cabins	Rates
Silver Cloud	148	102	$850*/**	none	N/A

* *Average rates provided by the cruise line*

** *All-inclusive, including airfare*

FLEET NOTES The all-suite cabins on the *Silver Cloud* and *Silver Wind* have walk-in closets and marble bathrooms, with all the amenities you'd expect of a top-of-the-line ship.

World Explorer Cruises

555 Montgomery St., San Francisco, CA 94111-2544. ☎ ***800/854-3835.***

Type of cruise: *Evian and granola.*

Fran says: *Learn while you cruise.*

THE EXPERIENCE While her size and number of public rooms dictate that she go in this chapter, this line's only ship, the *Universe Explorer,* could also fit well into the alternative category, because her focus is on wildlife education and giving passengers the experience of learning about other cultures.

Universe Explorer *(Photo: World Explorer Cruises)*

The ship is budget all the way, but her staff of naturalists and experts on each region the ship visits is among the best in the business. The line also recruits top lecturers from universities across the United States to lead seminars and provide lectures that are both entertaining and informative. Topics on an Alaska cruise, for example, might include culture, history, geology, glaciers, flora, and fauna. Shore excursions are also well planned, geared toward education, and include soft adventure experiences.

The *Universal Explorer* once sailed as the *Enchanted Seas* for Commodore (it's still owned by Commodore, and chartered by World Explorer) and as the *Veendam* for Holland America. It's a ship that looks as much old as it does classic.

Passengers on the ship tend toward the mature and are usually experienced travelers who enjoy the ship's low-key style. Families are also welcome.

Service, like the atmosphere, is warm and informal. Meals are simple, with selections limited.

The *Universe Explorer* brings aboard top-notch entertainers from around the world to perform both classical and folk entertainment.

In months when she is not carrying passengers, the *Universe Explorer* hosts college students for Semesters at Sea.

SPECIAL FEATURES The library, located in what used to be the ship's casino, has 15,000 titles, many on Alaskan topics, as well as scads of other research materials. There's also a computer room for passenger use.

SPECIAL DEALS Early-booking discounts of 25% and discounts for third and fourth passengers are available.

World Explorer Fleet Specifications

Ship	Itinerary	Year Built	Passengers	Crew	Size	Length
Universe Explorer	Alaska (s) Car. (w)	1957	739	330	23,500	617

World Explorer Cabins & Rates

Ship	Outside Cabins	w/Veranda	Rates	Inside Cabins	Rates
Universe Explorer	290	none	$160–$256	78	$149–$192

FLEET NOTES The *Universe Explorer's* cabins are comfortable, and most are good-sized.

New Ships in the Sea

Two cruise companies are due to join the Caribbean scene for the first time in 1998. **Mediterranean Shipping Cruises,** 420 Fifth Ave., New York, NY 10018 (☎ **800/666-9333**), is a four-ship line (a subsidiary of a large Swiss shipping company) that offers what its officials call "classic Italian cruising." The line's Caribbean ship, the *Melody,* might be familiar to some travelers: Formerly called *StarShip Atlantic,* she was until mid-1997 operated as one of "The Big Red Boats" by Premier Cruises. The *Melody* sails on 12-night Western Caribbean and West Indies itineraries in the winter, returning to Europe for the summer and fall seasons. Brochure rates start at $111 per person, per day, for an inside cabin, and $181 for an outside cabin. (Built: 1982; Size: 36,500 GRT; Length: 671 ft.; Passengers: 1,076; Crew: 535; Outside cabins: 392; Inside cabins: 157.)

Classical Cruises, 132 E. 70th St., New York, NY 10021 (☎ **800/252-7745**), operates small luxury yachts and is known mostly for its Mediterranean itineraries. In early 1999, however, the line will introduce a new state-of-the-art ship, *Le Levant,* that will operate exclusively in North America. The 90-passenger vessel, which is being built in France, will offer large staterooms appointed in elegant fabrics, and public rooms that include a wood-paneled library, a gymnasium, and two restaurants. It will also feature a platform on its stern from which guests will be able to swim, snorkel, and scuba dive. The ship will spend winters in the Caribbean; spring and fall in South America; and summers in New England, Canada, and the Great Lakes. Fares will range from $2,995 to $7,195 per person for weeklong sailings.

Chapter 6

The Alternative Ships

In This Chapter

- All the small cruise ships in the North American market, rated and reviewed
- Notes on the small-ship cruising experience

If big cruise ships are mostly for people who want every resort amenity—casinos, nightclubs, swimming pools, spas, state-of-the-art gyms, dining options, room service, full activities rosters, and cabins with all the comforts of home—then the ships in this chapter are for people who care about none of the above, and probably don't like big ships very much, or glitz either, for that matter.

In using the term *alternative,* I'm not talking loud, harsh music, baggy pants, and mosh pits. What these alternative ships offer instead is a casual, crowd-free cruise experience that gives passengers a chance to get up close and personal with the natural surroundings of the destinations they visit. In most of the cases, the destination, more than the ship itself, is what passengers come for (an exception being The Delta Queen Steamboat Company line, whose paddlewheelers are really destinations unto themselves).

Thanks to their smaller size, these ships can go places where larger ships simply can't, their shallow drafts allowing them to travel on rivers and canals and into tight waterways. When they're at sea, these ships tend to hug the coast, stopping at ports on a daily basis—including out-of-the-way places that larger ships can't get to, such as uninhabited islands and nature areas, as well as smaller ports that tend to cater to yachts. And they have the flexibility to change their itineraries as opportunities arise—say, to follow a whale.

The alternative-ship experience comes with a sense of adventure (although it's usually of the "soft" rather than rugged sort) and fosters a lot of camaraderie with fellow passengers, facilitated by small passenger capacities, close quarters, and open seating at meals (and, in some cases, meals served family style).

Cabins on these ships only sometimes offer TVs or telephones and tend to be very small, and in some cases, downright spartan. Activity-wise, instead of aerobics and pool games like on the big ships, these ships might offer a deck power walk or an opportunity to swim off the side of the boat. And the alternative ships are more likely to feature expert lectures on marine biology, history, and other intellectual pursuits than instruction in the fine art of line dancing.

There are no stabilizers on most of these smaller ships, and the ride can be bumpy in stormy weather (a problem more at sea than on inland waterways). Often, there are no elevators, either, making cruises on most of these ships a bit difficult for travelers with disabilities. And the alternative-ship lines do not offer activities or facilities for children, although you will find a few families on some of these vessels.

Alaska's Glacier Bay Tours and Cruises

520 Pike St., No. 1400, Seattle, WA 98101. ☎ ***800/451-5952.***

Type of cruise: *Evian and granola.*

Fran says: *Alaska, casual and close-up.*

THE EXPERIENCE Alaska's Glacier Bay Tours and Cruises is the best-equipped line in terms of its ability to share the intriguing past of the native people of Southeast Alaska. That's because the 11-year-old line is, in fact, owned by members of the Tlingit people. The line was purchased in 1996 by Goldbelt, Inc., a Native Alaskan corporation based in Juneau, and the company has been growing ever since, adding a ship a year and making plans for more.

Wilderness Adventurer *(Photo: Alaska's Glacier Bay)*

The line acquired the 78-passenger *Wilderness Adventurer* in 1997, adding a second adventure-class vessel (the first is its 36-passenger *Wilderness Explorer*) that gives passengers an opportunity to walk through lush forests, beachcomb on secluded shores, and sea kayak (no experience is required) in remote areas of

Alaska's Inside Passage. Both ships are outfitted with a flotilla of two-person kayaks to allow quiet and unobtrusive observations of wildlife areas, as well as Zodiac landing craft. Onboard naturalists lead passengers on guided shore walks, and shore excursions are included in the cruise fare.

The line also operates the 49-passenger *Executive Explorer,* a more luxurious vessel, as its name implies. And for the 1998 season, it introduced the 86-passenger *Wilderness Discoverer,* formerly American Ca7nadian Caribbean's *Mayan Prince.* Both have onboard historians/culturalists to share the region's colorful history and lead shore excursions, and in 1999 the *Wilderness Discoverer* will be outfitted with kayaks and other gear that will allow it to sail on soft-adventure itineraries.

Ahoy, Mateys!

Alaska's Glacier Bay sounds pretty Alaska-specific, right? That's why the line's new cruises to Mexico's Sea of Cortez—and any other non-Alaska destinations they visit—will be marketed under the name Voyager Cruise Line when they begin running in January 1999.

The *Executive Explorer's* itinerary from Ketchikan or Juneau includes visits to the remote Kake, an Alaska Native village (population 600) located on Kupreanof Island. The *Wilderness Discover's* shore excursions include a visit to the remote village of Tenakee Springs.

All the ships offer a comfortable and casual environment, with meals served family-style, at one seating, on an unassigned basis, and the windowed observation lounge and large observation decks serving as the main gathering places.

SPECIAL FEATURES The firm that owns Alaska's Glacier Bay Tours and Cruises is also the authorized concessionaire of Glacier Bay National Park. All the cruises include a day in the park, and special pre- or post-cruise packages to the Glacier Bay Lodge are offered. The *Executive Explorer* offers color TV and VCRs in the cabins for viewing movies and naturalist presentations.

SPECIAL DEALS Early-booking discounts are available, as are special rates for third persons sharing a room with two full-fare passengers.

Alaska's Glacier Bay Fleet Specifications

Ship	Itinerary	Year Built	Passengers	Crew	Size	Length
Executive Explorer	Alaska (sp/s)	1986	49	20	98	98
Wilderness Adventurer	Alaska (sp/s) Mexico (w)	1983	78	20	89	157
Wilderness Discoverer	Alaska (sp/s) Mexico (w)	1993	86	22	95	169
Wilderness Explorer	Alaska (sp/s)	1969	36	13	98	112

Alaska's Glacier Bay Cabins & Rates

Ship	Outside Cabins	w/Veranda	Rates	Inside Cabins	Rates
Executive Explorer	25	none	$474–$590	none	N/A
Wilderness Adventurer	30	none	$381–$421	5	$329
Wilderness Discoverer	37	none	$400–$499	6	$359
Wilderness Explorer	18	none	$293–$306	none	N/A

FLEET NOTES The *Wilderness Adventurer* and *Wilderness Discoverer,* both former American Canadian Caribbean Line vessels, have their former owner's patented bow-ramp design, which allows passengers to disembark right onto shore. The *Wilderness Adventurer* also has a custom-designed kayak-launch platform. Cabins are small, but modern and comfortable. The smaller *Wilderness Explorer* is called a "cruising base camp," its cabins with their upper and lower berths (bunk beds) a comfortable place to crash after a busy day of kayaking, hiking, and exploring.

The more plush *Executive Explorer* is built on a streamlined catamaran design that allows it to travel faster and visit more ports than the other vessels. According to the cruise line, the ship has the largest regular stateroom viewing windows of any small U.S. flag cruise ship.

Alaska Sightseeing / Cruise West

4th and Battery Bldg., Suite 700, Seattle, WA 98121. ☎ ***800/426-7702.***

Type of cruise: *Evian / prune juice and granola.*

Fran says: *Small is beautiful.*

THE EXPERIENCE On an Alaska Sightseeing / Cruise West ship, you can sit so close to the water that you can feel the spray—and that's just the kind of experience line-founder Chuck West was going for. West, who earlier created Alaska-Westours, a firm he sold to Holland America in the early 1970s, wanted to present a genuine and close-up view of Alaska, and the line's small, yacht-like vessels, operating on imaginative itineraries, provide just that.

Spirit of '98 *(Photo: ASCW)*

Passengers on Alaska Sightseeing / Cruise West vessels tend to be older, well-educated, independent-minded, and financially sound. The atmosphere on board the ships is casual and relaxed, with no luxurious accouterments or white-glove service—and that's the way most of the passengers who choose this line want it.

Because these ships are small, they can navigate tight areas, visit tiny ports, and scoot close to wildlife. Passengers tend to congregate in each vessel's open-bow area or windowed forward lounge to get the best views.

Binoculars are provided for guest use, with wildlife sightings announced over the intercom system.

The young, friendly, and energetic crew members do multiple tasks; the same person might carry your bags, serve you at dinner, and make your bed. A cruise coordinator on each trip is knowledgeable about Alaska's flora, fauna, geology, and history; and Forest Service rangers, local fishermen, and Native Alaskans often come aboard to share their knowledge as well.

Do-it-yourself entertainment is provided by the crew or fellow passengers, and there are a couple of exercise machines (generally, a Stairmaster and an exercise bike) available on each ship for those looking for a workout.

All the ships offer two public areas: a Grand Salon Lounge and a dining room. Home-style American meals are served in one open seating, using fresh products purchased at the ports along the way.

SPECIAL FEATURES The *Spirit of '98* has an elevator; the others do not. The ships' bridges are usually open for visits. Some of the ships have movies to borrow for in-room viewing. The line offers pre- and post-cruise tours to Denali National Park, Fairbanks, and Anchorage.

SPECIAL DEALS Early-booking and third- and fourth-passenger discounts are offered.

Alaska Sightseeing / Cruise West Fleet Specifications

Ship	Itinerary	Year Built	Passengers	Crew	Size	Length
Spirit of '98	Alaska (sp/s) Calif. (f)	1984	98	23	96	192
Spirit of Alaska	Alaska (s) Oregon (sp/f)	1980	82	21	97	143
Spirit of Columbia	Wash./Can. (sp/f) Alaska (s)	1979	78	21	98	143
Spirit of Discovery	Alaska (sp/s) Oregon (f)	1971	84	21	97	125
Spirit of Endeavor	Alaska (sp/s) Calif. (f) Mexico (w)	1983	107	30	100	207
Spirit of Glacier Bay	Alaska (sp/s) Wash. (f)	1976	54	16	94	166

Alaska Sightseeing / Cruise West Cabins & Rates

Ship	Outside Cabins	w/Veranda	Rates	Inside Cabins	Rates
Spirit of '98	49	none	$429–$548	none	N/A
Spirit of Alaska	27	none	$353–$453	12	$293–$313
Spirit of Columbia	27	none	$361–$418	12	$306–$322
Spirit of Discovery	43	none	$371–$540	none	N/A
Spirit of Endeavor	51	none	$429–$548	none	N/A
Spirit of Glacier Bay	14	none	$379	13	$297

FLEET NOTES The *Spirit of '98* is a replica of a 19th-century steamship and is decorated in a Victorian decor that carries through to its comfortable cabins. There's even a player piano in the lounge. No doubt attracted by the look, Kevin Costner's *Wyatt Earp* filmed one of its final scenes on board.

The *Spirit of Endeavor* is the line's flagship and is the luxury ship of the fleet, boasting larger cabins with picture windows. The *Spirit of Discovery* has a streamlined, modern appearance. Cabins are snug but comfortable. The *Spirit of Columbia, Spirit of Alaska,* and *Spirit of Glacier Bay* were all built by American Canadian Caribbean Line; the *Columbia* features that line's patented bow ramp, which allows passengers to disembark directly onshore, while the other two ships use a gangplank-like bow ladder for disembarkation. The *Columbia* is a slightly smaller ship than the *Discovery,* and offers seven suites among its cabins, including a large owner's suite with picture windows overlooking the bow. The *Alaska* is almost identical to the *Spirit of Columbia,* but without the suites. The *Glacier Bay* is the smallest of the ships and also has the smallest cabins.

The line's cabinless yacht, *Sheltered Seas,* also offers cruise-tours, cruising during the day and putting passengers up in shore-side hotels at night.

American Canadian Caribbean Line

461 Water St., Warren, RI 02885. ☎ ***800/556-7450.***

Type of cruise: *Prune juice and granola.*

Fran says: *The ship and the destination are the things with these inexpensive cruises.*

THE EXPERIENCE Given that this line's founder, Luther Blount, is a ship builder, perhaps it's no surprise that American Canadian Caribbean Line's ships are innovative and offer some of the most unusual cruise experiences and itineraries available.

The unique ship design and the destinations the design can take you to are the main attractions of this no-frills offering. These vessels sail places usually accessible only to private yachts. And thanks to their design, the ACCL boats are able to put their bow right up to the shore so you can walk directly off the ship onto, say, a pristine, deserted beach.

There is no luxury and little pampering on these ships, whose prices are among the lowest in the industry. What there is instead is camp-like, family style roughing it.

Grande Caribe *(Photo: ACCL)*

Decor is very simple, and cabins are minuscule. But people love these vessels, and the line has probably the highest number of repeat passengers in the industry. Passengers tend to be older, adventure-oriented, and rather conservative. And you'd better like them, as you'll be trapped with them in very close quarters for several days, including taking meals together family-style. Staff members tend toward the warm and perky, and most are from New England.

No alcohol is served on the ships, but you can bring your own.

Activities include a card game here or there in the dining room and lectures offered both on the ship and at destinations such as bird-watching venues.

Evening amusement is do-it-yourself and very low-key, and might include a marshmallow roast or songfest, and sometimes visits by local performers.

SPECIAL FEATURES The ACCL vessels have a retractable pilot house that can be lowered so the ships can pass underneath low-slung bridges, and they each have a stern dock for swimming. They also have glass-bottom launches so guests can easily view marine life, and chairlifts for passengers for whom stairs are a challenge.

SPECIAL DEALS Discounts for back-to-back cruises and for third passengers sharing a cabin with two full-fare passengers.

American Canadian Caribbean Line Fleet Specifications

Ship	Itinerary	Year Built	Passengers	Crew	Size	Length
Grande Caribe	Intracoastal (sp) Erie Canal, Canada (s/f) Panama, Central Am. (w)	1997	100	20	98	182
Grande Mariner	Erie Canal, Canada (s/f) Car., Panama (w/sp)	1998	100	20	98	182
Niagara Prince	U.S. South, Midwest, NE, NY (sp/f) Car., Central Am. (w)	1994	84	15	92	175

American Canadian Caribbean Line Cabins & Rates

Ship	Outside Cabins	w/Veranda	Rates	Inside Cabins	Rates
Grande Caribe	42	none	$187–$232	none	N/A
Grande Mariner	42	none	$184–$201	8	$99
Niagara Prince	40	none	$204–$208	2	$122–$193

FLEET NOTES The $7.5 million *Grande Caribe,* with a lounge-bar in addition to the dining room, is the biggest and most technologically advanced of the ships. Its sister ship, *Grand Mariner,* is due to be introduced in May 1998 (replacing the *Mayan Prince*).

Clipper Cruise Line

7711 Bonhomme Ave., St. Louis, MO 63105. ☎ ***800/325-0010.***

Type of cruise: *Evian/prune juice and granola.*

Fran says: *For those who like to explore in comfort.*

THE EXPERIENCE Passengers on Clipper ships get an adventure experience as they explore rivers, uninhabited islands, and fjords, yet these are hardly roughing-it cruises. The ambiance on the ships is informal and relaxed, with no glitter or Las Vegas glitz, but the interiors are well-maintained and decorated in pleasing soft colors and burnished woods. There are two main public rooms on each of the ships: an observation lounge and a dining room.

Yorktown Clipper *(Photo: Clipper Cruise Line)*

All the cabins are outside and are small but comfortable, and most have picture windows. Some have doors that open to the promenade deck rather than to an inside corridor.

Service is delivered by a young and personable American staff.

Most of the passengers are affluent, older, retired folks—seasoned travelers who are not too demanding. They tend to be both adventurous and intellectually curious, and they want a comfortable, hassle-free cruise experience without sequins and glitz. They don't like crowds and don't need an extravagant roster of onboard activities. Consequently, Clipper's approach to activities and excursions is unregimented.

Rather than entertainers, the Clipper line features "enlighteners," naturalists, historians, and other experts who offer informal lectures and lead expeditions to sites of natural beauty and historical or cultural interest. Stops at ports of call might include swimming, snorkeling, a hike in a wildlife preserve, a museum visit, a folk performance, or other options. Nights spent at port give passengers a chance to mingle with the locals.

SPECIAL FEATURES Extensive reference materials are sent to passengers before each cruise. Golf is offered when courses are within easy access of a port, and swimming and snorkeling are offered directly off the sides of the ships.

SPECIAL DEALS Special rate for third passengers sharing a cabin with two full-fare passengers.

Clipper Cruise Line Fleet Specifications

Ship	Itinerary	Year Built	Passengers	Crew	Size	Length
Nantucket Clipper	NE/Canada, NY (s/f) Car. (w) U.S. South (sp)	1984	102	32	1,471	207
Yorktown Clipper	Car., Panama (w) Alaska (sp/s) Pacific N.W. (f)	1988	138	40	2,354	257

Clipper Cruise Line Cabins & Rates

Ship	Outside Cabins	w/Veranda	Rates	Inside Cabins	Rates
Nantucket Clipper	51	none	$375	none	N/A
Yorktown Clipper	69	none	$375	none	N/A

FLEET NOTES The *Nantucket Clipper* and *Yorktown Clipper* are both American-built ships, with all-American crews and officers. They are similar in design, but the *Yorktown Clipper* is slightly larger.

In addition to the *Nantucket Clipper* and *Yorktown Clipper,* the line recently acquired a third ship, the 122-passenger ship *Clipper Adventurer,* an ocean-going vessel equipped with stabilizers and an ice-hardened hull that allows her to navigate in rugged natural environments. In 1998, she will offer cruises to areas such as Antarctica, with only one North American itinerary, a 22-day cruise from Canada to Florida.

The Delta Queen Steamboat Company

Robin St. Wharf, 1380 Port of New Orleans Place, New Orleans, LA 70130-1890.
☎ ***800/543-1949.***

Type of cruise: *Domestic wine and cheese.*

Fran says: *You might not see Tom Sawyer, but you will see Americana.*

THE EXPERIENCE The Delta Queen Steamboat Company is the oldest U.S. flag cruise line, tracing its roots to 1890, a time when riverboats were a primary form of transportation. The firm offers an experience it appropriately likes to call "steamboatin'" rather than cruising.

The *Delta Queen,* a national historic landmark, and her much newer and much larger siblings, the *American Queen* and *Mississippi Queen,* ply the Mississippi and other great rivers of the American South and Midwest, leaving from 12 port cities and bringing passengers to quaint communities where town officials just might be on hand to shake their hands and where they can head to the five-and-dime for a soda.

American Queen *(Photo: Delta Queen Steamboat Co.)*

The paddlewheelers are all done up in Victorian finery, and the "steamboatin'" experience is definitely laid-back. Passengers can sit in a rocker and do needlepoint or watch the world go by. The ships pass stately antebellum mansions and important Civil War sites and plow through the Mississippi's famous muddy water.

Perhaps attracted by the nostalgic nature and calm pace of these voyages, passengers tend to be 60 years old and older, but some folks bring along the kids to experience a taste of river life. Also, there's a good share of international travelers looking for a chance to learn about America.

There's no casino on any of the ships, but there is Dixieland jazz, and passengers enjoy diversions like flying kites from the sundeck, playing card games, and engaging in sing-alongs. A "Riverlorian" on each ship offers lectures and is available to answer questions.

American and Southern specialties are served in the ships' dining rooms by a cheerful staff.

The line's itineraries feature 20 themed cruises, including an Elvis Years cruise with a stop at Graceland and guests such as Marian Cocke, Elvis's nurse; Joe Esposito, his road manager and best man at his wedding; the Jordanaires, a vocal group that performed with the King for years; and, of course, an Elvis impersonator or two to bring the experience home.

Also new in 1998 is a Red River cruise that features lectures by Civil War experts who also accompany passengers on several shore visits. Stops include Shreveport, Louisiana, site of Fort Humbug Memorial Park, and Alexandria, Louisiana, home of Alexandria National Cemetery.

SPECIAL FEATURES All the ships have calliopes (steam-powered keyboard instruments), and guests are welcome to try their hand at playing. The *American Queen* has a library with more than 600 books, including many 1890s volumes.

SPECIAL DEALS Passengers booking at least 8 months in advance receive free round-trip airfare on most cruises of 7 nights or more, or airfare of $200 per person on cruises of 6 nights or less.

Delta Queen Fleet Specifications

Ship	Itinerary	Year Built	Passengers	Crew	Size	Length
American Queen	Miss. and other U.S. rivers (yr)	1995	436	180	3,707	418
Delta Queen	Miss. and other U.S. rivers, Intracoastal (yr)	1927	174	81	3,360	285
Mississippi Queen	Miss. and other U.S. rivers (yr)	1976	414	156	3,364	382

Delta Queen Cabins & Rates

Ship	Outside Cabins	w/Veranda	Rates	Inside Cabins	Rates
American Queen	166	24	$388–$457	56	$235–$318
Delta Queen	87	none	$150–$457	none	N/A
Mississippi Queen	135	104	$388–$457	73	$150–$318

FLEET NOTES The *Delta Queen* is much like a Victorian bed-and-breakfast, with her original fixtures including Tiffany-style, stained-glass windows; rich, hardwood paneling; brass fixtures; the only ironwood floor aboard a steamboat; and a dramatic grand staircase.

The larger *Mississippi Queen's* cabins include many with private verandas. She also features a lounge done up in 1890s saloon decor. The *American Queen* is the world's largest steamboat and is furnished largely with antiques and vintage artwork.

Over the next several years, Delta Queen plans to build up to five non-paddlewheel but still neato-cool historic-looking coastal steamers for use in the Pacific Northwest and along the Eastern seaboard. The first is to be introduced in the spring of 2000. The experience aboard the new ships is expected to be of the soft-adventure variety, with the line going after a younger demographic than its usual over-65 crowd.

Special Expeditions

720 Fifth Ave., New York, NY 10019. ☎ ***800/762-0003.***

Type of cruise: *Evian and granola.*

Fran says: *A casual experience for fit adventure types.*

THE EXPERIENCE Special Expeditions specializes in environmentally sensitive soft-adventure cruises. The line was founded by second-generation adventure travel pro Sven-Olof Lindblad, whose father, Lars-Eric Lindblad, pioneered the field.

Sea Lion *(Photo: Special Expeditions)*

The line's cruises are exploratory in nature; passengers tend to be younger and physically active, as well as intellectually curious.

Like the other small ships, these vessels don't have casinos or discos or, in this case, even TVs. Days are spent learning about and exploring the great outdoors with the help of experienced expedition leaders trained in botany, anthropology, biology, and geology. Shore excursions are included in the cruise fare.

Both the *Sea Bird* and *Sea Lion* have two public rooms: the observation lounge, which serves as each ship's nerve center, and the dining room.

Meals are simple, hearty, American fare and are served at open seatings. Pretty much everyone on these ships goes to bed early to catch enough sleep to be ready for the next day's adventures.

In addition to the *Sea Bird* and *Sea Lion,* the line also operates the *Caledonian Star,* which sails in Europe (among other places), and the *Polaris,* which cruises most of the year in the Galapagos but also offers some cruises in Panama and Costa Rica.

SPECIAL FEATURES Educational films and slide presentations are sometimes shown prior to shore excursions. Each ship has a reference library located in a closet in the lounge. Zodiac craft are used for shore excursions.

SPECIAL DEALS Early-booking and repeat-passenger discount fares are available, as is free airfare, offered on select sailings only.

Special Expeditions Fleet Specifications

Ship	Itinerary	Year Built	Passengers	Crew	Size	Length
Sea Bird	Alaska (s) Columbia River (sp/f) Mexico (w)	1982	70	22	100	152
Sea Lion	Alaska (s) Columbia River (sp/f) Mexico (w)	1981	70	22	100	152

Special Expeditions Cabins & Rates

Ship	Outside Cabins	w/Veranda	Rates	Inside Cabins	Rates
Sea Bird	37	none	$403–$590	none	N/A
Sea Lion	37	none	$403–$590	none	N/A

FLEET NOTES The *Sea Lion* and *Sea Bird* are identical right down to their casual decor and furnishings. The cabins are tiny, with a minuscule bathroom (the toilet is opposite the shower nozzle). All cabins are outside and have picture windows that open to let in breezes and fresh air.

New Ships in the Sea

Alaska Yacht Safaris, 1724 W. Marine View Dr., Seattle, WA 98201 (☎ **800/325-6722**), offers flexible 7-night itineraries through Alaska's Inside Passage aboard 2 intimate 12- to 14-passenger luxury yachts. The small size of the ships allow expeditions to boardwalked cannery towns and Tlingit villages, where local people receive guests more personally and gracefully than they might the hordes from a larger ship. For even more up-close experiences, each vessel carries a naturalist who leads passengers via Zodiac or kayaks (carried aboard ship) to investigate shoreline black bears or otters, or to navigate fjords packed with ice floes and lolling seals.

Six crew members cheerfully fuss over the passengers, adjusting lunchtime dishes or making elaborate cocktails from the open bar (they've even been known to call the next port to pick up a passenger's favorite beer), and the chef assails guests with multiple-course meals and clever snacks when he isn't bartering with a fishing boat for the catch of the day.

Public spaces are intimate and homey, yet luxurious, and four or five prime vantages for spotting wildlife (one is a hot tub) ensure as little or as much privacy as you desire. Cabins are comfortable and clean, with large, firm beds, adequate light, and decorative art (some good, some so-so). Showers provide a steady but not spectacular stream of reliably hot water. Unlike most other lines, the ships anchor at night, making for somewhat quieter sleeptime than if they were sailing.

The *Obsession* sails 7-night routes between Juneau and Sitka and the *Golden Mystique* sails 7-night routes between Vancouver and Juneau, both from May to September. Per-person, per-diem rates, including alcoholic beverages, shore excursions, kayaking, transfers, and (on *Obsession* only) a bush-plane expedition, range from $421 to $564 in early May to $707 to $850 from June into September. Tips, tax and port charges ($175), and airfare are not included.

Chapter 7

A Tall Ship & a Star to Steer By: Ships with Sails

In This Chapter

- All the sailing cruise ships in the North American market, rated and reviewed
- Notes on the ways of the wind and water, and the ships and people who ply them
- Previews of what's on tap from all the cruise lines

For those who have dreamed of going to sea like in the movies (think of Errol Flynn positioned proudly on a wooden deck, face dramatically pointing into the wind), there's nothing like the lure of a sailing ship. You might not be wearing a sword tucked in your belt (or a billowy shirt, for that matter), and there might not be a pirate ship flying a skull and crossbones on the horizon, but tall ships today do give passengers a chance to experience the romance of the sea. You can watch the huge sails flapping in the wind and breathe in the salt air while you talk halyards and flukes with your shipmates.

The tall ships plying the waters of the Caribbean are all casual in approach but offer facilities that range from very rustic (you can experience what sailors of yore experienced) to ultra luxury (you can sail like royalty did—and does), with price variations to match. Some of the ships are real historic vessels, while others are reproductions. They hold as few as 30 passengers and as many as 400.

What these tall ships all have in common, however, is those glorious sails. Some are still manually operated, with all the ceremony that entails, while some are computer-operated, and some ships sail entirely on wind power, while others are mostly motor-driven and have the sails as much for show as for locomotion. Whatever their relative usefulness, though, they're all glorious to look at and are graceful reminders of days gone by.

Unlike big cruise ships, sailing ships intrinsically offer a sense of adventure. Both because they are aware of this aura and because the small size of these ships makes it possible, the tall-ship cruise lines carefully pick itineraries that go beyond the norm. These ships can slip into quiet coves and up to remote islands, and some even make minor itinerary changes weekly based on the winds and weather.

And speaking of wind and weather, some of the ships can rock and roll as much as they did in the olden days, so they might not be appropriate for passengers who tend to get seasick.

The tall-ship experience tends to create a spirit of camaraderie among passengers, many who get into talking nautical, and some who are or will become nautical-history buffs. On some of the ships, passengers can actually help with the unfurling of the sails and such if they so choose.

You won't need a tux on any of these ships, and you won't find any fancy Las Vegas–type showrooms. And, in all but the more upscale ships, you also might not have TV in your cabin, or a swimming pool, gym, or spa.

People come on these ships to sail and relax. When the ships anchor, playtime includes exploring the islands and enjoying a variety of watersports, such as snorkeling, scuba diving, and water-skiing.

In this chapter, I review all the major tall-ship companies operating around North America. For additional offerings in areas a little farther off the beaten path, see chapter 25, "Cruising Around: Other Ports of Call."

Club Med Cruises

40 W. 57th St., New York, NY 10019. ☎ ***800/4-LESHIP.***

Type of cruise: *Evian and granola.*

Fran says: *Viva la France.*

THE EXPERIENCE Take the casual, all-inclusive Club Med–resort experience, turn it up a notch or two in the luxury and style department, add five masts and seven computer-operated sails to tune into the romance of the sailing experience (but not the inconvenience), and you've got the *Club Med II.*

The ship is one of a pair of the largest cruise ships with sails afloat today, each high-tech versions of historic clipper ships, the impressive sails more for show than anything else (the ships are really motor-operated). *Club Med II's* sister ship, *Club Med I,* became part of the Windstar fleet in March. *Club Med II* is also rumored to be for sale, but officials have indicated they aren't planning to part with her anytime soon.

Club Med being a French company and all, it's not surprising that the ship offers a French ambiance, with a good share of the passengers being either

French or Francophiles (the official language on board is French, but announcements are made in English and German as well). Passengers tend to be affluent, sports- and fitness-conscious, and into informality. They range in age from 28 to 55. Older kids are allowed but not encouraged (kids under 10 are not allowed).

Club Med II *(Photo: Club Med Cruises)*

Activities are conducted, as at Club Med resorts, by a delightful corps of young, English-speaking *gentils organisateurs* (GOs), who lead deck games and other organized events with great enthusiasm. At night, the GOs perform in the nightclub, with a small casino, piano bar, and late-night disco providing additional entertainment options. The ship also has a gym and spa.

Although food is not *Club Med II's* top attribute, dinner on the ship, as is the custom in France, is enjoyed as a big social event and can last up to 3 hours. It is served in one seating in the ship's two dining rooms on a sit-where-you-please basis.

The *Club Med II* has a private marina that hides in its stern; when opened, it gives passengers access to watersports such as windsurfing, water-skiing, and snorkeling. Gear for these activities is provided free as part of Club Med's all-inclusive pricing (which also includes tips).

SPECIAL FEATURES A weekly event on the *Club Med II* is Carnival Night, when passengers dress up in costumes provided by the staff. Since Club Med really is a club, passengers have to join for a one-time initiation fee of $30 per family, which includes travel-insurance coverage.

SPECIAL DEALS A third passenger in any cabin pays 80% of the ship's lowest per-person, double-occupancy fare.

Club Med Fleet Specifications

Ship	Itinerary	Year Built	Passengers	Crew	Size	Length
Club Med II	S. Car. (w)	1990	386	188	14,983	617

Club Med Cabins & Rates

Ship	Outside Cabins	w/Veranda	Rates	Inside Cabins	Rates
Club Med II	191	none	$270–$340	none	N/A

FLEET NOTES The standard cabins on *Club Med II* are all outside and nearly the same, offering good-sized accommodations with a variety of nice amenities. The ship also has five suites.

Star Clippers

4101 Salzedo St., Coral Gables, FL 33146. ☎ ***800/442-0553.***

Type of cruise: *Evian and granola.*

Fran says: *History without the hassle (in casual comfort).*

THE EXPERIENCE The twins *Star Flyer* and *Star Clipper* are replicas of the big, 19th-century clipper sailing ships (or *barkentines*) that once circled the globe. Their tall, square rigs carry enormous sails and are glorious to look at and a particular thrill for history buffs.

But these ships are not just window-dressing. The *Star Clipper* and *Star Flyer* were constructed using original drawings and the specifications of a leading 19th-century naval architect, but they have been updated with modern touches so that today they are the tallest and among the fastest clipper ships ever built (they've reached speeds of more than 19 knots).

Star Flyer & Star Clipper *(Photo: Star Clippers)*

The atmosphere on board is akin to being on a private yacht rather than a mainstream cruise ship. It's casual in an L. L. Bean sort of way and friendly—somewhere between the barefoot ambiance of sailing competitor Windjammer and the more upscale ambiance of Windstar.

Activities on the ships tend toward the nautical, such as visiting the bridge, watching the crew handle the sails, and taking classes in skills such as knot-tying.

When the ships stop at ports of call, it's usually in the late morning. In port, guests enjoy watersports like scuba diving and snorkeling before a sunset sail-away to the next port. Local entertainment is sometimes brought on at night, and the ships also have a piano player and a makeshift disco in the Tropical Bar. Movies are piped into passenger cabins.

Passengers generally fall into the 30-to-60 age range and include a good number of first-time cruisers. These cruises are also appropriate for older kids, and the chance it affords them to relive maritime history is downright educational.

Despite stabilizers, movement of the ships might be troublesome to those who get seasick.

SPECIAL FEATURES Each of the line's tenders accommodate 52 passengers and are powered by underwater jets rather than propellers, allowing them to run right up onto a beach. At the end of the visit, the tenders are backed into the water with a stern-mounted anchor. For an extra fee, both the *Star Clipper* and *Star Flyer* offer PADI-approved scuba diving and snorkeling, including instruction. Water-skiing is also available.

Star Clippers Fleet Specifications

Ship	Itinerary	Year Built	Passengers	Crew	Size	Length
Star Clipper	S. Car. (f/w)	1991	172	70	2,298	360

Star Clippers Cabins & Rates

Ship	Outside Cabins	w/Veranda	Rates	Inside Cabins	Rates
Star Clipper	78	none	$253–$353	6	$210–$239

FLEET NOTES Decor is conservative on both ships, with touches of mahogany and brass. Cabins are small, but the teak deck space gives passengers much more room than usual to spread out and enjoy the sea breezes. The *Star Clipper* sails Caribbean itineraries in the fall and winter; the *Star Flyer* remains in Europe and the Far East year-round.

Tall Ship Adventures

1389 S. Havana St., Aurora, CO 80012. ☎ ***800/662-0090.***

Type of cruise: *Bread and water.*

Fran says: *Yo ho ho and a bottle of rum.*

THE EXPERIENCE If you've ever wanted to sail on a real antique clipper ship, experiencing what 18th- and 19th-century sailors experienced, this is the cruise for you.

Tall Ship Adventures' only ship, the *Sir Francis Drake,* is the real thing—one of fewer than 100 remaining tall ships. And there's no pretending otherwise. This is not a ship with a lot of amenities and organized activities. There are none. This is a ship for people who want to sail with the wind, feel the waves, and spend their days enjoying the sailing experience and scenery.

With only 30 passengers on board, you have to hope you get along. Passengers tend to be a pretty undemanding lot, though, young—at least at heart—and very interested in talking nautical (knowing your halyards from your scuppers on this cruise is helpful). You don't have to pitch in with the work of sailing the ship, but the opportunity is there if you want it.

Because people on the *Sir Francis Drake* usually like to sail, the ship does just that most mornings, with lunch either served on board or on a beach, and

Sir Francis Drake *(Photo: Tall Ship Adventures)*

afternoons spent exploring the sparsely populated islands the ship targets for its ports of call. Snorkeling is a popular activity, and the ship also has water skis, a sea kayak, Sunfish, and assorted other watersports apparatus available for guest use.

The ship sails again around dusk and then anchors for the night when the sun goes down. Entertainment on the *Sir Francis Drake* is recorded calypso music, free rum punch, and that's about it, though the ship also stops some evenings within close proximity to isolated bars and marinas, where passengers can hobnob with the yachting set (the only others with access to the spots).

Food includes fresh fish and produce purchased along the way, but no pretense is made about it being fancy. Everyone on board is served the same meal (meaning you don't get to choose).

SPECIAL FEATURES Itineraries change slightly from week to week based on the winds and weather. A popular activity is diving into the water from the ship's jutting bowsprit for a swim. Agile guests can ask the captain for access to the crow's nests, located in the ship's three masts, for the best views.

SPECIAL DISCOUNTS There's a 20% discount for early bookings made more than 8 weeks in advance.

Tall Ship Adventures Fleet Specifications

Ship	Itinerary	Year Built	Passengers	Crew	Size	Length
Sir Francis Drake	Virgin Islands (w/sp) Grenadines (s/f)	1917	28	14	450	128

Tall Ship Adventures Cabins & Rates

Ship	Outside Cabins	w/Veranda	Rates	Inside Cabins	Rates
Sir Francis Drake	14	none	$142–$170	none	N/A

FLEET NOTES The ship is small—very small—and not for those who get claustrophobic. Cabins are tight and spartan, including the ship's one suite, but then again, that's part of the whole authentic experience.

Windjammer Barefoot Cruises

P.O. Box 190120, Miami Beach, FL 33119-0120. ☎ ***305/672-6453.***

Type of cruise: *Beer and pretzels.*

Fran says: *Taste the salt air and wiggle your toes while you get to know your fellow passengers.*

THE EXPERIENCE The Windjammer experience is very different than a megaship experience, and the line is very proud of that fact. These ships are about sailing, soft adventure, making friends, and barefoot fun—you don't need to pack much more than T-shirts, shorts, and a bathing suit or two.

The fleet is made up of classic sailing vessels and one motorized vessel, and the small size of the ships allows them to anchor in out-of-the-way Caribbean harbors that bigger ships can't get near.

The pricing is inexpensive, but then again, amenities are minimal.

On a typical Windjammer cruise, passengers will visit an island for a day and have plenty of time to lie on the beach, snorkel, swim, and test the local cuisine before the ship sets sail in the late afternoon or evening.

Polynesia *(Photo: Windjammer Barefoot Cruises)*

Captain Mike Burke, founder of the line, has amassed the largest fleet of tall ships in the world, buying up vessels that had seen better days and restoring them to their former glory. Each has its own interesting history and, like Burke, has been associated with the rich and famous: The *Fântome* was once owned by Aristotle Onassis; Gloria Vanderbilt asked Burke to take extra care of the *Yankee Clipper,* which had once been her family's private yacht; the *Polynesia* was the subject of the book *The Quest of the Schooner Argus,* by Allen Villers; and the *Mandalay* was once owned by E. F. Hutton. The *Flying Cloud,* meanwhile, was decorated by Charles de Gaulle for sinking Japanese submarines, while the newest vessel, the *Legacy,* was used as a research vessel by the French government.

Windjammer has a reputation for attracting party-hearty types, and there are those who relish the free Bloody Marys served at breakfast and don't stop until way after the free rum drinks come out at dinner. But the tone of any given Windjammer cruise is really set by the passengers aboard. Some cruises are more sedate than others, with the specially themed nude, singles, gay, and swingers cruises the most active. Windjammer used to advertise in magazines such as *Forum, Screw,* and *Hustler* but has gone much more mainstream under the leadership of Burke's daughter, Susan, who is now president of the line. Older kids are even welcome on the ships.

On Windjammer vessels, basically anything goes. There are no set activities. Guests can help hoist the sails if they want to, but they don't have to. Relaxing, checking out the gorgeous scenery, and telling stories are the favorite pastimes. The attitude on the ships is that everyone is part of a big happy family, and that's exactly what Cap'n Mike was going for. He wants passengers to leave at the end of their vacation with tears in their eyes.

Windjammer delivers what it promises; the line has an impressive 40% repeat rate, with very frequent passengers known as *jammers.* One older fellow, known as *Big John,* is legendary for having sailed on Windjammer more than 90 times.

Some people complain that the ships are rocky and not suited to those who get seasick, but the line begs to differ.

Plans are to expand the Windjammer fleet beyond the Caribbean in the next few years and to introduce additional ships.

SPECIAL FEATURES The itineraries of Windjammer ships are very much determined by the call of the winds. Working with a selection of islands, Windjammer captains pick stops based on weather conditions and island events. Itineraries, therefore, change from week to week. Theme cruises include trips for singles, gays, nudists, and swingers.

SPECIAL DEALS If you book back-to-back cruises, you can stow away on the ship for free for 2 nights. Children under 12 who share a cabin with 2 adults pay 50% of the adult fare.

Windjammer Barefoot Cruises Fleet Specifications

Ship	Itinerary	Year Built	Passengers	Crew	Size	Length
Amazing Grace	E. Car. (yr)	1955	94	40	1,585	254
Fântome	E. Car. Honduran Bay Islands (yr)	1927	128	45	676	282
Flying Cloud	E. Car. (yr)	1935	66	25	400	208
Legacy	E. Car. (yr)	1959	120	43	1,165	294
Mandalay	E. Car. (yr)	1923	72	28	420	236
Polynesia	E. Car. (yr)	1938	126	45	430	248
Yankee Clipper	E. Car. (yr)	1927	64	29	327	197

Windjammer Barefoot Cruises Cabins & Rates

Ship	Outside Cabins	w/Veranda	Rates	Inside Cabins	Rates
Amazing Grace	47	none	$90–$104*	none	N/A
Fântome	54	none	$170–$178*	10	$153
Flying Cloud	8	none	$153–$170*	25	$137–$153
Legacy	61	none	$145–$183*	none	N/A
Mandalay	36	none	$119–$146*	none	N/A
Polynesia	17	none	$153–$170*	40	$116–$153
Yankee Clipper	32	none	$137–$170*	none	N/A

**Average rates provided by the cruise line*

FLEET NOTES The ships in the fleet are all tall ships, with the exception of the motorized *Amazing Grace,* which carries both passengers and supplies for the other fleet ships (some areas are off-limits to passengers) and tends to attract an older clientele than the other vessels.

The Adventures of Captain Mike

There's a real-life swashbuckler in the cruise industry, and his name is Captain Mike Burke. The salty sea dog founder of Windjammer Barefoot Cruises is like no other cruise-industry executive.

He lives in a castle in Miami—a real castle—complete with a shark-inhabited moat and gargoyles, towers, and suits of shining armor. As befits a man whose cruise line once promised passengers they'd get a "bang" out of their vacation, he's still notoriously randy with the ladies. And this grandfather of 16 still sails the seven seas, though mostly these days on his private boat, *Tondeleyo* (which he says is Polynesian for "white whore"), rather than on the ships in his fleet, where he was a fixture for nearly 50 years.

Burke's creation of the cruise line is the stuff of legends. He says he ended up with his first boat in 1947 after an all-night bender that cost him his muster pay from the Navy. He aptly named the 19-foot wreck *The Hangover,* fixed the boat up, and after unsuccessful attempts to use it as a cargo boat, got the idea of using it to carry passengers. Offering bring-your-own-lunch cruises, Burke was able to save enough to upgrade from *The Hangover* and then upgrade again, until he found himself with a virtual collection of tall ships.

The whole attitude of the Windjammer lines stems from Burke himself, who likes to dress casually and barefoot and who enjoys a drink or two. He's a free spirit who told this interviewer that he didn't set out to create a cruise line, he just wanted "to be a happy captain, carry a lot of pretty girls around, and enjoy the benefits—the fringe benefits."

With a satisfied smile, he added, "Nothing could be happier than to earn a living doing that."

Cabins on all the ships are tiny and offer no frills. On the *Amazing Grace,* shower and toilet facilities are on a shared basis. The other ships provide showers in the cabins, but hot water might be limited. Some of the ships offer dormitory accommodations for those seeking to cut costs.

Windstar Cruises

300 Elliott Ave. W., Seattle, WA 98119. ☎ ***800/258-7245.***

Type of cruise: *Evian and granola.*

Fran says: *These ships are pretty enough to be in the movies and luxurious enough to host movie stars in laid-back splendor.*

THE EXPERIENCE Nothing rustic here. The *Wind Star, Wind Spirit,* and *Wind Song* ships might have 21,489 square feet of Dacron flying from their 4 masts (the masts themselves are as tall as 20-story buildings), but they operate as smoothly as the very best modern yachts, owing to the million-dollar computers that control not only the sails but also the stabilizers, ensuring a smooth ride.

Wind Spirit *(Photo: Windstar Cruises)*

These might look like sailing ships of days of yore, but they're really floating luxury resorts, complete with all the amenities. We're talking "Lifestyles of the Rich and Famous" here, complete with top-notch service and incredible cuisine.

In 1998, Windstar adds the *Wind Surf,* formerly the *Club Med I,* similar to the other ships (they were all built at the same French shipyard) but with more public areas (including a 10,000-square-foot spa—bigger than on the other ships), more suites (she has 31 as compared to 1 on the other ships), a dedicated conference center, and an alternative dining restaurant.

There's no set regime on the Windstar ships, unless you consider pampering a regime. Most of the passengers are well-heeled and sophisticated couples, ranging in age from 30 to 70, and are the kind of people who are perfectly happy entertaining themselves. This is definitely not your megaship crowd.

A watersports platform at the stern provides for a variety of activities when the ships dock. Creative island tours are also offered. Nighttime entertainment is low key, with a pianist and sometimes a vocalist. Local entertainment is sometimes brought aboard at ports of call, and the ships also have small casinos.

The cuisine on Windstar ships is certainly something to write home about and is just about the best at sea. It's overseen by Joachim Splichal, renowned Los Angeles chef/restaurateur, and includes a good number of healthy options.

SPECIAL FEATURES Passengers can visit the bridge whenever they please to see the sophisticated computer technology that sends the sails unfurling. All cabins have VCRs and CD players, with tapes and CDs available from the ship's library.

SPECIAL DEALS Windstar offers an early-booking discount with savings up to 50% off brochure rates. If a special promotion occurs after the booking is made, the line honors the lowest available fare.

Windstar Cruises Fleet Specifications

Ship	Itinerary	Year Built	Passengers	Crew	Size	Length
Wind Song	Costa Rica (f/w)	1987	148	88	5,350	440
Wind Spirit	Virgin Islands (f/w)	1988	148	88	5,350	440
Wind Star	Costa Rica (f/w), S. Car. (sp/s)	1986	148	88	5,350	440
Wind Surf	SE Car. (f/w)	1990	312	163	14,745	617

Windstar Cruises Cabins & Rates

Ship	Outside Cabins	w/Veranda	Rates	Inside Cabins	Rates
Wind Song	74	none	$507–$531	none	N/A
Wind Spirit	74	none	$507–$531	none	N/A
Wind Star	74	none	$507–$531	none	N/A
Wind Surf	156	none	$522	none	N/A

FLEET NOTES The *Wind Song, Wind Star,* and *Wind Spirit* are identical, with all outside cabins (featuring large portholes) and impressive teakwood-decked bathrooms. The *Wind Surf* was built at the same shipyard and is nearly identical to the other ships, but it has the added offering of 31 suites.

Part 3

From Booking to Boarding: Cruise Planning Practicalities

Okay. You've filled out your quiz in chapter 3 and read through the ship reviews in chapters 4 to 7, and you've probably found at least a couple that look to fit you to a T. So, you now have an idea of what you want to spend, where and when you want to go, what your interests and special needs are, and what cruise line and ship might be right for you. Now you're ready for the big step: booking your trip.

The quiz questions happen to be the same types of questions a good travel agent should ask you. In chapter 8, I'll advise you how to find just such a good travel agent and explain why a good agent can save you both time and money. I'll also show you how to do additional research on the Internet. Then, I'll get into the nitty-gritty of the booking process and offer advice on deciding what kind of cabin you should choose and how to pick your dining-room seating preference.

In chapter 9, I'll let you know what else you'll have to take care of before your cruise and give you full details on what you'll need to pack, what documents you'll need to bring along, and how much cash you'll need.

Chapter 8

Booking Your Cruise

In This Chapter

- Tips for booking your cruise through a travel agent
- Tips for finding a specialist and avoiding scams
- Strategies for booking the best cabin
- Strategies for booking your dining options

Do I hear you asking a question? Do I hear you asking, "Do I really need a travel agent? Can't I get just as good a cruise deal on my own?"

Here's my answer: Yes, you need one, and no, you can't!

If that seems like a blatant plug for the travel-agent community, read on.

Why an Agent?

Do you represent yourself in court? Perform surgery on your own abdomen? Tackle complicated IRS forms without seeking help? If so, then maybe you're the rare type who doesn't need a travel agent. Most of us, however, are better off working with one.

A good agent can offer you expert advice to make sure you're getting the cruise that's right for you, and he or she can also save you time. You don't have to hassle with calling cruise lines for brochures; agencies have them in stock.

Plus, agents usually work for you for free (they are paid by the cruise lines).

Such a bargain!

True, booking a cruise is not brain surgery, but it is a complicated process. That's why more than 95% of cruise passengers book through agents.

The cruise lines are happy with the system, have only small reservations staffs (unlike the airlines), and actually discourage direct sales. Even if you do try to call a cruise line to book yourself, you might be advised by the line to contact an agent in your area (the cruise line might even offer you a name from its list of preferred agencies).

In addition to directing you to the right ship, the agent will help you make decisions in the following areas (see more on these later in this chapter):

- Cabin type
- Dining-room seating preference
- Cruise-line airfare offerings
- Pre- and post-cruise land offerings
- Insurance

As you'll see, there are really no advantages to trying to book yourself, even through the Internet.

Plus, consider this: If you do try to do it yourself and screw up, who are you going to blame?

Unless you're a total control freak, working with an agent is really the way to go. A good travel agent will make you a happy camper—or should I say, happy sailor?

Finding the Agent of Your Dreams

You're probably best off finding a travel agent in your local area. Big companies that advertise with 800 numbers in the Sunday newspaper might seem to have tempting offers (see "Brokers & Discounters," later in this chapter), but they don't necessarily offer the experienced staff, hands-on service, or variety of products your local agent can provide. Your local agent will also be more accessible if you encounter any problems.

If you haven't used an agent before, ask some friends for advice on who they use, but try to find an agent who is experienced in selling cruises and who has, in fact, cruised before (preferably on some of the ships you're considering). It's perfectly okay to ask agents questions about their experience, such as how many cruises they have taken.

The easiest way to make sure that you get help from someone with experience in booking cruises is to work with a **cruise-only agency** (which means the *agency* specializes in cruises) or a **cruise specialist** (which means the *agent* specializes in cruises).

It's important to realize that not all agents sell all cruise lines. In order to be experts on what they sell, and to maximize the commissions the lines pay them (they pay more based on volume), some agents might limit their product to, say, one luxury line, one mid-priced line, one mass-market line, and so on. Your agent should still offer enough variety, however, to steer you in the right direction.

How Agents Can Save You Money

Agents, especially those who specialize in cruises, are in frequent contact with the cruise lines, who alert them by computer or fax about the latest and greatest deals and special offers the lines have. The cruise lines tend to hit their top agents first about such deals and offers before they clue in the general public, and some of these deals and special offers will never appear in your local newspaper at all.

But What's Included?

Make sure when you're discussing price with agents that you understand what's included in the amount they're quoting. Are they giving you a price that includes the cruise fare, port charges, airfare, taxes and fees, and insurance; or are they quoting a cruise-only fare? One agent might break out the charges in a price quote, another might bundle them all together. It's important to know what's included when making price comparisons. This will also help ensure that no last-minute fees or charges creep in when you book your trip.

Depending on the agency you choose, you might run across additional incentives for booking through an agent:

- **Group rates:** Some agencies buy big blocks of space on a ship in advance and offer it to their clients at a group price available only through that agency. *Group*, in this case, means savings, not that you have to hang around with the other people booking through the agency.
- **Agency rebates or incentives:** Some agencies are willing to give back to the client a portion of their commissions from the cruise line in order to close a sale. This percent might be monetary, or it might take the form of a perk, such as a free bottle of champagne or a cabin upgrade.
- **Newsletters:** Some agencies publish their own newsletters or have other means, such as postcards or e-mail, to alert clients quickly about specials so they can get first dibs (they might charge a slight fee for the service).

- **Match the price:** Some agencies are willing to negotiate, especially if you've found a better price somewhere else. It never hurts to ask.
- **Back-office systems:** Once you make your booking, some agencies have back-office systems that check updated deals as they come in to make sure the rate you got is the best rate (and if it's not, they'll try to make adjustments accordingly).

They Don't Call 'Em Specialists for Nothin'

A good and easy rule of thumb to ensure that you find someone experienced and don't get ripped off is to book cruises with agencies that are members of the **Cruise Lines International Association (CLIA)** (**☎ 212/921-0066**) or the **National Association of Cruise Oriented Agents (NACOA)** (**☎ 305/663-5626**). Members of both groups are cruise specialists, and the groups monitor the ethics of their members.

Membership in the **American Society of Travel Agents (ASTA)** (**☎ 800/275-2782**) similarly ensures that the agency is monitored for ethical practices, although this does not in itself designate cruise experience.

You might also run across cruise specialists with the **Certified Travel Counselor (CTC)** designation. This means they have completed a professional-skills course offered by the Institute of Certified Travel Agents (ICTA) and is another guarantor of in-depth knowledge of the industry.

You can tap into the Internet sites of these organizations for easy access to agents in your area:

ASTA	www.asta.net.com
CLIA	www.ten-io.com/clia
ICTA	www.icta.com
NACOA	www.nacoa.com

Brokers & Discounters

These are the high-volume operations you see advertised in the Sunday newspaper.

If you choose to book through a broker or discounter, don't expect a high level of personal attention and service. Their deals might sound good, and in fact might be good, but they tend to be last-minute offers, and when you call the 800 number, you might find that only limited departure dates, cabin types, and dining-room choices are available.

Remember: With these companies, price and volume are the focus, not necessarily service.

Scam Alert!

The travel business tends to attract more than its share of scam operators trying to lure consumers with incredible come-ons.

If you get a solicitation that just doesn't sound right or are uneasy about an agent you're dealing with, call your state consumer protection agency or local office of the Better Business Bureau. Or you can check with the cruise line to see whether they've heard of the agency in question.

The American Society of Travel Agents also offers the following recommendations for avoiding the bad apples in the crop:

- Be extremely skeptical about postcard and phone solicitations and e-mail come-ons that say you've been selected to receive a fabulous vacation.
- Never give out your credit-card number unless you initiate the transaction and are confident about the company with which you are doing business.
- You should receive complete deals in writing about any trip prior to payment. These details should include the total price and any applicable cancellation and change penalties. They should also include specific information about all components of the package.
- If you call a 900 number in response to a travel solicitation, understand that there are charges for the call, and know the risks.
- Walk away from high-pressure sales presentations that don't give you time to evaluate the offer or that require you to disclose your income.
- Be suspicious of companies that require you to wait at least 60 days to take your trip.

Surfing the Net to Cruise the Seas

The Internet is a good source for gathering information on cruises. Most major lines have their own sites, and the Cruise Lines International Association also has a site with hot links to the major lines.

The cruise lines' sites typically offer information on cabin configurations and public rooms, and some feature a virtual tour of specific ships. Some offer interactive programs to help you match your interests and preferred travel dates to a particular cruise. On most of the cruise lines' sites, you can also find links to that line's preferred travel agents.

Most of the sites do not allow for on-line booking. You might find sporadic special deals offered at the sites, but these are usually the same deals your travel agent can get you.

Here's a list of recommended cruise line sites:

Alaska's Glacier Bay	www.glacierbaytours.com
Alaska Sightseeing	www.smallship.com
American Canadian Caribbean Line	www.accl–smallships.com
American Hawaii Cruises	www.cruisehawaii.com
Cape Canaveral	www.capecanaveralcruise.com
Carnival Cruise Lines	www.carnival.com
Celebrity Cruises	www.celebrity-cruises.com
Clipper Cruise Line	www.clippercruise.com
Commodore Cruise Line	www.commodorecruise.com
Costa Cruise Lines	www.costacruises.com
Cunard	www.cunardline.com
Delta Queen Steamboat Co.	www.deltaqueen.com
Disney Cruise Line	www.disney.com/DisneyCruise
Holland America Line	www.hollandamerica.com
Norwegian Cruise Line	www.ncl.com
Premier Cruises	www.premiercruises.com
Princess	www.princesscruises.com
Radisson Seven Seas Cruises	www.asource.com/radisson
Regal Cruises	www.regalcruises.com
Royal Caribbean International	www.royalcaribbean.com
Royal Olympic Cruises	www.royalolympiccruises.com
Seabourn	www.seabourn.com
Star Clippers	www.star-clippers.com
Tall Ship Adventures	www.asource.com/tallship
Windjammer Barefoot Cruises	www.windjammer.com
Windstar Cruises	www.windstarcruises.com
World Explorer Cruises	www.wecruise.com

Another good source for cruise information accessible to users of America Online is **Cruise Critic.** Type in **cruises** as the keyword.

Choosing a Cabin—From Coffins to Penthouses

Once you and your agent get an idea of what kind of ship and itinerary you want, the biggest decision you're going to have to make, and on which your travel agent can give you some advice, is what kind of cabin is right for you. After all, if you were shopping for a house, you wouldn't decide you wanted to live in, say, Cincinnati, and then take any old house just because it's there.

Since some of today's megaships are just about as big as Cincinnati (or at least seem that way), the same rules apply.

The cruise lines have improved things a bit since Charles Dickens said his stateroom reminded him of a coffin, but you can still find cramped, windowless spaces. On the other hand, you can also find penthouse-sized suites with expansive verandas, Jacuzzis, and hot-and-cold–running butler service.

So what kind of cabin is right for you?

Price will likely be a big factor here. But so should the vacation style you prefer. Do you plan to spend a lot of quiet time in your cabin? Or are you the type who will be so busy you'll just use the cabin to change your clothes and to collapse in at the end of the day?

Manfred Ursprunger, vice president of customer satisfaction for Celebrity Cruises, says "A lot of people come on board and never get out of their room. They want a very relaxed vacation, to watch some nice movies, to read a book on the veranda." These folks, he says, should choose the biggest stateroom they can afford.

Meanwhile, he says, there are "Very active guests [who] spend very little time in their room and want to see every activity, every show." They would probably be just as happy with a smaller cabin.

You *Can* Always Get What You Want

Most cabins on cruise ships today have a private bathroom with a shower and twin beds that can be converted into a queen-size bed. Some cabins have bunk beds, which are obviously not convertible.

Many ships have rooms designed for three or four people and include bunks. In some rooms, it is possible to put in a fifth, portable bed. Some lines offer special cabins designed for families of four or five. Families might also be able to book connecting cabins, although they'll naturally have to pay for two cabins to do so.

Most cabins (but not all) have televisions. Some also have extra amenities, such as safes, mini-refrigerators, VCRs, bathrobes, and hair dryers.

A bathtub is considered a luxury on ships and usually is offered only in more expensive rooms.

Brochures: More Than Just Pretty Pictures

The typical ship offers several types of cabins, as outlined by **deck plans** in the cruise line's brochure. (For reference, see the sample deck plan in this chapter.) The cabins are usually described by price (highest to lowest), category (words such as *suite, deluxe, superior, standard,* and *economy* are used), and furniture configuration ("sitting area with two lower beds," for example). Cabin diagrams are typically included.

The cabins will also be described as being **inside** or **outside.** That might sound confusing, but it doesn't mean that you have a choice of sleeping

Reading a Ship's Deck Plan

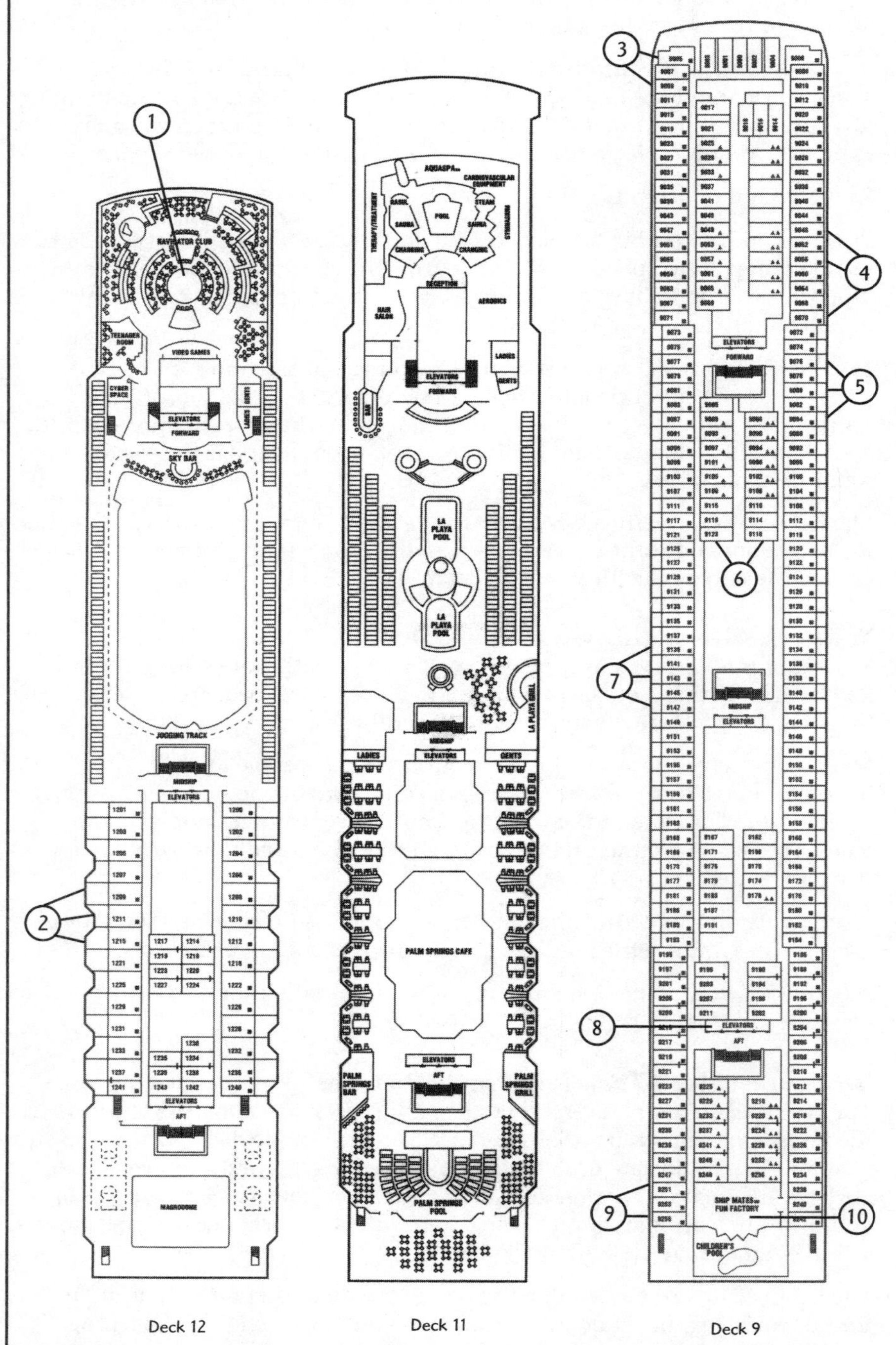

Deck 12

Deck 11

Deck 9

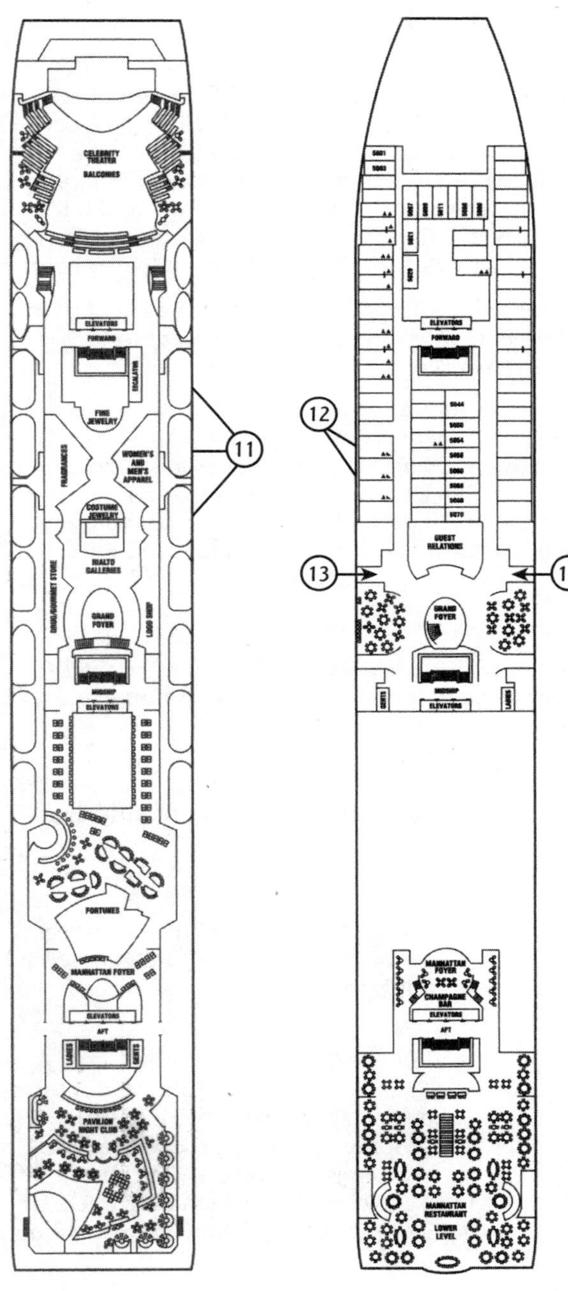

Deck 7

Deck 5

Decks

1 2 3 4 5 6 7 8 9 10 11 12

Some Cabin Choice Considerations:

1. Note the position of the ship's disco and other loud public areas, and try not to book a cabin that's too close or underneath. This disco is far from any cabins—a big plus.

2. Cabins on upper decks can be affected by the motion of the sea. If you're abnormally susceptible to seasickness, keep this in mind.

3. Ditto for cabins in the bow.

4. Outside cabins without verandas appear as solid blocks of space.

5. Outside cabins with verandas are shown with a line dividing the two spaces.

6. Inside cabins (without windows) can be a real money-saver.

7. Cabins amidships are the least affected by the motion of the sea, especially if they're on a lower deck.

8. Cabins that adjoin elevator shaftways might be noisy. (Though proximity makes it easier to get around the ship.)

9. Cabins in the stern can be affected by the motion of the sea, and tend to be subject to engine vibration.

10. Cabins near children's facilities may not be the quietest places, at least during the day.

11. Check that lifeboats don't block the view from your cabin. The ones in this example adjoin public rooms, and so are out of sight.

12. Cabins for people with disabilities are ideally located near elevators and close to the ship's entrances (#13).

(Thanks to Celebrity Cruises for use of the *Mercury*'s deck plan) under the stars in the ocean breeze. Simply put, inside cabins do not have windows, and outside cabins do. As most people consider windows to be a good thing, the outside cabins are more expensive.

Windows allow light into the cabin and might allow ocean views, but be careful here: That view might be obstructed (usually by a lifeboat) or look out onto a public area, which is an issue if you crave privacy. The deck plans in the cruise-line brochures give you some idea of whether either of these is the case, but even if you see lifeboats drawn in where your window should be, that doesn't *necessarily* mean they're blocking the view—they could, for example, be positioned above or below the sightlines of your window. This is another area in which your travel agent's experience with the ship can help.

I personally like a window, because it creates a feeling of openness. But if you do not plan to spend a lot of time in your cabin, you might want to forgo the window. You'll save bucks in the process.

Usually, the higher on the ship the cabin is located, the more expensive and nicer the cabin is. This is true even if there are cabins of the same size on lower decks (in which case, the decor changes). Luxury suites are usually on upper decks. Here's a quirky fact about cabin pricing, though: You might get that king-of-the-hill feeling on the upper decks, but in rough seas, you'll notice the pitch and roll much less in the cabins in the middle and lower parts of the ship.

Measuring Up

The size of a cabin is described in terms of square feet. This number might not mean a lot unless you want to mark it out on your floor at home, but to give you an idea, consider these guidelines:

- 120 square feet and less is low-end and cramped.
- 180 square feet is mid-range (and the minimum for people with claustrophobia).
- 250 square feet and larger is suite-size.

Smooth Sailing

The most-expensive and least-expensive cabins on any given ship tend to sell out first, so if you're looking at either of these options, book early.

Of course, how crowded the cabin seems depends on its furniture configuration and how many people are sharing a room.

A recent and popular innovation on cruise ships is cabins with verandas (or *balconies,* as most people call them). These spaces give you private outdoor space to enjoy sea breezes, but they vary in size and tend to demand big bucks. If you're looking to do more than stand on

Model Cabin Layouts

Typical Outside Cabin Configurations

- Twin beds (can often be pushed together)
- Upper berths for extra passengers fold into walls
- Bathrooms usually have showers only (no tub)
- Usually (but not always) have TVs and radios
- May have portholes or picture windows

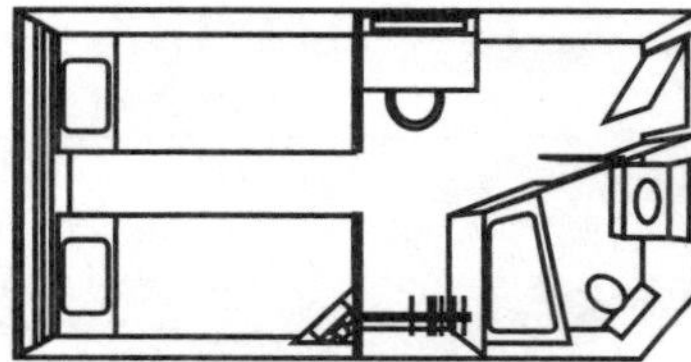

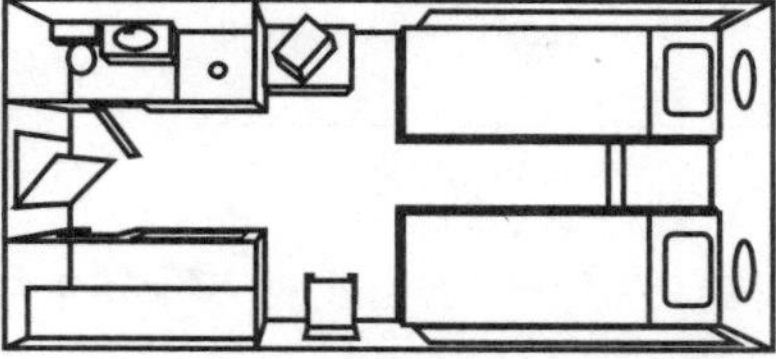

Typical Suite Configurations

- Queen-size or double beds
- Sitting areas (sometimes with sofa beds for extra passengers)
- Large bathrooms, usually with tub
- Refrigerators (sometimes stocked, sometimes not)
- Stereos and TVs with VCRs are common
- Large closets
- Large windows or outside verandas

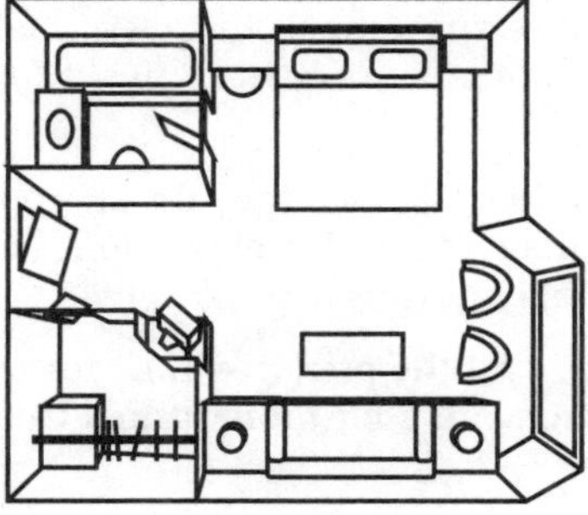

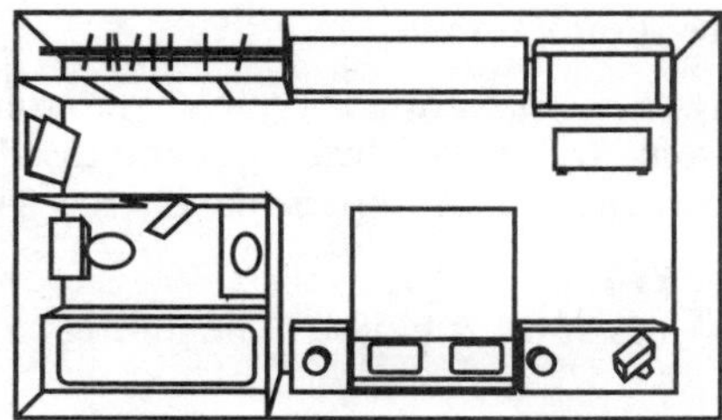

your balcony (sit in a lounge chair, dine, or make whoopee there), make sure the outdoor space is big enough to accommodate your plans.

The Sounds of Silence

Noise can be a factor that influences your cabin choice. Consider that if you take a cabin on a lower deck, you might hear engine noises, and if you're in the back of the ship, thruster noises (one cruise line official jokes that these cabins are great for honeymooners, because the vibrations caused by the noise have basically the same effect as Magic Fingers). A cabin near an elevator might bring door-opening and closing sounds, and a cabin above or below the disco might pulse until all hours of the night.

If noise is a consideration for you, make your cabin choice accordingly.

Video Cruising

Still not sure? In addition to brochures, many lines offer videos of their product. While the videos still use those beautiful-people models, they might give you a better idea than print pieces about the ship's size, space, and other offerings. Your travel agent might have videos you can borrow, or you might be able to order a video directly from the cruise line. You can also place an order with **Vacations on Video** (☎ **602/483-1551**), a major distributor, which offers videos for virtually all the major lines. The videos vary in length and go for an average price of $7.95, plus shipping charges.

Choosing Your Dining Option: Seating Times & Table Sizes

Another decision your travel agent will help you make is requesting your preferred meal time and table assignment.

The Sounds of the Dinner Bell

Because most ship dining rooms are not large enough to accommodate all passengers at once, ships typically offer two seatings (or sittings), especially for **dinner.** Typically, except on some of the smaller or ritzier ships, all table space is on a reserved basis.

Early or main seating is typically at around 6pm; late seating falls at around 8:30pm. There are advantages and disadvantages to both times, and it basically comes down to personal choice. Typically, it runs like this:

- **Early seating** is usually less crowded and the preferred time for families and the elderly. The dining experience is a bit more rushed (the staff needs to make way for the next wave). But food items don't have to sit for hours under warmers and might be fresher. You can see a show right after dinner and have first dibs on other nighttime venues as well. And you just might be hungry again in time for the midnight buffet.

- **Late seating** gives you time for a good long nap or a late spa appointment before dinner. Dinner is not rushed at all. You can sit as long as you want, enjoying after-dinner drinks—unless, that is, you choose to rush off to catch the 10pm show. You probably won't be hungry again at midnight, but you can go and laugh at all those who are.

If you choose to also eat **breakfast** and **lunch** in the dining room instead of at the more casual venues on the ship, you are, in theory at least, also supposed to eat at assigned times as well. I've found, however, that most ships aren't hard and fast on this. Crowds in the dining room are typically only an issue at dinner. If you show up at other than your assigned time at breakfast or lunch and your assigned table is full, the staff will probably just seat you elsewhere.

Typical Meal Times

Early Seating

- Breakfast: 7 or 8am
- Lunch: noon
- Dinner: 6 or 6:30pm

Late Seating

- Breakfast: 8:30 or 9am
- Lunch: 1:30pm
- Dinner: 8:15 or 8:30pm

Intimate Table for Two or Algonquin Round Table?

Do you mind sitting with strangers? Are you looking to make new friends? Do you want to be at a table for 1, 2, 4, 8, 10, or 12?

Rather than waiting for the luck of the draw, you can indicate your seating preference in advance through your travel agent. Based on your request, you will be assigned a table. Some lines indicate this assignment in advance on your tickets. Others give you your table assignment when you arrive at the ship.

In either case, don't worry if you don't like your assignment, because you'll probably be able to change it. Just tell the dining-room maitre d' if you're not happy, and he'll review the seating charts for an opening. (Of course, a little palm-greasing will probably help.)

In some cases, you can also request in advance of your cruise your preference for either a smoking or nonsmoking section of the dining room. (Though some cruise lines—including Carnival, Celebrity, Princess, and Royal Caribbean—have banned smoking completely in their dining rooms, making this a moot point.)

Let Your Agent Do the Walking—and the Calling, and the Paperwork . . .

Beyond helping you choose the where and in-what-style aspects of your cruise, your agent can help with some of those other little planning matters—just to make your life (and your vacation) that much easier.

Air Add-Ons

I discussed cruise-line airfare offerings in detail in chapter 2, "Can I Afford a Cruise?: Tips on Discounts & Deals," but your agent can help you decide what works best for you: taking the airfare offered by the cruise line or booking on your own.

Transfers from the airport to the pier are usually included in air/sea offers, but even if you book on your own, you might still be able to make arrangements for transfer through the cruise line—though you'll have to pay a fee, of course. Ask your agent for details.

Pre- and Post-Cruise Offerings

Some of the ports you'll sail from (and back to) are really fun places to explore (see details in chapters 10 and 11), but just as with airfare, you'll need to decide whether you want to buy a land package from the cruise line or make arrangements on your own.

When evaluating a cruise line's package, make sure you review it carefully to see what's included. Some questions to ask include:

- Does the cruise line offer a transfer from the airport to the hotel? From the hotel to the cruise ship?
- Do they use a hotel I'll be happy with? Is it centrally located?
- Are escorted tours included? Admission to local attractions? Meals?
- Is there a rental-car deal offered if I want to explore on my own?

Insurance

Your agent can also advise you on travel-insurance options (see chapter 2).

Deposits

Once you've made all your choices, kicked the tires, and looked at your trip's profile in the mirror a few more times, you'll be asked by your travel agent to make a deposit. The amount will either be a fixed amount or be based on a percentage of your total cruise cost. Later, you'll receive a receipt in the mail from the cruise lines. You'll be asked to pay the remaining fare usually no later than 2 months before your departure date.

Phew! Now the hard part's behind you. The cake is baked. It's time now to get out the icing and put the finishing touches on your dream cruise vacation.

Chapter 9

Tying Up the Loose Ends

In This Chapter

- A word on getting your documents in order
- The money situation at sea
- Budgeting for your cruise
- Advice on packing
- A last-minute checklist

OK, now you've made most of the hard decisions you'll have to make. The rest of your vacation planning should be relatively easy, because the cruise lines take over much of the arranging work, particularly if you've booked a package that includes airfare.

You should carefully read the brochure of your chosen cruise line (make sure your agent gives you one), because most include sections that address commonly asked questions. Just to be on the safe side, though, in this chapter, I'll run through the major questions that apply to almost every cruise.

Papers, Please!: Passports & IDs

For most of the itineraries described in this book (the Caribbean, Mexico, Alaska, Canada, and Hawaii), you do not need a passport. If you have one, however, bring it along, because it will help speed your way through customs and immigration as the preferred form of identification.

Here's some ID facts to consider:

- ➤ If you do not have a passport, you are required to bring a photo ID *and* proof of citizenship, such as a birth certificate (or a certified copy) or a voter-registration card.
- ➤ A driver's license is not considered enough ID.
- ➤ It's important to carry your ID with you. If you're flying, keep it in your hand luggage—not in your suitcase.
- ➤ You will not be allowed to board the ship without proper ID. This applies to everyone, including infants and children.
- ➤ If a child is traveling with someone other than his or her parents or legal guardian—a grandparent, for example—or with only one parent, you will also be required to have written permission from the absent parent(s) for the child to make the trip.
- ➤ If you are not a U.S. citizen but live in the United States, you have to carry your alien-registration card and passport. Non–U.S. citizens visiting from their home countries also have to carry a passport (and in some cases may be required to have a visa).
- ➤ If you take a cruise to Europe, Asia, or another part of the world, you'll be required to have a passport and possibly a visa as well. You'll need to apply for either well in advance of your trip. Check with your travel agent for advice.

Cold Hard Cash

I've never encountered any form of travel that, as far as money is concerned, is as easy as taking a cruise.

You've already paid the lion's share of your all-inclusive vacation when you get on board the ship. Then, when you check in at the cruise terminal, the cruise line folks will ask for a major credit card, to which all your onboard expenses will be billed at the end of your cruise. You also have the option of paying your account with cash, traveler's checks, or in some cases, a personal check (check the cruise line's brochure for specific rules on this). You might be asked to leave a deposit if you'll be paying with cash—usually, $250 for a 1-week sailing.

Smooth Sailing

If you need information about passports, call the U.S. Department or State **Office of Passport Services** information line at ☎ **202/ 647-0518.**

Here's how the whole thing works: With most ships, the folks at the check-in counter will give you a special ship charge card that you will use for the length of your cruise. (On some of the small-ship lines, such cards are unnecessary—there are so few people aboard that all you need to do is give your name and cabin number the first time, and after that the staff usually remembers you.) From this point, on most ships, your time on board is virtually cashless—at least until the end of the cruise, when you pay tips to the staff. (Although some lines now allow passengers to charge tips as well. See more on tipping in chapter 26, "The Last Details.") The only other time cash changes hands on most ships is in the casino.

The special ship charge card, which will probably double as your boarding card and on some ships as your room key, too, is what you use to pay for bar drinks, shore excursions, items in the gift shop, massages, beauty services, and so on.

You will need some cash on hand for when you stop at a port to pay for cabs, make small purchases, buy sodas, and tip your tour guides. Having bills smaller than $20 might be useful here. (You can usually exchange large bills for small at the purser's desk.)

United States dollars, along with major credit cards, are accepted at pretty much all the ports described in this book. If you prefer to deal in local currency, however, there are exchange counters and banks close to most of the docks. There are also ATMs at many port stops, but a word of advice here: The ATM will give you cash in the local currency, so don't take more than you need for that day.

To check ATM locations that are part of the widely used **Cirrus** network, call ☎ **800/4-CIRRUS.** For other networks, check with your local bank.

Some ships have their own ATMs aboard, most often located, not surprisingly, in the casino. These give out U.S. dollars.

Ships don't usually offer currency-exchange services on board except on European or Asian itineraries.

It's recommended that you not leave large amounts of cash unguarded in your room. All ships have some sort of safes available, either in the cabins or at the purser's desk, and passengers are wise to use them. Ditto for your plane ticket and passport or ID papers (you might need to retrieve these, however, when you leave the ship at non–U.S. ports).

The Little Things Add Up: Budgeting for Your Cruise

Before your trip, you might want to make a tentative budget.

Cruise folks I've talked to advise that passengers set aside between $40 and $50 a day per person, not including tips (which should run you at least $56 per person for a weeklong cruise). But you can plan for more or less based on your specific wants and needs.

Areas that should be included in your planning are bar drinks, dry cleaning, phone calls, massage and other spa services, beauty-parlor services, photos, wine at dinner, and souvenirs, as well as shore excursions. Remember to also include any port taxes, fees, or other charges.

Life Preservers

Port charges, taxes, and other fees are sometimes (but not always) included in your cruise fare, and these charges can add as much as $125 onto the price of, say, a 7-day Caribbean cruise. Make sure you know what's included when you're calculating your overall expenditures. Your travel agent can assist you on this score. Most cruise-line brochures list port charges and indicate whether they are included in the cruise fare.

There are other extras as well, such as the purchase of caviar at the champagne bar (if your ship has one) or cigars at the cigar bar (if your ship has one). Some ships charge extra for afternoon ice cream sundaes. All ships that offer baby-sitting (as opposed to the organized kids' programs) charge for it, and there might be fees associated with use of the golf simulator (if your ship has one) or other special activities.

Keeping Tabs on Your Tab

I suggest that you keep careful track of your onboard expenses to avoid an unpleasant surprise at the end of your cruise. Some ships make this tracking particularly easy by offering interactive TV. By pushing the right buttons, you can check your account from the comfort of your own stateroom. On other ships, you have to go the purser's or guest-relations desk to review your account. You can do so as often as you choose, but you might encounter lines of others doing the same.

Best, I think, to do it yourself.

On the last night of your cruise, a final bill will be slipped under your door. If everything is okay and you're paying by credit card, you don't have to do anything but keep the copy. If there's a problem on the bill, or if you are paying by cash, traveler's checks, or personal check, you will have to go down to the purser's or guest-relations desk and wait in what will likely be a very long line.

The Mind Is Strong, But the Flesh Is Weak: Budget-Breakers

Don't underestimate in your budget-planning the lure of items in the **gift shop.** The shops offer frequent sales and are especially attractive venues during days at sea (when you can't shop in port). Think you won't want that

$100 windbreaker with the line's logo stitched on? Just wait till you pass it in the shop window for the tenth time.

Also do not underestimate the lure of the **photos** that the ship's photographer takes. These are snapped on board on a posed basis and are offered not only in flat versions but also as keychains and other nifty souvenirs. Even if you're a reluctant poser, they'll get you at some point—trust me.

Lastly, beware the **casino.** A few spins of the roulette wheel or a whirl on the slots might not seem like too much of an investment, but watch yourself: It's very easy to get sucked into the scene.

Reading Your VIPs (Very Important Papers)

About 1 month before your cruise (and no later than 1 week before), you should receive in the mail your **cruise documents,** including your airline tickets (if you purchased them from the cruise line), a boarding document with your cabin and dining choices on it, boarding forms to fill out, luggage tags, and your prearranged bus-transfer vouchers from the airport to the port (if applicable). Also included will likely be a description of shore excursions available for purchase once on board, as well as additional material detailing things you need to know before you sail.

A Shot in the Arm

None of the itineraries mentioned in this book require any sort of inoculation, but if you have concerns, ask your doctor for advice.

All this information is important. Read it carefully. Make sure your cabin category and dining preference are as you requested. Also check your airline tickets to make sure everything is okay in terms of flights and arrival times. Make sure there is enough time so you can arrive at the port no later than a half hour before departure time, and preferably a lot earlier.

When the date of your sailing arrives, these documents should be hand-carried by you to the port. You cannot easily board without them.

Stowing Your Gear: A Cruise-Packing Primer

Some people tend to agonize over what to pack for a cruise vacation. You don't have to.

Except for the addition of a formal night or two, a cruise vacation is really no different than any resort vacation. And in some cases, it's much more casual. I was recently entertained while eating at the outside grill on one ship by a guy walking by with his tray, clad only in what looked like Calvin Klein jockeys. Perhaps the poor fellow forgot his bathing suit. Or perhaps there's a fashion trend I've missed. But I think the fact that he was comfortable dressing in such a manner is a prime example of how virtually anything goes on cruise ships—at least poolside.

But seriously, folks, knowing your ship's dress code will save you embarrassment and make you at least *look* like an experienced cruiser, even if you aren't one (yet).

The Basic Philosophy

Obviously, the weather and your choice of itinerary will be a factor in what you pack. During the day on a Caribbean cruise, very casual wear is perfectly okay. Shorts and T-shirts are the most popular, along with bathing suits and a cover-up.

Slightly warmer casual wear, like sweatshirts and jeans or jogging outfits, is the norm in Alaska during the summer months. In the shoulder season (May and September), you'll also want a waterproof jacket and maybe a sweater.

Ahoy, Mateys!

To check **weather** for destinations on your itinerary in advance of your trip, you can watch The Weather Channel, or for a fee of 95¢ per minute, call ☎ **900/ WEATHER,** a service operated by The Weather Channel that provides weather reports and forecasts for more than 900 cities.

Puttin' on the Ritz

Don't feel that you have to go out and buy "cruisewear." Unless you're just really excessively proper (in which case, you probably already *own* cruisewear), dinner is the only dress-up time you'll need to prepare for on ships. Cruise lines publish their dress code in their brochures, and information on the number of dressy occasions is provided before your trip.

Generally, ships describe proper dinner attire in their daily bulletins as **formal, informal,** or **casual.**

There are usually 2 formal nights and 2 informal nights during a 5-day to 7-day cruise, with the rest casual. There will usually be 1 formal night on a 2- to 4-day cruise.

- **Formal** means a tux or dark suit with tie for men; and a nice cocktail dress, long dress, gown, or dressy pants suit for women. (Black anything is particularly in, so if you really want to stand out, wear something bright.)
- **Informal** is a jacket, tie, and dress slacks, or a light suit for men (jeans are frowned upon); and a dress, skirt and blouse, or pants outfit for women. (The little black dress is appropriate here.)
- **Casual** at dinner does *not* mean shorts. Men should wear a sports shirt or open dress shirt with slacks (some will also wear a jacket); women should wear a dress, pants outfit, or skirt and blouse.

Men who don't own a **tuxedo** might be able to rent one in advance through the cruise line's preferred supplier (who will deliver the tux right to the ship). In some cases, the ship will keep a limited supply on board. Information on this service will often be sent with your cruise documents. If not, check with the cruise line for specifics.

Men tend to forget to pack cufflinks and cummerbunds, as well as black shoes, so here's your reminder:

Don't forget your cufflinks, cummerbund, and black shoes!!!

If you forget anyway, you can usually buy replacements at the ship's gift shop.

Special Wingdings

Most ships also have at least one casual theme night—country and western, Caribbean, the sixties, and so on. There also might be a masquerade party and/or a talent show that you might want to have a costume for. You can find out in advance from the cruise line what's on tap for your sailing and pack accordingly.

The Nitty-Gritty: Packing Specifics

What you choose to bring obviously involves a lot of personal choice, but here are some specific tips I hope will help.

The first rule is: **DON'T OVERPACK!!!** Even though cruise lines don't usually restrict how much you can bring on board, airlines usually do (check with your carrier for specifics). And remember, storage space in many staterooms is limited. What you pack, you have to live with (and step over) for the length of your cruise.

Here are some tips to keep in mind when you have the suitcase open on your bed and are getting ready to toss the closet in. It might help to chant these catch phrases like a mantra, just to calm your mind and prevent you from committing packing sins you'll regret later:

1. **Pack your clothes in bags that are tough!**

   Pack your clothes in bags that are sturdy enough to withstand not only airport baggage handlers but also those at the port.

2. **And don't forget that you'll buy some stuff!**

   You'll probably want to buy some items along the way—straw hats are a great buy in Key West, for example. So, try to leave a little room, or stow an extra lightweight bag in your luggage.

3. **Pack permanent press, so you'll always look dandy!**

   It's generally recommended that you avoid, whenever possible, packing clothes that need frequent ironing, although if the ship does have a guest laundry room, there will likely be an iron you can use for touch-ups. If I have an item I'm afraid will wrinkle, I carefully fold it around a dry-cleaning bag (tissue also works). I've found that this helps.

4. **And remember, the laundry service is handy!**

   Take into consideration that ships offer dry-cleaning and/or laundry services (for a fee, of course), and some even offer coin-operated laundry facilities. If you sweat out a T-shirt in the gym, you can easily get it washed.

5. **Bring one basic color, so you'll always shine!**

   A little tip for women: Choose one basic color to wear during the cruise. This allows you to avoid having to pack multiple pairs of coordinating shoes. You can take a simple long black dress and a short black dress and accessorize them with jackets, jewelry, and scarves so they'll look like different outfits each night. The same kind of rule applies to men. Make it easy on yourself and stick with clothes that all go together.

6. **And mind the climate, so you'll always feel fine!**

   For warmer climates, especially during the day, you might want to stick with breathable cotton fabrics. For colder climates, you're best off taking a layering approach. Even in the summer, temperatures in Alaska might not go much higher than the 50s or 60s, although they sometimes go into the 70s or even 80s. Having layers to peal off or toss on is the most convenient approach.

Suggested Checklist for a 1-Week Caribbean or Other Warm-Climate Cruise

Women

- ☐ Two bathing suits (one if you don't plan to actually get wet)
- ☐ A cover-up
- ☐ Two pairs of shorts
- ☐ Four tops (T-shirts are okay)
- ☐ Two sundresses or casual skirt or pants outfits

- ☐ Two formal outfits
- ☐ Two or three nice but less formal dresses or outfits
- ☐ Dress shoes
- ☐ Accessories
- ☐ A light sweater or jacket (for air-conditioning or evening deck strolls)
- ☐ A night shirt or pajamas (some cruise lines provide robes)
- ☐ One pair of sandals (that can be worn with dresses)
- ☐ One pair of walking shoes or rubber-soled sandals
- ☐ Extra nylons
- ☐ Undies
- ☐ A light raincoat and/or umbrella
- ☐ Gym clothes and sneakers, if you plan to exercise
- ☐ A sun hat
- ☐ Sunscreen (SPF 15 or higher)
- ☐ Toiletries, including toothpaste (most, but not all ships provide shampoo). Don't forget bug spray for tropical climates and condoms if you plan to indulge.
- ☐ Sunglasses
- ☐ A camera and film
- ☐ A good novel and/or magazines

Men

- ☐ Two bathing suits (one if you don't plan to get wet)
- ☐ Two pairs of shorts
- ☐ Four polo shirts or T-shirts
- ☐ Two pairs of lightweight slacks (one pair can be jeans)
- ☐ One pair of walking shoes
- ☐ Gym clothes and sneakers, if you plan to exercise
- ☐ Pajamas (some cruise lines provide robes)
- ☐ One pair of sandals
- ☐ A tux or dark business suit (plus appropriate shirts, ties, cufflinks, cummerbund, and accessories)
- ☐ Two belts, one dressy and one casual

- ☐ A sports coat
- ☐ Two or three pairs of dress slacks
- ☐ A light suit (optional)
- ☐ Dress shoes
- ☐ Three dress shirts
- ☐ Undies
- ☐ A hat
- ☐ Sunscreen (SPF 15 or higher)
- ☐ Toiletries, including toothpaste (most ships, but not all, provide shampoo). Don't forget bug spray for tropical climates and condoms if you plan to indulge.
- ☐ Sunglasses
- ☐ A camera and film
- ☐ A good novel and/or magazines

Suggested Checklist for a 1-Week Alaska or Colder-Climate Cruise

Women

- ☐ A lightweight, waterproof coat or jacket (waterproof is key here, as Alaska can be quite rainy)
- ☐ A sweater or warm vest
- ☐ A warm hat and gloves
- ☐ Two or three pairs of pants or jeans
- ☐ Several polo shirts, blouses, and/or light sweaters
- ☐ A blazer
- ☐ A warm-up suit
- ☐ Gym clothes and sneakers, if you plan to exercise
- ☐ A night shirt or pajamas (some cruise lines provide robes)
- ☐ A bathing suit
- ☐ Walking shoes (two pairs, preferably, in case one pair gets wet)
- ☐ Three assorted dresses (for informal or casual nights) or skirt and pants outfits
- ☐ Two formal-night outfits
- ☐ Accessories

- ☐ Undies
- ☐ Dress shoes
- ☐ Extra nylons
- ☐ A warm coat (optional, if you can layer instead)
- ☐ Toiletries, including toothpaste (most ships, but not all, provide shampoo). Surprisingly, you will need bug spray; bring condoms if you plan to indulge.
- ☐ Sunscreen (SPF 15 or higher)
- ☐ Sunglasses
- ☐ A camera and film
- ☐ A good novel and/or magazines

Men

- ☐ A lightweight, waterproof coat or jacket
- ☐ A hat and gloves
- ☐ Three or four pairs of casual slacks or jeans
- ☐ Several polo shirts and sweaters
- ☐ Two pairs of dress slacks
- ☐ A tux or dark business suit (plus appropriate shirts, ties, and accessories)
- ☐ A sports coat
- ☐ A necktie or neckties
- ☐ Three dress shirts
- ☐ Two belts—one dressy and one casual
- ☐ A warm coat (optional, if you can layer instead)
- ☐ Pajamas (some cruise lines provide robes)
- ☐ A warm-up suit
- ☐ Gym clothes and sneakers, if you plan to exercise
- ☐ A bathing suit
- ☐ Undies
- ☐ Walking shoes (two pairs, preferably, in case one pair gets wet)
- ☐ Sunscreen (SPF 15 or above)
- ☐ Binoculars

- ☐ Toiletries, including toothpaste (most ships, but not all, provide shampoo). Surprisingly, you will need bug spray; bring condoms if you plan to indulge.
- ☐ Sunglasses
- ☐ A camera and film
- ☐ A good novel and/or magazines

Additional Packing Tips

- I recommend packing a few hangers, just in case there aren't enough in your cabin. And if you don't like light filtering into your room in the morning, you might find that a few large safety pins come in handy for keeping the curtains closed.
- You'll also want to pack an extra bag to hold all those souvenirs you swear you won't buy (some lines provide tote bags free of charge, or sell them in the gift shop).
- Having a beach bag or something that can double for one (I like a backpack) is handy for beach excursions. You generally don't need to pack a beach towel, since the line should provide towels to take ashore (unless, of course, you have a favorite towel you prefer).
- Even in colder-weather climates, I take a backpack on shore excursions to carry my camera and other items.
- If you plan to bring along your own golf clubs, tennis racket, or scuba gear, you might want to check with the airlines for the best way to ship those items.
- You might not have to bring a hair dryer. Some ships provide them (though they're rarely very powerful). You can check this in advance.
- Most ships have standard 100 AC outlets, so you shouldn't have trouble plugging in your hair dryer or electric shaver.
- Some people prefer to bring their own travel alarm clocks. Most ships offer a telephone wake-up service for those who don't want to.
- If you plan on taking pictures, you'll want to bring along plenty of film, as it's not usually a cheap item in tourist destinations.
- Another word of advice, as I made this mistake on a recent cruise: Don't pack new shoes, unless you also pack Band-Aids for the blisters.
- If you plan to participate in the talent show and have a special costume you wear in your act, don't forget to pack that. Ditto if you want to dress up appropriately for theme night (you can call the cruise line in advance to check on what themes will be offered during your sailing).
- Big, important one: Remember to pack prescription medicine, passport or other ID, cruise documents, credit cards, money, traveler's checks,

house and car keys, claim checks for airport parking, and airplane tickets *in your carry-on luggage only.* Don't ever pack these items in baggage that you're going to check.

What to Carry in Your Carry-On

Remember, the following items should go in your hand luggage only: prescription medicine, passport or other ID, cruise documents, credit cards, money, traveler's checks, house and car keys, claim checks for airport parking, and airplane tickets. You are also advised to hand-carry any valuables, including jewelry, binoculars, cameras, and video equipment. You might also want to pack in your hand luggage a change of clothes (just in case your bags get delayed), your eyeglasses, some reading material, sea-sickness medication (in case you have a bumpy flight), and chewing gum.

A Word on Jewelry & Other Valuables

Okay, it's hard to resist taking along the family jewels for the formal night, but remember, you do so at your own risk. Keep the jewels in your in-room safe or in the purser's safe when you're not wearing them.

You should also carry a receipt for really expensive items. Otherwise, you might get stuck paying duty when you go through customs at the end of your cruise. (Officials might think the item is a little something you picked up on your trip.) Same goes for cameras and other valuables.

Confirming Your Flight

Since arrival and departure times are sometimes subject to change, you might want to confirm your flight a day before departure (or 3 days before departure for international flights).

Don't forget to also call the airline the day of your flight to make sure it's operating on time.

Plan to arrive at the airport 1 hour before departure for domestic flights and 2 hours before departure for international flights.

A Last-Minute Checklist

OK, your bags are packed and you're ready for the big trip. What's left? Here's a checklist of things people usually forget:

- ☐ Have the Post Office hold your mail or have a friend take it in for you.
- ☐ Stop your newspaper delivery or have a friend take it in for you.

- ☐ Refill your medical prescriptions with an appropriate supply, and bring them with you.
- ☐ Photocopy your passport or ID, airline tickets, and any credit cards you plan to use, and either pack these in a separate place from the actual documents or leave them with a friend.
- ☐ If you carry traveler's checks, remember to keep a separate record of the numbers. If you do lose them, you'll be required to report the numbers.
- ☐ Make photocopies of your itinerary to leave with a friend.
- ☐ Put a card with your name and address inside the luggage you plan to check in with the airline (in case your luggage tags fall off).
- ☐ Make sure your luggage tags are on your bags.
- ☐ Leave the ship's phone number, which should be included in your cruise documents, with a friend or relative. They can reach you at ☎ **800/SEA-CALL,** an expensive service run by AT&T that connects the caller to the ship's operator.
- ☐ Lastly, remember to read the material provided by the cruise line for ship-specific suggestions that might not be included here.

Checking In Luggage

After you have packed your bags, put one of the luggage tags that arrived with your cruise documents on each bag. Make sure you correctly fill in the tags with your departure date, port, cabin number, and so on. You can find all this information in your cruise documents. Put a luggage tag on your hand baggage as well.

If you've booked your airfare through the cruise line, you should be able at your departure airport to check your properly identified luggage through all the way to the ship, where it will be delivered straight to your cabin. Once you're on the ship, don't panic if your bags are not at your cabin when you arrive, since getting all the bags on board is a rather slow process. If it gets close to sailing time and you're concerned, call guest relations or the purser's office. They'll probably tell you it's on the way.

If you've booked your own air, you will have to check in your bags at the airline and retrieve them in baggage claim as normal, and then check them in with the cruise line at the port or, if you've separately arranged pickup with the cruise line, at the airport.

Part 4

Taking Passage: The Ports of Embarkation

As I suggested earlier, you might want to consider coming into the city your cruise leaves from at least a day or two ahead of your cruise departure date. This will give you time to check out the local attractions and alleviate any fears you might have about your plane getting delayed—worrying that you'll miss the boat is not a fun way to start your vacation. If you're traveling between coasts, arriving early also gives you a chance to catch up from jet lag and adjust to the time difference.

In chapter 10, I'll highlight things to do and places to stay at the major ports for cruises to the Caribbean and Mexico, and I'll do the same for Alaska cruises in chapter 11. Some small ships might depart from other ports, which you'll find described in part 6.

Chapter 10

Jump-Off Points to Fun in the Sun

In This Chapter

- Where to stay, what to see, and where to eat at your port of embarkation
- Maps of all the major embarkation ports for cruises in the Caribbean and Eastern Mexico

Keep in mind that most ships to the Caribbean and Mexico don't start boarding or embarkation until the afternoon and don't depart until after 4pm. So, if you plan right, you can get at least a half-day of sightseeing in on your departure day.

The main port cities for Caribbean cruises are all tourist destinations unto themselves, and as such, most lines offer a precruise hotel package, usually 2 to 4 days, as well as a post-cruise package for those who want to stretch their vacation a few days at the end of the cruise. If, however, you choose to go it alone, you can get an idea of the city's hotel offerings by checking out my suggestions in this chapter. I'll also offer a smattering of where-to-eat and where-to-play options and run through the sightseeing highlights.

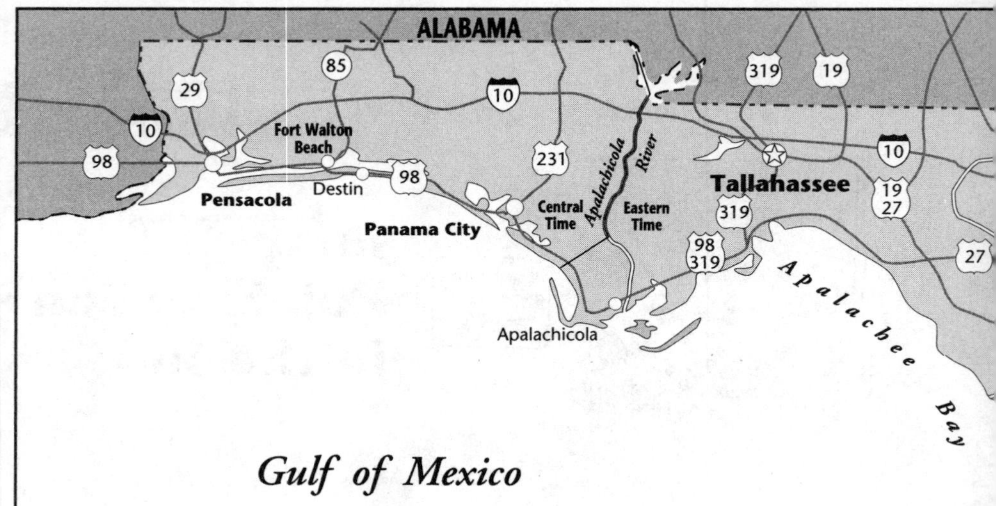

Cruise Line Home Ports	
Port of Miami *(Miami)*	Carnival Cunard Norwegian Premier Royal Caribbean
Port Everglades *(Fort Lauderdale)*	Celebrity Costa Holland America Mediterranean Shipping Cruises Princess Royal Olympic Seabourn
Port Canaveral *(Cape Canaveral)*	Cape Canaveral Carnival Disney Premier Royal Caribbean
Tampa	Carnival Holland America

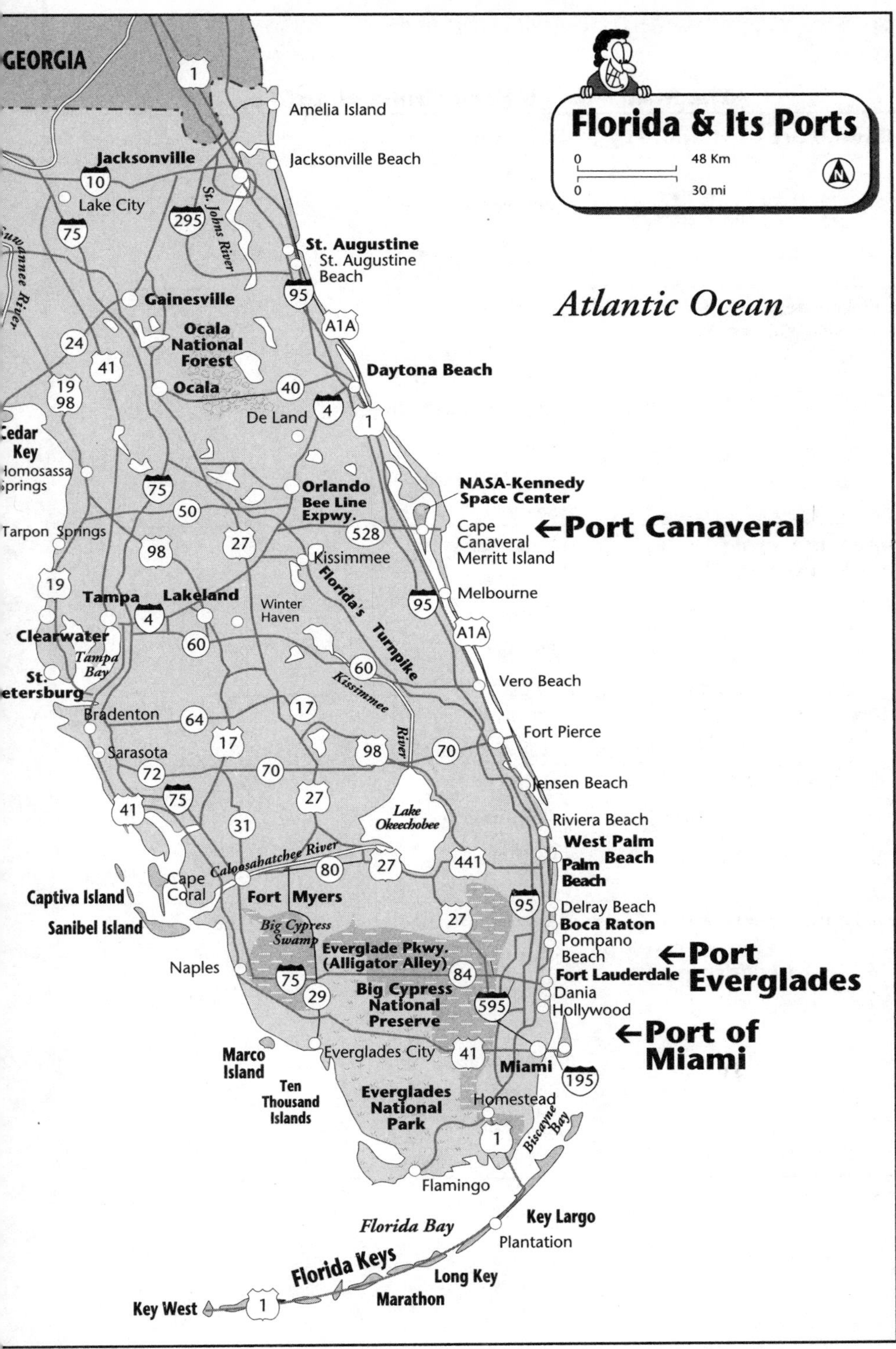

Florida & Its Ports
0
48 Km
0
30 mi
GEORGIA
Atlantic Ocean
Amelia Island
Jacksonville Beach
Jacksonville
Lake City
St. Johns River
St. Augustine
St. Augustine Beach
Gainesville
Ocala National Forest
Ocala
Daytona Beach
De Land
Cedar Key
Homosassa Springs
Orlando
Bee Line Expwy.
NASA-Kennedy Space Center
Cape Canaveral
Merritt Island
←Port Canaveral
Tarpon Springs
Kissimmee
Florida's Turnpike
Melbourne
Tampa
Lakeland
Winter Haven
Clearwater
Tampa Bay
St. Petersburg
Kissimmee River
Vero Beach
Bradenton
Fort Pierce
Sarasota
Jensen Beach
Lake Okeechobee
Riviera Beach
West Palm Beach
Palm Beach
Caloosahatchee River
Cape Coral
Fort Myers
Captiva Island
Sanibel Island
Big Cypress Swamp
Delray Beach
Boca Raton
Pompano Beach
←Port Everglades
Everglade Pkwy. (Alligator Alley)
Naples
Fort Lauderdale
Dania
Hollywood
Big Cypress National Preserve
←Port of Miami
Marco Island
Everglades City
Miami
Ten Thousand Islands
Everglades National Park
Homestead
Biscayne Bay
Flamingo
Florida Bay
Key Largo
Plantation
Florida Keys
Long Key
Marathon
Key West

The Main Ports & Their Cruise Lines*

Port	Cruise Lines
Miami, Port of Miami, FL	Carnival Cunard Norwegian Premier Royal Caribbean
Fort Lauderdale, Port Everglades, FL	Celebrity Costa Holland America Mediterranean Shipping Cruises Princess Royal Olympic Seabourn
Cape Canaveral, Port Canaveral, FL	Cape Canaveral Carnival Disney Premier Royal Caribbean
Tampa, FL	Carnival Holland America
New Orleans, LA	Carnival Commodore Crystal Holland America
San Juan, Puerto Rico	American Canadian Caribbean Line Carnival Celebrity Holland America Norwegian Princess Radisson Royal Caribbean

The following lines also sail ships from these smaller ports:

American Canadian Caribbean Line: St. Lucia; St.Thomas; Ponce, PR

Clipper: St. Thomas, Grenada

Club Med: Martinique

Cunard: St. Thomas, Barbados

Norwegian: Houston

Premier: Aruba, Santo Domingo

Radisson: Aruba

Regal: Port Manatee, FL

Royal Olympic: Galveston, TX

Star Clippers: Antigua, Barbados

Tall Ship Adventures: Tortola, St. Lucia

Windjammer: Fajardo and Ponce, PR; Trinidad; St. Maarten; Tortola; Grenada; Antigua; Nassau, Bahamas

Windstar: St. Thomas; Barbados

**Information provided by* Travel Weekly's Official Cruise Guide.

Miami

The Port of Miami is located at 1015 N. America Way, in central Miami. You can reach it via a five-lane bridge from the downtown district. For information, call ☎ **305/371-PORT.**

The Port of Miami is the primary port in the cruise world. Among the more than 15 cruise vessels berthed here are several of the world's largest cruise ships. Some 4 million cruise passengers are expected to pass through the port in 1999.

To handle all the traffic, officials have created a dozen bi-level terminals, all offering duty-free shopping, customs clearance, and easy car access. Plans to add 4 additional terminals and a 53-acre waterfront park, with shops, restaurants, museums and, entertainment offerings, are underway.

For now, passengers just have to cross the bridge (by shuttle) to access Bayside Marketplace, a restaurant and shopping complex.

Getting There

BY PLANE Flying to Miami, you'll arrive at the huge **Miami International Airport,** which is located about 8 miles from downtown and the Port of Miami. A cab ride to the port should cost about $15. Lower-cost options include public **Metrobus** service (☎ **305/638-6700**).

If you choose to rent a car, Avis, Budget, Dollar, Hertz, National, and Value all have counters in the airport's baggage-claim area.

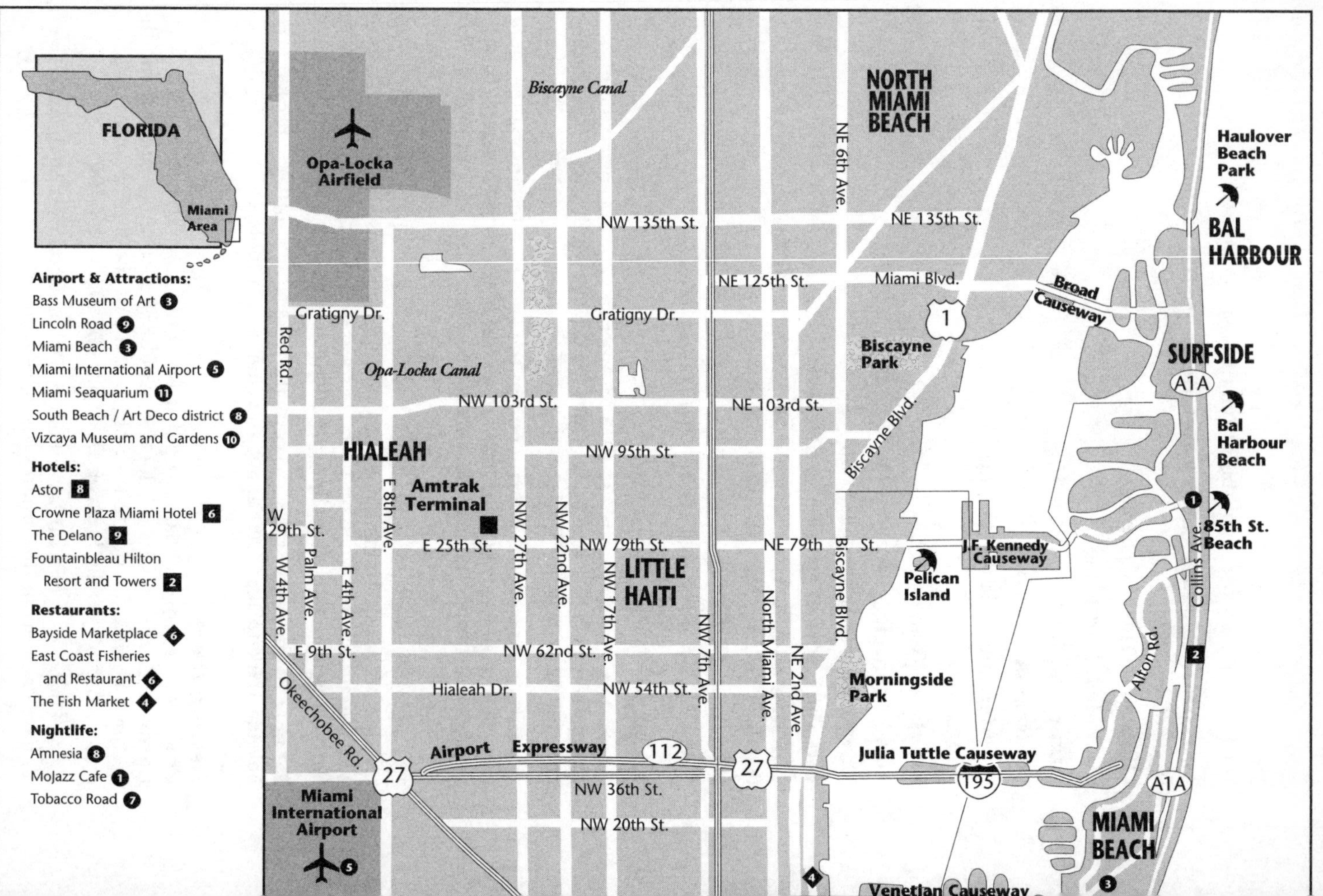
FLORIDA
Miami Area
Airport & Attractions:
Bass Museum of Art 3
Lincoln Road 9
Miami Beach 3
Miami International Airport 5
Miami Seaquarium 11
South Beach / Art Deco district 8
Vizcaya Museum and Gardens 10
Hotels:
Astor 8
Crowne Plaza Miami Hotel 6
The Delano 9
Fountainbleau Hilton Resort and Towers 2
Restaurants:
Bayside Marketplace 6
East Coast Fisheries and Restaurant 6
The Fish Market 4
Nightlife:
Amnesia 8
MoJazz Cafe 1
Tobacco Road 7
Biscayne Canal
Opa-Locka Airfield
NORTH MIAMI BEACH
Haulover Beach Park
BAL HARBOUR
NW 135th St.
NE 135th St.
NE 6th Ave.
NE 125th St.
Miami Blvd.
Broad Causeway
Gratigny Dr.
Red Rd.
Biscayne Park
SURFSIDE
A1A
Opa-Locka Canal
NW 103rd St.
NE 103rd St.
Biscayne Blvd.
Bal Harbour Beach
HIALEAH
NW 95th St.
Amtrak Terminal
W 29th St.
E 8th Ave.
E 25th St.
NW 27th Ave.
NW 22nd Ave.
NW 79th St.
NE 79th St.
J.F. Kennedy Causeway
85th St. Beach
Collins Ave.
Pelican Island
LITTLE HAITI
NW 17th Ave.
W 4th Ave.
Palm Ave.
E 4th Ave.
North Miami Ave.
NE 2nd Ave.
NW 7th Ave.
E 9th St.
NW 62nd St.
Alton Rd.
Okeechobee Rd.
Hialeah Dr.
NW 54th St.
Morningside Park
Airport Expressway
112
27
Julia Tuttle Causeway
195
A1A
NW 36th St.
Miami International Airport
NW 20th St.
MIAMI BEACH
Venetian Causeway

836
836
395
95
SOUTH BEACH
MacArthur Causeway
Collins Ave.
Alton Rd.
5th St.
A1A
Lummus Park Beach
First Street Beach
Fisher Island
Port of Miami
NW 7th St.
West
Flagler St.
SW 42 Ave.
Beachcom Blvd.
SW 17th Ave.
SW 12th Ave.
SW 1st St.
SW 7th St.
SW 8th St.
South Miami Ave.
Brickell Ave.
41
41
Tamiami Trail
Le Jeune Rd.
Ponce de Leon Blvd.
SW 37th Ave.
SW 27th Ave.
CORAL GABLES
DOWNTOWN
Coral Way
SW 22nd St.
Brickell Ave.
Rickenbacker
Causeway
Virginia Key
US 1 South Dixie Highway
S. Bayshore Dr.
Red Rd.
Bird Rd.
Bird Ave.
COCONUT GROVE
1
Hardee Ave.
Biscayne Bay
Atlantic Ocean
Hobie Beach
Crandon Park Beach
KEY BISCAYNE
Bill Baggs Cape Florida State Park
Miami Area
0
2 mi
0
3.2 Km
Airport
Beach
Cruise Ship Terminal

Ahoy, Mateys!

For additional visitor information, call the **Greater Miami Convention and Visitors Bureau** at ☎ **800/283-2707** or 305/539-3063.

BY CAR If you're driving, take the Florida Turnpike (a toll road) or I-95 from the north, or I-75 or U.S. 27 from the northwest. Parking at the port is available for $8 a day.

Not to Be Missed

- **Miami Beach:** The 300-foot sandy stretch runs for about 10 miles from the south of Miami Beach to Haulover Beach Park in the north. A wooden boardwalk runs about 1½ miles between 21st and 46th streets.
- **South Beach:** Home of the city's **Art Deco district,** this area was made famous during "Miami Vice" days, gained more notoriety as the setting for the movie *The Birdcage,* and gained infamous status as the scene of the real-life murder of designer Gianni Versace.
- **Shopping on South Beach's Lincoln Road:** An 8-block pedestrian mall that runs between Washington Avenue and Alton Road, it's filled with antique shops, galleries, restaurants, and coffee shops.

Other Recommended Attractions

- At the **Bass Museum of Art,** 2121 Park Ave. (☎ **305/673-7533**), you can see old masters and more.
- The **Vizcaya Museum and Gardens,** 3251 S. Miami Ave., Coconut Grove (☎ **305/250-9133**), is a 70-room villa in the Italian Renaissance style. (Thirty-four rooms are open to the public.)
- The **Miami Seaquarium,** 4400 Rickenbacker Causeway, Key Biscayne (☎ **305/361-5705**), has killer whale and dolphin shows, a shark feeding, and more.

Hotels, Eating & Nightlife

HOTELS The good thing about Miami is that it's fairly compact, so you can stay virtually anywhere and be within 20 minutes of the cruise port.

In South Beach, try **The Delano,**1685 Collins Ave. (☎ **305/672-2000**), which is very hip and numbers Madonna among its investors, or the art deco coral-pink **Astor,** 956 Washington Ave. (☎ **305/531-8081**).

Elsewhere, the **Crowne Plaza Miami Hotel,** 1601 Biscayne Blvd. (☎ **800/2-CROWNE** or 305/374-4000), is located above the Omni International Shopping Mall and was renovated by none other than Carnival Cruise Lines. Or if you're looking for a Miami resort experience, the venerable **Fountainbleau Hilton Resort and Towers,** at 441 Collins Ave. (☎ **800/548-8886** or 305/538-2000), should fit the bill.

RESTAURANTS **Bayside Marketplace,** 401 Biscayne Blvd., has a variety of restaurants, with offerings ranging from Spanish tapas to the burgers at the Hard Rock Cafe.

The Fish Market (☎ **305/374-0000**) at the Crowne Plaza Miami Hotel, is known as one of Miami's best restaurants.

East Coast Fisheries and Restaurant, 360 W. Flagler at South River Drive (☎ **305/372-1300**), has an enormous variety of fresh-fish preparations.

NIGHTLIFE Definitely head to South Beach, where there are both straight and gay offerings. One of the leading straight discos is **Amnesia,** 136 Collins Ave. (☎ **305/531-5535**). For jazz, head to **MoJazz Cafe,** 928 71st St. (☎ **305/865-2636**). For blues, head to the landmark **Tobacco Road,** 626 S. Miami Ave. (☎ **305/374-1198**).

Fort Lauderdale & Port Everglades

Port Everglades is located on State Road 84, east of U.S. 1, about a 5-minute drive from the airport. For information, call ☎ **954/523-3404.**

Not quite as busy a port as Miami, Port Everglades has the distinction of being home to more upper-end and luxury ships than any other port in the world.

The port is close to the airport and offers nine modern cruise terminals with comfortable seating areas and snack bars. On the downside, there's not much else around.

Getting There

BY PLANE The **Fort Lauderdale / Hollywood International Airport** is much lower-key than Miami's airport, and it's located less than 2 miles from Port Everglades.

A taxi ride to the port costs about $5 to $10 a person. Most cruise lines provide bus service on a prearranged basis.

BY CAR By car, you can enter the port on Spangler Boulevard, Eisenhower Boulevard, or Eller Drive.

Car-rental firms that provide shuttle service from the port to their rental sites include Avis, Budget, National, and Dollar.

Parking at the port is $7 for each 24-hour period.

Ahoy, Mateys!

For additional visitor information, call the Greater Fort Lauderdale **Convention and Visitors Bureau** (☎ **954/765-4466**).

Not to Be Missed

- **Fort Lauderdale Beach:** This 2-mile strip gained fame as a setting for spring break in the 1950s and 1960s with the movie *Where the Boys*

Are. The crowds of partying college kids have since moved elsewhere, mostly because they were advised by the city's fathers (and mothers) that they were no longer welcome.

➤ **The Fort Lauderdale Beach Promenade:** This area has been renovated to the tune of $20 million. If you don't want to lie on the beach, you can also bike or rollerblade here.

Other Recommended Attractions

➤ At the **Museum of Discovery and Science,** 401 SW Second St. (☎ **954/467-6637**), you can interact with various science displays or catch a giant IMAX movie.

➤ The **Museum of Art,** 1 Las Olas Blvd. (☎ **954/763-6464**), showcases modern art.

➤ **Butterfly World,** 3600 W. Sample Rd., Coconut Creek (☎ **964/977-4400**), has butterflies. Lots of butterflies. 150 different varieties of butterflies.

➤ **A sightseeing boat trip, dinner cruise, or water-taxi ride.** After all, it's not for nothing that the city is known as "the Venice of the Americas": It has 300 miles of navigable waterways and artificial canals.

Hotels, Eating & Nightlife

HOTELS There are plenty of hotel choices in Fort Lauderdale, ranging from dumpy motels to luxurious resorts.

Most major chains with offerings here include two Marriott properties, the **Fort Lauderdale Marina Marriott,** 1881 SE 17th St. (☎ **800/433-2254**), and the **Marriott in Harbor Beach,** 3030 Holiday Dr. (☎ **800/222-6543**), as well as **The Hyatt Regency Fort Lauderdale** at Pier 66 marina, 2301 SE 17th St. Causeway (☎ **800/233-1234**), a circular landmark with a famous revolving bar on its roof.

RESTAURANTS **Burt & Jacks,** which is co-owned by Burt Reynolds, is located at Berth 23, right at Port Everglades (☎ **954/522-2878**). It's open for dinner only. **Cap's Place,** 2765 NE 28th Court in Lighthouse Point (☎ **954/941-0418**), is the area's famous old-time seafood joint.

NIGHTLIFE **The Piertop Lounge** in the **Hyatt Regency** at Pier 66 (☎ **954/525-6666**) is the area's most famous bar. There's a dance floor and floor shows Tuesday through Saturday.

Cheers, 941 E. Cypress Creek Rd. (☎ **954/771-6337**), features acoustic blues on some nights, rock 'n' roll on others, and yes, it's named Cheers because of the TV show. A trendy place to hear live blues and jazz is **O'Hara Pub and Sidewalk Cafe,** 722 E. Las Olas Blvd. (☎ **954/524-1764**).

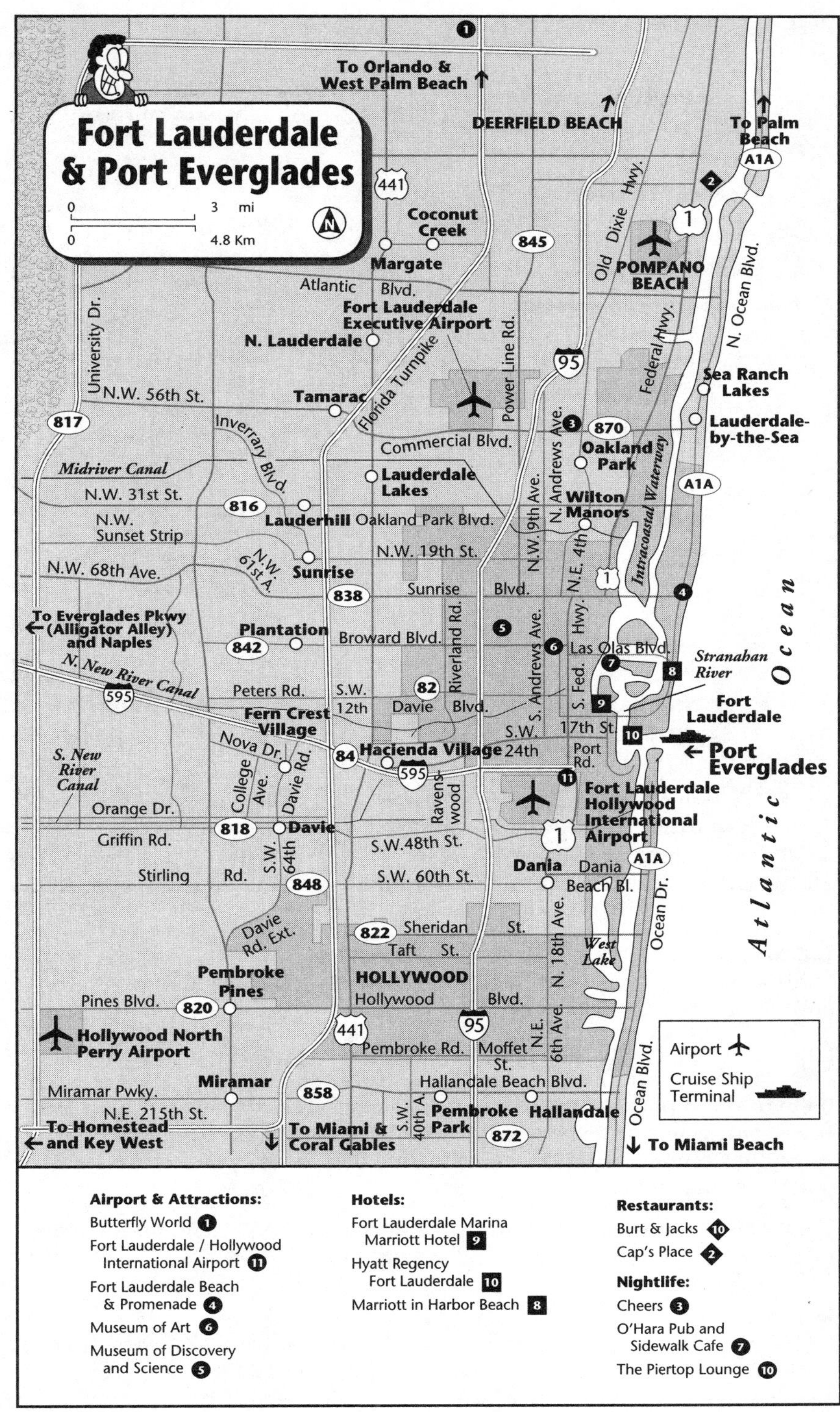
Fort Lauderdale & Port Everglades
0 3 mi
0 4.8 Km
To Orlando & West Palm Beach
DEERFIELD BEACH
To Palm Beach
A1A
441
Coconut Creek
Margate
845
Old Dixie Hwy.
1
POMPANO BEACH
N. Ocean Blvd.
Atlantic Blvd.
Fort Lauderdale Executive Airport
N. Lauderdale
Power Line Rd.
95
Federal Hwy.
University Dr.
Florida Turnpike
Sea Ranch Lakes
N.W. 56th St.
Tamarac
Lauderdale-by-the-Sea
817
Inverrary Blvd.
870
N. Andrews Ave.
Commercial Blvd.
Oakland Park
Midriver Canal
Lauderdale Lakes
N.W. 9th Ave.
Intracoastal Waterway
A1A
N.W. 31st St.
Wilton Manors
816
N.W. Sunset Strip
Lauderhill
Oakland Park Blvd.
N.E. 4th
N.W. 19th St.
N.W. 68th Ave.
N.W. 61st A.
Sunrise
838
Sunrise Blvd.
To Everglades Pkwy (Alligator Alley) and Naples
Plantation
842
Broward Blvd.
Riverland Rd.
S. Andrews Ave.
Hwy.
Las Olas Blvd.
Stranahan River
Atlantic Ocean
N. New River Canal
595
Peters Rd.
S.W. 12th
82
Davie Blvd.
S. Fed.
Fort Lauderdale
Fern Crest Village
S.W. 17th St.
Nova Dr.
84
Hacienda Village
24th
Port Rd.
Port Everglades
S. New River Canal
College Ave.
Davie Rd.
595
Ravenswood
Fort Lauderdale Hollywood International Airport
Orange Dr.
818
Davie
1
Griffin Rd.
S.W. 64th
S.W.48th St.
Dania
Dania Beach Bl.
A1A
Stirling Rd.
848
S.W. 60th St.
N. 18th Ave.
Ocean Dr.
Davie Rd. Ext.
822
Sheridan St.
Taft St.
West Lake
Pembroke Pines
HOLLYWOOD
Pines Blvd.
820
Hollywood Blvd.
441
95
N.E. 6th Ave.
Hollywood North Perry Airport
Pembroke Rd.
Moffet St.
Ocean Blvd.
Airport
Cruise Ship Terminal
Miramar Pwky.
Miramar
858
Hallandale Beach Blvd.
N.E. 215th St.
S.W. 40th A.
Pembroke Park
Hallandale
To Homestead and Key West
To Miami & Coral Gables
872
To Miami Beach
Airport & Attractions:
Butterfly World 1
Fort Lauderdale / Hollywood International Airport 11
Fort Lauderdale Beach & Promenade 4
Museum of Art 6
Museum of Discovery and Science 5
Hotels:
Fort Lauderdale Marina Marriott Hotel 9
Hyatt Regency Fort Lauderdale 10
Marriott in Harbor Beach 8
Restaurants:
Burt & Jacks 10
Cap's Place 2
Nightlife:
Cheers 3
O'Hara Pub and Sidewalk Cafe 7
The Piertop Lounge 10

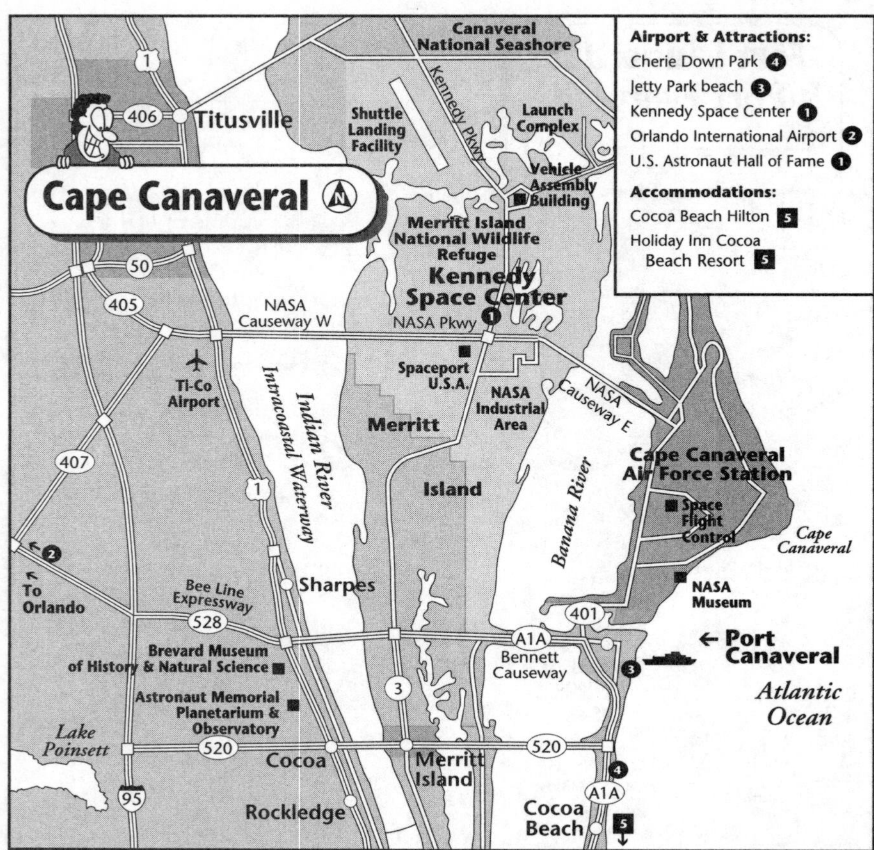

Cape Canaveral / Port Canaveral

Port Canaveral is located at 200 George King Blvd. in Cape Canaveral. For information call ☎ **407/783-7831.**

Port Canaveral is home not only to cruise ships but to the region's fishing fleet. The juxtaposition of the fishing vessels and cruise ships already made the port stand out among Florida cruise venues, but the new, private **Disney terminal,** where passengers will be sprinkled with pixie dust before they board the vessels of the Disney Cruise Line fleet, adds even more to the port's unusual allure.

The facilities at the port include terminals that are stylish and up-to-date and offer easy access to nearby bars and restaurants.

Getting There

BY PLANE The nearest airport is **Orlando International Airport,** about a 45-minute drive from Port Canaveral on Highway 528 (the Bee Line Expressway).

Sea Stories

When you think *cruising*, you think Texas, right? Well, if a couple of cruise lines have their way, that might be the case in a few years. Norwegian Cruise Line is trying to establish Houston as an alternative port for Western Caribbean sailings, and Royal Olympic Cruises is doing the same for Galveston by basing its *Stella Solaris* there for its Western Caribbean itinerary.

There is no public bus service from the airport to the docks, so most passengers arrange to take the vans or buses offered by the cruise lines. If you haven't arranged this, call the **Cocoa Beach Shuttle** (☎ **800/633-0427**), which offers shuttle service from the airport to the port for $20 per person each way.

If you want to rent a car for a day or two, you might be best off doing so in Cocoa Beach, through Budget or Americar.

BY CAR Port Canaveral and Cocoa Beach are accessible via Route 1 or I-95, or from Orlando, Highway 528 (the Bee Line Expressway). Parking at the port is $7 a day.

Not to Be Missed

The big attraction here is space exploration. Some people will probably miss it, preferring to spend their pre- or post-cruise time at Disney World or Universal Studios, but those who do choose to stay on the **Space Coast** will not be disappointed.

Ahoy, Mateys!

For additional visitor information, call the **Cocoa Beach Chamber of Commerce** (☎ **407/459-2200**).

- **The Kennedy Space Center:** At State Road 405 E., Titusville (☎ **407/452-2121**), this has been the departure point for all U.S.–manned space missions since 1968, including man's first trip to the moon and the current space shuttle launches. Offerings at special visitor centers include movies, IMAX presentations, interactive exhibits, and an actual Apollo / Saturn V moon rocket. And the center offers bus tours past real space shuttle launch pads, which often have real space shuttles in residence. You can easily spend a full day at the center.

Other Recommended Attractions

- The **U.S. Astronaut Hall of Fame,** located at the entrance to the Kennedy Space Center, State Road 405, 6225 Vectorspace Blvd. (☎ **407/269-6100**), was founded by the Mercury and Gemini astronauts and contains plenty of memorabilia about the Space Age.
- The **Space Coast** beaches include the popular **Jetty Park,** at 400 E. Jetty Rd. For a quieter beach setting, try **Cherie Down Park,** at 8492 Ridgewood Ave. **Lori Wilson Park,** 1500 N. Atlantic Ave., has a children's playground, while **Robert P. Murkshe Memorial Park,** SR A1A and 16th Street, in Cocoa Beach, offers the area's best surfing.

Hotels, Eating & Nightlife

HOTELS There are plenty of chain hotels in the area, including the **Cocoa Beach Hilton,** 1550 N. Atlantic Ave. (A1A) (☎ **800/HILTONS** or 407/799-0003), and the **Holiday Inn Cocoa Beach Resort,** 1300 N. Atlantic Ave. (☎ **800/2BOOKUS** or 407/783-2271).

For those looking for something different, **The Inn at Cocoa Beach,** 4300 Ocean Beach Blvd. (☎ **800/343-5307** or 407/700-3460), has more of a large-scale bed-and-breakfast atmosphere.

RESTAURANTS **Lloyd's Canaveral Feast,** 610 Glen Cheek Dr. (☎ **407/784-8899**), is a waterfront seafood restaurant, where on some days, you can watch cruise ships from the outdoor tables.

Bernard's Surf Restaurant, 2 S. Atlantic Ave. (☎ **407/783-2401**), is a seafood joint that has played host not only to real-life astronauts but to the cast of *I Dream of Jeannie*. The show was supposed to be based in Cocoa Beach but was in fact filmed mostly in Hollywood. Actors from the show really did come to town in 1969, however, to film a special show, and the name of this restaurant made its way into a script or two.

For a more sophisticated dining ambiance, try **The Mango Tree,** 118 N. Atlantic Ave. (☎ **407/799-0513**).

NIGHTLIFE **The Pier,** 401 Meade Ave. (☎ **407/783-7549**), is an entertainment complex with several venues, including **Marlin's Sports Bar.** You can find live jazz at **Heidi's Jazz Club,** 7 N. Orlando Ave. (☎ **407/783-6806**).

Tampa

The Port of Tampa is located at 811 Wynkoop Rd., near Ybor City, Tampa's historic Latin Quarter. For information, call ☎ **813/272-0555.**

The Port of Tampa offers a modern terminal, known as **Seaport Street Terminal,** anchoring a 30-acre site that also includes the Florida Aquarium, a large complex of shops and restaurants, and an entertainment venue.

Getting There

BY PLANE **Tampa International Airport** is located 5 miles northwest of downtown Tampa. The port is a 15-minute cab ride from the airport; the cost should be about $10 to $15. Central Florida Limo (☎ **813/396-3730**) runs a minivan service to the pier for $7.50 a person.

Car-rental companies with kiosks at the airport and offices downtown include Avis, Dollar, National, Budget, Hertz, Alamo, Thrifty, and Value.

BY CAR Tampa is easily accessible from I-275, I-75, I-4, U.S. 41, U.S. 92, U.S. 301, and many state roads. Parking at the port is $6 a day.

Ahoy, Mateys!

For additional visitor information, call the Tampa/Hillsborough **Convention and Visitors Association** (☎ **800/44-TAMPA**).

Not to Be Missed

- **Busch Gardens:** Busch Gardens (☎ **813/987-5171**) is the big attraction here, despite its steep admission prices ($36.15 for adults, $28.75 for children). The park, designed to be reminiscent of turn-of-the-century Africa, offers thrill rides, animal habitats (it's ranked as one of the top zoos in the U.S.), live entertainment, shops, restaurants, and games.

Other Recommended Attractions

- The **Florida Aquarium,** 701 Chanelside Dr. (☎ **813/273-4000**), is home to more than 5,300 marine animals and plants, all of which are native to the Florida region.
- The **Henry B. Plant Museum,** 401 W. Kennedy Blvd. (☎ **813/254-1891**), is modeled after the Alhambra in Spain. Check out the 13 silver minarets.
- The **Tampa Museum of Art,** 600 N. Ashley Dr. (☎ **813/274-8130**), offers 8 galleries with rotating exhibits, as well as a 7-acre riverfront park and sculpture garden.
- The **Salvador Dali Museum,** 1000 Third St. S., St. Petersburg (☎ **813/823-3767**), offers a surreal experience, housing the world's largest collection of the renowned painter's works.

Hotels, Eating & Nightlife

HOTELS **The Don CeSar Beach Resort and Spa,** 3400 Gulf Blvd., St. Petersburg (☎ **800/282-1116**), is big and pink and listed on the National Register of Historic Places. It's also kinda pricey, with double rooms up in the $300 range.

Other options include the chains. **Doubletree Guest Suites,** 11310 N. 30th St. (☎ **800/222-TREE**) offers, as its name implies, all suite

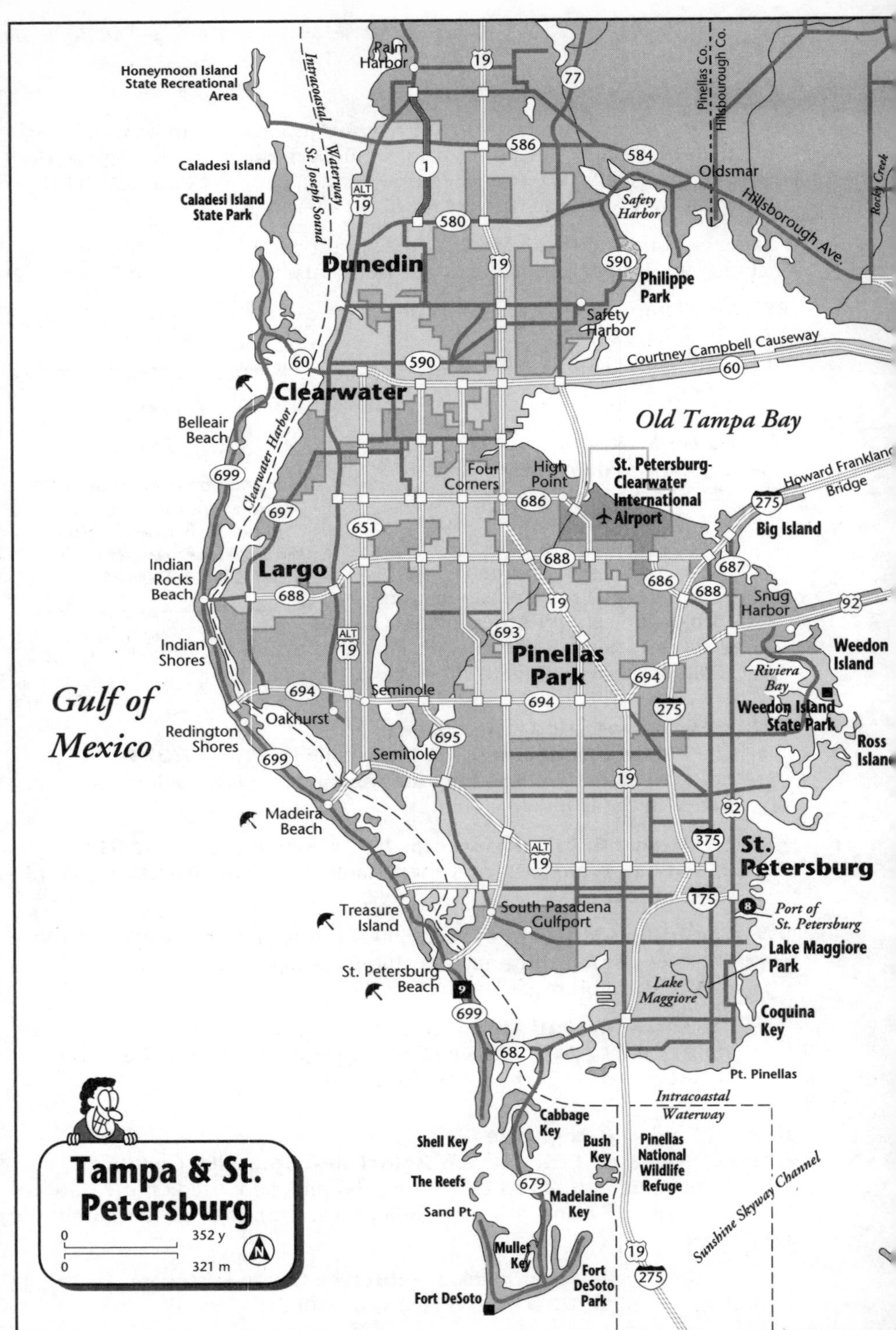
Tampa & St. Petersburg
Honeymoon Island State Recreational Area
Caladesi Island
Caladesi Island State Park
Intracoastal Waterway
St. Joseph Sound
Palm Harbor
Dunedin
Safety Harbor
Philippe Park
Oldsmar
Pinellas Co.
Hillsborough Co.
Hillsborough Ave.
Rocky Creek
Courtney Campbell Causeway
Clearwater
Clearwater Harbor
Old Tampa Bay
Belleair Beach
Four Corners
High Point
St. Petersburg-Clearwater International Airport
Howard Frankland Bridge
Big Island
Largo
Indian Rocks Beach
Indian Shores
Snug Harbor
Weedon Island
Riviera Bay
Weedon Island State Park
Pinellas Park
Gulf of Mexico
Seminole
Oakhurst
Redington Shores
Ross Island
Madeira Beach
St. Petersburg
Treasure Island
South Pasadena
Gulfport
Port of St. Petersburg
Lake Maggiore Park
Lake Maggiore
St. Petersburg Beach
Coquina Key
Pt. Pinellas
Cabbage Key
Bush Key
Pinellas National Wildlife Refuge
Shell Key
The Reefs
Sand Pt.
Madelaine Key
Mullet Key
Fort DeSoto
Fort DeSoto Park
Sunshine Skyway Channel
0 352 y
0 321 m

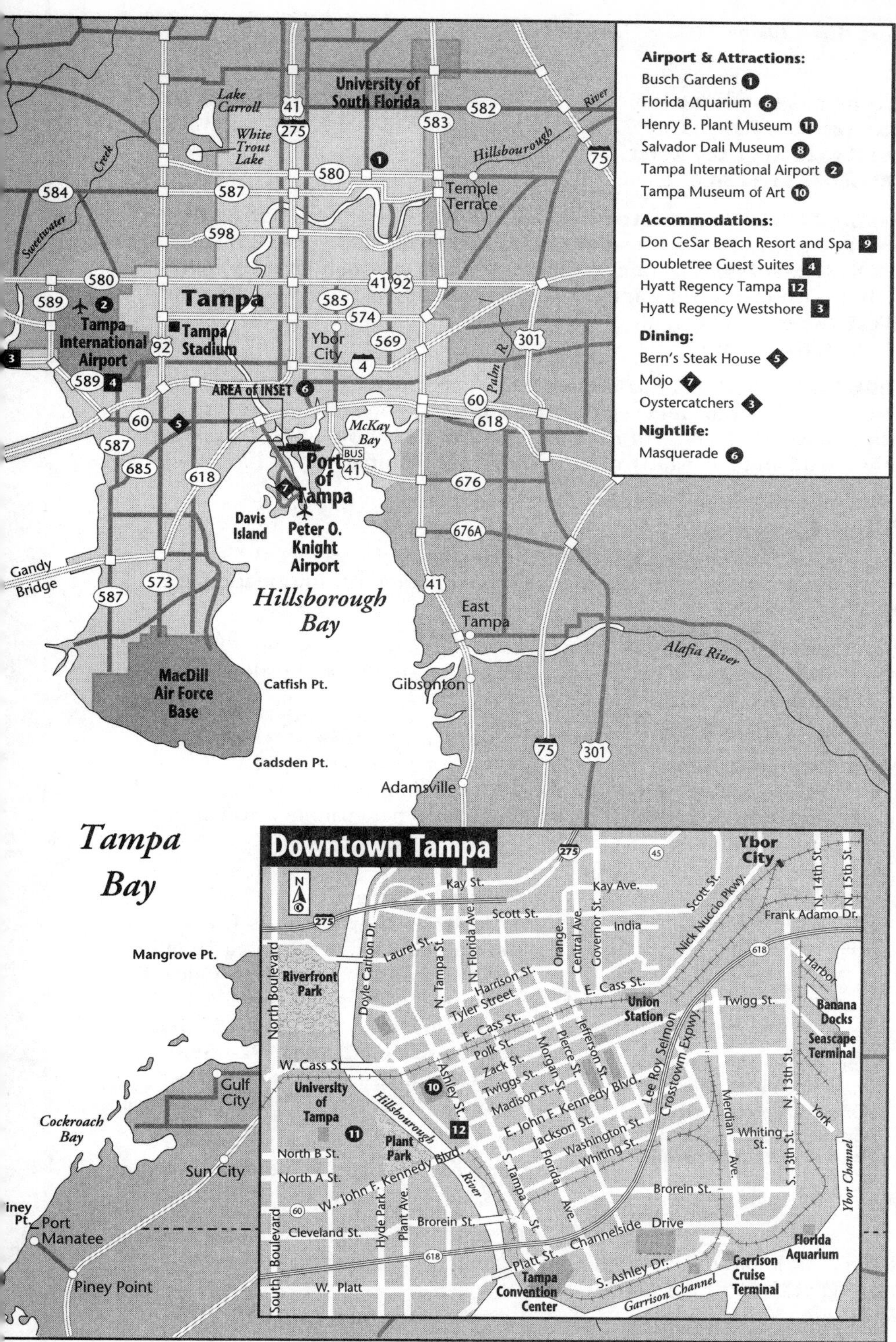
Airport & Attractions:
Busch Gardens 1
Florida Aquarium 6
Henry B. Plant Museum 11
Salvador Dali Museum 8
Tampa International Airport 2
Tampa Museum of Art 10
Accommodations:
Don CeSar Beach Resort and Spa 9
Doubletree Guest Suites 4
Hyatt Regency Tampa 12
Hyatt Regency Westshore 3
Dining:
Bern's Steak House 5
Mojo 7
Oystercatchers 3
Nightlife:
Masquerade 6
University of South Florida
Lake Carroll
White Trout Lake
Tampa
Tampa International Airport
Tampa Stadium
Ybor City
Temple Terrace
Hillsborough River
Sweetwater Creek
AREA of INSET
McKay Bay
Port of Tampa
Davis Island
Peter O. Knight Airport
Gandy Bridge
Hillsborough Bay
East Tampa
Alafia River
MacDill Air Force Base
Catfish Pt.
Gibsonton
Gadsden Pt.
Adamsville
Tampa Bay
Mangrove Pt.
Gulf City
Cockroach Bay
Sun City
Port Manatee
Piney Point
Downtown Tampa
Ybor City
Kay St.
Kay Ave.
Scott St.
India
Frank Adamo Dr.
N. 14th St.
N. 15th St.
Nick Nuccio Pkwy.
Laurel St.
Riverfront Park
North Boulevard
Doyle Carlton Dr.
N. Tampa St.
N. Florida Ave.
Orange
Central Ave.
Governor St.
Harrison St.
Tyler Street
E. Cass St.
Union Station
Twigg St.
Harbor
Banana Docks
Seaside Terminal
Polk St.
Zack St.
Twiggs St.
Madison St.
Morgan St.
Pierce St.
Jefferson St.
E. John F. Kennedy Blvd.
Lee Roy Selmon Crosstown Expwy.
W. Cass St.
University of Tampa
Hillsborough River
Ashley St.
Jackson St.
Washington St.
Whiting St.
Merdian Ave.
N. 13th St.
Whiting St.
York
North B St.
North A St.
Plant Park
W. John F. Kennedy Blvd.
S. Tampa St.
Florida Ave.
Brorein St.
S. 13th St.
Ybor Channel
Hyde Park
Plant Ave.
Brorein St.
Cleveland St.
Channelside Drive
Platt St.
South Boulevard
W. Platt
Tampa Convention Center
S. Ashley Dr.
Garrison Channel
Garrison Cruise Terminal
Florida Aquarium

accommodations. And there are two Hyatts in town, the **Hyatt Regency Tampa,** Two Tampa City Center (☎ **800/233-1234** or 813/225-1234), and the **Hyatt Regency Westshore,** 6200 Courtney Campbell Causeway (☎ **800/233-1234** or 813/874-1234).

RESTAURANTS **Bern's Steak House,** 1208 S. Howard Ave. (☎ **813/251-2421**), has the best steaks in town; and **Mojo,** 238 E. Davis Blvd. (☎ **813/259-9949**), features Caribbean cuisine in a flamboyantly charming setting. Fish-lovers will want to try Oystercatchers in the **Hyatt Regency Westshore Hotel** complex, 6200 Courtney Campbell Causeway (☎ **813/874-1234**).

NIGHTLIFE Head to **Ybor City,** the city's century-old Latin Quarter, for music, ethnic food, and even poetry readings. A popular club here is **Masquerade,** 1503 E. 7th Ave. (☎ **813/247-3319**), where the DJs play the music loud and live bands are also sometimes featured.

New Orleans

The Port of New Orleans is located at 1350 Port of New Orleans Place, a 5-minute walk from the edge of the French Quarter. For information, call ☎ **504/522-2551.**

New Orleans is one of the busiest ports in the nation, but cruise ships are just a fraction of the activity that goes on here amidst the hustle and bustle of commercial shipping.

Cruise passengers generally board their ships at the **Julia Street Cruise Ship Terminal,** which was originally developed as part of the 1984 Louisiana World Exposition. But some southbound passengers might board at the **Robin Street Wharves,** which is also where paddle wheelers begin their upriver cruises.

Ahoy, Mateys!

For additional visitor information, call the New Orleans Metropolitan **Convention and Visitors Bureau (☎ 504/566-5011)**.

Getting There

BY PLANE **New Orleans International Airport** is located 10 miles northwest of the Port of New Orleans. A cab ride to the port takes about 20 minutes and costs about $21. **Airport Shuttle** (☎ **504/592-0555**) offers van rides for a cost of $10 per passenger each way (children under age 6 are free).

Car-rental agencies at the airport include Avis, Budget, Dollar, and Hertz.

BY CAR Take Highway I-10, U.S. 90., U.S. 61, or Louisiana 25 (the Lake Pontchartrain Causeway) into the city. Parking at the port is $6 to $10 a night.

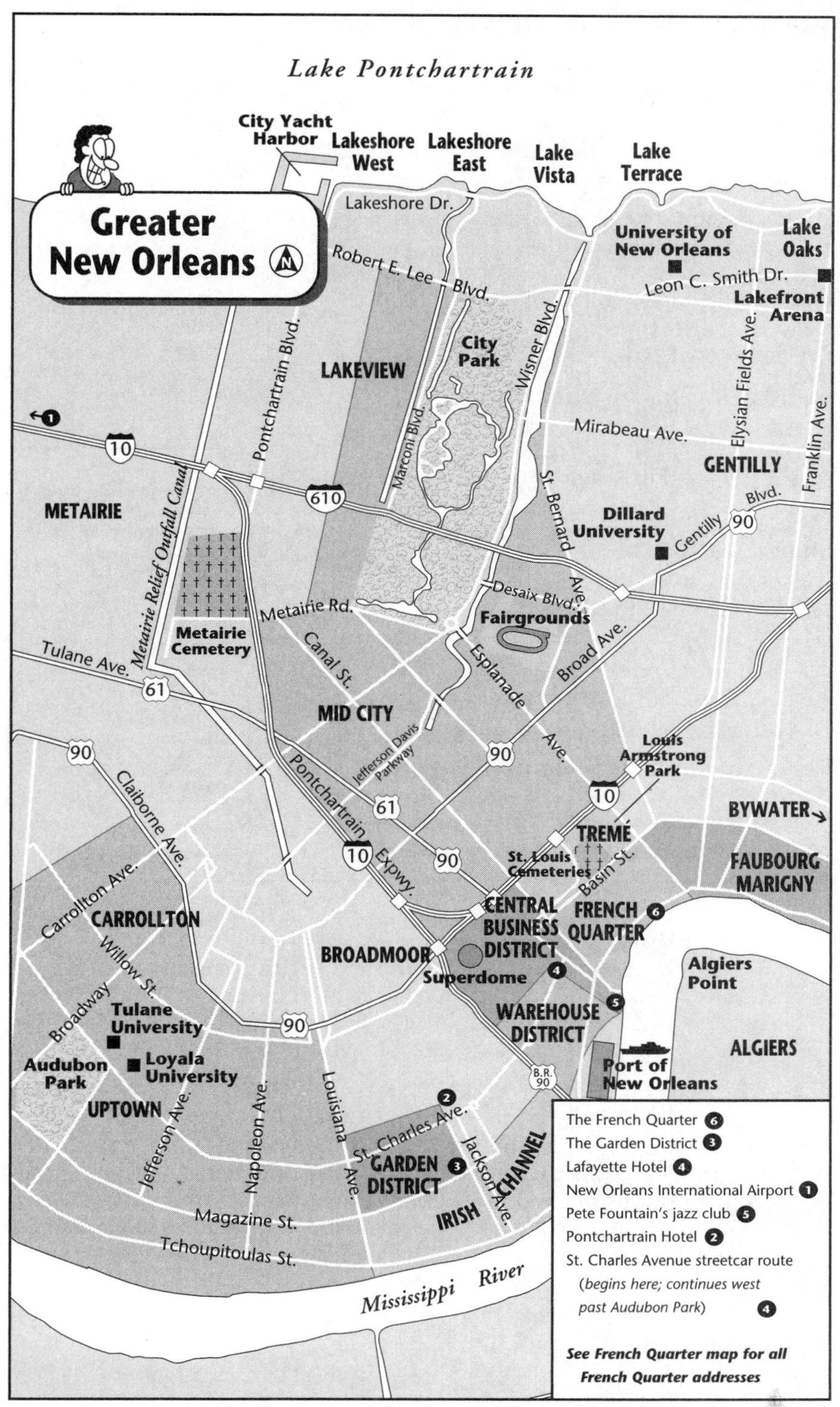
Greater New Orleans
Lake Pontchartrain
City Yacht Harbor
Lakeshore West
Lakeshore East
Lake Vista
Lake Terrace
Lakeshore Dr.
University of New Orleans
Lake Oaks
Robert E. Lee Blvd.
Leon C. Smith Dr.
Lakefront Arena
Pontchartrain Blvd.
LAKEVIEW
City Park
Wisner Blvd.
Elysian Fields Ave.
Franklin Ave.
Marconi Blvd.
Mirabeau Ave.
GENTILLY
METAIRIE
Metairie Relief Outfall Canal
St. Bernard Ave.
Dillard University
Gentilly Blvd.
Desaix Blvd.
Metairie Rd.
Fairgrounds
Metairie Cemetery
Tulane Ave.
Canal St.
Esplanade Ave.
Broad Ave.
MID CITY
Jefferson Davis Parkway
Louis Armstrong Park
Claiborne Ave.
Pontchartrain Expwy.
BYWATER
TREMÉ
St. Louis Cemeteries
Basin St.
FAUBOURG MARIGNY
Carrollton Ave.
CARROLLTON
CENTRAL BUSINESS DISTRICT
FRENCH QUARTER
BROADMOOR
Superdome
Algiers Point
Willow St.
Broadway
Tulane University
WAREHOUSE DISTRICT
ALGIERS
Audubon Park
Loyala University
Port of New Orleans
UPTOWN
Jefferson Ave.
Napoleon Ave.
Louisiana Ave.
St. Charles Ave.
Jackson Ave.
CHANNEL
GARDEN DISTRICT
IRISH
Magazine St.
Tchoupitoulas St.
Mississippi River
The French Quarter 6
The Garden District 3
Lafayette Hotel 4
New Orleans International Airport 1
Pete Fountain's jazz club 5
Pontchartrain Hotel 2
St. Charles Avenue streetcar route (begins here; continues west past Audubon Park) 4
See French Quarter map for all French Quarter addresses

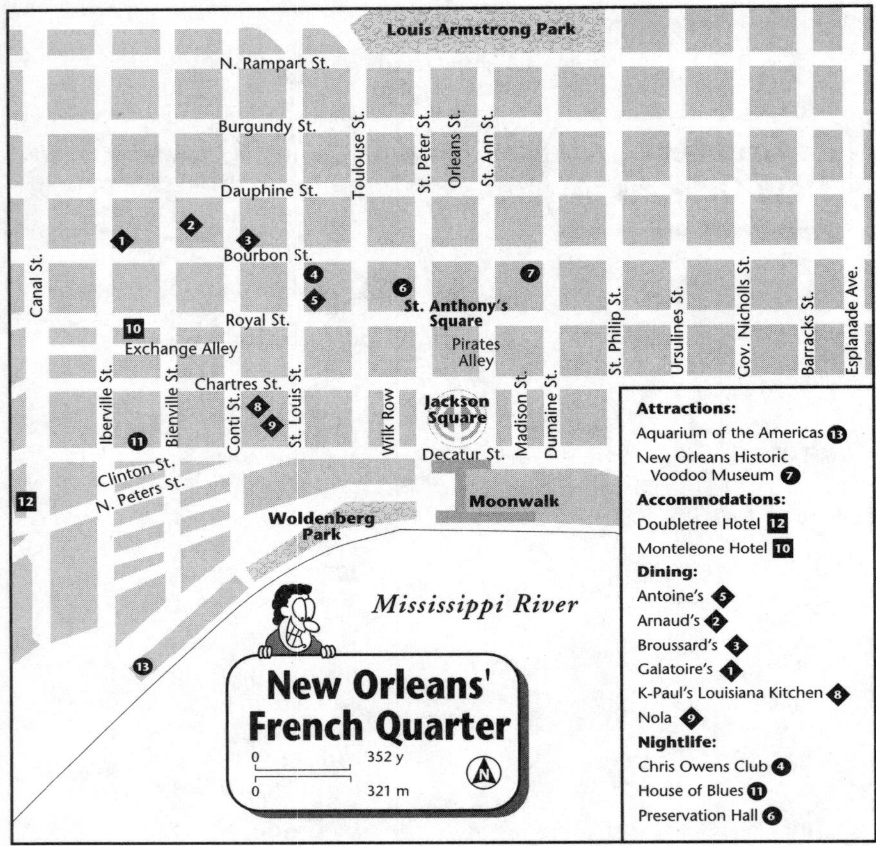

Not to Be Missed

- **The French Quarter:** The historic and slightly naughty French Quarter is so popular and such an attraction in itself that some visitors never bother to venture outside. The area offers 18th- and 19th-century architecture, museums, jazz clubs, shops, and great food.
- **The Garden District and Environs:** For those who do want to see more of the "Big Easy," the Garden District offers impressive homes and great restaurants, and the area spreading loosely among the Garden District, the Quarter, and the Mississippi River—including the Warehouse District and the Lower Garden District—offers art galleries, historic sites, shopping, and one of the hippest urban experiences around.

Other Recommended Attractions

- The **Aquarium of the Americas,** 1 Canal St., at the Mississippi River (☎ **504/861-2537**), offers a million gallons of marine fun, an IMAX theater, an underwater tunnel, and the always-popular penguin exhibit.
- The **New Orleans Historic Voodoo Museum,** 724 Dumaine St. (☎ **504/523-7685**), offers visitors a somewhat theatrical yet fun intro to voodoo lore. A guided voodoo walking tour of the French Quarter departs from the museum at 1pm daily.
- Board the **St. Charles Avenue streetcar** at the corner of Canal and Carondelet streets in the French Quarter for a ride through town. There's no more New Orleanian way to see the place.

Hotels, Eating & Nightlife

HOTELS Located near both the pier and the French Quarter is the **Doubletree Hotel,** 300 Canal St. (☎ **504/581-1300**). For history buffs, about 7 blocks from the pier is the **Monteleone Hotel,** 214 Royal St. (☎ **504/523-2341**), the grande dame of the French Quarter. The **Lafayette Hotel,** 600 St. Charles Ave., at Lafayette Square (☎ **800/733-4754** or 504/524-4441), and the **Pontchartrain Hotel,** 2031 St. Charles Ave. (☎ **504/524-0581**), provide upscale options.

RESTAURANTS There are more great restaurants in 10 square blocks of New Orleans than in most other major American cities, but among the well-established, old, tried-and-true French favorites are **Antoine's,** 713 St. Louis St. (☎ **504/581-4422**), established in 1840; **Broussard's,** 819 Conti St. (☎ **504/581-3866**), established in 1920; **Arnaud's,** 813 Bienville St. (☎ **504/523-5433**); and **Galatoire's,** 209 Bourbon St. (☎ **504/525-2021**).

K-Paul's Louisiana Kitchen, 416 Chartres St. (☎ **504/524-7394**), tends to have lines of patrons stretching halfway down the street waiting to get in to sample its Cajun cuisine. Cajun is also the influence at **Nola,** 534 St. Louis St. (☎ **504/522-6652**).

NIGHTLIFE **Preservation Hall,** 726 St. Peter St. (☎ **504/523-8939**), is the top of the mountain for Dixieland jazz fans. Dixieland is also the thing at **Pete Fountain's,** at the New Orleans Hilton, 2 Poydras St. (☎ **504/523-4374**), where clarinet maestro Pete Fountain personally performs several nights a week.

For more jumpin' music offerings, try the **House of Blues,** 225 Decatur St. (☎ **504/529-1421**), and for the crop of New Orleans' brass bands, try **Donna's,** at 800 N. Rampart St. (☎ **504/596-6914**), at the very top of the French Quarter, across from Louis Armstrong Park. At **Chris Owens Club,** 500 Bourbon St. (**504/523-6400**), Ms. Owens does a one-woman cabaret act, singing with whatever band is in the house. Jazz legend Al Hirt performs here several nights a week.

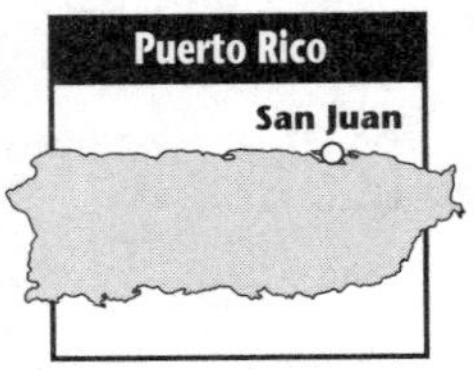

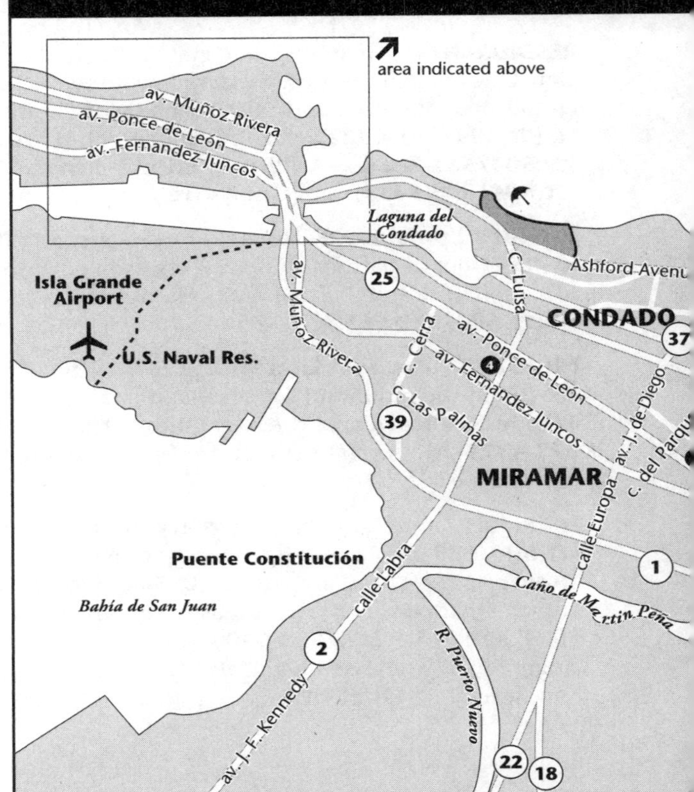

Airport & Attractions:
Luis Munoz Marin International Airport ❽
For attractions, see San Juan map under Ports of Call, chapter 23

Accommodations:
El Convento 1
El San Juan Hotel and Casino 7
Galeria San Juan 2
Wyndham Old San Juan Hotel and Casino 3

Dining:
See San Juan map under Ports of Call, chapter 23

Nightlife:
Amadeus Disco ❼
Copa ❻
Egipto ❹
Krash ❺
Palm Court ❼

OLD SAN JUAN & PUERTO DE TIERRA

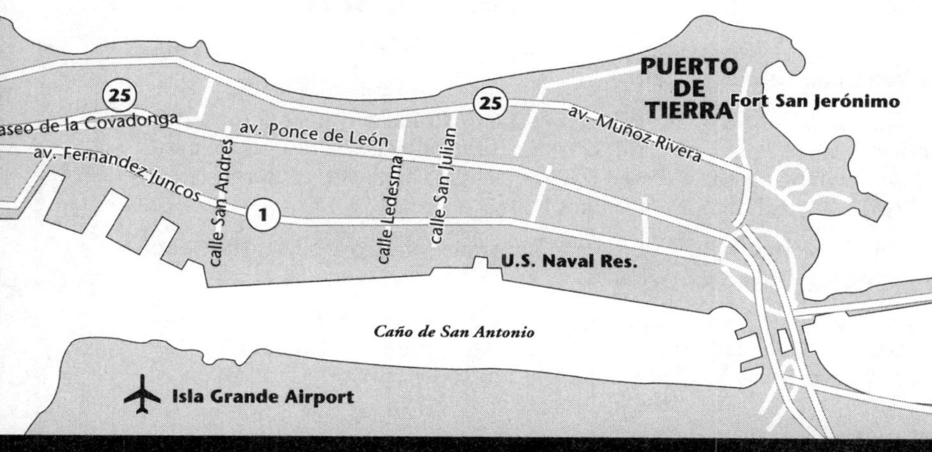

MIRAMAR, CONDADO, SANTURCE, OCEAN PARK & ISLA VERDE

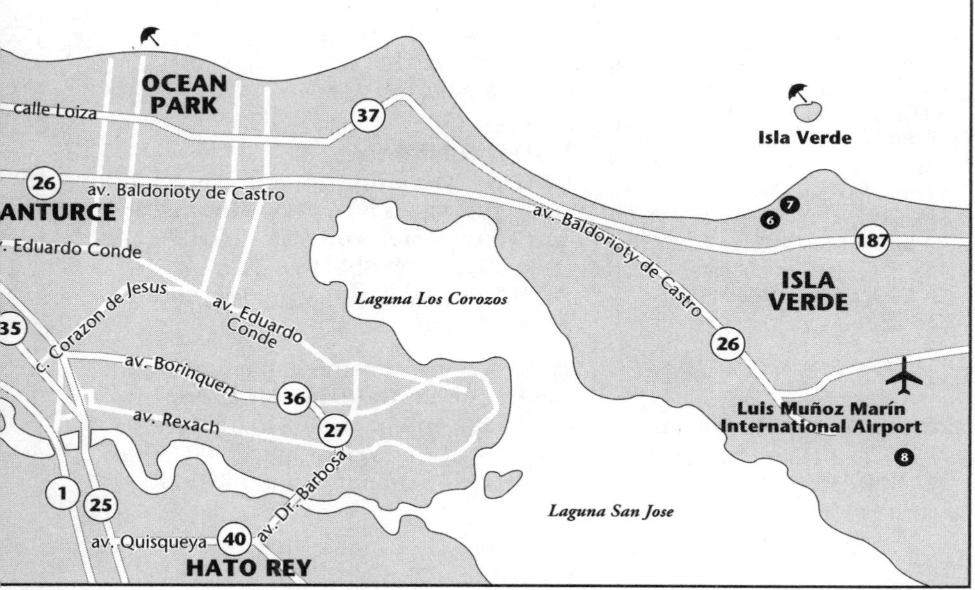

San Juan & the Port of San Juan

Most cruise ships dock on the historic south shore of Old San Juan beside piers that stretch between Plaza de la Marina and the Puerto Rican capitol building. For information, call the Port of San Juan at ☎ **787/723-2260.**

San Juan is the top cruise port in the Caribbean and serves both as a port of embarkation and a port of call.

The newer piers, 1 and 4, as well as pier 3, are all located near shops and attractions in San Juan's historic district. Close to pier 3, a radical renewal project is revitalizing the Barrio de la Marina pier area, the centerpiece of which is the Wyndham Old San Juan Hotel.

Passengers at piers 5, 6, 7, and 8 are a 10-minute walk or so past the Spanish colonial fortress of San Cristóbal.

Occasionally, on days of exceptionally busy cruise ship traffic, less convenient piers are activated, but in these cases the cruise lines generally will offer passengers some kind of transportation to Old Town.

Getting There

BY PLANE Visitors from overseas arrive at **Luis Munoz Marin International Airport,** which is about 7½ miles from the port. Taxis offer a fixed fare of $16 to the port, with the ride taking about a half hour, depending on traffic. There is no easy access to parking at the port.

Ahoy, Mateys!

For additional visitor information, call the **Puerto Rico Tourism Company** offices in New York at ☎ **800/223-6530** or 212/599-6262; in Los Angeles at ☎ **800/874-1230** or 213/874-5991; or in Florida at ☎ **800/815-7391** or 305/445-9112. In Canada, call ☎ **800/667-0394** or 416/368-2680.

Not to Be Missed

Since San Juan is also a major port of call, I deal with its attractions and restaurants in chapter 23, "The Ports of Call: Caribbean & Mexico."

Hotels & Nightlife

HOTELS The most convenient hotel for cruise passengers is the **Wyndham Old San Juan Hotel and Casino,** 101 Calle Marina (☎ **800/996-3426** or 787/721-5100), a luxury property located right at the docks.

Those seeking something different might want to stay at **Galeria San Juan,** Calle Norzagaray 203–206 (☎ **787/722-1808**), an inn created in one of the city's oldest private residences. The landmark **El Convento** hotel, 100 Cristo St. (☎ **800/468-2779** or 787/723-9020), is only a 5-minute cab ride from the cruise piers.

If you want beaches, the **El San Juan Hotel and Casino,** Isla Verde Avenue (☎ **800/468-2818** or 787/791-1000), is closer to the airport but the place to be for fun in the sand.

NIGHTLIFE You can find some of the area's best music for dancing at **Krash,** 1257 avenida Ponce de León (☎ **787/722-1390**), which has a large gay following. **Egipto,** avenida Roberto H. Todd 1 (☎ **787/725-4664**), offers a young crowd Spanish and American dance music in an Egyptian setting. No jeans are allowed.

On the beach strip, Las Vegas–style revues are offered at **Copa** in the Sands Hotel and Casino, Isla Verde Avenue (☎ **787/791-6100**). Meanwhile, those seeking a quiet drink in a beautiful setting might want to check out the **Palm Court** in the El San Juan Hotel and Casino, Isla Verde Avenue (☎ **787/791-1000**). Live music is offered in an adjoining room after 9pm Thursday through Saturday, and the hotel has a popular disco, **Amadeus Disco,** as well.

Chapter 11

North to Alaska!

In This Chapter

- Where to stay, what to see, and where to eat in your port of embarkation
- Maps of the major embarkation ports for cruises in Alaska

Most Alaska cruises operate between Vancouver, British Columbia, and Anchorage/Seward, Alaska, sailing through the Inside Passage, either round-trip from one or the other port or one way, either northbound or southbound. Some small, adventure-type vessels run regularly between Seattle and Juneau, and a few sail from smaller Alaska ports, including Skagway, Ketchikan, and Valdez. (For information on these towns, see chapter 24, "Ports of Call: Alaska.")

Because Alaska, unlike the Caribbean, also has fascinating places to see in areas that are not near the water—Denali National Park, Fairbanks, and Nome, for example—Alaska cruises, both for 1 week and shorter, are offered with optional land tours that combine to make a 1- or 2-week land/sea vacation. You can purchase these tours on an escorted-group or individual basis, including hotels and transportation (train or motorcoach, and sometimes plane or ferry), and you might have the option of purchasing meal packages.

Both Holland America Line–Westours and Princess Cruises own their own hotels to accommodate guests on land.

I recommend arriving at least 1 day before your Alaska sailing and taking time to explore, especially if you've come from a long distance to get here. This will also give you a chance to catch up from jet lag and avoid that awful "I'm going to miss the boat!" feeling you'll get if your plane is running late.

In addition to the land tours, the cruise lines offer a variety of pre- and post-cruise tours, usually of 2 to 4 days. If, however, you choose to go it on your own in Vancouver, Anchorage, Seward (the port of Anchorage), or Juneau, see my following recommendations for hotels, restaurants, and must-see attractions.

As in the Caribbean, most ships start embarkation in the early afternoon and depart between 4 and 5:30pm. (See chapter 13, "Sittin' on the Dock of the Bay," for more on this.)

The Main Alaska Ports & Their Cruise Lines*

Port	Cruise Lines
Anchorage/Seward	Carnival Celebrity Holland America Norwegian Princess Radisson World Explorer
Juneau	Alaska's Glacier Bay Alaska Sightseeing / Cruise West Clipper Special Expeditions
Vancouver	Carnival Celebrity Crystal Holland America Norwegian Princess Royal Caribbean World Explorer

The following lines also sail ships from these smaller ports:

Alaska's Glacier Bay: Ketchikan (AK), and Seattle (WA)

Alaska Sightseeing: Whittier (AK), and Seattle (WA)

Clipper: Ketchikan and Seattle

Crystal: San Francisco (beginning June 1999)

Radisson: Nome (AK)

Special Expeditions: Sitka (AK)

**Information provided by* Travel Weekly's Official Cruise Guide.

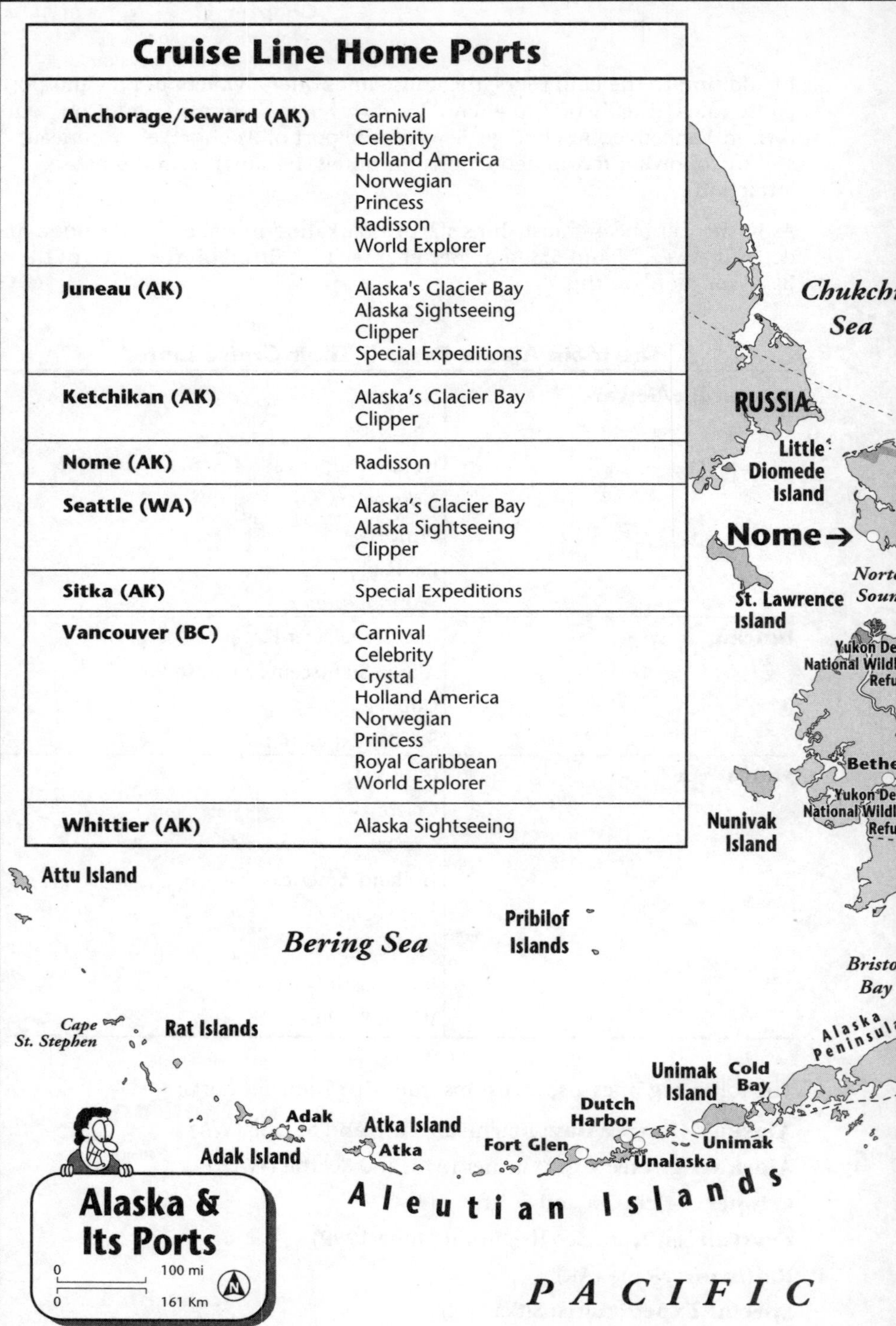

Cruise Line Home Ports	
Anchorage/Seward (AK)	Carnival Celebrity Holland America Norwegian Princess Radisson World Explorer
Juneau (AK)	Alaska's Glacier Bay Alaska Sightseeing Clipper Special Expeditions
Ketchikan (AK)	Alaska's Glacier Bay Clipper
Nome (AK)	Radisson
Seattle (WA)	Alaska's Glacier Bay Alaska Sightseeing Clipper
Sitka (AK)	Special Expeditions
Vancouver (BC)	Carnival Celebrity Crystal Holland America Norwegian Princess Royal Caribbean World Explorer
Whittier (AK)	Alaska Sightseeing

Paved Road
State or Provincial Route
Dirt Road
Arctic Ocean
Beaufort Sea
Barrow
Prudhoe Bay
Deadhorse
Cape Krusenstern National Monument
Brooks Range
Noatak National Preserve
Anaktuvuk Pass
Dalton Hwy.
Arctic National Wildlife Refuge
Brooks Range
United States
Canada
Kobuk Valley National Park
Gates of the Arctic National Park and Preserve
Kotzebue
Bettles
Arctic Circle
Dempster Hwy.
Bering Land Bridge National Preserve
Fort Yukon
Yukon Flats National Wildlife Refuge
Circle
Chena Hot Springs
CANADA
Galena
Yukon-Charley Rivers National Preserve
Manley Hot Springs
Unalakleet
Fairbanks
North Pole
Eagle
YUKON
Nenana
Yukon River
Delta Junction
Dawson City, Yukon
Denali National Park
McGrath
Alaska Range
Mt. McKinley
Tok
Kuskokwim River
Talkeetna
Glennallen
Wrangell Mts.
Willow
Wasilla
Palmer
McCarthy
Whitehorse, Yukon
Anchorage
Valdez
Lake Clark National Park and Preserve
Kenai
Whittier
Soldotna
Cordova
Wrangell-St. Elias National Park and Preserve
Seward
Dillingham
Cook Inlet
Homer
Halibut Cove
Prince William Sound
Yakutat
Skagway
BRITISH COLUMBIA
Haines
King Salmon
Seldovia
Kenai Fjords National Park
Glacier Bay National Park and Preserve
Juneau
Katmai National Park and Preserve
Alaska Marine Highway
Gustavus
Admiralty Island National Monument
Gulf of Alaska
Chichagof Island
Admiralty Island
Kodiak
Petersburg
Baranof Island
Sitka
Wrangell
Kodiak Island
Prince of Wales Island
Aniakchak National Monument and Preserve
Craig
Ketchikan
Misty Fjords National Monument
Prince Rupert, B.C.
OCEAN
To Vancouver & Seattle

Anchorage

Cruise ships usually dock in Seward, about 125 miles from Anchorage on the east coast of the Kenai Peninsula, to avoid the extra day that cruising all the way to Anchorage adds to itineraries.

Most visitors will use Anchorage as a hub, because thanks to the international airport, it's where Alaska links with the rest of the world. You can spend a day or two here before heading off on a cruise from Seward or a land adventure.

Getting There

BY PLANE The Anchorage International Airport is located within the city limits, 10 to 15 minutes from downtown. Taxis run about $14 for the trip downtown. Or two airport shuttles charge $6 a person: the **Borealis Shuttle (☎ 907/276-3600)** and **Mom's Shuttle (☎ 907/344-6667)**.

Ahoy, Mateys!

For additional visitor information, call the **Anchorage Convention and Visitor Bureau (☎ 907/276-4118)**.

Most major rental-car companies operate at the airport, including Alamo, Avis, Budget, Dollar, Hertz, and National. A midsize car costs about $55 a day, with unlimited mileage. Advance bookings are recommended. (See appendix B, "Car-Rental Agencies Contact Information.")

BY CAR There's only one road into Anchorage from the rest of the world: the Glenn Highway. The other road out of town, the Seward Highway, leads to the Kenai Peninsula.

Not to Be Missed

The downtown area is pleasant, if a bit touristy. For a better sense of what Alaska's all about, you'll want to get outside a bit, maybe on one of the trails that run through and around town.

- **A walk on the Tony Knowles Coastal Trail:** This paved trail runs 10 miles along the water, from the western end of Second Avenue to Kincaid Park. You can hop on the trail at several points, including via Elderberry Park, at the western end of Fifth Avenue.
- **A walking tour of downtown:** If you're in town on a weekday from June to August, you can join one of the historic tours hosted by Alaska Historic Properties (**☎ 907/274-3600**). Meet in the lobby of the old City Hall (524 W. Fourth Ave., next to the log-cabin visitor center) at 1pm. Tours cost $5 for adults, $4 for seniors, and $1 for children. The tours cover about 2 miles and take 1 hour.
- **A bike ride around town:** You can rent a bike from **CycleSights**

(☎ **907/344-1771** or 907/227-6109) right in Elderberry Park (at the western end of Fifth Avenue) for $15 per half day, $25 per full day. Bike tours are also offered.

➤ **A walk in the Chugach Mountains:** If you have a little time, head out to the surrounding Chugach Mountains, which are easily accessible and as beautiful as any mountains you're likely to see. Stop by the Alaska Public Lands Information Center at 605 W. Fourth Ave., Suite 105 (☎ **907/271-2737**) for info on getting out there.

Other Recommended Attractions

➤ The **Anchorage Museum of History and Art,** 121 W. Seventh Ave. (☎ **907/343-4326**), has a gallery with displays on the history and anthropology of the state, and also a series of art galleries that feature contemporary Alaskan works.

➤ The **Alaska Zoo,** 4731 O'Malley Rd. (☎ **907/346-3242**), is about 6 miles south of downtown and is home to delegates from many of the state's native animal species, plus a few foreign dignitaries.

Hotels, Eating & Nightlife

HOTELS Chain hotels can be found here, including the **Anchorage Hilton,** Third Avenue and E Street (☎ **800/245-2527** or 907/272-7411). For history and charm, try the **Anchorage Hotel,** right next to the Hilton on E Street (☎ **800/544-0988** or 907/272-4553). The **Westmark Anchorage,** which is owned by Holland America Line, is at 720 W. Fifth Ave. (☎ **800/544-0970** or 907/276-7676); and the grandest hotel in the city and probably in all of Alaska is **Hotel Captain Cook,** Fourth Avenue and K Street (☎ **800/843-1950** or 907/276-6000).

RESTAURANTS **Club Paris,** 417 W. Fifth Ave. (☎ **907/277-6332**) offers beef and seafood and a smoky, classy atmosphere. The **Marx Brothers Cafe,** 627 W. Third Ave. (☎ **907/278-2133**) offers cuisine ranging from Asian to Italian, served in a casually elegant setting. Favorites include Caesar salad prepared at your table.

NIGHTLIFE The **Long Branch Saloon,** 1733 E. Dimond Blvd., east of the New Seward Highway (☎ **907/349-4142**), has country music every night and serves great burgers to boot. **Mr. Whitekey's Fly By Night Club,** on Spenard Road south of Northern Lights Boulevard (☎ **907/279-SPAM**), has drinks and a nightly 8pm show (Tuesday to Saturday) featuring the proprietor and his crude brand of humor. Some 43 beers are on tap at **Humpy's,** at Sixth Avenue and F Street, which also offers live acoustic music every night.

Seward

Seward is the main northern embarkation and disembarkation port for cruise ships exploring the Inside Passage and Gulf of Alaska. Most cruise ships dock about a half mile from downtown. For information, call ☎ **907/224-2424.**

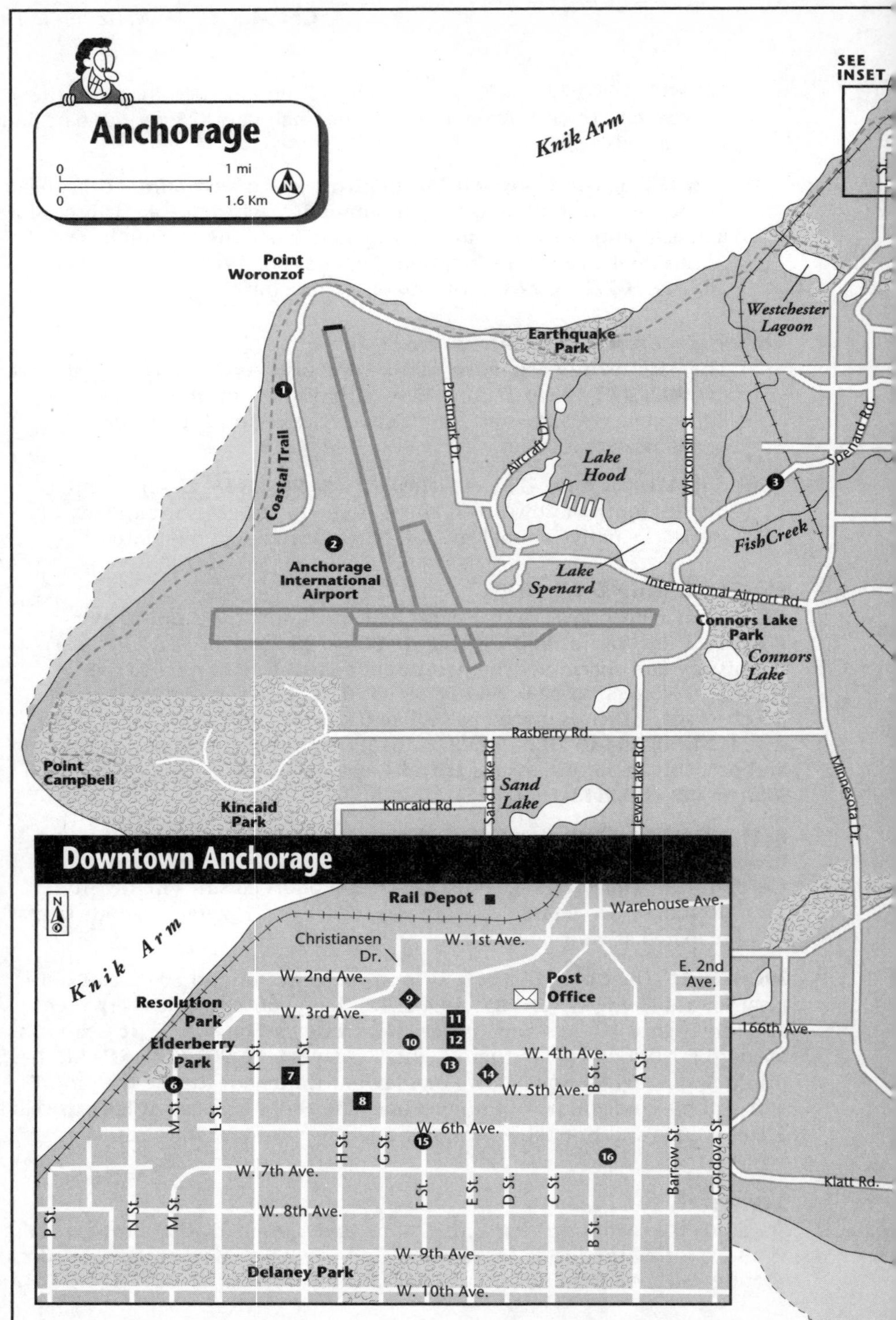

Anchorage
0
1 mi
0
1.6 Km
N
Knik Arm
SEE INSET
L St.
Point Woronzof
Westchester Lagoon
Earthquake Park
Postmark Dr.
Coastal Trail
Aircraft Dr.
Lake Hood
Wisconsin St.
Spenard Rd.
Anchorage International Airport
Lake Spenard
Fish Creek
International Airport Rd.
Connors Lake Park
Connors Lake
Rasberry Rd.
Point Campbell
Sand Lake Rd.
Sand Lake
Jewel Lake Rd.
Kincaid Park
Kincaid Rd.
Minnesota Dr.
166th Ave.
Klatt Rd.
Downtown Anchorage
Rail Depot
Warehouse Ave.
Knik Arm
Christiansen Dr.
W. 1st Ave.
W. 2nd Ave.
E. 2nd Ave.
Post Office
Resolution Park
W. 3rd Ave.
Elderberry Park
W. 4th Ave.
W. 5th Ave.
W. 6th Ave.
W. 7th Ave.
W. 8th Ave.
W. 9th Ave.
W. 10th Ave.
Delaney Park
K St.
I St.
M St.
L St.
H St.
G St.
F St.
E St.
D St.
C St.
B St.
A St.
Barrow St.
Cordova St.
P St.
N St.

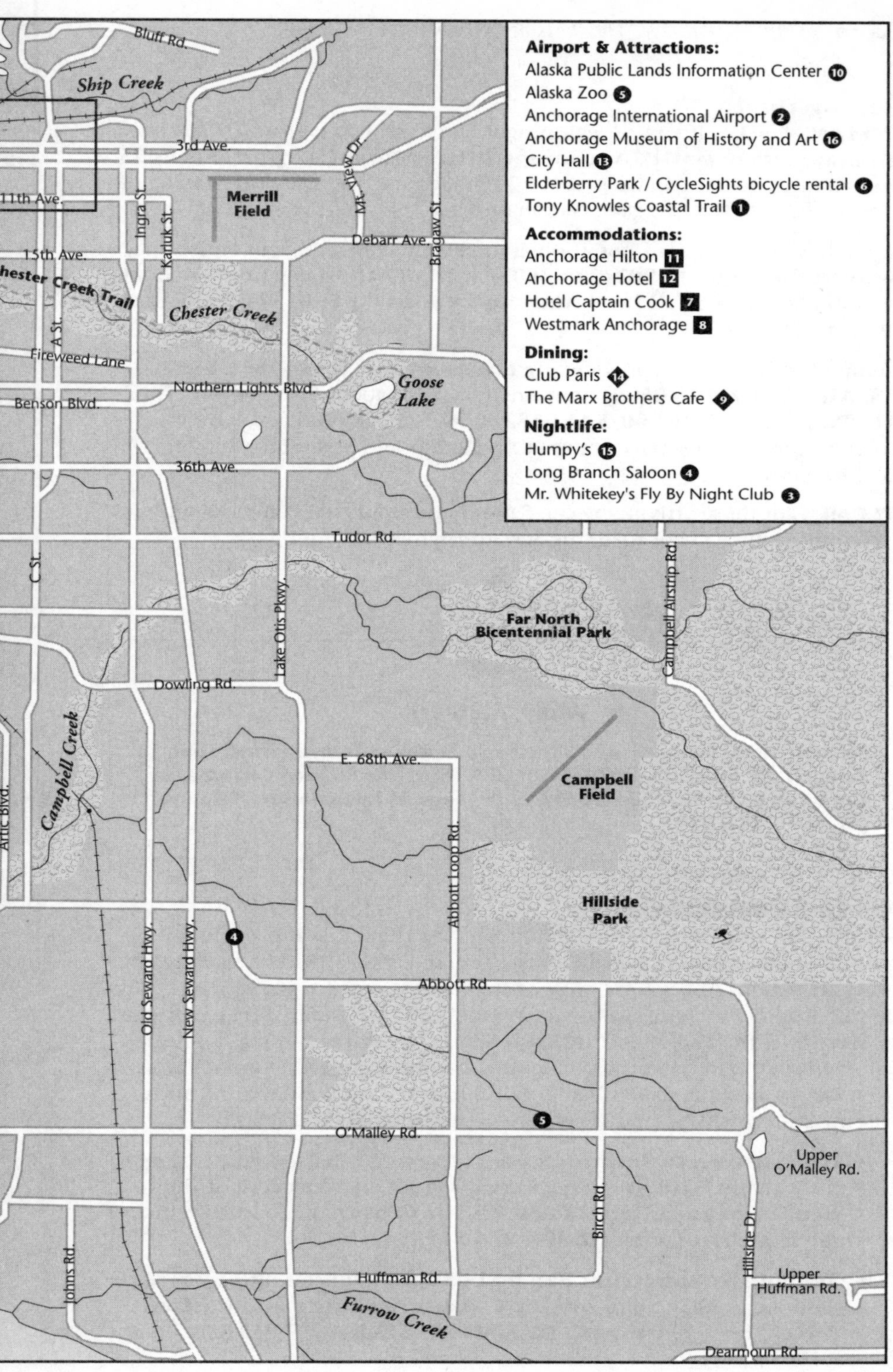
Airport & Attractions:
Alaska Public Lands Information Center 10
Alaska Zoo 5
Anchorage International Airport 2
Anchorage Museum of History and Art 16
City Hall 13
Elderberry Park / CycleSights bicycle rental 6
Tony Knowles Coastal Trail 1
Accommodations:
Anchorage Hilton 11
Anchorage Hotel 12
Hotel Captain Cook 7
Westmark Anchorage 8
Dining:
Club Paris 14
The Marx Brothers Cafe 9
Nightlife:
Humpy's 15
Long Branch Saloon 4
Mr. Whitekey's Fly By Night Club 3
Bluff Rd.
Ship Creek
3rd Ave.
11th Ave.
Merrill Field
Mt. View Dr.
Ingra St.
Karluk St.
Bragaw St.
Debarr Ave.
15th Ave.
Chester Creek Trail
Chester Creek
A St.
Fireweed Lane
Goose Lake
Northern Lights Blvd.
Benson Blvd.
36th Ave.
Tudor Rd.
C St.
Lake Otis Pkwy.
Campbell Airstrip Rd.
Far North Bicentennial Park
Dowling Rd.
Campbell Creek
E. 68th Ave.
Campbell Field
Artic Blvd.
Abbott Loop Rd.
Hillside Park
Old Seward Hwy.
New Seward Hwy.
Abbott Rd.
O'Malley Rd.
Upper O'Malley Rd.
Birch Rd.
Hillside Dr.
Johns Rd.
Huffman Rd.
Upper Huffman Rd.
Furrow Creek
Dearmoun Rd.

Getting There

BY PLANE & BUS If you're beginning your cruise, you'll arrive by bus from the nearest major airport, **Anchorage International Airport,** some 125 miles away. The bus trip takes about 3 hours, but it's a pretty ride, taking passengers through the Chugach National Forest.

If you haven't made transportation arrangements through your cruise line, **Seward Bus Line (☎ 907/224-3608)** offers one trip a day from Anchorage for $30 one way. **Gray Line's Alaskan Express (☎ 800/544-2206)** does the same for $40.

Commuter air service is provided by **Era Aviation (☎ 800/866-8394)** or **F.S. Air (☎ 907/248-9595)** from Anchorage for about $75 one way. The **Alaska Railroad (☎ 800/544-0552** or 907/265-2494) offers extraordinarily scenic train service between Anchorage and Seward for $55 one way ($82 round-trip).

BY CAR For those arriving by car, Seward and the Kenai Peninsula are served by a single major road, the Seward Highway.

Ahoy, Mateys!

For more visitor information, call the Kenai Peninsula **Tourism Marketing Council (☎ 800/535-3624** or 907/283-3850), the **Seward Chamber of Commerce (☎ 907/224-8051)**, or the **Seward Information Helpline (☎ 907/224-2424)**.

Not to Be Missed

Seward's big attraction is Resurrection Bay and the access it provides to the rest of Alaska, as well as Kenai Fjords National Park. Until very recently, the other attractions in the town were of the modest, small-town variety, but the newest attraction might put the town more solidly on tourist maps. Opened in May 1998, the $50 million **Alaska Sea Life Center** is a major research aquarium that also hosts the public. It was funded mostly by money won from Exxon after the Exxon Valdez oil spill. Seals, sea lions, marine birds, and the scientists who study them are expected to be on display.

- **Hiking around Seward:** Seward's environs offer several excellent hiking trails. Visitors can get a complete list and directions at the **Kenai Fjords National Park Visitor Center**, on Fourth Avenue, at the small-boat harbor (**☎ 907/224-3175**).
- **Touring Resurrection Bay by boat:** Several firms offer tours of the Resurrection Bay fjords by boat. **Coastal Kayaking and Custom Adventures Worldwide (☎ 800/288-2134** or 907/258-3866) offers

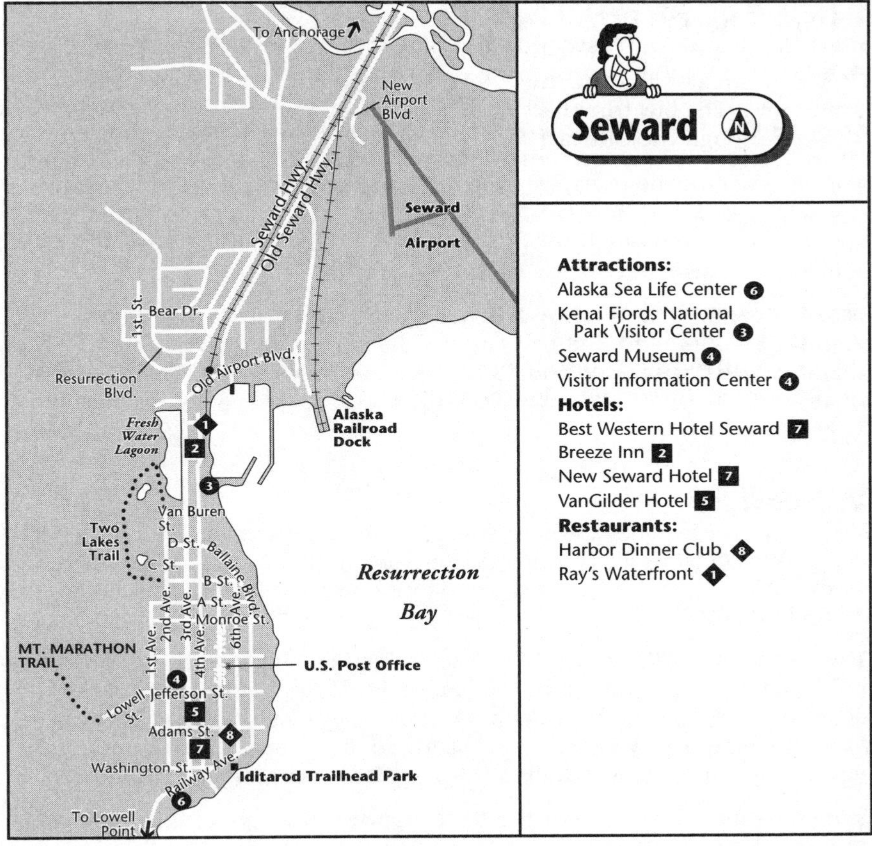

kayaking day trips in Resurrection Bay for $95, as well as longer trips into Kenai Fjords National Park.

➤ **A walking tour of downtown:** You can explore Downtown Seward with the help of a walking-tour map available from the Chamber of Commerce visitor information kiosk located at the cruise ship dock and in the old Alaska Railroad car at the corner of Third Avenue and Jefferson Street, downtown.

Other Recommended Attractions

➤ **The Seward Museum,** at Third Avenue and Jefferson Street, offers historical memorabilia, including a display about the Russian ships built here in the 18th century.

➤ **Iditarod dogsled tours,** Old Exit Glacier Road, 3.7 miles out the Seward Highway (☎ **800/478-3139** or 907/224-8607), offers dogsled demonstrations and rides on a wheeled dogsled.

Hotels, Eating & Nightlife

HOTELS The **Best Western Hotel Seward,** 217 Fifth Ave. (☎ **800/478-4050** or 907/224-2378), is a good choice, particularly if you book a room in front (the back ones just have a view of another hotel). The **New Seward Hotel** (☎ **907/224-8001**) is connected by a lobby to the Best Western and shares an owner too, but the rooms are smaller and less expensive. The **Breeze Inn,** 1306 Seward Hwy. (☎ **907/224-5237**), is located at the boat harbor. The **VanGilder Hotel,** 308 Adams St. (☎ **907/224-3525**), is the historic property in town, built in 1916. The rooms vary more than somewhat, so ask to see a few before you choose.

RESTAURANTS The **Harbor Dinner Club,** 220 Fifth Ave. (☎ **907/224-3012**), is an old-fashioned family restaurant with a diverse menu that includes fine seafood and $3 hamburgers. **Ray's Waterfront,** at the small boat harbor (☎ **907/224-5606**) is a local favorite where salmon is a specialty.

Vancouver

Vancouver is the main southern embarkation and disembarkation port for cruise ships exploring the Inside Passage and Gulf of Alaska. Most cruise ships dock at Canada Place at the end of Burrard Street. For information, call ☎ **604/666-6068.**

The pier terminal **Canada Place** is a landmark in the city, noted for its five-sail structure that reaches into the harbor. It's located at the edge of the downtown district and is just a quick stroll from **Gastown** and **Robson Street,** where trendy fashions can be found. Right near the pier are hotels, restaurants, and shops, as well as the **Tourism Vancouver Infocentre.**

Ships also sometimes dock at the **Ballantyne** cruise terminal, a 5-minute cab ride away.

Getting There

BY PLANE **Vancouver International Airport** is located 8 miles south of downtown Vancouver. The average taxi fare from the airport to downtown is about CAN$25/US$17.50. This is a set fee, but some cabs will try to charge you more. **YVR Airporter** buses (☎ **602/244-9888**) offer service to the city for CAN$9/US$6.30 per person for adults one way (less for seniors and kids). **AirLimo** (☎ **604/273-1331**) offers flat-rate limousine service for CAN$26/US$18.20 (about the same as a cab).

Rental-car agencies with local branches include Avis, Budget, Hertz Canada, and Thrifty.

Not to Be Missed

➤ **Strolling around Gastown:** Named for "Gassy" Jack Deighton, who built a saloon here in 1867, the area offers charming cobblestone streets, historic buildings, gaslights, street musicians, and a touch of

Bohemia. It's so close to the ship pier that it's a must-see. There are boutiques, antique and art shops, and lots of touristy stuff, along with restaurants, clubs, and cafes.

- **Visiting Chinatown:** Vancouver's Chinatown is one of the largest in North America, and like Gastown, is also a historic district. Chinese architecture and the **Dr. Sun Yat-sen Garden,** 578 Carrall St. (**☎ 604/689-7133**), are among the attractions, along with great food and shops selling Chinese wares.

Other Recommended Attractions

- The **shopping** is good on **Robson Street** for trendy fashions or **Granville Island** for crafts and kids' items (especially since the U.S. dollar is worth more than the Canadian dollar).
- **Stanley Park** is a 1,000-acre retreat just north of the downtown area and includes within its environs the **Vancouver Aquarium** (**☎ 604/682-1118**)—the third-largest in North America—as well as rose gardens and hiking trails.
- The **Vancouver Art Gallery,** 750 Hornby St. (**☎ 604/682-5621**), holds a large collection of both Canadian and international art, and also features a special gallery geared toward kids.
- The **Vancouver Museum,** 1100 Chestnut St. (**☎ 604/736-4431**), presents a history of the city, from prehistoric times to the present day. Of particular interest to cruise passengers is the exhibit that allows you to walk through the steerage deck of a 19th-century immigrant ship.

Life Preservers

In Vancouver, it's advised not to wander off the tourist path. Only a block or two from Gastown, for example, you can encounter needle parks and other places tourists don't want to wander into.

Hotels, Eating & Nightlife

HOTELS Conveniently located right at Canada Place are the upscale 23-story **Pan-Pacific Hotel Vancouver,** 300–999 Canada Place (**☎ 604/662-8111**), and the similarly lofty **Waterfront Centre Hotel,** 900 Canada Place (**☎ 604/691-1991**). Both offer rooms with spectacular views. The grande dame of hotels in the city is **Hotel Vancouver,** 900 W. Georgia St., a few blocks from the pier (**☎ 604/684-3131**); it sports all stone walls, a copper roof, marble interiors, and massive proportions.

While virtually all downtown hotels are within walking distance of shops, restaurants, and attractions, for safety reasons, if you plan to go out at night it's best to avoid these places around Hastings and Main. Granville Street

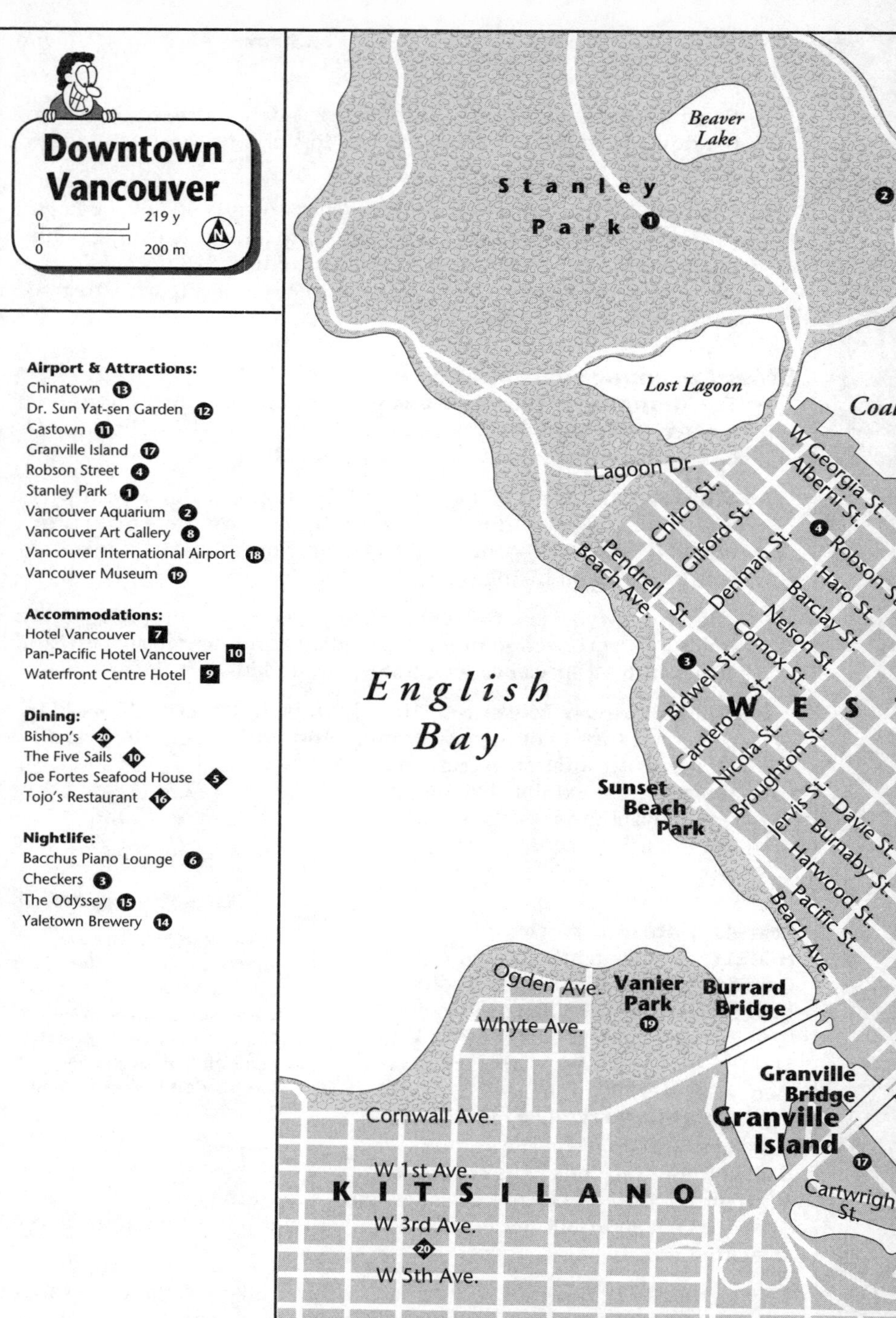

Downtown Vancouver
0
219 y
0
200 m
N
Airport & Attractions:
Chinatown 13
Dr. Sun Yat-sen Garden 12
Gastown 11
Granville Island 17
Robson Street 4
Stanley Park 1
Vancouver Aquarium 2
Vancouver Art Gallery 8
Vancouver International Airport 18
Vancouver Museum 19
Accommodations:
Hotel Vancouver 7
Pan-Pacific Hotel Vancouver 10
Waterfront Centre Hotel 9
Dining:
Bishop's 20
The Five Sails 10
Joe Fortes Seafood House 5
Tojo's Restaurant 16
Nightlife:
Bacchus Piano Lounge 6
Checkers 3
The Odyssey 15
Yaletown Brewery 14
Beaver Lake
Stanley Park
Lost Lagoon
Coal
Lagoon Dr.
W Georgia St.
Alberni St.
Chilco St.
Gilford St.
Robson St.
Pendrell St.
Beach Ave.
Denman St.
Haro St.
Barclay St.
Nelson St.
Comox St.
Bidwell St.
Cardero St.
Nicola St.
Broughton St.
WEST
English Bay
Sunset Beach Park
Jervis St.
Davie St.
Burnaby St.
Harwood St.
Pacific St.
Beach Ave.
Ogden Ave.
Vanier Park
Burrard Bridge
Whyte Ave.
Granville Bridge
Granville Island
Cornwall Ave.
W 1st Ave.
KITSILANO
Cartwright St.
W 3rd Ave.
W 5th Ave.
W 7th Ave.
W. Broadway
Post Office
Information

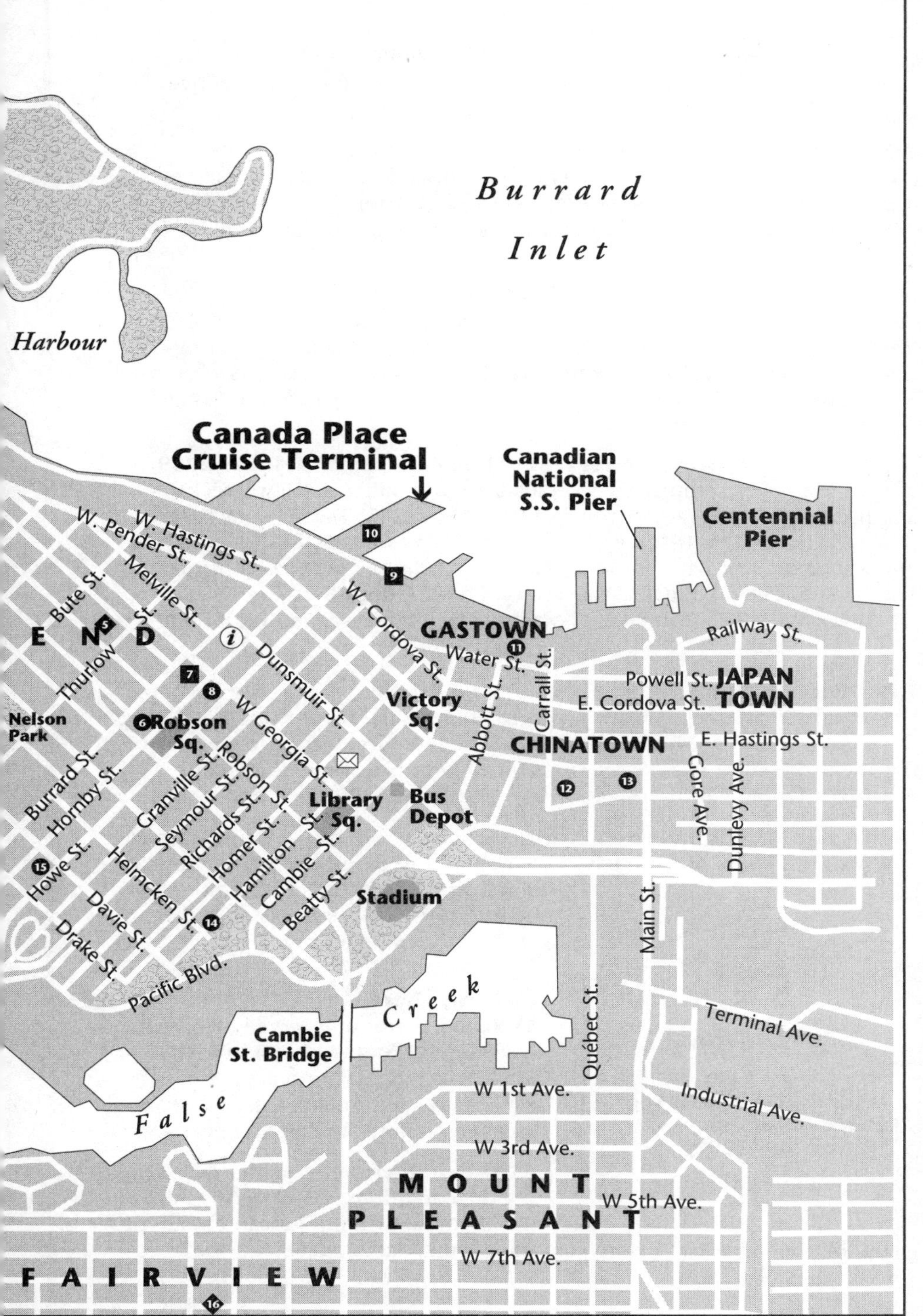
Burrard
Inlet
Harbour
Canada Place
Cruise Terminal
Canadian
National
S.S. Pier
Centennial
Pier
W. Hastings St.
W. Pender St.
Melville St.
Bute St.
St.
E N D
Thurlow
Nelson
Park
Robson
Sq.
Dunsmuir St.
W Georgia St.
Robson St.
W. Cordova St.
GASTOWN
Water St.
Railway St.
Powell St.
E. Cordova St.
JAPAN
TOWN
Victory
Sq.
Abbott St.
Carrall St.
CHINATOWN
E. Hastings St.
Gore Ave.
Dunlevy Ave.
Burrard St.
Hornby St.
Granville St.
Seymour St.
Richards St.
Homer St.
Hamilton St.
Cambie St.
Beatty St.
Library
Sq.
Bus
Depot
Howe St.
Helmcken St.
Davie St.
Drake St.
Stadium
Main St.
Pacific Blvd.
Creek
Cambie
St. Bridge
Québec St.
Terminal Ave.
Industrial Ave.
W 1st Ave.
False
W 3rd Ave.
M O U N T
P L E A S A N T
W 5th Ave.
W 7th Ave.
F A I R V I E W

downtown is an area that's being "cleaned up" and is now home to some lower-end, boutique-type hotels. It's an area that has clubs and an active nightlife that attracts a young set, but also panhandlers.

RESTAURANTS The **Five Sails** in the Pan-Pacific Hotel, Canada Place (☎ **604/878-9000,** ext. 480) offers views and food that can both be described as spectacular. **Joe Fortes Seafood House,** 777 Thurlow St. (☎ **604/669-1940**), is a best bet for seafood and views of successful Vancouverites.

In central Vancouver is the famous **Bishop's,** 2183 W. Fourth Ave. (☎ **604/738-2025**), which has gained an international reputation as being the finest restaurant experience in town. Sushi lovers, including visiting celebrities, flock to **Tojo's Restaurant,** 777 W. Broadway (☎ **604/872-8050**), for what's supposed to be the best sushi in Vancouver. (Some say it's the best in North America.)

NIGHTLIFE **Yaletown Brewery,** 1110 Hamilton St. (☎ **604/681-2739**), offers a tasty range of microbrews, plus darts and billiards. Classic rock and people-watching are the thing at **Checkers,** 1755 Davie St. (☎ **604/682-1831**); and **The Odyssey,** 1251 Howe St. (☎ **604/689-5256**), is a popular gay dance spot with live entertainment, including male go-go dancers. The Bacchus Piano Lounge at the **Wedgewood Hotel,** 845 Hornby St. (☎ **604/689-7777**), features Wes Mackey playing blues guitar most nights.

Juneau

Juneau is used as an embarkation port by some of the small-ship lines. Cruise ships usually dock at **Marine Park** or at the old ferry dock, also known as the Cruise Ship Terminal. Some ships (notably Princess) use the **South Franklin Dock.** For information, call ☎ **907/586-2201.**

Marine Park and the old ferry terminal are both within easy walking distance to downtown shops and attractions. Sometimes ships use the South Franklin Dock, which is about a fifth of a mile away. Shuttle-bus service is offered from all 3 locations for $1 round trip.

Ahoy, Mateys!

For additional visitor information, call **The Davis Log Cabin Visitor Center** (☎ **907/586-2201**).

Getting There

BY PLANE Juneau is served by **Alaska Airlines** (☎ **800/426-0333** or 907/789-9791), with daily nonstop flights from Seattle and Anchorage, as well as several commuter and air-taxi operators.

Because weather can wreak havoc with landing conditions, it's especially advisable if you're flying to Juneau to plan on being there a day or two before your cruise embarkation date.

A cab from the airport to downtown will cost about $20. The **Island Waterways** van (☎ **907/780-4977**) charges $8 a person to major hotels. The **Capital Transit city bus** (☎ **907/789-6901**) offers hourly service for $1.25, but your luggage has to sit at your feet.

Major car-rental companies have offices at the airport.

Not to Be Missed

Since Juneau is also a major port of call, I've covered its attractions and restaurants in chapter 24, "Ports of Call: Alaska." (See that chapter for a map of the town as well.)

Hotels & Nightlife

HOTELS **Baranof Hotel,** 127 N. Franklin St. (☎ **800/544-0970** or 907/586-2660), belongs to Westmark (Holland America Line), and has a lovely, meandering lobby and the feel of a grand old hotel (it was built in 1939). **Westmark Juneau,** 51 W. Egan Dr. (☎ **800/544-0970** or 907/586-6900), is a more modern alternative. A lower priced alternative, right on the waterfront, is the **Prospector Hotel,** 375 Whittier St. (☎ **800/331-2711** or 907/586-3737).

NIGHTLIFE The **Red Dog Saloon,** 278 S. Franklin St., is a place of legends. It offers sawdust floors and stuffed animal heads on the walls, as well as live music and crowds (mostly tourists). Real Alaskans can be found at other bars, including the one at the **Alaskan Hotel,** 167 S. Franklin St., which features blues, jazz, and folk music.

Part 5

The Cruise Experience: What to Expect

So what's it really like to vacation on a cruise ship? Here's where we'll get into it all, from the Technicolor whoopee of the onboard activity offerings to the Fellini-esque food presentations to the luxurious spa treatments.

In the following 10 chapters, you'll pick up gambling tips; hear what the captain's table is all about; learn nautical-speak; be briefed on what you can expect in the way of food, activities, and entertainment; find out how to find quiet when you want quiet; and pick up recipes for popular shipboard drink concoctions. I've even included special chapters for you singles, bargain-hunters, and families with kids.

Fasten your seat belts—or, more aptly, hook up your life jackets: You're in for a fun ride.

Chapter 12

How to Pass Yourself Off as a Veteran Cruiser

In This Chapter

- Tips on telling the guy who steers the ship from the one who serves your dinner
- A glossary of seagoing terms
- Dumb questions to avoid asking
- Cruise do's and don'ts
- Tips on dressing for the occasion

Just because you're a first-time cruiser doesn't mean you have to act like one. Knowing a little background information about cruising and the sea and having the right attitude can make you seem like an expert even before you get on board for your cruise vacation.

To help, I've prepared a quick lesson in who's who on the ship, a brief dictionary of nautical terms for you to throw into conversations, and a list of do's and don'ts. And, just in case, I've also noted some dumb questions not to ask.

Who's Who in the Crew?

Ships have enormous staffs. You won't find a staff or crew member for every guest, but you will often find one for every two guests. What that means is that a ship of 1,800 passengers might have a crew of 900. You won't come into contact with all of them, though, because there are two kinds of crew categories: **front-of-the-house** and **back-of-the-house.** Only front-of-the-house staff members have contact with guests.

Out to Sea

Some ships hire retired gentlemen to entertain single ladies (usually of the older variety) with their dance ability and witty conversation—as Walter Mattheau and Jack Lemmon did in the movie *Out to Sea*. These **gentlemen hosts** (also known as *guest hosts*) may also, in some cases, accompany single women on shore excursions. In exchange for their services, these men travel for free. They are not allowed to take tips, and they're not allowed to make whoopee with passengers, either.

With the exception of lecturers, who have full passenger privileges and sleep in regular passenger cabins, the staff sleeps in cabins in the lower decks of the ship—decks to which passengers do not have access. They eat in staff dining rooms and relax in staff recreation areas.

You can tell the **top officers** by the number of stripes on their uniforms. Those with four stripes are the top dogs—the captain, the chief engineer, the hotel manager, and the staff captain.

Anyone who has seen the TV show *The Love Boat* knows that ships have a captain, a purser, a cruise director, a doctor, and a bartender, but their main jobs are not to find love matches for passengers. Here's what these people really do:

Captain: The big boss; may also be referred to as "The Master."

Staff Captain: The second in command; usually in charge of navigation and safety.

Hotel Manager: In charge of all passenger services, including restaurants, bars, and sleeping accommodations.

Chief Engineer: In charge of all the machinery on board, including the engines.

Purser: In charge of information and financial matters.

Chief Steward: In charge of cleaning and maintenance of cabins and public rooms.

Cruise Director: In charge of activities and entertainment; also acts as the ship's emcee.

Doctor: In charge of medical care.

Head Chef or Chef de Cuisine: In charge of the kitchen (galley), including menus.

Shore-Excursion Director: In charge of land tours; often doubles as the port lecturer.

Entertainment Director: In charge of the show staff.

Maitre d': In charge of the dining room operation.

Cabin Stewards: The people who clean the cabins.

Dining Stewards: A fancy name for waiters.

Talk Like a Sailor

On most modern cruise ships, you're not expected to know your halyard from your fluke, but reviewing the following list will let you throw out just enough nautical terms so you'll sound like an experienced cruiser.

> **Which Side Is Which?**
>
> Here's an easy way to remember which is the port side of the ship and which is the starboard: When facing the front, port is the left side—and the words *port* and *left* both have four letters. Remember that, and you're set.

abeam: Located off the side of the ship

aft: The back of the ship

ahead: Located in front of the ship's bow

alongside: Said of the ship when it's beside another vessel or a pier

amidships: Toward the middle of the ship (also *midship*)

ashore: On land

astern: Behind the ship

beam: Widest part of the ship

bearing: Compass-point direction into which the ship is headed

below: Anything beneath the main deck

berth: A bed; also a space to anchor or moor (tie up) the ship

bilge: Lowest inner part of the ship's hull

blast: Sound of the ship's horn

bow: Front of the ship

bridge: Where the captain and officers control the ship

bulkhead: Any wall aboard the ship

buoy: A floating marker moored to the bottom of the sea or tied to an anchor

cabin: A passenger guest room; also called a *stateroom*

cast off: To release the lines that tie the ship to the pier

chart: A nautical map to guide the ship

come about: Turn the ship around

course: Direction in which the ship is headed

davit: Device for raising and lowering lifeboats

deck: Floor or level (usually the higher up the cabin, the more expensive)

disembark: To leave the ship (also *debark*)

dock: Where the ship is tied up; the landing wharf or pier

draft: Measure of the space between the bottom of the ship and the water's surface

embark: To get on board the ship

fore: Front of the ship

galley: Ship's kitchen

gangway: Ramp used to board or disembark from the ship

head: Bathroom

heavy seas: Rough water

helm: Ship's steering mechanism

hold: Ship's cargo area

hull: Frame of the ship

keel: Bottom of the ship

knot: 1 nautical mile per hour; equal to about 1.15 land miles per hour.

leeward: Direction toward which the wind is blowing

lines: Ropes that tie the ship to the dock

midships: In the center position

muster: Assembly

nautical mile: 6,080.2 feet (compared to a land mile of 5,280 feet)

pitch: Rise-and-fall motion of the ship in heavy seas

port side: Left side of the ship when facing the front

roll: Side-to-side motion in heavy seas

starboard: Right side of the ship when facing the front

stateroom: Guest cabin

stern: Back of the ship

tender: A small boat used to transport passengers to shore

wake: Waves produced by a ship's movement in water

windward: The side exposed to the wind, or moving toward the direction from which the wind is blowing

Sea Stories

The Carnival *Elation,* which began service in March 1998, is the first cruise ship to feature the new **Azipod propulsion system,** which unlike conventional systems, *pulls* a ship through the water rather than pushes it. Azipod eliminates the need for traditional propeller shafts, rudders, and stern thrusters. It occupies less space on board, makes the ship easier to steer and maneuver, reduces propulsion noises and vibration, and provides fuel savings. It's the propeller system we'll be seeing more of in the future.

Dumb Questions Not to Ask

Some people say there are no dumb questions, just dumb answers, but cruise directors and other cruise officials I've talked to swear they've been asked the following questions in real life. I think they qualify in the D-word category. If any of them confuse you, see the responses that follow.

Questions

1. Does the crew sleep on the ship when we're at sea?
2. Does the ship have its own supply of electricity?
3. What time is the midnight buffet?
4. Does the elevator go forward?
5. Is the trapshooting held outside?
6. Why does the ship rock only when we're at sea?
7. Will I get wet if I go snorkeling?
8. What do you do with the ice carvings after they melt?
9. Is there water all around the island?
10. How will we know which photos (taken by the ship's photographers) are ours?

Answers

1. No, there are separate little boats that follow the big cruise ship, and the crew climbs on board when they're needed.

Ahoy, Mateys!

An outside cabin is not outside, literally—it just has a window. And it's more expensive than an inside cabin, which is in fact inside.

2. No. The ship plugs into a big cord at the terminal and drags the cord wherever it sails.
3. Duh!
4. Maybe on Pluto.
5. No. We like to do it in the casino so we can scare as many passengers as possible.
6. Because that's when it's most excited.
7. Only if you get in the water.
8. Can you say d-r-a-i-n?
9. Why don't you try driving home, and we'll see?
10. Just look for the person wearing your clothes.

Dress for Success

A surefire way to look like a cruise veteran is to make sure you're properly dressed for the part. So, to review what you learned in chapter 9, "Tying Up the Loose Ends," you can wear very casual clothes during the day, and at night, something from one of these categories:

- **Formal** for men means a tux or dark suit with a tie; for women, it's a nice cocktail dress, a long dress or gown, or a dressy pants suit.
- **Informal** for men is a jacket and tie and dress slacks, or a light suit (jeans are frowned upon); for women, a dress, skirt and blouse, or pants outfit is right on (the little black dress is appropriate here).
- **Casual** at dinner does not mean shorts—for either men or women. Men should wear a sports shirt or open dress shirt with slacks (some will also wear a jacket); women should wear a dress, pants outfit, or skirt and blouse.

Remember to read through the program that will be delivered to your room each evening to check the appropriate dress for the next day.

Cruise Do's and Don'ts

If you want to look like a cruise pro right from the start of your cruise, here are a few pointers:

- **DO whip out your onboard charge card and pay for a round of drinks at the poolside bar.** Casually sign your name to the bill. It'll impress your new friends.

- **DON'T try to use cash at the bar, gift shop, and so on.** Remember that the system on the ship is cashless except in the casino. Use your onboard charge card. Similarly, you don't have to tip the crew member who escorts you to your cabin as soon as you step aboard.
- **DO order yourself champagne, in advance.** (See the order form with your cruise document.) That way, you can invite people to your cabin for a bon voyage party.
- **DON'T try to tip the staff every time service is provided.** You'll get them at the end of the cruise. A tip is automatically added to bar bills, but it's okay to slip the bartender a buck if he or she has a bowl or jar out for tips.

Why Monrovia?

You might notice when you arrive at the docks that your ship is flagged or registered to some country that has nothing to do with the cruise line's home base. That's because most flags are based on financial considerations and other matters of convenience to the cruise lines. Panama and Liberia have very liberal rules governing unions and so on, so you'll see a lot of cruise ships registered there. Other common flags include Monrovia, The Bahamas, Bermuda, and the Netherlands Antilles.

- **DO have your ID and boarding card ready when you board the ship.** Fumbling for them is uncool.
- **DON'T wear a sailor suit or admiral's cap.** You'll look like a dope. Dress in comfortable, casual clothes for your first day.
- **DO book your shore excursions and your salon and beauty services the first night.** The prime tours tend to sell out. Reading the literature provided by the cruise line in advance of your cruise will help. Similarly, the most desirable spa treatments might sell out fast.
- **DON'T play hopscotch on the deck's shuffleboard markers.** The markings might look similar, but you'll look silly. There are no hopscotch markers on any ship. Trust me.
- **DO confirm your dining-room seating assignments.** Remember, the best tables go first. If you're not happy with your assignment, slip the maitre d' $20 to make the situation better.

- **DON'T show up at formal night dressed in a sweatshirt.** You'll look really, really out of place and, more important, you'll feel that way, too.
- **DO pack an extra set of clothes in your carry-on.** You'll look fresh and spiffy, even if your luggage doesn't show up in your cabin for a while.
- **DON'T smoke** in areas designated as nonsmoking.
- **DO explore the ship immediately upon your arrival.** You can then offer directions to others. You should be able to find a map either in your room or at the purser's office.
- **DON'T leave a towel or magazine on a prime deck chair to reserve it for later.** This is less a cruise-veteran thing and more of common-courtesy thing. It's just rude.
- **DO know in which direction the ship is sailing,** and where you're cruising to, for that matter. That way, you can go up on deck and point out landmarks.
- **DON'T steal the towels.** This is another one of those just-plain-rude things to avoid.
- **DO remember** that doorway thresholds in your stateroom, bathrooms, and some public rooms are often slightly raised.
- **DON'T** trip.

(For tips on dining-room do's and don'ts, see chapter 15, "My Dinner with Andre . . .")

Chapter 13

Sittin' on the Dock of the Bay

In This Chapter

- Getting from the airport to the seaport
- What to do if your flight is delayed
- How to check in at the dock
- What to do if you (gasp!) miss the boat
- Diversions to keep you busy while you wait to board
- What to do as soon as you get on the ship
- The lowdown on the lifeboat drill
- Tips on how to spend your first evening at sea

It's travel time! That welcome-aboard party is right around the corner, but before you get on board you'll have to deal with the inevitable lines. In this chapter, I offer advice on how to avoid the biggest lines, and I also provide some diversions that I hope will ease the tension. I also let you know what you can expect of your first afternoon and evening on board, from lifeboat drills to letting the good times roll.

Airport Rigmarole

Your bags are packed, and you're ready to go. The bags you will check in at the airport are properly tagged with your name and address. If you're checking the bags through to the ship, they're also wearing the appropriate cruise line tags, with your ship name, cabin number, and sailing date filled in.

You have your carry-on, and in it are all your cruise documents, passport (and/or other ID), airline tickets, house keys, jewelry and other valuables, medications, and so on (as described in chapter 9, "Tying Up the Loose Ends"). You might also want to have an extra set of clothes in your carry-on so you can freshen up when you get aboard ship, even if your other bags haven't yet arrived.

Make sure you call the airport to see whether your flight is on time. And get there in plenty of time to check in your bags.

If You Booked Your Air and/or Your Transfers with the Cruise Line . . .

Start looking around either when you get off the plane or at the baggage area: You should see a **cruise line representative** holding a card with the name of the line. Check in with this person.

If you're on a precruise package, the details of what to do at the airport are described in the cruise line's brochure.

Smooth Sailing

If your cruise leaves from Canada or another country, and you arrive there on a flight from the U.S., you need to clear **Customs and Immigration.** Follow the appropriate signs. When you get through, a cruise line representative will meet you outside the Customs area or at the baggage-claim area.

If your bags are checked through to the ship, you will be directed right to waiting transportation (most likely buses or vans) that will take you to the pier. If not, you will have to reclaim your luggage, and the cruise line representative will then direct you to the transportation area. Don't forget to put your cruise line's luggage tags on all your bags, properly filled out (with your ship's name, your cabin number, and sailing date), as this is probably the last you'll see of your luggage until it arrives at your stateroom.

You'll have to turn over the **transportation voucher** you received with your cruise documents to the bus driver, so have it handy. Depending on the amount of time it takes to get to the pier, your driver might give you a small "tour"; if so, think about slipping him a small tip when you arrive.

If You Booked Your Air on Your Own . . .

If you're flying on your own, claim your luggage at the baggage area and proceed to the pier by cab or whatever arrangements you've made. (See chapters 10 and 11 for info on getting to the piers from the airport.) And again, remember to put the luggage tags provided by the cruise line on your bags at this point, because when you get to the pier your bags will be taken from you by a porter for loading onto the ship. Ditto if you're driving to the pier.

The porter at the pier who takes your bags might expect a tip of $1 per bag. Some will be more aggressive than others in asking for it.

Also, if you're on your own, make sure you get to the right ship at the correct pier. That might sound silly, but in cities with multiple piers, it can get confusing, and cab drivers don't always know their way around the docks.

What to Do if Your Flight Is Delayed

First of all, tell the airline personnel at the airport that you're a cruise passenger with a sailing date that day. They might be able to put you on a different flight. Second, have the airline folks call the cruise line to advise them of your delay. There should be an emergency number included in your cruise documents. Keep in mind that you might not be the only person delayed, and the line just might hold the ship until your arrival.

Checking In

What happens as you enter the terminal depends on the cruise line and the size of the ship, but generally at this point you can expect to wait in line. Despite the best efforts of the cruise line, the scene at the pier might be zoo-like.

You will not be able to board the ship before the scheduled embarkation time, usually about 2 or 3 hours before sailing. That's because the ship has likely disembarked passengers from the previous cruise earlier that day, and the crew needs time to clean and prepare and take care of the various paperwork and customs documents that need to be completed.

You have up until a half hour (on some ships, it's 1 hour) before the departure to board, but there are some advantages to boarding earlier, like getting first dibs on prime dining-room tables and spa-treatment times. Plus, if you get on early enough, you can eat lunch on the ship—depending on the ship and departure time, lunch may be served until 3 or even 4pm the first day.

On the downside, crowds tend to be longer earlier into the embarkation process, so if you have time to spare or are a "type A" personality who can't stomach lines, you might want to check out local attractions, shops, or watering holes if there are any nearby the pier (and there sometimes aren't—see chapters 10 and 11 for some suggestions). In any event, it might be impossible to avoid some sort of line at boarding.

What to Do if You Miss the Boat

Don't panic. Go directly to the cruise line's port agent at the pier. You might be able to get to your ship via a chartered boat or tug, or you might be put up in a hotel for the night and flown or otherwise transported to your ship's next port the following day. If you booked your flight on your own, you'll likely be charged for this service.

Tips

- Before you start to board, make sure all the documents you've been sent in advance by the cruise line have been correctly filled out.
- Now is also the time to make any phone calls you need to make. Calls from the ship are expensive ($6.95 to $15 a minute), even when the ship is docked.
- Fix your hair and tidy yourself up a bit (you, fella, tuck in your shirt!), since the ship's photographer will almost certainly waylay you for a picture when you're stepping aboard.

Test Your Nautical Verbiage

Every ship name is officially preceded by an abbreviation that identifies the kind of propulsion it uses—for example, SS *United States,* MV *Galaxy,* and so on. Can you identify these nautical abbreviations?

(a) DS ______
(b) MS ______
(c) MTS ______
(d) MV ______
(e) NS ______
(f) RHMS ______
(g) RMS ______
(h) SAPV ______
(i) SPV ______
(j) SS ______
(k) SSC ______
(l) STR ______
(m) SV ______
(n) TS ______
(o) TSS ______
(p) USS ______

Answers: (a) diesel ship, (b) motor ship, (c) motor-turbine ship, (d) motor vessel, (e) nuclear ship, (f) Royal Hellenic Mail Ship, (g) Royal Mail Ship, (h) sail-assisted power vessel, (i) sail passenger vessel, (j) steamship, (k) semi-submersible craft, (l) steamer, (m) sailing vessel, (n) twin screw, (o) turbine steamship, and (p) United States ship (U.S. Navy).

Cruise Lingo Word-Find

You may have a little while to wait until you can board the ship, so here's an educational way to pass the time. Study the list of nautical lingo from chapter 12 and the names of the various cruise lines and ports, then try to pick 'em out of this word-find.

ACCL (American Canadian Caribbean Line)
Aft (the back of the ship)
Alaska
Anchorage
Bridge
Cabin
Captain
Caribbean
Carnival
Celebrity
CLIA (Cruise Lines International Association)
Crew
Cruise
Cunard
Davit (the winches used for lowering lifeboats)
Deck
Disney
Galley (the ship's kitchen)
Gangway
HAL (Holland America Line)
Keel (the bottom of the ship)
Lido (as in "the Lido Deck")
The Love Boat
Megaship
Norwegian
Ocean
Pool
Port (the left side of the ship, facing forward; also, the places you go)
Porthole
Princess
RCCL (Royal Caribbean Cruises, Ltd.)
Scuba
Snorkel
Spa
Starboard (the right side of the ship, facing forward)
Tender (the small boats that often bring you into port)
Titanic
Windjammer

And Now, a Poem

Don't do word-finds (or finished it and still have time to wait)? How about testing your knowledge of nautical terminology by interpreting this little ditty by my friend Bill Poling, who used more nautical terms in his poem than most of us have ever heard.

Drunk on a Nautical Dictionary, Harry Builds a Yacht

For the *Bream Slake*, Harry conjured
scuppers, halyards, flukes, ferrules,
three trident masts, sheets of crewel
and a wheel house raked on stilts.
In blueprint, gimbaled davits drooped abaft the mizzen,
while copper cringles fluttered from his yawl
and peerless winches coiled his braided spume.
But in schooner trim, the *Bream Slake* pitched
hard for the scalloped beach
and sank in the heaving brine
like a steel-toed shoe.
And my uncle sailed a fathom, maybe two.

Standing in Line—Again

Either right before or right after you get to the check-in desk, you will likely have to pass through an X-ray machine like those at the airport. Put all your bags, including pocketbooks, on the moving belt, empty your pockets of any metal objects (turn them over to the security officials for examination), and walk through the screening gate as indicated.

At the check-in desk, you'll probably be asked to stand in line alphabetically, based on the first letter of your last name. If you have booked a suite, you might get priority boarding at a special desk. Passengers with special needs—such as those with mobility problems—might also be processed separately.

Ship personnel will check your boarding tickets and ID and collect any documents you've been sent to fill out in advance. Any unpaid port taxes or fees will also be collected at this point, and you'll be given a **boarding card.**

Depending on the cruise line, you might establish your **onboard-credit account** at this point by turning over a major credit card to be swiped or making a deposit in cash or traveler's checks (usually $250—see info about this in chapter 9). You might also be given your **cabin key** at this time. In some cases, your onboard credit card doubles as your room key and boarding card.

On other ships, you need to report to the purser's office once on board to establish your onboard-credit account. Also on some ships, your cabin key will be waiting for you in your cabin instead of being given to you before boarding.

Protocol for establishing your **dining-room table assignment** also varies by ship. You might be given your assignment in advance of your sailing (on your tickets), advised of your table number as you check in, or informed of your table number via a card in your stateroom. If you do not receive an assignment by the time you get to your stateroom, you will be directed to a maitre'd's desk set up in a convenient spot on board. This is also the place to go to make any changes if your assignment does not meet with your approval. Make sure your seating time (early or late) and table size are as you requested and that you are in the smoking or non-smoking section you requested (where applicable). Most requests will be met, but not always. You can make a loud stink if you're not happy, though.

No Visitors, Please

Visitors are not allowed on the ship except on a limited, prearranged basis. Check with your travel agent for how to arrange this. Your guests will have to show a photo ID to board.

You also can confirm **special dietary requests** at this time.

A bevy of cruise line employees will be on hand to make sure your check-in goes smoothly. Don't be afraid to ask them questions.

After you clear the check-in area, you'll be asked—and in some cases, forced—to pose for the **ship's photographer.** These pictures sell for about $5 to $8 and will be displayed later for your perusal at the ship's photography shop. You are under no obligation to buy them.

You are also under no obligation to buy the **drinks** you might be offered as soon as you board the ship. And the keyword here is *buy.* Just because they're being pressed into your hands doesn't mean they're complimentary; in fact, they rarely are.

Shipboard at Last

As you walk up the gangplank and onto the ship, a crew member will escort you to your cabin, probably offering to help carry your hand luggage. No tip is required for this service.

Either immediately or a short time later, your **steward**—the person responsible for the upkeep of your cabin—will stop by to introduce him- or herself. Your steward points out the various cabin amenities and controls (such as air-conditioning and light switches), advises you on how to reach him or her when necessary (usually by phone or buzzer), and answers any immediate questions you have. The steward will also make you aware of the ship's safety-drill procedures and tells you the location of your muster (assembly) station for the lifeboat drill.

Now is not the time to quiz your steward about where he or she is from and so on, because he or she probably has to do this cabin tour for some 20 other guests. You'll have plenty of time to talk later in your voyage.

It's important to alert your steward immediately if you spot any problems with your cabin—such as the beds not being configured to your liking. If the cabin itself is not what you thought you booked, go right to the hotel manager with your complaint. You can ask your cabin steward where to find the manager.

You can also make the steward aware of any special needs you have, such as a preference for foam as opposed to feather pillows (extra pillows and blankets should already be in your closet).

In your cabin, you'll find a **daily program** detailing the day's events, meal times, and so on, as well as important information on the ship's safety procedures.

There might also be a hotel-like notebook filled with a **menu of services** (including room-service options) and a **phone directory.** Your room should also be outfitted with a Do Not Disturb sign (important for nappers), order forms for room-service breakfast (if offered), and forms and bags for dry-cleaning and laundry services.

You might want to try out the TV, safe, and other gadgets to see how they work, check out the bathroom, and so on. The loud *whoosh* of the toilet is normal (most ships use a vacuum system). Note that you are not supposed to put any objects other than paper in the bowl.

Bottled water might be provided in your cabin (although the water on most ships is perfectly drinkable). Just because the bottles are there, though, doesn't mean they are free. If you don't know, ask before you open them. Items in the minibar are not free, and their cost should be indicated on a handy price card.

There should be directions near the phone telling you how to make calls to other passengers and to ship personnel, as well as how to request wake-up calls. There should also be directions on dialing outside the ship, via satellite. Note the cost of outside calls, which is *really* expensive (usually $6.95 to $15 a minute). I've rung up bills of well over $100 just by checking my answering machine during a cruise.

Your **luggage** probably won't have arrived yet, but if it has, go ahead and unpack. After you've exhausted your tour of your room, I recommend checking out the rest of the ship.

Before you do this, though, don't forget to put your cash, ID, air tickets, and other valuables in the safe. If there is no safe in your room, take this all down to the purser's desk, where there will be one available. Don't forget to take your shipboard credit card (in case you want to buy a drink) and stateroom key with you.

You might find a **deck map** of the ship in your cabin. If not, you should be able to get one at the purser's office, so find your way there. Usually, deck plans and directional signs are posted at main stairways and elevators. (Note that if you haven't already established you onboard credit account at check-in, now's the time to do that.) You probably won't need the map after the first day (part of the fun of being on a big ship is getting lost, anyway), but it's a good way to establish the layout in your mind.

I usually begin my tour up on the top deck and work my way down, checking out the main public rooms. That way, I can stop for lunch rather quickly at the **welcome-aboard buffet,** which is usually set up in the casual dining area, near the pool deck.

If you're planning to use the **spa services,** stop by and make appointments so you can get your preferred times (the best times go fast, and some popular treatments sell out). The spa staff might be offering an introductory tour. Also stop by at the **gym,** especially if you're planning on taking fitness classes. The fitness staff will likely be on hand to pass out schedules and answer any questions you have.

Another advantage to taking your ship tour early is that cabin doors may be open, awaiting guests, and you can peek inside to compare their cabins to yours.

Note that the ship's **casino** and **shops** are always closed when the ship is in port, and that the swimming pool(s) will also likely be tarped. They will later be filled with either fresh or salt water.

Some ships offer **escorted tours** of the public rooms. If you aren't comfortable roaming on your own, check the daily program in your cabin for details.

Better Safe than Soggy: Attending the Lifeboat / Safety Drill

In your room, you will find bright-orange **life jackets** waiting on your bed, in your closet, or in a drawer. If you are traveling with kids, there should be special jackets for them (if not, alert your steward).

Ships are required by law to conduct safety drills the first day out. Most do it either right before the ship sails or shortly thereafter. Attendance is mandatory. You will be alerted as to the time in both the daily program and in repeated public announcements (and probably by your steward as well).

A notice on the back of your cabin door will list the procedures and your assigned muster station, as well as how to get there. Directions to the muster station also are posted in the hallway.

To start the drill, the ship broadcasts its **emergency signal.** At this time, you'll be required to return to your cabin, grab your life jacket, and report to your assigned muster station (this will be in a lounge, the casino, or some other public room).

Some drills last only a few minutes, while others are quite detailed. At the muster station, a crew member will review how to put on your life vest. He or she will also point out the features of the vest, including the whistle to call for help (it's considered bad form to try it out here) and the light that turns on when the jacket hits the water. The drill might also include a visit to the lifeboats and even a discussion of how to jump into the water.

In some cases, guests will be required to put on their life jackets so that crew members can check to make sure it's being worn correctly. Some other ships don't even encourage guests to put on their life jackets at all; guests are just required to bring the jackets with them.

The crew is supposed to take attendance to make sure everyone attends the drill. After the drill, return to your cabin and put your life jacket back in its place.

If you have any additional questions about safety procedures, you can address them to a crew member or officer at this time. On some ships, in addition to the drill, a safety video will also be broadcast on the TV in your cabin.

What to Do if You Think Your Bags Are Lost (Or if They Really Are)

Before you start to panic, keep in mind that on big ships, as many as 4,000 bags need to be loaded and distributed. If your ship has sailed, though, and you're getting concerned that your luggage hasn't shown up, don't hesitate to call the guest-relations desk or the purser's desk.

If your luggage really does get lost, the cruise line customer relations folks are supposed to spring into immediate action. They, not you, will contact the airline and ground operators to see what's what. Usually, missing bags will arrive at the ship the next day, having been driven or flown to the first port of call.

If your baggage is lost, the cruise line will likely provide an overnight kit with items such as a toothbrush and toothpaste. Also, as the first night of a cruise is always casual dress, you don't have to worry about showing up to dinner wearing what you have on.

If your baggage is still lost the next day, your baggage insurance, if you purchased it, will kick in and you get to go shopping in the ship's shops for proper attire. If you do not have insurance, the line may, at its discretion, offer you cash compensation (usually $50 a day).

If the second night is a formal night, the line might be able to provide a tux for a man and might also have a small selection of clothes available that a woman can borrow.

Cruise officials say it's very rare, however, for luggage to be lost for more than a day.

Bon Voyage!

Most people like to be out on deck as the ship sails, many with drinks in hand. There will likely be live music on the pool deck (Princess Cruises' ships first play a prerecorded version of *The Love Boat* theme song) and a lively party atmosphere. Some lines offer complimentary champagne toasts, but most charge for the drinks.

If I have a balcony in my cabin, I like to cast off with a few friends in a private party there, waving at smaller ships as we pass by in the harbor and to those seeing us off on shore.

The Rest of the First Day

How you spend the rest of the first day is up to you. Depending on my mood, I usually choose between a nap or a drink at one of the bars, where musical entertainment will probably be featured. Or you might want to get over jet lag with a soothing massage.

In the evening, there will probably be a special **getting-to-know-you party** for single passengers, and the first night is often singles night in the disco as well. Families traveling with kids might be invited to a get-together to hear about youth and teen program offerings.

The ship will offer a special **welcome-aboard show** in the show lounge, emceed by the cruise director, although it won't be a particularly elaborate production the first night. A movie probably will be shown somewhere on board as well.

Smooth Sailing

Get to the **ship's library** early for first dibs on the hot new releases (you might be able to find books here that are waiting-list-only at your public library). It will open sometime the first evening. Ditto for the video library, if there is one. The best movies go first.

Dinner will be casual attire the first night, but not without the formalities (as described in chapter 15, "My Dinner with Andre . . .").

Expedition Time!: Choosing Your Shore Excursions

At some point during the early-evening hours of your first day on board, there will be a discussion of shore excursions (tours offered by the cruise line at the ports of call, usually at additional cost). The briefing, run by a shore-excursions manager or the cruise director, is basically a sales pitch for the sightseeing tours (which you probably also received a brochure about with your cruise documents) and is usually held in the show lounge and often rebroadcast on your in-cabin TV as well. There might be useful information provided as well, such as availability of transportation and any safety concerns you need to consider.

You usually aren't required to make a decision about the tour offers your first night, but you might want to. Some of the excursions are offered on a limited basis, and all are offered on a first-come, first-served basis. The most popular ones might sell out fast. (For more information on shore excursions, see chapter 22, "Hitting the Beach: The Port Scene.")

Your shore-excursion briefing might be combined with a **port lecture.** These "lectures" are ostensibly designed to help you make the most of your time in port and are typically offered a day or two before a port visit, with the lecture conducted either by the cruise director or, in rare cases, by a real expert on the area you'll visit.

Typically, these lectures quickly gloss over the main sights at the port of call and then focus heavily on shopping. In some cases, the cruise line gets advertising fees for recommending certain shops (usually jewelry stores), so be aware of this when you consider the suggestions. But also be aware that the shops that are recommended may be the ones less likely to rip you off (as they are beholden to the cruise line for their business). See chapter 19, "Shop Till You Drop," for details.

Chapter 14

The Typical Cruise Week

In This Chapter

- The lowdown on how the typical week plays out, both in the Caribbean and in Alaska
- Examples of typical itineraries
- A rundown of the typical activities over the course of a cruise week
- Tips on getting the news, sending the mail, and attending religious services on board
- Recipes for some favorite cruise ship drinks

When we look at a typical week, here's where the kind of ship you choose and its itinerary come into play.

If you're on a 1-week cruise on a big ship in the Caribbean, you'll likely be stopping at 3 to 5 popular islands and maybe even at a private island owned by the cruise line. On some itineraries, Key West, Florida, and Mexico might be included as well. And you'll have 1 to 3 days at sea, during which you can participate in all the shipboard activities or just relax.

On a smaller ship in the Caribbean, you might stop at more islands and will certainly stop at some off the main tourist path, and you will likely have less time at sea.

In Alaska, on a big ship, you will likely visit the popular ports of Skagway, Juneau, and Ketchikan, and you will have several days at sea to enjoy the glorious glaciers, fjords, and wildlife, as well as participate in shipboard activities and relax.

On a smaller ship in Alaska, you might also visit several smaller ports of call and head into wildlife areas that cannot accommodate larger vessels.

Below, I've included some sample itineraries as examples of how your cruise might be structured:

A Western Caribbean Itinerary (Celebrity Cruises)

Day	Arrive	Depart
Sun (first day)	Fort Lauderdale	5:30pm
Mon	Key West, 7am	1:30pm
Tues	Calica, 10am	7pm
Wed	Cozumel, 7am	7pm
Thurs	At sea (all day)	
Fri	Grand Cayman, 8am	4pm
Sat	At sea (all day)	
Sun	Fort Lauderdale, 7am	

An Eastern Caribbean Itinerary (Holland America Line)

Day	Arrive	Depart
Sat	Fort Lauderdale	5pm
Sun	Nassau, Bahamas, 7am	noon
Mon	At sea (all day)	
Tues	San Juan, 9am	midnight
Wed	St. John, 7am	7:30am*
Wed	St. Thomas, 8:30am	5pm
Thurs	At sea (all day)	
Fri	Half Moon Cay,** Bahamas, 8am	4:30pm
Sat	Fort Lauderdale, 8am	

* *Service call: The ship disembarks passengers taking certain shore excursions (such as snorkeling). The passengers then meet up with the ship later in St. Thomas.*

** *Private island*

A Southern Caribbean Itinerary (Carnival Cruise Lines)

Day	Arrive	Depart
Sat	San Juan	10pm
Sun	St. Thomas, 7am	5:30pm
Mon	St. Maarten, 7am	4pm
Tues	Dominica, 8am	4pm
Wed	Barbados, 8am	10pm
Thurs	Martinique, 8am	5:30pm
Fri	At sea (all day)	
Sat	San Juan, 7am	

An Alaska Itinerary (Princess Cruises)

Day	Arrive	Depart
Sat	Vancouver, B.C.	5:30pm
Sun	At sea (all day)	
Mon	Ketchikan, 6:30am	2pm
Tues	Juneau, 6:30am	11pm
Wed	Skagway, 7am	7:30pm
Thurs	At sea (all day)	
Fri	At sea (all day)	
Sat	Anchorage (Seward), morning	

One if by Land!

On days in port, you'll want to have a battle plan for what you want to see, keeping in mind when your ship leaves and other such practicalities as whether you want to eat lunch on the ship or at a local restaurant (see chapters 22 to 25 for more on ports of call).

At some ports, your ship will dock at the pier, meaning you can walk right off on a gangplank. At others, the ship will be required to tie up offshore, and you'll have to take a *tender* (a small boat) to get to the pier. In the latter case, you'll likely be called to assembly in a lounge area and given a number for an assigned tender. Getting to the lounge early will get you a quicker assignment but might require you to get in a long line. Those who have signed up for shore excursions are given priority disembarkation.

You are not required to get off the ship at every port of call. I always like to at least take a walk and get some exercise, but plenty of people stay behind on the ship to lounge in the sun (the pool itself might be closed), take spa treatments, use the gym equipment (the gym is less crowded on port days), play cards, or just enjoy some quiet time.

The number of organized activities offered on days when the ship is in port might be dramatically reduced but will not be nonexistent. There will probably be a movie showing, and music poolside, as well as some lectures and sports competitions.

One if by Sea!

On days at sea, there will be so many activities to choose from that you might be downright overwhelmed, especially in the Caribbean. In Alaska, you will have lots of scenery and sights to enjoy during your days at sea, with wildlife and glacier experts offering commentary. Activity offerings might be reduced at times when the ship is scheduled to, for instance, pass one of the state's famous glaciers.

Here's a sample of the offerings available on a 1-week Caribbean cruise (information courtesy of "The Fun Ship," *Carnival Destiny*):

- Captain's Welcome Aboard party
- Movies
- Port lectures
- Megacash jackpot
- Bingo
- Rum Swizzle party
- Las Vegas / Broadway revues
- Art auctions
- Trivia quizzes
- Sing-along
- Horse racing
- Cellulite seminar
- Bridge tournament
- Golf Putting contest
- Hairy Chest contest
- Couples and Lovers party
- Singles party
- Adult comedy special
- Jogging
- Swimming
- Bad Hair demonstration
- Eat More to Weigh Less seminar
- Shore excursions
- High-impact/low-impact aerobics
- Step workout
- Body-toning and stretch class
- Gaming lessons
- Pool games
- Spa treatments
- Lido Deck party
- Teen movie screening
- Deck games
- Musical entertainment
- Gambling
- Shopping
- Mexican folkloric show
- Casino raffle

In-cabin movies
The Great Balloon Toss
Learn the Art of Massage seminar
The Marriage Show
Food and Beverage lecture
Karaoke
Guacamole & Salsa party
Country Western night
Disco
Skincare demo
Talent show
Blackjack tournament
Male Nightgown competition
Twist contest
Bridge tour
Galley tour
Camp Carnival (kids' program)
Farewell Appreciation party
The Mr. and Mrs. Show

Other Things You Should Know About

In the next several chapters, I'll describe in great detail what you can expect in the way of dining options, activities, children's offerings, entertainment, gambling options, spa services, shopping opportunities, and mating opportunities, as well as offerings at the various ports of call. But here's a few more items you should know about.

Religious Services

Depending on the ship and the clergy on board, some ships offer Catholic mass every day. Most ships offer a nondenominational service on Sunday and a Friday-night Jewish Sabbath service, usually run by a passenger. On holidays, whether Jewish or Christian, clergy is typically aboard large ships to lead services. These services are usually held in the library or conference room.

Getting Married On Board

Though most cruise ship captains conduct marriage ceremonies only in movies and on TV, the new *Grand Princess* is an exception; it has its own wedding chapel and a captain who is able and willing to lead the proceedings.

What's more common is for ships to bring on board a clergyman or other official, usually at a port of call, to lead the ceremony. Several lines, including Princess, offer wedding and marriage vow-renewal packages that include a ceremony, flowers, music, cake, champagne, and other niceties. Consult your travel agent or the cruise line directly about the offerings.

Mailing Postcards

If you want to send mail from the ship, you should be able to find both stamps and a mailbox at the purser's office. Remember, since you will likely be traveling to other countries, you'll have to use local postage, not the U.S. stamps you might have carried from home. The purser's office should have the appropriate postage available.

Getting the News

Newshounds don't have to feel out of touch on a cruise ship. Most newer ships offer CNN on their in-room TVs, and nearly every ship will post the latest news from the wire services outside the purser's office. Some lines even excerpt information from leading newspapers each day and deliver the news to your room.

Yo Ho Ho and a Bottle of Rum: Special Cruise Concoctions

The bar scene is an important aspect of shipboard life, especially on the bigger ships, where you'll find the bars open nearly all the time. The *Carnival Destiny,* for one, has more than 20 lounges and service bars where 100,000 drinks are prepared each week. Ships also usually feature a drink (or two) of the day, specially priced at less than $3.

Even if you're a teetotaler (and it is possible to enjoy a cruise without drinking), it's fun to people-watch at the bar near the pool or at those in the various lounges. Some lines have lately introduced martini bars, champagne bars, and cigar bars for those looking for upscale hobnobbing, but fruit drinks are the mainstay of most lines and are often sold on board in souvenir take-home glasses.

Ahoy, Mateys!

Meetings of **Alcoholics Anonymous** are offered on some ships, with their times discreetly listed in daily programs or available at the guest-relations desk.

Now, here's an added bonus for those of you who want to re-create your fruity cruise-drink experience once you get home: Carnival Cruise Lines gave me the skinny on the secret ingredients in some of its most popular concoctions, and I'm passing 'em your way. Just don't forget the little paper umbrella (packages available at a liquor store near you).

For those of you who want more, Carnival recently introduced a little recipe booklet featuring dozens of exotic drink recipes. The line's own speciality "fun drinks"—such as Caribbean Breeze, Ultimate Suntan, Goombay Smash, and Carnival's popular signature drink, the Fun Ship Special (featured below)—are included, along with nonalcoholic options. *Carnival Cocktails* is available in the bars and lounges aboard the line's "Fun Ships" or by calling Carnival's Bon Voyage department at ☎ **800/522-7648.** The cost is $3.95, and a hangover.

"Fun Ship" Special

1 oz. rum

½ oz. vodka

¼ oz. amaretto

¼ oz. apricot brandy

5 oz. fruit punch

Mix in a blender and pour over ice in a 10 oz. collins glass. Garnish with a cherry and orange slice.

Yellow Bird

1 oz. rum

¼ oz. Galliano

¼ oz. Crème de banana

2½ oz. orange juice

1 oz. pineapple juice

Blend ingredients in a mixer and serve over ice in a 10 oz. collins glass. Garnish with an orange slice and a cherry.

Tropical-Island Smoothie

1½ oz. 151-proof rum

4 oz. mango nectar

4 oz. pineapple juice

6 oz. coconut cream

Combine ingredients in a blender with crushed ice. Serve in an extra-large glass.

Chapter 15

My Dinner with Andre (and Jackie, and Julie, and Pete, and that Couple from Omaha)

In This Chapter

- Typical schedules for shipboard feasting
- A quick intro to cruise menus
- Tips on what kind of wine to order with your meal
- How to rid yourself of unwanted dinner companions
- A word on special diets, another on etiquette at the captain's table, and a third on alternative dining
- Dining room do's and don'ts

Meals are an important part of the cruise experience, adding greatly to the sense of luxury and pampering, and dinner in the dining room is an experience of much pomp and circumstance and much ritual, especially on bigger ships. Breakfast, lunch, and midnight buffets are more casual but are often extravagant enough to be scenes in a Fellini movie.

Even if you meticulously watch your calories the rest of the year, there will be something to entice you at every food venue. And you *will* be hungry (it has something to do with the salt air).

Some people claim that they gain 3 to 8 pounds on a 1-week cruise. For tips on how to avoid this by working off those extra calories, see chapter 18, "Meet Me at the Spa, Dahling: The Spa & Fitness Scene."

All the Food That's Fit to Eat

You never, ever have to worry about going hungry on a cruise. On almost any given ship, it's possible to eat more in 1 day than a supermodel probably eats in a week.

Just look at this typical meals listing from Carnival and you'll see why:

Early risers: 6:30am; coffee and Danish

Buffet breakfast: 8–10:30am; including daily specials, sweet rolls, eggs, bacon, cereal, yogurt, croissants, coffee, juice, and tea

Breakfast in the dining room: 6:45–7:45am (main seating), 8 or 9am (late seating); full breakfast including juices, fruits, yogurt, fish, hot and cold cereals, omelettes, eggs, French toast, pancakes, breakfast meats, and potatoes

Mid-morning snack: 10am; coffee, tea, sweet rolls, and muffins

Buffet lunch: 11:30am–2:30pm; full hot and cold lunch offerings, including salad bar and pasta station

Lunch in the dining room: noon (main seating), 1:30pm (late seating); full luncheon from a changing menu of hot dishes, salads, sandwiches, pastas, grill selections, and desserts

Afternoon tea: 3:30–5pm; tea and cake

Snack time: all afternoon; ice cream, fat-free frozen yogurt

Dinner in the dining room: 6pm (early seating), 8:15pm (late seating); gourmet cuisine, including international and American favorites served in 7 courses, including desserts

Midnight buffet: around midnight; an extravagant spread, including hot and cold entrees, desserts, salads, cold meats, breads, cheeses, and fruit

Late-night minibuffet: 1:30am (on nights at sea); some of the same items as the midnight buffet, along with items from the breakfast menu

Still hungry? Don't worry. Your ship might also have a pizza parlor where you can grab a slice and probably also offers 24-hour room service, including at the very least, a selection of sandwiches, beverages, desserts, and fruits. You won't go hungry between meals. And the room service is usually free, like all the other meals.

Other Niceties

Not wanting you to feel they've left anything out, the newer and bigger ships are adding additional food venues such as coffee bars, which might also offer sweets; champagne bars, where caviar with all the trimmings is available (for an extra charge); and ice cream parlors. And some ships offer hot canapés to compliment before-dinner drinks in the bars and lounges.

Dinner Is Served

Dinner on most ships is one of the main social events of the day. You should be elegantly served, delightfully entertained by your tablemates, and despite any vows you made prior to your arrival at the table, stuffed to the gills.

The table setup is likely to be quite formal, with china, silver, fresh flowers, and starched linens. Make yourself comfortable. Your meal will go on for at least an hour and a half, the service purposely timed at a relaxed pace.

What's Cookin'?

Most cruise cuisine is continental or international, with regional specialties at dinner appropriate to the cruise venue, such as salmon in Alaska, jerk spices in the Caribbean, and Maine lobster in New England.

The cruise ship chefs aren't just guys off the street. Many were trained at world-famous restaurants (the more expensive the cruise, the more extensive the training).

Signature dishes will be among the offerings and are often good bets. If the chef is Italian, definitely try the pasta. If the chef is French, try the sauces and don't pass up the desserts.

Five- to seven-course dinners are the norm. These consist of an appetizer, soup, salad, main course (with starch and vegetables), sorbet, dessert, and fruit and cheese.

Typically the dinner menus feature at least one "healthy" selection in each category, with fat and salt content and calories listed. Some ships also feature a daily pasta and vegetarian selection.

On some ships, 1 night during a weeklong cruise will feature menus built around a theme, such as Caribbean or Italian night. And on almost every ship, there will be one dinner featuring Baked Alaska, a flaming ice cream dessert that has become traditional to cruise ships and that will be paraded around by the dining-room staff to musical accompaniment and usually much applause from the passengers.

You can make a culinary request if you have an urge for something in particular, but keep in mind that the chef can prepare only from the ingredients available in the larder (you're at sea, after all). Such a request is also best made the day before, so the chef has time to prepare—remember, the kitchen is putting out as many as 2,000 or 2,500 passenger meals each evening.

Some Wine, Monsieur? (What Goes with What)

OK, admit it: When handed a wine list by your waiter, you probably open it, scan the selections, say "hmmmm" in the most knowledgeable, educated tone you can muster, and then take a wild stab in the dark about what will go with your dinner. I'm guessing most of us are in this boat (so to speak), and for that reason I've included a few pointers to help you get through the ordeal.

First, a few general rules to point you in the right direction:

- **Generally, the heavier the food, the sturdier the wine**—meaning a nice, solid red to go with that 5-pound steak, but a light white (or light red) for that healthful poultry dish.
- **Champagne** is mostly consumed only as an aperitif, with dessert, or to toast just about anything at all. You would not use champagne to wash down a big platter of jalapeño nachos.
- **Sweet wines** work best at the end of the meal, for the same reason you don't eat dessert first: It would spoil your appetite.
- **If you're having several different wines** with your meal, it's usually best to work up from light to heavy. (Usually, this works well for complementing your food, as appetizers are generally lighter than your main course.) Your dessert wine doesn't count in this equation. Dessert is, after all, a completely separate phenomenon.

The Moment of Truth: Matching Wine with Food

Here's where you get to look erudite—or like a dope, if you're not prepared. To save you potential embarassment, I've included the following chart, which makes suggestions as to which types of wine go with some common cruise ship foodstuffs.

Barbequed Meats	Medium-bodied reds (Chianti, Shiraz, Zinfandel)
Beef (roasted or grilled)	Full-bodied reds (Merlot, Pinot Noir, Cabernet Sauvignon, Bordeaux)
Caviar	Champagne (or—even better—iced vodka)
Chicken (in cream sauce)	Chardonnay
Chicken (roasted or grilled)	Red or white (almost any variety)
Clams	Dry whites
Crabs (solf-shell)	Chardonnay or German Riesling
Desserts	Sweet wines (Sauternes, Barsac) or Champagne
Duck	Merlot or Pinot Noir
Fish (grilled or steamed)	Light reds (Beaujolais, Rioja) or light whites (Fumé Blanc, Pinot Grigio, Soave, Muscadet)
Fish, full-flavored (red snapper, striped bass, etc.)	Full-bodied whites (Chardonnay, French Burgundies)
Fish (in butter sauce or white sauce)	Full-bodied whites (Chardonnay, white Burgundy)
Fish, the meatier type (salmon, tuna, swordfish)	Merlot, Pinot Noir, or Cru Beaujolais

Ham	Light reds or rosés (Beaujolais); also Chardonnay, Pinot Noir Blanc, or red burgundy
Hamburgers	Zinfandel, Chianti, Correas Syrah, Pinot Blanc, Beaujolais-Villages
Lamb	Full-bodied reds (Cabernet Sauvignon, Merlot, Rioja, Zinfandel)
Lasagna	Medium- to full-bodied reds (Barbera, Barolo, Zinfandel)
Lobster	Champagne, California Chardonnays, white Burgundy, Bordeaux, Chablis
Mexican Food	Pinot Noir Blanc, White Zinfandel, or a nice Rosé
Oysters	Champagne, Chablis, white Bordeaux, Fumé Blanc, Muscadet
Pasta Alfredo	Soave, Chadonnay
Pasta Primavera (or with other cream sauces)	Red Beaujolais, Soave, or other light and fruity wines
Pasta (with garlic or pesto)	Pinot Grigio, Chardonnay
Pasta (with seafood sauce)	Sauvignon, Verdiccio, Soave
Pasta (with shellfish)	Reds (Cabernet Sauvignon, Merlot) or whites (Sauvignon Blanc, Muscadet, Pinot Grigio)
Pasta (with tomato sauce)	Chianti, Barbera, red Zinfandel
Pork Roast	Light reds or rich whites
Prime Rib	Cabernet Sauvignon, Chianti, Shiraz, full-bodied Rioja
Salads (with herb or fruit dressing)	Sauvignon Blanc, Sancerre, Fumé Blanc
Salads (with vinegar dressing)	None
Salmon (fresh)	White Burgundy
Salmon (smoked)	Champagne, Sauvignon Blanc, Sancerre
Seafood	Sauvignon Blanc, Sancerre, Fumé Blanc, Muscadet, Soave
Shrimp (boiled)	Chardonnay
Shrimp (grilled)	Sauvignon Blanc, Fumé Blanc
Shrimp Scampi	Chardonnay, French Chablis
Sole	Light whites
Steak	Full-bodied reds (Cabernet Sauvignon, Chianti, Shiraz, Zinfandel)
Tex-Mex	Rosés

Turkey	Red or white (almost any variety)
Veal (chops or scallopini)	Medium-bodied reds (Bordeaux, Merlot, Cabernet Sauvignon, Pinot Noir)
Veal (in cream sauce)	Rich whites (California Chardonnay, French Burgundy)

Thumbs Up or Thumbs Down? Tasting the Wine

After you've ordered, your wine steward will bring your selection and offer a sample for approval. What do you do? Do you revert to the old "Hmmm" and the sage nodding? Do you just fake your way through it? No need. Here's the skinny on wine tasting:

First, remember that *not liking the wine is not a good enough reason to send it back*. What you're looking for are serious flaws in the wine, not flaws in your selection process. Here are the steps to take:

- **Test the cork:** If it's dry there's a good chance air might've leaked into the bottle and ruined the wine.
- **Swirl the wine around:** Wine experts say this is a way of opening the wine up to oxygen and releasing its full flavor, but I think they do it just to look cool. What do I know, though? It couldn't hurt. Swirl away.
- **Check the color:** If it's any kind of neon shade, you have problems. (Honestly, though, look for red wines to have a clarity to their color and for white wines, conversely, to have a richer hue.)
- **Give it a sniff:** This is a pretty obvious one. If it smells like vinegar, it is vinegar, so send it back. If, however, you stick your nose in and reel back from pleasure, that's a good sign.
- **Take a swig:** But don't just gulp it down. Take your time. Roll the wine around on your tongue. Is it pleasurable? Any hints of the wine having turned? This isn't always as apparent as you'd think. I was on a ship recently and a tablemate noted in tasting that the wine showed the barest hint of having started over the edge. The wine steward tested it, tested it again, then complimented the gentleman on his educated palate. He was exactly right.

When to Send It Back

Only a few really valid reasons here:

1. If it's not the wine you ordered.
2. If it smells musty because of a bad cork.
3. If the wine has turned.
4. If it's not correctly chilled. (Be nice about it, though; just ask for an ice bucket and chill it down yourself.)

What's for Breakfast & Lunch?

Breakfast and lunch in the dining room are also multicourse events, and the service is not rushed. Menus generally change daily.

If you're in a hurry or just don't want to deal with the formalities, you almost always have the option of a casual buffet, usually located near the pool deck, where you can serve yourself, and where the offerings and choices will be even more bountiful.

How Much Food Do Cruise Passengers Really Eat?

The following are the weekly store suppliers for the 1,950-passenger *Mercury*, the newest Celebrity ship:

21,600 lb. beef	2,500 lb. rice
5,040 lb. lamb	1,500 lb. cereal
3,360 lb. pork	600 lb. jelly
1,680 lb. sausages	1,650 lb. coffee
4,200 lb. chicken	1,600 lb. cookies
4,200 lb. turkey	42,000 tea bags
11,760 lb. fish	300 lb. herbs and spices
675 lb. crab	3,400 bottles assorted wines
3,250 lb. lobster	200 bottles champagne
21,500 lb. potatoes	200 bottles gin
16,800 lb. fresh fruit	290 bottles vodka
2,500 gal. milk	350 bottles whiskey
250 qt. cream	150 bottles rum
600 gal. ice cream	45 bottles sherry
103,800 eggs	600 bottles assorted liqueurs
4,200 lb. sugar	10,100 bottles or cans beer

Ditching the Dinner Companion from Hell

Your dinner companions can make or break your cruise experience, and if you don't like your companions, it's perfectly okay to ask the maitre d' for a change. You can even decide to dine alone. Generally, I find that sitting at a table with six to eight seats gives you enough variety so that you don't get bored and also lets you steer clear of any one individual you really don't like.

Alternative Dining

If after a few days, you get sick of all the dining-room pomp and circumstance, the slow pace, or the dining room itself, your ship might also have a smaller gourmet restaurant that you can visit (sometimes for a small service fee) on a reservations-only basis. These restaurants usually focus on one type of ethnic cuisine; Italian, Japanese, and Chinese are the most popular.

There might also be a casual option to eating in the dining room—a venue that operates on an open-seating, no-reservations-required basis. And if you really get sick of nighttime dining formalities, you can eat in your stateroom (although the room service menu might be limited).

The Captain's Table

Seating at the captain's table is on an invitation-only basis and should be considered an honor.

These tables typically seat 8 to 10 people and are placed prominently in the dining room. Those at the table are carefully chosen and expected to behave. Guests will include personal friends of the captain, repeat passengers, celebrities, people who have booked the expensive suites, executives of the cruise line, travel writers, and some regular passengers. Other senior officers also sometimes host their own tables.

If you'd like to be considered for inclusion, you can write the line—via your travel agent—before the cruise, including a brief biography of yourself (no, I'm not kidding). On board, you can also ask the maitre d' for an invitation. Honeymooners and others celebrating important events (and singles) might make it to the top of the list faster than others.

If you do get an invite, dress up, even if it's one of the ship's casual dress nights. Men should wear a jacket and tie, women a dress.

The captain usually will provide wine for his table. It's considered good etiquette to enjoy the food that night and verbally applaud it for the captain's benefit.

Could I Have a Kosher, Vegetarian, Low-Salt, Macrobiotic Meal, Please?

Probably. If you have any special dietary needs, the preferred time to inform the cruise line is when you make your reservation for the trip. You might also want to check in with the maitre d' on your first day out to make sure the kitchen got your request. If you failed to make previous arrangements, though, most lines will still be able to accommodate you. Some lines offer kosher menus, and all will have vegetarian, low-fat, low-salt, or sugar-free options available.

Dining-Room Do's and Don'ts

Ah, protocol. What you're dealing with aboard a ship is centuries of passenger ship etiquette and even more centuries of plain old dining etiquette all rolled up into one big room. Here's some pointers:

Chatting with a Celebrity Chef

I recently had occasion to chat with Michel Roux—culinary and wine consultant for Celebrity Cruises and one of the most famous chefs in England—about the eating habits of cruise passengers.

"Beef and lobster or lobster and beef," he said, when I asked about the most popular dinner selections. He said at a typical dinner on a Celebrity cruise, 1,100 out of 1,600 passengers will order one or the other.

But, he said, menu variety and options are also important. "We might 'sell' 75 pork chops, but it's a nice little dish, and the people that take it will be happy with it."

Roux, who personally visits the Celebrity ships about five times a year and also sends his son on inspections, said he's somewhat restricted as to what he can offer on board, based on staffing—even though there are dozens of chefs in the kitchen, they are preparing more than 1,000 meals. Cost of supplies also plays a factor in menu preparation, since he works from a fixed budget based on a portion of the cruise fare and cannot charge extra for a special item.

Roux said he also is not always able to get ingredients he might want to use in the great bulk needed to serve so many passengers and has to make adjustments accordingly.

Speaking of ingredients, a trick in preparing cruise cuisine is in using the most perishable ingredients early on in the cruise and the more hearty later. Fresh fish will be on the menu at the beginning of the cruise and might be replaced by frozen later in the voyage (although some lines also pick up supplies along the way).

Roux said the kitchen is always accommodating to people's needs in terms of special requests.

"I don't know how many illnesses there are that involve foods, but we take care of it: lactose-free, salt-free, sugar-free, fat-free, etc."

And what about those midnight buffets? Do people really indulge, or is it all for show?

"'I'm just going to take a look' ends with a dinner plate that's full."

- **DO arrive in the dining room on time.** (Dining hours are listed in the daily program.)
- **DON'T show up dressed incorrectly for the evening.** Check the dress code for the evening and dress accordingly: casual, informal, or formal.
- **DO wait until everyone has arrived** before you order.
- **DON'T put the napkin around your neck.** It belongs on your lap.

- 👍 **DO understand the staffing pecking order:** Order from the waiter, not the bus boy.
- 👎 **DON'T use the incorrect piece of silverware.** Implements should be used from the outside in. The first fork on the left is the one you use for the first course.
- 👍 **DO offer wine to the others at your table if you order a bottle.** One of your tablemates should then order the next night's bottle.
- 👎 **DON'T feel you have to eat a meal you don't like.** It's okay to send it back and ask for another selection.
- 👍 **DO ask for your wine to be recorked if you don't finish it.** It can then be held for you for the next night.
- 👎 **DON'T try to smoke in a no-smoking section**—or, even worse, in a no-smoking dining room.
- 👍 **DO take the waiter's suggestion** if he or she whispers in your ear something good to try.
- 👎 **DON'T start eating until everyone at your table is served.**

The Best Ships for Discriminating Palates

What are the top ships for foodies? In my opinion it's the luxury lines: **Cunard, Crystal, Radisson, Seabourn, Silversea,** and **Windstar.** If these lines are out of your league price-wise—and they are for many of us—I'd go with **Celebrity** or **Costa.**

Chapter 16

Let's Get Busy: Onboard Activities & Entertainment

In This Chapter

- An intro to the daily bulletin
- A typical day's activities
- Tips on where to whoop it up and where to lay low
- The lowdown on cruise ship theater—glimmer, shimmy, and all
- The best ships for spectacular entertainment

You won't get bored! You won't, really! There's more to do on a cruise ship than at nearly any other vacation location. And best of all, you can choose between doing SOMETHING and doing NOTHING, and no one will hassle you about your choice.

Allan King, cruise director on Celebrity's *Mercury,* is in charge of keeping some 1,900 people a week enlivened and enlightened while they're on the ship with a virtually nonstop roster of entertainment and activities. But even King said in a recent interview that if he had his druthers and a week off, he'd probably not be looking for a single activity to do.

"I'd want to lie here and have quiet at the pool," King said.

In fact, he said a big part of his job is finding a democratic middle ground, where people who just want quiet can find quiet and people who want morning-to-evening offerings of bingo games, conga lines, and identify-your-husband-while-blindfolded-by-feeling-all-these-guys'-hairy-chests contests (okay, they don't really offer that on Celebrity ships, but I like that example) can have that, too.

There's something for everyone in the cruise ship world.

On the bigger ships, there's enough space so that you won't usually hear the steel band playing "Hot, Hot, Hot!" by the pool if you're lounging on the stern. On the smaller ships, they don't have steel bands playing dance music, but they might have an enticing lecturer to pull you off your lounge chair.

The cruise lines are proud of saying that a cruise vacation is about choices, and that rings true. You choose the ship that's right for you, the type of cabin, the dining options, whether to take shore excursions, and the activities that suit your tastes.

Extra! Extra! Read All About It!

All the cruise ships have a **daily bulletin** that's distributed to your cabin in the evening and highlights the next day's activities schedule, along with entertainment offerings, hours of operation for the bars and shops, and the evening dress code. The bulletin also usually offers details about ports of call (such as must-see attractions) or, if the ship is spending the day at sea, offers facts about the region you'll be sailing through.

The bulletin is also frequently loaded with advertisements for the ship's shops, and sometimes shops in ports as well, and might include a schedule of exercise classes, a list of TV and movie presentations, and a flyer with hints on how to play casino offerings. Sometimes ships also include a rundown of the day's top news stories from the real world, gleaned from wire services or top newspapers, for those who want to stay informed.

To give you an idea as to what the activity schedules look like, here's a sampling of the activities available during a day at sea in August 1997 aboard Norwegian Cruise Line's *Norwegian Dream* (then called by her former name, the *Dreamward*):

8am	Cards and games available
9am	Step It Up advanced step aerobics
9am	Test your trivia knowledge
9am	Walk a Mile with a Smile
9–10am	Coffee and Danish with Michelle to discuss future cruising opportunities
9–10am	Library open for book checkout
9am–6pm	Shuffleboard and golf-driving equipment available
9am–midnight	Duty-free shops open
9:15am	Marine life slide presentation with Dive-In instructors
10am	Live gaming tables open in the casino
10:15am	Stretch and Relax class
10:30am	Trapshooting with a Norwegian officer (fee charged)

10:45am	Two for Bingo game
11am	Skin Clinic: Learn the ultimate in European skin care
11am	Circuit training
11am	Kids Crew performs "Circus at Sea"
11am	Golf putting clinic with golf pro
11am	Vegetable-carving demonstration
Noon–3pm	Enjoy the musical sounds of Roots Link poolside
1pm	Putting tournament with golf pro
1pm	The Match Game
1pm	Service-club meeting
1–2pm	Lottery tickets available
2:30pm	Rehearsal for passenger talent show
2:30pm	Team Trivia contest
2:30–4:30pm	Art show and auction
3pm	Napkin-folding demonstration
3pm	Norwegian Olympic Games registration
3–6pm	Basketball play available
3:15pm	Olympic Games begin
3:15pm	Cha-cha dance classes
4–6pm	Roots Link performs at poolside
4:15pm	Trapshooting
4:30pm	Jackpot bingo
5–6pm	Library open
5:15–6pm	Join entertainer David Williams for piano melodies
5:30pm	Jewish Sabbath Eve services
5:30pm	Golf social
6:45–7:30pm	Enjoy a cocktail while listening to Cross My Heart
7:30pm & 9:15pm	"Sea Legs at Sea" show
7:45–8:30pm	Evening melodies with David Williams
8pm–10pm	Redeem lottery tickets
10pm–close	David Williams plays your favorite songs
10pm–close	Dance into New York in the After Hours Nightclub
10pm–close	Party the night away with Cross My Heart
10:30pm	Passenger talent show
11:30pm–12:30am	Chocoholics buffet

The activities roster might seem overwhelming, but remember that the activities are there to keep everyone happy—no one person could possibly attend them all. The idea of the bulletin is to let you know all your options. What you do is your choice. Pick and choose what sounds good or chuck the whole thing in the trash, grab a book, and head for the nearest lounge chair. Some people will do the latter for the first few days and then loosen up and join in the festivities as the week goes on, but it's always up to you how much or how little you do. And remember, if you exhaust yourself at pool volleyball, there's no one telling you that you can't take a snooze for a while to recuperate. As a matter of fact, Royal Caribbean's *Enchantment of the Seas* actually lists the 2 to 4pm slot in its bulletin as "Naptime: No Skill Required."

Activities on cruise ships are offered from early morning until late at night—or, perhaps more aptly, from the early morning power walk to the line-dancing at the midnight buffet.

Show Me Where the Action Is!: Daytime Diversions

Given the amount of eating that takes place on cruise ships and our cultural obsession with gaining weight, it's not surprising that some of the most popular activities on cruise ships take place in the gym and spa. (I cover these separately in chapter 18, "Meet Me at the Spa, Dahling: The Spa & Fitness Scene.") Even if you're not going on a cruise to exert yourself, there's still plenty of things to do that won't strain anything, except perhaps your eyes. Let's run through some shipside hot spots.

Hangin' at the Pool

The hub of activity of most ships, especially in the Caribbean, is the pool area. On the bigger ships, you're best off getting there early in the day so you can stake out the best lounge chair. From the vantage point of your chair, you can watch and/or participate in pool or poolside games and contests, listen to a live band, sip a piña colada, and work on your tan. And, of course, you can check out all your fellow passengers in their bathing suits.

Be warned, though: The pool area is not necessarily a quiet place to relax or read a book. And, depending on the size of the pool, actual swimming (as opposed to dunking or standing poised on the side with your drink) might not really be an option—there simply isn't room.

Quiet Diversions

For those seeking a less rowdy time, **libraries** are offered on nearly all ships. The better ones stock everything from classics to the kind of hot new releases you'd have to wait for on a long waiting list to borrow from your public library.

You can borrow a book from the library by showing the staff member in charge your onboard credit card (you will not be charged unless the book is not returned). Most of the ship libraries allow books to be taken out only during set hours, with the book cases locked at other times, so check your bulletin for hours of operation.

Some libraries also have **video movies** and **CDs** that guests can borrow.

Usually adjacent to the library is the ship's **card room,** a quiet place for people to play, with Bridge usually the top attraction. On some sailings, a Bridge instructor might be on hand, and tournaments might be offered. The card rooms usually provide decks of cards, but if you want to be sure you're playing with a full one, you can bring your own or purchase one at the ship's gift shop.

Board games like **Monopoly** and **Scrabble** are also sometimes available in either the card room or library for guests to borrow and play in their cabins or up on deck.

Film buffs will find **movie theaters** on the bigger ships, and some even offer free popcorn. On smaller ships, movies might be shown in a bar or lounge (not always in the most comfortable arrangement). The movies might be recent releases, although they won't be current releases. Still, it's a good opportunity to catch up on a film you might have missed.

If the movie theater isn't showing something that appeals to you, you might find just the ticket on your in-room TV. Check the bulletin or separate TV guide for listings. While these movies are usually free, on some of the newer ships there might also be pay-per-view TV movie options.

On your in-room TV, depending on the ship, you might also find CNN, ESPN, and special programming, such as The Nature Channel. Occasionally, you might also be offered local TV programming from the area you're passing, pulled off a satellite. And you might also be able to entertain yourself by watching your fellow passengers or yourself enjoying activities, as some of the ships now provide TV productions during the sailing to make sure no one misses anything. You might even be able to see yourself from the night before doing the conga with a pineapple on your head.

If you prefer your small screens to be interactive, many ships have **video arcades** (some restricted to the under-21 set), and a new offering is **computer learning centers.**

Esoterica, Oddities & Enlightenment: Classes and Demonstrations

In the spirit of enlightenment, cruise ships offer myriad demonstrations and classes. You can learn the fine art of **wine tasting** (usually for a fee of $5 to $10) or **mixology,** see how the kitchen staff makes vegetables look like flowers, and learn how to fold napkins so they look like birds.

You can take in a demonstration on **makeup** or **hair styling,** and maybe even serve as a volunteer. I did this one time and came out of the session looking like a Las Vegas showgirl, but what the heck: It washes off.

Experts such as historians, marine biologists, and U.S. forest rangers might join the cruise to offer **lectures** for those seeking more intellectual learning opportunities.

On Princess ships, while you cruise you can also take classes to earn your **scuba certification** from the *Professional Association of Diving Instructors* (PADI).

On some ships, the onboard photography crew will offer photography tips, artists will hold drawing and painting classes, and authors will talk about their books.

It's Art

A lot of big ships are spending big bucks—as in millions—on their onboard art collections, including pieces by well-known artists that might be worth more than a passing glance as you head to the pool or dinner. The purser's office might organize a tour of the collection on a group basis or offer a printed description and map so you can take the tour on your own.

On **small ships,** there might be fewer activities, but less can be more. For example, you're more apt to find an ex-astronaut or TV news anchor such as Walter Cronkite giving a lecture on a Seabourn or Silversea ship than aboard a Carnival megaliner.

Some small ships also offer an **open-bridge** policy, which allows passengers to check in with the officers almost anytime they see fit.

Another popular shipboard diversion offered on both large and small ships is a **galley tour,** a behind-the-scenes look at the ship's food-preparation area. And, once during each cruise, Norwegian and Holland America offer a midnight buffet in the galley, giving passengers a chance to raid the fridge on a grand scale.

After Dark: Bring on the Technicolor Whoopee!

When the sun goes down, cruise ships come alive with the sound of music, and that sound takes many forms. There are the grand production shows, intimate cabarets, piano bars, sing-alongs, dance bands, and even karaoke. The offerings and the quality varies greatly from line to line and even ship to ship.

Many cruise line executives consider entertainment to be one of the four more important things about a ship, right up there with food, service, and ambiance. While some people are content to head for bed after dinner, hit the casino, or just stroll the deck, most passengers do, in fact, prefer some sort of entertainment.

The Really Big Show

On most cruise ships today, sequins and feathers have been joined by high-tech laser lighting and video production as staples of the big stage shows. With all the special effects, live performance sometimes takes a back seat to computers, but on nearly all cruise ships, live big bands wail, dancers prance, and singers belt out hits from Broadway, the movies, and the worlds of pop and rock. Well, okay, they *try* anyway—some more successfully than others.

The large ships all feature at least 2 show productions during any 1-week cruise. Some even offer 2 on a 4-night cruise. These shows are offered in a show lounge, which usually means tiered seating with tables for drinks, but on some ships, it actually means a traditional theater setup, sans tables. Some of the newer ships offer multilevel theaters, and some even have a second-show lounge.

Show productions are offered twice each night: once for those at the main dinner seating and again for those at the late dinner seating. Ships that have only one seating usually stage their shows after dinner.

The live band that plays in the show lounge (sometimes from an orchestra pit) usually consists of little more than a handful of musicians armed with the latest in electronic gadgetry, MIDI equipment, and digital sequencers to give the impression you're listening to a 20-piece orchestra. Many of the dancers will also be lip-synching to a recording.

Some lines rely more heavily on prerecordings than others, and some cruise directors have come to joke about this. When Majesty Cruises owned the *Royal Majesty* (now the *Norwegian Majesty*), there was a distinct difference in the sound quality between the music in the production shows and the competent but tinny-sounding live sextet that opened and closed the show. At the end of every performance, the cruise director could not resist urging "And let's hear it for the Majesty Orchestra."

It should be noted that the use of the recordings really has nothing to do with the ability of the musicians—it's just a way for the cruise lines to fill out the sound without hiring a lot more of them. Ship musicians are professionals, and many have toured with big bands, backed big-name performers, and taught before heading out to sea. They usually sign on for 3-to-6-month stretches, and more than a few have been known to make cruise ships a way of life.

Who's Who in the Review

Cruise ships have replaced the old "straw hat" circuit as a place for musical performers to work while waiting for their big break in New York theater or on the Big Screen.

Those fabulous and mostly young faces you see up on the ship's stage may come from anywhere in the world, although many are American or British. Most have some sort of stage credits, some have worked in TV commercials, some at theme parks, while others are fresh from college. And most are quite talented, a far cry from the early days of cruising, when dance routines had more in common with Las Vegas showgirl kick lines than with Broadway shows.

Choreography is frequently a strong suit in ship productions, but you can also find lead vocalists that are of a recording caliber.

Most smaller ships forego the glitzy productions in favor of smaller cabaret shows, sometimes with dancers, sometimes just a vocalist with a combo. There's no high-tech fuss on these vessels, just old-fashioned music without the frills. Like the musicians mentioned earlier, the performers here sign on for 3-to-6-month stretches aboard ship, and some stay on for several contract renewals. In a business where the vast majority of practitioners spends more time waiting tables, doing temp work, and teaching rather than performing, cruise ships provide steady, fulfilling employment at decent wages (with food and lodging included).

Variety Acts

On nights when show productions aren't offered, cruise ships prove that Vaudeville never died, it just went to sea. You'll find a collection of acrobats and jugglers (and people who can do both) and circus performers, some from Asia and Eastern Europe, as well as comedians, ventriloquists, magicians, singers, impressionists, and instrumentalists. Some ships will also offer big-name performers, second-tier performers, has-beens, wannabes, and talented journeymen who might be better than all of these people but just haven't yet gotten their big break. The quality of these acts varies, with the performances sometimes hitting a home run and other times falling flat.

Lounge Lizards

Lounge entertainment also varies not only from ship to ship but from lounge to lounge on the same ship. This isn't always a bad thing, however, since the tastes of people on any given cruise are bound to vary.

Some of the lounge performers seem to suffer from the old lounge-lizard syndrome, though, looking a bit bored as they sing yet another rendition of *Mack the Knife*. Still, you can discover hidden gems among the lounge performers—say, a talented pianist at the piano bar or a really good jazz combo performing in a dark, cushy lounge.

On most ships, at any given time of the evening, you can find a place to dance to live music as well as to the pulsating tunes spun in the disco. You might also find a place where you can sing along in popular nighttime offerings such as Name That Tune contests and karaoke.

In addition to the main stage and lounge offerings, night owls on some ships can find midnight nightclub shows. These might feature the main-stage performers taking a second turn with some new material or a second-tier "name" performer or up-and-comer.

Do-It-Yourself Entertainment

Virtually all large ships have **passenger talent shows.** Acts are chosen at an audition and usually perform later the same day, either in the main show lounge or in a smaller lounge. If you've fantasized about being the next Sinatra or Madonna, here's a chance to test your skill before a live audience.

If you need accompaniment, it's a good idea to bring along sheet music in your desired key. If you don't know your key, the piano player might be able to help out. If you don't know what a key is, you might be better off watching than performing.

If your routine requires a costume or props, don't forget to pack them.

And remember, it's important to know your audience. Don't try telling X-rated jokes to a G-rated crowd.

A Ham Served My Ham

Some lines let the staff get into the entertainment act even if they weren't specifically hired as performers. Don't be surprised if, during one night of your cruise, you find your waiter parading around the room singing a heavily accented version of *When the Saints Go Marching In* as he and his fellow waiters light up the room with flaming plates of gooey Baked Alaska.

Most cruise ships have at least one **theme night** during a 1-week cruise, such as country and western, Caribbean, the fifties, Italian, or Greek. The staff might dress appropriately on these nights (your waiter wearing a cowboy hat, for example), and you might be encouraged to do the same. And there will be a musical performance and/or dance opportunity reflecting the night's theme.

The Best Ships for Razzle-Dazzle Entertainment

Carnival and **Royal Caribbean** are the best afloat when it comes to production shows, nightclub acts, lounge performances, and audience-participation entertainment.

In the luxury tier, **Crystal** gets high marks for shows and nightclub and lounge performances.

One of the best and most unusual shipboard lounge acts I've found was on **Celebrity's** *Mercury* during its inaugural season. It's Hit and Run, a male a cappella quartet that combines comedy and music as they stroll around the ship in search of gatherings that need a shot of adrenaline. I can't guarantee they'll be aboard when you are, but you can hope.

Silversea wins accolades for its popular Disco Night, when the hotel manager plays music from his private collection.

Princess Cruises offers well-produced shows; some feature circus performers from Eastern Europe and Asia, who perform some pretty incredible feats.

Norwegian offers the best theme cruises, with performances by big bands, country music, jazz, and blues performers.

Chapter 17

I'm Shocked! Shocked to Find Gambling Going on Here!: The Casino Scene

In This Chapter

- An intro to shipboard gambling
- The rules, hours, and protocol of ship casinos
- All the games people play, with rules, illustrations, and tips

According to Carnival's Bob Dickinson, typically only about 30% of cruise passengers gamble in the ship's casino, with more people tending to hang out there just to watch. Few people actually take a cruise for the sole purpose of hitting the slots or tables.

Like me, a lot of the "gamblers" on cruise ships are really teetotalers. We come in with $10 (I have one friend who visits the casino with only 25¢) and leave after the $10 bucks (or 25¢) has been lost, chalking it up to the cost of an evening's entertainment. On one ship, I actually left the casino with $11, having done well at the slots that night and having traveled with an impatient friend who didn't want to wait until I could lose the money.

Since my knowledge of casinos is limited, I turned to my friend and fellow writer Mark Chapman to write this chapter. Take it away, Mark . . .

Las Vegas on the High Seas

I always had this nagging feeling that shipboard slot machines were lagging behind their shoreside cousins in the benevolence department. That is, it seemed like a roll of coins would last a lot longer in Las Vegas than aboard a cruise ship.

But that was before I hit a mini-winning streak. That convinced me that shipboard gaming parlors actually were *more* apt to pay out than those at, say, Foxwoods casino in Connecticut, where, if my guess is right, they actually use the old cruise ship slot machines—the ones that never seemed to pay out.

Of course, what I was really experiencing was luck.

Most shipboard slot machines are just as loose as those at Foxwoods, Las Vegas, Atlantic City, or any of the other gaming halls around the world. Many of the onboard casinos are, in fact, operated by major land-based gaming companies that are bound by the rules and regulations of the Nevada State Gaming Commission.

There was a time when cruising was one of the lone alternatives to Las Vegas for folks looking to dance with Lady Luck. Those days are over. Unlike cruisers as recently as 10 years ago, many of today's vacationers, living as many of us do within a few hours' drive of land casinos, are casino savvy and have learned to put up with old equipment and infrequent payouts.

Vincent Dale has worked in the casino business on land and sea, most recently with Royal Caribbean Cruises Ltd. Soon after RCCL bought Celebrity Cruises in the summer of 1997, Dale was placed in charge of the casino on the latter's new *Mercury,* a ship with an upscale, sophisticated clientele. He says the rules and regulations of all casinos in the U.S., including those off the coast on ships, are pretty standard now.

"People won't play otherwise," Dale said.

Several cruise lines, however, still run their own casino operations and are not bound by the rules of gaming commissions. Celebrity was one of those lines until its merger with Royal Caribbean. Royal Caribbean runs its own casinos and Celebrity's, but because there are investor ties between RCCL and the Hyatt hotel chain, and Hyatt is involved in Las Vegas gaming, the cruise line must adhere to Vegas rules and standards. Crystal Cruise's gaming is operated by Caesar's. Carnival, Princess, and Norwegian run their own operations.

No matter who is running the show, though, it is the more knowledgeable customer who is shaping today's cruise casino experience.

The Layout

Casinos on ships can sometimes get packed but are more frequently not. Depending on the cruise line and the itinerary, it's sometimes possible to actually walk from one end of the casino to the other without feeling like you've stumbled into a half-off sale at Macy's.

On some ships, nongamblers have to make that walk along with gamblers, and the routing is a point of aggravation for some cruisers, who resent the cruise ship design practice of making it inconvenient for passengers to avoid the casino if they so choose. See, on many ships, the casino is in the middle of the ship on the same deck as the theater and, in several cases, the dining room. The most direct route from dinner to the show is thus through the casino, which invariably takes up the entire width of the ship.

Celebrity's Dale said it should take 5 minutes to get through the casino, but this statement is somewhat astounding, considering that covering the distance unimpeded on even the biggest ships would take maybe 20 seconds. The thing is, many ships' designs—particularly aboard Carnival and Royal Caribbean—incorporate narrow entranceways, ramps, multiple levels, gaudy displays, and lots of twists and turns. One entrance to the casino on Royal Caribbean's *Grandeur of the Seas* and *Enchantment of the Seas* features a glass-top pit filled with sunken treasure and underwater flotsam, convincingly lit and displayed. When I was on the ship, it gave me pause when I caught this scene with my peripheral vision, and it nearly caused me to stumble in an effort to not fall into the pit. OK, so the pit is covered, but just the same, I found myself hesitating each time I walked into the casino.

A Different Game

Once in the shipboard casino, players will find important differences from casinos on land. As anyone who has toured Atlantic City knows, sprawling landside gaming halls aren't the friendliest places to be. They are often crowded by people in a hurry, people bent on making every second count, people on gambling junkets who have only two things on their mind: Get the free meal that came with the bus ticket and pump as many quarters as possible into as many machines as can be reached from one spot. Table-game attendants and cashiers at land-based casinos can be surly, too. And just try holding up a blackjack game to ask the dealer whether you should split the pair of eights or stand pat.

On cruise ships, by contrast, customer service is considered key, and dealers are hired for their people skills as much as anything else.

"Anyone can come up and have the dealer talk them through a game," explained Celebrity's Dale. "The way we keep people in the casino is customer service. We aren't hard-core gambling. It's a vacation."

Of course, just because they are people people doesn't mean the cruise ship dealers are a bunch of neophytes on the job. To ensure top-flight service and a thorough knowledge of the games, most lines recruit experienced dealers from shoreside casinos. They then put them through training in the way cruise ships do business. The casino staffs are international, with a heavy European presence.

The Rules, the Hours & a Word on Freebies

There are a few things to be aware of. First of all, you must be 18 to gamble at sea. This is a hard-and-fast policy, never to be violated, just like "no talking at the mandatory lifeboat drills," "bringing your own liquor on board is not allowed," and Holland America's "no tipping required."

But, y' know, some rules are made to be broken.

Underage passengers are allowed in the casino to watch, and I've never seen anyone actually get carded at the slots. So if you take your teenager along and want to introduce her or him to the wonderful world of gambling, you have a good chance of pulling it off. On the other hand, if you would prefer to keep your teen blissfully innocent of legalized gaming, then keep your eyes on him or her at all times.

Second, don't expect the Vegas-type beverage freebies. Land-based casinos have a vested interest in keeping their patrons at the table or machines for extended periods, and free booze is a time-honored way of accomplishing that goal. Cruise ships, however, have you trapped. If you want to gamble, you have to do it there. If you want a drink, you have to buy it there. And while some ships offer a cocktail hour with free or cheap drinks, the lines generally try to avoid having drunk customers in the casino.

Third, if you want to gamble, plan your time wisely. Casinos are not open in port (with a few locally negotiated exceptions). Typically, casinos are open until 3am; on port-call days, they open after the ship clears local waters. On sea days, they open at 10 or 11am.

What to Expect

Cruise ship casinos vary as much as the ships themselves, each catering to a different crowd. But they tend to fall into three main categories:

Very Sparkly

A few years ago, there was a delightful movie called *Rain Man,* starring Tom Cruise and Dustin Hoffman. Slick, yuppie Cruise took his autistic/savant brother Hoffman to a casino to take advantage of his math wizardry at the blackjack table. Hoffman's take on the casino experience: "Very sparkly."

Carnival Cruise Lines aggressively pushes its casinos, which are garish, gaudy, bright, and totally seductive to anyone who loves the Vegas atmosphere. They might not have cornered the neon market, but they have come close.

Right up there alongside Carnival when it comes to flash and dash is **Royal Caribbean.** Surprisingly, **Holland America Line's** casinos also have a carnival-like atmosphere. HAL caters to an older, more sedate crowd, but you'd never know it from these gaming halls. **Princess, Norwegian,** and **Costa** would fit into this category as well.

Slightly Sophisticated

OK, so none of them will ever replace the black-tie elegance of the European salons of yesteryear, but the more upscale lines tend to play down the glitz and go for a more refined air.

The small-ship, ultra-luxury lines—**Seabourn, Silversea, Windstar,** and **Radisson Seven Seas**—come the closest to European elegance. Larger-ship, ultra-luxury lines **Crystal** and **Cunard** are also more understated and refined, as are high-end premiums like **Celebrity.**

While you might find a touch of neon here and there, you are more apt to find etched glass and crystal, with no glowing denizens of the deep leering over the slots and no glass-top treasure pits in the floor.

Casino à la Denny's

Ya gets watcha pay for, so it was no surprise when I wandered into the casino on **Regal Cruises'** *Regal Empress* and found a room that was at once dysfunctional and reminiscent of a Prohibition-era speakeasy. Dark, dingy, and smoky, but teaming with gamblers. So the banks of slots are crammed together, so the restaurant waiting line winds back into the casino and mingles with the players, so it's nearly impossible at night to work your way back to the bar and table-game area. This is no-frills gambling, and there's a whole lotta people who like it that way. OK?

The Games People Play

Slots

Slot machines are the nonthinking person's game. Just drop in a coin or five, pull the handle (or push a button) and let luck take over. Slots are the

This payout table tells you what symbols need to line up and how much you win when they do.
The reels spin simultaneously, but each one stops individually.
This is a winning combination of symbols, lined up on the payline.
Lucky Lady II
$1,0020.56
1ST COIN
2ND COIN
3RD COIN
PAYLINE
Lucky Lady II

What pays what? Check the payout table to see.

It can pay to play the max number of coins.

If you play a second coin, a winning combination will win on either the top or the center payline.
With only one coin in, you have to line the symbols up on this center payline.
When you play three coins, a winning combination on any payline wins.
Big Money
$1,029,357.68
$ 500.03
2 COIN PAYLINE
$10000
1 COIN PAYLINE
$5000
3 COIN PAYLINE
BIG MONEY
2ND
1ST
3RD
BAR
$1
Big Money!

quickest way for a small-stakes player to make a lot of money. They are also the surest way to lose a fistful of coins in a very short period of time.

I've lost. Of course, on the other hand, I once won more than $100 on a ship without ever breaking open a second roll of quarters.

There are some great stories of people hitting it big on slot machines. And this usually happens on **progressive slots,** where jackpots increase based on the amount of play.

Norwegian Cruise Line is one line that offers progressive-slot jackpots on their ships, but the pots are not linked throughout the fleet. Carnival, on the other hand, has its ships—and those sailing under Carnival's Holland America brand—linked together to pay **progressive jackpots.** The pot depends on how much is played fleetwide and keeps growing until someone hits it.

In 1994, three lucky passengers made huge scores on Carnival slots. In March of that year, someone hit the progressives for just over $1 million. A month later, someone hit for $130,000, and in October, a vacationer rang up a $514,000 jackpot.

Most of the time, though, payouts are much smaller—smaller, in fact, than in land-based casinos.

Slots fans will usually find in the ship's casino a good variety of the latest quarter machines, some half-dollar machines, and plenty of dollar slots. I've always found it easy even at busy times to find a dollar machine; quarter machines are most popular, and the cruise lines provide plenty.

Machines that are not linked to progressive pots display a chart of potential winnings, usually ranging from a few thousand to $10,000. Read the chart carefully and remember to play the maximum number of coins the machine allows, or you'll risk hitting a winning combination that will be worth a lot less than advertised.

PLAYING TIP Forget all the hype about "hot" machines, machines at the end of rows being more apt to pay out, and all the other tall tales. Today's slot machines are run by microprocessors that continuously generate hundreds of random combinations every second that the machines are turned on, even when they are not being played. The combination that will be displayed on the winning line is the one that was chosen at the split second you made your play. It's entirely random.

Blackjack

Blackjack, or 21, is a skill game best tried after reading an instructional booklet or watching a video, both provided on most ships. In fact, a cruise ship is the ideal place to learn this game because the dealers are more helpful, and fellow passengers are apt to be more tolerant than in a land-based casino. Some ships offer smoking and nonsmoking tables, and most have low minimums ($5).

The object of the game, played with multiple-card decks shuffled together, is to come as close to **21** as possible without going over, or **busting.** Cards are worth their face value; face cards are worth 10 points, and an ace can be 11 or 1, player's choice. Up to 7 people sit at a semicircular table and play against the dealer.

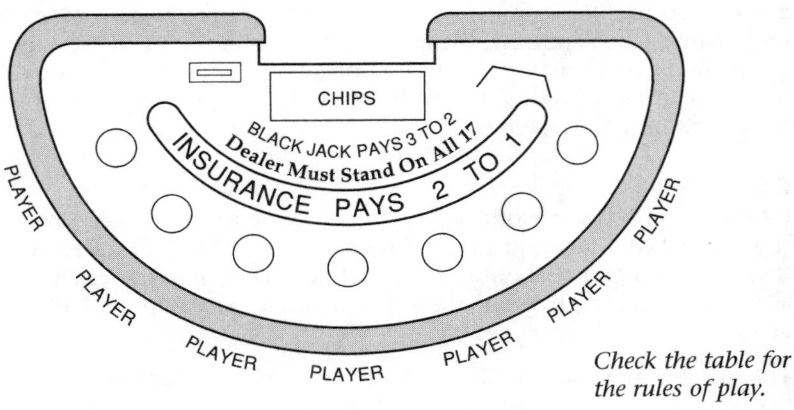

Check the table for the rules of play.

All players place their initial bet, and the dealer deals each a card, face up. The dealer takes one face down. Each player then gets a second card face up, and the dealer gets another face down, then turns one up.

Players decide whether to **hit** or **stand**—that is, whether to take another card or leave well enough alone. The dealer must stand with a total of 17 or more; 16 or less requires the dealer to take another card.

If the dealer busts, all players with cards totaling 21 or less are winners. If the player busts, the bet is lost. And if the dealer is still in after the player elects to stand, the higher hand wins.

Always use hand signals to declare hit or stand. To hit, tap your cards with a finger. To stand, wave your hand over the cards.

If you get 21 on 2 cards **(blackjack),** you automatically win. Payoff odds are 3–2. All other bets are paid off at 1–1.

Blackjack always beats a 21 reached by 3 or more cards. And if a player and dealer both have blackjack, it's a **push,** and no money changes hands.

There are a few other plays to complicate matters. If your first two cards match you can split them and play two hands. This is always done with a pair of aces, never with a pair of face cards or 10s.

Doubling down is making a second wager up to the amount of the first and can only be done after receiving the first two cards. After you double down, you may take only one more card. This is a good play to consider when you have 10 or 11 showing, and the dealer has less.

There's also an **insurance bet.** If the dealer's up card is an ace and you think he might have blackjack, place an insurance bet of one-half your original bet. If the dealer has blackjack, you get paid at 2–1.

PLAYING TIP A good memory helps. If you know how many decks are in use, you can multiply that number by 16 to get the number of 10-point cards and by 4 to find the number of aces. Try to keep track to give yourself the best chance when splitting, hitting, and staying. Also, if you hit a losing streak, don't try to make it back all at once. A frequent player once told me his secret to success: After a winning streak is broken by losing three straight hands, it's time to walk away. Or at least to change tables.

Roulette

Here's a modified game of chance; that is, if you are observant, you can work the odds in your favor, just like with blackjack. Unlike blackjack, though, there's nothing finite about roulette. While blackjack has a certain number of aces and face cards, the roulette ball can land on any number and any color at any time.

The thing is, the ball is unlikely to land on a red number five times in a row, just as it is unlikely to land on an odd number five times in a row. Of course, it can also do just that. That's why it's called gambling.

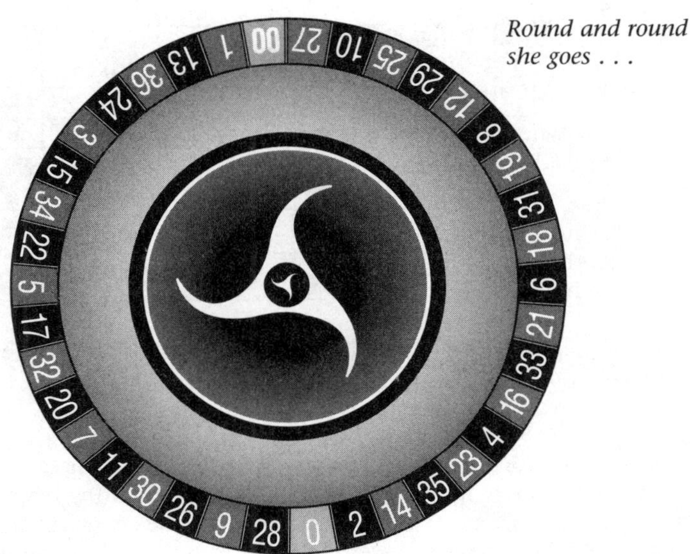

Round and round she goes . . .

You can play this game lots of ways, with the most daring bets paying off best and the safest bets paying 1–1. Make as many bets as you want on each spin.

Bet	**Odds**
A single number	35–1
2 adjoining numbers	17–1
A street (3 adjoining numbers on the board)	11–1
A 5-number bet (there's only 1 combination for this one)	6–1
A line of 6 consecutive numbers	5–1
A dozen numbers (there are 3 groups paying off)	2–1
A corner of 4 adjoining numbers	8–1
A column (3 combos)	2–1
High-low money (first 18 or last 18)	even
Odd-even	1–1
Red/black	1–1

Bets, made with special chips that are color-coded to each player, must be placed precisely on the table. A **split bet,** for example, is made by placing a chip on a line between two numbers. If the chip is not squarely on the line, it will be taken as a straight-up bet.

PLAYING TIP Make a mental note about how many times either black or red comes up and how many odd or even numbers come up. Because there is an equal number of both, the odds favor the bettor playing whichever

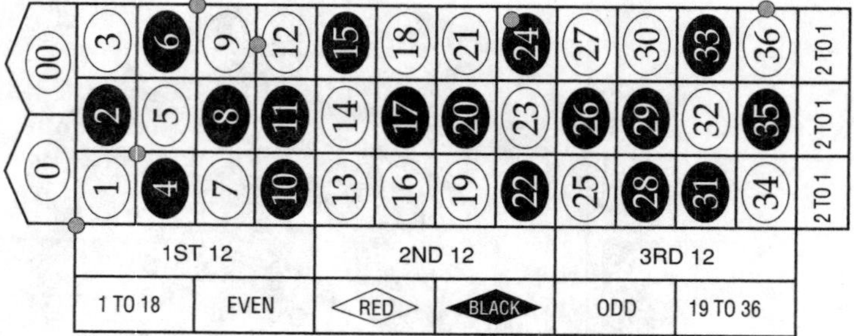

The layout of the roulette betting table.

number or color set is trailing. An occasional daring play on these 1-to-1 bets can net you a nice profit.

Craps

This dice game moves fast, can be confusing, and offers more excitement than any other game. Remember Nathan Detroit's floating crap game in the Broadway and movie musical *Guys and Dolls?* This is what all those camped-up Damon Runyon gangsters were flocking to New York for. Shipboard casinos offer their own floating crap games, but they are perfectly legal.

Because the game is convoluted, players should take advantage of free lessons generally offered by the casino. At the very least, watch the in-cabin video offered on most ships.

Here's the basics of how it works: All bets are made, and the dice are presented to the **shooter,** who is one of the players. The shooter throws the dice hard enough for them to bounce off the wall at the end of the table. The shooter continues until he or she rolls a 7 or until a decision has been made on the point.

If the shooter throws a 7 or 11 on the first roll—the **come-out roll**—he's an automatic winner and retains the dice. If the first roll is a 2, 3, or 12—all

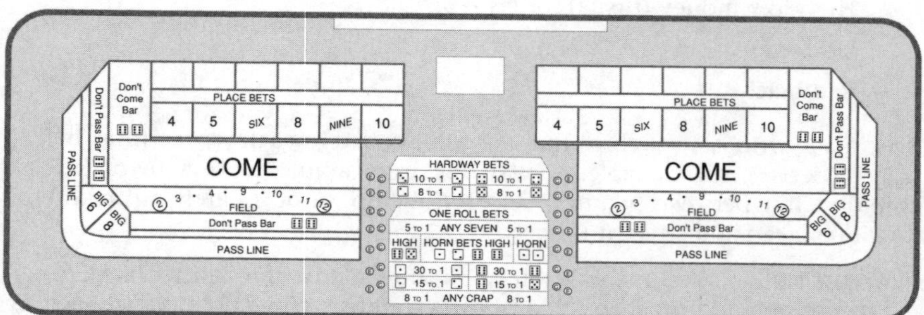

The mysterious craps table.

known as **craps**—he loses. He does, however, keep control of the dice, because he hasn't yet rolled a 7.

If the shooter rolls a 4, 5, 6, 8, 9, or 10 on the first roll, the number becomes the **point.** The shooter's objective is then to roll that number again, called **making point,** before rolling a 7. The bet is on whether or not the shooter makes point.

Number Rolled	How Many Ways to roll the Number?	True Odds	Winning Combinations
Two	1	35 to 1	⚀ ⚀
Three	2	17 to 1	⚀ ⚁ · ⚁ ⚀
Four	3	11 to 1	⚀ ⚂ · ⚂ ⚀ · ⚁ ⚁
Five	4	8 to 1	⚀ ⚃ · ⚃ ⚀ · ⚁ ⚂ · ⚂ ⚁
Six	5	6.2 to 1	⚀ ⚄ · ⚄ ⚀ · ⚁ ⚃ · ⚃ ⚁ · ⚂ ⚂
Seven	6	5 to 1	⚀ ⚅ · ⚅ ⚀ · ⚁ ⚄ · ⚄ ⚁ · ⚂ ⚃ · ⚃ ⚂
Eight	5	6.2 to 1	⚁ ⚅ · ⚅ ⚁ · ⚂ ⚄ · ⚄ ⚂ · ⚃ ⚃
Nine	4	8 to 1	⚂ ⚅ · ⚅ ⚂ · ⚃ ⚄ · ⚄ ⚃
Ten	3	11 to 1	⚃ ⚅ · ⚅ ⚃ · ⚄ ⚄
Eleven	2	17 to 1	⚄ ⚅ · ⚅ ⚄
Twelve	1	35 to 1	⚅ ⚅

There are simple ways to bet on this game, and there are complicated, reckless ways. The basic bet is a line bet—**pass** or **don't pass.** You place this bet before the come-out roll. Bet on the pass line, and you are betting that the shooter rolls a 7, 11, or point number on the come-out; if the number is point, you are betting that the shooter hits point before 7. "Don't pass" is, predictably, the opposite.

Come or **don't come** bets are made after point has been set. Place a come bet, and the next roll sets your come number. If your number comes up before the shooter rolls 7, you win. If the 7 turns up, you lose. If the shooter makes point, no money changes hands. "Don't come" is, again, the opposite—a bet against the shooter.

All those bets are even-money wagers. There is also something called an **odds bet,** which pays off at true odds. After point is set, make an odds bet (you must make a pass / don't pass or come / don't come bet first) of equal value. The odds bet is parallel to your first bet; that is, you are betting the same thing twice. The odds bet, though, pays off at 2–1 if the winning roll is a 4 or 10, 3–2 if it's 5 or 9, and 6–5 if it's 6 or 8.

Confusing? I told you so.

PLAYING TIP There are other bets available on the table, but they are long shots, and it's best to avoid them until you master the basics.

Caribbean Stud Poker

Poker has long been a favorite game of gamblers everywhere, but this version seems to be the most popular on cruise ships. It's easy to play, and the payoffs vary from average to terrific.

The table looks like a blackjack table at first glance, but the markings are different and there are slots for bets into a progressive jackpot.

Everyone makes his initial bet, or **ante,** before the cards are dealt. Then the dealer doles out five cards, face down, to each player. After all cards are dealt, the dealer flips over his last card for all to see. You then decide whether to drop out, or **fold,** or to continue with your hand, which requires a **call** bet equal to twice the original ante. The dealer then reveals his hand and must have at least an ace and a king, or any other card combination that ranks above those cards, such as one pair, for the game to continue. If not, anyone still in the game is paid even money on his ante only.

If the dealer can continue, her hand is compared with each player's hand. If your hand beats the dealer, your ante is paid off at even money, and your call bet is paid off according to the odds, which increase depending on the strength of the hand. A chart should be displayed at the table (and I've included one here, to study up on). If you win with 1 pair, your call bet is paid off at even money; 2 pairs earn 2–1 odds, a full house nets 7–1 odds, and a royal flush pays 100–1.

PLAYING TIP Always play the progressive jackpot. The progressive jackpot pays separately for certain hands, and payoffs vary according to what's in the pot. Draw a straight flush (5 consecutive cards of the same suit) or royal flush (10, jack, queen, king, and ace of the same suit) and make serious money on just a $1 bet. On Royal Caribbean's *Enchantment of the Seas,* for example, the jackpot is advertised as always worth in excess of $20,000.

Jackpot in Bed

Never heard of this game? It's a cruise ship original. Thanks to TV's *The Love Boat,* there are plenty of single people booking cruises in hopes of hitting the romantic jackpot, and on some cruise lines, you can literally hit the jackpot in bed—but I'm talking casino jackpots.

Through the wizardry of electronics, it's now possible to play video slots on some stateroom TVs using your remote control. Just punch it up, purchase credits on your shipboard account, and have a ball without getting out of bed. Winnings are applied to your onboard account and are paid (and losses collected) at the end of the cruise.

There is a lockout feature to keep youngsters from gaining access to in-cabin gaming.

Bingo

A cruise without bingo is like a trip to Disney World without the mouse ears. It's cliché, it's corny, but it's true. Bingo is legendary on cruise ships. There

Royal Flush A♥ K♥ Q♥ J♥ 10♥	A, K, Q, J and 10 all of the same suit.
Straight Flush Q♣ J♣ 10♣ 9♣ 8♣	Five cards in sequence and all of the same suit (such as Q, J, 10, 9, 8 of clubs).
Four of a Kind Q♥ Q♣ Q♦ Q♠ 3♦	Four cards of the same rank.
Full House K♣ K♦ K♥ 2♦ 2♠	Three of a kind, plus a pair.
Flush Q♠ 10♠ 9♠ 6♠ 4♠	Five cards of the same suit.
Straight 10♦ 9♠ 8♣ 7♥ 6♥	Five cards in sequence. (Ace can be high or low.)
Three of a Kind J♣ J♠ J♦ 7♣ 2♦	Three cards of the same rank.
Two Pair K♣ K♥ 7♠ 7♣ A♦	Two cards of one rank and two cards of another rank.
Jacks or Better J♥ J♦ A♣ 10♥ 3♠	A pair of jacks, queens, kings, or aces.

The hierarchy of poker hands.

are devoted players who wouldn't miss a game, as well as casual players who take the occasional fly at making a few dollars. And while progressive jackpots—often called **snowball jackpot bingo**—can reach several thousand dollars by the end of a cruise, most winners take out less than $100.

The setup of the bingo card.

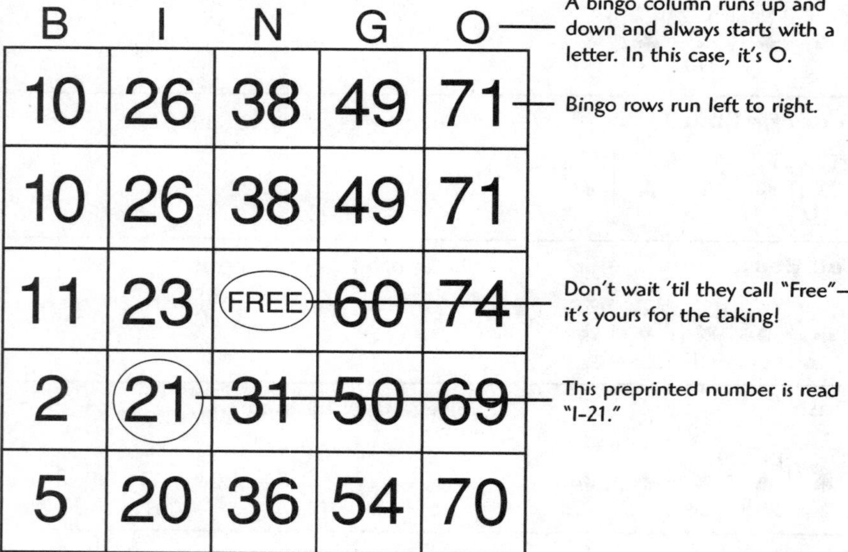
B I N G O
10 26 38 49 71
10 26 38 49 71
11 23 FREE 60 74
2 21 31 50 69
5 20 36 54 70
A bingo column runs up and down and always starts with a letter. In this case, it's O.
Bingo rows run left to right.
Don't wait 'til they call "Free"—it's yours for the taking!
This preprinted number is read "I-21."

Players buy into the game for varying amounts, often around $5 for 3 cards. Members of the entertainment staff call out numbers randomly chosen by a machine, and the numbers are posted on an electronic board, with the games held daily, usually in the mid-afternoon.

While no one gets rich at bingo, it's a relatively cheap diversion that offers just enough chance at making some money to keep things interesting.

Horse Racing

You're probably wondering just where they keep the horses on board a ship, right? Never fear, we're talking toys here.

Shipboard horse racing is about as silly an activity as there is at sea, and therein lies its popularity. The toy horses are mounted on poles and moved by players along a "track" according to rolls of the dice. A member of the entertainment staff calls the race just like they do at the real tracks. Passengers bet on the outcome and cheer their steeds on to victory.

The big event is the **owners' race,** typically on the final day at sea. Passengers form syndicates or buy 1 of the 6 horses outright, usually for around $100, paying into a pot that goes to the winning owner. Owners typically dress up their horses in gaudy fashion and give them exotic names. Some get so involved in the process they will even take their horses with them to dinner. There's usually a best-dressed horse competition, with the winner earning 10% of the pot.

Passengers make $5 wagers on the winner; payoff is dictated by the amount of play. For example, on one of my cruises, a $5 wager earned $40; the pot was $600, with the winning owner taking $540 ($60 went to the best-dressed horse).

Ridiculous? You bet. Fun? Yep. Yell, scream, jump up and down. Remember: You'll probably never see any of these people again.

Live Horse Events

No, no horses on the ship here either, but in late 1997, Carnival became the first cruise line to offer live video simulcasts of top thoroughbred horse races, introducing them on the *Holiday.*

The races are broadcast in the ship's casino and operate much the same as pari-mutuel betting on land. After selecting the horse of choice, a guest's wagers are transmitted via satellite directly to the host track, and confirmation, in the form of a betting slip, is received back at the ship in a matter of seconds. Racing odds and payouts are identical to those at the host track, and winning bets are cashed at the ship's casino window.

Just like at a typical shoreside track, passengers can try to gain a competitive handicapping edge by viewing the horses prior to the race through live video feeds of the paddock area and starting gate.

And Carnival's passengers aren't limited to wagering on the races shown on the parlor's seven video monitors. Detailed information on a wide variety of races taking place that day is also provided, allowing guests to wager on any horse at a participating track at any time.

Chapter 18

Meet Me at the Spa, Dahling: The Spa & Fitness Scene

In This Chapter

- What to expect at the shipboard spa: treatments, prices, and protocol
- A rundown of the services available in the beauty salon
- An intro to shipboard exercise, from pumping you up to slimming you down
- The best spas and gyms afloat

Back in the old days, a spa on a ship, if there was one, was a tiny, cramped room off the beauty parlor, barely big enough for a massage table, and probably located in the bowels of the ship. The gym, meanwhile, would be a dark, closet-size room with an implement of torture or two. Of course, they also offered shuffleboard, if you can consider that exercise . . . or a sport . . . or if you consider it at all.

Boy, have times changed. Today on the high seas, you can exercise on state-of-the-art equipment and get the latest and greatest in beauty and relaxation treatments in nearly deck-size spaces where windows let in light and views, TVs, and sound systems provide entertainment as your sweat flows. You can get advice from a personal trainer and even have your body composition analyzed by little electrodes. And if you haven't been following an exercise program before now, this might be the best time to start—after all, it's convenient, you have the time, and the gym staff is there to help.

As more and more people have embraced healthy lifestyles, spas and gyms have become a major marketing feature of ships; some people even choose ships based on these offerings. And in their newest vessels, cruise lines have invested millions in impressive facilities that even rival land-based offerings.

Consider Celebrity, which had to go through all sorts of architectural rigmarole to offer clients access to a 115,000-gallon fresh seawater thalassotherapy pool on its newest ships, the *Century, Galaxy,* and *Mercury.* Was it worth it? You bet. The relaxing pools with their warm water and massaging jets, done up in Japanese design on the *Century* and *Galaxy* and Moorish design on the *Mercury,* have proven to be popular offerings.

"The whole industry has changed," says Michele Warshaw, executive vice president of Steiner Transocean Limited, a firm that has cornered the cruise ship spa market, operating the gyms and spas on nearly 100 vessels as an outside vendor, with mostly British-trained staffers.

Of course, there are still older ships with small spa and gym spaces. Warshaw said Steiner's smallest operation has 3 to 5 staffers (the largest has 23). But in even the smallest venues, facials, massages, and beauty-parlor services (cut, perm, color) are on the spa menu.

The age of the ship doesn't necessarily mean the spa is smaller. The *QE2,* for example, has a large spa and a spa staff of 19, one of the largest staffs at sea.

Operating a ship spa and gym requires a creative use of whatever space the ship has allotted for that purpose. You won't often find multiple exercise rooms, for example; instead, there's usually one large, open, mirrored room where aerobics and other classes are offered. Staffing numbers are limited to how many crew beds are available.

Still, Warshaw wants to provide her customers, especially first-timer spa-goers, with no less than "a lifestyle change."

"I'm sure that we do that for many Americans. For some people to walk into a land-based facility, it is quite difficult to go to have your first facial or massage. When you're on a ship you can try these things."

All the Steiner treatments are done with European ingredients. And all the ships with Steiner spas sell Elemis and La Therepie products (on some ships, the selling is more aggressive than on others).

Celebrity offers cruise passengers special book-in-advance spa packages that include a number of treatments, and Princess is planning a similar offering.

Don't Overdo It

With eating being one of the most popular activities on ships, you are, even if you are extremely careful, bound to pig out at least once. But killing yourself at the gym the next day is not the answer—especially if you haven't been following an exercise regimen before stepping aboard. Besides the fact that it'll just make you hungrier at your next meal, it can be downright dangerous. Be sure you exercise at a reasonable pace, and one your body can handle.

Some of the services offered by Steiner on the ships are not available anywhere else in America, such as Ionithermie, a detoxification process that, it's claimed, reduces cellulite. Among the most unusual treatments is the highly popular Rasul, offered on Celebrity ships (see "And the Gold Medal Goes To . . .," later in this chapter).

According to Warshaw, her company is constantly looking for new and fabulous treatments to offer cruise passengers.

What to Expect at the Spa

On the first day of the cruise, the spa staff usually offers free demos to show exactly what the various treatments involve, and as Warshaw explained, "to help people get over the fear of what may happen to them." If you've never been to a spa before, you might want to watch these free demos. You might even be able to volunteer as a test subject.

You will be required to **make a reservation** for any treatments you're interested in. It's good to do this as soon as you can after you've boarded the ship, as popular treatments tend to sell out fast. The same goes for beauty appointments (there's usually a beauty parlor adjacent to the spa), as the prime time slots, such as hair and nail appointments in the afternoons before formal nights, tend to go quickly.

When making your appointment, be sure you take into consideration your planned meal time and potential conflicts with shore excursions. The spa and beauty parlor remain open when the ship is at port, and this is often a nice, quiet time to book treatments if you're not planning to go ashore.

When you check in at the spa for your treatments, you will be assigned a locker and given a bathrobe and towel. You do not have to wear any specific clothes to the spa. In fact, you are encouraged to wear nothing at all, except a swimsuit in the spa's pool areas (if there are any). If you are uncomfortable going into a treatment room naked, you can request disposable undergarments (so your own don't get soiled by the mud, seaweed, oil, or other ingredients used in the treatments).

Before your treatment begins, you will be requested to fill out a form that will ask questions about your general health, lifestyle, and other things that might impact the kind of treatment delivered. If your treatment involves water therapy, you might also be interviewed by a nurse, since hot water can effect your blood pressure.

After you've been interviewed, your therapist will escort you to a private treatment area, which will be a small room, often with a shower (to wash off mud or seaweed), a bedlike treatment table, a sink, bottles of formulas, and a sound system to play relaxing (and often New Age) tunes. Don't be put off by the fact that it looks more than a bit like a doctor's examination room. The goal here is to make you relax.

Most of the treatments are offered on an individual basis. Celebrity's Rasul is an exception, as is the couples' Partner-Teach Massage therapy session offered by Crystal Cruises. The session ($100 per couple) is taught by a therapist and consists of about 30% theory and 70% practical, hands-on training. Couples are instructed to use the techniques on each other to relieve stress and tension, reduce pain, boost energy, and rejuvenate muscles.

Warshaw said her staff is trained with the understanding that a lot of passengers have never had these treatments before.

"We want to make our passengers feel as comfortable as possible," she said. "Everyone we see is on vacation and we want everyone to have a good time in our spa, a great relaxing experience, and fun as well. We want them to experience mud treatments, baths, and things that they wouldn't do in everyday life," Warshaw added.

Note: From personal experience, I can tell you that after some of these treatments, you will feel like butter. You might be so relaxed that you don't recognize yourself. Plan some quiet time after the treatment so you can enjoy the moment.

While there are some male therapists, the staff tends to be female. This goes for those offering treatments to women as well as to men. And by the way, there's a strict no-fraternizing policy on all ships.

Menu of Spa Services

Here are some of the more standard Steiner spa treatments. Specific offerings and prices may vary from ship to ship:

Aromatherapy Massage Massage for the back, neck, shoulders, and backs of legs. 25 minutes, $35.

Massage of Full Body Using Aromatherapy Oils 50 minutes, $70.

Personal Training An experienced and qualified fitness instructor will help you develop a personalized exercise program to achieve your fitness goals. 1 hour, $35.

Reflexology An energizing massage on the soles of the feet based on traditional Chinese techniques. Relieves stress and creates harmony throughout the body. 45 minutes, $70.

La Therapie Facial Focusing on the face and eye area, the treatment helps alleviate signs of stress and tiredness. Restores moisture to the skin and drains impurities. 55 minutes, $69.

La Therapie Intensif A facial concentrating on the eye and neck areas. 80 minutes, $99.

Ionithermie Slimming Treatment Uses active ingredients, including sea kelp, ivy, and clay, for a firmer appearance in problem areas (due to cellulite, muscular problems, or water retention). 55 minutes, $80.

Aromatherapy & Seaweed Mask Treatment Improves the metabolism using mineral-rich seaweed and sea water to nourish skin cells and aid in reducing water retention. Three types of seaweed masks are offered to relax and de-stress, firm and tone, or detoxify and cleanse. $80.

Elemis Sinergistic Therapy Combines reflexology, *Shiatsu* (a type of finger massage), and pressure-point massage techniques, as well as aromatherapy oils. The massage is from the soles of the feet up to the face and scalp. 105 minutes, $150.

Body-Fat Composition Analysis / Fat Test Measures the body's lean and fat tissue and provides guidelines for determining fitness goals. $25.

Menu of Beauty Salon Services

Prices for these services may vary from ship to ship, though haircuts should run about $30, manicures around $20, and pedicures around $35.

- Hair cuts for men and women, with shampoo and blow dry
- Styling (including formal-night hairstyles)
- Permanent waves
- Coloring
- Makeup consultation
- Manicure
- Pedicure
- French-spa hand treatment (facial for the hands) $35

Cruise lines that offer Steiner spa services include Carnival, Celebrity, Costa, Crystal, Cunard, Disney, Holland America, Norwegian, Premier, Princess, Radisson, Royal Caribbean, Seabourn, and Silversea.

Pumping Iron

I've seen exercise machines on ships that I've never seen anywhere else—that's how up-to-date some of these seagoing gyms are. There generally are several exercise bikes, rowing machines, Stairmasters, and treadmills for your **aerobic conditioning** and a selection of **weight machines** for toning. Some ships even offer an assortment of **free weights** and benches for you Schwarzenegger types. Some ships offer complete Nautilus setups.

The ship gyms are usually open from early morning well into the evening hours. Because of the popularity of some machines, there might be sign-up sheets and perhaps time limits on use of the aerobics machines. Check with the staff in the gym for your ship's specific rules in this regard.

For a fee, you might be able to book the services of a **personal trainer** for a day or an entire week, and on some ships you can have your body-fat composition electronically analyzed and get advice on ways to bring the number down.

Towels are generally available in the gym, there's usually a water fountain, and a few ships even have juice bars.

Life Preservers

The location of the gym is one thing to look for in a ship's deck plan when you're booking your cabin, as an early-morning high-impact aerobics class held right above your head would pretty much put the kibosh on sleeping late. Maybe that's why a lot of ships put crew quarters right below the gym floor—no excuse for those crewmen being late for work!

Additional facilities on some ships include **tennis courts,** a **sports deck** where you can play basketball and volleyball, and (coming soon on Royal Caribbean) an ice-skating rink, roller-skating rink, and rock-climbing wall. Ping-Pong tables and dartboards can also commonly be found, and many ships feature a padded jogging track.

And, of course, I can't think of any ship that doesn't offer shuffleboard.

Tee Time

There was a time when golf fanatics had to content themselves on cruise ships with driving golf balls off the stern into the sea, an ecologically unsound and now banned practice (those fishies didn't liked getting whacked in the head). Alternatively, these golfers could try to quench their urges by participating in hit-the-ball-in-the-plastic-cup contests.

Lately, though, recognizing the popularity of the sport, cruise lines have developed much more sophisticated programs to make sure golf fans will be happy on their cruise vacations and will not be able to use their love of the game as an excuse not to take a cruise.

Cruise ships can, in fact, get golfers into some of the top golf courses in the world, and cruise passengers can get tips from some of the world's top players on board some ships.

And we're not just talking golf simulators, which allow players to drive a ball against a film screen showing a hole on a famous course. They are hardly the real thing. The lines recognize that purists want to play on 18 holes with real grass and carts or caddies, and several lines have established relationships with golf courses in Bermuda, the Caribbean, Hawaii, the eastern U.S., and Mexico to offer golfers just that, with tee times scheduled to coincide with the hours the ship is in the port of call. Based on season and course, fees range from $50 to more than $170 per round.

Royal Caribbean, as the official cruise line of the PGA (it sponsors the Royal Caribbean Classic of the Senior PGA tour), can get passengers tee times at championship courses such as **Paradise Island** in The Bahamas and **St. George's** in Bermuda. The line has contracts with 31 courses in all as part of its Golf Ahoy program.

On its *Legend of the Seas* and *Splendour of the Seas,* the line also offers an 18-hole golf course right on top of the ship, a miniature putting green without windmills, but with water hazards, sand traps, and of course, fabulous ocean views.

Crystal Cruises arranges tee times at ports of call and offers golf clinics on board, led by pro players. Both the *Crystal Symphony* and *Crystal Harmony* are equipped with two driving cages and a putting green.

Costa Cruise Lines offers a Golf Academy at Sea on the *CostaRomantica* and *CostaVictoria* in the Caribbean, with a PGA instructor on board who joins passengers in play at **Sandals Resort** in Jamaica, the **Links at Safe Haven** in Grand Cayman, Nassau's **Cable Beach,** and other fine courses. Lessons are also offered on board for a fee, with a videotape of the session available for an additional fee.

Holland America Line offers rounds on Caribbean sailings at the courses listed above as well as at **Royal St. Kitts,** Aruba's **Tierra del Sol,** and others.

Seabourn offers supplementary golf itineraries for a fee above the cruise fare. One such itinerary includes **Kingsmill Resort** and other famous courses in the eastern U.S.

American Hawaii Cruises offers a Floating Greens of Hawaii package that allows passengers to play some of the best courses on the islands.

Group Sweat

If exercise classes are your thing, on most of the bigger ships you'll find plenty of offerings such as **aerobics, step aerobics, dance classes, thigh classes,** and **stretch-and-relaxation classes,** all conducted by perky and well-trained recent college graduates. Some ships also offer **water aerobics** and other exercise activities in the swimming pools, and some offer **health lectures,** such as talks on nutrition. Special classes for seniors also might be offered, including suggestions for those who can best exercise from a sitting position.

The **schedule of classes** is usually listed in the ship's bulletin, and there may be separate sheets available at the gym as well.

Several lines offer an incentive program on their ships for people to attend exercise classes and participate in other active group events, such as **walk-a-mile** (on the promenade deck). You can earn T-shirts, water bottles, and other paraphernalia for your participation, with the gifts awarded at the end of your cruise.

Prizes are not awarded for my favorite shipboard exercise activity, which is avoiding the elevators and running or fast-walking up the stairs. (Hey, it burns calories!)

And the Gold Medal Goes To . . .

Here are my picks of the cruise lines with the best gym and spa programs:

Celebrity The three newer Celebrity ships—*Century, Galaxy,* and *Mercury*—all have 10,000-square-foot AquaSpas offering the latest and greatest. The gyms offer state-of-the-art equipment and free weights; golf simulators are located in a separate area; and spa facilities on each ship include a thalassotherapy pool, whirlpools, hydrotherapy pools, saunas, mud baths, massage rooms, Turkish baths, a gym, an aerobics area, and a beauty salon. Plus, the ships are the only ones to offer the mysterious Rasul.

What Is the Mysterious Rasul?

Nope, it's not a new event at the winter Olympics. Rasul is a mud-and-seaweed treatment that evolved from a ceremony found in the Sultan's harem during the Ottoman Empire. It was designed to purify and cleanse a bride before her wedding—physically, mentally, and spiritually. After a hot shower with seaweed soap, mud is applied over the entire body and face. Then you take a bowl of seasalt into an herbal steam bath where you relax before reentering the shower to wash the mud away. The treatment concludes after an aromatic potion is applied to your body. On the Celebrity ships, you can book the treatment solo ($35) or with a partner ($60). In the latter, a staff member will assist with the application of the mud only if you request it. Otherwise, you get to do it yourselves.

Carnival The newer "fun ships" have Nautica Spas with wonderful gyms, equipped with free weights and Keiser exercise machines; and plenty of massage and spa treatment rooms; as well as saunas, steam rooms, and whirlpools. The best are the 12,000-square-foot offerings on the line's Fantasy-class ships (*Ecstasy, Fantasy, Fascination, Imagination, Inspiration,* and *Sensation*) and on the *Destiny,* which has 15,000 square feet of gym and spa space, including a juice bar. Classes include low-impact and advanced aerobics and weight circuit training. Some of the ships also have jogging tracks.

Norwegian The *Norway* offered the first real European spa at sea, built quite far down on the ship and hard to find, but offering 16 treatment rooms, a small "aquasize" pool, hydrotherapy baths, and saunas. The gym, which is in a separate location, has floor-to-ceiling windows and an indoor pool and is equipped with Cybex and Bally fitness machines; it also has steam rooms and saunas, as well as body-jet showers and a whirlpool.

Princess This line's grand-class ships (the *Dawn Princess, Sun Princess,* and upcoming *Sea Princess* and *Grand Princess*) all have beautiful facilities, including stunning glass-walled health centers and four swimming pools (five on the *Grand Princess*), including a lap pool. Princess offers a daily Cruisercise program that includes walk-a-mile, stretch and tone, high- and low-aerobics, and aquacise. Sports decks offer basketball, volleyball, badminton, and table tennis.

Chapter 19

Shop Till You Drop

In This Chapter

- Tips for shopping in the ports: finding a treasure, getting a deal, and avoiding scams
- Tips for shipboard shopping: what to expect and what (and when) to pay for it
- The skinny on art auctions and port lectures
- Customs regulations and how to deal with them

If shopping's your bag and you're worried that you won't be able to get your fix while at sea, fear not: You'll never be far away from shopping on a big cruise ship. That's because the ships have their own shops (some so large and varied they almost qualify as shopping malls) and all ports of call offer plenty of shopping opportunities.

The people in the islands, towns, and cities you'll visit realize the value of the tourist dollar, and they want you to buy, Buy, BUY. In many cases you, the tourist, are the location's main source of income. As you visit the various ports, you will be offered items you can't resist and deals that are too good to be true. Problem is, sometimes the items are junk, and sometimes the "deals" are really rip-offs.

Fran's Philosophy of Shopping

Before we get into the most common scams, let's establish that beauty is in the eye of the beholder, and so is the item's worth. If that "Horny in Alaska" T-shirt is irresistible to you at $12, then it's a good deal. If that Mexican silver necklace is worth $20 to you whether or not it turns out to be real silver, it's a good deal, too.

I've found that some of my most cherished souvenirs are inexpensive craft items that remind me of my journeys but didn't cost me an arm and a leg.

Before you start shopping on your cruise, think about what you want. Are you looking for diamonds and other luxury items or snow globes and refrigerator magnets? After that, set a tentative budget. Nothing can ruin a vacation memory more than getting a huge credit-card bill full of charges for things you didn't mean to buy and probably have little use for.

Many people get caught up in the idea of finding a bargain and don't think hard about what an item might cost at home. If you're in the market for a high-ticket item, you might want to do some comparison shopping before you leave home. Check prices of jewelry at your local jewelry store. And if you're in the market for a camera or other electronics item, check the prices at the discount stores.

Ahoy, Mateys!

Museum shops are great places to find interesting and inexpensive items, and a portion of the proceeds usually goes to support the museum's programs.

Of course, you might come across that item on your trip that really is an unbelievable value. On a cruise I went on a few years ago, the people I was with went on and on about the great jewelry prices. I resisted until I saw not one but two rings, one with sapphires, the other with rubies, that I just had to have. I couldn't choose between the two, so I bought both, negotiating a price of $550.

When I got home, I felt extremely guilty and didn't even tell my husband about my purchase for 2 days. When I finally did tell him, I assured him the rings would cover his holiday and birthday gifts to me for the next year, and he was fine with it. He was even more fine when I later had the rings appraised at $1,290.

Yes, travelers can find bargains.

Customs & Duties

There are limits on how much in the way of goods you can bring back to the U.S. from an international destination. Also, when you get home, you might have to pay a U.S. Customs duty of 10% (or less, depending on the destination) if you go over the set limit. (See chapter 26, "The Last Details," for more on this.)

For Customs reasons, it's important that you save receipts from all your purchases.

She Shops Ship Shops by the Seashore

The shops on most ships are operated mostly by outside concessionaires. That's why you might find the same brands on different ships—only the logo on items such as T-shirts and sweatshirts has been changed, so that on Princess you'll find a Princess logo sweatshirt, and on Celebrity, you'll find the same sweatshirt with a Celebrity logo.

A Carnival spokesman said cruise lines get big bucks from their onboard shopping operations. He said Carnival operated its own shops until the late 1980s but found it could make even more money by having a professional organization running the show. The ship shop operators are the same firms that do airport concessions, and they buy in bulk, he explained.

Still, Royal Caribbean, which does its own buying, has the best shopping offerings afloat. The Royal Caribbean ships sell excellent merchandise, with its megaships offering a dozen shops each, their inventories including booty from local ports of call and items such as jewelry, liquor, perfumes, and collectibles at discounted prices that are even better than what you'll find ashore.

And Royal Caribbean also makes it more relaxing for its passengers to shop at ports by offering, in several locations, **Crown and Anchor Clubs**—hospitality centers with sofas, chairs, and rest rooms where you can take a break, have a drink at the bar or snack bar, and leave your packages before you're ready to return to the ship.

Norwegian Cruise Line's *Norway* is also a shopper's dream with its vast selections, including boutiques selling resort wear, gold and jewelry, T-shirts, stylish clothing items, and logo souvenirs.

Typically on the big cruise ships, there will be a gift shop with items both generic (such as the ship-logo wear mentioned) and regional, such as smoked salmon in Alaska. There's also usually a jewelry store that sells collectibles, a liquor store, and a fine-clothing shop that might have items as diverse as perfume, makeup, fine shoes, and a good selection of evening wear.

Small Ship Shopping

If you're sailing on a small ship, don't expect extensive onboard shopping options. The "shop," such as it is, might consist of nothing more than a glass case on the wall of a public room, and its stock might be little more than the odd logo-wear T-shirts, sweatshirts, caps, and jackets. Small-ship cruising is just not oriented to the "shop till you drop" crowd. (Though of course, there's still plenty of booty to be had in the ports.)

Ship Shopping Tips

Here's a few tips on the ins and outs of onboard shopping:

- **Shop early:** You're best off visiting the shops early in your cruise to check the prices so you can compare them to those at the ports. Usually items such as liquor, jewelry, and perfume are competitively priced, but you might be able to get a better deal on Kahlua in Mexico, or rum on one of the Caribbean islands that produces the product.
- **Don't shop duty-free for instant gratification:** Duty-free liquor and cigarettes purchased on the ship are not for consumption on the ship. To ensure this, your purchases will be delivered to your cabin at the end of the cruise. If you want a supply of booze in your room, you can buy liquor at port and sneak it back to your room, but you're not supposed to. Be discreet (and if you're caught, don't tell them I told you to do it).
- **Hit the sales:** Keep in mind that all ship shops hold sales, especially toward the latter part of the cruise, including discounted gold-by-the-inch bargains and a "T-Shirt Blowout." These sales will be advertised in the ship's daily bulletin.
- **Mind the shops' open hours:** The shops on the ship are closed in port to encourage people to patronize stores at the port destination. They also close on disembarkation day, so if you have your eye on something, be sure you buy it by the last night of your cruise.
- **Decide you don't like it? Exchange it:** If you buy an item at a ship shop and later decide you don't like it, you might be able to exchange or return it. The shops generally guarantee quality and might also guarantee lowest prices on some items.
- **Shop the private islands:** Cruise lines that operate their own private islands in the Caribbean offer shopping on these islands as well. At Holland America Line's Half Moon Cay, for example, passengers can visit the West Indies Shopping Village and Market, which features contemporary men's and women's fashions, an art gallery with Bahamian artwork, and a straw market.

Art Auctions

Many ships also now offer art auctions, which are fun and entertaining, but not necessarily guaranteed to give you a bargain price. Outside concessionaires run the auctions, with artwork selling for anywhere from $50 to $85,000 or more.

These auctions are held in one of the ship's public rooms and usually feature works by both up-and-coming artists and world-famous names, such as Peter Max, Walt Disney, Salvador Dali, Marc Chagall, and Pablo Picasso. I've seen some really nice pieces at auctions and some deeply awful dreck, but even if you don't bid on a piece, the auctions can be a fun way to pass an afternoon, allowing you to pretend you're a rich heir or heiress taking passage on the high seas, sipping your drink while fine art is paraded by for your appraisal.

If you do bid on a piece, and win, you'll be required to ship your purchase home (for a fee, of course), and it will take a few weeks to arrive. Framing is optional, at an extra charge.

On Princess ships, you can also buy some of the art that's displayed aboard the ship, if something really takes your fancy.

Port Lectures & Shop Promotions

Shops at the ports might have deals with your cruise line to offer promotions on board, such as a giveaway at the cruise director's port lecture. Also, the cruise director might make direct recommendations of shops you should visit. You might even be offered a list of the cruise line's recommended shops.

The cruise lines charge a fee for these shops to be promoted, and as a buyer, you should be aware that these recommended shops might not have the lowest prices. They do, however, generally promise the cruise line they will guarantee the satisfaction of all the line's customers who make purchases there. What that means is that if you buy from one of these recommended shops, and there's a problem with a product (such as a jewelry appraisal that's less than you were promised), you might be able to return it within 30 days for a refund. "Buyer's regret" is not considered an acceptable reason for a refund, however.

Think Before You Buy

Before you buy any particularly large or fragile item, consider how you're going to get the item home. Is it breakable? Will it fit in the overhead compartment of the airplane? How much will it cost to have it shipped?

Also keep in mind that you probably can't return items purchased on your cruise if you later change your mind.

The staff on some ships will also offer recommendations of the best shops in a given port if you ask. And in some cases, you can get real deals by following the crew, who have visited these ports many times and tend to head right to the places where the deals are.

Shopping Shoreside: The Ports of Call

No matter how many shops your ship might have, the selection can't hope to compete with what you'll find at your ports of call, where the whole local economy might, in fact, be built on cruise passengers' dollars. In this section, I clue you in to some of the best buys in the Caribbean and Alaska, and tip you off to the most common scams.

Shopping in the Sun: The Caribbean

The Caribbean is a shopper's paradise, where luxury items are imported from all over the world for your shopping pleasure—leather from Italy, perfume from France, linens from China, emeralds from Colombia, and so on. Cruise passengers can save 10% to 50% on luxury items such as designer watches, jewelry, loose precious stones, perfume, china, porcelain, crystal, high fashion, liquor, cameras, electronics, and imported linens purchased duty-free on the islands and in Mexico. The exact discount depends on the item and where you buy it.

Life Preservers

Keep in mind that no matter how loudly or often anyone shouts the term **duty-free** at you, it still doesn't necessarily mean you'll get the best deal or a guaranteed bargain price—it just means there's no duty added by the country in which you purchase the item.

Such savings are not guaranteed, however, and you can sometimes do just as well buying the items in the U.S.—an exception, of course, being handicraft items and products made on the islands. For that reason, I offer the following list as *popular* buys rather than *best* buys. Keep in mind that many of the following items might also be available at the shops on the ship, where their quality is more likely to be guaranteed.

Popular Buys

Country	Purchases
Antigua	English linens and woolens, local straw work, Antiguan rum, fabrics with hand-printed designs, shell curios, bead necklaces
Aruba	Delft blue pottery, Edam and Gouda cheeses from Holland
Barbados	Cameras, watches, crystal, gold jewelry, bone china, British-made sweaters, liquor, tobacco products

British Virgin Islands	British goods, including china
Cozumel & Playa del Carmen	Handicrafts, Mexican jewelry, Yucatan ceramics, loose stones such as topaz
Curaçao	French perfume, Delft blue items, woven Italian silks, cameras, jewelry, silver, Swiss watches, linens, leather goods, liquor, cheese, lace work
Freeport/Lucaya	African handicrafts, Chinese jade, British china, Swiss watches, Irish linens, Colombian emeralds, straw products
Grand Cayman	Silver, china, crystal, Irish linen, British woolen goods, black-coral jewelry, rare Caymanian stamps
Grenada	Spices, British products
Guadeloupe	Anything French, including perfume, cosmetics, and crystal, as well as straw hats and dolls
Jamaica	Arts and crafts, watches, fine jewelry, crystal, perfume, china, silverware, linens, Italian handbags, cashmere sweaters, liquor (*Note:* There is a 10% general-consumption tax on all items purchased.)
Key West	Straw hats, sportswear, T-shirts, sunglasses, books on Hemingway
Martinique	French luxury imports such as perfume, fashions, Vuitton luggage, Lalique crystal, Limoges china
Nassau	China, crystal, fine linens, jewelry, leather goods, cameras, watches, perfume
St. Barts	Liquor, French perfume, sportswear, crystal, porcelain, watches
St. Croix	Handmade items, jewelry, items for the home
St. Kitts	Local handicrafts including goatskin items, baskets, and coconut shells; clothing and fabrics
St. Lucia	Bone china, jewelry, perfume, watches, liquor, crystal, local pottery and straw items
St. Maarten / St. Martin	Original artwork, jewelry, swim wear, handicrafts
St. Thomas & St. John	Fine art, jewelry, crystal, china, watches, perfume, black coral, handicrafts, leather goods, watches, cameras, fabrics, clothing
San Juan	Handicrafts, artwork, clothing, jewelry, watches, linens, lace work

A NOTE ON PRICES In most cases, you'll find prices in the shops on the islands quoted in U.S. dollars, but you might also find prices quoted in Eastern Caribbean (EC) dollars or, in Mexico, in new pesos. By way of comparison, 1 U.S. dollar generally equals EC$2.70. The Mexican peso has fluctuated so much in recent years that it's best to check its worth close to the time of your trip. If you're hooked into the Internet, one handy place to find currency conversions is CNN's web site at **www.cnn.com/TRAVEL/CURRENCY**.

SCAMS & SHADY DEALINGS There are several schemes to lure travelers at the ports, such as flyers that offer giveaways based on your cabin number (allegedly, if your cabin number is on their list, you win). These are not always legit, so be wary if you're handed a flyer as you get off the ship.

Street vendors in the Caribbean and Mexico offer cheap prices and are willing to haggle (in fact, the prices are usually inflated so that you have to haggle), but their wares come with no verification of authenticity. That silver necklace might really be tin, that shell necklace really plastic. Think before you buy.

Shopping in Bed

A fairly new innovation on some ships is shopping via the ship's interactive TVs. Essentially, it's an oceangoing version of the Shopping Channel, whereby you can purchase items from brand-name stores, such as the Nature Company. The items are then shipped to your home and charged directly to your credit card.

Shopping in the Great Land: Alaska

In Alaska, you'll find some of the same upscale stores selling jewelry and watches as you'll find in the Caribbean, such as Little Switzerland. These shops have basically followed the cruise ships from the Caribbean hoping to scoop up some of this destination's tourism dollars. Also moving in are vendors of cheaper souvenirs. In fact, in some port towns it's hard to find a shopkeeper who's actually a year-round resident, as many come for the summer tourist season only and then scoot back home before it gets cold.

Alaska doesn't offer the shopping bargains that the Caribbean does, but you can still can find some funky items. **Native woodcarvings** are some of the more distinctive items you'll find, but they can often be prohibitively expensive. The same goes for other handmade native items, such as drums, sculptures, baskets, and paintings. There are bargains, though, like the beautiful signed and numbered native print a friend found for $40 in Juneau. Certain other items are most commonly seen in certain towns. Ketchikan, for example, has more **fish art** than you'll find most anywhere else. (And believe me, there's *lots* of fish art in Alaska.) In Juneau, there are Red Dog Saloon items, and Petersburg is a good stop for **Norwegian sweaters** and other woolens.

If your cruise starts or ends in Vancouver, you'll be able to take advantage of the Canadian dollar (worth about two-thirds of the U.S. dollar) to get deals on fashion, art, and other items. Canada charges a stiff goods-and-services tax (GST), but as a tourist you are eligible to have the tax rebated on purchases of $100 or more. You need to take your receipts to a rebate office (there's one at the Hotel Vancouver) or mail them to the Canada Customs department. Ask for details at the shop or your hotel.

SCAMS & SHADY DEALINGS In Alaska, there's a large market in fake Native Alaskan art. In 1995, for example, the *Anchorage Daily News* reported that villages in Bali were turning out Eskimo masks and other carvings using materials from Alaska and designs found in books. There have even been cases in which shopkeepers' assistants were spotted removing "Made in Taiwan" stickers from "art" objects with razor blades.

Before you buy a piece of native art, ask the art dealer for a biography of the artist and whether the artist actually carved the piece (rather than lending his or her name for knock-offs). Most dealers will tell you where a work really comes from if you ask. But you have to ask.

Price should be a tip-off to fakes. It's rare for a work of native art to be priced at less than $500. An elaborate mask, for example, should be priced at $3,000, not $300.

Be particularly weary of soapstone carvings, as most are not made in Alaska.

Two marks are used to identify Alaska products: a Made-in-Alaska polar-bear sticker, which means the item was at least mostly made in the state, and a silver-hand sticker that indicates authentic native art. An absence of the label, however, does not mean the item is not authentic—it might simply mean the artist doesn't like labels.

Chapter 20

Love on the High Seas: Cruising & the Single Man or Woman

In This Chapter

- Tips on the best cruises for singles, whatever your situation
- Best spots on board for doing the singles thing
- The lowdown on gentlemen hosts, singles parties, and flirting with the officers

Taking a cruise hoping to meet Mr. or Ms. Right? Hoping to take a stroll down the promenade deck, dressed in your finest, and see the spouse of your dreams standing alone by the rail, staring soulfully out to sea?

You've been watching *The Love Boat* (or *Titanic*) too much.

Still, it is a fact that cruise ships are inherently romantic places, and it's also a fact that one in four cruise passengers today is single—so, statistically speaking, the odds of meeting other singles works in your favor. Times have changed a bit since Windjammer all but assured in its advertising that travelers would get a "bang" out of their vacation, yet cruising remains a social experience where people, whether single or married, are usually more than willing to make new friends.

Some lines, like Windjammer, offer special singles cruises, where you can literally go cruising while cruising, and most other ships offer singles mixers during the first day of your cruise to let you know who else is in the same boat you are (so to speak). But no matter what ship you're on, there will be plenty of opportunities to meet other singles. The smaller the ship, the fewer the people (and choices), but the even greater chance to mingle.

Rest assured: As a single cruise passenger, you'll never have to sit alone in the dining room (arranged seating will see to that) or explore ports alone (thanks to group shore excursions), and you'll never lack for group activities. Will you meet that special someone? I offer no guarantees. What I will say is that with the moon, the breeze, and the glimmering stars over the ocean, you could choose many worse places to go looking.

Choose the Right Cruise

Knowing which ship attracts which kind of singles will make it more likely you'll find what you're looking for. You can get some hints in the ship reviews in chapters 5, 6, and 7, but here are a few facts to consider:

- **Carnival** tends to attract young singles—the kind who like to work out in the gym.
- **Premier Cruises** goes after single parents.
- **Royal Caribbean** gets singles in the 35-to-50 age range who might have been married before.
- **Holland America** is a good bet for older singles.
- **Windjammer** is for those who want to experience the '60s free-love mentality.

Theme cruises, like those offered by Norwegian Cruise Line, are a particularly good way to meet other single people who share your particular area of interest.

Safety First

Because they provide controlled environments (those who misbehave have nowhere to hide) and because they're heavily staffed, cruise ships have a big safety advantage over land-based singles venues.

And while we're on the subject of safety, condoms are usually available in the ship's gift shop.

Hoping to Meet an Officer?

Again, you have to remember that *The Love Boat* is fiction. On the other hand, it is true that a captain of the *Pacific Princess* met his wife at sea. I've spotted more than a couple of officers in the disco late at night, after their shifts end.

Gentlemen Hosts

Women will always have a dance partner if they pick a ship that has gentlemen hosts. These mostly retired gentlemen travel for free in exchange for being ready, willing, and able to dance with you at the disco and other dance venues. They are not, however, allowed to fraternize.

Where to Hang Out to Meet the Love of Your Life

There are so many people-meeting opportunities on cruise ships that it's almost hard to list them all. You can even start off making new friends with people while you're in line checking in for your cruise. Try an introductory line like "Is this your first time?"

Sea Stories

On *The Love Boat,* Captain Stubing meets and falls in love aboard ship with Emily (Marion Ross) and gets married. According to *Travel Weekly,* real-life *Pacific Princess* Capt. John Crichton also met his wife during a cruise.

Most big ships offer at least one **singles party,** usually on the first night of the cruise, so that singles know right away what the companion options are.

In the **dining room,** there might be a table designated for singles. Ask the maitre d' for advice. If your ship has open seating, of course, you can sit anywhere you want, so if you see someone who perks your interest, ask him or her if you can join them for a meal.

Some crew members will go out of their way to help you meet other singles, most notably the cruise director and social hosts, so don't be afraid to ask for their help. But don't expect them to serve as your personal dating service, either.

Some more great places to meet other singles include:

- **The poolside bar and deck chairs.** "Excuse me, is this seat taken?" is a tried-and-true favorite, as is the ever-popular (and very direct) "Would you mind helping me put this suntan lotion on my back?"
- **The spa and health club.** "Excuse me, could you show me how to use this machine? I can't seem to get it right," is a good one, as is "My God, how do you *bend* like that?"
- **The disco and casino.** Think Travolta for the former, James Bond for the latter.
- **The card room and library** (especially if you're an older single).
- **Sports bars.** "Go Patriots!"
- **Lectures.** Try this: "So, do you think his theory of solar alignment in Mayan architecture holds any water?"

- **Any areas with live music.** Boogie down, baby. Shake your booty.
- **Participatory activities,** such as sports contests. Can you think of anything that promotes free and easy mixing more than pool volleyball? I can't.
- **Deck parties and midnight buffets.** "Isn't that ice sculpture a real work of art?"
- **Shore excursions.** After a long day of climbing up ziggurats or hiking through Alaskan forests, what could be more relaxing than some quiet time in the martini bar? "Would you like to join me?"

You can also create your own singles activity by hosting a party in your cabin or putting together a group for a private tour excursion. ("So, what are you doing tomorrow?")

Just remember if you get lucky that the ship's lifeboats are only used as mating venues in the movies, and that the promenade deck is a public place.

Be Prepared & Be Impressive

One way to impress your fellow single passengers is with your knowledge. Read about a port of call in advance and share the facts you've learned on the subject. Become a 2-minute expert on constellations or glaciers, or learn about your destination's wildlife or geography, then position yourself on deck to point out the sights.

Ain't Misbehavin'

On some big ships, it might be possible to get lost in the crowd, but then again, if you burn bridges, you might just run into that person again. All told, it's best to behave. And if someone says no, they mean no.

One-Stop Shopping

Like the proprietors of a small-town general store, cruise lines have stocked their shops with all the provisions you'll need for romance at sea.

- If you've got a hot date and nothing to wear, the shops keep a selection of formal wear on hand. It ain't cheap, but it might be worth it.
- If you've got a *really* hot date and nothing to, um, wear, the shops also stock condoms.
- If you fall in love, you might be able to find engagement rings for sale in the onboard shops, and you certainly will at the ports of call.

Ahoy, Mateys!

If you do meet someone you like, ask for his or her cabin number so you can give a call.

And remember, there's nothing more romantic than having room service deliver champagne to your cabin.

Pick-Up Lines from Hell

Earlier in this chapter, I gave you some nice subtle pick-up (or getting-to-know-you) lines, but if you really want to hit someone over the head, here's a few I've gleaned from the Internet joke-sharing contingent (and updated with a cruise angle, of course):

- "I might not be the best-looking guy [gal] on this ship, but I'm the only one talking to you."
- "If you're going to regret this in the morning, we can skip breakfast and sleep until the afternoon."
- "Excuse me, do you have your cabin number? I seem to have lost mine."
- "I'm new on this ship. Could I have directions to your cabin?"
- "I lost my cabin. Can I borrow yours?"
- "Do you have $6.95 [or whatever the going ship-to-shore phone rate is]? My mom told me to call if I met the gal [or guy] of my dreams."

Chapter 21

But What's the Kid Gonna Do?: Activities for Children & Teens

In This Chapter

- Information on kids' and teens' programs—what they are, what they involve, and where to find them
- Finding baby-sitting on board
- Tips on safety
- The best ships for kids and teens

Cruise lines have recognized as much as any other vacation providers that baby boomers like to bring the kids along on vacation, and that some, in fact, won't leave home without them. The lines have also been smart enough to realize that parents, while they want to keep their kids happy and entertained, also want a chance to relax and unwind—in other words, they want the perfect family vacation.

The industry has responded to the family market by building ships that have great facilities for kids, from toddlers to teens, as well as supervised and well-organized day and evening programs designed to keep the kiddies occupied and the parents free to do their own thing. The lines are investing big bucks in these programs, with part of the philosophy being that the young cruisers of today will be the cruisers of tomorrow.

The newer ships of the mass market and premium brands—Carnival, Royal Caribbean, Celebrity, and Princess included—offer particularly extensive facilities for kids of all ages. Selections include playrooms, ball jumps, splash pools, teen centers, kiddy theaters, climbing apparatus, ice cream parlors, and video arcades. Even some luxury operators such as Cunard and Crystal offer extensive children's programs on a seasonal basis and special facilities for the younger set.

The response of family travelers has echoed *Field of Dreams:* If you build it, we will come. Carnival alone said it expects more than 160,000 kids (ages 2 to 17) on its ships in 1998.

But that's not to say that all ships are kid-friendly. There are some ships where kids are welcomed, but only if they are seen and not heard. There are other ships where kids are not welcome at all (see "The Best of the Crop," later in this chapter, to get information on particular ships).

Kid-Friendly Cruise Lines

What are the best cruise lines for kids? Based on the quality of their supervised children's programs and on special onboard play areas and facilities, the rug-rat cruise contenders are:

- Carnival
- Celebrity
- Costa
- Disney
- Holland America
- Norwegian Cruise Line
- Premier
- Princess
- Royal Caribbean

Parents will find plenty of choices, though, when it comes to family-friendly ships, and at various price levels (budget brands tend to offer kids' programs, but not always with separate facilities). Children's activities are all included in the cruise fare, except for baby-sitting, shore excursions, and occasional other extras, and they often go beyond the standard arts and crafts and movies-on-video offerings parents might expect. Many ships offer the kinds of unique experiences that become cherished vacation memories.

What's There to Do?

Children's programs on ships generally divide the kids into categories based on age, sort of like at summer camp, so 12-year-olds won't find themselves with 6-year-olds, and 6-year-olds won't be stuck with a bunch of babies. The best programs are run by specially trained youth counselors.

Kid-UNfriendly Cruise Lines

Some lines actively discourage you from bringing your kids along, while others have actual rules against it. **American Canadian Caribbean Line** permits no kids under 10; **Club Med** permits no kids under 12; and **Silversea** and **Seabourn** are just too adult for any kid to have any fun at all aboard their ships. I wouldn't recommend these lines for kids, especially young kids.

The programs start at age 2 or 3. Ships really aren't equipped to deal with infants, and Princess, for one, doesn't even allow infants under 12 months on board. Some programs require toddlers to be potty-trained.

On various lines, kids can cuddle with such big-name cartoon favorites as Mickey Mouse and Bugs Bunny, sports-loving kids can learn to snorkel and even meet well-known sports heroes, and computer geeks can hone their skills and even go online using services that are just starting to be introduced on ships.

Smooth Sailing

Children not traveling with both parents, even if the parents are divorced, must have a letter from both parents saying it's okay for them to leave the country.

Kids can also learn a language, take science classes and dance lessons, get photography tips, tour the bridge, and learn about the inner workings of the ship. And on some ships, they can even get a chance to perform in a circus or talent show.

Both American Hawaii (in Hawaii) and Holland America (in Alaska) even offer special shore excursions for youngsters so they can learn, at their level, about the destinations they are visiting. Several lines also offer special activities for kids on their private islands.

At night, ships offer pizza parties, movies, and other entertainment, timed to give parents a chance to dine alone or take in a show.

Baby-Sitting

Most ships offer private baby-sitting in your cabin, and some even guarantee that sitters will be available. Rates are generally about $10 an hour for 2 children, and there might be a 4-hour minimum. Group baby-sitting might also be offered, usually at a rate of about $6 an hour for 2 kids.

What to Ask when Looking for a Family Cruise

Since no two ships are created equal, parents are well advised to do some homework to find the ship that best matches their needs and those of their children.

Is the Program Year-Round or Seasonal?

The most important thing to ascertain is whether the children's program operates year-round, or at the least, whether it will it be in operation during the period when you want to cruise. Some programs operate only during the summer and holiday periods, which is when most families travel, and on some ships, programs for a specific age category might operate only if there are 15 or more kids of that age on the cruise. Nothing is more frustrating than thinking your ship will have a family program for your kids and finding otherwise once you get on board.

During What Hours Is the Program in Operation?

You will also want to know what hours the program operates. Some programs do not run during days at port. This means that if you want to take a shore excursion, you'll have to bring along the kids—and doing so can be pricey. Most lines do not offer discounts on shore excursions for kids.

Some lines also close their children's programs at meal times to encourage families to dine together.

Are There Special Programs for Teens?

If you have a teen, you'll also want to make sure there's a special program for that age group, even if your teen is reluctant to participate in an organized activity. Ships that do have teen programs offer dances, parties, and other opportunities for teens to stay up late with their peers and away from adult crowds—a bonus for all concerned.

Price & Space Considerations

Above and beyond all that, you'll want to consider how good a deal you can get as a family on price and how cramped you're going to be in the cabin. It's a pretty safe bet the answer to the latter will be "very," but don't worry: None of you will probably spend much time in the cabin anyway. But if this is an area of concern, and you have the bucks, you might look at what kind of deal you can get on two cabins.

Safety Concerns

Obviously, with the big blue sea below, safety is going to be on the mind of every cruising parent.

Although children are limited in the amount of trouble they can get into on a ship, given that it's a confined environment, parents still need to instill some basic safety rules into their children before setting sail. The biggest rule is, of course, **don't lean on the railings of open decks and balconies** (most railings are high enough to not be of major concern for nonclimbing little kids, but it's best to just make a strict rule about it).

Parents should be sure their children **understand the information provided in the onboard safety drill,** and check to be sure that the cabin is equipped with appropriately sized life jackets.

Parents should also have their children **learn their cabin and deck numbers** in case they become separated from them during the voyage.

And Parents Should Remember . . .

Parents should keep in mind that most of the children's programs are designed more so kids can come and go than as day care. The youth counselors might assume older kids can leave the program whenever they want. If this is a problem for you, and you have concerns about your child wandering around the ship unsupervised, make your position clear.

On most ships, parents are responsible for their children's safety in swimming-pool areas. Most children's programs do not take kids to the swimming pool for safety reasons, but they might offer supervised time in a splash pool.

Prompt and capable health care is available on cruise ships, but parents should bring along any items they think they will need, such as prescription medications, special formulas, and even a first-aid kit, including a thermometer.

Teens particularly enjoy the freedom that being on a ship presents. Most parents will let them do their thing on their own, but these pre-adults should be warned that the casino is off limits. The ship might also have a policy limiting their visiting the spa, gym, disco, and/or certain bars and nightclubs.

The Best of the Crop

The best lines for family travelers offer not only great supervised programs for kids, but also special play areas and facilities.

Carnival Cruise Lines Carnival carries more families than anyone in the industry, and it shows. It has the largest staff of trained counselors of any line, and its Camp Carnival program runs on a year-round basis.

Recognizing the popularity of its kids' offerings, Carnival added a second playroom on its fantasy-class vessels (*Ecstasy, Fantasy, Fascination, Imagination, Inspiration, Sensation,* and new for 1998, the *Paradise* and *Elation*), and introduced a new 2-level, indoor/outdoor 1,300-square-foot playroom on the Carnival *Destiny.* The *Elation* and *Paradise* not only offer expanded kids' play areas and expanded teens' programs but also a high-tech Virtual World video game center. The *Holiday* has also been outfitted with a $1 million entertainment center with virtual-reality games and 60 state-of-the-art video and arcade games.

Camp Carnival divides its activities groups into Toddlers, ages 2 to 4 (offered on all ships except the *Tropicale*); Intermediates, ages 5 to 8; Juniors, ages 9 to 12; and Teens, ages 13 to 17 (the newer ships all have teen clubs). Private baby-sitting is offered.

Cabins suitable for families—featuring twin beds and one or two upper berths—are available on most of the line's ships. Carnival also has roll-away beds and cribs available.

Onboard restaurants offer children's menus, and kids can get hot dogs and ice cream at informal eateries.

Celebrity Cruises This is the line for children who are really into computers. The line's newest ships—the *Century, Galaxy,* and *Mercury*—offer an array of Sony computers and game facilities for both kids and grown-ups.

The line's children's program is offered on summer and seasonal sailings or whenever more than 12 children are on board, and the program is supervised by a youth staff.

The kids are divided into four age categories. The Ship Mates program, for kids ages 3 to 6, offers cartoons, face painting, jungle gym, snowflake fun, and music. Celebrity Cadets, for children 7 to 10, features T-shirt painting, relay races, movies, and line-dancing lessons. Ensigns, for children 11 to 13, and Teens, for those 14 to 17, include activities such as karaoke, stargazing, basketball, scavenger hunts, and disco dancing. Computer classes, Junior Olympics, magic lessons, and a midnight film festival are sometimes offered as well.

The Ship Mates Fun Factory playroom on the ships features giant animal sculptures for the younger set to climb on. The *Mercury* also has a ball pit for kids to jump in.

Group baby-sitting is available on Celebrity ships from 10pm to 1am every night for kids ages 3 and older.

Children can eat together at the Celebrity Breakfast Club, and kids' menus are available at dinner.

Many cabins on Celebrity ships can hold three or four passengers, and cribs are available.

Costa Cruise Lines The Costa Kids Club offers programs for kids 3 to 12, and the Costa Teens club is for kids 13 to 17, depending on the number of teens on board.

There is one full-time youth counselor on each ship year-round, as well as additional counselors in the summer, during holidays, and when more than 12 children are on board. Nintendo competitions, bridge and galley tours, Italian lessons, and "Coke-tail" parties are featured offerings. The *CostaVictoria* has a teen center with a disco floor and video games.

Group baby-sitting is available for children 3 and older on most cruises.

Some cabins on Costa ships can accommodate up to two additional passengers.

Pizza and Italian ice cream are available on the ships. There is no set children's menu.

Disney Cruise Line Family cruising gets a big push in summer 1998 with the arrival of the *Disney Magic* and, soon after, with the launch of its twin, the *Disney Wonder.* Both ships will offer extensive programs designed to appeal to specific ages and interests. They'll also both feature a whopping 15,000 square feet of dedicated children's space (nearly an entire deck), with playrooms, various high-tech offerings, a designated teen club, a children's pool area, and a special family lounge.

Kids on Disney ships run into costumed Disney characters, of course, and they are entertained by more children's counselors than on any other ship—presumably because the line expects to host more kids than other ships.

Kids are divided into 3 categories: 3 to 8, 9 to 12, and teens. The younger kids can explore a pirate-themed play space, the 9- to 12-year-olds are offered a more high-tech environment with video games and computers with Internet access, and teens can enjoy their own coffee bar and video arcade. Parents and children are given linked beepers so they can locate each other at any time.

The line offers evening group baby-sitting as well as private baby-sitting.

Budding scientists can visit the "Bill Nye the Science Guy" sea-life lab on Disney's private island, Castaway Cay, where a variety of other kids-oriented activities are also offered.

The line's cabins all sleep three and many can sleep six.

Disney, of course, also combines its cruises with a visit to Disney World, to every child's delight.

Holland America Line Club HAL is the name of this line's year-round kids program, which features not only supervised activities on board, but special kids' shore excursions at some ports as well.

The newer Holland America vessels have special children's facilities including playrooms, video-game areas, and wading pools. The *Rotterdam* also has a teen disco.

Club HAL divides kids into 3 age groups: 5 to 8, 9 to 12, and teens.

Holland America dining rooms offer kiddy menus, with families encouraged to eat together. Baby-sitting is also offered.

Cabins that can accommodate three and four passengers on a foldaway sofa bed are available. Cribs are limited, so parents with infants are advised to reserve a crib when booking their cruise.

Norwegian Cruise Line Family attractions on this line's ships include Circus at Sea, a program that turns the kids into circus performers. Kids are also offered opportunities to visit the bridge and have a "Coke-tail" with the captain. Some theme cruises include autograph-signing sessions with professional athletes.

The children's program, designed for children ages 3 to 17, is supervised by trained youth counselors. A Kids Crew program for children ages 3 to 5 is available year-round only on the *Norway.* On the other vessels, the program for younger kids is available during summer months and on major holidays, with limited hours. Programs for the older kids are offered on all the ships, year-round.

The *Norwegian Wind, Norwegian Dream,* and *Norwegian Star* all have a playroom, a video arcade, and a teen activity center.

The *Norway* and *Norwegian Sea* feature video games and SEGA games. The *Leeward* also has a playroom where games and activities are offered.

The line puts out a daily bulletin just for kids, so they can keep track of all the activities.

The line guarantees that baby-sitters will be available from noon to 2am.

Cabins that can accommodate a third or fourth passenger are available on all the ships. Deluxe suites that can sleep up to six passengers are available on the *Norwegian Dream* and *Norwegian Wind.*

Premier Cruises Before there was Disney, there was *The Big Red Boat,* an industry innovator in the area of family cruising. The ship continues to offer one of the industry's most extensive kids' programs on a ship that's virtually a big, floating kids' playground. And it offers 3- and 4-day cruises to The Bahamas, which can be combined with a visit to an Orlando-area theme park to make a 1-week package—a good choice for families who have never cruised before with children and don't want to risk a full 7 days at sea. You can get your feet wet, so to speak.

Even with the Premier name now on six ships, as part of various corporate mergers and acquisitions, family cruising continues to be an area of focus for the line. All the ships offer activities year-round, with trained youth counselors, and the *SeaBreeze* and *OceanBreeze* have joined *The Big Red Boat* in hosting a bunch of Looney Tunes characters on every sailing. Kids can pal around with Bugs Bunny, the Tasmanian Devil, Sylvester, Tweety Bird, and Yosemite Sam, and for an extra fee, you can even have the characters visit your kids' cabin to tuck them into bed.

On *The Big Red Boat,* the kids' program is divided into 5 age levels: First Mates for ages 2 to 4, Kids Call for ages 5 to 7, Starcruisers for ages 8 to 10, Navigators for ages 11 to 13, and Wave Runners for ages 14 to 17.

The activities are led by trained youth counselors and are offered from early morning until late at night. Private baby-sitting is not available, but children ages 2 to 12 can spend a few hours or even stay overnight (from 10pm to 9am) in the Pluto's Playhouse area.

Cabins on *The Big Red Boat* accommodate two to five passengers with upper berths and sofas that convert to beds.

Kids' menus are available aboard all the line's ships.

On the line's other ships, the kids' program is divided into 2 age groups: a Youth program for 3- to 8-year-olds, and a Junior Cruisers program for 9- to 15-year-olds, with age-appropriate activities. Cabins on these ships accommodate 2 to 5 passengers.

Princess Cruises Princess ships built since 1990 (the *Crown Princess, Regal Princess, Dawn Princess, Sun Princess,* and upcoming *Sea Princess, Ocean Princess,* and *Grand Princess*) all offer entertainment centers for children, the most extensive being on the line's grand-class ships, the *Sun Princess, Dawn Princess,* and upcoming *Sea Princess, Ocean Princess,* and *Grand Princess.* The *Grand Princess,* which debuted in May as the largest ship afloat, has not only a video-game center and teens-only disco (also offered on the ships listed earlier) but also a whirlpool spa and sundeck area just for teens. Teens also have access to a virtual-reality center and video studio.

Well-trained youth counselors lead Love Boat Kids program activities year-round for 2- to 17-year-olds on the line's newer ships as well as on Princess' private island, Princess Cay. Programs are offered on the other ships when at least 15 kids are aboard.

For younger kids, facilities include a Fun Zone with a splash pool, ball jump, fairy-tale castle, and life-size doll's house.

On the older *Sky Princess* there are youth centers and teen centers with a video arcade, arts-and-crafts center, game tables, and kiddy pool. And the *Regal Princess* and *Crown Princess* also offer facilities for kids.

On Princess ships, children are encouraged to dine with their parents. Group baby-sitting is available on some ships.

The ships offer poolside grills, with popular fare such as hot dogs and hamburgers.

Many cabins can accommodate three and four passengers in close quarters.

Royal Caribbean International The Royal Caribbean Adventure Ocean program is designed for kids ages 3 to 17 and is one of the best programs offered on the high seas.

The well-established program divides kids into Aquanauts, 3 to 5 years; Explorers, 6 to 8 years; Voyagers, 9 to 12 years; and Navigators, 13 to 17 years. The line's children's offerings are available year-round on all the line's ships (the *Song of America* does not have a program for 3- to 5-year-olds).

Kids receive their own daily-activities calendar in the cabin to keep track of the goings-on. Activities offered include golf putting, midnight basketball, special shore tours, dance classes, pizza parties, and arts and crafts. Mad Science shows are offered during summers and holidays, which teach children about science by featuring such popular fare as slime and rockets.

The line's children's facilities, which vary from ship to ship, are extensive, featuring children's playrooms and teen discos and video arcades. Some of the ships even have special teen nightclubs.

Smooth Sailing

Royal Caribbean offers a special deal for which you pay $15 in advance for your kids to drink all the soda they want during the cruise, instead of paying $1.25 each time they're thirsty. You pay at the purser's office when you first get on board.

Group baby-sitting is offered for children who are 3 or older and are potty-trained.

Some cabins can hold third or fourth passengers in upper berths, and some six-person family suites also are available.

Children eat with their families or at special group meals. Kids' menus are available.

Part 6

Land! I See Land!: Visiting the Ports of Call

If shipboard life is your chance at vacation nirvana, the ports of call are your chance to see the world, albeit in quick snippets.

The opportunity to visit a variety of exotic destinations is a big part of the cruise experience. Instead of staying at a land-based resort in one spot, your floating resort takes you to many. In the Caribbean, ships even stop at places you can't get to any other way, like the private islands in the Bahamas that some cruise lines operate. And in Alaska, they take you to places that are just plain hard to get to on your own, like Juneau, the only U.S. capital that can't be reached by car.

Cruise lines carefully arrange their itineraries to visit places that offer a little something for everyone, whether your thing is bar-hopping, museum-hopping, or not hopping at all. At the ports of call, you can learn a little something about the destination's culture and history, eat interesting foods, view and explore the location's natural beauty, and enjoy sports activities—and you'll have the opportunity to shop to your heart's delight.

In chapter 22, I'll give you a brief rundown of the way cruise ships do the port thing, and in chapters 23 to 25, I'll review the ports of call both to help you pick a cruise that stops at places you find interesting and to help you decide how to spend your time in the ports once you arrive.

Chapter 22

Hitting the Beach: The Port Scene

In This Chapter

- The scoop on shore excursions
- Doing the port scene on your own
- What to bring with you
- Tips and essentials for a safe and happy port experience

When the ship gets into port, you have three choices: Go on a shore excursion organized by the cruise line, go it alone, or, if you just want to relax, stay on the ship. The shore excursions are designed to help you make the most of your limited time at each port of call, to get you to the top museums and other attractions, and to make sure you get back to the ship on time. But make no mistake about it: Shore excursions are also a money-making area for the cruise line, and the offerings can add a hefty sum to your vacation costs. Whether you choose to take a prearranged sightseeing trip is a matter of both personal preference and pocketbook concerns.

Of course, you are in no way required to get off the ship at every port of call. The ship's restaurants remain open (even if you do get off, you can come back to eat), activities are offered (but usually on a limited basis), and you always have the option of just sitting and relaxing.

The What, When & Where of Shore Excursions

Shore excursions typically (but not always) involve buses and lots of people. There's a guide on each bus, and the excursion price includes admission to all the attractions and sometimes a meal, a dance, or a musical performance.

The commentary is sometimes hokey and other times quite educational, and the tours usually involve at least one obligatory stop at a souvenir stand—especially in the Caribbean. The guide will usually expect a tip (how much is at your discretion, but I usually give about 10% of the cost of the trip).

Pros & Cons

In some ports, it's both cheaper and more fun to explore on your own, and exploring on foot might be the best way to see the sights anyway. Plus, this way you can at least *try* to steer clear of the crowds. However, in ports where there's not much within walking distance of the docks and it's difficult to find a cab or other transportation, the cruise line's program might be your best and most cost-effective option.

Another area in which shore excursions are really worth the money is **sports and adventure offerings,** such as kayaking, biking, golf, fishing, snorkeling, and scuba diving; and in **helicopter and flightseeing tours.** These usually involve small groups of passengers, and by booking through the cruise line, you save having to make advance reservations on your own (these offerings also are available to land-based vacationers and may sell out). You also have the advantage of vendors who have been screened by the cruise line. By booking the ship's package, you should be able to avoid going aloft with Mad Dog Mike and his Barely Flying Machine or diving with Dave "The Shiv" Jackson. The extra few bucks you pay will be worth it.

What's It Cost?

The organized shore excursions usually range in price from about $15 for an hour-long bus tour to more than $250, per person, for an elaborate offering such as helicopter sightseeing.

Ahoy, Mateys!

You might be in port long enough to book more than one excursion option, and you might very well find that you want to take a prearranged shore excursion at one port and go it on your own at the next. Be flexible!

Do Your Homework

The best way to decide which shore excursions you want to take is to do some research on a particular port city in advance of your trip. The cruise line will probably send you a description of the shore excursions offered by your ship with your cruise documents. Review this information carefully.

In chapters 23 and 24, I offer information on the major ports in the Caribbean and Alaska, detailing the typical shore-excursion offerings as well as top sights and transportation available at the ports to help you decide what to do at each stop. In chapter 25, "Cruising Around: Other Ports of Call," I detail the ports and regions that are sailed on cruises to Bermuda, Central America, and some more uncommon destinations. For additional research before your trip, I suggest you consult one of the comprehensive Frommer's guides for the region in which you'll be traveling.

Decide what you want to see, if anything, at each port, calculate admission and transportation costs, and compare this to what the cruise line offers in its shore-excursions brochure.

Making the Shore Excursion Decision

When making the decision about whether to book a shore excursion or go it on your own, consider the following:

- What's within walking distance of the ship and what's not?
- How easy is it to find a cab, and how reliable are they if you find one?
- Am I the type of person who minds seeing the sights on buses and with crowds?
- How much does it cost to get in to see the attractions?
- Are reservations required?
- Are there things I want to see that are not on the organized tours? Will I still have time to see them if I take the tour?

Opting for the Excursion & Signing Up

If you do choose to take a shore excursion, look for the order form. There will probably be one in your cabin when you first arrive at the ship; if not, you can get one at the purser's desk or at the shore-excursions lecture offered on the first day of your cruise. (See "Expedition Time!: Choosing Your Shore Excursions," in chapter 13, "Sittin' on the Dock of the Bay.")

Most cruise lines do not allow you to book shore excursions in advance of arriving at the ship. An advantage of this is that you can ask questions of the ship's tour staff before you make your decision (keeping in mind, of course, that their role is to get you to buy the ship's tours).

Remember, the most popular excursions sell out fast. For that reason, you're best off booking your shore excursions the first or second day of your cruise.

To make your reservation, check off the appropriate places on the shore-excursions order form, sign the form (being sure to include your cabin number), and drop it off as directed, probably at the ship's shore-excursion desk or the purser's office. Your account is charged, and tickets are sent to your cabin before your first scheduled tour. The tickets include information on where and when to meet for the tour. Carefully note the time: If you're not at the right place at the right time, the tour may very well leave without you.

Debark, Debarking, Debarked: Getting off the Ship

When the ship arrives at the port, it will either dock at the pier or anchor slightly offshore. You might think that in the former case, you can walk right off the ship as soon as it arrives at port. Well, you can't. Before the gangway is opened to the public, clearance must be given by local authorities and lots of papers must be signed, a process that can take as long as 2 hours. Don't bother to go down to the gangway until you hear an announcement saying the ship has been cleared.

A Tender Moment

If your ship anchors instead of docking, you will go ashore in a small boat called a **launch** or **tender.** It usually takes about 5 to 15 minutes to get to shore on the boats, and the ride can be quite choppy. If you suffer from seasickness, you might want to sit near an open area on the tender.

Getting on the tender might require a helping hand from the crew members assigned to that task. The small boat ties up next to the cruise ship, and the waves might keep the tender swaying, sometimes requiring passengers to jump a bit to get on board. Travelers with disabilities should alert the crew in advance of going ashore, as they will need special assistance getting on and off the tender.

Before you go down to the tender, you will be required to gather in a public place, usually a lounge, where you will be given a boarding number. Those on shore excursions are given priority disembarkation. If you're not on an excursion, getting to the lounge early will assure you of a quicker tender assignment, but also of a long wait. You might be better off waiting an hour and spending your time doing something more enjoyable.

The tenders will operate all day, so you can return to the ship at any time (including, if you choose, for lunch). It might sound silly, but when boarding a tender for your return, be sure that you are on the tender for *your* ship. Boats from several anchored ships might be departing at the same time, and it can get confusing.

Smooth Sailing

Before you reboard from your port of call, you might want to use the phones at the docks to call home. It'll be much cheaper than making the call from the ship.

Shoreside Essentials

You must bring your ship **boarding pass** and/or **shipboard ID** with you when you disembark or you will have trouble getting back on board. And also don't forget to bring some cash—although your ship operates on a cashless system, the ports do not (although credit cards are widely accepted at stores and restaurants). However, don't bring too much cash, as pickpockets can be a problem in some locations. Remember to keep any valuables you leave on the ship in a safe.

At beach destinations, your ship might have **beach towels** available to borrow as you leave the ship. **Bottled water** might also be for sale. You may want to buy a bottle (or bring one from your cabin), particularly if you're going into an area where the quality of the drinking water might be questionable. You might not be able to find a recognizable brand of bottled water for sale once you're on land.

Doing the Ports on Your Own

Here are a few important points if you are exploring on your own:

- Plan out carefully what you want to see and approximately how long it will take you to see it. The shore-excursions people and cruise director can help in this regard.
- If you want to do an activity such as golf, tennis, scuba diving, kayaking, horseback riding, or fishing and don't want to book it through the ship, consult with the shore-excursions staff or cruise director as to whether you will need reservations. Remember, the same facilities and offerings might be full from people on land-based vacations as well as from passengers who booked through your ship and other cruise ships.
- If you want to eat at a particular restaurant, you might want to make a reservation in advance or when you first arrive at the dock.
- Don't accept a ride in a taxi that's not marked. Joe, who says he'll show you the best of the island, might provide a perfectly good tour, but you never know. Just because you're on vacation doesn't mean you want to go on vacation from safety and sensibility.
- You might want to try the local cuisine (in fact, I encourage you to do so), but it's a good rule of thumb to eat in restaurants rather than to grab items from stands on the street. And if you're not sure about the tap water, don't drink it (and remember to avoid ice, as well).
- If you go to the beach for the day, arrange for the cab driver who brings you there to also pick you up.
- Consider splitting the cost of a cab with some other folks on your ship.
- Get back to the ship on time.

Hold the Boat!

Cruise lines are very strict about sailing times. These are posted both in the daily bulletin that's delivered to your room and at the gangway. You are required to be back at the dock at least a half hour before the ship's scheduled departure—otherwise, it's possible for you to miss the boat. Shore excursions are an exception. If they run late, the ship accepts responsibility and won't leave without those passengers. If you're on your own, however, you're on your own, and you could get stuck.

If you do miss the boat, immediately contact the cruise line representative at the port. You'll probably be able to catch your ship at the next port of call, but you'll have to pay your own way to get there.

Chapter 23

The Ports of Call: The Caribbean & Mexico

In This Chapter

- The best attractions, shopping, and fun at 21 Caribbean ports
- Tips on the best shore excursions in each port
- The lowdown on the cruise line's private islands
- Which cruise lines go where

There's a good reason why the Caribbean is the number one cruise destination in the world: The region is a sun-lover's paradise, and that sun is nearly always shining. The Caribbean's islands boast white-sand beaches, swaying palms, and colorful tropical birds, as well as rain forests, waterfalls, rivers, mountains, lush gardens, and even volcanoes. Add to that the region's clear turquoise-blue waters, plentiful with marine life, and you have a place where beach lovers, scuba divers, and watersports enthusiasts will never be disappointed.

The region has an intriguing history that will delight history buffs, with reminders left by early native cultures, explorers (including Christopher Columbus), shipwrecked sailors, conquering navies, and pirates. There are museums, forts, ancient ruins, historic homes, churches and synagogues, and since several islands are either colonies or are/were otherwise attached to European nations, you might even find touches of Britain, France, Holland, Sweden, or Spain.

Shoppers will find the Caribbean a paradise, with duty-free opportunities galore and options ranging from handicrafts at local markets to world-class jewelry offerings in glitzy showrooms.

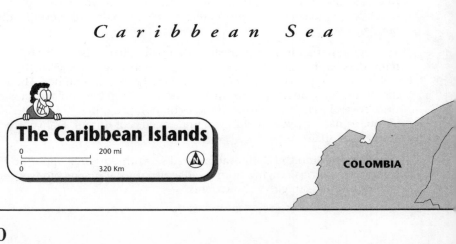

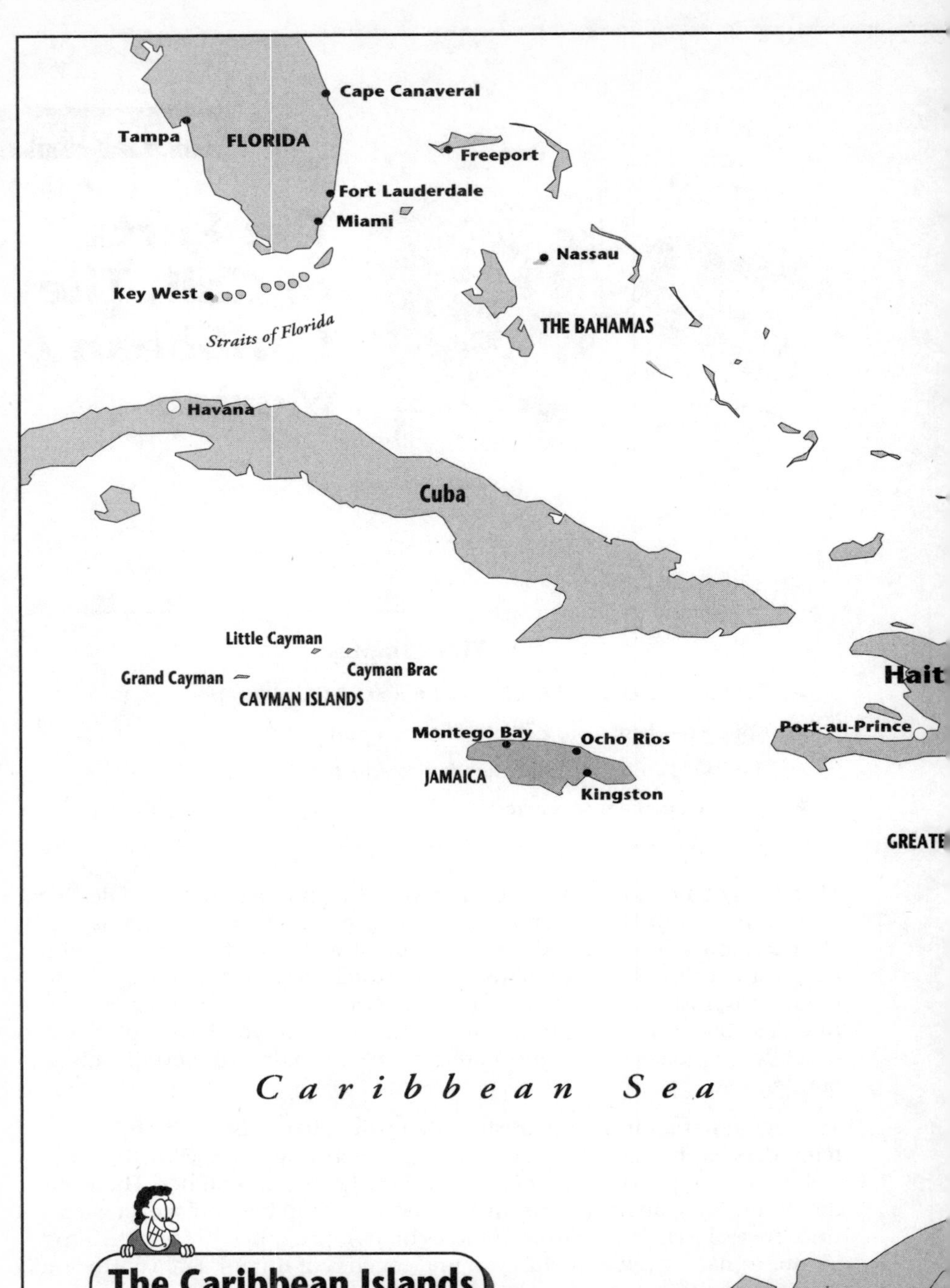
Cape Canaveral
Tampa
FLORIDA
Freeport
Fort Lauderdale
Miami
Nassau
Key West
Straits of Florida
THE BAHAMAS
Havana
Cuba
Little Cayman
Cayman Brac
Grand Cayman
CAYMAN ISLANDS
Hait
Port-au-Prince
Montego Bay
Ocho Rios
JAMAICA
Kingston
GREATE
Caribbean Sea
The Caribbean Islands
0
200 mi
0
320 Km
N
COLOMBIA

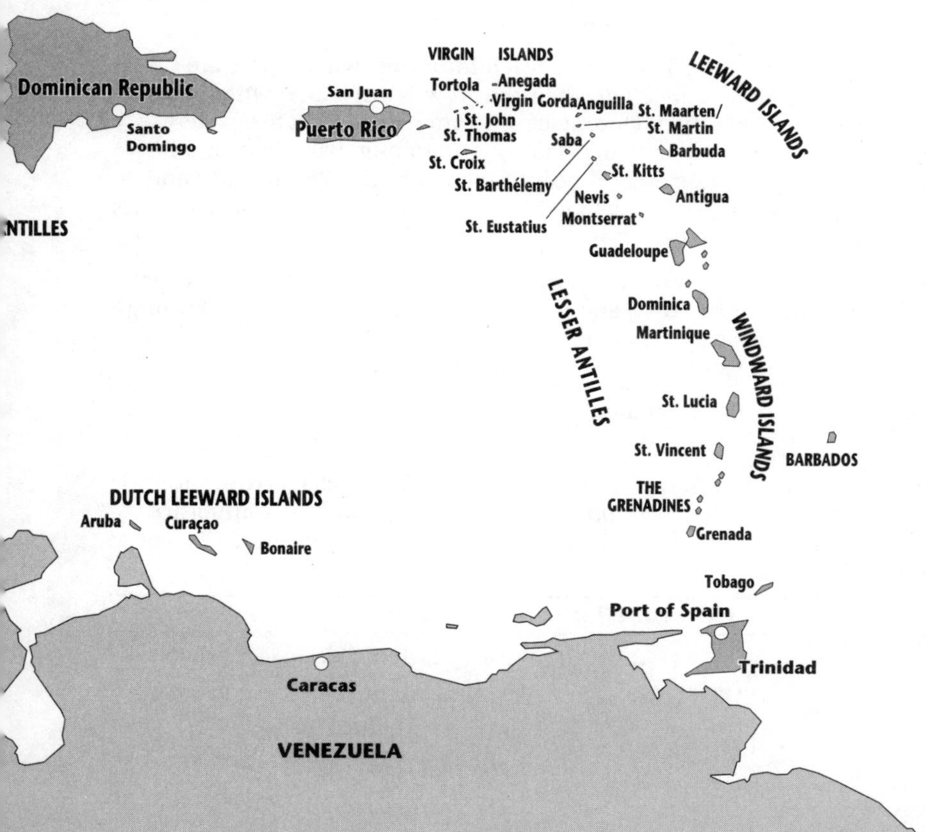
Atlantic
Ocean
TURKS AND CAICOS ISLANDS
Dominican Republic
Santo
Domingo
NTILLES
San Juan
Puerto Rico
VIRGIN ISLANDS
Tortola
Anegada
Virgin Gorda
St. John
St. Thomas
St. Croix
Anguilla
St. Maarten/
St. Martin
Saba
Barbuda
St. Kitts
St. Barthélemy
Nevis
Antigua
Montserrat
St. Eustatius
LEEWARD ISLANDS
Guadeloupe
Dominica
Martinique
LESSER ANTILLES
WINDWARD ISLANDS
St. Lucia
St. Vincent
BARBADOS
THE
GRENADINES
Grenada
Tobago
Port of Spain
Trinidad
DUTCH LEEWARD ISLANDS
Aruba
Curaçao
Bonaire
Caracas
VENEZUELA

And there are plenty of enticements on the various islands for golfers and gamblers as well.

On many of the islands, you can hit the major sightseeing attractions pretty easily on your own. If nature is your thing, you'll want to get out of the crowded tourist meccas that some of the ports have become, and I'll offer transportation suggestions to help you do that.

In some cases, booking a shore excursion offered by the cruise line is your best bet. I suggest you book active tours such as snorkeling, scuba diving, and sportfishing through the cruise line to ensure that space is available and that you're dealing with a reputable vendor. The same goes for golf and tennis.

The best attractions and other offerings at 21 Caribbean ports are featured in this chapter. Prices are approximate and based on 1998 rates.

Psst, Buddy—Wanna Buy an Island?

Several cruise lines operate their own Bahamas islands or other private beaches—fantasy places where you can play Gilligan, albeit with hundreds or thousands of other Skippers, Professors, and Mary Anns.

Ships usually spend a full day at these beach locations, where there are extensive facilities that come alive when the crowds arrive and where guests can enjoy activities aplenty, including beach games and, for a fee, water-sports offerings such as water-skiing, sailing, parasailing, banana-boat and paddleboat rides, and snorkeling in beautiful coral heads. Beach walks and special activities also might be included for kids. And, in some cases, facilities include a playground.

In the center of it all, calypso bands play, bartenders shake drinks, chefs prepare barbecues and other feasts, and vendors sell items like tropical clothing and beach goods. The atmosphere is that of a big beach party; the operative words are "Hot, Hot, Hot!"

Some of the settings also offer a quieter beach you can reach by walking or taking a tram.

The cruise lines spend millions to maintain the private-beach settings to make sure you have a chance to put your feet in the clear-blue Caribbean water away from local crowds and land-locked vacationers in more of a controlled environment.

The Cruise Lines & Their Islands

Celebrity	Private beach in Dominican Republic
Costa	Private beach in Dominican Republic
Disney	Disney's Castaway Cay
Holland America	Half Moon Cay
Norwegian	Great Stirrup Cay

Premier	Salt Cay
Princess	Princess Cays
Royal Caribbean	CocoCay

Norwegian Cruise Line started the trend in 1977, purchasing a tropical island called **Great Stirrup Cay** (pronounced *key*), an uninhabited 2.5-by-1.5 mile stretch located about 120 nautical miles east of Fort Lauderdale.

In short order, Royal Caribbean set up a private beach on Little Stirrup Cay, renaming its setting **CocoCay.** Royal Caribbean later added to its private-beach inventory by buying 260 acres with 5 beaches on a secluded stretch of Haiti's north coast, far away from that country's political turmoil.

Princess set up a private beach in the Grenadines for a few years, upgrading in 1992 to **Princess Cays,** located on the southwest coast of Eleuthera.

In late 1997, Holland America inaugurated its new **Half Moon Cay,** marking a $16 million investment. The line decided only to develop 2% of the 2,400-acre island, maintaining the rest as a wild-bird reserve for the Bahamian National Trust. There's a network of hiking trails guests can use to explore the setting and watch the birds, which include several varieties of terns, shearwaters, and Bahamian pintails.

In 1998, Disney opened a private-island destination known as **Disney's Castaway Cay,** formerly Gorda Cay.

Costa and Celebrity both offer a private-beach experience for guests in the Dominican Republic at government-owned beach facilities designated for cruise ships, while Premier offers guests a chance to visit the island of **Salt Cay,** located about 3 miles off Paradise Island.

Visits to the private-beach settings usually involve taking a tender from the ship, although Disney built its facility with a pier so the *Disney Magic* and *Disney Wonder* can dock right at Castaway Cay.

Antigua

You'll never be wanting for beaches on Antigua (*an-TEE-guah*), where there are more than enough sugar-white sand beaches to keep the most serious of sun worshippers busy. Antigua also has something for history buffs: English Harbour, where smaller cruise ships may anchor, is home to the Nelson Dockyard Park, one of the Caribbean's top historical attractions.

Passengers on larger ships come ashore at Deep Water Harbour Terminal, about 11 miles from English Harbour and less than a mile from sleepy St. John's.

THE CRUISE LINE SITUATION Crystal, Holland America, Norwegian, Royal Caribbean, Seabourn, Star Clippers, and Windjammer all make port calls here.

Caribbean Port Calls by Cruise Line

Cruise Line	Private Islands & Beaches	Antigua	Aruba	Barbados	Cozumel/ Playa del Carmen	Curaçao	Freeport	Grand Cayman
American Canadian Caribbean						•		
Cape Canaveral							•	
Carnival			•	•	•		•	•
Celebrity	•		•	•	•	•		•
Clipper								
Club Med				•				
Commodore					•			•
Costa	•				•			•
Crystal		•			•			
Cunard			•	•	•	•		•
Disney	•							
Holland America	•	•	•	•	•	•		•
Mediterranean Shipping				•	•			•
Norwegian	•	•	•	•	•	•		•
Premier	•		•	•	•	•		•
Princess	•		•	•	•	•		•
Radisson			•			•		
Regal					•			
Royal Caribbean	•	•			•			
Royal Olympic			•	•	•	•		•
Seabourn		•			•			
Silversea								
Star Clippers		•						
Tall Ship Adventures								
Windjammer		•					•	
Windstar			•			•		
World Explorer					•			•

Information for this chart courtesy of Travel Weekly's Official Cruise Guide.

	Grenada	Guadeloupe	Jamaica	Key West, Fla.	Martinque	Nassau	St. Barthélemy	St. Croix	St. Kitts	St. Lucia	St. Maarten/ St. Martin	St. Thomas & St. John	San Juan	Tortola & Virgin Gorda
										•		•		•
				•										
	•	•	•	•	•	•	•	•		•	•	•	•	
	•		•	•	•	•				•	•	•	•	
	•								•	•		•		•
	•						•		•		•	•	•	•
			•											
			•	•		•			•		•	•	•	•
						•						•	•	•
	•	•		•		•	•		•	•	•	•	•	
						•								
	•	•	•	•	•	•			•	•	•	•	•	
	•	•	•	•	•	•						•		•
			•	•		•		•	•	•	•	•	•	
	•	•	•	•	•	•		•		•	•	•	•	
	•		•		•					•	•	•	•	•
							•				•	•	•	•
			•	•					•				•	
			•	•		•		•			•	•	•	
	•		•	•		•	•				•	•	•	
				•		•	•					•		•
				•		•	•							•
					•		•		•	•	•	•		•
					•					•				
	•				•	•	•		•	•	•	•		•
	•				•		•			•	•	•		•
			•			•								

THE MONEY SITUATION The **Eastern Caribbean dollar (EC$)** is the official currency here, but prices are nearly always quoted in U.S. dollars. (US$1 = EC$2.70)

THE LANGUAGE SITUATION The official language is English.

Antigua Self-Tour

The Antigua and Barbuda Department of Tourism, located at Long and Themes streets in St. John's, is open Monday through Friday for basic information. While it is easy to get around Antigua, it is recommended that travelers not rent cars and instead stick to the ship's shore excursions or taxis. Bus service is available, but it is geared more toward the schedules of locals, not for sightseeing. Taxi drivers double as guides, and the cost for the service is low.

Money Makes the World Go 'Round

In most cases, you'll find prices in the ports you visit quoted in U.S. dollars (which is what I've used for all prices in this book), but you might also find prices quoted in Eastern Caribbean dollars (EC$), in another local currency, or, in Mexico, in new pesos. I've noted in each port review the currency in use there. By way of comparison, 1 U.S. dollar generally equals EC$2.70. The Mexican peso has fluctuated so much in recent years that it's best to check its worth close to the time of your trip. If you're hooked into the Internet, a handy place to find currency conversions is CNN's web site at **www.cnn.com/TRAVEL/CURRENCY**.

Within Walking Distance

While St. John's itself is a bit ragged around the edges, several interesting historical destinations are close to the main dock. The **market** in the southern part of St. John's gives travelers a sense of the local flavor, especially on Saturday morning, when locals bargain, gossip, and ply their trades. Located at the lower end of Market Street.

Duty-free shopping is close to the docks at **Heritage Quay** and **Redcliffe Quay.**

The **Museum of Antigua and Barbuda** is located in the old Court House building, which is nearly 250 years old, and offers a history of the area. Located at Long and Market streets. Admission is $2.

At **St. John's Cathedral**, an Anglican church dating back to 1683, you can learn about the tragic history of the church itself (it's been damaged twice by earthquakes). Located between Long and Newgate streets at Church Lane.

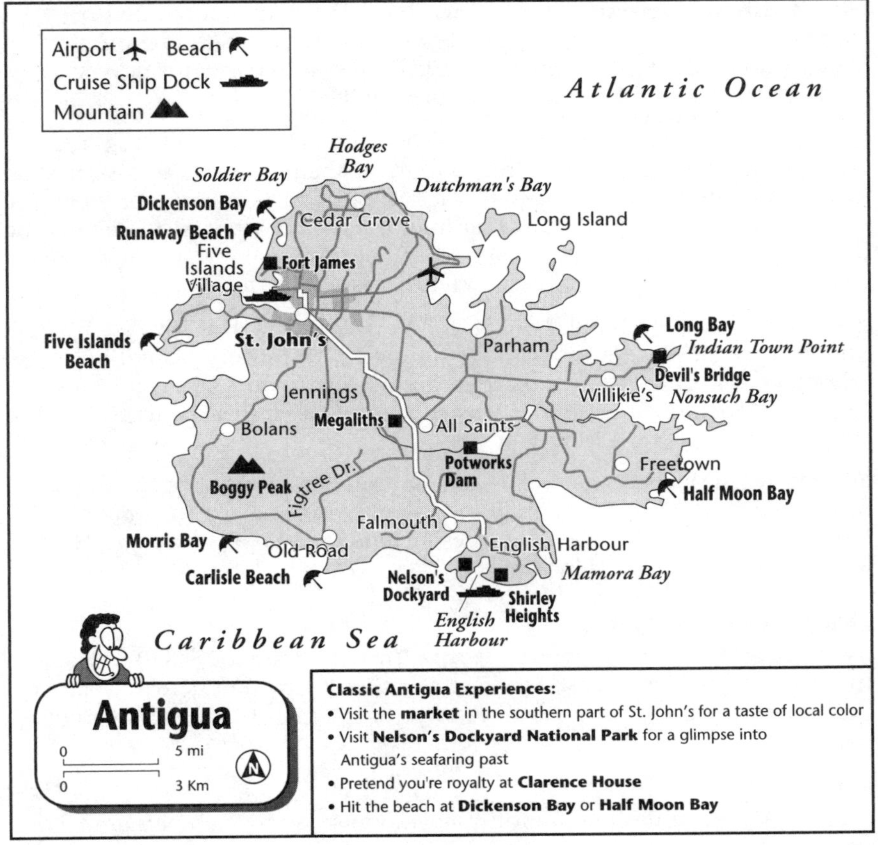

Beyond Walking Distance

You can get a true feel for Antigua's link to its seafaring past, from naval battles to pirates laying low, at **Nelson's Dockyard National Park,** accessible from St. John's by taxi or shore excursion. It's known as the Williamsburg of the Caribbean. The dockyard offered refuge from hurricanes for English ships as far back as 1671 and was headquarters to Britain's Admiral Horatio Nelson from 1784 to 1787. The dockyard also played a role in the pirate times of the 1800s. It costs $5 per person to tour the dockyard; children under 13 are admitted free.

Clarence House at English Harbour is a house fit for a king. It was built for Prince William Henry, who stayed there while serving as commander of H.M.S. *Pegasus* in 1787. The prince later was crowned King William IV. The house, which was also where Princess Margaret and former husband Lord Snowman spent part of their honeymoon, is open to the public on days when the governor of Antigua and Barbuda is not in residence. It's customary to tip the caretaker for taking the time to give a tour.

Dow's Hill Interpretation Center, about 2½ miles east of English Harbor, offers a multimedia presentation of the island's history, from the occupation by the British military to the local connection with slavery. Admission is $5 for adults, $3 for children under 16.

For scenery, have your taxi driver take you back to St. John's via **Fig Tree Drive** (fare negotiable). It's a circular route of about 20 miles across Antigua's main mountain range. It's steep in places, a bit rutty in others, but you'll get the best view of the lush tropical settings, the fishing villages, and a sense of the island's coast. Remember that on Antigua, "fig" is the word for banana, so don't expect to see fig trees as you might know them.

About a 40-minute cab ride from St. John's, **Harmony Hall** in Brown's Bay Mill, near Freetown, offers a partially restored 19th-century plantation house and sugar mill, and is a good place to find Caribbean arts and crafts and to stop for a lunch of Green Island lobster or some other local delicacy. The cab ride there should cost $20 to $30.

You can reach the best beaches by cab, but remember to arrange with your driver to pick you up, or you might get stuck. Also, sticking to populated beach areas is advisable. Good choices include **Dickenson Bay** and **Half Moon Bay.** (See map for locations.)

The Best Shore Excursions

Nelson Dockyard & Clarence House Tour (3 hours, $25–$40): Visits to these two major sights make up the major shore excursion here (see earlier descriptions). On the way, you'll see some of the island's lush countryside.

Aruba

Aruba is a popular destination for honeymooners, sun worshipers, and fanciers of a little action at the gaming table. Unfortunately, the island's growing popularity has seen it move from traditional Caribbean quaintness to overbuilding.

Sun is almost guaranteed here, since Aruba receives only about 17 inches of rain a year. The island is also outside the hurricane path that often batters Caribbean points to the north. Instead of clouds, get ready for crowds here, especially at the island's casinos.

You'll find plenty of shopping within walking distance of the Aruba Port Authority in downtown Oranjestad, with its Spanish and Dutch architectural influences.

Aruba's beaches, which stretch for some 7 miles along the island's west coast, are notable for the absence of the types of vendors that make sunbathing such a hassle on other islands. There also is little of the racial tension that is present on Jamaica, for example, so safety concerns aren't as high, meaning the chance of getting mugged is minimal.

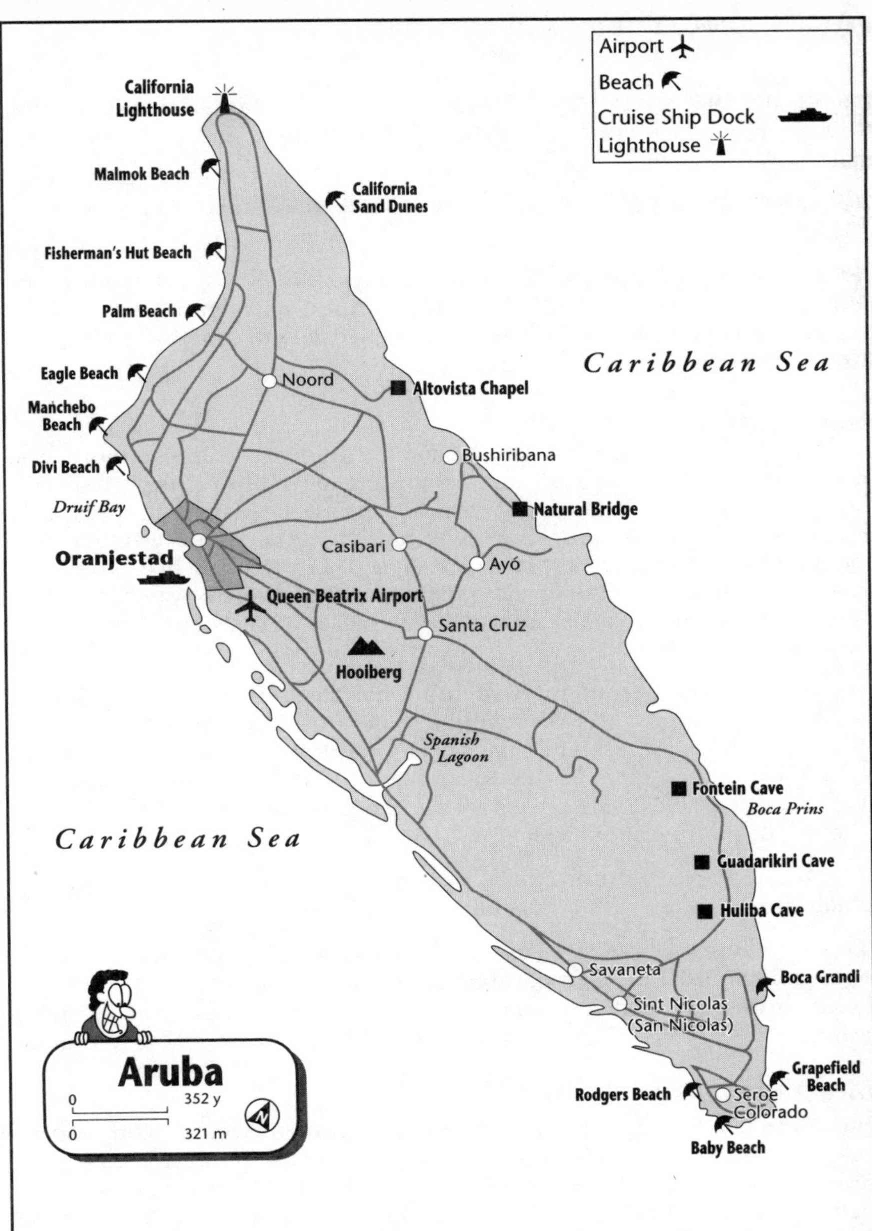

Classic Aruba Experiences:

- Go shopping in **Schooner Harbor** or up Lloyd G. Smith Boulevard
- Head to the top of **Hooiberg**, from which you can see Venezuela on a clear day
- Visit the mysterious rocks of **Ayo** and **Casibari** or the Arawak cave artwork at **Savaneta**
- Try your luck at the **Royal Cabana Casino**
- Take a trip on an **Atlantis Submarine** or a **Glass-Bottom Boat**

THE CRUISE LINE SITUATION Carnival, Celebrity, Cunard, Holland America, Norwegian, Premier, Princess, Radisson, Royal Olympic, and Windstar all make port calls here.

THE MONEY SITUATION The currency is the **Aruba florin (AFl).** (US$1 = 1.77 AFl)

THE LANGUAGE SITUATION The official language is Dutch, but nearly everybody speaks English. You'll also hear Spanish and Papiamento, a regional dialect that combines Dutch, Spanish, and English with Amerindian and African dialects.

Aruba Self-Tour

The Aruba Port Authority is a very modern facility. After coming ashore, stop by the **information booth** inside for touring ideas. **Shopping** is a short 5-minute walk away up Lloyd G. Smith Boulevard, the main road that runs from Queen Beatrix Airport along the waterfront up to Palm Beach, but you'll find that most travelers cross the street to Caya G. F. Betico Croes, which leads to a wide array of shopping. Items such as Swiss watches, German and Japanese cameras, French perfume, and English bone china are available.

Mopeds are a popular way to get around Aruba and cost about $37 to $40 a day. A taxi ride from the cruise terminal to most beach resorts runs between $8 and $12, with a maximum 4-passenger limit. If you use a taxi to get to a remote part of the island, be sure to arrange with the driver for a return ride at a designated time. Some drivers are also excellent tour guides, with a 1-hour tour running about $35.

It's also easy to rent a car on Aruba, with Hertz, Budget, and Avis among the rental-car companies with offices here.

The local bus service is easy to use and inexpensive, with schedules available at the Arubus Office on Zoutmanstraat. Buses stop across the street from the cruise terminal, and you can take them to the beach, hotel resorts, and casinos.

Within Walking Distance

One of the first things you'll see is **Schooner Harbor,** where colorful boats are docked and locals display their goods in little open stalls. Up the beach, fresh seafood is available to buy right off the boat. The Dutch influence is highlighted by **Wilhelmina Park,** which honors Queen Wilhelmina of the Netherlands and includes a tropical garden and a statue of the queen.

Beyond Walking Distance

Hooiberg, often called "The Haystack," about 15 miles southeast of Oranjestad in the center of the island, is a prominent 541-foot hill of diorite boulders. On a clear day, it's possible to see Venezuela from its top.

To the northeast, you'll find boulders the size of buildings at **Ayo** and **Casibari.** You can see Amerindian drawings on the rocks at Ayo. Casibari, open daily 9am to 5pm, features rocks that have been shaped through the years into the likenesses of prehistoric birds and animals.

In **Savaneta**, located on the east side of the island and a 25-minute cab ride from Oranjestad, you can see caves with Arawak artwork—the oldest traces of humans on the island. The area was also an industrial center dating back to the days of phosphate mining in the late 19th century, and later was where the town of San Nicolas was developed and where an Exxon oil subsidiary refinery operated until 1985. A great reason to head for San Nicolas is **Charlie's Bar and Restaurant** Main Street (**☎ 297/8-45086**). It dates back to 1941, is crammed with a pennants, banners, trophies, and other memorabilia, and offers two-fisted drinks and decent food.

The **Turquoise Coast** on the western and southern shores is a magnet for sunseekers. An $8 ride from the cruise terminal will get you to **Palm Beach** and **Eagle Beach,** two of the best on the island.

Gamblers will want to try their luck at one of the hotel casinos. **Royal Cabana Casino,** at La Cabana All-Suite Beach Resort & Casino, is Aruba's largest, with 33 tables and games and 320 slot machines.

The Best Shore Excursions

Island Tour (3 hours, $25): Most ships offer this trip around the island, but it's usually pretty dull.

Atlantis Submarine Trip (3 hours, $32 children, $69 adults): This is a much better bet than the island tour, and it's a great chance to see the underwater life on a coral reef.

Glass-Bottom Boat Trip (1½ hours, about $25): If submersibles are a bit much for you, here's another way to view life underwater, and without getting wet.

Barbados

Barbados is a destination that has it all, from fine dining to pink-and-white sandy beaches. The locals on this former British colony call themselves *Bajans,* speak with an English accent, and refer to their island as "an England in the tropics," only with much better weather. Barbados has afternoon tea, cricket, small cottages with well-kept gardens, and old parish churches. The northeast part of the island is hilly, with a morning mist that helped it earn the nickname "The Scotland District."

You'll find plenty of shopping, but Bridgetown—near where you come ashore—is noisy, dry, dirty, and jammed with honking traffic. It's best on this island to head for the beach. Bardadians brag that their island has a beach for every day of the year. Beaches on the western side, where luxury resorts make up the Gold Coast, offer calmer waters compared to the pounding surf on the Atlantic side of the island, a favorite of windsurfers.

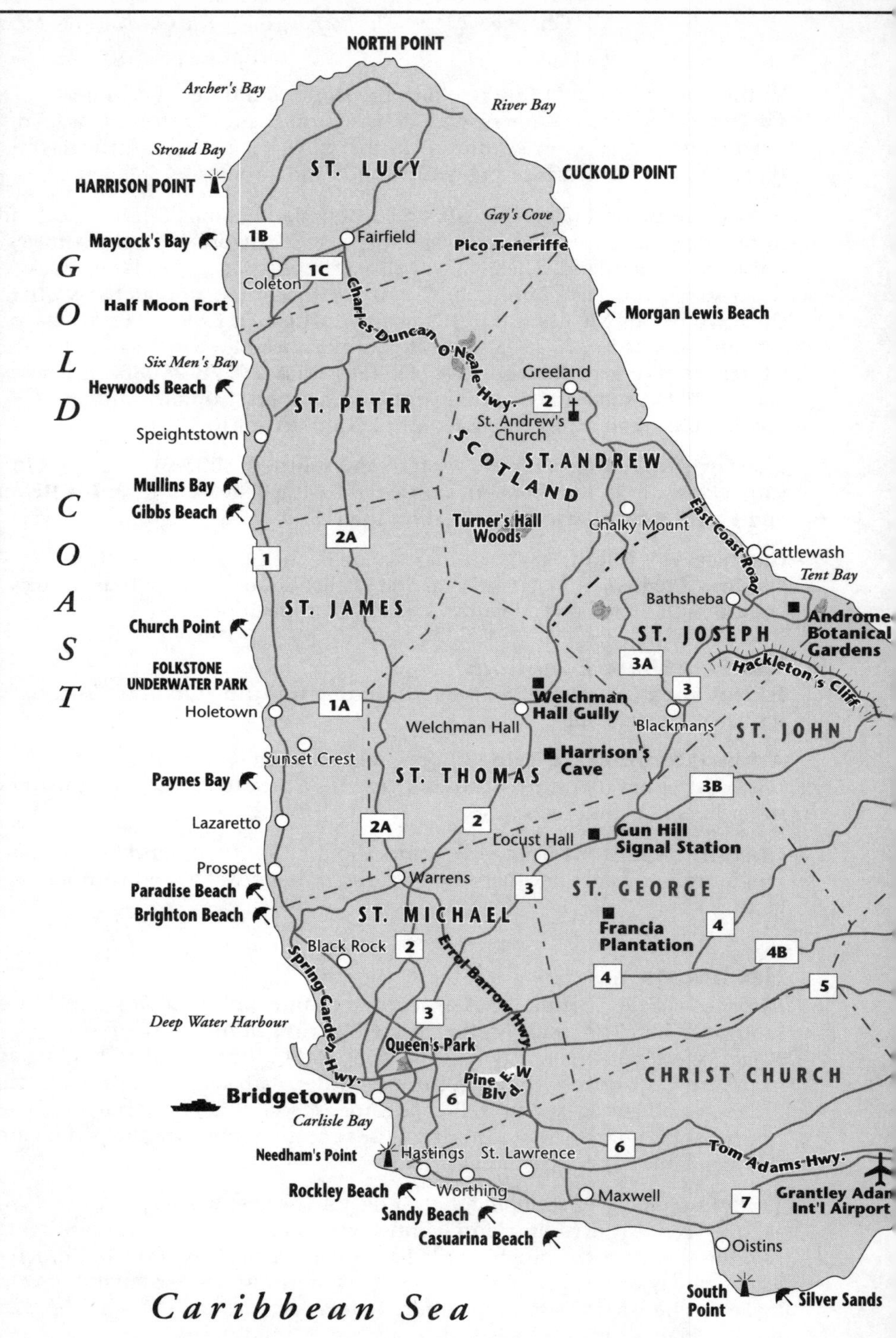
NORTH POINT
Archer's Bay
River Bay
Stroud Bay
HARRISON POINT
ST. LUCY
CUCKOLD POINT
Gay's Cove
1B
Fairfield
Pico Teneriffe
Maycock's Bay
G
Coleton
1C
Charles Duncan O'Neale Hwy.
Half Moon Fort
O
Morgan Lewis Beach
L
Six Men's Bay
Greeland
Heywoods Beach
2
D
ST. PETER
St. Andrew's Church
Speightstown
SCOTLAND
ST. ANDREW
Mullins Bay
Gibbs Beach
C
Chalky Mount
East Coast Road
Turner's Hall Woods
2A
O
1
Cattlewash
Tent Bay
A
ST. JAMES
Bathsheba
Andromeda Botanical Gardens
Church Point
ST. JOSEPH
S
FOLKSTONE UNDERWATER PARK
3A
Hackleton's Cliff
T
Welchman Hall Gully
3
Holetown
1A
Welchman Hall
Blackmans
ST. JOHN
Sunset Crest
Harrison's Cave
Paynes Bay
ST. THOMAS
3B
Lazaretto
2
2A
Locust Hall
Gun Hill Signal Station
Prospect
Warrens
3
ST. GEORGE
Paradise Beach
Brighton Beach
ST. MICHAEL
Francia Plantation
4
Black Rock
2
Spring Garden Hwy.
Errol Barrow Hwy.
4B
4
5
3
Deep Water Harbour
Queen's Park
Pine E. W Blvd.
CHRIST CHURCH
Bridgetown
6
Carlisle Bay
6
Needham's Point
Hastings
St. Lawrence
Tom Adams Hwy.
Rockley Beach
Worthing
Maxwell
Grantley Adams Int'l Airport
7
Sandy Beach
Casuarina Beach
Oistins
South Point
Silver Sands
Caribbean Sea

Classic Barbados Experiences:

- Explore the underworld at **Harrison's Cave**
- Revel in floral splendour at **Flower Forest** or **Andromeda Botanical Gardens**
- Take the view from the **Gun Hill Signal Station**
- Do the history thing at **Francia Plantation** or the historic **Synagogue**
- Descend to your own undersea world on the ***Atlantis II* submarine**

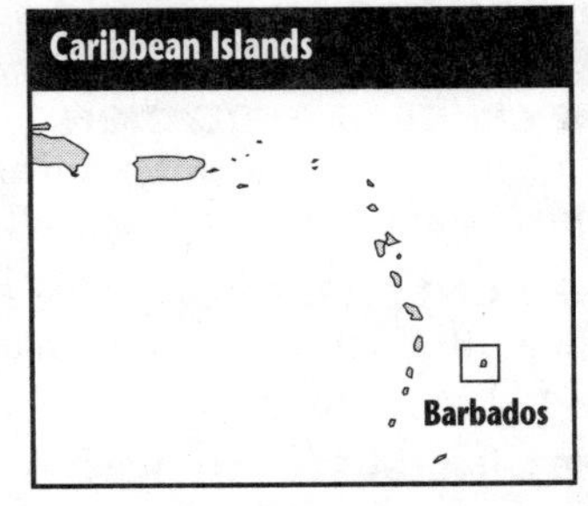

Airport Beach Church Lighthouse Cruise Ship Dock

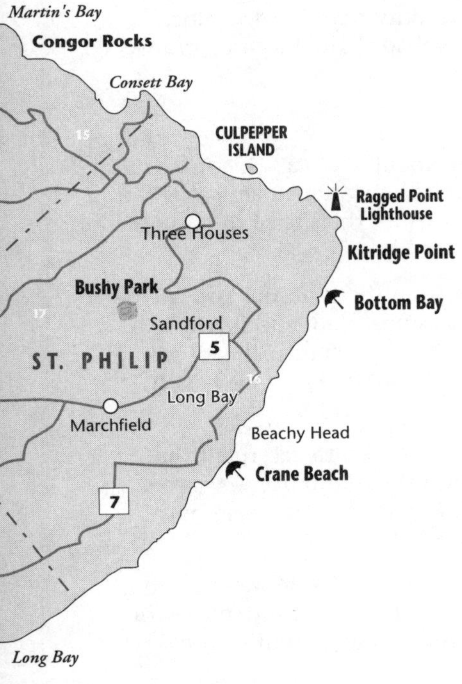

THE CRUISE LINE SITUATION Carnival, Celebrity, Club Med, Cunard, Holland America, Mediterranean Shipping Cruises, Norwegian, Premier, Princess, and Royal Olympic all make port calls here.

THE MONEY SITUATION The **Barbados Dollar (BD$)** is the official currency, although most stores take traveler's checks or U.S. dollars. (BD$1 = US50¢)

THE LANGUAGE SITUATION English is spoken here.

Barbados Self-Tour

There's a **tourist information office** right in the huge, modern cruise terminal, where you can obtain information on how to get around Barbados. The walk into Bridgetown is a dusty 30-minute affair. Catch a cab ($3 to $4 one way).

Since Barbados is so spread out and has bad roads, renting a car is not advisable. Taxis, motor scooters (starting at around $30.50 a day, with a $100 deposit), or bicycles ($10 a day, $50 deposit) are a better way to go.

Within Walking Distance

There's not much within walking distance from the terminal except shopping. The $6 million cruise facility is home to 20 duty-free shops, 13 local retailers, and smaller venders. Goods made on Barbados are duty-free, from black-coral jewelry to Barbados rum and liquors.

Beyond Walking Distance

The Synagogue, Synagogue Lane, Bridgetown, about a $4 cab ride from the cruise terminal, is one of the oldest synagogues in the western hemisphere. The current building dates back to 1833 and stands on the site of the original synagogue, built by Brazilian Jews in 1654.

Welchman Hall Gully, located about 9 miles from the terminal and reachable by bus, offers a lush tropical garden that has some plant specimens dating back to when English settlers first arrived in 1627, including breadfruit trees said to come from the seedlings made famous in *Mutiny on the Bounty.* Admission is $5 for adults, $2.50 for children (under 5 free).

Harrison's Cove, Welchman Hall, St. Thomas, about a $15 cab ride from the cruise terminal, is the top tourist attraction on the island. Here, visitors view an underground world via an electric tram and trailer. There are both stalactites and stalagmites aplenty. Admission is $7.50 adults, $3.75 children.

Flower Forest, 12 miles from the cruise terminal and $15 one way by cab, is an old sugar plantation located on the western edge of the Scotland district and is considered one of the most scenic sites on Barbados. Admission is $5 adults, $2.50 children.

Gun Hill Signal Station, 12 miles from the port and $17.50 for a one-way cab ride, is one of a chain of signal stations built in the early 1800s and once used by British troops stationed there. It's located on the highland of

St. George and offers a panoramic view. Admission is $4 adults, $2 children under 14.

Andromeda Botanical Gardens is located on a cliff overlooking Bathsheba on the east coast. The garden contains a variety of orchids, hibiscus, ferns, and more than 100 species of palms. Keep a close lookout for an occasional mongoose or monkey. Admission is $5, children under 12 free.

Francia Plantation, St. George, a 20-mile ride from the terminal. Descendants of the original owner still own and live in this house, located on a wooded hillside overlooking the St. George Valley. The house is filled with antique maps and prints, including a West Indies map printed in 1522. Admission is $4.

Good beach bets include **Paynes Bay** on the West Coast and **Sandy Beach** on the South Coast.

The Best Shore Excursions

***Atlantis II* Submarine Trip** (2 hours, $80): Board this air-conditioned submersible and view colorful underwater life, including tropical fish, plants, and an intact shipwreck.

British Virgin Islands

There's a lot to do in this chain of some 40 islands that once served as a haven for pirates and other scoundrels. Most of the islands are tiny, with the largest being **Tortola, Virgin Gorda** (or "Fat Virgin"—the name dates back to Christopher Columbus, who thought the island's mountain resembled a protruding stomach), and the less-visited island of **Jost Van Dyke.**

Literary buffs will get a charge out of **Norman Island,** rumored to be similar to the island used in Robert Louis Stevenson's *Treasure Island,* a story inspired by a ditty about pirate leader Blackbeard. It says that Blackbeard stashed a bottle of rum and marooned 15 men at Deadman Bay on neighboring Peter Island. Yo ho ho.

THE CRUISE LINE SITUATION American Canadian Caribbean, Clipper, Club Med, Costa, Crystal, Mediterranean Shipping Cruises, Princess, Radisson, Seabourn, Silversea, Star Clippers, Windjammer, and Windstar all make port calls at Tortola and Virgin Gorda.

THE MONEY SITUATION The **U.S. dollar** is the legal currency.

THE LANGUAGE SITUATION English is what you'll hear; English is what you'll use.

BVI Self-Tour

Passengers disembark via tenders at **Road Town,** the capital of Tortola. The pier is about a 5-minute walk from Main Street. Instead of heading for Tortola, some smaller ships anchor outside of Virgin Gorda. In either case, if you want to visit Virgin Gorda, you have to take a tender.

The **BVI Tourist Board Office** is in the center of Road Town near the dock south of Wickhams Cay 1.

The **bus service** on Tortola is not convenient for cruise passengers to use, so even though the roads are bad, and most travelers must adjust to driving on the left (this is a British colony, after all), renting a car to explore the island is an option here. Budget, Hertz, and Avis all have offices on Tortola. Reservations may be required (see appendix B, "Car-Rental Agencies Contact Information," for reservations numbers).

Taxis also line up to meet every visiting cruise ship.

Within Walking Distance

A short walk from the pier onto Main Street in Tortola brings passengers to a shopping area that's pretty quiet by Caribbean standards, but offers good buys on duty-free British goods, such as English china.

Beyond Walking Distance

Mount Sage National Park, on Tortola, covers 92 acres and reaches heights of 1,780 feet. The park offers the lush feel of a tropical rain forest. Hikers will enjoy the Rain Forest Trail and the Mahogany Forest Trail. Any taxi driver can take you to the mountain. Before going, stop at the tourist office for a brochure with a map of the park's trails.

For something entirely different, a good bar scene on Tortola can be found at **Bomba's Surfside Shack** at Cappon's Bay near the West End. It's a shack filled with junk and covered with Day-Glo graffiti and other stuff that's all tied together into a fun party palace.

Most folks particularly enjoy a visit to **Cane Garden Bay** on the northwest shore, where you can veg out on the palm-lined, white, sandy beach and get everything from food to a freshwater shower at **Rhymer's.** You might find that you want to stay there all day.

Over on Virgin Gorda (which you can reach by tender from Tortola), **the Baths** is the most popular beach destination. Huge boulders have fallen on each other over the years to form saltwater grottoes for exploring and pools for swimming.

Follow a path away from the Baths for about 15 minutes through boulders and dry coastal vegetation and enjoy **Devil's Bay National Park.** There's good snorkeling at nearby **Spring Bay.**

The Best Shore Excursions

Cruise ships don't offer excursions themselves but deal through local operators. The cost for a 2½-hour **guided tour** of Tortola will run $45 to $60 for up to 3 people (sharing a cab or car).

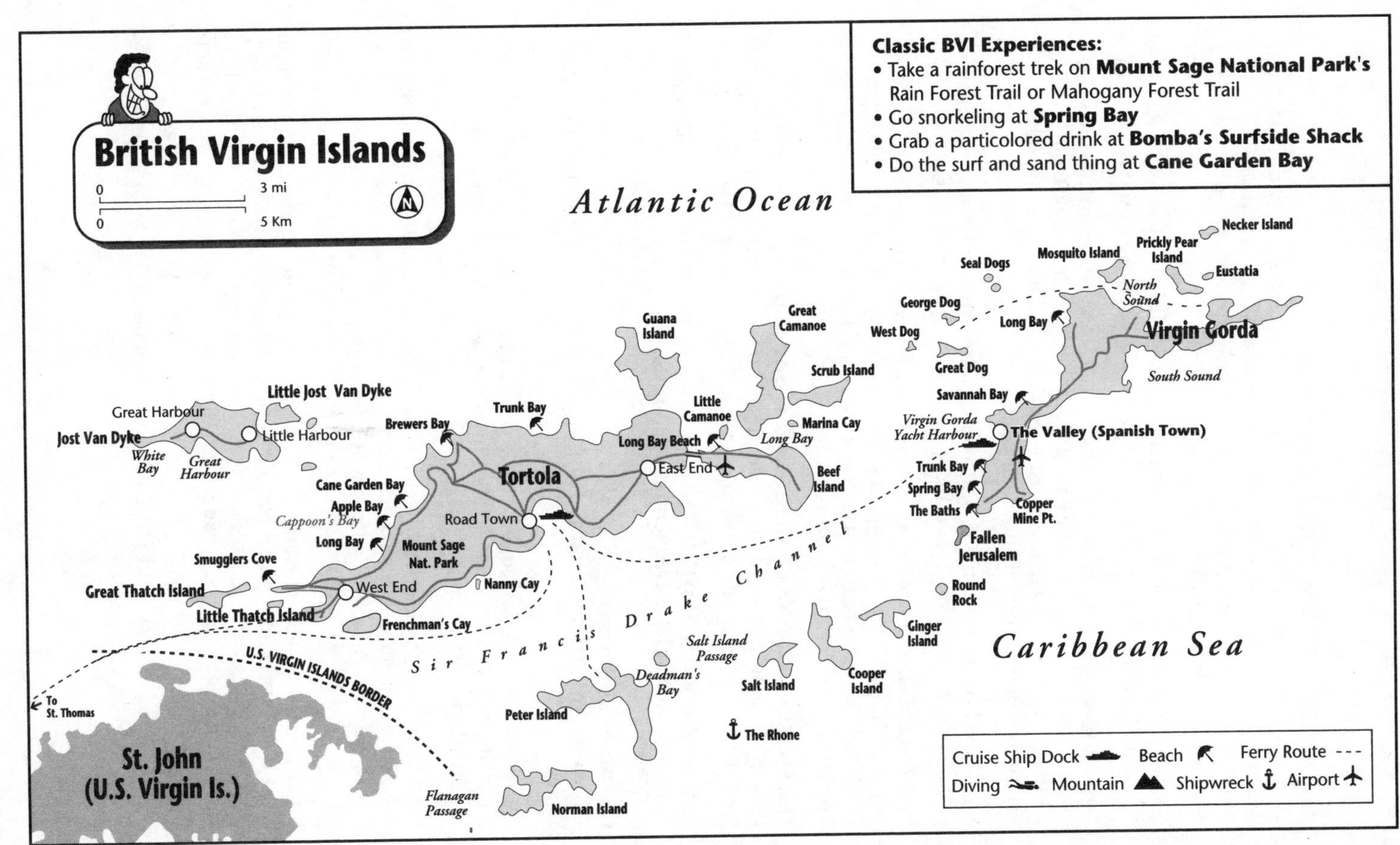
British Virgin Islands
0
3 mi
0
5 Km
N
Classic BVI Experiences:
• Take a rainforest trek on **Mount Sage National Park's** Rain Forest Trail or Mahogany Forest Trail
• Go snorkeling at **Spring Bay**
• Grab a particolored drink at **Bomba's Surfside Shack**
• Do the surf and sand thing at **Cane Garden Bay**
Atlantic Ocean
Caribbean Sea
Sir Francis Drake Channel
Jost Van Dyke
Great Harbour
Little Harbour
White Bay
Great Harbour
Little Jost Van Dyke
Brewers Bay
Trunk Bay
Tortola
Cane Garden Bay
Apple Bay
Cappoon's Bay
Long Bay
Mount Sage Nat. Park
Road Town
Smugglers Cove
Great Thatch Island
Little Thatch Island
West End
Frenchman's Cay
Nanny Cay
Guana Island
Little Camanoe
Great Camanoe
Long Bay Beach
East End
Long Bay
Marina Cay
Scrub Island
Beef Island
Peter Island
Deadman's Bay
Salt Island Passage
Salt Island
The Rhone
Cooper Island
Ginger Island
Norman Island
Flanagan Passage
U.S. VIRGIN ISLANDS BORDER
To St. Thomas
St. John (U.S. Virgin Is.)
George Dog
West Dog
Great Dog
Seal Dogs
Mosquito Island
Prickly Pear Island
Necker Island
Eustatia
North Sound
Long Bay
Virgin Gorda
South Sound
Savannah Bay
Virgin Gorda Yacht Harbour
The Valley (Spanish Town)
Trunk Bay
Spring Bay
The Baths
Copper Mine Pt.
Fallen Jerusalem
Round Rock
Cruise Ship Dock
Beach
Ferry Route
Diving
Mountain
Shipwreck
Airport

Cozumel & Playa del Carmen

A stop at the island of Cozumel offers cruise passengers a chance to see the **Mayan ruins** at Tulum and Chichen Itza (on shore excursions), as well as to enjoy the island's own alabaster beaches and turquoise waters, which are ideal for snorkeling and scuba diving.

Some ships spend a day in Cozumel and then the next in nearby Playa del Carmen, which is on the Yucatan Peninsula and closer to the ruins.

San Miguel is Cozumel's only town, and a lot of its quaintness has disappeared in favor of familiar fast-food restaurants such as Kentucky Fried Chicken, Subway, Pizza Hut, Hard Rock Cafe, and a smattering of Mexican offerings—plus plenty of shops, of course.

Still, travel outside the town, and you can find deserted beaches and abundant wildlife, including armadillos, tropical birds, and lizards.

THE CRUISE LINE SITUATION Carnival, Celebrity, Commodore, Costa, Crystal, Cunard, Holland America, Mediterranean Shipping, Norwegian, Premier, Princess, Regal, Royal Caribbean, Royal Olympic, Seabourn, and World Explorer all make port calls here.

THE MONEY SITUATION The **Mexican nuevo peso** is the currency of choice, though it's rare to find a vendor who won't accept dollars. If you do want to exchange money, several banks are clustered near the docks.

THE LANGUAGE SITUATION Spanish is the common tongue, but English is spoken in most places frequented by tourists.

Cozumel Self-Tour

The **Tourism Office** is located at Plaza del Sol, the main square in San Miguel.

Ships either tender passengers to the center of San Miguel or dock at the international pier, which is 4 miles from San Miguel and very close to Cozumel's beaches.

Taxi service is available around the clock from both locations and is inexpensive. Cruise passengers have been known to be overcharged, so settle on fares before the ride. A **taxi** ride from San Miguel to most resorts and beaches costs around $4.50, and trips to more remote locations run about $12.

Other popular modes of transportation include **mopeds,** available for about $25 a day. When riding on a moped, look out for heavy traffic, hidden stop signs, and roads with potholes. If you rent a car, make sure it's a four-wheel drive vehicle, as the roads leading to ruins and remote beaches are particularly rough.

Ferries link Cozumel and Playa del Carmen, and one-way fares range between $4 and $5 per person.

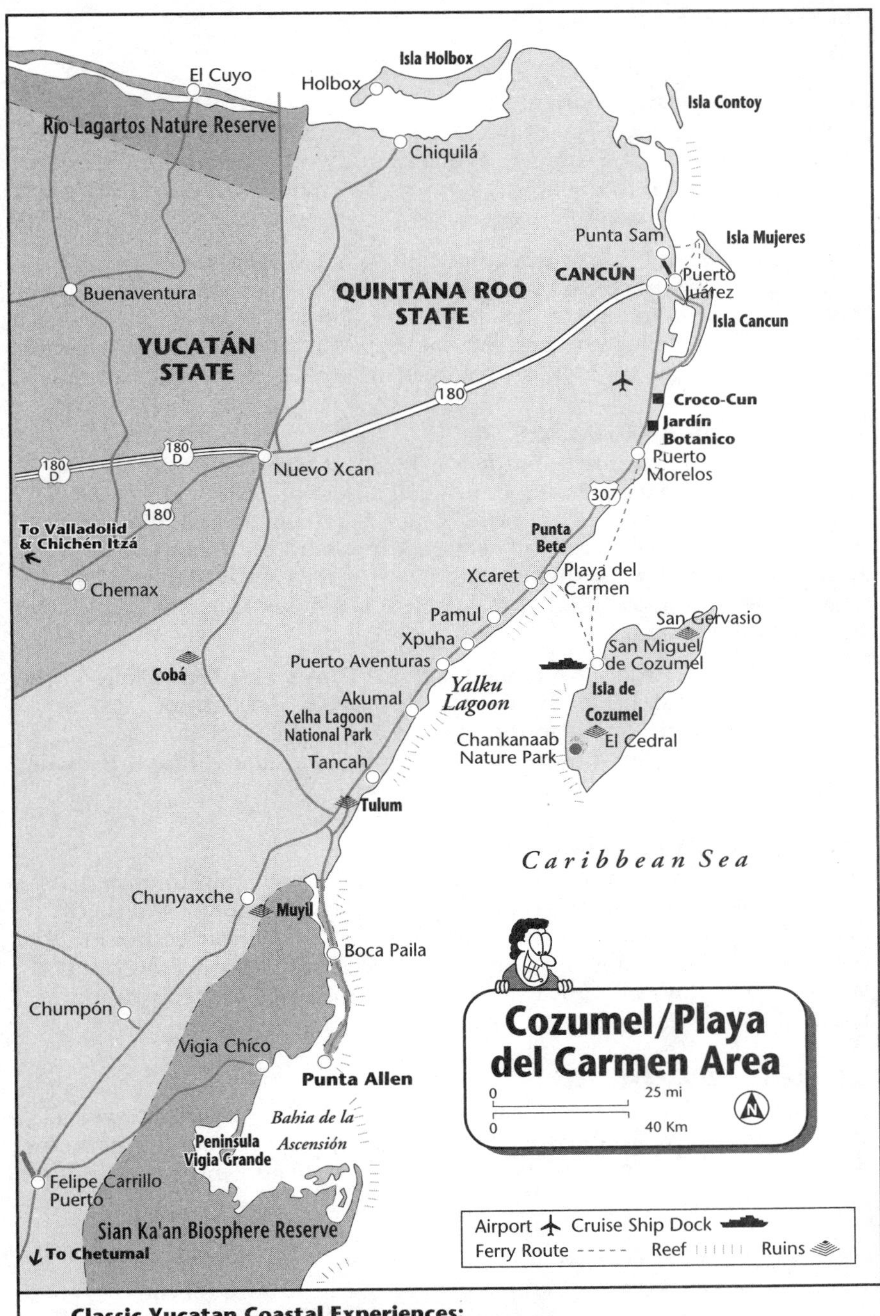

Classic Yucatan Coastal Experiences:

- Visit the Mayan ruins at **Chichen Itza, Tulum**, or **San Gervasio**
- Take in the botanical garden or hit the water rides at **Xcaret**
- **Rent a moped** and zip around for the afternoon
- Shop for handicrafts at **Rincon del Sol**
- Hit the beach at **Playa San Francisco**, **Playa del Sol**, or **Playa Bonita**

Within Walking Distance

The town of San Miguel is small and easy to get around on foot. The real attractions here are the shops and restaurants, with a good selection within walking distance from the downtown pier. Most are on **Avenida Rafael Melgar** (the main street, running along the waterfront) and **Plaza del Sol.**

Three blocks from the downtown pier, on Rafael Melgar between Calles 4 and 6 North, is **Museo de la Isla de Cozumel,** which offers two floors of historical exhibits in a space that was earlier Cozumel's first luxury hotel. The exhibits, which include swords and nautical artifacts, start in pre-Hispanic times and continue through the colonial era to the present. Admission is $3.

Beyond Walking Distance

A 10-minute, $5 taxi ride from the Muelle Fiscal pier takes you to **Chankanaab Nature Park,** an unusual attraction well worth a visit. The setting offers an archeological park, botanical garden, and wildlife sanctuary, as well as a saltwater lagoon, a beautiful white-sand beach, and offshore reefs for snorkeling and scuba diving (equipment rentals are available). There is also a restaurant and snack bar and some small shops. Admission is $7, free for children 9 and under.

Cozumel's best powdery white-sand beach is **Playa San Francisco** on the southwestern coast. It's a cab ride from downtown and right near the international pier. About a mile to the south is one of the more popular and crowded beaches, **Playa del Sol.** A less-crowded option is **Playa Bonita,** which you can reach via a taxi or car.

Playa del Carmen Self-Tour

Plans are underway to build a pier in Playa del Carmen, but for now, passengers reach it via tenders. Some ships spend 1 day in Cozumel and then another here, because the Mayan ruins are more easily reached from Playa del Carmen. The town is small and easily accessible by foot. Taxis can take you wherever you want, but you can walk to the heart of the town, the beach, and most major shops from the pier.

Within Walking Distance

Besides the crowds and brilliant white beach, this city can offer you excellent snorkeling and opportunities for turtle-watching. You can stroll to **Rincon del Sol,** a Mexican colonial–style, tree-lined courtyard, where you will find an array of stores selling handicrafts.

Beyond Walking Distance

When docked in Playa del Carmen, most passengers head for the ruins (see the following section). Other options include hitting the beach or visiting **Xcaret,** a 250-acre ecological theme park. Four miles south of Playa del Carmen, the park contains water rides, a dive shop, and a botanical garden. The admission price is $30, and the park is accessible via the frequent bus service from Playa Del Carmen. A taxi costs $4.

The Best Shore Excursions

Chichen Itza (by plane from Cozumel, $185; by bus from Playa del Carmen, $79 to $85): Located on the mainland, Chichen Itza is the largest of the Mayan ruins in the Yucatan, covering 7 square miles. It was first inhabited in A.D. 445. Best known of the ruins is the pyramid Castillo of Kukulcan, an astronomical clock, with 365 steps (1 for each day) ascending to the top platform. Shore excursions from Cozumel are by plane, with the flight taking about 45 minutes. Ships docking at Playa del Carmen offer bus tours that take approximately 12 hours (excursion price includes a box lunch). You can explore only a portion of Chichen Itza in 1 day. *Note:* If you want to videotape your visit, you must pay a fee of $8.

Tulum (6 hours, $69 to $72, including a box lunch, from Playa del Carmen): The walled city of Tulum, 80 miles south of Cancun, is the single most visited Mayan ruin, and the only Mayan city built on the coast.

San Gervasio (4 hours, $36): If you don't want to travel quite as far as Tulum or Chichen Itza to see ruins, you can instead visit Cozumel's own minor site, San Gervasio, once the capital of Cozumel and a ceremonial center.

Curaçao

When you enter Willemstad's harbor, a floating bridge swings aside, inviting you into a narrow channel, and your eyes turn to the island's rows of pastel-colored Dutch homes. Legend has it that one of the first governors of Curaçao suffered from terrible headaches because of the sun reflecting off the white houses, and to accommodate him, all the homes were painted with vibrant colors.

The fairy-tale ambiance of the island is captured in its Dutch-colonial architecture, with the rest of its landscape more reminiscent of America's desert-like Southwest.

THE CRUISE LINE SITUATION American Canadian Caribbean, Celebrity, Cunard, Holland America, Norwegian, Premier, Princess, Radisson, Royal Olympic, and Windstar all make port calls here.

THE MONEY SITUATION The official currency is the **Netherlands Antillean florin (NAf),** also called a guilder. (NAf1 = US56¢). Canadian and U.S. dollars are accepted for purchases.

THE LANGUAGE SITUATION Dutch, Spanish, and English are spoken, along with Papiamento, a regional dialect that combines these three major tongues with Amerindian and African dialects.

Curaçao Self-Tour

Cruise ships dock at the terminal just beyond the Queen Emma Pontoon Bridge. It is a 6- to 10-minute walk to the heart of Willemstad from the terminal, and taxis are available.

The **Curaçao Tourist Board** is located at Pietermaai 19.

If you opt to take a **taxi,** agree on a fare prior to the ride, because taxis aren't metered. You don't need to tip drivers. The best spot to catch a taxi is on Otrobanda.

Yellow buses run from Wilhelmina Plein (near the shopping center) to most parts of the island. You can flag a bus at any designated bus stop.

Within Walking Distance

At the **Floating Market,** located a few minutes' walk from the pontoon bridge, schooners from Venezuela, Columbia, and other areas dock alongside the canal. The vendors sell fruits, spices, and fresh fish, and there's always a flurry of activity. Nearby, on Van den Brandhof Street, in a newly-renovated mansion that was once a bordello, you'll find one of the island's newest attractions, the **Curaçao Maritime Museum,** where exhibits trace the island's history. Admission is $8.50 for adults, $4.50 for students and children under 12.

The **Mikve Israel-Emanuel Synagogue,** at the corner of Columbusstraat and Hanchi Snog, dates from 1651 and houses the oldest Jewish congregation in the New World. The floor of the building is covered in white sand, symbolic of the desert of the early Israelites. The **Jewish Historical and Cultural Museum** next door displays ritual, ceremonial, and cultural objects, many dating back to the 17th and 18th centuries. Admission is $2.

Art lovers can visit the **Curaçao Museum** on Van Leeuwenhoekstraat, which is home to paintings, objets d'art, and antique furniture. An art gallery is located on the museum grounds. Admission is $2 for adults, $1 for children.

The **Curaçao Seaquarium,** off Dr. Martin Luther King Boulevard, features a display of more than 400 species of fish and plant life. A standout feature is a "shark and animal encounter" in which divers, snorkelers, and experienced swimmers get to feed, film, and photograph sharks, stingrays, lobsters, and other marine life in a controlled environment. Nonswimmers can see but not touch the underwater life from a 46-foot semisubmersible observatory. The seaquarium also boasts the island's only full-facility, powder-white, palm-shaded beach. Admission is $12.50 adults, $7 for children under 15.

Beyond Walking Distance

About a 45-minute taxi ride from Willemstad is the 4,500-acre **Christoffel National Park,** where you will find an abundance of flora and fauna and, ascending from the desert-like landscape, the 1,230-foot-high Mount Christoffelberg. Several hiking trails can take you to the top. Along the route, you will find Arawak paintings and Piedra di Monton, a rock formation created by the slaves who cleared this former plantation. Admission is $9.

Next door to the park is **National Park Shete Boka** (Seven Bays), a turtle sanctuary. Admission is $1.50.

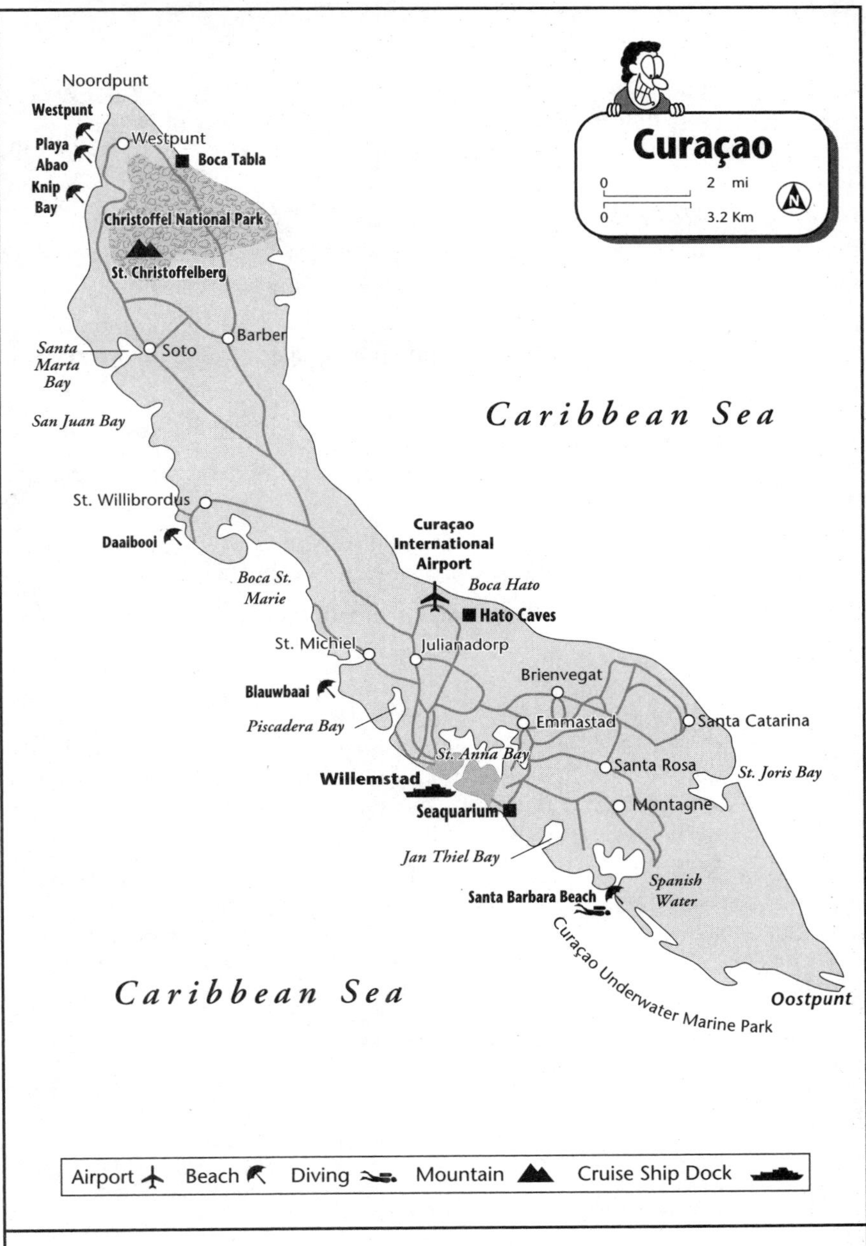

Classic Curaçao Experiences:

- See how people sailed the area in times past at the **Curaçao Maritime Museum**
- See 400 species of fish and plant life at the **Curaçao Seaquarium**
- Hike to the top of St. Christoffelberg in **Christoffel National Park**
- Take a **Countryside Tour** and visit Westpunt, St. Christoffelberg, and other spots
- Visit the 350-year-old **Mikve Israel-Emanuel Synagogue**
- See what lurks belowground at the **Hato Caves**

If you want to explore the island's deeper side, check out **Hato Caves,** filled with stalagmites, stalactites, and underground pools. It was once used as a hiding place for runaway slaves. Admission is $6.25 for adults, $4.75 for children.

Curaçao has 38 beaches, and among the better ones are **Santa Barbara Beach** and **Blauwbaai (Blue Bay).** If you take a cab (fares are negotiable), make arrangements for the driver to pick you up at a specific time.

Note: Watch out for sea urchins that lurk in these waters. Stepping on one is quite unpleasant, and locals suggest applying vinegar or lime juice to ease the discomfort.

The Best Shore Excursions

You can tour the town on your own in about 2 or 3 hours, with plenty of time for sunbathing and swimming.

Countryside Tour (3 hours, $29): Many cruise lines offer a countryside tour that visits Westpunt, Mount Christoffel, and other spots.

Submarine Trip (3 hours, $39): This short trip includes a visit to the Seaquarium.

Freeport/Lucaya

Grand Bahama Island is brimming with hordes of tourists and teeming with sports, sun, and nightlife. There is an air of glitz and glamour here because of the casinos and discos, but there's also a more natural side you can discover by visiting the island's many parks and gardens.

Other ways to spend your day include checking out the nearly 100 shops at the International Bazaar, diving with a dolphin, golfing at a championship golf course, taking a parasailing adventure, or just having a drink at Pusser's and sampling the conch (pronounced *konk*)—either by eating a conch salad, conch chowder, conch fritters, or other delicacies.

THE CRUISE LINE SITUATION Cape Canaveral, Carnival, New SeaEscape, and Windjammer make port calls here.

THE MONEY SITUATION The legal tender is the **Bahamian dollar (B$1),** but both U.S. and Bahamian dollars are accepted on an equal basis. (B$1 = US$1)

THE LANGUAGE SITUATION English is the official language.

Freeport/Lucaya Self-Tour

The **Grand Bahama Tourism Board** is located at the International Bazaar in Freeport. There is also a booth at Port Lucaya.

On Grand Bahama Island, cruise passengers disembark at the west end of the island in the middle of nowhere. It's about a $10 taxi ride to Freeport and the International Bazaar, the center of most action on the island. Taxis are metered and the rates are fixed by law.

Other ways to explore the island include renting a car ($45 to $60 a day), bicycle ($12 for a half day, $20 for a full day), or moped ($40 a day). Buses run from the International Bazaar to downtown Freeport and from the Pub on the Mall to the Lucaya area. The fare is 75¢, and bus drivers do not give change.

Within Walking Distance

Gotta be honest here: Nothing of interest is within walking distance of the pier itself.

Beyond Walking Distance

In the center of the waterfront restaurant and shopping area of Port Lucaya is **Count Basie Square,** where you can hear the best live music on the island nightly. The square, of course, honors great jazzman Count Basie, who used to have a home on the island.

There's no place for shopping in The Bahamas quite like the **International Bazaar,** at East Mall Drive and East Sunrise Highway, which has been described as a shopper's theme park. Nearly 100 shops sell just about any trinket your little heart desires. You can find Bahamian items at the **Straw Market,** next door to the Bazaar.

Garden of the Groves in the East End, 7 miles east of the International Bazaar, is the prime attraction of the island, an 11-acre garden honoring Wallace Groves, the founder of Freeport/Lucaya. The scenic setting features waterfalls and flowering shrubs, as well as some 10,000 trees that attract a variety of tropical birds. Admission is $5. Located at the intersection of Midshipman Road and Magellan Drive.

Lucaya National Park, on Sunrise Highway, also on the East End about 12 miles from Lucaya, is a 40-acre park filled with mangrove, pine, and palm trees. A wooden path winds through the woods and takes visitors to caves and freshwater springs. Admission is free.

If nature is not your thing, you can try your luck at the **Princess Casino** at the Bahamas Princess Resort, at the Mall at West Sunrise Highway, adjacent to the International Bazaar.

Other worthwhile adventures on Grand Bahama Island include the **Dolphin Experience** operated by the *Underwater Explorers Society* (UNEXSO). You can get up close and personal with dolphins for $36. Diving with a dolphin in the ocean costs $130, and reservations are essential (call ☎ **800/992-DIVE** in the U.S.). UNEXSO also offers daily reef trips, shark dives, wreck dives, and snorkeling excursions.

Most of the **beaches** on Grand Bahama Island are in Lucaya, where the major resort hotels are located, but a favorite is **Xanadu Beach** at the Xanadu Beach Resort, which is in Freeport.

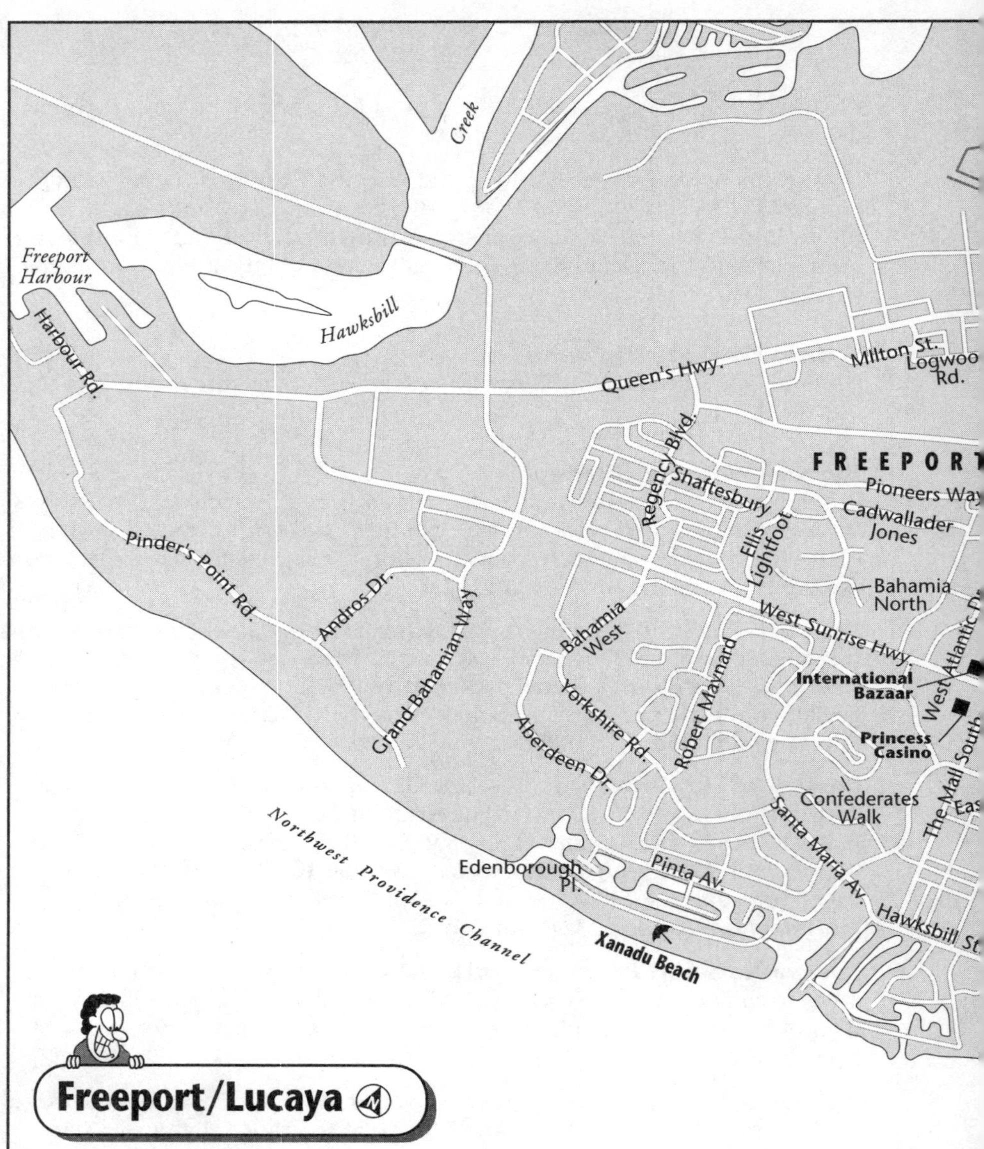

Classic Freeport/Lucaya Experiences:

- Shop, Shop, SHOP at the **International Bazaar**
- Take in the waterfalls, trees, and tropical birds at the **Garden of the Groves**
- Try your luck at the **Princess Casino**
- Take a hike through **Lucaya National Park**
- Swim with the fishes at UNEXSO's **Dolphin Experience**

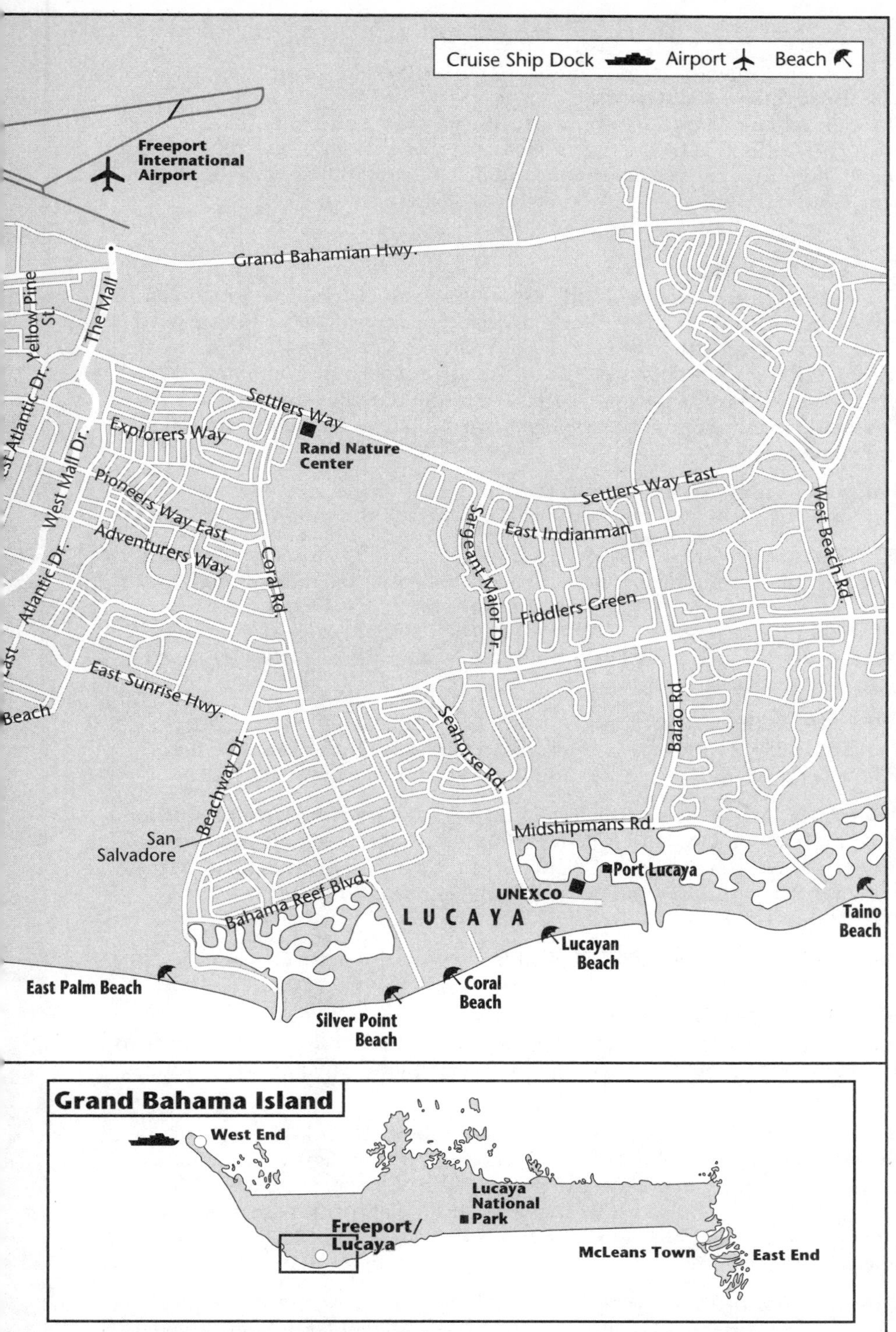
Cruise Ship Dock
Airport
Beach
Freeport
International
Airport
Grand Bahamian Hwy.
Yellow Pine
St.
The Mall
Atlantic Dr.
West Mall Dr.
Atlantic Dr.
Settlers Way
Explorers Way
Rand Nature
Center
Pioneers Way East
Adventurers Way
Coral Rd.
Settlers Way East
Sargeant Major Dr.
East Indianman
West Beach Rd.
Fiddlers Green
East Sunrise Hwy.
Beach
Seahorse Rd.
Balao Rd.
Beachway Dr.
Midshipmans Rd.
San
Salvadore
Port Lucaya
UNEXCO
Bahama Reef Blvd.
LUCAYA
Taino
Beach
Lucayan
Beach
East Palm Beach
Coral
Beach
Silver Point
Beach
Grand Bahama Island
West End
Lucaya
National
Park
Freeport/
Lucaya
McLeans Town
East End

The Best Shore Excursions

Garden of the Groves/International Bazaar Tour (3 hours, $12): Most ships offer this trip, but be forewarned that you probably will only spend 30 minutes at the nature site and be led like cattle around the shopping complex. Both can really be better explored on your own.

Grand Cayman

The largest of the Cayman Islands, Grand Cayman is one place where you can go to Hell and back (see "Beyond Walking Distance," later in this section), and still have time to snorkel or go diving. There's probably more to see underwater than on land. There's also championship shopping that lines the streets around the port in George Town, the island's capital. Grand Cayman has more than 500 tax-advantaged offshore banks for the financially secure.

Cruise ships ferry passengers into George Town to a pier that is along Harbour Drive and is conveniently in the center of the shopping district.

The area was first home to shipwrecked sailors and buccaneers in the 16th and 17th centuries. The real British connection occurred later, though, when Scottish fishermen arrived, setting the slow pace of local life. Columbus referred to the islands as *Las Tortugas,* or *The Turtles,* because of the large number of green sea turtles in surrounding waters. Those turtles are now an endangered species.

THE CRUISE LINE SITUATION Carnival, Celebrity, Commodore, Costa, Cunard, Holland America, Mediterranean Shipping, Norwegian, Premier, Princess, Royal Olympic, and World Explorer all make port calls here.

THE MONEY SITUATION The legal tender is the **Cayman Islands dollar (C.I.).** Canadian, U.S., and British currencies are accepted, but you'll save money if you exchange your U.S. dollars for Cayman Islands dollars. Many restaurants and shops quote prices in Cayman Islands dollars. ($1 C.I. = US$1.25)

THE LANGUAGE SITUATION English is the official language.

Grand Cayman Self-Tour

After disembarking at the pier in George Town, head to the **Department of Tourism** in the Pavilion Building in Cricket Square, which is open Monday to Friday.

It's easy to get around Grand Cayman by car once you adjust to driving on the left. Rentals are available through several franchise agencies, including Avis, Budget, and Hertz. Expect to pay between $35 and $55 a day. Bicycles and motorcycles are a nice alternative given the flat roads, with scooters about $25 a day and bikes about $15. Taxis typically run $10 to $12 for a one-way fare.

Duty-free shopping can be found right across the street from the pier. Stores offer a variety of quality goods, from black-coral jewelry and a variety

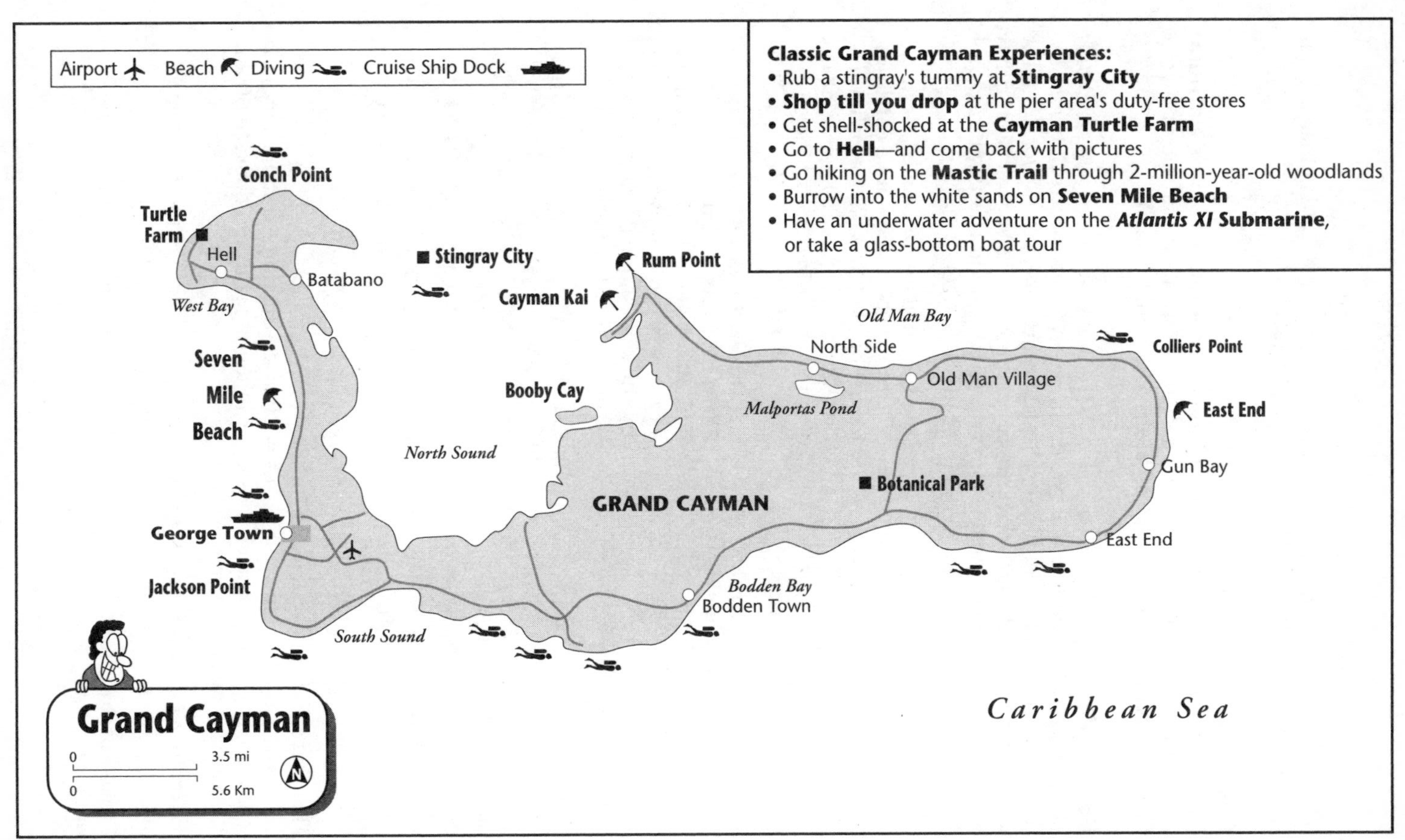
Airport Beach Diving Cruise Ship Dock
Classic Grand Cayman Experiences:
• Rub a stingray's tummy at Stingray City
• Shop till you drop at the pier area's duty-free stores
• Get shell-shocked at the Cayman Turtle Farm
• Go to Hell—and come back with pictures
• Go hiking on the Mastic Trail through 2-million-year-old woodlands
• Burrow into the white sands on Seven Mile Beach
• Have an underwater adventure on the Atlantis XI Submarine, or take a glass-bottom boat tour
Conch Point
Turtle Farm
Hell
Batabano
West Bay
Stingray City
Rum Point
Cayman Kai
Seven Mile Beach
Booby Cay
Old Man Bay
North Side
Old Man Village
Colliers Point
Malportas Pond
East End
North Sound
Gun Bay
Botanical Park
GRAND CAYMAN
George Town
East End
Jackson Point
Bodden Bay
Bodden Town
South Sound
Caribbean Sea
Grand Cayman
0
3.5 mi
0
5.6 Km

of turtle products to Irish linens, British woolens, silver, and china. Be forewarned that turtle products can't be brought back to the U.S.

Within Walking Distance

Located in the island's former courthouse, the **Cayman Islands National Museum** on Harbour Drive offers a variety of Caymanian artifacts collected by Ira Thompson from the 1930s. Adults $5, children $2.50.

Beyond Walking Distance

The **Cayman Turtle Farm** at Northwest Point is the world's only green–sea turtle farm. Its aim is to both supply quality turtle meat to the local market and also to help replenish the turtle population to local waters. Visitors have the opportunity to view turtles from eggs to 600-pound adults. Admission is $5 for adults, $2.50 for children 6 to 12 (under 6 free).

Life Preservers

Remember that U.S. law prohibits the importation of the kind of turtle products you'll see sold in the Caymans.

The tiny mail outpost called **Hell,** at Northwest Point, includes a coral-reef formation that looks like a Dali interpretation of the place's namesake. The signposts pointing toward the area make for a nifty snapshot.

The **Queen Elizabeth II Botanic Park,** off Frank Sound Road, North Side, allows you a 1-hour walk through rugged, wooded land, wetlands, swamp, dry thickets, and mahogany trees. Adults $2.50, $1 children over 5.

At **The Mastic Trail,** west of Frank Sound Road, a 45-minute drive from George Town, a restored 200-year-old footpath takes you through a woodland area in the center of the island that is estimated to be 2 million years old. It's easy to get lost on your own. The 3-hour tours offered are a better bet and cost $30 per person. Reservations are required (☎ **809/949-1996**).

Seven Mile Beach, which begins north of George Town, offers white sands with a backdrop of Australian pines and is an easy cab ride from the cruise dock.

The Best Shore Excursions

Stingray City (2 hours, $28): This popular destination for snorkelers and scuba divers gives you the chance to swim among and feed between 30 and 50 relatively tame stingrays.

***Atlantis XI* Submarine Trip** ($55 minutes, $72): If you want to view undersea life while remaining dry, this is the trip for you.

Glass-Bottom Boat Tour (1 hour, $29): A short intro to the underwater world of Grand Cayman.

Grenada

The Grenada of today is a peaceful place to enjoy the Caribbean experience. There's great snorkeling, sailing, and fishing, especially along Grand Anse Beach (considered among the best in the Caribbean), and there's no sign of the political turmoil of the late 70s and early 80s, which included an invasion by U.S. troops to rescue American medical students.

As fragrant as it is picturesque, a stop in Grenada offers a great chance to buy many favorite spices. Among the items that can be purchased at the waterfront Carenage (the main street) in the capital, **St. George's,** are nutmeg, mace, cocoa, ginger, cloves, and cinnamon. The island is covered in lush foliage, including palms, oleander, bougainvillea, purple and red hibiscus, bananas, breadfruit, and ferns.

St. George's is located in a deep crater of an old, dead volcano and flanked by several old forts. Georgian colonial buildings with wrought-iron balconies line steep, narrow streets.

THE CRUISE LINE SITUATION Carnival, Celebrity, Clipper, Club Med, Cunard, Holland America, Mediterranean Shipping, Premier, Princess, Royal Olympic, Windjammer, and Windstar all make port calls here.

THE MONEY SITUATION The official currency is the **Eastern Caribbean dollar (EC$).** (EC$1 = US37¢)

THE LANGUAGE SITUATION English is commonly spoken here.

Grenada Self-Tour

There's a **tourist information center** at the pier in St. George's, where some ships dock (others bring their passengers ashore by tender). You easily can cover St. George's on foot. It's not particularly easy to get around by car, but car rentals are available. Taxi drivers offer their services as guides for around $15 an hour, but make sure you negotiate a price before starting out. The most economical way to travel is by bus (40¢ to $2.20). Water-taxi service ($4) is an ideal way to both soak in the scenery and get to Grand Anse Beach.

Within Walking Distance

The main street, known as the **Carenage,** is a short walk from the pier. A wide range of shopping awaits you there.

Connected to the Carenage by the Sendall Tunnel is the **Esplanade** on the Outer Harbour, a scenic and market area.

Grenada National Museum, at the corner of Young and Monckton streets, is a small facility located in the foundations of an old French army barracks and prison dating back to 1704. Among the more interesting items are two bathtubs: One is a wooden barrel used by the fort's prisoners; the second is a carved marble tub used by Josephine Bonaparte when she was a young girl in Martinique. Admission is about 90¢.

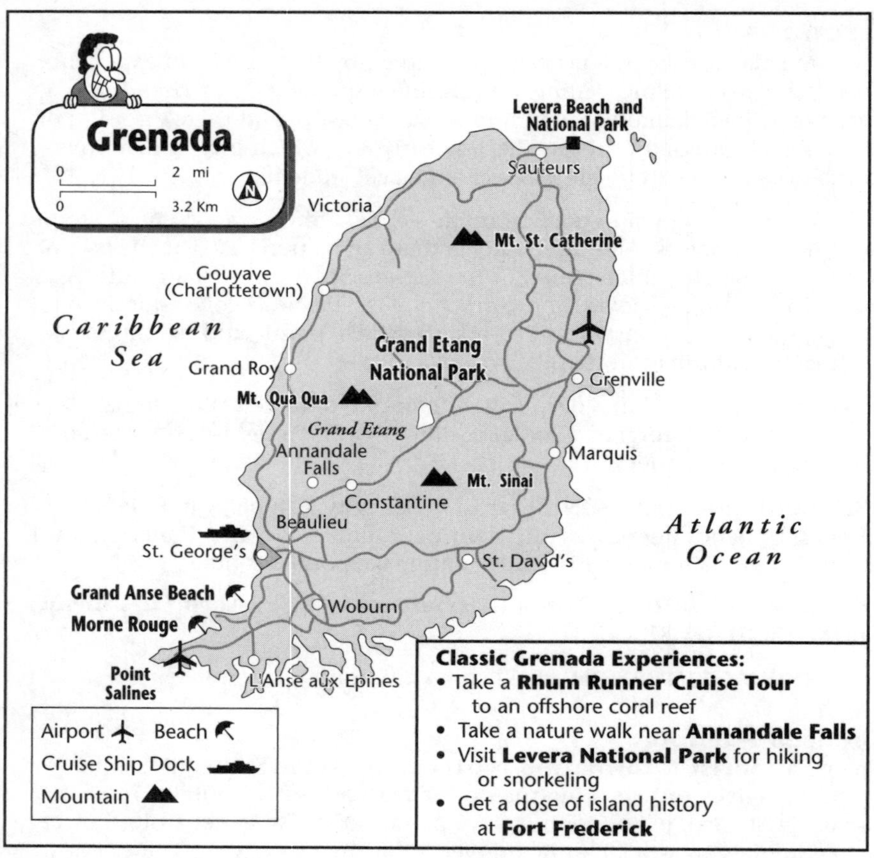

Beyond Walking Distance

Fort Frederick, a short taxi ride up to Richmond Hill, was begun by occupying French forces in 1779 and completed by the British, who recaptured the island in 1793. The fort's battlements offer a great view of the harbor and yacht marina.

Annandale Falls, a 15-minute drive into the mountains northeast of St. George's, is a great place for a picnic or nature walk through lush tropical surroundings that feature liana vines, elephant ears, and other native plants.

Levera National Park, 15 miles from St. George's harbor—reachable by taxi, bus, or water taxi—has white, sandy beaches and opportunities for snorkeling among offshore coral reefs and seagrass beds. Be aware, though, that the surf can be rough. Hikers will enjoy walking around the mangrove swamp, lake, and bird sanctuary.

Betty Mascoll's Morne Fendue, at St. Patrick's, is a plantation house built in 1912 and located about 25 miles north of St. George's. It's a great place to dine on such old-time island recipes as yam-and-sweet-potato casserole, curried chicken, corn coo coo, and pepperpot stew, a savory concoction that includes pork and oxtail. Call ahead (☎ **473/442-9330**).

One of the best beaches in the Caribbean is **Grande Anse Beach,** located about 10 minutes and a $10 taxi ride from the pier (you can also take a water taxi there for $4). The beach offers 2 miles of sugar-white sands, and most of the island's best resorts are within walking distance.

The Best Shore Excursions

Rhum Runner Cruise Tour (3 hours, $26): This trip aboard a glass-bottom boat offers a view of marine life and coral reefs offshore, as well as all the rum you want to consume.

Grenada Tour (3 hours, $25 to $30): This highlights tour of the interior and coastal regions includes a visit to Grand Anse Beach. You also get to see part of Grenada's rain forest, a nutmeg-processing station, and small hamlets along the way.

Guadeloupe

Guadeloupe is shaped like a butterfly, and its wings are individual islands separated by a narrow channel, the Riviere Salee.

The eastern island, Grande-Terre, boasts sugar plantations and rolling hills. The western island, Basse-Terre, is mountainous, with the active 4,800-foot volcano, La Soufriere, towering above its rain forest and waterfalls.

During the day, you can find a lively crowd throughout the capital, Pointe-a-Pitre. Shops close for long, leisurely lunches, and at the open-air markets, vendors wear colorful headdresses. When the sun sets, the town grows quiet and the crowds disappear.

French is the official language of the island. Creole is the second language, and English is spoken only in the major tourist areas.

THE CRUISE LINE SITUATION Carnival, Cunard, Holland America, Mediterranean Shipping Cruises, and Premier all make port calls here.

THE MONEY SITUATION The official currency is the **French franc (Fr).** Most restaurants quote prices in francs, but shops around the cruise dock generally have prices in both francs and U.S. dollars, with rates lower than the official exchange rate. (1 Fr = approximately US16.3¢)

THE LANGUAGE SITUATION The official language is French, and Creole is commonly spoken as well. English is spoken only in the tourist centers.

Guadeloupe Self-Tour

The **Office Departmental du Tourisme** is located at 5 Square de la Banque.

Ships dock at Centre St.-Jean-Perse at Pointe-a-Pitre on Grande-Terre. Duty-free shopping, open-air markets, a bank, and phone booths are located right at the pier.

To get around the island, most people take **taxis.** Settle on a price before taking a trip; although the fares are supposed to be regulated by the government, some taxis charge whatever they can. It is possible to go sightseeing with a group via a taxi and negotiate the fare. Renting a car and catching a bus are other options.

You will need to take a car or taxi to visit Basse-Terre.

Within Walking Distance

A lively **covered market** is located at the corner of rue Frebault and rue Thiers. If you want to relax in the shade, head to the town center, **Place de la Victoire,** a park filled with palm trees and poincianas that offer relief from the sun.

In the city, French items are the best shopping buy; local goods can be found on the back streets.

Beyond Walking Distance

On **Grande-Terre,** you can head to **Gosier,** the major resort area where the beach stretches for nearly 5 miles, and to **Fort Fleur d'Epee,** where the 18th-century site provides views over the bay.

Other points of interest on the island include the **Edgar Clerc Archaeological Museum La Rosette,** Parc de la Rosette, Le Moule, which exhibits collections of Amerindian artifacts. Admission is $2.20.

The **Aquarium de la Guadeloupe,** at the tourist complex of Bas du Fort, 2 miles east of Pointe-á-Pitre, near Gosier, is the largest and most modern aquarium facility in the Caribbean and home to tropical fish, coral, huge sharks, and other sea creatures. Admission is about $8.35 for adults, $4.40 for children 12 and under. It's just off the main highway near Bas-du-Fort Marina.

On **Basse-Terre,** you'll find several good beaches, including **Clungy Beach** and **Grande Anse.**

Parc Naturel de Gaudeloupe covers nearly one-fifth of the island and is an attraction for nature lovers. The park offers small exhibition huts spotlighting the island's volcano; the forest; and coffee, sugarcane, and rum. A variety of tame birds and animals—such as the wood pigeon, turtledove, and *titi* (a raccoon that is the island's official mascot)—make their homes here.

The Best Shore Excursions

Most ships offer a trip exploring scenic **Grande-Terre** (3 hours, $40), and some include even more scenic **Basse-Terre.**

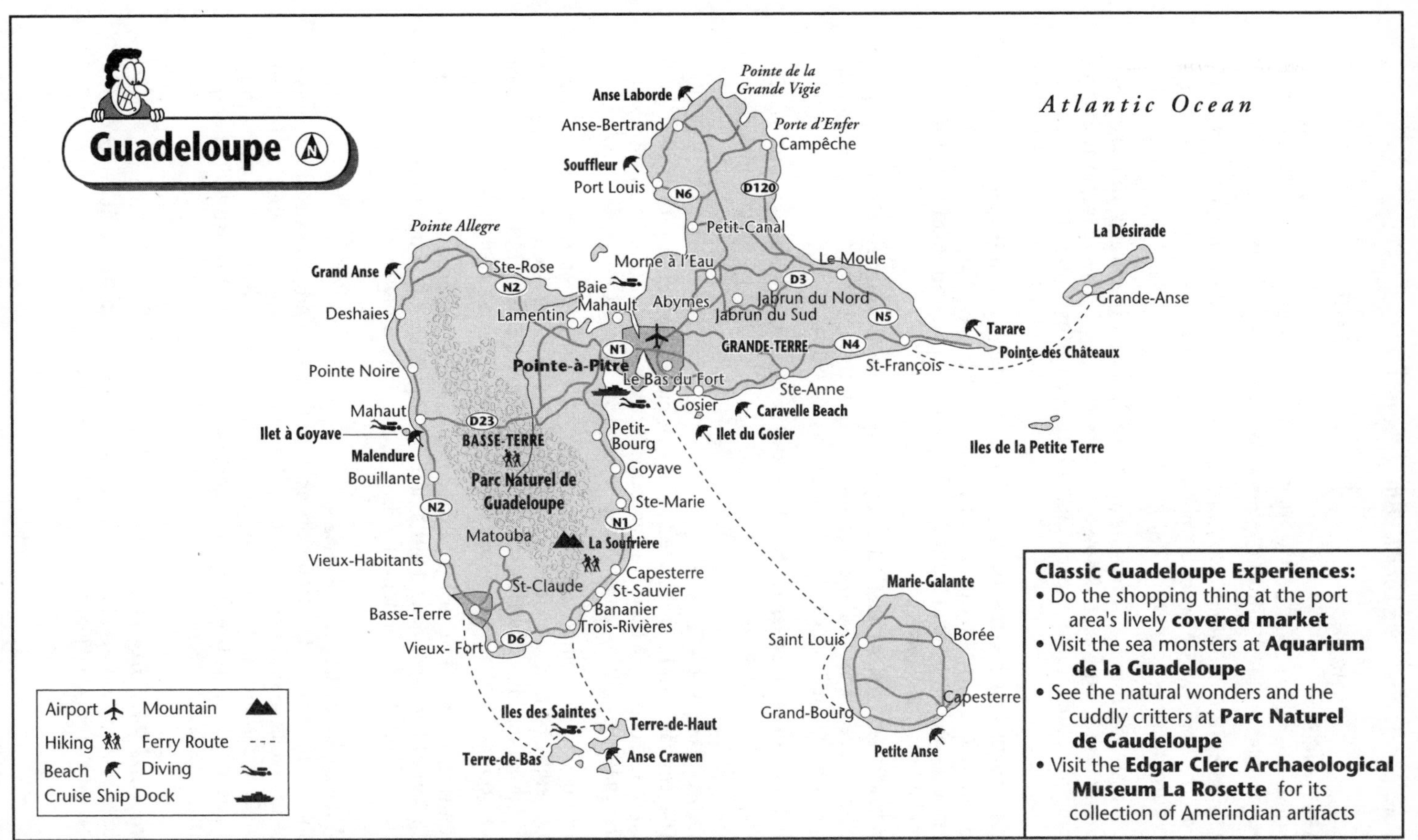
Guadeloupe
Atlantic Ocean
Pointe de la Grande Vigie
Anse Laborde
Anse-Bertrand
Porte d'Enfer
Campêche
Souffleur
Port Louis
N6
D120
Petit-Canal
Pointe Allegre
La Désirade
Grande-Anse
Grand Anse
Ste-Rose
N2
Morne à l'Eau
Le Moule
D3
Baie Mahault
Abymes
Jabrun du Nord
Jabrun du Sud
N5
Deshaies
Lamentin
Tarare
GRANDE-TERRE
N4
Pointe-des Châteaux
N1
Pointe-à-Pitre
Le Bas du Fort
St-François
Pointe Noire
Ste-Anne
Mahaut
Gosier
Caravelle Beach
Ilet à Goyave
D23
Petit-Bourg
Ilet du Gosier
Iles de la Petite Terre
BASSE-TERRE
Malendure
Goyave
Bouillante
Parc Naturel de Guadeloupe
Ste-Marie
Matouba
La Soufrière
Vieux-Habitants
Capesterre
St-Claude
St-Sauvier
Bananier
Basse-Terre
Trois-Rivières
Vieux- Fort
D6
Marie-Galante
Saint Louis
Borée
Capesterre
Grand-Bourg
Petite Anse
Iles des Saintes
Terre-de-Haut
Terre-de-Bas
Anse Crawen
Airport
Mountain
Hiking
Ferry Route
Beach
Diving
Cruise Ship Dock
Classic Guadeloupe Experiences:
• Do the shopping thing at the port area's lively covered market
• Visit the sea monsters at Aquarium de la Guadeloupe
• See the natural wonders and the cuddly critters at Parc Naturel de Gaudeloupe
• Visit the Edgar Clerc Archaeological Museum La Rosette for its collection of Amerindian artifacts

Jamaica

Jamaica is the land of Bob Marley and Blue Mountain coffee, where Red Stripe beer and jerk chicken offer a taste of the local flavor.

The island's most notable features are its natural ones. The island sparkles with brilliant white beaches, plush green terrain blankets the region, and a mountain peak soars to 7,400 feet above sea level.

Most ships drop their anchors at **Ocho Rios** on the northern coast, but many also head west to **Montego Bay** (Mo Bay). The attractions and shopping are comparable at each city, so there's really no need to visit more than one.

THE CRUISE LINE SITUATION Carnival, Celebrity, Commodore, Costa, Holland America, Mediterranean Shipping Cruises, Norwegian, Premier, Princess, Regal, Royal Caribbean, Royal Olympic, and World Explorer all make port calls here.

THE MONEY SITUATION The currency is the **Jamaican dollar (J$).** Most places accept U.S. dollars, but always determine whether a price is being quoted in Jamaican or U.S. dollars. (J$1 = US3¢)

THE LANGUAGE SITUATION English is the official language, but most Jamaicans speak a rich patois.

Ocho Rios Self-Tour

The **tourist office** is located at the Ocean Village Shopping Centre. Ships dock at the port, which is near Dunn's River Falls and only a mile away from the major shopping area, Ocean Village Shopping Centre.

You need to negotiate for taxi fares. You can also arrange to have a taxi take you sightseeing for a negotiated rate. Taxis that are licensed by the government are equipped with red Public Passenger Vehicle (PPV) plates. The ones without such plates are gypsy cabs, and you should avoid taking them.

Renting a car in Jamaica is not recommended, because Jamaica has a combination of bad drivers and left-sided driving. Also, you have to reserve a car in advance, and leave a deposit when you do. It's a big hassle.

Within Walking Distance

Shopping's the main attraction here, but be warned: The street vendors in Ocho Rios are known for being quite aggressive when it comes to hawking their merchandise. *Ganja*—locally grown marijuana—will be among items being hawked on the street, but just because it's readily available doesn't mean it's legal. It's not.

Beyond Walking Distance

Shore excursions are the best way to see popular sights such as **Dunn's River Falls** (see "The Best Shore Excursions").

The **Columbus Park Museum** is located in a spacious open area between the main coast road and the sea at Discovery Bay. Items on display include a canoe made from a single piece of cottonwood and a planter's strongbox. Admission is free.

Art lovers can head to **Harmony Hall,** which houses a gallery and restaurant. Works by local artists are on display there.

Firefly, about 20 miles east of Ocho Rios, was the home of Sir Noël Coward and his longtime companion, Graham Payn. The house and grounds are open to visitors, who can also visit Coward's grave site. Admission is $10.

If you want to be dazzled by one of Jamaica's beaches, stop at **Mallards Beach** (the most crowded) and **Turtle Beach** (more private).

The Best Shore Excursions

Dunn's River Falls Tour (3½ hours, $35): This is the most popular offering (and thus, the most often crowded), visiting (and climbing, if you wish) a waterfall that cascades 600 feet to the beach. The tour also visits **Shaw Park Botanical Gardens,** the rain forest called **Fern Gully,** and other local sites. You need to wear a bathing suit for this offering. A portion of the tour is reserved for shopping.

Prospect Plantation Tour (4 hours, $39): This tour takes you to a real working plantation.

Brimmer Hall Plantation Tour (3 hours, $49): This trip includes a trip to the countryside. You see the Great House and crops of banana and pimento, and as an added bonus, you pass the estates of James Bond author Ian Fleming and playwright Noël Coward.

Snorkeling Adventure (2 hours, $25): This trip takes you to the coral reef near the cruise pier.

Glass-Bottom Boat Tour (1 hour, $16): Undersea life, without the annoyance of getting soggy.

Montego Bay Self-Tour

The **visitor center** is at Cornwall Beach, St. James. Ships dock at the modern cruise facility, which offers duty-free stores, telephones, and tourist information. The port is not at the center of town, however, so you have to take a $5 taxi ride to get to the heart of "Mo Bay."

In either town, you need to negotiate for taxi fares. You can also arrange to have a taxi take you sightseeing for a negotiated rate. Taxis that are licensed by the government are equipped with red *Public Passenger Vehicle* (PPV) plates. The ones without such plates are gypsy cabs, and you should avoid taking them.

Renting a car in Jamaica is not recommended.

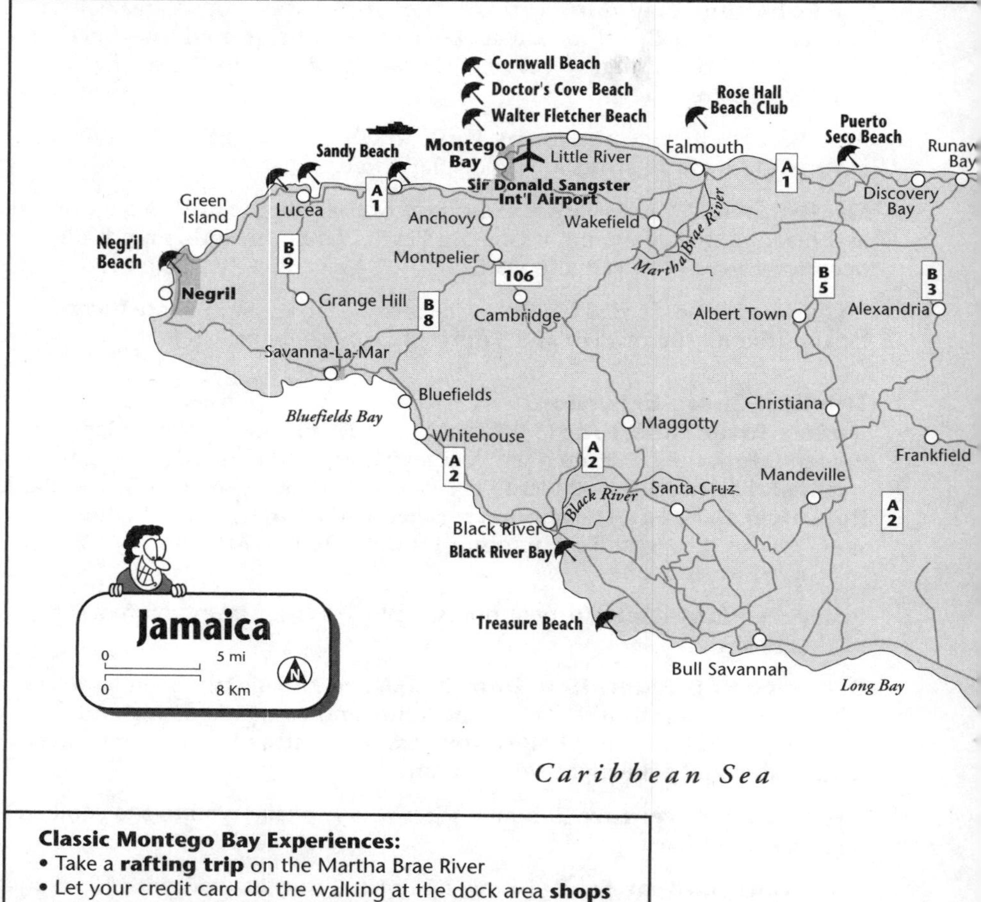

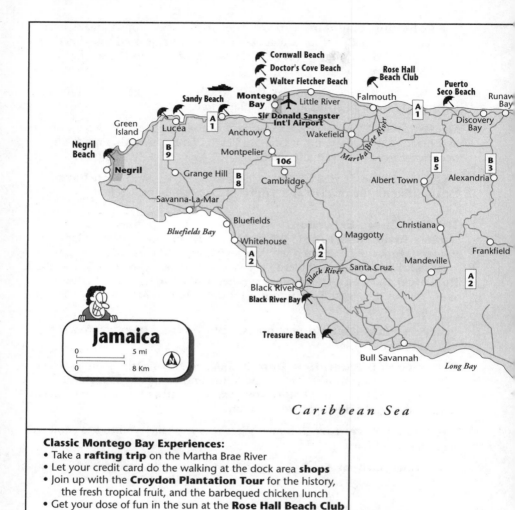

Classic Montego Bay Experiences:

- Take a **rafting trip** on the Martha Brae River
- Let your credit card do the walking at the dock area **shops**
- Join up with the **Croydon Plantation Tour** for the history, the fresh tropical fruit, and the barbequed chicken lunch
- Get your dose of fun in the sun at the **Rose Hall Beach Club**

Within Walking Distance

Like Ocho Rios, there isn't much here except shopping. The primary shopping districts are **Montego Freeport,** located near the pier; **City Centre,** which has duty-free shopping, and **Holiday Shopping Centre.** For arts and crafts items, head to **Old Fort Craft Park** and the **Crafts Market.**

Beyond Walking Distance

Skip the public beaches, and go to the **Rose Hall Beach Club,** about 11 miles east of the city, for fun in the sun. It is equipped with a restaurant, two beach bars, a covered pavilion, an open-air dance area, showers, rest rooms,

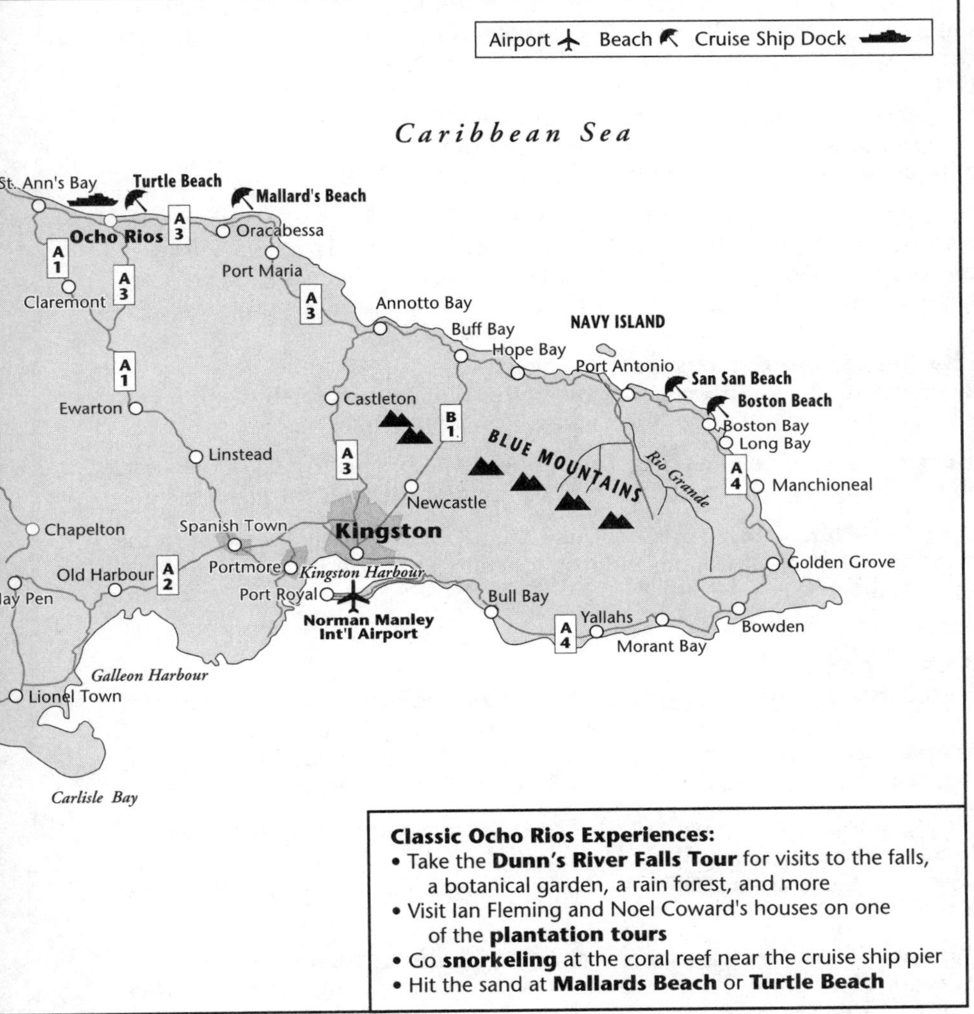

Classic Ocho Rios Experiences:

- Take the **Dunn's River Falls Tour** for visits to the falls, a botanical garden, a rain forest, and more
- Visit Ian Fleming and Noel Coward's houses on one of the **plantation tours**
- Go **snorkeling** at the coral reef near the cruise ship pier
- Hit the sand at **Mallards Beach** or **Turtle Beach**

and changing areas. You can also participate in watersports and beach volleyball and check out the live entertainment. Admission is $15 adults, $10 children.

Rose Hall Great House, 9 miles east of Montego Bay, is a restored home steeped in history and notoriety. It was built by John Palmer nearly 2 centuries ago, but it was the second mistress of the house who made it famous. "Infamous Annie" Palmer, wife of the builder's grandnephew, supposedly experimented with witchcraft and took slaves as her lovers, then killed them when she grew bored of them. On the ground floor, Annie's Pub has been opened. Admission is $15 adults, $10 children.

A historic house of a different sort is **Greenwood Great House,** about 14 miles east of Montego Bay. The house is of Georgian design and was the residence of Richard Barrett, a relative of Elizabeth Barrett Browning. On display is the original library of the Barrett family, with rare books dating from 1697, as well as oil paintings of the family and specially made Wedgwood china. There's also a rare exhibition of musical instruments and a fine collection of antique furniture. Admission is $15 adults, $10 children.

Nature lovers can visit **Rocklands Wildlife Station,** about a mile outside Anchovy on the road from Montego Bay, where you can have a Jamaican doctor bird rest on you finger or feed small doves and finches from your hand. Admission is $6.25.

The Best Shore Excursions

Be prepared: The excursions available in this port are not much to write home about. You might be better going it on your own.

Martha Brae River Rafting Trip (4 hours, $45): This trip takes the river aboard 30-foot, 2-seat bamboo rafts. In all honesty, it's not the greatest trip.

Croydon Plantation Tour (half day, $55): This tour includes a visit to the plantation, tasting pineapple and tropical fruits in season, and a barbecued chicken lunch.

Key West

Legendary for its sunsets, nightlife, and famous residents (including Ernest "Papa" Hemingway), Key West beckons visitors to have fun mixing with its colorful cast of characters and attractions. Key West is the final link in a chain of islands extending 103 miles from the Florida mainland.

Since you will probably have limited time here, avoid the crowded cruise docks and touristy Duval Street for a stroll through secluded byways such as Olivia or William Street. Golfing, snorkeling, and scuba diving are also great at this port.

Ships dock at **Mallory Square** or at nearby **Truman Annex,** and almost everything (shopping, bars, restaurants, and attractions) are either right there or a short ride away.

THE CRUISE LINE SITUATION Cape Canaveral, Carnival, Celebrity, Costa, Cunard, Holland America, Mediterranean Shipping Cruises, Norwegian, Premier, Regal, Royal Caribbean, Royal Olympic, Seabourn, and Silversea all make port calls here.

THE MONEY SITUATION The **U.S. dollar** is the money of choice.

THE LANGUAGE SITUATION It's Florida, so it's English.

Key West Self-Tour

The **Greater Key West Chamber of Commerce** is located at 402 Wall St., near the cruise docks. The island is 4 miles long and 2 miles wide, and

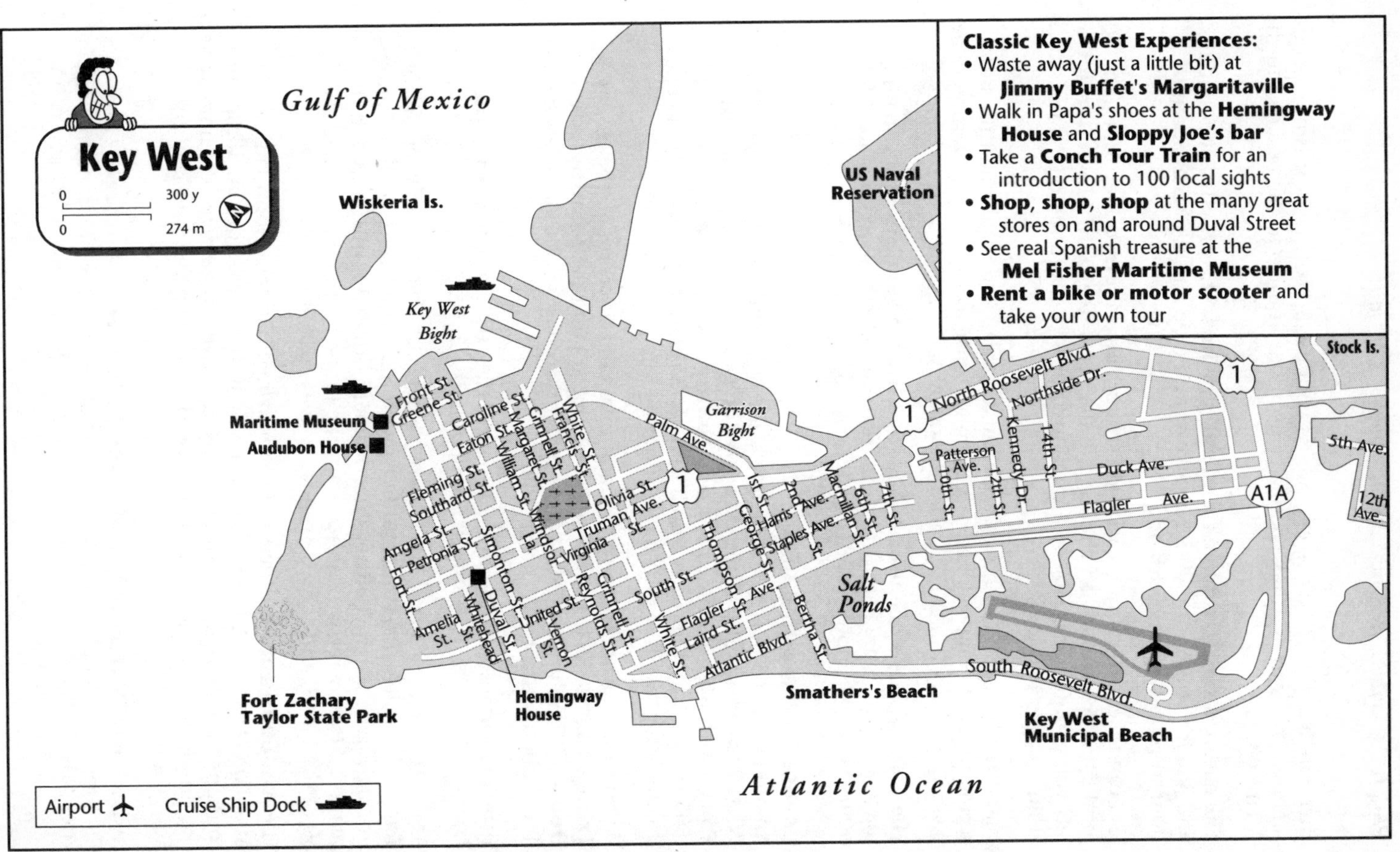

Key West
0 300 y
0 274 m
Gulf of Mexico
Wiskeria Is.
Key West Bight
Maritime Museum
Audubon House
Front St.
Greene St.
Caroline St.
Eaton St.
Margaret St.
Grinnell St.
William St.
Francis St.
White St.
Fleming St.
Southard St.
Olivia St.
Truman Ave.
Windsor La.
Angela St.
Petronia St.
Simonton St.
Virginia St.
Fort St.
Amelia St.
Whitehead St.
Duval St.
United St.
Vernon St.
Reynolds St.
Grinnell St.
South St.
White St.
Palm Ave.
Garrison Bight
Thompson St.
George St.
1st St.
Harris Ave.
2nd Ave.
Staples Ave.
Macmillan St.
6th St.
7th St.
Flagler Ave.
Laird St.
Atlantic Blvd.
Bertha St.
Salt Ponds
US Naval Reservation
North Roosevelt Blvd.
Northside Dr.
Patterson Ave.
10th St.
12th St.
Kennedy Dr.
14th St.
Duck Ave.
Flagler Ave.
A1A
Stock Is.
5th Ave.
12th Ave.
South Roosevelt Blvd.
Fort Zachary Taylor State Park
Hemingway House
Smathers's Beach
Key West Municipal Beach
Atlantic Ocean
Airport
Cruise Ship Dock
Classic Key West Experiences:
• Waste away (just a little bit) at Jimmy Buffet's Margaritaville
• Walk in Papa's shoes at the Hemingway House and Sloppy Joe's bar
• Take a Conch Tour Train for an introduction to 100 local sights
• Shop, shop, shop at the many great stores on and around Duval Street
• See real Spanish treasure at the Mel Fisher Maritime Museum
• Rent a bike or motor scooter and take your own tour

therefore it is pretty easy to explore on your own. Renting a car is not recommended. You can even take public transportation to go to the beaches on the Atlantic side.

The cheapest way to explore the island is by **bus.** The price is 75¢ for adults and 35¢ for seniors and children 6 years and older. It only takes about an hour to ride around the island.

You can take a 90-minute narrated **Conch Tour Train** trolley tour past 100 local sites—$14 adults, $6 children (under age 3 free). **Old Town Trolley** lets you get off and on at top attractions. Tours cost $15 for adults, $6 for children ages 4 to 12.

Island **taxis** operate 24 hours a day but are small and insufficient for sightseeing tours. If you use a taxi service to go to the beach, arrange a time to be picked up. Taxi rates are uniform; the meter starts at $1.40.

The island also is a fine place to tour by **bike,** and aside from the main roads, the streets are fairly free of traffic. You can rent a bicycle for $4 for 8 hours. A 3-hour motor-scooter rental costs $12; all day is $14.

Within Walking Distance

An old-fashioned pub crawl is a quick and easy initiation for visitors to Key West. You can start by hitting **Sloppy Joe's** (201 Duval St.), **Captain Tony's Saloon** (428 Green St.), and **Jimmy Buffett's Margaritaville** (500 Duval St.). At all three you'll find good times, fast food, killer margaritas, and maybe a dose of Papa Hemingway lore.

If you would rather take a more traditional (and drier) route, the **Harry S Truman Little White House** (111 Front St.) and the **Hemingway House** (907 Whitehead St.) are good places to start your tour. Be aware that lines at both attractions can get long.

Truman's former vacation home is part of the 103-acre **Truman Annex.** There's a museum in the small house. Admission is $7.

At the Hemingway House, you can see where Papa wrote *For Whom the Bell Tolls* and *A Farewell to Arms* and lived with his second wife, Pauline. Among the highlights are the Pulitzer Prize winner's original furnishings and the *polydactyl* (many-toed) cats that roam the property. Hemingway had nearly 50 of these cats, and their descendants live on. Admission is $6.50.

The **Audobon House** is devoted to renowned naturalist John James Audobon. The ornithologist did not reside in the three-story building, but it contains his engravings. Surrounded by lush tropical gardens, the home gives you an idea of how rich sailors lived on the island in the 19th century. Admission is $7.50.

Jessie Porter's Heritage House and Robert Frost Cottage (410 Caroline St.) offer a glimpse into the life of Jessie Porter Newton, known as Miss Jessie to her friends. She was the grande dame of Key West and counted many celebrities as friends. Some of the people she entertained here include Tennessee Williams, Gloria Swanson (a childhood girlfriend), and Robert Frost (a family friend who stayed in a cottage out back). The house is filled with antiques and many other items that the Porter family accumulated over six generations. Admission is $6; children under 12 free.

Other notable attractions include the 21-acre **Key West Cemetery,** where you can find gravestones inscribed with such memorable phrases as "I Told You I Was Sick" and "At Least I Know Where He Is Sleeping Tonight."

The **Mel Fisher Maritime Museum** (200 Greene St.) shows the treasure from shipwrecked Spanish galleons collected by treasure-hunter Mel Fisher. There are long-lost Spanish jewelry, doubloons, and silver and gold bouillon on display. Admission is $6.50.

Nancy Forrester's Secret Garden (1 Free School Lane, off Simonton between Southard and Fleming streets) offers more than 130 species of palms, palmettos, climbing vines, and ground covers. An ideal way to spend time is to have a picnic lunch at one of the tables in the garden. Admission is $6.

If your ship leaves late enough, you might get a chance to partake in one of Key West's most celebrated rituals: **watching the sunset from Mallory Dock.** Sunset-watching creates a carnival-like atmosphere at the square.

Beyond Walking Distance

Beaches are not a strong point here. Most are manmade, with sand brought in from the Bahamas or mainland Florida. If you're set on some sun time, though, **Fort Zachary Taylor State Beach** is close to the docks. The beach is fine for sunbathing, but rocks make it a bit difficult to swim.

The Best Shore Excursions

Key West is easy to access by foot or public transportation, so you'll save time and money by heading out on your own instead of signing up for a shore excursion.

Martinique

First impressions are deceiving when it comes to Martinique. Upon landing at the Maritime Terminal in the capital of **Fort-de-France,** there's a choice of a long, hot walk into town through some fairly unappealing scenery or haggling with a taxi driver bent on overcharging his fare. Get beyond this initial experience, though, and you'll find yourself in one of the most beautiful locations in the region. There's a New Orleans–French Riviera feel in Fort-de-France, from flower-covered, iron-grilled balconies to houses lining narrow, steep streets. The island attractions include miles of white, sandy beaches south of Fort-de-France and gray, sandy beaches to the north; five bays and coves; top-drawer shopping; Creole cuisine; and Mount Pelée, which rises to 4,656 feet in the rain forest of the northern region.

The island's links to France date back to 1763, when France gave up rights to Canada in exchange for the French West Indies. That was also the year that the future Empress Josephine was born here, and Louis XIV's mistress, Madama de Maintenon, also lived here for a time in the fishing village Le Precheur.

Sea Stories

Martinique is not a colony of France but a *departement,* meaning the people here are full-fledged French citizens.

THE CRUISE LINE SITUATION Carnival, Celebrity, Holland America, Mediterranean Shipping Cruises, Premier, Princess, Star Clippers, Tall Ship Adventures, Windjammer, and Windstar all make port calls here.

THE MONEY SITUATION The **French franc (Fr)** is the legal tender here. (US$1 = Fr 6.14)

THE LANGUAGE SITUATION French is the official language and is spoken by almost everyone. English is spoken occasionally in the major tourist areas.

Martinique Self-Tour

There's a tourist information office at the Maritime Terminal, but it has a reputation for being less than helpful to travelers. Some cruise lines, instead of docking here, will anchor in the **Baie des Flamands** and transport passengers to the heart of Fort-de-France via tender. Otherwise, you have a choice between a hot walk to downtown or an overpriced $8 (or more) cab ride.

There are two kinds of **bus service** available to travelers: *grand busses* go anywhere within Fort-de-France for 85¢ to $1.35, while privately owned minivans called *taxis collectifs* travel outside the city for a one-way fare of around $5. *Note:* These are both crowded and uncomfortable.

Taxis are probably the best way to get around, but they can be expensive, especially between 8pm and 6am, when a 40% surcharge is added. A 5-hour tour by taxi can run up to $220.

Car rentals ($40 to $60 a day) are available from Avis, Budget, or Hertz. Consider getting a collision-damage waiver as protection against the island's hordes of reckless drivers.

Traveling by **ferry** is the cheapest way to get between quai d'Esnambuc in Fort-de-France and Pointe-du Bout, the main tourist zone. The one-way fare is $2.50.

Within Walking Distance

La Savane, a garden of palms and mangoes with a statue of Napoleon's Josephine facing her birthplace in Trois-Ilets, lies in the center of Fort-de-France.

Macouba
Grand Rivière
Basse-Pointe
Leyritz
Le Lorrain
N1
Montagne Pelée
Ajoupa-Bouillon
Le Marigot
Le Prêcheur
Le Morne Rouge
Ste-Marie
Tartane
Chateau Dubuc
St-Pierre
Morne des Esses
Caravelle Peninsula
Trinité
Musée Gaugin
Le Carbet
Gros-Morne
N2
N3
N4
Balata
Bellefontaine
St-Joseph
Case-Pilote
Lamentin
Le François
Fort-de-France
Lamentin International Airport
Pointe du Bout
Anse Mitan
Mt. Vauclin
N6
N5
Vauclin
Anse à l'Ane
Trois-Ilets
D7
Grande Anse
Anses-d'Arlets
D37
Le-Diamant
Rivière-Pilote
Le Marin
Ste-Luce
D18A
Diamant
Diamond Rock
Ste-Anne
Cap Chevalier
Petrified Forest
Plage des Salines

Atlantic Ocean

Caribbean Sea

Airport
Beach
Cruise Ship Dock
Mountain

Classic Martinique Experiences:

- Take a tour to **The Pompeii of Martinique** and visit what's left of St. Pierre
- Visit the Empress Josephine's birthplace at **Trois-Ilets**
- Get in touch with Arawak and Carib history at the **Musee Departemental de la Martinique**
- Visit the tropical botanical park and restored Creole house at **Jardin de Balata**
- Hit the beach at **Point du Bout**, **Anse Mitan**, or **Plage des Salines**

St. Louis Roman Catholic Cathedral, rue Victor-Schoelcher, is the island's religious centerpiece, dating back to 1875.

Bibliotheque Schoelcher, 21 rue de la Liberté, was named in honor of 19th-century hero Victor Schoelcher, who worked to free the slaves. The library's structure was displayed at the Paris Exposition in 1889.

Musee Departemental de la Martinique, 9 rue de la Liberte, contains relics left from the island's early settlers, the Arawaks and Caribs. Admission is $3.30 for adults, $2.20 for students, $1 for kids.

Beyond Walking Distance

Jardin de Balata, just north of the capital along Route N3, is a tropical botanical park built by Jean-Phillippe Thoze on former jungle land that was overgrowing at his grandmother's Creole house. The house has been restored and furnished with antiques and etchings. Admission is $7.70 for adults, $3.30 for children.

Le Carbet looks much as it did when Paul Gauguin painted the beach in his *Bord de Mer.* Gauguin lived here in 1887 before heading to Tahiti to paint his most famous works. Le Carbet was also the landing point of Columbus in 1502 and the first French settlers in 1635.

Centre d'Art Musee Paul-Gauguin, Anse Turin, features books, prints, letters, and other items to help remember Gauguin's brief stay in Le Carbet. Admission is $3.30.

Trois-Ilets (*Twaz-ee-lay*) is the birthplace of Marie-Josephe-Rose Tasher de la Pagerie in 1763, who became wife to Napoleon I and empress of France. It's a 20-minute taxi ride south of Fort-de-France. There's also a small museum devoted to Josephine in La Pagerie.

The best beaches include the white, sandy stretches of **Point du Bout,** where the island's major hotels are located, and **Anse Mitan** and **Plage des Salines** in the south.

The Best Shore Excursions

The Pompeii of Martinique (2½ hours, $40): This trip takes you through the lush countryside to St. Pierre, which was the cultural and economic capital of Martinique until May 7, 1902, when Mount Pelée erupted with fire and lava, killing 30,000 people. It's one of the most intriguing outings offered in the Caribbean. The Musee Volcanologique, included on the tour, offers pictures and relics excavated from the debris, including a clock that stopped at the exact moment the lava hit.

Nassau

One of Nassau's claims to fame is that, due to millions of government development dollars, 11 cruise ships can dock at the cruise port at one time. Nassau can also brag about its duty-free shopping, great entertainment, and powder-white beaches. Visitors will find the island has not lost its British colonial charms.

Cruise ships anchor near **Rawson Square,** the heart of the city and its main shopping district.

THE CRUISE LINE SITUATION Carnival, Celebrity, Costa, Crystal, Cunard, Disney, Holland America, Mediterranean Shipping Cruises, New SeaEscape, Norwegian, Premier, Royal Caribbean, Royal Olympic, Seabourn, Silversea, Windjammer, and World Explorer all make port stops here.

THE MONEY SITUATION The legal tender is the **Bahamian dollar (B$),** but both U.S. and Bahamian dollars are accepted on an equal basis. (B$1 = US$1)

THE LANGUAGE SITUATION English is the official language.

Nassau Self-Tour

The Ministry of Tourism is on Bay Street. You can find an **information booth** at Rawson Square, near the dock.

The ideal way to explore Nassau is on foot. Major attractions and stores, as well as Cable Beach and Paradise Island, are within walking distance.

The cheapest method of public transportation on the island is via the **jitneys** (buses). The fare is 75¢, and exact change is required.

Taxis are another option (especially for longer island trips). The taxis are metered, and fares start at $2 and then 30¢ for each quarter mile for the first two passengers. Additional passengers pay $2. You can hire five-passenger taxis for $23 to $25 an hour.

A more traditional way to see Nassau is by **horse-drawn carriage.** Settle on a fare before the ride (the average fare is $5 per person). The total capacity is 3 adults plus 1 or 2 children under the age of 12. The carriages operate daily from 9am to 4:30pm and can be found at Rawson Square.

Other popular modes of transportation include **ferries** and **mopeds.** The ferries run from Paradise Island to Rawson Square at a cost of $2 for a one-way trip. Mopeds cost $20 per hour or $30 for 2 hours, $40 for a half day, and $50 for a full day, plus $4 for insurance. A $10 deposit is required.

Within Walking Distance

Start your tour of historical Nassau at **Rawson Square,** home of the **Straw Market.** A short walk away is the native market on the waterfront, where Bahamian fishers unload fish and produce.

A great place to observe local life is under the Paradise Island Bridge at **Potter's Cay.** You'll see sloops bringing in the daily catch, including conch. Fresh herbs and vegetables are also sold here.

Fort Fincastle on Elizabeth Avenue, constructed in 1793 by Lord Dunmore, the royal governor, can be reached by climbing the **Queen's Staircase,** a

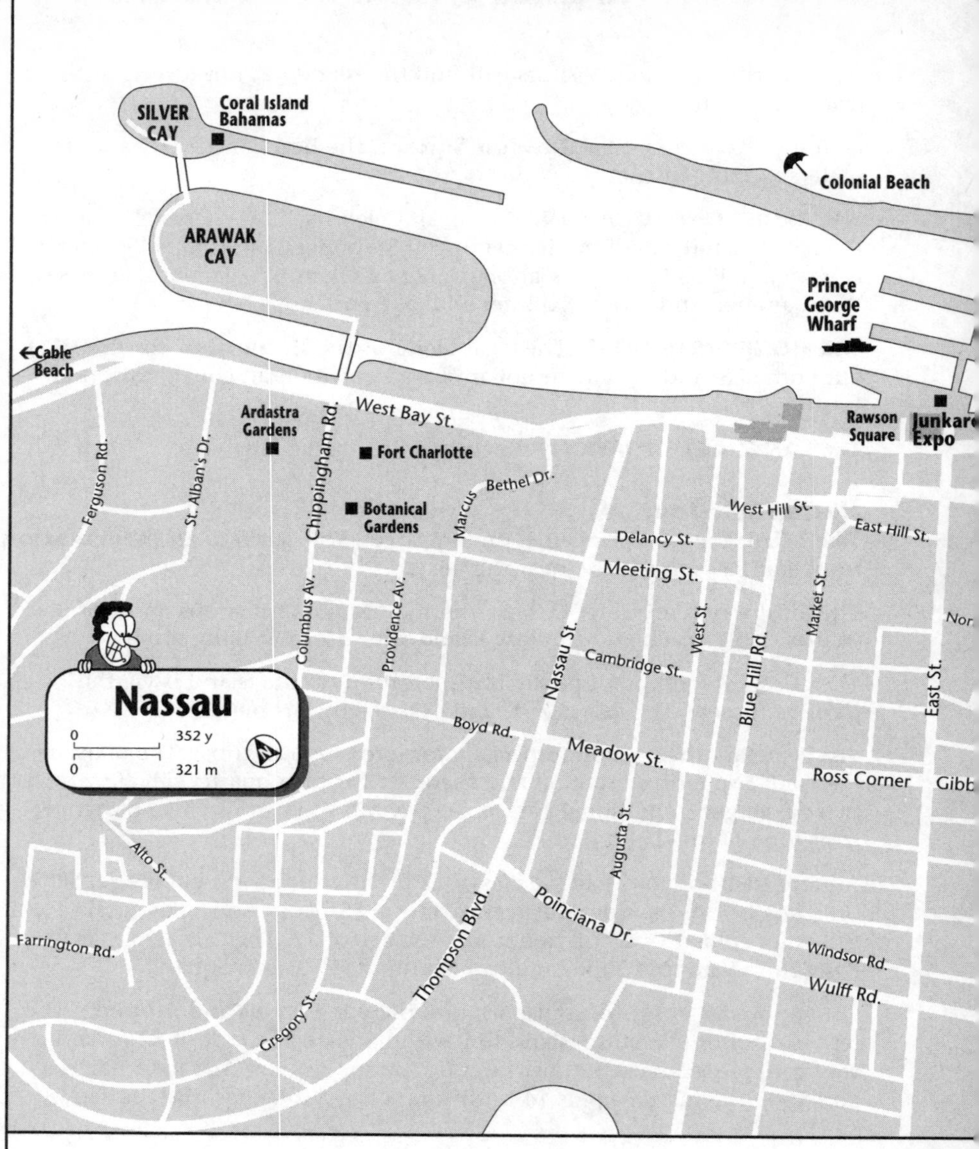

Classic Nassau Experiences:

- Bet the farm at the **Paradise Island Casino**
- Take a tour to the **Coral Island Bahamas marine park** for great undersea and above-ground views
- Go shopping at the **Straw Market**
- See the famous **Marching Flamingos** at Ardastra Gardens
- Head to **Cable Beach** for shops, casinos, restaurants, and water sports
- Take in the view from **Fort Fincastle** or leap into local color at the **Junkanoo Expo**

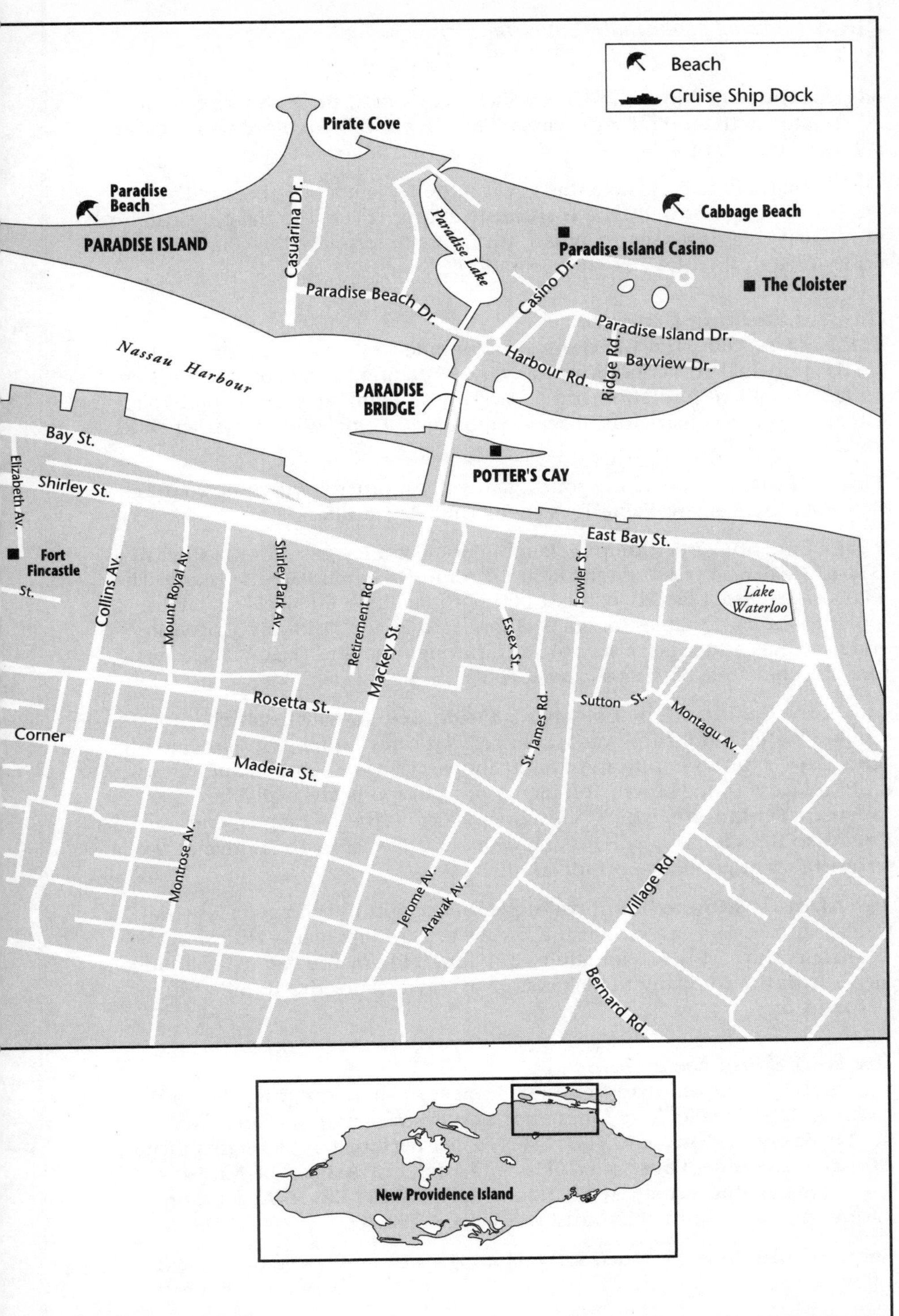

Beach
Cruise Ship Dock
Pirate Cove
Paradise Beach
Cabbage Beach
PARADISE ISLAND
Casuarina Dr.
Paradise Lake
Paradise Island Casino
The Cloister
Casino Dr.
Paradise Beach Dr.
Paradise Island Dr.
Nassau Harbour
Harbour Rd.
Bayview Dr.
Ridge Rd.
PARADISE BRIDGE
Bay St.
POTTER'S CAY
Elizabeth Av.
Shirley St.
East Bay St.
Fort Fincastle
St.
Collins Av.
Mount Royal Av.
Shirley Park Av.
Retirement Rd.
Mackey St.
Fowler St.
Essex St.
Lake Waterloo
Rosetta St.
St. James Rd.
Sutton St.
Montagu Av.
Corner
Madeira St.
Montrose Av.
Jerome Av.
Arawak Av.
Village Rd.
Bernard Rd.
New Providence Island

66-step landmark named for Queen Victoria. Once at the fort, you can take an elevator to the top for great views (or you can walk up more steps, if you still have the energy).

The annual Junkanoo parade starts at 2am on December 26 (Boxing Day), but if you miss it, stop by the **Junkanoo Expo.** Located in the old Customs warehouse on Prince George Wharf, this museum displays the colorful costumes used during the holiday celebration.

Beyond Walking Distance

At the 5-acre **Ardastra Gardens,** about a mile west of town, pink flamingos are the principal attraction. Known as the Marching Flamingos, the birds are trained to walk in formation and do so daily at 11am, 2pm, and 4pm. You can also see boa constrictors, macaws, monkeys, a crocodile, and other waterfowl.

The Retreat, an 11-acre unspoiled garden, is another worthwhile venture. Half-hour tours are available Tuesday to Thursday at noon.

If gambling, not garden touring, is more up your alley, head to the **Paradise Island Casino,** in the Atlantis Resort, Casino Drive, on Paradise Island. The 30,000-square-foot facility boasts 1,000 slot machines, 60 blackjack tables, 10 roulette wheels, 12 tables for craps, 3 for baccarat, and 1 for big six. While you're at the casino, make sure to stroll through the Bird Cage Walk, a mixture of restaurants, bars, and cabaret spots.

One of the Caribbean's best beaches is **Cable Beach,** which stretches for 4 miles. Watch out for the water; some days it can be quite tranquil, and on other days it turns choppy and rough. Shops, casinos, nightlife, and restaurants are close to the beach, and plenty of watersports are available. **Western Esplanade,** which is a short walk from the cruise pier, and **Paradise Beach** on Paradise Island (walk or drive across the bridge or take a ferry) are other popular spots for sun lovers.

***The Atlantis* submarine** provides another opportunity to go below the water's surface. You can get a fish-eye view of New Providence during a 2½-hour tour. The cost is $74 for adults, $37 for children. You can make arrangements with the company to pick you up at the dock for the 18-mile trip to **Lyford Cay.**

The Best Shore Excursions

You can see the downtown sites on your own, so shore excursions are not essential. If you are looking for an organized tour, sign up for one offered by the **Ministry of Tourism.** The cost is $2 per person, and highlights include **Adastra Gardens, Fort Charlotte,** and **Fort Fincastle.** The Ministry sells 3 separate tours that last 1½ hours. Call ☎ **242/326-9772** for more information, or stop by the tourist office on Bay Street.

Coral Island Tour (3 hours, $30 to $35): This trip takes you on a scenic boat ride to Silver Cay and the popular Coral Island Bahamas marine park.

Here you will find both a 100-foot aboveground and a 20-foot belowground observation area. The Underwater Observation Tower allows you to observe a coral reef and sealife, while the aboveground tower has two viewing decks and a bar offering sweeping views of Nassau, Cable Beach, and Paradise Island. There's also a Reef Tank (the largest manmade living reef) and Shark Tank, as well as the Marine Gardens Aquarium. Enhancing the setting are nature trails, waterfalls, and lush foliage.

You can also catch a ferry to the marine park on your own for about $25.

Glass-Bottom Boat Tour (1½ hours, $30): This short trip takes visitors to the colorful marine world off New Providence Island.

St. Barts

A favored playground of the very rich and famous, St. Barts (full name: St. Barthélemy) offers a little something different from other Caribbean destinations, all with a touch of Normandy and Sweden, from its language, lifestyle, and food.

Visitors are encouraged to forget about historical sites and watersports here and get into relaxing on the beach and perhaps catching a view of a familiar famous personality. The best month for celebrity-viewing is February.

St. Barts was discovered by Christopher Columbus in 1493, and its residents today are descended from Breton and Norman fishermen, with a dash of Swedish, as evidenced by the fair skin, blond hair, and blue eyes that some of the natives have. The Swedish link is also strong in the capital of Gustavia, named after a Swedish king.

THE CRUISE LINE SITUATION Carnival, Club Med, Cunard, Radisson, Royal Olympic, Seabourn, Silversea, Star Clippers, Windjammer, and Windstar all make port stops here.

THE MONEY SITUATION The official currency is the **French franc (Fr),** but most stores and restaurants prefer payment in U.S. dollars. (1 Fr = US16¢)

THE LANGUAGE SITUATION The official language is French, but nearly everyone speaks English as well.

St. Barts Self-Tour

Small cruise ships are the only ones that visit here, anchoring off Gustavia and ferrying passengers to town. It's a short walk into the center of Gustavia and its restaurant and shopping district. The **Office du Tourisme** is located in the Town Hall on quai du General-de-Gaulle.

Taxis are plentiful and cheap for travelers coming ashore. Getting around in open-sided rental Mini-Mokes and Suzuki Samurais, which are in plentiful and colorful supply, is another option. The rentals are available from Budget, Hertz, and Avis, but reservations are required (allow a month in high season; see appendix B for reservations phone numbers). Prices begin at about $45 a day. Motorbike and motor-scooter rentals are available for $24 to $30 a day.

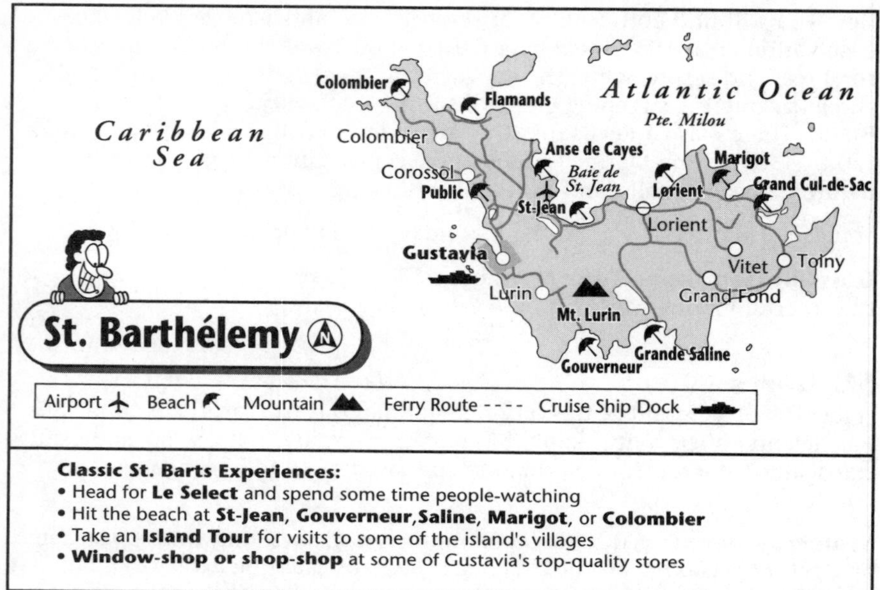

Classic St. Barts Experiences:

- Head for **Le Select** and spend some time people-watching
- Hit the beach at **St-Jean**, **Gouverneur**,**Saline**, **Marigot**, or **Colombier**
- Take an **Island Tour** for visits to some of the island's villages
- **Window-shop or shop-shop** at some of Gustavia's top-quality stores

Within Walking Distance

A lot of travelers enjoy just walking around Gustavia or browsing through the many top-quality shops of the capital. Prices on liquor and French perfume are among the lowest in the region.

Beyond Walking Distance

The best place to people-watch in Gustavia is **Le Select,** rue de la France, a simple cafe that attracts the likes of Jimmy Buffet and (if you're really lucky) Mick Jagger.

The best of St. Barts' secluded beaches include **Gouverneur** and **Saline** to the south and **Marigot** and **Colombier** to the north. Topless sunbathing is quite common.

The most famous beach is **St-Jean,** where rather than seclusion, you'll find watersports, beach restaurants, and a few hotels.

The Best Shore Excursions

Island Tour (1½ hours, $23): Most cruise ships offer a tour that takes in some of the island's 14 beaches and villages, including Carossol, a tiny fishing village where the locals make straw from lantana palms.

St. Croix, U.S. Virgin Islands

Ships dock at St. Croix in either the capital of **Christiansted** or the sleepy town of **Frederiksted.** The destination for shopping and viewing the island's Dutch influence is in Christiansted. In fact, the only time things happen in Frederiksted is when cruise passengers come ashore.

St. Croix's biggest attractions are its beaches, including white sand, palm trees, and snorkeling at Davis Bay, Cane Bay, and Cormorant Beach, and windsurfing at Reef Beach.

Traveling the 17 miles from Frederiksted to Christiansted is possible either by **taxi** or on air-conditioned **buses** ($1). It you opt for a taxi, negotiate the price ahead of time, since cabs are unmetered on St. Croix.

This island was another stop for Columbus in 1493. He didn't stay long, due to a harsh welcome by the locals. At various times, the island, once dominated by sugar plantations, was controlled by Spain, England, and France. The Dutch bought it from the French in 1773. The island came under control of the U.S. during World War I, and islanders now vote in national elections and send a nonvoting delegate to the U.S. House of Representatives.

THE CRUISE LINE SITUATION Carnival, Norwegian, Premier, and Royal Caribbean make port stops here.

THE MONEY SITUATION The **U.S. dollar** is the official currency.

THE LANGUAGE SITUATION English is the official language.

Christiansted Self-Tour

There's an **information center** at the pier that's a historic building in its own right: It was once used as the weighing house for all taxable items coming into or leaving the harbor.

Within Walking Distance

Christiansted is easily explored on foot.

The **Steeple Building,** St. Croix's first Lutheran church, was completed in 1753. Admission is $2, which includes admission to **Fort Christiansvaern.**

Fort Christiansvaern, which overlooks the harbor, is a historic monument maintained by the National Park Service. The **St. Croix Police Museum,** located in the fort, offers a history of police activities from 1800 to modern times.

Beyond Walking Distance

The **Salt River Bay National Historical Park and Ecological Preserve** is a 912-acre area approximately 4 miles northwest of Christiansted. It's pretty much in its natural state and includes the site of the original Carib village that was explored by Columbus. Salt River is the only known site where Columbus landed on what is now U.S. territory. At the time, Columbus was involved in a confrontation with hostile Caribs that prompted him to name this area of St. Croix "Cape of the Arrows." The St. Croix Environmental Association conducts tours of the area, which also contains the largest mangrove forest in the Virgin Islands. Call ☎ **809/773-1989** for details.

Beaches are one of the biggest attractions on the island, although they can be both difficult and expensive (by taxi) to get to. From Christiansted, you can head for **Hotel on the Cay,** a palm-shaded island in the harbor (you get there by ferry). You can also visit **Buck Island** by boat (see "The Best Shore Excursions," later in this section).

Frederiksted Self-Tour

There's an **information center** at the pier. Frederiksted is easily explored on foot.

Within Walking Distance

Fort Frederick is located next to the cruise pier at the northern end of the town. There are a courtyard and stables to explore as well as an exhibit area. Admission is free.

Beyond Walking Distance

The **Cruzan Rum Factory,** West Airport Road, Route 64, offers guided tours of this distiller of Virgin Islands rum. Call for reservations (☎ **809/692-2280**). Admission is $3.

The Great House at **Estate Whim Plantation Museum,** Centerline Road (2 miles east of Frederiksted), has 3-foot-thick walls of stone, coral, and molasses. There are ruins of the plantation's sugar-processing plant, a shop containing the estate's original kitchen, and a showroom where you can purchase reproductions of the Whim Plantation's furniture. Admission is $5 for adults, $1 for children.

St. George Village Botanical Garden of St. Croix, 4 miles east of Frederiksted, is a setting for lush tropical plants that surround the ruins of a 19th-century sugarcane workers' village. The garden itself is a feast for the eye, and there's a superintendent's house, blacksmith's shop, and other smaller buildings that have been restored as part of an ongoing project. Admission is $5 for adults, $1 for children.

The most convenient beach for passengers arriving in Frederiksted is **Sandy Point,** the largest beach in the U.S. Virgin Islands. If you want to spend the bucks to get there, **Cane Bay** on the north shore is a great beach locale.

The Best Shore Excursions

Buck Island National Park Snorkeling Excursion (4 hours, $40): On this trip, visitors can enjoy a tropical underwater experience of blue water and colorful coral reefs. Transportation is provided from the pier in Frederiksted to Christiansted, where a boat takes visitors to the island. An experienced guide provides snorkeling lessons.

Reef Party Cruise (3 hours, $29): This trip takes cruise passengers who prefer not to get wet on a double-decker, glass-bottom boat over sunken wrecks and reefs.

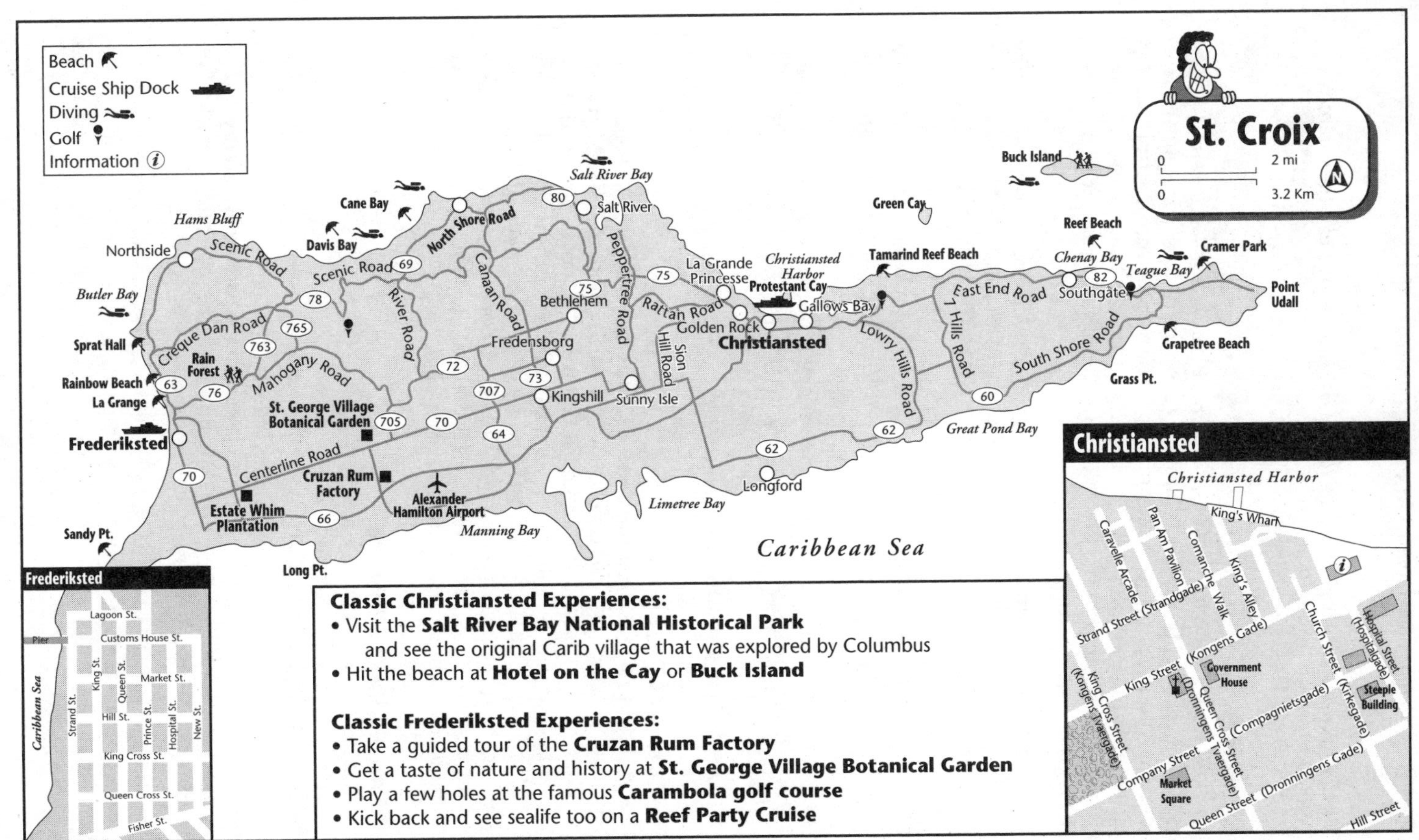
St. Croix
0 2 mi
0 3.2 Km
Beach
Cruise Ship Dock
Diving
Golf
Information
Salt River Bay
Cane Bay
Hams Bluff
Northside
Scenic Road
Davis Bay
North Shore Road
Salt River
Butler Bay
Sprat Hall
Rainbow Beach
La Grange
Frederiksted
Sandy Pt.
Long Pt.
Creque Dan Road
Rain Forest
Mahogany Road
St. George Village Botanical Garden
River Road
Canaan Road
Peppertree Road
Bethlehem
Fredensborg
Kingshill
Sunny Isle
Sion Hill Road
Rattan Road
Golden Rock
Christiansted
La Grande Princesse
Christiansted Harbor
Protestant Cay
Gallows Bay
Lowry Hills Road
7 Hills Road
East End Road
Southgate
South Shore Road
Centerline Road
Cruzan Rum Factory
Estate Whim Plantation
Alexander Hamilton Airport
Manning Bay
Limetree Bay
Longford
Great Pond Bay
Caribbean Sea
Green Cay
Tamarind Reef Beach
Buck Island
Reef Beach
Chenay Bay
Teague Bay
Cramer Park
Point Udall
Grapetree Beach
Grass Pt.
Frederiksted
Caribbean Sea
Pier
Lagoon St.
Customs House St.
Strand St.
King St.
Queen St.
Market St.
Hill St.
Prince St.
Hospital St.
New St.
King Cross St.
Queen Cross St.
Fisher St.
Christiansted
Christiansted Harbor
King's Wharf
Caravelle Arcade
Pan Am Pavilion
Comanche Walk
King's Alley
Strand Street (Strandgade)
King Street (Kongens Gade)
Government House
Church Street (Kirkegade)
Hospital Street (Hospitalgade)
Steeple Building
King Cross Street (Kongens Tvaergade)
Queen Cross Street (Dronningens Tvaergade)
Company Street (Compagnietsgade)
Market Square
Queen Street (Dronningens Gade)
Hill Street
Classic Christiansted Experiences:
• Visit the Salt River Bay National Historical Park and see the original Carib village that was explored by Columbus
• Hit the beach at Hotel on the Cay or Buck Island
Classic Frederiksted Experiences:
• Take a guided tour of the Cruzan Rum Factory
• Get a taste of nature and history at St. George Village Botanical Garden
• Play a few holes at the famous Carambola golf course
• Kick back and see sealife too on a Reef Party Cruise

Golf at Carambola ($83): This is one of the Caribbean's most famous courses. Fore!

St. Kitts

You will find wonderful beaches, restaurants, and shops here, and since St. Kitts generates the majority of its revenue from the sugar industry, not tourism, you'll be able to avoid the hordes of tourists that overrun so many other ports in the Caribbean. The island almost has a sleepy feel. Its real charm can be found in the old mills and plantation homes scattered throughout the island.

The port of **Basseterre** received a boost in 1997 when a deep-water cruise ship facility was finished, meaning large cruise ships can now dock here. You will find more to do on St. Kitts than on Nevis, the other half of this two-island federation.

THE CRUISE LINE SITUATION Clipper, Club Med, Costa, Cunard, Holland America, Norwegian, Regal, Star Clippers, and Windjammer all make port stops here.

THE MONEY SITUATION The local currency is the **Eastern Caribbean dollar (EC$),** although many shops and restaurants quote prices in U.S. dollars. (EC$2.70 = US$1)

THE LANGUAGE SITUATION English is the official language.

St. Kitts Self-Tour

The **St. Kitts / Nevis Department of Tourism** is located at Pelican Mall, Bay Road. The best way to reach Basseterre or **Brimstone Hill Fortress** (St. Kitts' major attraction) is to take a taxi from the dock. Most taxi drivers double as tour guides, and this is the most convenient way to tool around the island. Settle on a price beforehand (taxis are not metered), and ask whether the rates are quoted in U.S. dollars or Eastern Caribbean dollars. A 3-hour tour of the island will cost around $55. Renting a car is not a recommended option. Taxis are just a better idea.

Within Walking Distance

You'll need to take a cab to town.

Beyond Walking Distance

Basseterre sports 18th-century houses with toothpick balconies. The circular town square is home to the oft-photographed **Victorian Berkeley Memorial Clock.** People from the countryside come here with baskets of colorful fruit for sale (adding to the photographer's delight).

The **Brimstone Hill Fortress,** one of the Caribbean's largest and best-preserved landmarks, is a must-see attraction. Located 9 miles west of Basseterre, the citadel contains a series of bastions, barracks, and other struc-

tures cleverly grafted to the top and upper slopes of a steep hill. The British built the fort in the 17th century, and one of the largest military conflicts in the Caribbean took place there in 1782 when the French invaded. When the British recaptured the island the following year, they enlarged the fort and dubbed it "The Gibraltar of the West Indies." The fortress has been restored and is now part of a national park. It boasts nature trails and an abundance of plants and wildlife, including the green vervet monkey. You can take a self-guided tour of the complex, and there's a gift shop on its grounds.

If you're seeking a hiking adventure, head to **Mount Liamuiga,** a dormant volcano that had its last rumblings around 1962. A round-trip hike to the normally cloud-covered peak takes about 6 hours. The ascent is usually made from the Belmont Estate, on the north end of St. Kitts.

For an excursion of a different sort, you can tour the **Sugar Factory** and watch raw cane being processed into bulk sugar. The factory also makes *Cane Spirits Rothschild* (CSR), a light liqueur that locals use in a grapefruit concoction called *Ting*.

The narrow peninsula in the southeast, where St. Kitts' salt ponds are located, has the best powder-white **beaches.** All beaches are open to the public, but you must get permission and pay a fee if you want to use a resort's beach facilities.

The Best Shore Excursions

Brimstone Hill Fort Tour (2½ hours, $25): This trip takes you to the fortress (as described in "Beyond Walking Distance").

Ahoy, Mateys!

To introduce yourself to the sweeter side of St. Kitts, purchase a stalk of **sugar cane** (any farmer will sell you one), peel its hard exterior, and chew the tasty reeds to enjoy the nectar-sweet juice. It's also nice with ice and a splash of rum.

Beach Horseback Ride (1 hour, $35): This is your chance to look like you're in a TV commercial and ride well-trained horses on the beach at the Atlantic coast. Remember to toss your hair carelessly in the breeze.

Catamaran Adventure (3½ hours, $45): Featuring a 45-minute sail along the southern coast of St. Kitts, this trip also allots time for swimming or snorkeling.

St. Lucia

Sure it's a Caribbean island, but one look at the peaks of Petit Piton and Gros Piton, the white sandy beaches along the northwest coast, and the green mountains in its interior, and you might swear that St. Lucia is located in the South Pacific.

The capital, **Castries,** is built around an extinct volcanic crater. You'll notice that Castries has more of a modern feel than other regional capitals. That's because fires destroyed much of the French colonial and Victorian buildings that typify the region's architecture. Don't let the modern look fool you, though. Traditions are still alive here. Women from the countryside, who you can spot at the Saturday market on Jeremy Street, wear traditional headdresses, with the number of knotted points on top indicating their marital status.

THE CRUISE LINE SITUATION American Canadian Caribbean, Carnival, Celebrity, Clipper, Cunard, Holland America, Norwegian, Premier, Princess, Star Clippers, Tall Ship Adventures, Windjammer, and Windstar all make port stops here.

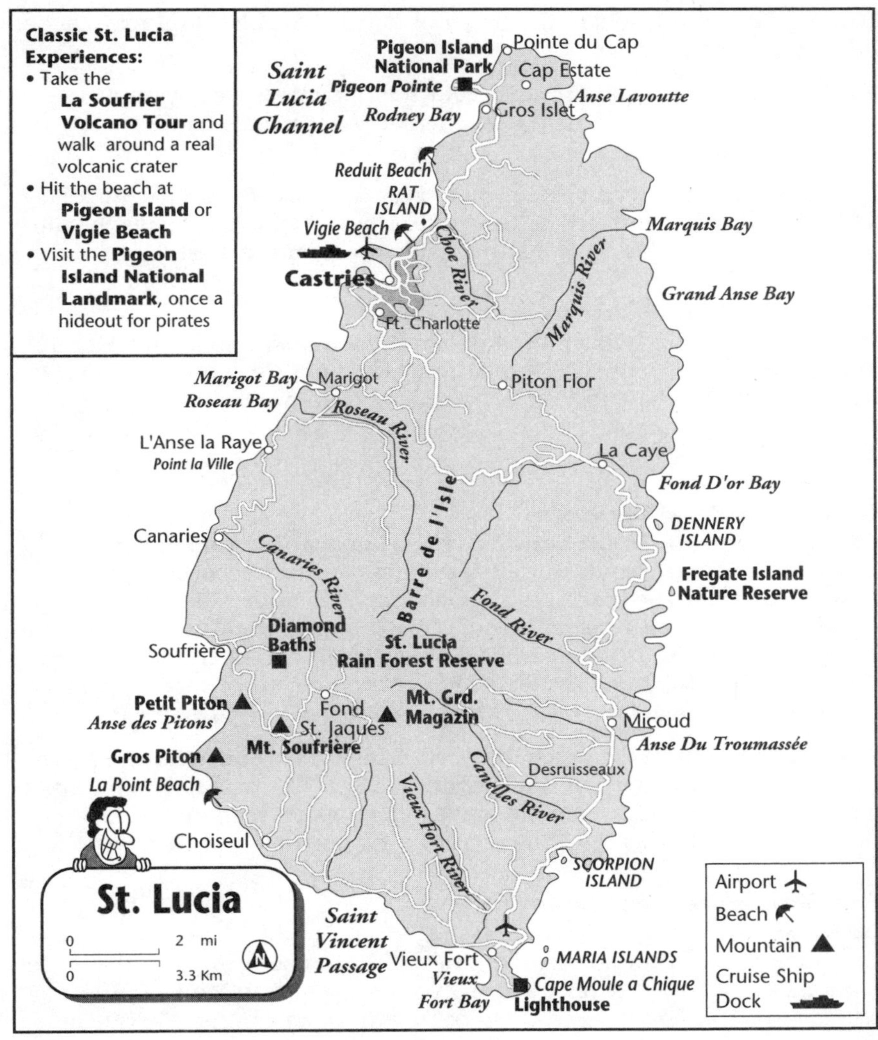

THE MONEY SITUATION The local currency is the **Eastern Caribbean dollar (EC$),** although many shops and restaurants quote prices in U.S. dollars. (EC$2.70 = US$1)

THE LANGUAGE SITUATION English is the official language.

St. Lucia Self-Tour

The pier at **Pointe Seraphine** offers everything from great shopping to information at a small visitor information bureau, and is a short cab ride from the center of Castries. There is also alternate docking at the **Elizabeth**

II pier, also a short walk to the center of Castries. Smaller ships may anchor off **Soufriere** and tender to shore.

Taxi drivers are trained to serve as guides and the rates are government-regulated. Make sure you figure out whether your driver is quoting a rate in U.S. or E.C. dollars.

If you want to **rent a car,** you need to get a St. Lucia driver's license for $12. Budget, Hertz, and Avis all have offices here. If you are driving, be sure to pay attention on the hilly, narrow switchbacks outside Castries.

Within Walking Distance
The main streets are William Peter Boulevard and Bridge Street. Up **Morne Fortune** (Hill of Good Luck) is the barracks of **Fort Charlotte,** including the "Four Apostles Battery," the nickname for four muzzle-loaded cannons. There is also a panoramic view of Castries harbor from this site and a small museum.

Beyond Walking Distance
Pigeon Island National Landmark, a national park, is flanked by the Caribbean and the Atlantic. A causeway joins it with the mainland, making it easier to get to. The island once served as a hideout for a peg-legged pirate named Jambe de Bois ("Leg of Wood"). The Interpretation Centre contains a number of artifacts, including some dating back to the Amerindian occupation of the year 1000. Admission is $1.90. *Note:* If you take a taxi here, remember to arrange for a return trip in time to get back to your ship.

If you opt for time at the beach, try the beaches at **Pigeon Island,** off the island's northern shore, or **Vigie Beach,** north of Castries Harbour. Keep in mind that the West Coast beaches have calmer waters than on the Atlantic side of the island, where swimming can be dangerous.

The Best Shore Excursions
La Soufriere Volcano Tour (8 hours, $43, including lunch): This excursion offers views of the spectacular Pitons, the twin pointed peaks that were formed by lava and were once actively volcanic; a visit to Mont Soufriere, referred to as the "drive-in" volcano because travelers can literally ride into an old crater and walk between sulfur springs and steam pools; and a stop at the Diamond Mineral Baths, where the waters are said to offer recuperative powers. *Note:* This excursion will only be offered if your ship will be in port for an extended period.

If you are on a small ship anchoring off La Soufriere, you might be able to take a 2-hour tour of the same sights ($28).

St. Maarten / St. Martin
It might be hard to believe, but two sovereign states peacefully coexist on this 37-square-mile island. How did the Dutch and French come to this

agreement, you wonder? Local lore says that a wine-drinking Frenchman and a gin-guzzling Dutchman walked around the island in 1648 to see how much territory they could claim. The Frenchman ended up with the most territory, but the Dutchman earned the better real estate.

St. Maarten is the Dutch side, and St. Martin is the French region. The only way you can tell that you have crossed from one to the other is by the *"Bienvenue Francaise"* signs marking the border.

Marigot, on the French side, has a cosmopolitan flair. The latest French fashions can be found in its shops, and charming bistros serve fresh croissants and pastries.

On the Dutch side, **Philipsburg** bustles with energy from the hordes of tourists exploring its shops and casinos.

The island is known as a duty-free shopping haven.

Both sides of the island weathered a tough beating from hurricanes in 1995, but everything has been rebuilt (with some rearranging courtesy of Mother Nature).

THE CRUISE LINE SITUATION Carnival, Celebrity, Club Med, Costa, Cunard, Holland America, Norwegian, Premier, Princess, Radisson, Royal Caribbean, Royal Olympic, Star Clippers, Windjammer, and Windstar all make port stops here.

THE MONEY SITUATION The legal tender in Dutch St. Maarten is the **Netherlands Antilles guilder/NAf** (NAf 1.80 = U.S. $1), but dollars are accepted here. French St. Martin uses the **French franc/Fr** (Fr 6.14 = US$1). Canadians should convert their money into U.S. dollars rather than francs.

THE LANGUAGE SITUATION The official languages are Dutch and French, but most people also speak English.

St. Maarten Self-Tour

The **Tourist Information Bureau** is located in the Imperial Building at 23 Nisbeth Road.

Taxis are unmetered, but Dutch St. Maarten law requires taxi drivers to list fares to major island destinations. There is a minimum rate for two passengers. Each additional passenger pays $2.

Buses are a crowded but fairly cheap way to get around the Dutch side of the island. Fares range from $1.15 to $2, and buses generally follow a specified route. The most popular run is from Philipsburg to Marigot on the French side.

Within Walking Distance

Smaller vessels can make their way into Margiot's harbor (on the French side), but most head to Philipsburg (on the Dutch side) and dock at

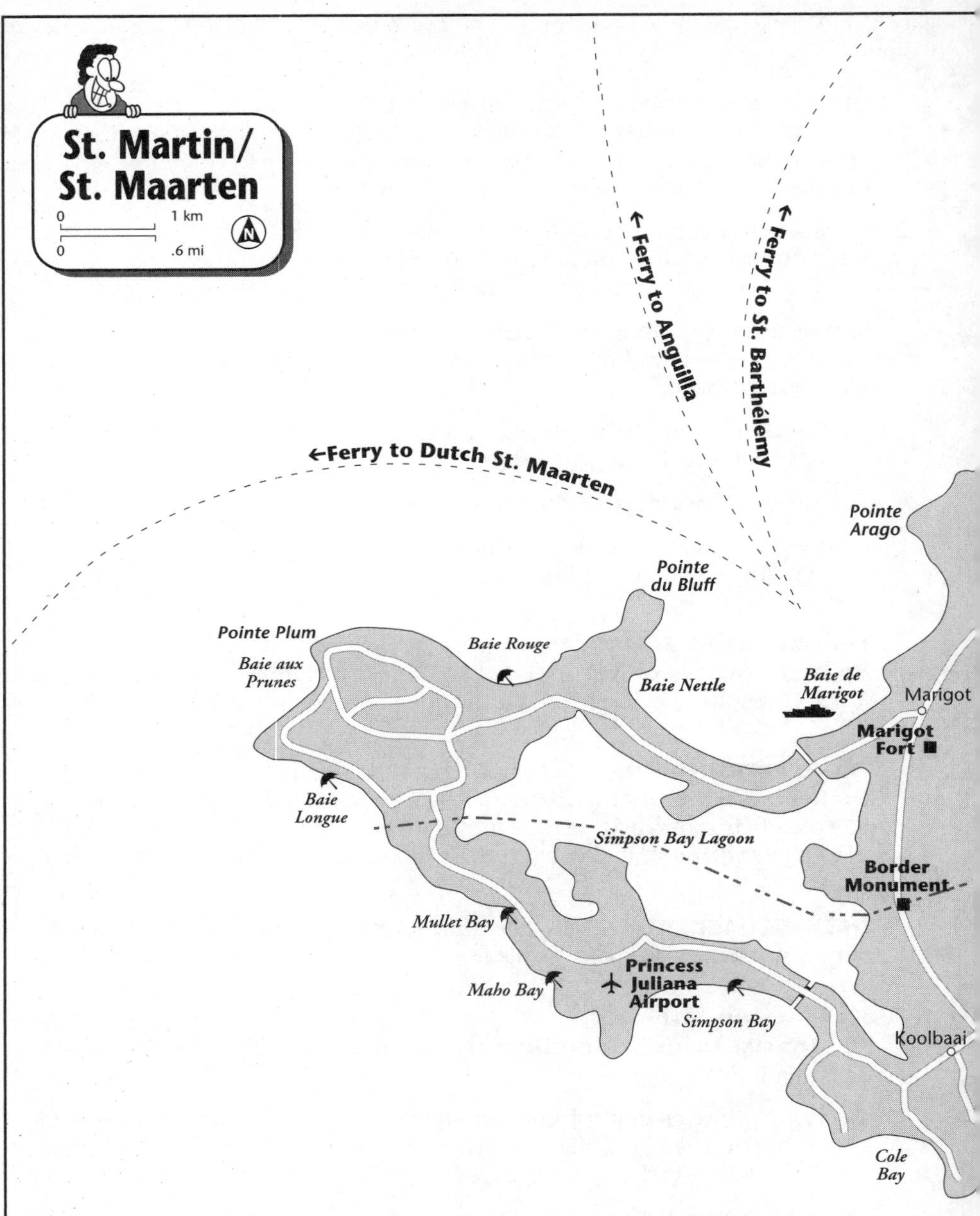

Classic St. Maarten Experiences:
- Have a **shopping adventure** on Front and Back streets
- Hang with the high-rollers at the **Coliseum Casino**
- Relax on one of St. Maarten's sugar-white **beaches**

Classic St. Martin Experiences:
- Take a snorkeling trip to **Pinel Island**
- **Hit the beach** (with clothes or without)
- Do the shopping thing at **Marina Port la Royale** or **the harbour**

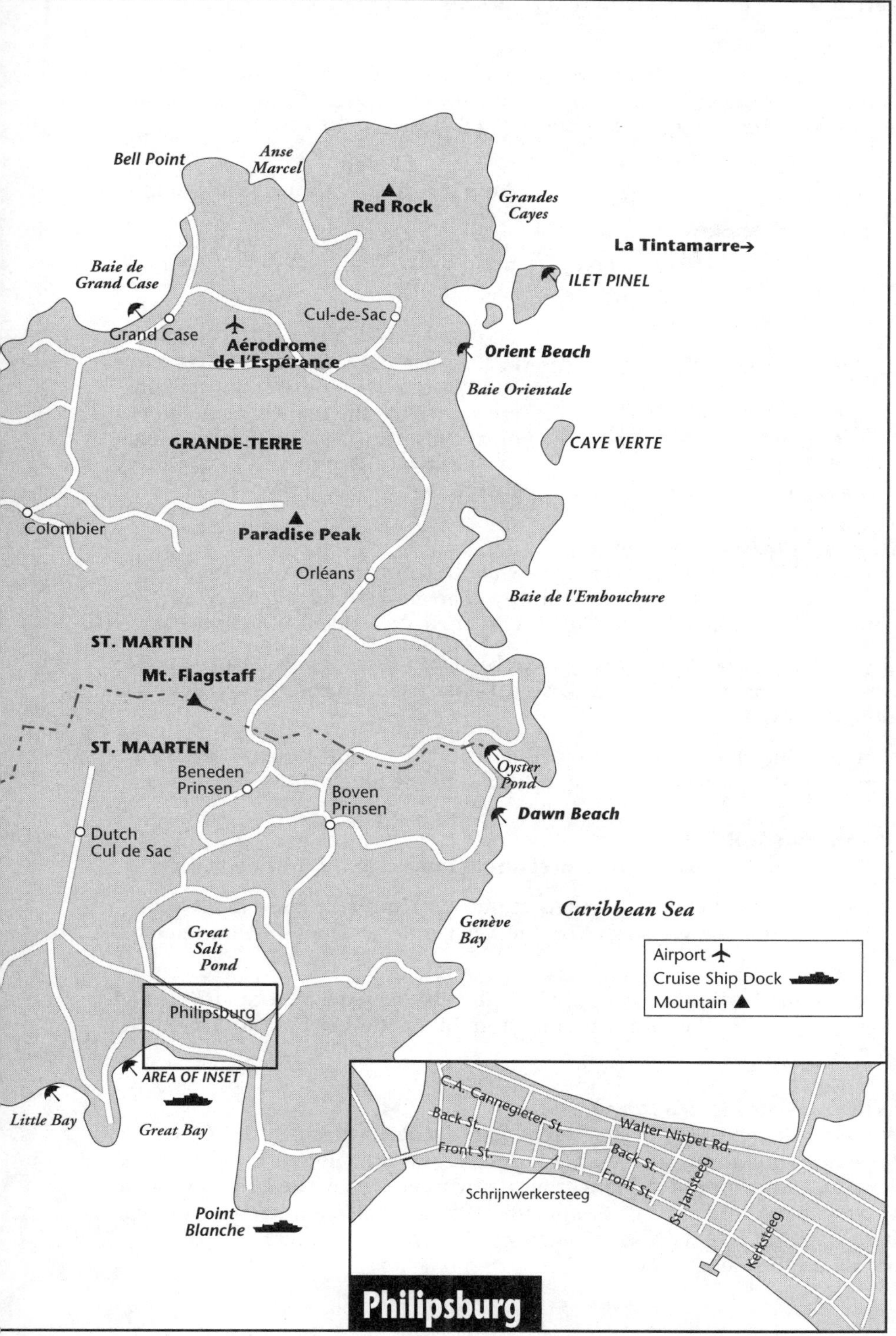
Bell Point
Anse Marcel
Red Rock
Grandes Cayes
La Tintamarre→
Baie de Grand Case
ILET PINEL
Cul-de-Sac
Grand Case
Aérodrome de l'Espérance
Orient Beach
Baie Orientale
GRANDE-TERRE
CAYE VERTE
Colombier
Paradise Peak
Orléans
Baie de l'Embouchure
ST. MARTIN
Mt. Flagstaff
ST. MAARTEN
Oyster Pond
Beneden Prinsen
Boven Prinsen
Dawn Beach
Dutch Cul de Sac
Caribbean Sea
Genève Bay
Great Salt Pond
Airport
Cruise Ship Dock
Mountain
Philipsburg
AREA OF INSET
Little Bay
Great Bay
Point Blanche
C.A. Cannegieter St.
Back St.
Walter Nisbet Rd.
Front St.
Back St.
Front St.
St. Jansteeg
Schrijnwerkersteeg
Kerksteeg
Philipsburg

A. C. Wathey Pier at Point Blance. It is located about a mile southwest of Philipsburg and not equipped with many facilities. Some ships also anchor and transport passengers via a tender to Little Pier in the center of Philipsburg.

Life Preservers

When touring St. Martin/St. Maarten, be aware that crimes against tourists (such as muggings and robberies) have been on the rise.

From the dock, taxis can take you into town or you can walk there. The main shopping area is along **Front and Back streets,** and you can find some boutique shops at the resorts.

If you want to check out the gaming action, visit the **Coliseum Casino** on Front Street. The Roman-themed gaming center has the highest table limits on St. Maarten—$1,000. You can walk to **Great Bay Beach** and **Little Bay Beach** from the center of town.

Beyond Walking Distance

The island is renowned for its sugar-white beaches, and between the two sides, you can pick from 37 to visit. If you are looking for topless or au naturel beaches, head to the French side; the Dutch side is more modest.

On the Dutch side, **Mullet Bay Beach, Maho Bay Beach, Simpson Bay Beach, Oyster Pond Beach, Dawn Beach,** and **Cupecoy Bay Beach** are all worth a visit.

Keep in mind that robberies have been reported at some isolated beach locations. You should avoid bringing valuables to the beach.

St. Martin Self-Tour

In St. Martin, the **Office du Tourisme** is located at the Port de Marigot.

Taxis are the most common means of transport and may also offer 2-hour sightseeing tours. Always agree on the rate before getting into an unmetered cab.

Buses on the French side are actually minivans operated by local drivers and typically cost $2. There's a departure from Marigot every hour to the Dutch side.

Within Walking Distance

A wide selection of European merchandise awaits day trippers to Marigot. Prices are commonly quoted in U.S. dollars, and the salespeople speak English. In the morning, Marigot bustles with energy at **the harbor,** where vendors hawk fruits, spices, and handicrafts at an open-air market. Another busy center of activity is **Marina Port la Royale,** the largest shopping arcade on the French side.

Beyond Walking Distance

Top-rated beaches on the French side are **Baie Longue, Baie Rouge, Grand Case Beach,** and **Pinel Island.** If you are seeking a stripped-down adventure, visit the famous clothes-optional **Orient Beach.**

The Best Shore Excursions

The island's most notable attractions are its beaches, so don't feel guilty if you pass on the 3-hour sightseeing trip. Better bets, if you want an organized excursion, are the **Pinel Island Snorkeling** tour on the French side (3 hours, $28) and the **Sun-and-Sea Cruise** (2 hours, $22). A **Sea-and-Island** tour (3½ hours, $40) combines the best of both offerings.

St. Thomas & St. John

When you come to St. Thomas, you enter the shopping capital of the Caribbean. **Charlotte Amalie,** which is also the island's capital, blends island charm and tackiness with its plethora of shops, restaurants, bars, resorts, and of course, crowds of tourists.

St. John presents a startling contrast to St. Thomas's frenzied pace. More than half of St. John is protected within the government-sheltered **Virgin Islands National Park.** Stretching along its jagged coastline are crescent-shaped bays and pearly white beaches. As you stroll around, you can observe the many birds and animals that make their homes there. Hiking trails snake through the park, lead you past the ruins of 18th-century Danish plantations, and offer breathtaking views.

The area was hit hard by the hurricanes of the mid-1990s, but shops, restaurants, and attractions are back in business.

Most vessels dock in Charlotte Amalie on St. Thomas, but some anchor off St. John. Most of the lines offer excursions to St. John, but even if yours doesn't, it's still easy to find your way there.

THE CRUISE LINE SITUATION American Canadian Caribbean, Carnival, Celebrity, Clipper, Club Med, Costa, Crystal, Cunard, Holland America, Mediterranean Shipping Cruises, Norwegian, Premier, Princess, Radisson, Royal Caribbean, Royal Olympic, Seabourn, Star Clippers, Windjammer, and Windstar all make port stops here.

THE MONEY SITUATION The **U.S. dollar** is the official currency.

THE LANGUAGE SITUATION English is the language of choice.

St. Thomas Self-Tour

The **U.S. Virgin Islands Division of Tourism** has offices at Tolbod Gade. A branch office also is located at Havensight Mall.

Most ships make port at **Havensight Mall,** 1½ miles from the eastern end of the Charlotte Amalie harbor. You will find a tourist booth, restaurants, duty-free shopping, a bank, a U.S. postal van, phones, and a bookstore there.

Renting a car is not the best idea here. The preferred mode of transport is the **taxi.** Taxis are unmetered, so settle on a fare before taking a ride. There is an official rate ($30) for 2 passengers taking a 2-hour sightseeing trip in a cab. Each additional passenger pays another $12. It is also possible for up to 12 people to share a van to see multiple attractions.

Another option is **Vitran buses,** which serve Charlotte Amalie and even go to Red Hook, a jumping-off point for St. John. Within Charlotte Amalie, the fare is 75¢; to other districts, it's $1.

"Taxi vans," a fleet of privately owned vans or minibuses, charge the same fares as Vitran buses. They are usually less comfortable, though, and the service is inconsistent.

Within Walking Distance

Once you hit the shopping capital of the Caribbean, you will, of course, find yourself caught in the barrage of tourists and stores. Sandwiched among the shops are key historical buildings, though, and you should try to check out some of these sites, including the so-called **Grand Hotel,** near the just-renovated Emancipation Park, which houses a visitors center and some shops.

Fort Christian, which dates back to 1672, dominates the center of the town. It was named after the Danish monarch Christian V and has served as everything from a governor's residence to a prison. Some of the cells have become part of the Virgin Islands Museum. Native American artifacts are also on display at the small facility.

If you came to the island to shop, by all means, jump right in. **Main Street** is the main shopping street, and to the north is fully-stocked **Back Street.** You can find other retail outlets along the **Waterfront Highway.** If you need even more stores, browse the side streets, alleys, and walkways between these principal streets.

Beyond Walking Distance

Coral World Marine Park and Underwater Observatory, the number one attraction on the island, was destroyed when Hurricane Marilyn hit there in 1995; however, it's being reconstructed to its original design and is scheduled to reopen in mid-1998. The marine complex is a 20-minute drive from downtown and is home to a three-story underwater observation tower that is 100 feet offshore. Admission is $17 for adults, $10 for children.

If you're not afraid of heights, check out the **Paradise Point Tramway.** The lift takes you from the Havensight area to Paradise Point atop a 697-foot peak for a breathtaking view of Charlotte Amalie harbor. A restaurant, bar, shops, and hiking trails are located at Paradise Point. The ride only lasts 3½ minutes at an inflated price tag of $10 per person, half off for kids, round-trip.

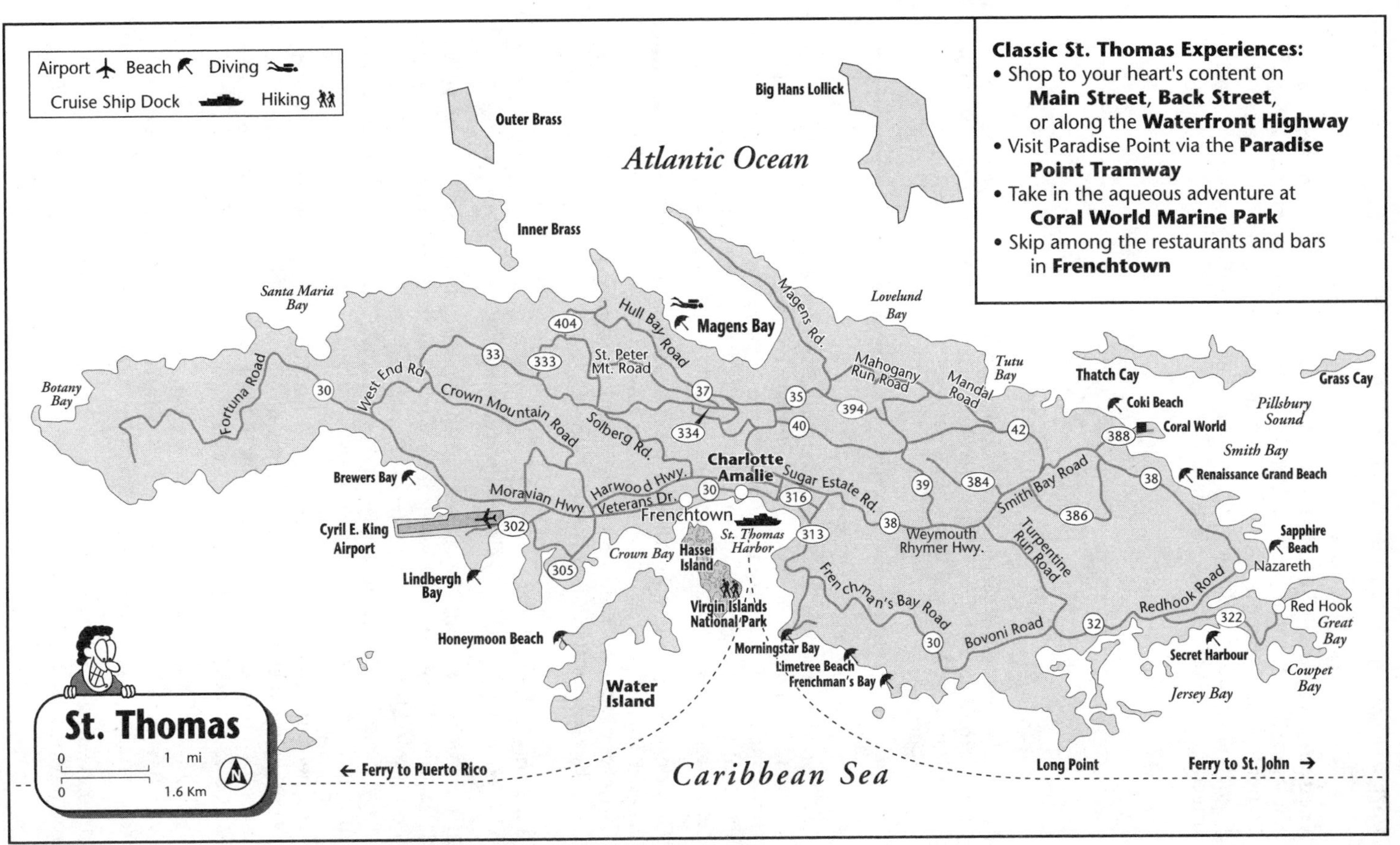
St. Thomas
0 1 mi
0 1.6 Km
Airport Beach Diving
Cruise Ship Dock Hiking
Classic St. Thomas Experiences:
• Shop to your heart's content on **Main Street**, **Back Street**, or along the **Waterfront Highway**
• Visit Paradise Point via the **Paradise Point Tramway**
• Take in the aqueous adventure at **Coral World Marine Park**
• Skip among the restaurants and bars in **Frenchtown**
Atlantic Ocean
Caribbean Sea
Outer Brass
Inner Brass
Big Hans Lollick
Santa Maria Bay
Botany Bay
Lovelund Bay
Tutu Bay
Thatch Cay
Grass Cay
Pillsbury Sound
Smith Bay
Magens Bay
Coki Beach
Coral World
Renaissance Grand Beach
Sapphire Beach
Nazareth
Red Hook
Great Bay
Cowpet Bay
Secret Harbour
Jersey Bay
Long Point
Ferry to St. John →
← Ferry to Puerto Rico
Brewers Bay
Cyril E. King Airport
Lindbergh Bay
Honeymoon Beach
Water Island
Crown Bay
Hassel Island
Virgin Islands National Park
St. Thomas Harbor
Charlotte Amalie
Frenchtown
Morningstar Bay
Limetree Beach
Frenchman's Bay
Fortuna Road
West End Rd
Crown Mountain Road
Solberg Rd.
Hull Bay Road
St. Peter Mt. Road
Magens Rd.
Mahogany Run Road
Mandal Road
Moravian Hwy
Harwood Hwy.
Veterans Dr.
Sugar Estate Rd.
Weymouth Rhymer Hwy.
Smith Bay Road
Turpentine Run Road
Frenchman's Bay Road
Bovoni Road
Redhook Road
30
33
333
404
37
334
35
40
394
42
388
38
39
384
386
316
313
302
305
32
322

Frenchtown, west of Charlotte Amalie, is a quaint fishing village that boasts many fun restaurants and bars. The town was founded by some French-speaking people who were uprooted when the Swedes invaded their homeland of St. Barts. Many of the people who currently reside here are direct descendants of those settlers.

Life Preservers

If you're visiting the beaches on St. Thomas, be sure to protect your belongings, as pickpockets and thieves have been known to strike. Also, to ensure that you don't miss the boat, you'll need to arrange for a cab to pick you up at a specific time.

St. Thomas's **beaches** are quite good and easy to reach via taxis. All are open to the public, but some charge a fee. **Sapphire Beach** on the East End is the island's most famous, and the one most popular with windsurfers. You can rent snorkeling gear and lounge chairs there, or you can stretch out on its white-coral sand and take in the sun and the awesome views of the bay.

Other notable beaches are **Magen Bay, Coki Beach,** and the **Renaissance Grand Beach Resort,** located on the North Side. **Morningstar, Limetree Beach, Brewer's Beach,** and **Lindberg Beach** are worth visiting. They are located on the South Side.

St. John Self-Tour

The **St. John Tourist Office** is located near the Battery at Cruz Bay.

If your ship docks on Charlotte Amalie, you can travel to St. John by **ferry.** Departures leave from the waterfront starting at 9am and running at 1- to 2-hour intervals until the final departure around 7pm. Returning, the last boat leaves Cruz Bay for Charlotte Amalie at 5:15pm. The ride lasts about 45 minutes and costs $7 each way.

Another ferry that runs from the Red Hook Pier on St. Thomas's eastern tip departs almost every half hour starting at 6:30am. The ride to Cruz Bay takes almost 20 minutes, and the last ferry departs Cruz Bay at 11pm. The one-way fare is $3 for adults and $1 for children under age 11.

To explore St. John, hop into one of its surrey-style **taxis.** Average fares from Cruz Bay are $3 to Trunk Bay, $3.50 to Cinnamon Bay, and $7 to Maho Bay. You can also take a 2-hour island tour by taxi for $30.

If you want a wind-whipping-your-hair experience, **rent a Jeep** and take full advantage of the island's uncluttered roads and expansive vistas. **Hertz**

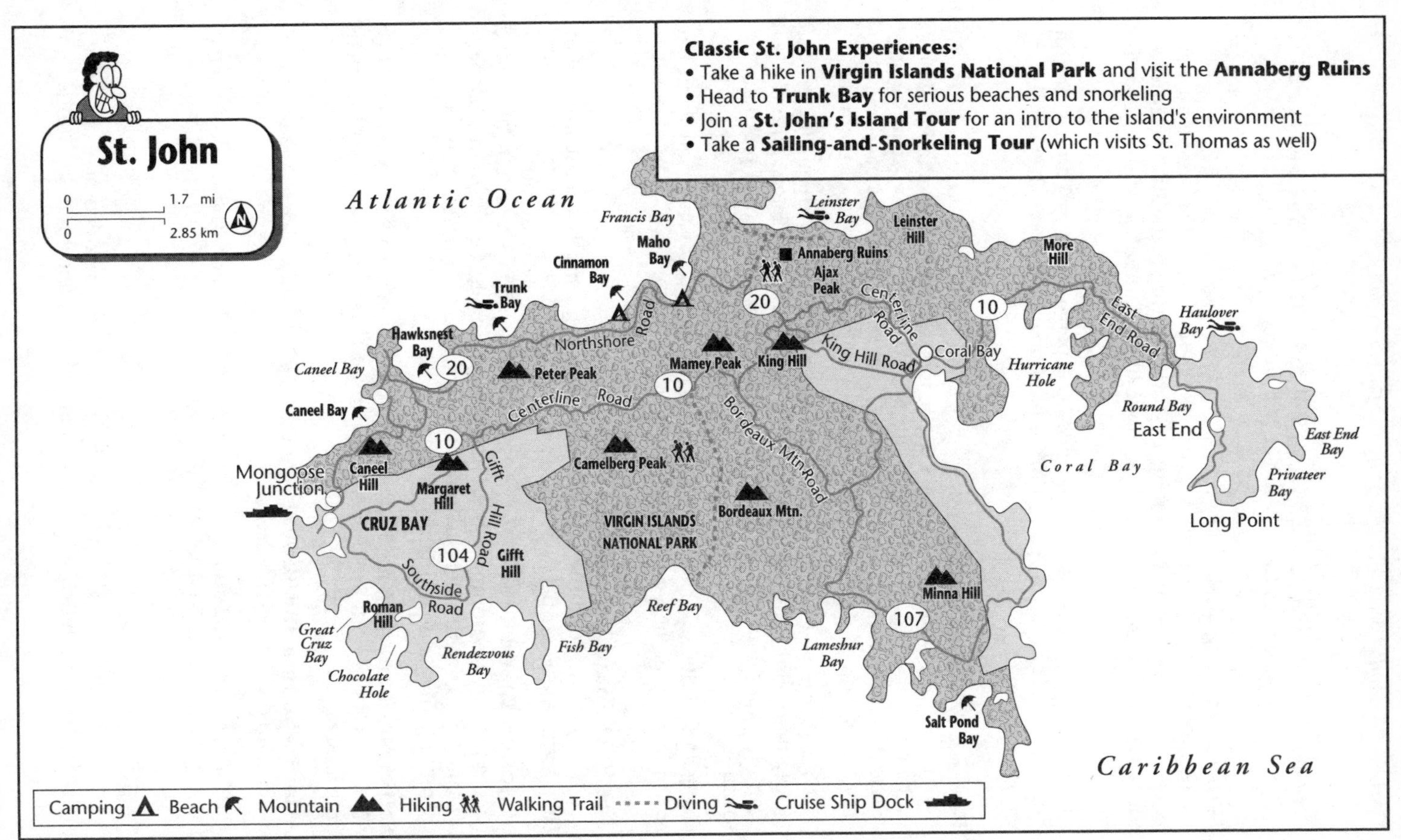
St. John
0 1.7 mi
0 2.85 km
Classic St. John Experiences:
• Take a hike in Virgin Islands National Park and visit the Annaberg Ruins
• Head to Trunk Bay for serious beaches and snorkeling
• Join a St. John's Island Tour for an intro to the island's environment
• Take a Sailing-and-Snorkeling Tour (which visits St. Thomas as well)
Atlantic Ocean
Francis Bay
Leinster Bay
Leinster Hill
More Hill
Maho Bay
Cinnamon Bay
Trunk Bay
Annaberg Ruins
Ajax Peak
Hawksnest Bay
Caneel Bay
Northshore Road
Centerline Road
East End Road
Haulover Bay
Peter Peak
Mamey Peak
King Hill
King Hill Road
Coral Bay
Hurricane Hole
Round Bay
East End
East End Bay
Privateer Bay
Long Point
Coral Bay
Mongoose Junction
Caneel Hill
Margaret Hill
Gifft Hill Road
Camelberg Peak
Bordeaux Mtn Road
Bordeaux Mtn.
CRUZ BAY
VIRGIN ISLANDS NATIONAL PARK
Gifft Hill
Southside Road
Roman Hill
Great Cruz Bay
Chocolate Hole
Rendezvous Bay
Fish Bay
Reef Bay
Lameshur Bay
Minna Hill
Salt Pond Bay
Caribbean Sea
10
20
104
107
Camping Beach Mountain Hiking Walking Trail Diving Cruise Ship Dock

(☎ **800/654-3001** or 340/693-7580) and **Avis** (☎ **800/331-1084** or 340/776-6374) have offices here. Reservations are required.

Within Walking Distance

Cruz Bay is a sleepy port village that boasts some nice bars, restaurants, boutiques, and pastel-painted homes. Worth visiting is the **Elaine Ione Sprauve Museum,** located at the public library and filled with local artifacts.

Although shopping is a must-see, must-do experience on St. Thomas, St. John offers more of an eclectic collection of boutiques and stores that are also worth browsing.

Beyond Walking Distance

If you can make your way to the **Virgin Islands National Park,** you'll find a maze of trails (head to the visitors center first) and the **Annaberg Ruins,** a former Danish plantation and sugar mill that dates back to 1719. On certain days of the week, park rangers give guided walks of the ruins.

Beach lovers should head to **Trunk Bay,** a beautiful but perpetually crowded facility manned by lifeguards. The beach is great for snorkelers, who can rent gear and explore its underwater trail near the shore. Beware of pickpockets roaming about.

Caneel Bay, Hawksnest Beach, Cinnamon Bay, Maho Bay, and Salt Pond Bay are all other good beach choices.

The Best Shore Excursions

You'll snooze through the St. Thomas sightseeing trips that most ships offer. Here are a few better bets:

St. John's Island Tour (4 to 4½ hours, $25 to $50): This trip focuses more on the natural environment than on shopping malls. On St. John, an open-air safari bus goes through the national park, allowing time for snorkeling, swimming, and sunbathing.

Sailing-and-Snorkeling Tour (3½ to 4 hours, $35 to $40): Most ships offer this tour of both St. John and St. Thomas via a single-hull sailing yacht or catamaran.

Atlantis Submarine Tour (1½ hours, $70): A quick dive to see the underwater sights while staying dry.

Scuba Adventure Tour (3 hours, $40 to $75): Explore the waters (though the trip might be limited to certified divers).

San Juan

With ruins that date back to when the Spanish empire ruled here, San Juan offers history on a much wider scale than other Caribbean destinations, but it's also a modern city with high rises and casinos, a glitzy beach strip, and other attractions and diversions.

San Juan is also the busiest cruise port in the West Indies, with more than 700 cruise ships bringing some 850,000 passengers to the island annually. Be ready for crowds.

THE CRUISE LINE SITUATION Carnival, Celebrity, Club Med, Costa, Crystal, Cunard, Holland America, Norwegian, Premier, Princess, Radisson, Regal, Royal Caribbean, and Royal Olympic all make port stops here.

THE MONEY SITUATION The **U.S. dollar** is the legal tender.

THE LANGUAGE SITUATION Spanish is the native tongue, but most people involved in the tourist industry speak English.

San Juan Self-Tour

Cruise ships normally dock at one of eight piers on the south shore of **Old San Juan,** the core of the city's historic district, first settled by the Spanish in the early 1500s. The **Tourist Information Center** is located near Pier 1 in Old San Juan, and the area's top tourist sites are within walking distance, so there's really no need for you to take an organized tour.

A walkway connects the piers to the cobblestone streets of the area and to some great shopping. Piers 1, 3, and 4 are the most convenient to shopping, but even passengers coming ashore at piers 5, 6, 7, and 8 will only have a walk of about 10 minutes. During the weekend, ships might have to use alternate docks, including Froitier Pier near the beaches at Candado and the Pan American Dock in Isla Grande across San Antonio Channel. In this case, you'll have to take a taxi or van to Old San Juan.

There's really no need to rent a car, and doing so can be a hassle, since San Juan is a congested urban area.

In Old Town, a free **trolley service** is offered.

The *Agua Expresso* **ferry** links Old San Juan to Hato Rey and Catano across the bay. The one-way fare is 75¢ to Hato Rey and 50¢ to Catano.

Taxis are priced at a $1 initial charge, and 10¢ for each thirteenth of a mile, with a minimum fare of $3. Riding the municipal bus costs 50¢ or less.

Within Walking Distance

You can get a feel of 5 centuries of history by walking the cobblestoned streets of Old San Juan. In the 7-block historic landmark area, you'll see many of Puerto Rico's top historical attractions. On a walking tour, you'll also find shops and cafes.

There are dozens of noteworthy attractions, but the must-sees include **El Morro** (Castillo de San Felipe del Morro), a fort believed for centuries to be impregnable. It was here that Spanish Puerto Rico defended itself against the navies of Great Britain, France, and Holland, as well as against hundreds

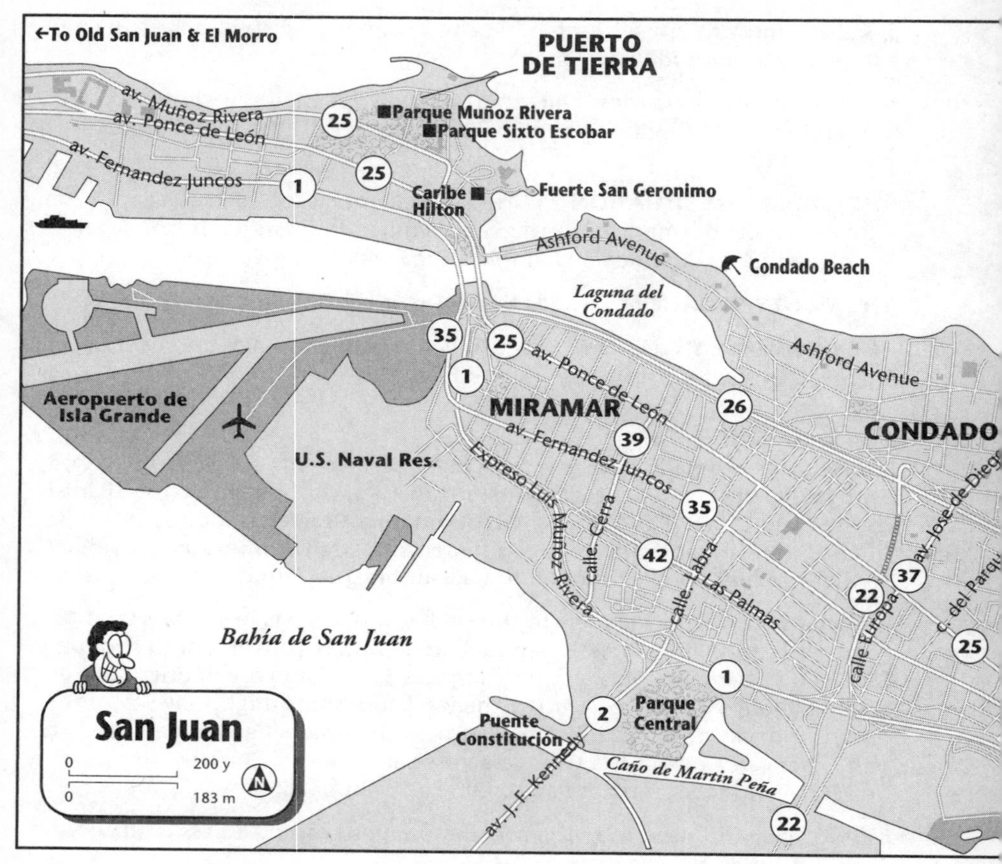

of pirate ships. The fortress walls are designed as part of a network of defenses that made San Juan a walled city. This is the city's top attraction.

Other recommended sights include **La Princesa,** once the most-feared prison in the Caribbean; **La Casa Blanca,** which was built by the son-in-law of Juan Ponce de León as the great explorer's island home, to El Morro; **La Fortaleza** and Mansion **Ejecutiva,** the centuries-old residence of the Puerto Rican governor; and **Plaza de Armas,** the most beautiful of the squares in Old Town, flanked by the neoclassic **Intendencia,** which houses offices of the State Department, and San Juan's historic **City Hall.**

Antiguo Monicomio Insular was built in 1854 as an insane asylum but now houses the **Puerto Rican Academy of Fine Arts.** Nearby is the stately neoclassical building **Asilo de Beneficias,** or "Home for the Poor," which dates back to the 1840s.

The monumental **Cuartel de Ballaja** houses the **Museum of the Americas** on its second floor. Nearby is **Plaza de San Jose,** which is

Classic San Juan Experiences:

- Visit the pretty-much impregnable **El Morro** fortress and the feared **La Princesa** prison
- Tipple through the **Bacardi Rum Plant Tour**
- Take a tour of the **El Yunque Rain Forest**
- Shoot for the stars at the **Caribe Hilton casino** or the **Casino at the Ritz-Carlton**
- Visit one of the dozens of **historic sights** within walking distance of the port (see Old San Juan map)

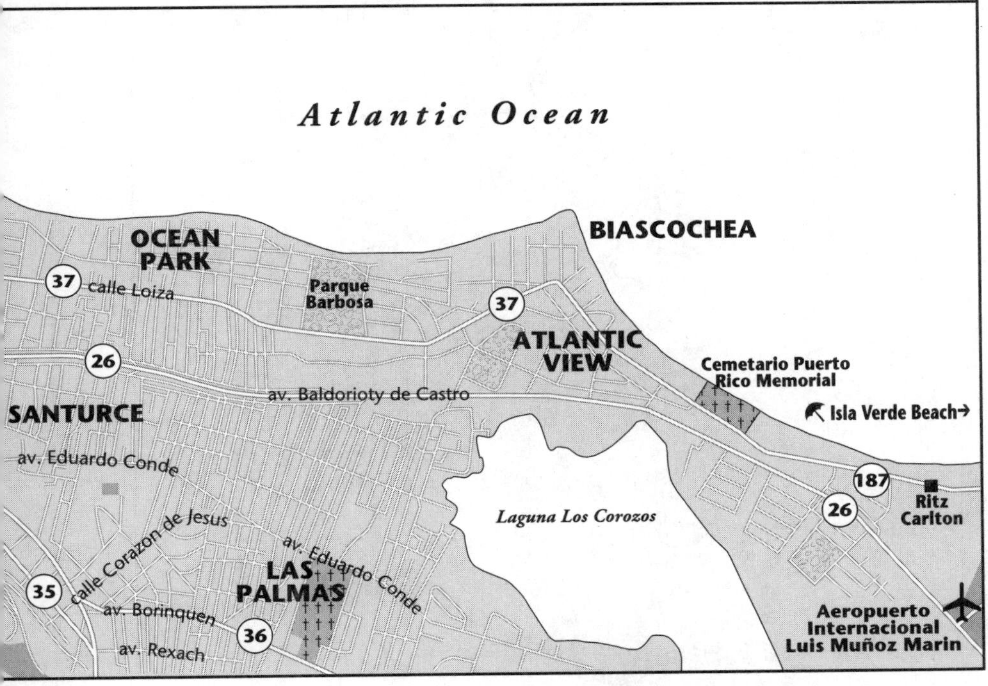

highlighted by a statue of explorer Juan Ponce de León that was cast from an English cannon captured during a naval battle in 1797. Among the buildings surrounding the Plaza de San Jose is the **Museo de Pablo Casals,** which honors the Spanish-born cellist who lived his final years in Puerto Rico. Another is the **Iglesia de San Jose,** a church established by the Dominicans in 1523.

Catedral de San Juan is Puerto Rico's most famous church. You might also want to visit **Capilla de Cristo** on the calle del Cristo, a tiny chapel that has a silver alter dedicated to the "Christ of Miracles."

Fort San Cristobal is the adjunct to the El Morro fortress, and like its sibling, is maintained by the National Park Service.

Beyond Walking Distance

Most casinos in Puerto Rico are open from noon to 4pm and again from 8pm to 4am. Among the better ones is the casino at the **Caribe Hilton.** The

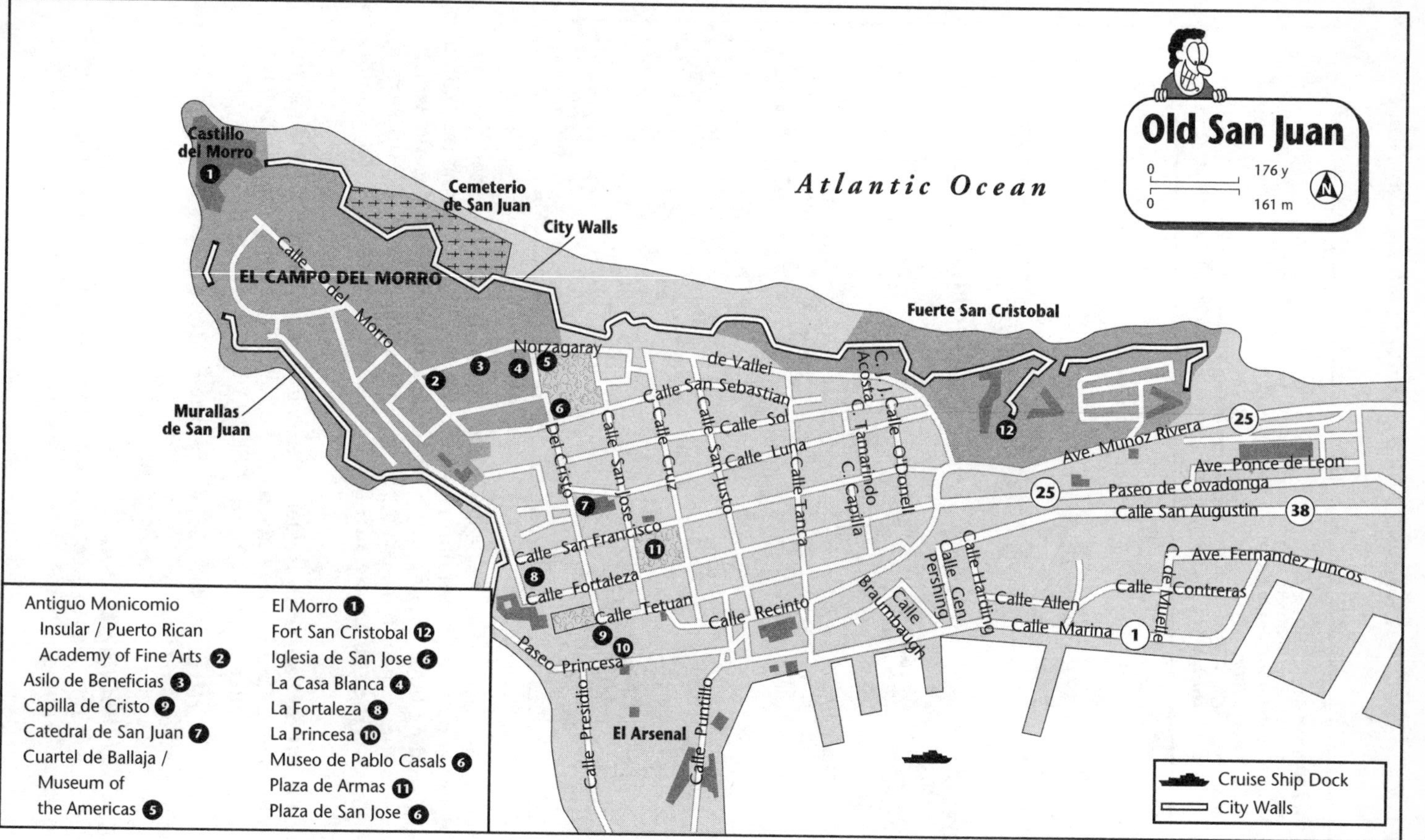

Old San Juan
0 176 y
0 161 m
Atlantic Ocean
Castillo del Morro
Cemeterio de San Juan
City Walls
EL CAMPO DEL MORRO
Calle del Morro
Murallas de San Juan
Fuerte San Cristobal
Norzagaray
de Vallei
Calle San Sebastian
Calle Sol
Calle Luna
Del Cristo
Calle San Jose
Calle Cruz
Calle San Justo
Calle Tanca
C. Capilla
C. Tamarindo
Acosta
C. J. J. Calle O'Donell
Calle San Francisco
Calle Fortaleza
Calle Tetuan
Calle Recinto
Paseo Princesa
Calle Presidio
El Arsenal
Calle Puntillo
Calle Braumbaugh
Calle Gen. Pershing
Calle Harding
Calle Allen
Calle Marina
Calle Contreras
C. de Muelle
Ave. Fernandez Juncos
Calle San Augustin
Paseo de Covadonga
Ave. Ponce de Leon
Ave. Munoz Rivera
25
38
1
Antiguo Monicomio Insular / Puerto Rican Academy of Fine Arts 2
Asilo de Beneficias 3
Capilla de Cristo 9
Catedral de San Juan 7
Cuartel de Ballaja / Museum of the Americas 5
El Morro 1
Fort San Cristobal 12
Iglesia de San Jose 6
La Casa Blanca 4
La Fortaleza 8
La Princesa 10
Museo de Pablo Casals 6
Plaza de Armas 11
Plaza de San Jose 6
Cruise Ship Dock
City Walls

largest, at 18,500 square feet, is at the **Casino at The Ritz-Carlton,** 6961 State Rd.

A good beach bet is **Isla Verde.** Good snorkeling is possible there, and rental equipment for watersports is available.

The Best Shore Excursions

Bacardi Rum Plant Tour (2 hours, $18): This trip includes a visit to the plant and distillery and a chance to sample the company's products, too.

El Yunque Rain Forest Tour (6 hours, $35): This tour takes you to lush vegetation and waterfalls. An observation tower offers spectacular views of the coast.

Chapter 24

Ports of Call: Alaska

In This Chapter

- The best attractions, shopping, and fun at the nine major Alaska ports of call
- The lowdown on glaciers and whale watching
- Tips on the best shore excursions in each port
- Which cruise lines go where

Alaska has become one of the top cruise destinations in the world, and when you're cruising through the calm waters of the Inside Passage it's easy to see why: The scenery is simply breathtaking.

Much of the coastline is wilderness, with snowcapped mountain peaks, immense glaciers, rain-forested islands, icebergs, fjords, soaring eagles, and the occasional whale all easily viewed from the comfort of your cruise ship deck chair.

The fact that a half million cruise passengers a year arrive in this last great frontier has had its impact, of course. Some towns have become such tourist meccas that vendors from outside come in only for the summer seasons to sell their imported tourist wares. Even so, the ports of call highlighted in this chapter are not without their rustic charms, and the state's history, native culture, geography, and wildlife is fascinating.

Nearly all the ports of call in Alaska offer shore excursions for those who want to get active, such as mountain-bike trips, fishing, and kayak voyages. They are bookable through the cruise lines as shore excursions and are

Alaska Port Calls by Cruise Line

Cruise Line	Haines	Juneau	Ketchikan	Petersburg	Sitka	Skagway	Valdez	Victoria	Wrangell
Alaska Sightseeing	•	•	•	•	•	•	•	•	•
Alaska's Glacier Bay	•	•	•	•	•	•			•
Carnival		•	•		•	•			
Celebrity	•	•	•		•	•	•	•	
Clipper		•	•	•	•			•	•
Crystal		•	•		•	•	•	•	
Holland America		•	•		•	•	•	•	
Norwegian	•	•	•			•		•	•
Princess		•	•		•	•		•	
Royal Caribbean	•	•	•			•			
Special Expeditions	•	•	•		•	•		•	
World Explorer		•	•		•	•	•	•	•

generally worth taking. The prices might be slightly higher than similar excursions offered by vendors at the port itself, but you can be assured the vendors the cruise lines work with are reputable.

Flightseeing trips, offered as shore excursions at many of the ports of call, are your chance to see the Alaskan landscape from the air. If you don't mind trips in small planes or helicopters and are willing to pay for the experience (it can be expensive), these trips are a fascinating way to round out your experience of the Great Land.

At most ports, the cruise lines offer guided **city tours,** usually by bus. Some are worthwhile, particularly those that take you outside the downtown areas. In most ports, the downtown area is small enough to view on your own, by foot, if you so choose.

In this chapter, I detailed some of the best shore-excursion offerings in Alaska's Southeast, along with advice on exploring on your own and tips on suggested attractions.

Prices listed here are for 1998 and may increase slightly in 1999.

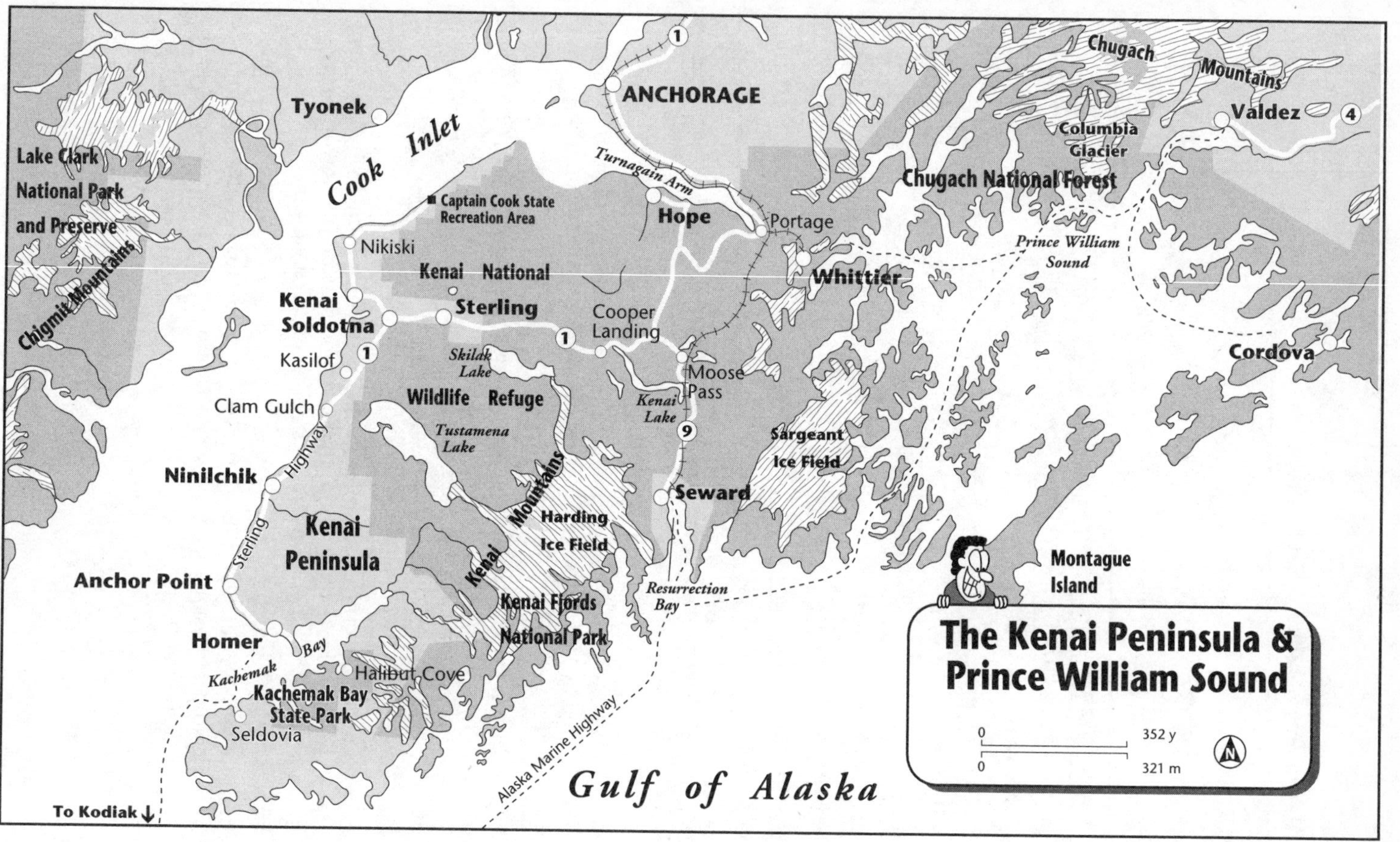
The Kenai Peninsula &
Prince William Sound
0
352 y
0
321 m
Tyonek
ANCHORAGE
Chugach
Mountains
Valdez
4
1
Lake Clark
National Park
and Preserve
Chigmit Mountains
Cook Inlet
Turnagain Arm
Columbia
Glacier
Chugach National Forest
Captain Cook State
Recreation Area
Hope
Portage
Prince William
Sound
Nikiski
Kenai National
Wildlife Refuge
Whittier
Kenai
Soldotna
Sterling
Cooper
Landing
Kasilof
Skilak
Lake
Moose
Pass
Cordova
Clam Gulch
Kenai
Lake
9
Tustamena
Lake
Sargeant
Ice Field
Ninilchik
Sterling Highway
Kenai Mountains
Seward
Harding
Ice Field
Kenai
Peninsula
Montague
Island
Anchor Point
Resurrection
Bay
Kenai Fjords
National Park
Homer
Kachemak Bay
Halibut Cove
Kachemak Bay
State Park
Seldovia
Alaska Marine Highway
Gulf of Alaska
To Kodiak

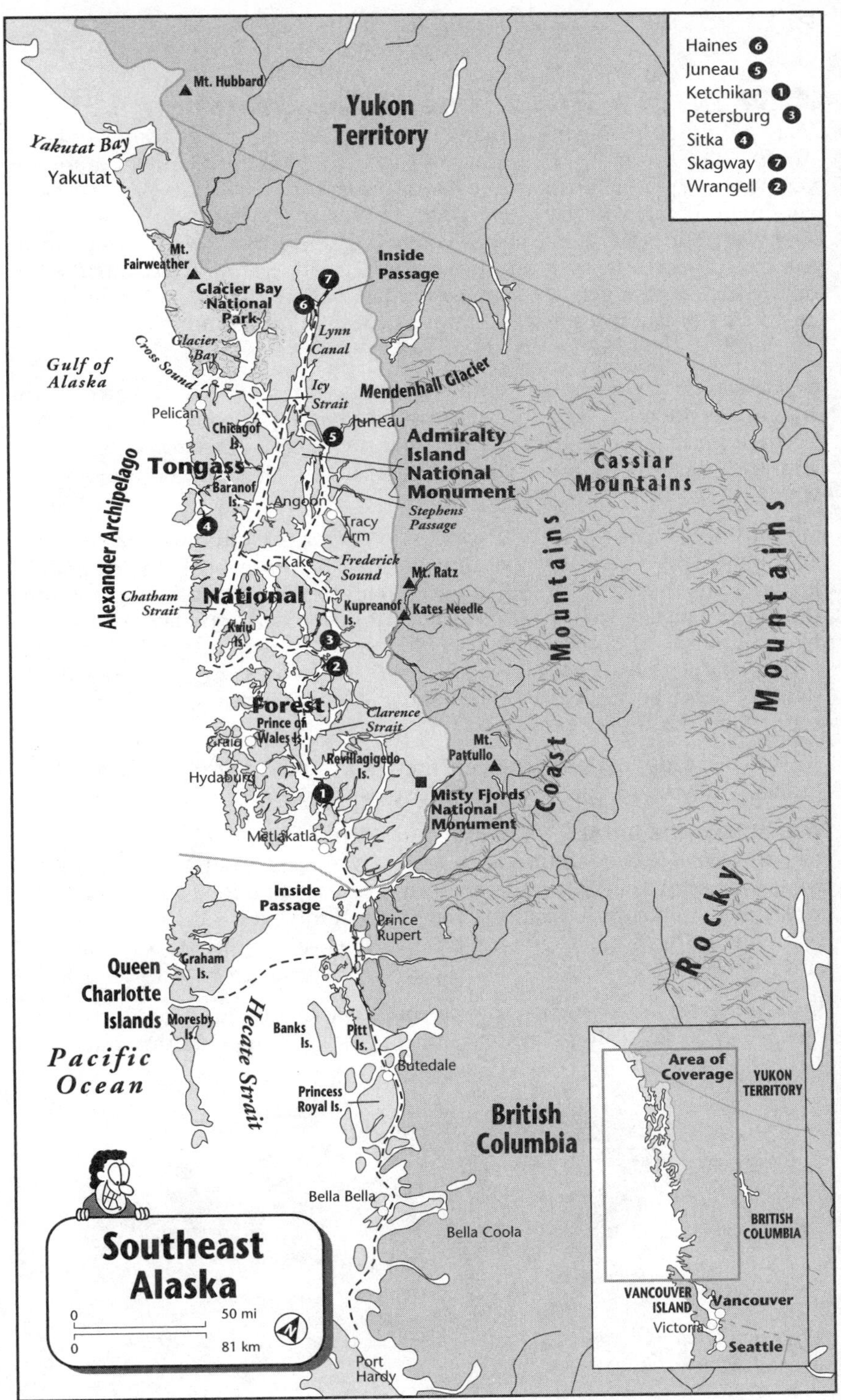
Haines 6
Juneau 5
Ketchikan 1
Petersburg 3
Sitka 4
Skagway 7
Wrangell 2
Mt. Hubbard
Yukon Territory
Yakutat Bay
Yakutat
Mt. Fairweather
Glacier Bay National Park
Inside Passage
Glacier Bay
Cross Sound
Gulf of Alaska
Lynn Canal
Mendenhall Glacier
Icy Strait
Pelican
Juneau
Chicagof Is.
Admiralty Island National Monument
Tongass
Cassiar Mountains
Baranof Is.
Angoon
Stephens Passage
Alexander Archipelago
Tracy Arm
Kake
Frederick Sound
Mt. Ratz
Chatham Strait
National
Kupreanof Is.
Kates Needle
Kuiu Is.
Coast Mountains
Rocky Mountains
Forest
Clarence Strait
Prince of Wales Is.
Craig
Revillagigedo Is.
Mt. Pattullo
Hydaburg
Misty Fjords National Monument
Metlakatla
Inside Passage
Prince Rupert
Queen Charlotte Islands
Graham Is.
Moresby Is.
Hecate Strait
Banks Is.
Pitt Is.
Pacific Ocean
Butedale
Princess Royal Is.
British Columbia
Bella Bella
Bella Coola
Southeast Alaska
0
50 mi
0
81 km
Port Hardy
Area of Coverage
YUKON TERRITORY
BRITISH COLUMBIA
VANCOUVER ISLAND
Vancouver
Victoria
Seattle

A Whale of a Good Time: Whale Watching 101

Imagine standing on deck, looking out onto the calm, silver waters of an Alaskan bay. Suddenly, the surface of the water pulls back, and an immense yet graceful creature appears, moving silently, the curve of its back visible for a moment before the water again closes over it. You wait for it to reappear. And wait. And wait. Then, just as you're beginning to think it's gone forever, the creature leaps straight out of the water, twisting around in midair before falling back with a gigantic *kersploosh!* that's followed a half-second later by an equally distinctive sound: That of a thousand cruise ship passengers saying "OOOH!" "AAAH!" and "Marty! Marty! Did you see *that*?!"

In Alaska, whale watching is serious business, and many cruisers arrive with a sighting as the main wish for their trip. Maybe it's the whales' size, maybe it's their grace, or maybe it's the fact that they tend to be elusive just when you want to see them most; whatever it is, it's a fact: Alaska cruisers are whale-crazy.

On most large cruise ships, the captain or officer on watch will make an announcement when they spot one, but the ship probably won't stop and linger. A few lines, though (mostly the small-ship lines), feature whale watching as a big part of their focus, so their ships will visit areas favored by whales and spend time waiting there for an encounter, or they will monitor marine-traffic radio broadcasts and deviate from course to go where whale sightings have been reported. Most ships will offer lectures about whales at some point during your cruise.

To get you ready for your whale encounter, I've prepared this little whale primer. Study up so you'll know what you're looking at.

THE HUMPBACK WHALE A part-time resident of Alaska that spends its winters in warmer waters around Mexico or Hawaii, the humpback is a baleen whale, meaning that instead of teeth, it has strips of bone-like baleen that strain tiny sea-creatures from the water. The humpback is distinguished primarily by its huge tail; the hump on its back, just forward of its dorsal fin; and its enormously long, armlike flippers, which can grow to 14 feet.

If you're really lucky, you'll get to see humpbacks breaching, or leaping completely out of the water. No one knows for sure why they do this, but I think

The humpback whale *Max. length: 53 ft.*

it's because they *can*. I watched a pair of humpbacks breaching for 10 minutes not long ago, after which they laid on their sides and slapped the water with their flippers. Territorial display? Warning sign? Feeding activity? Who knows? What I do know is that it's thrilling to watch.

Humpbacks tend to congregate to feed on the rich supply of krill off Point Adolphus and other spots in and near **Glacier Bay** and farther south around the Brothers Islands in **Frederick Sound.**

THE ORCA (KILLER WHALE) With their distinctive black-and-white coloring, they might look like aquatic panda bears, but don't be fooled: The orca really is a killer. One of the fastest creatures in the sea, capable of swimming at up to 25 knots, orcas typically hunt porpoises, seals, and other fish, but here's an interesting fact: There's never been a report of one attacking a human being. Why? In Tlingit legend, the orca was created by a great hunter who had been marooned on an island by his jealous brothers in law. Using his magic, the hunter fashioned the most fearsome monster he could imagine and sent the creature to kill those who had betrayed him. Once the task was done, the monster returned to the hunter, who said, "Now your job is completed, but since I am a man, and I created you, you will never again hunt for men." And that's why orcas don't attack people.

The top spot to see orca is **Robson Bight,** an area in Johnstone Strait (between Vancouver Island and mainland British Columbia), where they tend to cruise slowly near the shoreline, rubbing their bellies on the rounded stones of the sloping beach.

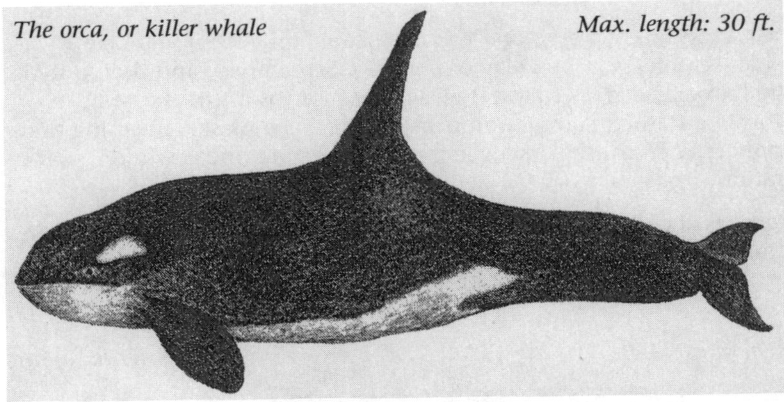
The orca, or killer whale *Max. length: 30 ft.*

THE BELUGA WHALE This small, white whale with the cute, rounded beak is one of only three types that spend all their lives in cold water rather than heading south for the winter. (The other two are the narwhal and bowhead.) Distinguished by their lack of dorsal fin and by the extraordinary range of sounds they can produce, the beluga is also the only whale that can turn its head and one of the few with good eyesight.

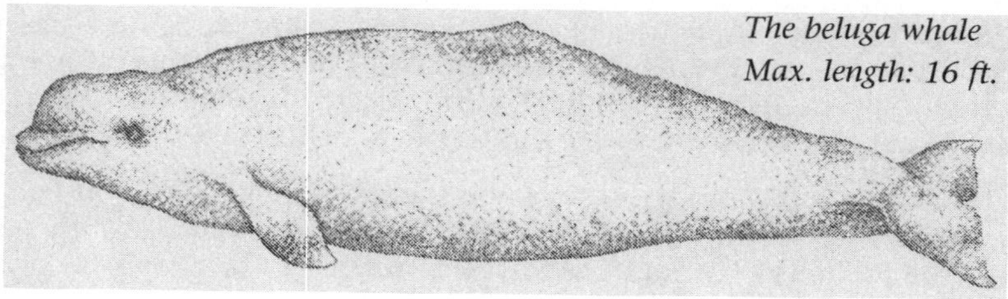

The beluga whale
Max. length: 16 ft.

Beluga frequently follow salmon to feed in **Turnagain Arm** near Anchorage; if your cruise starts or ends in Seward, you'll most likely take a bus transfer between Anchorage and Seward, driving along this arm a good portion of the way.

THE MINKE WHALE Also known as the piked whale, this is the smallest of the baleen whales—generally less than 30 feet long—and has a blackish-gray body with a white stomach. Along with the humpback and the gray whale, it is the only baleen commonly seen in Alaska waters.

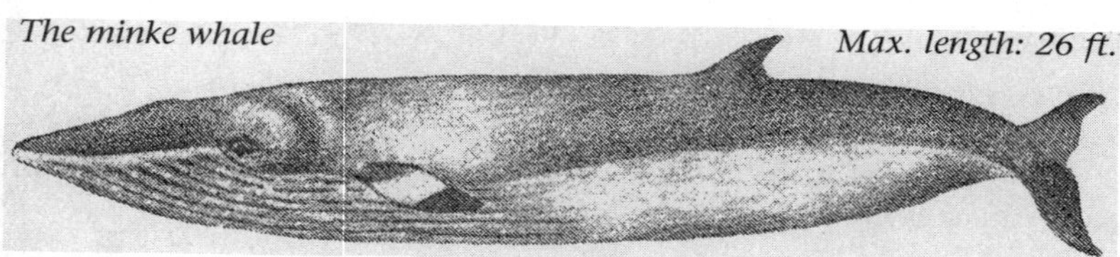

The minke whale *Max. length: 26 ft.*

THE GRAY WHALE Here's one you'll probably only see if you take a shoulder-season cruise (in May or very late September), and then only if you're lucky. The grays spend their winter months off the coast of California and their summer months off northern Alaska, meaning that the only chance cruise passengers have of spotting one is while it's on its migration.

The gray is about the same size as the humpback whale, though it lacks the humpback's huge flippers. Its head is pointed, and it lacks a dorsal fin.

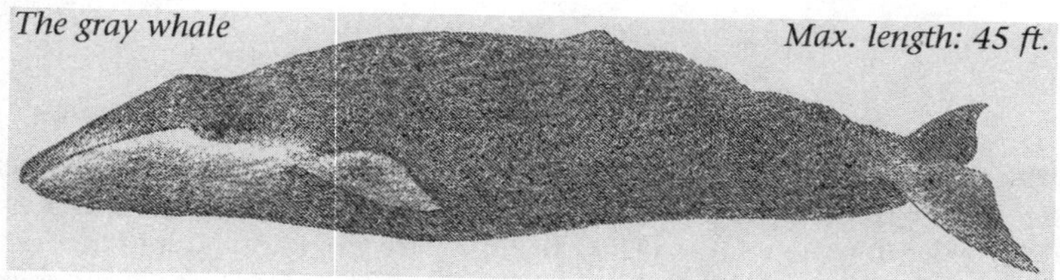

The gray whale *Max. length: 45 ft.*

Understanding the Ice: Glaciers 101

Along with whales, glaciers are the other really big draw of Alaska cruising, hanging there over the mountains, dipping down into the seawater, running through valleys they carved themselves, all those years ago, as they advanced. Every Alaska cruise makes a stop at one or another of the major glaciers in Alaska's Southeast, and while everyone knows the basics—they're ice; they're big—you'll be ahead of the game if you pick up a little glacial terminology before you go. With that in mind, I've prepared a glacier primer for ya. Read on.

HOW THEY FORM Think of that old refrigerator you have at home, the one that you have to defrost every month if you don't want the accumulated ice to consume your Popsicles. It's pretty much the same deal with glaciers. When extremely low temperatures prevent successive snowfalls from melting, the accumulated weight of the snow compresses the bottom layers into an extremely dense ice. Once this ice begins to accumulate, the law of gravity takes over, and the ice begins to seek the lowest point, flowing downhill through or over whatever stands in its way.

WHAT HAPPENS AS THEY MOVE Glaciers are constantly on the move, sculpting the landscape below, grinding the shale and other rocks, and pushing rubble and silt ahead and to the sides. This sediment is known as **moraine.** *Terminal moraine* is the accumulation of rubble at the front of a glacier; *lateral moraine* lines the sides of glaciers. A dark area in a glacier's center—seen when two glaciers flow together, pushing their ice and crushed rubble together—is *median moraine.*

Depending on temperature and rainfall, some glaciers may "gallop," surging either forward or backward as much as 10 to 150 feet a day, and some may recede or retreat—like the Mendenhall Glacier in Juneau, which is melting away at the rate of about 30 feet a year. Hubbard Glacier became a galloping glacier for a brief time in 1986, moving forward rapidly to block in Yakutat Bay for a few months.

THE DIFFERENT TYPES OF GLACIERS All glaciers begin in mountain icefields and move downhill. If they make it all the way to the sea, they become what are known as **tidewater glaciers,** which are the kind you'll probably see on your cruise. These glaciers run directly into the water, like very slow-moving lemmings. Once there, the various forces of gravity and water temperature force a process called *calving,* in which great chunks of the glacier wall split off with a thunderous crack and fall into the sea to form icebergs. This is a continual process, so you stand a good chance of seeing a good calving, no matter when you go.

The **icebergs** that remain after calving come in different sizes, and over the years, seamen have developed names to identify them (and their potential level of threat): Very large chunks are *icebergs,* pieces of moderate size are known as *bergy bits, growlers* are slightly smaller still, and *brash ice* is little chunks no more than 2 meters long.

The other types of glaciers you'll see are **mountain glaciers,** which develop in high mountains, flowing out of large icefields; **valley glaciers,** which, as their name implies, spill down through valleys, looking like the frozen rivers they are; **piedmont glaciers,** which occur when a valley glacier spills out and widens onto a flat plain; **alpine** or **cirque glaciers,** which occupy bowl-like hollows in high mountains; and **hanging glaciers,** which cling to the sides of steep mountains, flowing down almost like a man's beard.

THE GLACIERS YOU'LL SEE Some of the most-visited glaciers on the various cruise ship itineraries include the 16 tidewater glaciers of **Glacier Bay National Park and Preserve; Hubbard Glacier in Yakutat Bay; Mendenhall Glacier** outside Juneau; the **North and South Sawyer Glaciers** in Tracy Arm; and the many glaciers of **College Fjord.**

Haines

Remember Cicely on the TV show *Northern Exposure?* This town, surrounded by snowcapped peaks, could have been the model. It's quintessential small-town Alaska, and even a little quirky; a moose might feel perfectly at home wandering down the tiny, quiet Haines main street (except, perhaps, when a cruise ship is docked).

Shops and museums are located downtown, but Haines also offers another interesting area only a short walk away: **Fort William Seward,** a 1903 U.S. Army outpost, deactivated after World War II, which now houses an arts and cultural center featuring a famous dance troupe and wood-carvers. In the center of the fort's 9-acre parade grounds is a replica of a Tlingit clan house.

The area around Haines is also one of the best places in the world to view bald eagles, although the largest numbers (more than 3,000) gather in the fall and winter (noncruise) season.

THE CRUISE LINE SITUATION Alaska Sightseeing, Alaska's Glacier Bay, Celebrity, Norwegian, Royal Caribbean, and Special Expeditions make port calls here.

Haines Self-Tour

If you want to explore on your own, pick up a map at the kiosk at the end of the Port Chilkoot dock. From the dock, you can head up Portage Street to Fort William Seward or walk down Front Street to the Main Street area. Main Street is about three-quarters of a mile from the pier. Cruise ships usually provide shuttle service.

Within Walking Distance

Fort William Seward is the setting for the **Alaska Indian Arts Center** and the **Chilkat Center for the Arts.** The center features totem poles and a carver's workshop. The dancers, who have been a troupe since 1957 (they were formed as a Boy Scout project) and have since performed around the

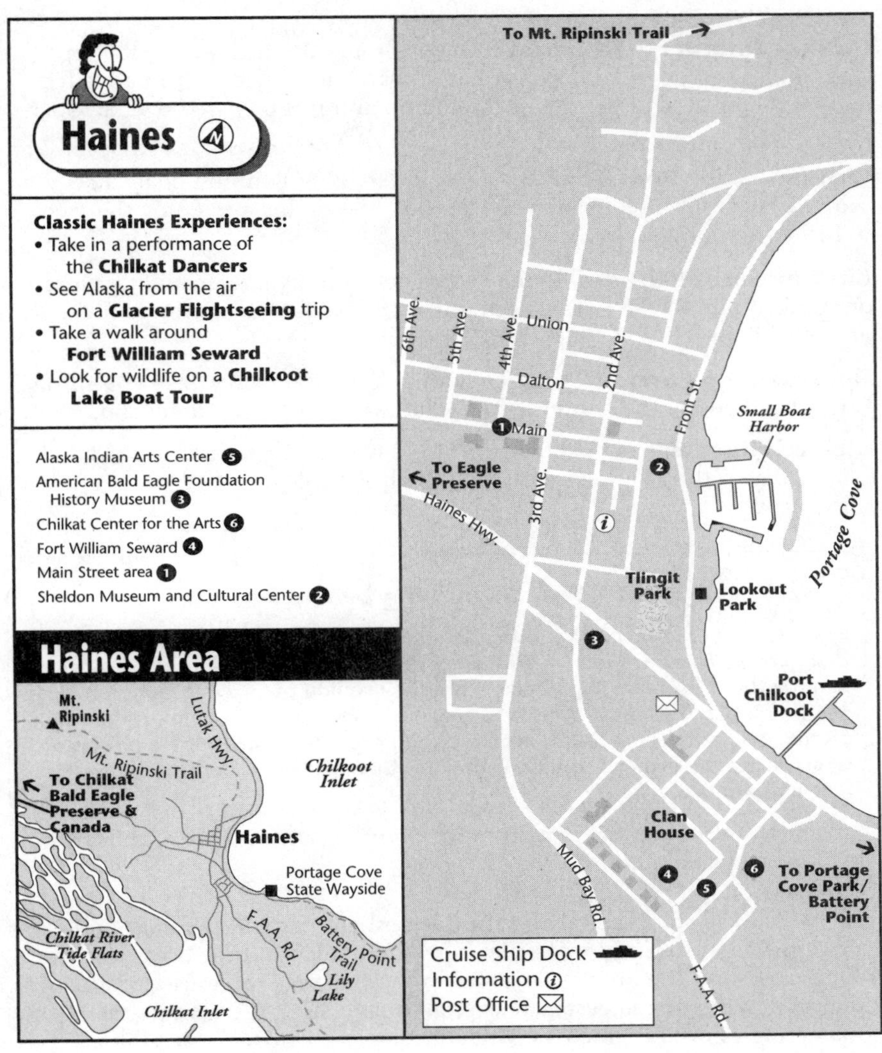

world, offer performances timed to cruise ship schedules (that is, when the dancers aren't on tour). Admission is $10 adults, $5 students, free for children under 4.

In the Main Street area, visitors will find the **Sheldon Museum and Cultural Center,** which highlights local history, including Tlingit art and cultural artifacts. Admission is $3 for adults, free for children under 17. The **American Bald Eagle Foundation History Museum** features a huge woodland diorama. Admission is free, but donations are accepted.

The Best Shore Excursions

Chilkat Dancers & Salmon Bake (3½ hours, $55): Guests visit a replica of a Chilkat native tribal house at Fort Seward, are regaled with native legends and dances, and then feast on salmon and ribs prepared over an open fire.

Chilkoot Lake Boat Tour (3 hours, $65 to $70): Pontoon boats take you across a beautiful lake, where you can look for wildlife and enjoy the views of the surrounding mountains and forests.

Chilkat Nature Hike (4 hours, $40): The 4.8-mile hike includes a narrative on Alaskan rain forests, and you might spot a bald eagle or two. Moderately difficult hiking.

Horse-Drawn Carriage Tour (1 hour, $25): Local guides take you through Fort Seward, along the Lynn Canal, and downtown at a leisurely clip.

Glacier Flightseeing (1½ hours, $125): Fly over the Juneau Icefield and Glacier Bay. If the weather's clear, you might be able to see Mount Fairweather.

What's That Swimming by the Bow?

If you stand in the bow of your ship and look down into the bow wake, there's every chance you'll see **Dall porpoises** swimming there, rushing along right by the side of the ship, looking as if they couldn't be having more fun. The Dall looks like a small killer whale—same black-and-white coloring, similar profile (except that the Dall lacks the orca's large dorsal fin)—but are possessed of a significantly milder disposition. Think of them as the surfers of the marine mammal world.

Juneau

Juneau, Alaska's state capital and third-largest city (after Anchorage and Fairbanks), is surrounded by ice fields on three sides and the ocean on one, which means it's the only state capital you can't drive to. It also has the distinction of being the largest state capital in land size—it encompasses 3,108 square miles, most of which are wilderness.

Despite its remote status, the hilly city is bustling; it's the most cosmopolitan place you'll see between Vancouver and Anchorage.

For cruise passengers, the town offers within easy walking distance from the pier a tramway and mountain hiking trails, charming historical architecture, shops (mostly of the tourist variety), a great museum, the state capitol building, and a real saloon or two. The blue-white Mendenhall Glacier is nearby, and the forests that surround Juneau offer hikers much variety.

The town's gold-mining history is evident as you get off the ship. Look up at the mountain near the Mount Roberts Tramway to see the ruins of the

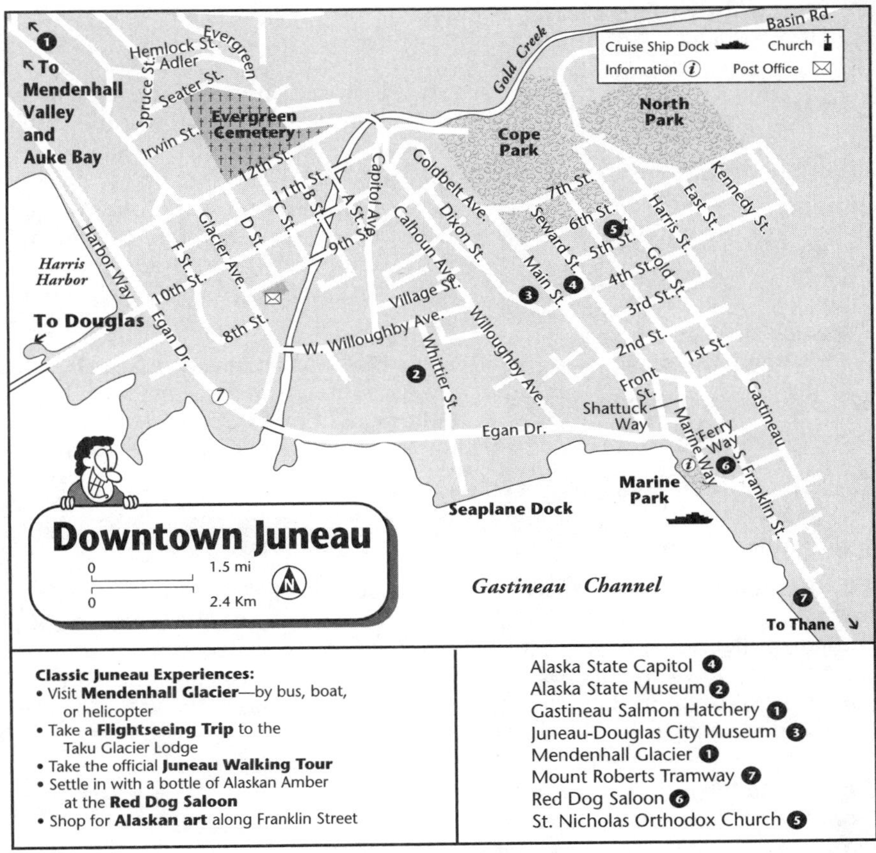

Alaska-Juneau Mill. Gold was found here in 1880 by Joe Juneau and Richard Harris, and the industry continued here into the 1940s.

THE CRUISE LINE SITUATION Alaska Sightseeing, Alaska's Glacier Bay, Carnival, Celebrity, Clipper, Crystal, Holland America, Norwegian, Princess, Royal Caribbean, Special Expeditions, and World Explorer all make port calls here.

Juneau Self-Tour

There's a **visitor information center** located at the cruise ship wharf, where walking maps and visitors' guides are available. Downtown is only a stone's throw up to the left as you stand on the dock, but a shuttle-bus service also is offered.

Within Walking Distance

The **Alaska State Museum,** 395 Whittier St., offers a huge collection of Alaska art and Alaska native and historical artifacts. Admission $3 adults, free for students and children 18 and under.

At the **Alaska State Capitol,** 4th between Main and Seward, photo murals depict the old days, and free tours are offered.

Life Preservers

Alaska is home to no less than 55 kinds of **mosquitoes.** Translation: Bring bug repellent or suffer the consequences.

The **Mount Roberts Tramway,** 490 S. Franklin St., right by the cruise ship docks, offers a 6-minute ride up the tramway (the wait to get on can take much longer), at the top of which is an observation area, restaurant, shops, and a series of nature trails offering great views. Tickets are $16.95 for a daylong pass.

St. Nicholas Orthodox Church, Fifth and Gold streets, is an octagonal chapel built in 1893 by local Tlingits and still run as an active Tlingit parish today.

The little **Juneau-Douglas City Museum,** Fourth and Main streets, has displays of artifacts from the city's history and gold-mining past. Admission is $2 adults, free for students and children 18 and under.

The Red Dog Saloon, 278 S. Franklin St., at the beginning of the downtown area, is a saloon right out of the movies, complete with sawdust floors, stuffed animal heads on the walls, and a devilish history. Okay, it's a bit touristy, but how can you not love a place where years ago one poor guy allegedly fell through the floor and wasn't discovered until the next day (his drinking pals were so drunk that no one noticed his absence).

Beyond Walking Distance

From the well-designed outdoor decks of the **Gastineau Salmon Hatchery,** 2697 Channel Dr. (about 3 miles from downtown), visitors can watch the whole process of harvesting and fertilizing salmon eggs.

Mendenhall Glacier, about 13 miles from downtown, is the easiest glacier to get to in Alaska and the most-visited glacier in the world. The U.S. Forest Service has a visitor center with glacier exhibits, a video, and rangers who can answer questions. There are several trails that bring you close to the glacier, the easiest being a half-mile nature trail.

The Best Shore Excursions

Glacier Helicopter Tour (2 to 3 hours, $160 to $165): You can actually walk on the face of either the Mendenhall or Norris Glacier (ice boots are provided), and you'll get the best views of the jagged peaks.

Gold History Tour (1½ hours, $30 to $35): Pan for gold near the ruins of a real mine while a guide tells you about the gold rush. Great for kids.

Mendenhall Glacier Float Trip (3½ hours, $100): Board 10-person rafts on Mendenhall Lake and pass icebergs as you travel into the Mendenhall River (special clothing is provided). The raft is guided by an experienced oarsman, the rapids are moderate, and the views are spectacular. You'll also be offered a snack of smoked salmon and reindeer sausage.

Wilderness Lodge Flightseeing Adventure (3 hours, $175 to $200): Flightseeing over an ice field and glaciers is combined with a visit to the Taku Glacier Lodge for a salmon bake and optional hiking on nature trails.

Ketchikan

Home of what could very well have been the best little whorehouse in Alaska, this picturesque place acts like a quirky little town but is actually Alaska's fourth-largest city (population 14,000).

The city offers much to cruise passengers. There's colorful Creek Street, the historic street where whorehouses were, in fact, located until they were put out of business by government degree in the 1950s; there's an active harbor, where fishermen set out in the calm waters to fish for salmon (Ketchikan has been deemed the "Salmon Capital of the World"); and there's more shopping than you can shake a stick at.

Ketchikan is also one of the best places to gain an understanding of Native Alaskan culture. The city has the largest concentration of Tlingit, Haida, and Tsimshian people in the state and is home to the world's largest collection of totem poles.

THE CRUISE LINE SITUATION Alaska Sightseeing, Alaska's Glacier Bay, Carnival, Celebrity, Clipper, Crystal, Holland America, Norwegian, Princess, Royal Caribbean, Special Expeditions, and World Explorer all make port calls here.

Ketchikan Self-Tour

Pick up a walking-tour map at the **Ketchikan Visitor Information Center** on the pier.

Within Walking Distance

Located only 1 block from the pier, **The Southeast Alaska Visitors Center,** 50 Main St., is a must-see museum offering a wonderful and informative series of dioramas dealing with local culture, history, flora, fauna, and industry. Admission is $3.

The colorful, boardwalked **Creek Street**—"Where the fish and fishermen go up the creek to spawn"—was once the city's red-light district and might take up a whole roll of your film. One of the homes, that of Big Dolly Arthur, at no. 24, has been turned into a museum called **Dolly's House.** Admission is $3.

Whale Park, at Mission and Bawden streets, is one of several sites in town where visitors can view totem poles. **The Totem Heritage Center,** 601 Deermount St., with its collection of antique Tlingit and Haida totem poles, has been given a National Landmark designation.

Deer Mountain Salmon Hatchery, 1158 Salmon Rd., offers visitors information on the life cycle of the fish. Admission is $3.

Tongass Historical Museum, 629 Dock St., a one-room museum, presents displays on the history and native heritage of the city. Admission is $2.

Mnemonic Salmon

Did you know there are five different kinds of salmon in Alaska? Did you also know you have in your possession, right now, the means of remembering their names? It's true, and here's how it works. Begin by holding up your left hand, palm toward you. Then, finger by finger, it goes like this:

- **Chum** is the first type of salmon; *chum* rhymes with *thumb.*
- **Sockeye** is the second type, and it's your index finger—the one you'd use to poke somebody in the eye.
- **King** is the third type, and your middle finger is the biggest one, the "king" finger.
- **Silver** is the fourth type, and your fourth finger is where you'd wear a silver ring.
- **Pink** is the fifth type, and what is your fifth finger if not your pinkie?

Now you know from salmon.

Beyond Walking Distance

Totem Bight State Historical Park, located about 10 miles outside of town on the North Tongass Highway (a short walk through the woods is involved), began as a New Deal project to save artifacts of the Tlingit culture and is run today by the Alaska Division of Parks. A clan house and outdoor totem poles are featured and can be viewed with the help of interpretive signs and a printed guide.

Saxman Totem Pole Park, located about 2½ miles south of Ketchikan on the South Tongass Highway in the Saxman Native Village, offers visitors a chance to view artifacts as well as accomplished carvers still at work. Two-hour tours are offered that include art demonstrations, a slide show, and dancing (note that there is no interpretive material for those looking to tour on their own). Admission is $30 for adults, $15 for children 12 and under.

The Best Shore Excursions

Misty Fjords Flightseeing (2 hours, $140 to $175): The floatplane is as common as a taxi in Ketchikan. The flightseeing trip offers views of fjords, waterfalls, forests, rugged mountains, and if you're lucky, wildlife.

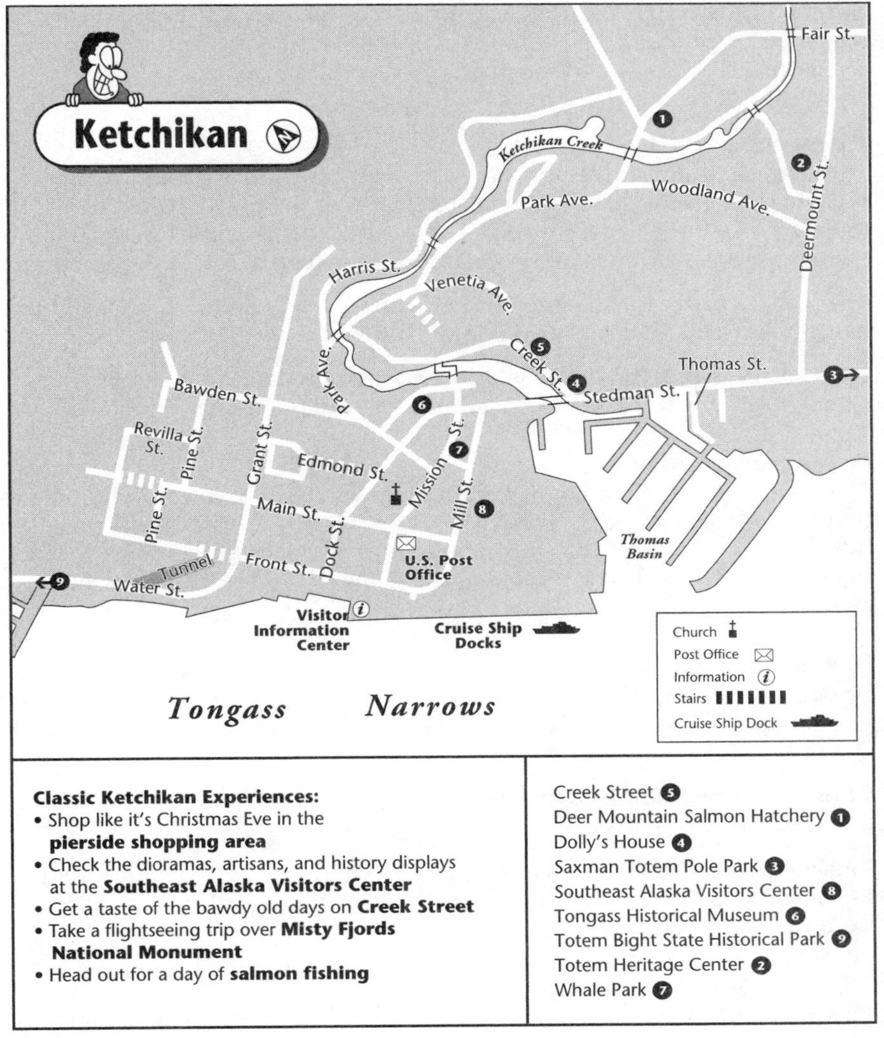

Saxman Native Village Tour (2½ hours, $45): The village is home to hundreds of Tlingit, Tsimshian, and Haida and is an arts and cultural center. The tour includes a native performance and a tour through the grounds to see totem poles and hear native stories. Craftsmen are usually on hand to offer totem-carving demonstrations.

Sportfishing (4 to 6 hours, $140 to $170): Charted fishing boats (complete with tackle, bait, and fishing gear) offer anglers a chance to catch salmon in one of the very best places to do it. They'll even ship it home for you (for a fee, of course). *Note:* $10 fishing license and $10 king-salmon tag are extra.

Totem Bight Historical Park Tour (2 to 2½ hours, $25 to $35): This tour takes passengers by bus through the Tongass National Forest to see a ceremonial clan house and totem poles. Walking is involved.

Petersburg

This town is decisively less touristy than other towns in Southeast Alaska, because its residents, many proud descendants of the town's Norwegian founders, like it that way. Fortunately for them, the harbor is too small for the big ships, and only three small-ship cruise lines make port stops here.

The main industry is fish, and that's evident at nearly every turn. One of the best things to do here is hang out at the harbor.

THE CRUISE LINE SITUATION Alaska Sightseeing, Alaska's Glacier Bay, and Clipper are the only three lines that make port calls here.

Petersburg Self-Tour

There are plenty of photo opportunities in town, but not much in the way of tourist attractions. Renting a bike is a good way to get beyond downtown (where everything is within walking distance), and you can do so for $3 an hour at **Northern Bikes,** located in the lobby of the **Scandia House Hotel,** 110 Nordic Dr.

Within Walking Distance

Hammer Slough, with its wood-frame houses built on stilts, is a good photo opportunity. To get there, turn right at the end of the dock parking lot and walk along the boardwalk streets.

Clausen Memorial Museum focuses on the town's history and fishing traditions, as well as on its Norwegian heritage.

Eagle's Roost Park often has bald eagles perched in the trees and swooping down to grab fish from the Wrangell Narrows. The best spot to watch is from the rocky beach.

The Best Shore Excursions

Commercial Trawling (3 hours, $100): The trip aboard Syd and Vara Wright's gillnetter allows a rare close-up view of commercial fishing. Trawl for shrimp, crab, and sole, which is then cooked up for an onboard feast.

LeConte Glacier Flightseeing (45 minutes, $125): A quick trip by floatplane visits the Stikine Icefield, the Coastal Mountains, and the LeConte Glacier.

Waterfront Walk (1½ hours, $10): Guides take you through Hammer Slough, Singh Lee Alley, the port area (including a stop at a seafood processing plant), and downtown, after which there's a stop at Eagle's Roost Park to watch the eagles feeding.

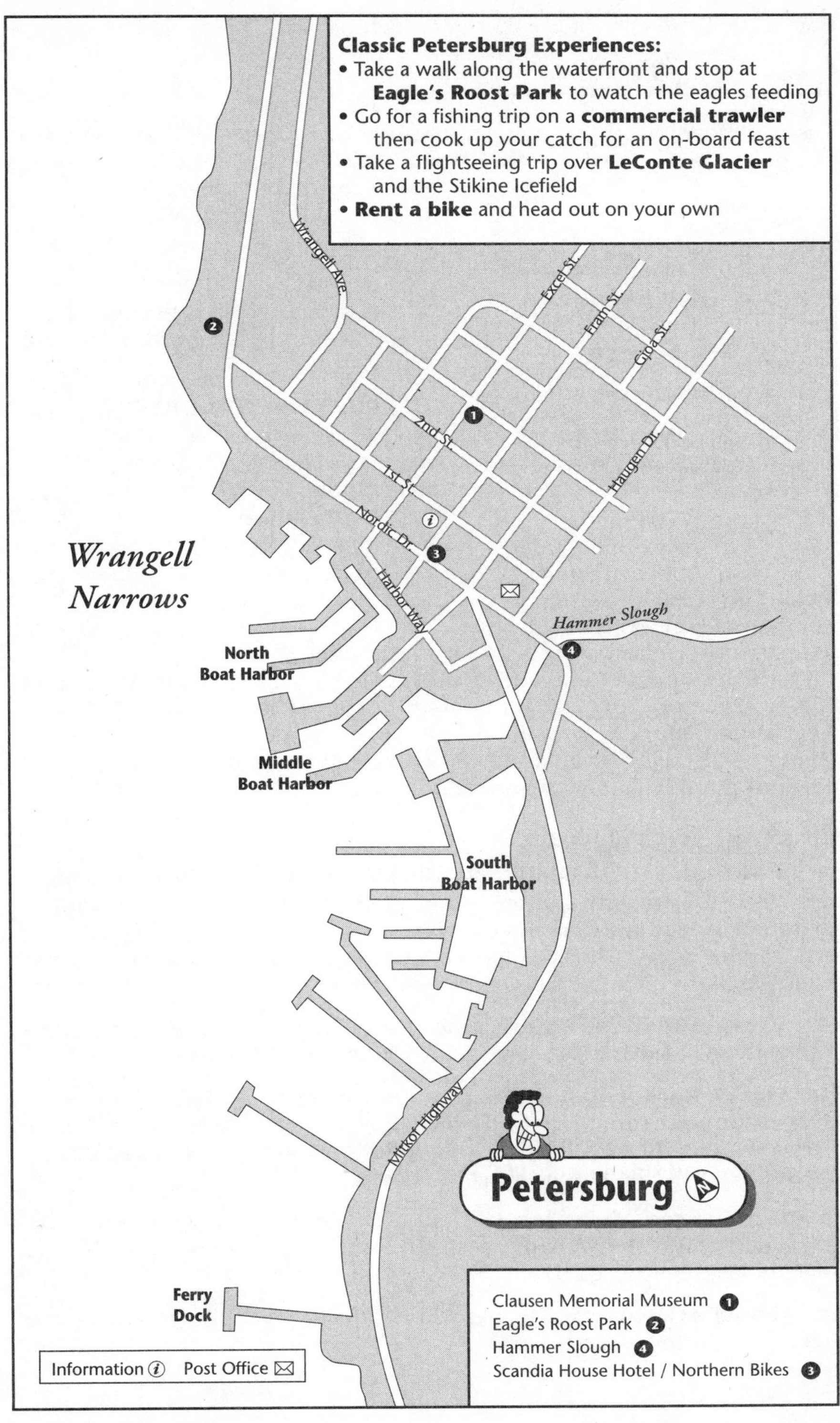
Classic Petersburg Experiences:
• Take a walk along the waterfront and stop at Eagle's Roost Park to watch the eagles feeding
• Go for a fishing trip on a commercial trawler then cook up your catch for an on-board feast
• Take a flightseeing trip over LeConte Glacier and the Stikine Icefield
• Rent a bike and head out on your own
Wrangell Ave.
Excel St.
Fram St.
Gjoa St.
2nd St.
1st St.
Haugen Dr.
Nordic Dr.
Harbor Way
Hammer Slough
Wrangell Narrows
North Boat Harbor
Middle Boat Harbor
South Boat Harbor
Mitkof Highway
Petersburg
Ferry Dock
Information
Post Office
Clausen Memorial Museum 1
Eagle's Roost Park 2
Hammer Slough 4
Scandia House Hotel / Northern Bikes 3

Sitka

Russian, American, and Tlingit culture and history merge in Sitka, a city that was purchased by the U.S. from Russia in 1867 and was earlier the site of a historic battle between the Russian invaders and the proud native Tlingit tribe.

Sitka offers visitors attractions of historical and cultural interest (including a totem park), combined with its natural beauty.

THE CRUISE LINE SITUATION Alaska Sightseeing, Alaska's Glacier Bay, Carnival, Celebrity, Clipper, Crystal, Holland America, Princess, Special Expeditions, and World Explorer all make port calls here.

Sea Stories

Here's a "bet you didn't know" kinda fact: The heart of a humpback whale is about the same size as a Volkswagen Beetle.

Sitka Self-Tour

Most passengers will arrive in Sitka by tender, because the harbor is too small to accommodate large ships. Pick up a map at the Sitka Convention and Visitor Bureau in the **Centennial Building** (which also houses the **Isabel Miller Museum** and an auditorium featuring performances by the **New Archangel Dancers,** a traditional Russian dance troupe), near the dock. Shuttle buses meet arrivals at the docks, but cabs are also available for a ride downtown for $3 (although you can also walk).

Within Walking Distance

Sitka National Historical Park, 106 Metlakatla St., is where the Tlingits and Russians battled for control of the island. Hiking trails are lined with a collection of incredibly tall totem poles, and there's an interpretive center that features native artifacts, films on Sitka history, and workshops offering demonstrations of native weaving, totem carving, and silver etching.

The Russian Bishop's House, Lincoln and Monastery streets, is a historical house operated as a museum by the National Park Service.

The **Alaska Raptor Rehabilitation Center,** 1101 Sawmill Creek Blvd., gives visitors a chance to see birds, including bald eagles and owls, close-up. They are brought here to be treated for injuries. Admission is $10 adults, $5 for children (it's a donation to a good cause).

Shelton Jackson Museum, 104 College Dr., is a state museum that offers a great collection of Alaska native artifacts. It's located on the campus of Sheldon Jackson College.

St. Michaels Cathedral, Lincoln and Cathedral streets, is a town landmark and houses historic icons.

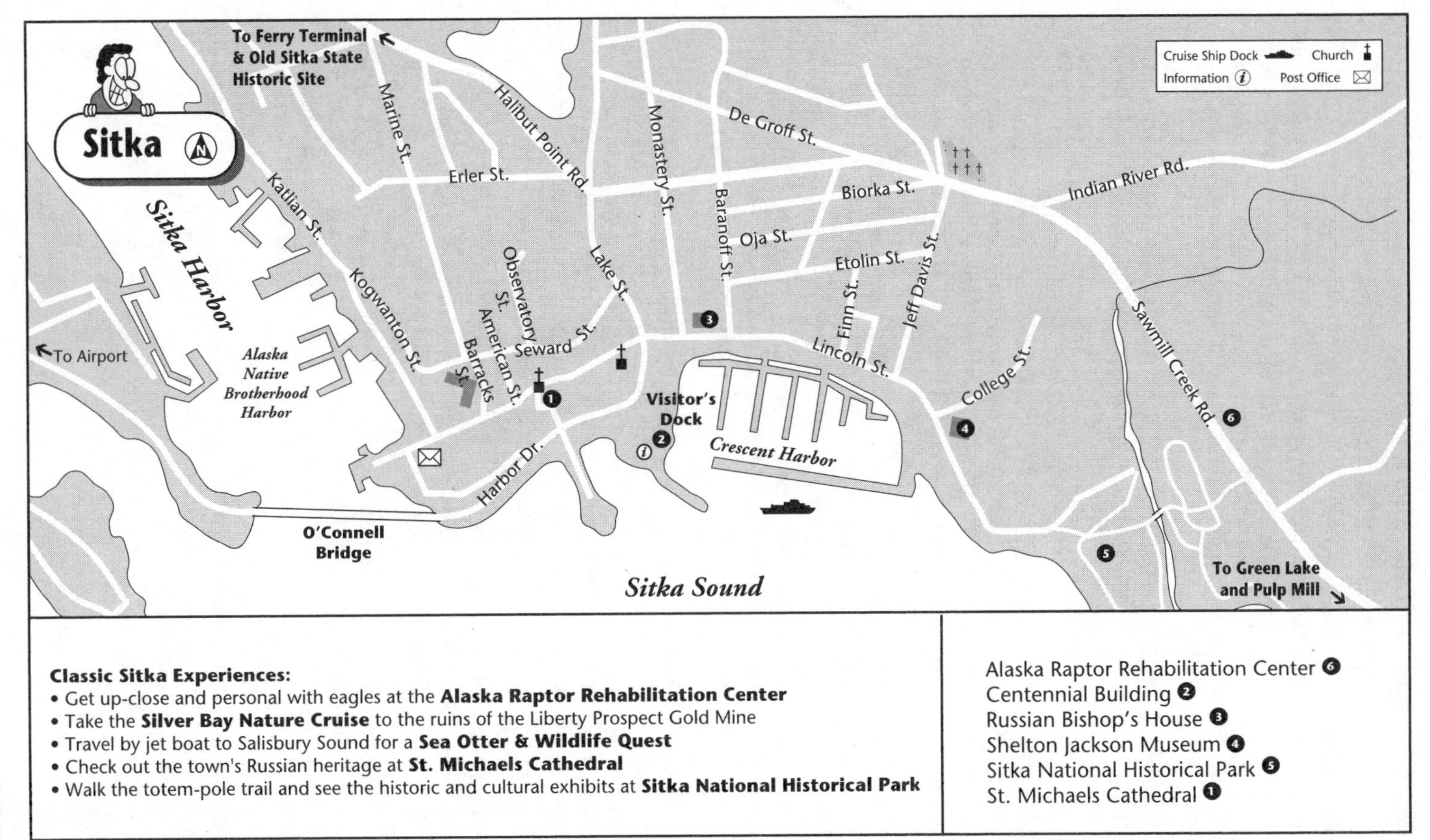

Classic Sitka Experiences:

- Get up-close and personal with eagles at the **Alaska Raptor Rehabilitation Center**
- Take the **Silver Bay Nature Cruise** to the ruins of the Liberty Prospect Gold Mine
- Travel by jet boat to Salisbury Sound for a **Sea Otter & Wildlife Quest**
- Check out the town's Russian heritage at **St. Michaels Cathedral**
- Walk the totem-pole trail and see the historic and cultural exhibits at **Sitka National Historical Park**

Alaska Raptor Rehabilitation Center 6
Centennial Building 2
Russian Bishop's House 3
Shelton Jackson Museum 4
Sitka National Historical Park 5
St. Michaels Cathedral 1

The Best Shore Excursions

Sea Otter & Wildlife Quest (3 hours, $92 to $100): A 50-mile trip by jet boat takes you to Salisbury Sound. The naturalist on board will point out the wildlife (which might include whales, bear, and otters) and explains the region's marine ecosystem. You might be offered a partial refund if no wildlife is spotted.

Silver Bay Nature Cruise (2 hours, $35): An excursion boat takes you through scenic Silver Bay to view wildlife, scenery, the ruins of the Liberty Prospect Gold Mine, and a salmon hatchery.

Skagway

This is definitely an Alaskan town that looks the part, albeit in an almost Disneyesque manner. The gold rush has given way to the tourism rush in Skagway, but a visit here is still fun and educational, in much the way that EPCOT is.

Skagway is probably the best-preserved gold-rush town in the U.S., thanks in good part to the National Park Service, which has restored the best of the older buildings and set them aside as a historic district.

THE CRUISE LINE SITUATION Alaska Sightseeing, Alaska's Glacier Bay, Carnival, Celebrity, Crystal, Holland America, Norwegian, Princess, Royal Caribbean, Special Expeditions, and World Explorer all make port calls here.

Skagway Self-Tour

It's a quick walk from the pier to downtown, but shuttle buses are also offered. The only street you really need to see is Broadway, which runs through the center of town. Stop into the **Skagway Convention and Visitors Bureau,** at Broadway and Fifth Avenue, and pick up one of its walking-tour maps.

Within Walking Distance

The **Klondike Gold Rush National Historic Park Visitor Center,** at the corner of Broadway and Second Avenue, offers free tours that visit the **White Pass & Yukon Railway Depot; Soapy's Parlor,** a preserved saloon once owned by the notorious Soapy Smith; **Moore House,** Skagway's original homestead house; and the **Mascot Saloon,** a tavern museum realistically done up with turn-of-the-century patrons frozen over their drinks. If you don't want to take the tour, you can easily explore these historical sites on your own.

The facade of the **Trail of '98 Historical Museum,** on Broadway between Second and Third streets, is covered with 20,000 pieces of driftwood and is one of the most photographed buildings in Alaska. Now a city-owned museum, it contains an interesting collection of gold-rush artifacts. Admission is $2 for adults, $1 for students and children.

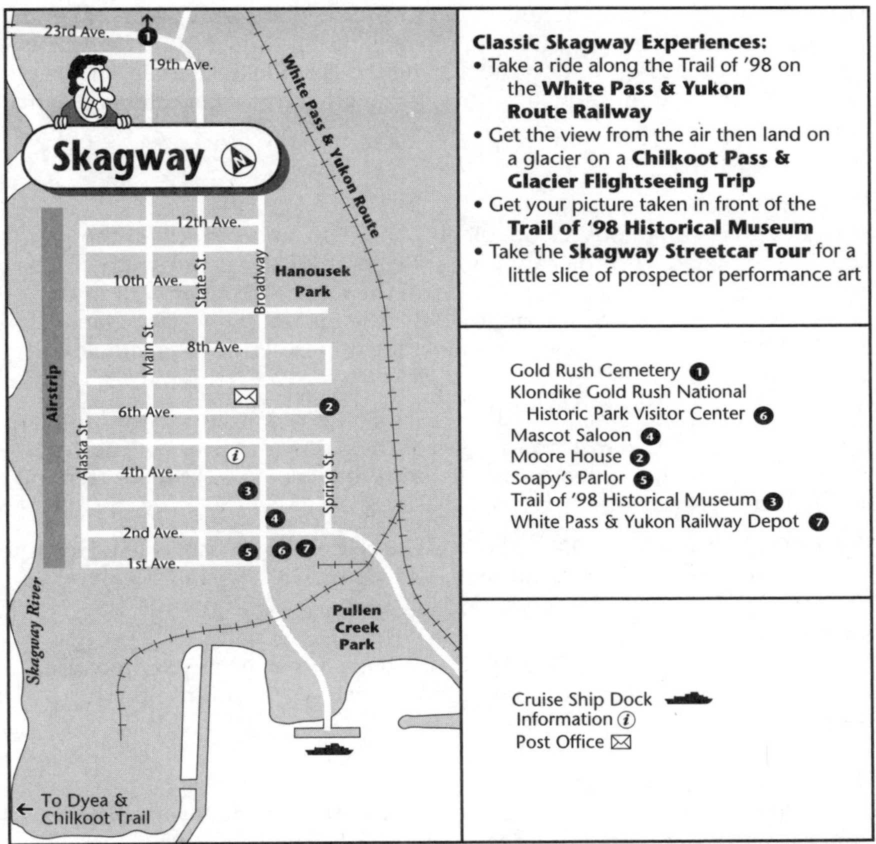

Beyond Walking Distance

The **Gold Rush Cemetery,** about 1½ miles from town up State Street, was used until 1908 and includes the graves of bad man Soapy Smith and the surveyor hero who finally shot him, Frank Reid. A map is available at the visitor center.

The Best Shore Excursions

Chilkoot Pass & Glacier Flightseeing (1½ hours, $150 to $165): You'll fly by helicopter over the prospectors' trail and then view glaciers in their high mountain peaks, and you even get to land on one.

White Pass & Yukon Route Railway (3 hours, $85): The railroad's vintage parlor cars take you up the famous narrow-gauge railway from the dock past waterfalls and parts of the Trail of '98 to White Pass Summit, the boundary between the U.S. and Canada. ***Note:*** *This trip is only worth the money if the weather is clear.*

Skagway by Streetcar (2 hours, $35 to $40): If you just want an entertaining take on the town, take this tour, offered aboard vintage 1937 Kenworth sightseeing limousines, where guides in period costume relate tales of the old days. It's pure theater—more like riding through a theme park than an actual town—but it's lots of fun.

Valdez

This little town is famous for oil, oil, and more oil, and as with all things, you take the good with the bad. Here's the good: Valdez is the southern terminus of the Alaska Pipeline and is where the tankers that carry oil to the Lower 48 tank up. Here's the bad: In 1989, the tanker *Exxon Valdez* ran ashore 23 miles from the port, spilling crude oil into Prince William Sound and poisoning the land.

Unless you're a real oil fan, you'd do much better to look away from the oil storage tanks and turn instead to views of the 5,000-foot peaks of the Chugach Mountains, which cause this town to be known as the Switzerland of the Alaska coast.

THE CRUISE LINE SITUATION Alaska Sightseeing, Celebrity, Crystal, Holland America, and World Explorer make port calls here.

Valdez Self-Tour

There's not that much to see here. Shuttle buses from the pier drop cruise passengers off at the Tourist Information Center, where you can pick up a map.

Within Walking Distance

The **Valdez Museum,** 217 Egan Ave., has exhibits on the town's history, from early white exploration up to the oil spill. Admission is $3.

The Best Shore Excursions

Canyon Rafting in Keystone Canyon (2¼ hours, $65 to $70): This mostly mild run offers stunning views of the sheer canyon walls and waterfalls pounding into the Lowe River. The trips are guided, and all the equipment you'll need is provided.

Helicopter Flightseeing Trip (1½ hours, $130 to $200): You'll zip over the Trans-Alaska Pipeline, the Columbia Glacier, Prince William Sound, Anderson Pass, and the old Valdez, which was destroyed by an earthquake in 1964 (it's about 4 miles from new Valdez). You'll also land on a beach at the face of Shoup Glacier.

Thompson Pass & Worthington Glacier Bus Tour (2½ to 3 hours, $35): This trip takes you past old Valdez (destroyed by an earthquake in 1964), through the narrow Keystone Canyon, and up to Thompson Pass for a look at where the Trans-Alaska Pipeline is located, as well as to the Worthington Glacier Recreation Site, a scenic viewing spot.

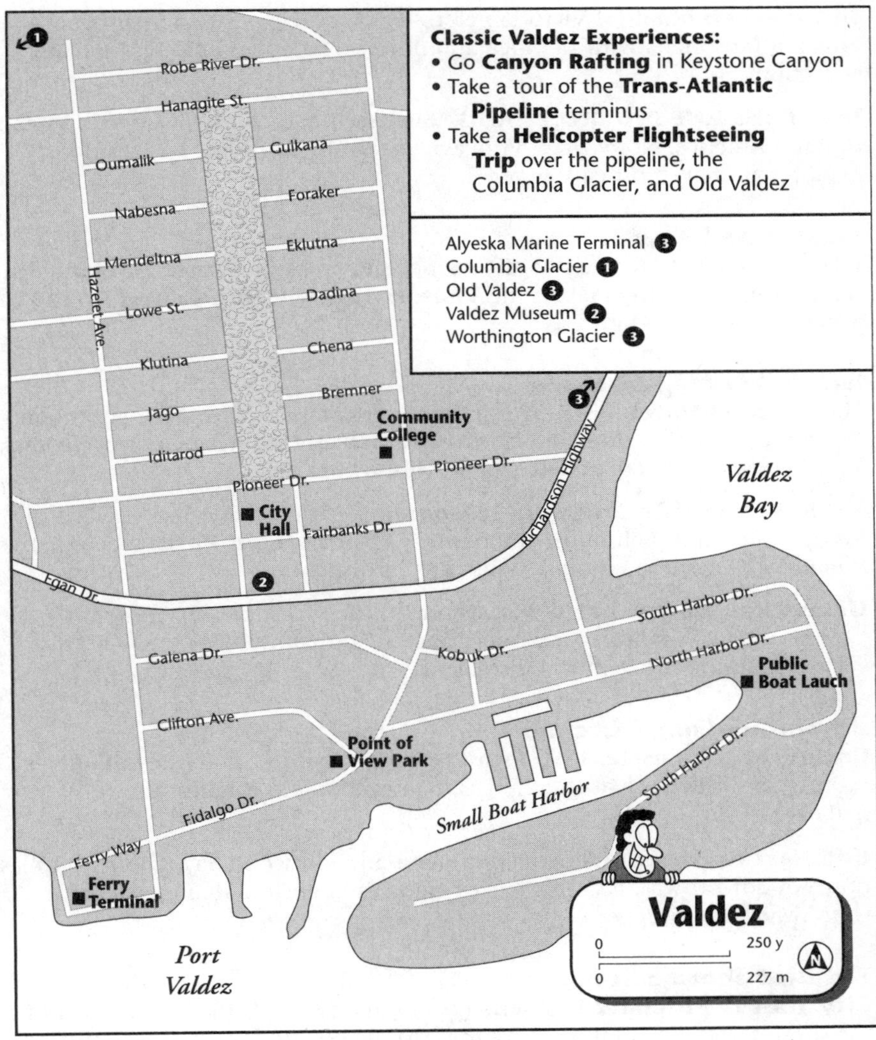

Trans-Atlantic Pipeline Tour (2 to 2½ hours, $25): For those interested in the pipeline project, this trip takes you to the storage tanks and tanker berths of the Alyeska Marine Terminal.

Victoria, British Columbia

Okay, I know it's in Canada, not Alaska, but cruises that start in Los Angeles or Seattle typically include Victoria on Vancouver Island as a port of call on the way up to Alaska.

The city offers beautiful Victorian architecture and an extremely proper British atmosphere, with high tea and flowering gardens among the main attractions.

THE CRUISE LINE SITUATION Alaska Sightseeing, Celebrity, Clipper, Crystal, Holland America, Norwegian, Princess, Special Expeditions, and World Explorer all make port calls here.

Victoria Self-Tour

Take the shuttle to the center of Victoria, known as the **Inner Harbor.** You can pick up a walking map at the **Visitors Information Center** on the waterfront at 812 Wharf St.

Within Walking Distance

The **Empress Hotel,** 721 Government St., is a famed setting for afternoon tea, complete with scones and clotted cream. (Reservations are recommended, and there is a dress code. Call ☎ **250/384-8111.**

The **Royal British Columbia Museum,** 675 Belleville, offers exhibits of historical interest. Behind the museum is **Thunderbird Park,** where native totem poles and a ceremonial house are on display.

Helmecken House, 10 Elliot St., is one of the oldest houses in British Columbia. It was home to a pioneer doctor, and painful-looking medical tools are among the items on display.

Beyond Walking Distance

Craigdarroch Castle, 1050 Joan Crescent, requires a cab ride but allows visitors an inside look at the lifestyle of a millionaire coal-mining magnate.

Butchart Gardens, 800 Benvenuto Ave., in Brentwood Bay (about 13 miles north of downtown), is a 130-acre estate with English, Italian, Japanese, water, and rose gardens.

The Best Shore Excursions

City Tour & Butchart Gardens (3½ hours, $30 to $40): A quick tour of the sites of Victoria is followed by the 13-mile bus trip out the Saanich Peninsula to the world-renowned gardens, where you'll have 2 hours to explore the 130-acre grounds.

City Tour with High Tea or Castle Visit (2½ to 3 hours, $20 to $30): This excursion on a double-decker bus includes the major sites of the Inner Harbor, downtown, and residential areas, with either a stop for high tea or a visit to Craigdarroch Castle.

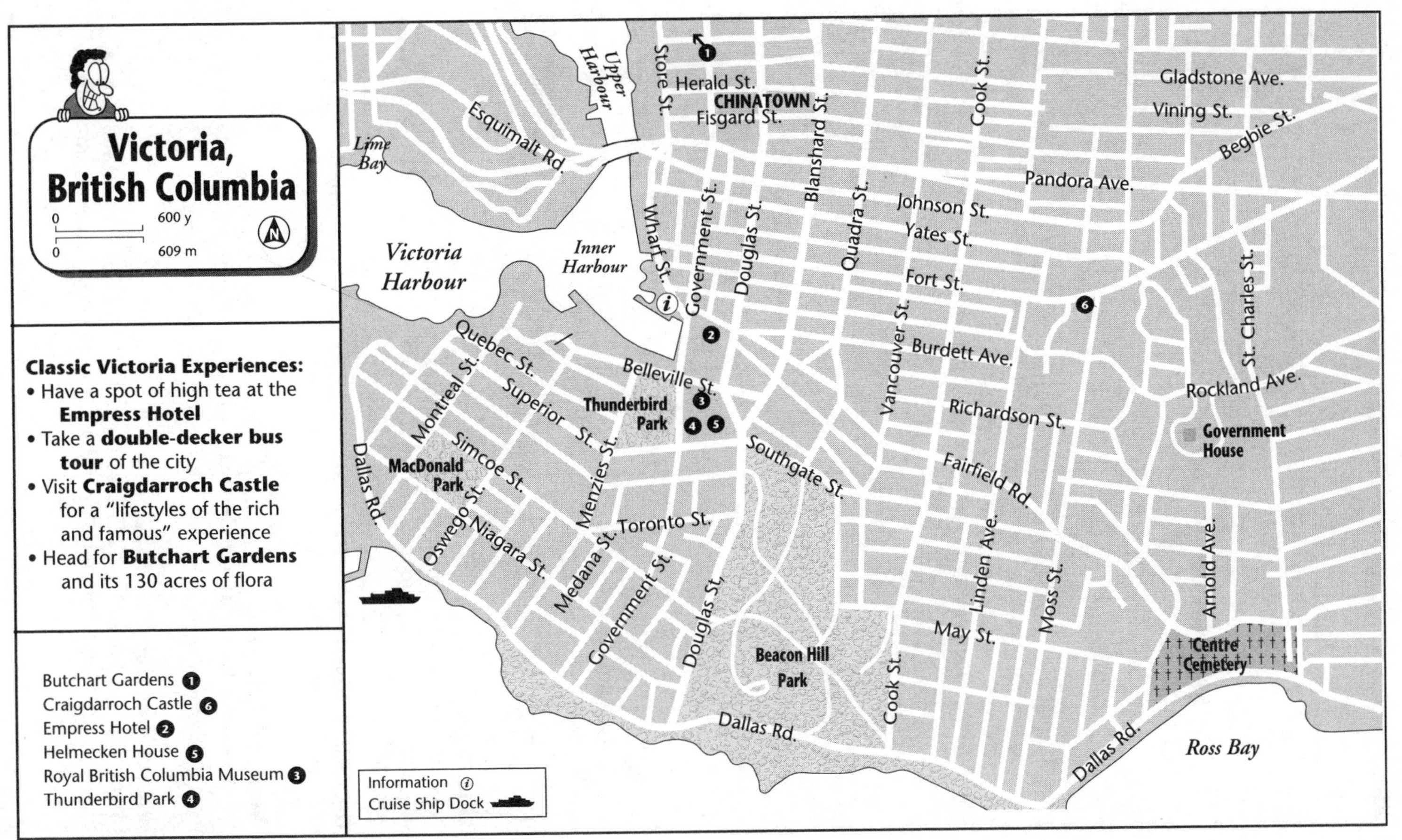

Victoria, British Columbia
0 600 y
0 609 m
N
Classic Victoria Experiences:
• Have a spot of high tea at the Empress Hotel
• Take a double-decker bus tour of the city
• Visit Craigdarroch Castle for a "lifestyles of the rich and famous" experience
• Head for Butchart Gardens and its 130 acres of flora
Butchart Gardens 1
Craigdarroch Castle 6
Empress Hotel 2
Helmecken House 5
Royal British Columbia Museum 3
Thunderbird Park 4
Information
Cruise Ship Dock
Lime Bay
Esquimalt Rd.
Upper Harbour
Victoria Harbour
Inner Harbour
Store St.
Herald St.
CHINATOWN
Fisgard St.
Blanshard St.
Cook St.
Gladstone Ave.
Vining St.
Begbie St.
Pandora Ave.
Johnson St.
Yates St.
Fort St.
Wharf St.
Government St.
Douglas St.
Quadra St.
Vancouver St.
Burdett Ave.
St. Charles St.
Rockland Ave.
Government House
Richardson St.
Fairfield Rd.
Quebec St.
Belleville St.
Thunderbird Park
Montreal St.
Superior St.
Menzies St.
Southgate St.
MacDonald Park
Simcoe St.
Oswego St.
Niagara St.
Toronto St.
Medana St.
Dallas Rd.
Beacon Hill Park
Linden Ave.
Moss St.
May St.
Arnold Ave.
Centre Cemetery
Ross Bay

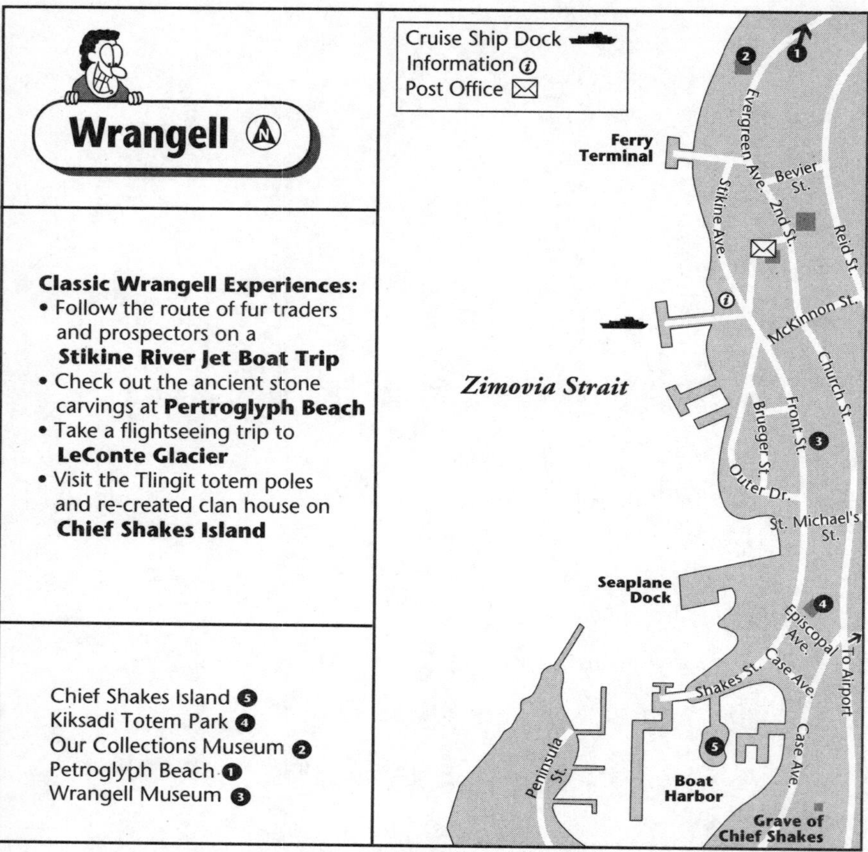

Wrangell

This one-time lumber-mill town has not been overtouched by tourists yet (it's mostly visited by smaller, adventure-type ships). In fact, it's still kind of blue-collar and homey.

THE CRUISE LINE SITUATION Alaska Sightseeing, Alaska's Glacier Bay, Clipper, Norwegian, and World Explorer make port calls here.

Wrangell Self-Tour

The **Visitor Information Center** is located at the Stikine Inn near the city dock. You can pick up a map there.

Within Walking Distance

Chief Shakes Island, off Shakes Street, is a tiny island that is home to a collection of Tlingit totem poles and a re-created clan house. Admission is

$1.50. You also can view totem poles a few blocks away at **Kiksadi Totem Park.**

The **Wrangell Museum,** 318 Church St., offers hodgepodge displays on the town's history and industry. Admission is $2.

Our Collections Museum, Evergreen Avenue, is a private and unusual museum showcasing 60 years of family and town memorabilia. Donations are accepted.

Petroglyph Beach, located about 1 mile north of town, has ancient geometric and animal designs chipped into the rocks on the beach (don't go within an hour of high tide).

The Best Shore Excursions

City Tour (1½ hours, $20 to $30): This bus trip stops at Petroglyph Beach to see the ancient rock carvings and at Chief Shakes Island to view the tribal house and totem poles. The bus also stops at the Wrangell Museum before returning to the ship.

LeConte Glacier Flightseeing (1½ hours, $130): This trip takes passengers by plane over the Coastal Mountains, the Stikine Icefield, and the LeConte Glacier. If weather permits, you'll descend toward the glacier face for a closer view of the blue crevasses.

Stikine River Jet Boat Trip (3 to 3½ hours, $135 to $145): Follow the route of fur traders and prospectors as you traverse open water, back sloughs, and clear tributaries to reach Shakes Lake, where the boat will navigate amid icebergs. Incredible views will thrill you and offer plenty of photo opportunities, too.

Chapter 25

Cruising Around: Other Ports of Call

In This Chapter

- Cruises to Bermuda
- Cruises to Central America and Mexico
- Cruises to Hawaii, Canada, and New England
- River and lake cruises, and cruises through the Panama Canal

While the Caribbean and Alaska are by far the most popular cruising regions in this part of the world, they are hardly the only ones. The overview of cruise options in this chapter includes offerings for people who prefer to cruise off the beaten path and offerings for people looking for a hassle-free way to visit several locations in a specific area, such as New England/Canada or the west coast of Mexico. There are even cruises for people with no interest in going to sea, with ships that instead cruise America's inland waterways.

I've included charts to help you easily determine who offers cruises in the region(s) you find most interesting. You can cross-reference these charts with the ship-review chapters to learn more about the cruise lines mentioned. For instances in which the lines are too small to have made the cruise-reviews chapter, I've included a phone number you can call for more information.

The Mighty Mississippi & Other Inland Waterways of the South and Midwest

Mark Twain discovered America's heartland while traveling down the Mississippi River, which he described as "the great Mississippi, the majestic, the magnificent Mississippi, rolling its mile-wide tide along, shining in the sun."

Cruise passengers can explore the Americana that so enticed the writer by traveling down the same water, and on the same mode of transportation as Twain: a paddlewheel steamboat.

The Delta Queen Steamboat Company operates three paddlewheelers year-round on the Mississippi and on other major rivers as well, including the Ohio, Tennessee, Cumberland, and Illinois.

Cruising the Great Lakes

Want to feel like you're on the ocean without being on the ocean? Take a cruise on the Great Lakes. Both **American Canadian Caribbean** and **Clipper Cruises** offer Great Lakes cruises, and the Traverse City, Michigan–based **Traverse Tall Ship Company** (☎ **800/678-0383**) also offers Windjammer sailings on Lake Michigan and Lake Huron.

The cruises take passengers to Civil War sites and other places of historic interest, past quaint towns and stately mansions, with departures from major cities including New Orleans, Memphis, St. Louis, Cincinnati, Louisville, and Pittsburgh.

A new company, **RiverBarge Excursion Lines** (☎ **888/650-5041**), is also starting year-round river cruises on waterways including the Mississippi, Cumberland, Ohio, and Missouri rivers in August 1998. The 4- to 10-day cruises are offered on 2 connected 295-foot hotel barges.

American Canadian Caribbean Line offers fall cruises on the Mississippi, Ohio, and Cumberland rivers; and also, farther east, on the Erie Canal. **Clipper Cruises,** also to the east, offers cruises on the Hudson River and Chesapeake Bay.

Bermuda

Cruises to Bermuda, an Atlantic-ocean island known for its pink sand and British ambiance, usually combine several relaxing and fun-filled days at sea with several relaxing and fun-filled days on the island.

Cruise passengers can spend their island time exploring by the preferred and fabulously fun means of transport—mopeds or scooters (rental cars are banned here)—and enjoy activities such as golf, tennis, horseback riding, beach-sitting, snorkeling, scuba diving, glass-bottom boat tours, and visits to museums and historic homes. There's also plenty of opportunity to shop, especially for British goods like wool sweaters and Wedgwood china, and to enjoy the lively pub scene.

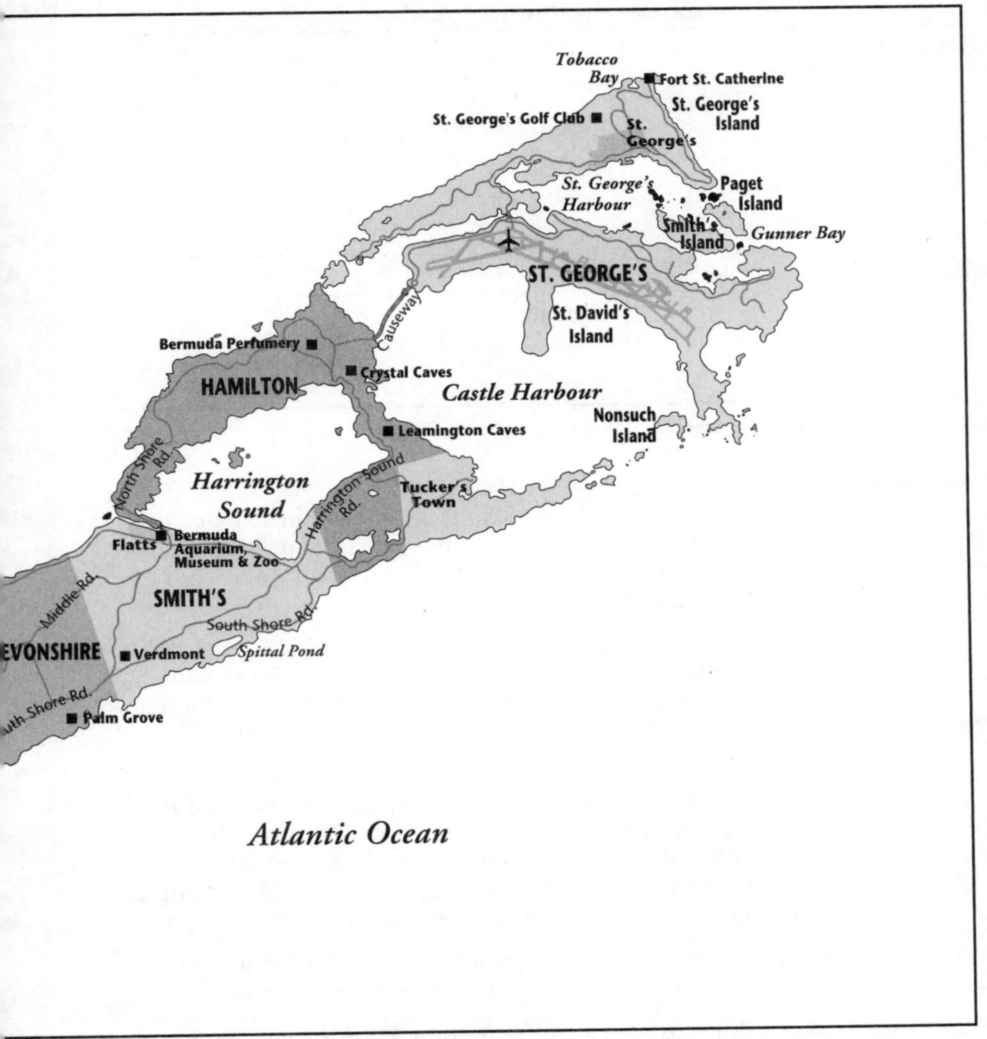

Cruises to Bermuda are offered weekly from late April to October, with most of the cruises departing from New York or Boston. Some ships also visit Bermuda as part of transatlantic crossings or in combination with coastal Atlantic itineraries.

Bermuda Ports of Call

Hamilton	Celebrity Cunard Holland America Norwegian Royal Caribbean Seabourn
King's Wharf	Celebrity
St. George's	Celebrity Norwegian Royal Caribbean

Information courtesy of Travel Weekly's Official Cruise Guide.

Costa Rica

The name means "Rich Coast" in Spanish, and this Central American country is, in fact, rich in lush rain forests, beaches, mountains, and wildlife, including hundreds of species of birds, mammals, and fish and thousands of varieties of insects, including butterflies.

Cruises here usually include exploration of wildlife areas, including the country's numerous national parks, with the aid of naturalists. Some ruins and other historical attractions of interest are available to visitors, and unlike some of its neighbors, Costa Rica has the advantage of being a politically stable environment.

Temptress Adventure Cruises (☎ **800/336-8423**) offers cruises of 3 to 7 days, year-round, on the country's Pacific coast, using its 99-passenger *Temptress Explorer.* The itineraries include visits to Corcovado and other national parks and remote wildlife habitats, with opportunities for passengers to hike in rain forests and enjoy remote beaches and a variety of watersports.

Windstar introduced a winter Costa Rica itinerary in 1998 using its *Wind Song,* which explores the country's Pacific coast, visiting several islands.

Other cruise lines offering Costa Rica cruises (but on a less-frequent basis) include **Clipper Cruise Line** and **Special Expeditions,** both of which combine a visit of several days to Costa Rica with a Panama Canal transit.

Many lines call on Costa Rica as part of Caribbean, Panama Canal, or Central America itineraries, stopping usually at Puerto Caldera on the Pacific coast or Puerto Límon on the Caribbean coast.

Costa Rica Ports of Call

Port	Cruise Line
Caño Island, Drake Bay	Temptress
	Windstar
Corcovado, Puntarenas	Temptress
Curu	Clipper
	Special Expeditions
	Temptress
Golfito	Norwegian
	Temptress
Golfo Dulce	Holland America
	Seabourn
Play Flamingo	Windstar
Puerto Caldera	Carnival
	Celebrity
	Clipper
	Crystal
	Holland America
	Norwegian
	Princess
	Radisson
	Royal Caribbean
	Seabourn
	Silversea
	Special Expeditions
	Windstar
Puerto Límon	Cunard
	Holland America
	Norwegian
	Premier
	Princess
	Regal
	Royal Olympic
	World Explorer
Puerto Quepos	Windstar
Tortuga	Temptress
	Windstar

Information courtesy of Travel Weekly's Official Cruise Guide.

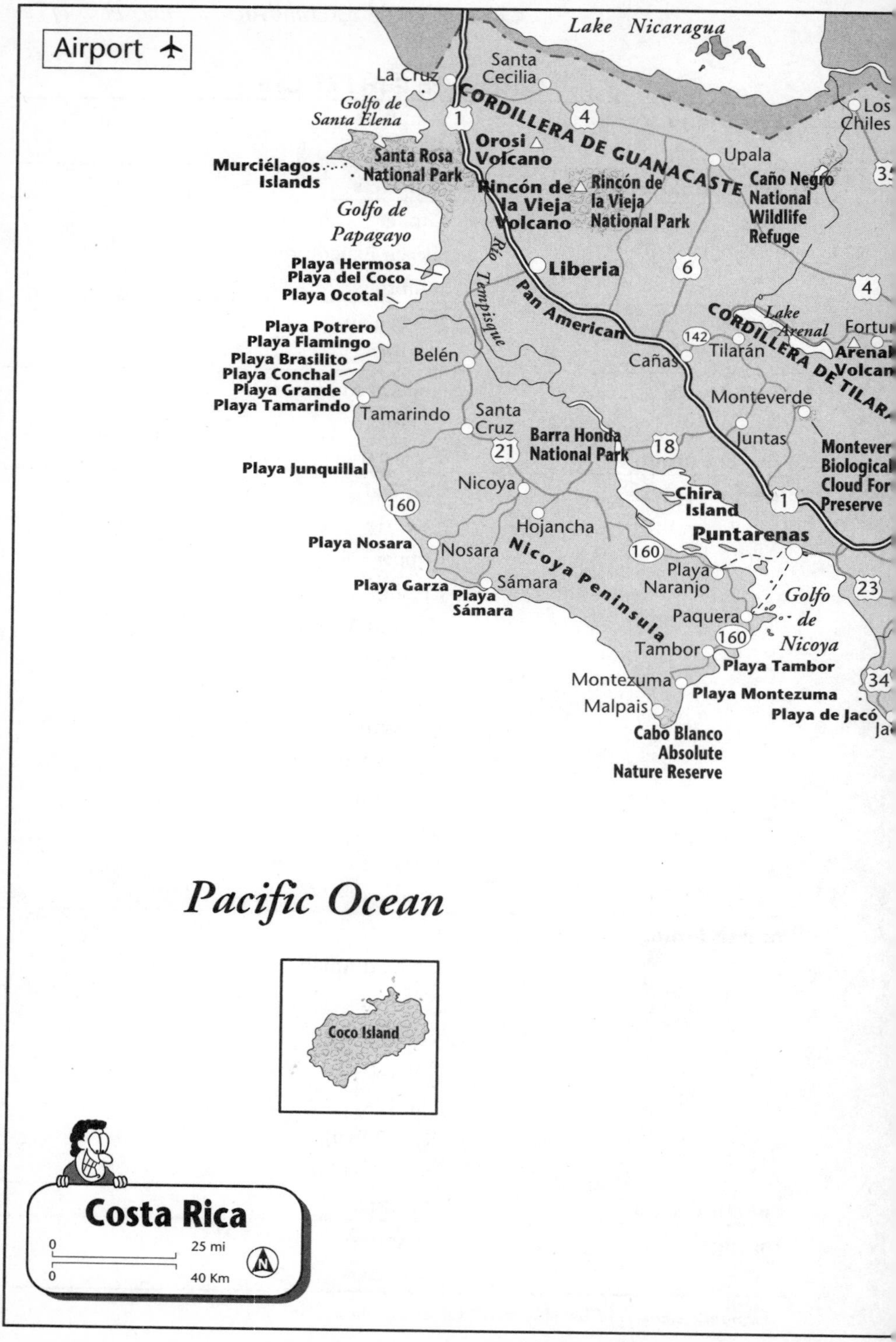

Airport
Lake Nicaragua
La Cruz
Santa Cecilia
Golfo de Santa Elena
CORDILLERA DE GUANACASTE
Los Chiles
Orosi Volcano
Murciélagos Islands
Santa Rosa National Park
Upala
Rincón de la Vieja Volcano
Rincón de la Vieja National Park
Caño Negro National Wildlife Refuge
Golfo de Papagayo
Liberia
Playa Hermosa
Playa del Coco
Playa Ocotal
Río Tempisque
Pan American
Lake Arenal
CORDILLERA DE TILARÁN
Playa Potrero
Playa Flamingo
Playa Brasilito
Playa Conchal
Playa Grande
Playa Tamarindo
Belén
Cañas
Tilarán
Arenal Volcano
Monteverde
Tamarindo
Santa Cruz
Barra Honda National Park
Juntas
Playa Junquillal
Nicoya
Chira Island
Montever Biological Cloud For Preserve
Hojancha
Puntarenas
Playa Nosara
Nosara
Nicoya Peninsula
Playa Naranjo
Playa Garza
Sámara
Playa Sámara
Golfo de Nicoya
Paquera
Tambor
Playa Tambor
Montezuma
Playa Montezuma
Malpais
Playa de Jacó
Cabo Blanco Absolute Nature Reserve
Pacific Ocean
Coco Island
Costa Rica
0 25 mi
0 40 Km

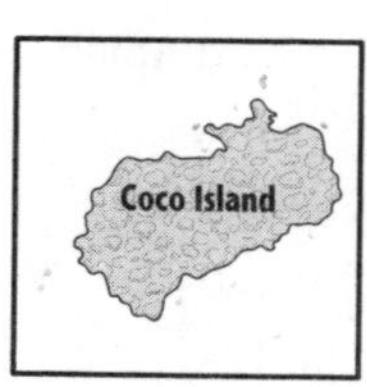

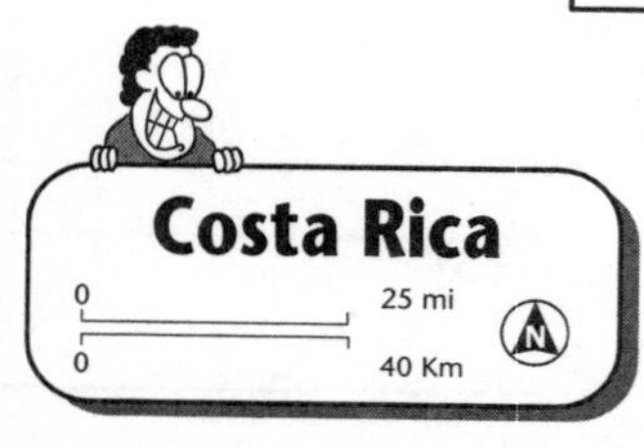

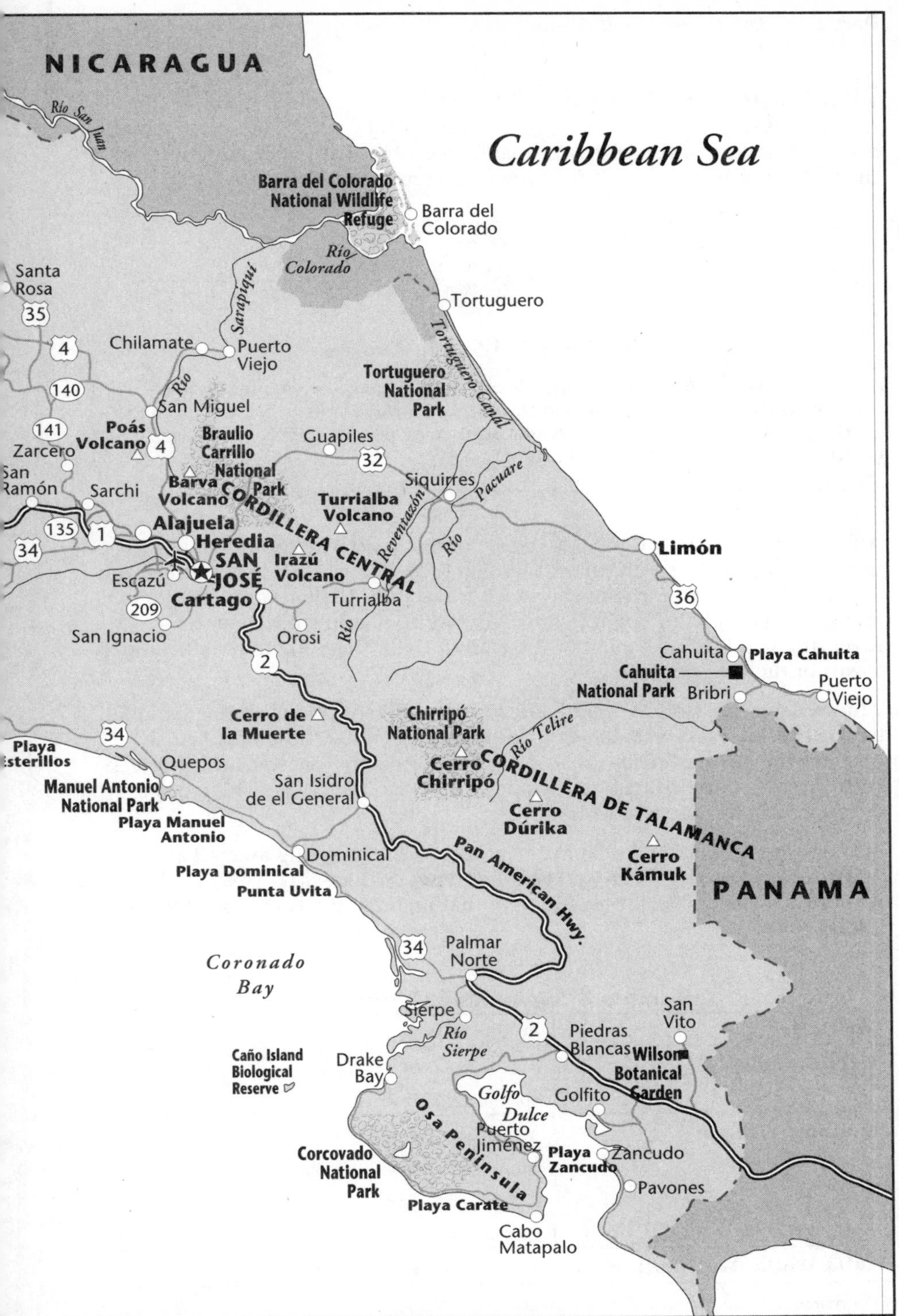

NICARAGUA
Caribbean Sea
Río San Juan
Barra del Colorado National Wildlife Refuge
Barra del Colorado
Río Colorado
Sarapiquí
Santa Rosa
35
Tortuguero
4
Chilamate
Puerto Viejo
Río
140
Tortuguero National Park
Tortuguero Canal
San Miguel
141
Poás Volcano
4
Braulio Carrillo National Park
Guapiles
Zarcero
32
San Ramón
Sarchi
Barva Volcano
Siquirres
Pacuare
Turrialba Volcano
Reventazón
CORDILLERA CENTRAL
135
1
Alajuela
Heredia
Río
34
Limón
Irazú Volcano
SAN JOSÉ
Escazú
Cartago
Turrialba
36
209
San Ignacio
Orosi
Río
2
Cahuita
Playa Cahuita
Cahuita National Park
Bribri
Puerto Viejo
Cerro de la Muerte
Chirripó National Park
Río Telire
34
Playa Esterillos
Cerro Chirripó
Quepos
CORDILLERA DE TALAMANCA
Manuel Antonio National Park
San Isidro de el General
Cerro Dúrika
Playa Manuel Antonio
Dominical
Cerro Kámuk
Pan American Hwy.
Playa Dominical
PANAMA
Punta Uvita
34
Palmar Norte
Coronado Bay
San Vito
Sierpe
Río Sierpe
2
Piedras Blancas
Wilson Botanical Garden
Caño Island Biological Reserve
Drake Bay
Golfo Dulce
Golfito
Osa Peninsula
Puerto Jiménez
Corcovado National Park
Playa Zancudo
Zancudo
Pavones
Playa Carate
Cabo Matapalo

The Columbia & Snake Rivers

If you've ever dreamed of exploring like Lewis and Clark, you can have your chance, thanks to a few cruise companies that have introduced offerings on the Columbia and Snake rivers in the U.S. northwest.

Northern California Cruises

Both **Alaska Sightseeing/Cruise West** and **Clipper** (see chapter 6) offer nice northern California cruises in the fall that include visits to Sacramento and the Napa Valley wine country. Alaska Sightseeing departs from San Francisco; Clipper departs from Redwood City

Attractions in the region include the Columbia itself (the second-largest river in the U.S.) and the spectacular Columbia River Gorge, with its waterfalls and forest trails. Cruises on the rivers, which travel from Oregon into Washington and sometimes Idaho, might include visits to the Bonneville Dam, Hood River (the windsurfing capital of the world), Hell's Canyon, and the historic towns of the Oregon Trail.

Cruises departing from Portland, Oregon, are offered spring, summer, and fall by **American West Steamboat Company** (☎ **800/720-0012**), which operates the 163-passenger *Queen of the West,* an authentic sternwheel-driven ship. The weeklong cruise also includes the Willamette River, with stops in Oregon, Washington, and Idaho.

Also offering Columbia and Snake river cruises in the spring and fall are **Alaska Sightseeing / Cruise West** and **Special Expeditions. Clipper** also offers a Pacific Northwest itinerary that includes the Columbia River in the fall.

Columbia & Snake River Ports of Call

Port	Cruise Line
The Dalles	American West
Hell's Canyon	Alaska Sightseeing Special Expeditions
Portland, Oregon	Alaska Sightseeing American West Clipper Special Expeditions
Walla Walla, Washington	Alaska Sightseeing

Information courtesy of Travel Weekly's Official Cruise Guide.

The Hawaiian Islands

Hawaii is becoming an increasingly popular place for cruise ships to visit, even though U.S. law does not allow ships not built in the U.S. (which means *most* ships) to sail directly here from the mainland. Instead, they must include in their itineraries Mexico, Canada, or another country. Some lines stop in Hawaii on their way across the Pacific to countries such as New Zealand and Tahiti.

Most of the itineraries are for more than a week (1-week, 1-way itineraries are offered by Holland America from Ensenada, Mexico) and include visits to several Hawaiian islands.

American Hawaii, a company with an American-built ship, sails here year-round, offering cruises that include Hawaii (The Big Island), Oahu, Maui, and Kauai.

The islands offer cruise passengers pristine beaches and incomparable natural beauty, including volcanic peaks, rugged coastlines, waterfalls, and lush forests. There also are opportunities to taste island culture at a traditional lu'au (Hawaiian feast), explore ancient places of worship and underwater reefs, go hiking and/or bird watching, enjoy a variety of watersports (including surfing!), and buy a colorful Hawaiian shirt.

Hawaii Ports of Call

Hawaii	American Hawaii
	Carnival
	Crystal
	Cunard
	Holland America
	Norwegian
	Princess
	Royal Caribbean
	Silversea
Kauai	American Hawaii
	Carnival
	Crystal
	Holland America
	Norwegian
	Princess
	Royal Caribbean
	Silversea

continues

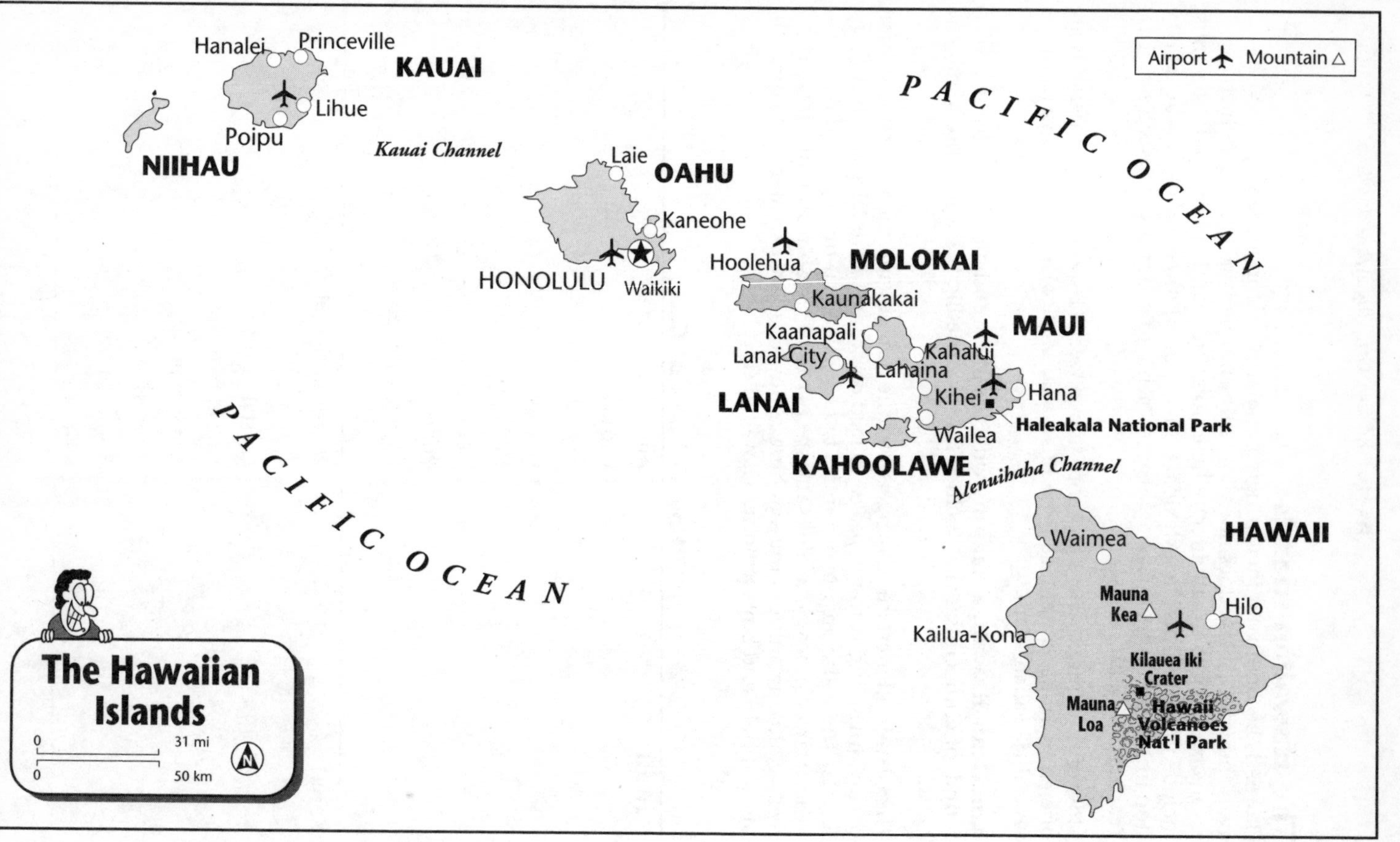

Airport
Mountain
PACIFIC OCEAN
NIIHAU
KAUAI
Hanalei
Princeville
Lihue
Poipu
Kauai Channel
OAHU
Laie
Kaneohe
HONOLULU
Waikiki
MOLOKAI
Hoolehua
Kaunakakai
MAUI
Kaanapali
Lahaina
Kahului
Kihei
Wailea
Hana
Haleakala National Park
LANAI
Lanai City
KAHOOLAWE
Alenuihaha Channel
PACIFIC OCEAN
HAWAII
Waimea
Kailua-Kona
Hilo
Mauna Kea
Mauna Loa
Kilauea Iki Crater
Hawaii Volcanoes Nat'l Park
The Hawaiian Islands
0 31 mi
0 50 km

Hawaii Ports of Call *(continued)*

Maui	American Hawaii Crystal Cunard Holland America Norwegian Princess Royal Caribbean
Oahu	American Hawaii Carnival Crystal Cunard Holland America Norwegian Princess Royal Caribbean Silversea

Information courtesy of Travel Weekly's Official Cruise Guide.

The Mexican Riviera

The west coast of Mexico is the western equivalent of the Caribbean, an area of scenic beauty and fun in the sun, with stops designed to appeal to tourists—*lots* of tourists—along the way.

Many of the historical features of this part of Mexico are hidden behind souvenir stands and fast food restaurants. But history is not why people take these cruises; the attraction here is more to the tune of miles of glorious white-sand beaches, golf and tennis, and watersports offerings that include parasailing, windsurfing, water-skiing, snorkeling, scuba diving, windsurfing, and deep-sea fishing, as well as glass-bottom boat tours to see marine life.

Cruises to the Mexican Riviera leave from Los Angeles, travel the Pacific Ocean, and last from 3 to 10 days, with the longer cruises usually including a stop in **Acapulco.** They are offered year-round, with winter being the top season.

On 1-week sailings, ships typically call at **Cabo San Lucas** at the southern tip of Baja, California, an area rich in marine life, including sea lions and gray whales. Further stops include the active seaport of **Mazatlán** and the ever-popular **Puerto Vallarta,** where visitors can travel 7 miles south to Mismaloya, where *Night of the Iguana* was filmed.

Shorter cruises might call at **Catalina Island** and **Ensenada.** Special Expeditions, Alaska Sightseeing, and Alaska's Glacier Bay Tours and Cruises

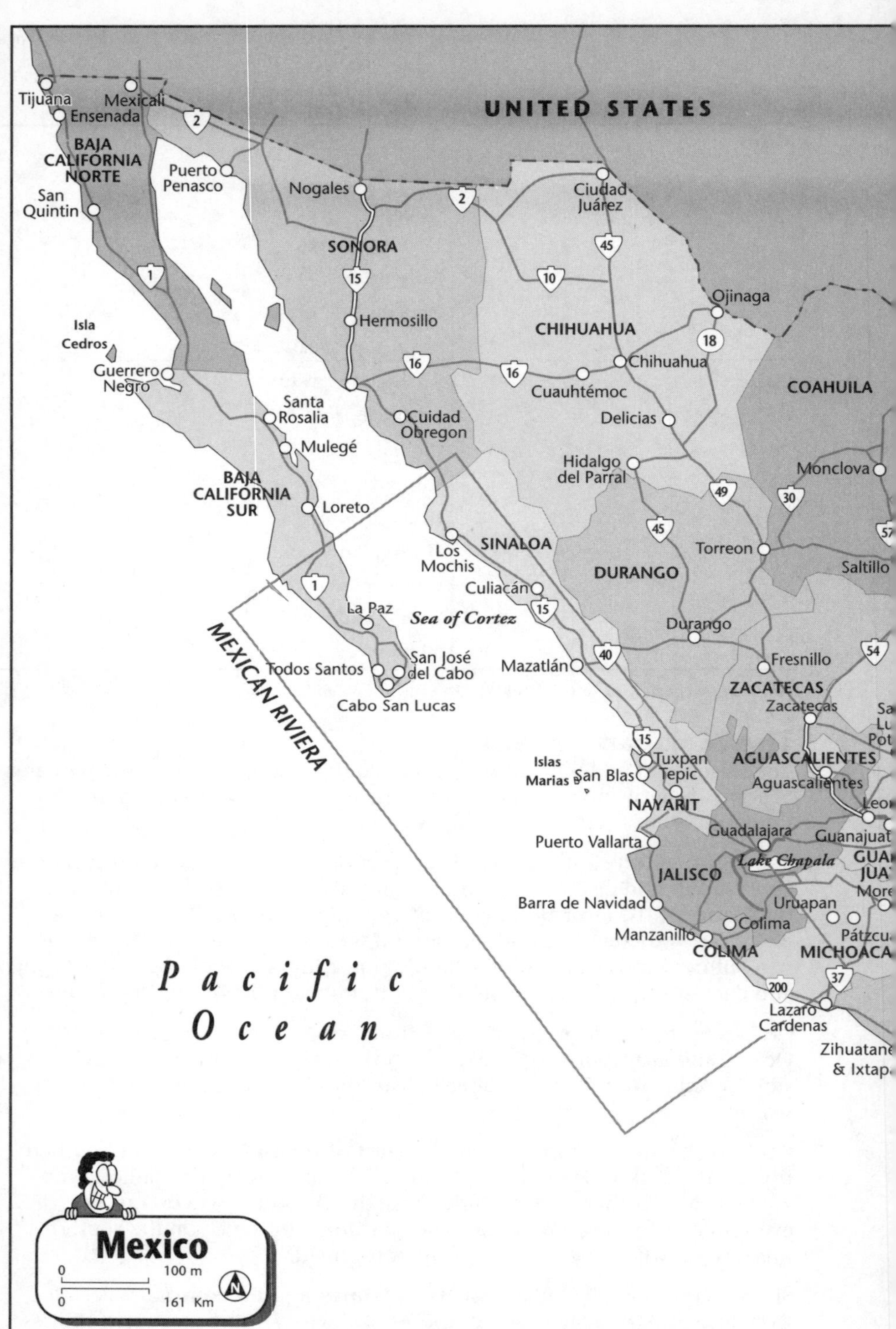
UNITED STATES
Tijuana
Mexicali
Ensenada
BAJA CALIFORNIA NORTE
Puerto Penasco
Nogales
San Quintin
Ciudad Juárez
SONORA
Hermosillo
CHIHUAHUA
Ojinaga
Isla Cedros
Chihuahua
Guerrero Negro
Cuauhtémoc
COAHUILA
Santa Rosalia
Cuidad Obregon
Delicias
Mulegé
Hidalgo del Parral
Monclova
BAJA CALIFORNIA SUR
Loreto
Los Mochis
SINALOA
Torreon
DURANGO
Saltillo
Culiacán
La Paz
Sea of Cortez
Durango
MEXICAN RIVIERA
Todos Santos
San José del Cabo
Mazatlán
Fresnillo
Cabo San Lucas
ZACATECAS
Zacatecas
Tuxpan
AGUASCALIENTES
Islas Marias
San Blas
Tepic
Aguascalientes
NAYARIT
Guadalajara
Puerto Vallarta
Lake Chapala
JALISCO
Barra de Navidad
Uruapan
Colima
Manzanillo
COLIMA
Pacific Ocean
Lazaro Cardenas
Mexico
0 100 m
0 161 Km
N

UNITED STATES
Piedras Negras
Nuevo Laredo
85D
Matamoros
180
85
TAMAULIPAS
Ciudad Victoria
Gulf of Mexico
Ciudad Mante
Tampico
SAN LUIS
POTOSÍ
QUERÉTARO
Tuxpan
Poza Rica
HIDALGO
180
Pachuca
Mexico City
Jalapa
TLAXCALA
Tlaxcala
Veracruz
Bay of
Campeche
Puebla
Orizaba
MORELOS
PUEBLA
Catemaco
Tehuacán
VERACRUZ
TABASCO
Villahermosa
95
Coatzacoalcos
190D
175
Chilpancingo
Acapulco
Oaxaca
186
Tuxtla
Gutierrez
San Cristóbal de las Casas
200
OAXACA
CHIAPAS
Salina
Cruz
Comitan
Puerto Escondido
Huatulco
Puerto Angel
Gulf of
Tehuantepec
200
Tapachula
GUATEMALA
Río Lagartos
Isla
Mujeres
Progreso
Valladolid
Cancún
Celestún
180
Merida
YUCATÁN
Playa del
Carmen
Cozumel
Campeche
QUINTANA
ROO
Punta
Allen
CAMPECHE
Bacalar
261
Escarcega
Chetumal
Xcalak
Peninsula
186
Caribbean Sea
BELIZE
HONDURAS
EL
SALVADOR

are among the firms offering more exotic Mexico itineraries, including sailing in the tranquil waters of the **Sea of Cortez.**

Mexican Riviera Ports of Call

Cabo San Lucas	Carnival Celebrity Crystal Holland America Norwegian Princess Royal Caribbean Silversea Special Expeditions
Ensenada	Carnival Cunard Holland America Norwegian Royal Caribbean Silversea
Mazatlán	Carnival Crystal Cunard Princess Royal Caribbean Silversea
Puerto Vallarta	Carnival Celebrity Crystal Cunard Holland America Norwegian Princess Royal Caribbean Silversea

Information courtesy of Travel Weekly's Official Cruise Guide.

New England & Canada

Okay, I'm biased because I live in New England, but I've got to tell you: This is one of my favorite regions to cruise. Why? Because the port stops are decisively less touristy and more quaint than, say, the Caribbean, and because the scenic coastal beauty of this region is unmatched anywhere in the world, especially during the fall foliage season.

Cruises of New England and Canada typically start in New York or Boston, or, coming down the coast the opposite way, from Montreal or Quebec City. The ships sail the Atlantic Ocean, with the itineraries usually one way and 1 week, or 10 days or longer and round-trip.

The itineraries usually include a chance to take in the historic **Freedom Trail** in Boston; a stop in a New England town, such as **Newport, Rhode Island,** with its gorgeous turn-of-the-century mansions, or **Bar Harbor, Maine,** with its equally gorgeous hiking trails and scenic vistas; a stop in the Canadian coastal provinces of **Nova Scotia, New Brunswick** and/or **Newfoundland;** and a visit to **Quebec City** or **Montreal,** two Canadian cities with a French flair and much in the way of historic interest.

Some smaller ships include Canada's **St. Lawrence and Saguenay rivers,** others go as far up the coast as Labrador, and some include stops at other lovely New England towns, including Boothbay Harbor, Maine; Provincetown, Massachusetts; and the scenic islands of Nantucket and Martha's Vineyard.

A favorite of mine is **St. Andrews, New Brunswick,** a town so quaint it looks like Disney artists created it as the quintessential coastal Canadian village.

Also in New England, you can take a rustic, fun cruise vacation on board a schooner, with a fleet of **tall ships** based in Rockland or Camden, Maine, and sailing from May to October in the scenic Penobscott Bay, the precise itineraries depending on the wind and weather. The fleet of schooners includes the historic *Stephen Tabor* (☎ **800/999-7352**) and *Victory Chimes* (☎ **800/745-5651**).

New England / Canada Ports of Call

Boston, Massachusetts	Clipper
	Holland America
	Norwegian
	Princess
	Radisson
	Royal Caribbean
	Silversea

continues

New England / Canada Ports of Call *(continued)*

Halifax, Nova Scotia	American Canadian Caribbean Clipper Cunard Holland America Norwegian Princess Radisson Regal Royal Caribbean Seabourn Silversea
Maine	American Canadian Caribbean Clipper Cunard Holland America Norwegian Princess Regal Royal Caribbean Seabourn Stephen Tabor Victory Chimes
Montreal	American Canadian Caribbean Clipper Holland America Norwegian Princess Seabourn Silversea
New Brunswick	Clipper Cunard Norwegian Princess Royal Caribbean
Newport, Rhode Island	American Canadian Caribbean Clipper

Newport, Rhode Island ***(continued)***	Cunard Holland America Norwegian Princess Radisson Regal Seabourn
Quebec City	American Canadian Caribbean Clipper Cunard Holland America Norwegian Princess Radisson Regal Royal Caribbean Seabourn Silversea

Information courtesy of Travel Weekly's Official Cruise Guide.

Panama Canal

Ships pass through this eighth wonder of the world as part of one-way repositioning cruises in the late fall and early spring, as the cruise lines move their vessels from the Alaska market to the Caribbean market and vice versa. Some lines also include the Panama Canal as part of longer Caribbean, Central American, and South American itineraries in the winter.

The reasons are both practical and scenic. Use of the canal trims some 8,000 nautical miles off a trip from, say, New York to San Francisco, because without the continental passageway ships would have to go way south around Cape Horn, the tip of South America.

Crossing through the 51-mile canal takes just 9 hours, with the ships literally lifted and lowered 85 feet through a series of locks, gates, and dams. The experience is so fascinating that some cruise lines do partial canal crossings just to give passengers a taste.

Panama Canal cruises might include stops at Central American ports, the best being the **San Blas Islands,** home of the Cuna Indians, who are known for their colorful needlework. Other calls might include the nature lover's paradise of **Costa Rica,** or **Guatemala,** home of the Mayan ruins of Tikal, the largest such site yet uncovered. The cruises also usually include stops in the **Caribbean** or **Mexican Riviera.**

Panama Canal Ports of Call

Full Canal	American Canadian Caribbean
	Carnival
	Celebrity
	Clipper
	Crystal
	Cunard
	Holland America
	Norwegian
	Princess
	Radisson
	Regal
	Royal Caribbean
	Royal Olympic
	Seabourn
	Special Expeditions
	Windstar
Partial Canal	American Canadian Caribbean
	Carnival
	Celebrity
	Cunard
	Holland America
	Norwegian
	Premier
	Princess
	Radisson
	Regal
	Royal Olympic
	Seabourn
	Windstar
	World Explorer
Guatemala	American Canadian Caribbean
	Crystal
	Holland America
	Norwegian
	Royal Olympic

Information courtesy of Travel Weekly's Official Cruise Guide.

Part 7

All Good Things Must Come to an End: Wrapping up Your Cruise

During your cruise vacation, you've experienced days of bliss, doing nothing or everything, depending on what choices you have made. But now it's time to get ready to say good-bye to your cozy little home away from home, your new friends, and that fabulous crew that served you so well.

In this section, I'll give you tips on last-minute issues such as tipping the crew, settling your shipboard account, and packing, and take you through the process of disembarkation.

Chapter 26

The Last Details

In This Chapter

- Info on disembarkation procedures
- Tips on tipping the crew: who gets what, how much to give, and when to do it
- How to settle your shipboard account
- Tips on packing up and getting your bags off the ship
- A checklist of last-day bugaboos
- Getting off the ship and clearing customs

Sad but true: At some point, you'll have to get off the ship. If you're like me, by the time you've been on board for 5 or 7 days, you'll have begun to feel so at home that the thought of leaving is almost traumatic. Separation anxiety begins to set in. "Home" seems like a relative concept. You'd gladly trade house and hearth to stay on board.

That's an option, of course (if you're rich as hell), but for most of us, reality begins to set in at some point. Cheer up and think about it this way: Once you disembark, you're not a first-time cruiser anymore. You're a veteran. You know your stuff. Now you can start planning for your *next* cruise . . .

In this chapter, I take you through the nuts and bolts of actually getting off the boat.

Everybody Off!: The Disembarkation Talk

On the last full day of your cruise, the cruise director will offer a disembarkation talk covering areas such as tipping, settling your onboard account, packing, dealing with Customs and Immigration, and following the disembarkation procedures, all as they apply to your specific ship.

You or a member of your party should attend the talk, particularly if you are a first-time cruiser. You might also be able to catch a broadcast of the session on your in-room TV, and procedures will also be printed in your daily bulletin, but the talk is your chance to ask any questions you might have. Some lines even offer a prize drawing to encourage your attendance at the session.

Tips on Tipping

Tipping is an area that some people find confusing. First, let's establish that on almost all lines (the exceptions being the ritzy Seabourn and Radisson), you are expected to tip the crew—in particular your cabin steward, waiter, and busboy—and to not do so is bad form. But how much you tip the crew is totally up to you. The cruise line will make suggestions in the daily bulletin and in the cruise director's disembarkation briefing. Keep in mind that these are just suggestions.

Tip-Free Cruising

A few lines—for example, HAL, most Cunard ships, Windstar, and Radisson—have a no tipping required policy, meaning you're under no obligation, though staff on these ships will gratefully accept any tips proffered. Some other lines, however, have a no tipping *allowed* policy, among them Seabourn, Silversea, and Cunard's *Sea Goddesses* vessels.

I think the minimum tip you should consider for the folks mentioned here is $3 per adult passenger, per day, for both your room steward and waiter, and $1.50 to $2 per adult passenger, per day, for your busboy. It's okay to give half of that for a child passenger.

That totals up to about $56 for a 7-night cruise (you do not have to include disembarkation day).

Again, that's what I see as a minimum. You can give more. In fact, the cruise line might even recommend more (I've seen suggestions of up to $4.50 a day for the waiter and cabin steward and about half that for the busboy).

When deciding what to tip, keep in mind that these people are extremely underpaid, their salaries largely dependent on tips. Some lines pay their room stewards as little as $45 a month. And many of these crew members support families back home on their earnings.

A Tip on Tipping

To get a little perspective on your tipping, try to imagine what you might tip if you'd had the same kind of waiter service in your local restaurant that you had night after night on the cruise. All in all, you're getting a real bargain.

The lines are not shy about encouraging you to tip, and you might even be given envelopes printed with the titles of crew members to show you who to tip. On some ships (many small ships, in particular) you might be asked to submit your tips in a single sum that the ship will distribute appropriately. But generally, you reward people individually.

You will also be encouraged to tip the dining room maitre d', head waiter, and other better-salaried employees. Whether to tip these folks or not is your decision. The same goes for other staff members who have done you a good turn.

Bar bills automatically include a 15% tip, but if the wine steward, for example, served you exceptionally well you can slip him or her a bill, too.

If you have spa or beauty treatments you can tip that person at the time of the service (you can even do it on your shipboard charge account), but otherwise, tips are usually given on the last night of your cruise. Most lines suggest that you tip in cash, but some also have means to allow you to tip via your shipboard account.

Usually, when ships operate on a no-tipping-required basis, the staff will still accept a tip, but on some very upperscale lines, tipping is strictly forbidden.

Don't *ever* tip the captain or other officers. They are salaried employees and might actually be insulted by the gesture.

The porters who carry your luggage at the pier will likely expect a tip.

If a staff member is particularly great, a written letter to a superior is always good form and might earn that person an "employee of the month" honor and maybe even a bonus.

Settling Up

Your shipboard account will close in the wee hours before departure, but prior to that time you will receive a preliminary bill in your cabin.

If you are settling your account with your credit card, you don't have to do anything but make sure all the charges are correct. If there's a problem, you will have to report to the purser's office, where you will likely encounter a long line.

Smooth Sailing

On some modern ships, you can keep track of your onboard expense account through your interactive TV system. This allows you to both budget yourself as you go along and to spot any problems with billing before the last minute.

If you are paying by cash or traveler's check, you'll be asked to settle your account either during the day or night before you leave the ship. This will require you to report to the purser's office.

A final invoice will be delivered to your room before departure.

Keeping receipts for shipboard purchases during your cruise will help you with your tallying efforts and also ensures that you're not surprised when the bill arrives.

Last-Day Checklist

On the last full day of your cruise, remember to:

- ☐ Redeem your fitness points for prizes.
- ☐ Place any last-minute liquor and cigarette orders from the duty-free shop (they will be delivered to your cabin that night).
- ☐ Alert the purser's office if you have an early flight the next day.
- ☐ Buy any other items you've had your eye on in the ship's shops, and check out the sales (the shops will close that night and not open again during your cruise).
- ☐ Pick up any photos you've ordered from the photographer.
- ☐ Check the lost and found in the guest-relations area if you've misplaced anything.
- ☐ Check out the repeat-passenger offerings. If you plan on cruising with the line again, you might be able to book on the spot and receive discounts for future cruises.
- ☐ Be sure to return any books or games you borrowed from the library.
- ☐ Fill out the passenger questionnaire/comment card (if any). A prize drawing (using the returned questionnaire) might be held to encourage you to do so.

Pack It Up!

With thousands of suitcases to deal with, big ships have established the routine of requiring guests to pack the night before departure. You'll be asked to leave your bags in the hallway before you retire for the night (or at least by midnight). While you sleep, the bags will be picked up and moved to a baggage area, then be removed from the ship before passengers are allowed to disembark. You'll see your bags again in the cruise terminal, where they'll most likely be arranged by deck number.

It's important to make sure that your bags are tagged with the **luggage tags** that will be given to you by the cruise line the night before disembarkation. These are not the same tags you arrived with. They are color-coded to indicate deck number and disembarkation order. If you need more tags, alert your cabin steward.

A good rule of thumb is to begin packing before dinner. Usually the last night of your cruise will be a casual night to make things easier.

When packing, remember to leave out any clothes and toiletries you will need the next day, and don't pack your valuables, breakables, travel documents, or medication. Be sure that everything you're keeping out fits in your overnight bag.

Pack all your purchases made during the trip in one suitcase. This way, you can easily retrieve them if you are stopped at Customs (see "Clearing Customs & Immigration," later in this chapter).

If you end up partying late and put your bags out after other bags on your deck have already been collected, notify the purser's office so they can send someone to get them.

If you don't leave your bags in the hall, you will have to carry them off the ship yourself.

Disembarkation Rigmarole

You'll know it's the day you have to get off the ship because loudspeaker announcements will start blaring particularly early in the morning.

You won't be able to get off the ship until it is cleared by Customs and other authorities, a process that usually takes 90 minutes. Rarely have I seen a ship actually begin unloading passengers before 9am.

Even so, in most cases you will be asked to vacate your cabin by 8am so the crew has time to prepare the space for the next load of passengers. I usually leave my overnight bag in a corner of the cabin anyway so I don't have to lug it around, but whether you do so or not is up to you.

Before you leave the cabin, be sure you check all the drawers to check that you're not leaving anything behind.

On disembarkation day, breakfast might be served earlier than usual, and there might be limited room service or no room service at all. Check your daily bulletin for details.

On the last night of the cruise (or thereabouts), you'll be given a departure number that dictates the order in which you will leave the ship. Those with earlier flights will be allowed to leave first. It takes about 2 hours to get everyone off the ship, and everyone will want to leave the ship at the same time, but unless you have an early number, you don't have to rush. Grab a book and head up to the deck, catch a movie or another ship offering, or find another way to occupy yourself.

Ahoy, Mateys!

If you're booked on back-to-back cruises, you don't have to go through customs, but instead will be given an "In Transit" pass.

Clogging the hallways doesn't help anyone get off faster.

If things drag on and you're concerned about missing your flight, tell a crew member.

Above all, be patient. Disembarkation always takes longer than anyone thinks it should.

Clearing Customs & Immigration

When your ship arrives at the port, non–U.S. citizens, including Canadians and green card holders, will be required to meet with U.S. Immigration authorities, usually in a lounge or theater. You will have to bring your passport receipt with you, and all family members must attend.

U.S. citizens usually do not have to pass through a formal immigration process, but you should have your passport or ID handy when you disembark, just in case.

Everyone will have to fill out a **Customs Declaration form** (one per family) that will be delivered to your cabin the evening before departure. Before you disembark, you will be required to indicate on the form whether you are bringing in more than your set allowance of foreign goods.

Read the Customs form carefully. You do not have to list individual purchases on the form unless you have gone way over the limit.

Standard Customs allowances for U.S. citizens are $400 in goods duty-free, including 1 liter of alcohol per person over age 21 and 1 carton of cigarettes. The same goes for green card holders and non–U.S. residents staying more than 72 hours in the U.S.

There are exceptions to the allowances, however, for several Caribbean islands. If you purchased your goods in the U.S. Virgin Islands, for example, you can bring back $1,200 in goods duty-free. No customs are collected on goods in any amount from San Juan, and some products from Mexico are also duty-free.

Is the Earth Moving, or Is It Me?

When you get off the ship, and especially when you close your eyes, you might experience a feeling of rocking, as if you're still on the water. Don't worry—this is perfectly normal and should go away by the next day.

You don't have to pay duty on fine works of art and some other luxury items.

Does this all sound really complicated? It is.

The Customs service knows this, and to help you understand the rules, it publishes a booklet called *Know Before You Go,* available by writing the Department of the Treasury, U.S. Customs Service, Washington, DC 20229.

If you do go over your limit you will have to report to a Customs official (either on the ship or when you get off) and may be subject to a duty of 10% (or less, depending on where you purchased the goods).

If you are in doubt about whether you have gone over the limit, you can ask a Customs officer for help in filling out the form.

Inspections of passenger baggage are rare, but customs officers may do random and not-so-random checks (see the sidebar on page 432).

If you go over your allowance, fail to declare it, and get caught, you can get in a heap of trouble, and you might have to pay stiff fines.

Remember that fruits, seeds, animals, plants, and meat are not allowed ashore (this is a Customs rule rather than a ship rule). This includes any leftovers from the fruit basket in your cabin.

More Baggage

If you booked air travel through the cruise line, when you disembark and after you clear Customs, you might be able to check in your luggage for your flight right at the cruise terminal. You will collect your bags (there should be porters to help), turn them over to an airline representative, and receive your claim checks. You might even be able to get your flight-boarding passes at the cruise terminal. You will then proceed to a bus that will take you to the airport.

If you booked your own air travel, you're on your own. Retrieve your bags and catch a cab to the airport or your next destination.

If you're on a post-cruise tour, special instructions will be given to you by your cruise line.

The Customs of Customs

The U.S. Customs Service has been streamlining its entry procedures for cruise passengers, using computer-tracking systems to target certain passengers for inspections, based on information from law enforcement and other databases. Ships are also required to submit a "big spender" list from the onboard gift shop.

Random inspections of passengers not based on this database information are rare. But if your things are inspected, you might have to show the officer all the goods you have purchased. Here's when having the items in one suitcase saves time and aggravation. It also pays to have your receipts handy so you can show what you paid for the items—otherwise, inspectors will value your purchases based on U.S. prices.

If you disagree with a Customs determination, you can contest it later, in writing.

Try to Relax

From waiting in line at the purser's office to settling your bill, to waiting to disembark, to the chaos you might encounter at the terminal, this is not the most laid-back and relaxing part of your trip. Breathe deep and go with the flow. And remember, the crew might be tense too, since they have only a few hours to prepare the ship for the next flock of passengers.

Pat Yourself on the Back

You're now a veteran cruiser! Congratulations. I hope you had an even better time than you'd expected. Now go home and try not to think about work. (If possible, I like to take an extra day off before I start back, just to decompress.) Also, don't be concerned if you feel a little woozy for the first day or so—it sometimes takes a while to get used to the world *not* rocking under your feet.

Finally, remember: There are a million ships in the sea, and you've already started accumulating more vacation time. Where do you want to sail to next?

Appendix A

Cruise Line Contact Information

Alaska Sightseeing / Cruise West
4th and Battery Building, Suite 700, Seattle, WA 98121 (☎ **800/426-7702;** www.smallship.com)

Alaska's Glacier Bay Tours and Cruises
520 Pike St., No. 1400, Seattle, WA 98101 (☎ **800/451-5952;** www.glacierbaytours.com)

American Canadian Caribbean Line
461 Water St., Warren, RI 02885 (☎ **800/556-7450;** www.accl-smallships.com)

American Hawaii Cruises
1380 Port of New Orleans Place, Robin Street Wharf, New Orleans, LA 70130-1890 (☎ **800/543-7637;** www.cruisehawaii.com)

Cape Canaveral Cruise Line
101 George King Blvd., Suite 6, Cape Canaveral, FL 32920 (☎ **800/910-SHIP;** www.capecanaveralcruise.com)

Carnival Cruise Lines
3655 NW 87th Ave., Miami, FL 33178-2428 (☎ **800/CARNIVAL;** www.carnival.com)

Celebrity Cruises
5201 Blue Lagoon Dr., Miami, FL 33125 (☎ **800/437-3111;** www.celebrity-cruises.com)

Classical Cruises
132 E. 70th St., New York, NY 10021 (☎ **800/252-7745**)

Clipper Cruise Line
7711 Bonhomme Ave., St. Louis, MO 63105 (☎ **800/325-0010;** www.clippercruise.com)

Club Med
40 W. 57th St., New York, NY 10019 (☎ **800/4-LESHIP**)

Commodore Cruise Line
4000 Hollywood Blvd., South Tower, Suite 385, Hollywood, FL 33021 (☎ **800/237-5361;** www.commodorecruise.com)

Costa Cruise Lines
World Trade Center, 80 SW 8th St., Miami, FL 33130-3097 (☎ **800/462-6782;** www.costacruises.com)

Crystal Cruises
2121 Avenue of the Stars, Suite 200, Los Angeles, CA (☎ **310/785-9300**)

Cunard
6100 Blue Lagoon Dr., Suite 400, Miami, FL 33126 (☎ **800/5CUNARD;** www.cunardline.com)

The Delta Queen Steamboat Company
Robin Street Wharf, 1380 Port of New Orleans Place, New Orleans, LA 70130-1890 (☎ **800/543-1949;** www.deltaqueen.com)

Disney Cruise Line
210 Celebration Place, Suite 400, Celebration, FL 34747-1000 (☎ **800/951-3532;** www.disney.com/DisneyCruise)

Holland America Line–Westours
300 Elliot Ave. W., Seattle, WA 98119 (☎ **800/426-0327;** www.hollandamerica.com)

Mediterranean Shipping Cruises
420 Fifth Ave., New York, NY 10018 (☎ **800/666-9333**)

Norwegian Cruise Line
7665 Corporate Center Dr., Miami, FL 33126 (☎ **800/327-7030;** www.ncl.com)

Premier Cruises
901 S. America Way, Miami, FL 33132 (☎ **800/373-2654;** www.premiercruises.com)

Princess Cruises
10100 Santa Monica Blvd., Suite 1800, Los Angeles, CA 90067 (☎ **800/421-0522;** www.princesscruises.com)

Radisson Seven Seas Cruises
600 Corporate Dr., Suite 410, Fort Lauderdale, FL 33334 (☎ **800/477-7500;** www.asource.com/radisson)

Regal Cruises
4199 34th St. S., St. Petersburg, FL 33711 (☎ **800/270-SAIL;** www.regalcruises.com)

Royal Caribbean International
1050 Caribbean Way, Miami, FL 33132 (☎ **800/ALL-HERE;** www.royalcaribbean.com)

Royal Olympic Cruises
1 Rockefeller Plaza, Suite 315, New York, NY 10020 (☎ **800/872-6400;** www.royalolympiccruises.com)

Seabourn Cruise Line
55 Francisco St., Suite 710, San Francisco, CA 94133 (☎ **800/929-9595;** www.seabourn.com)

Silversea
110 E. Broward Blvd., Fort Lauderdale, FL 33301 (☎ **800/722-9055**)

Special Expeditions
720 Fifth Ave., New York, NY 10019 (☎ **800/762-0003**)

Star Clippers
4101 Salzedo St., Coral Gables, FL 33146 (☎ **800/442-0553;** www.star-clippers.com)

Tall Ship Adventures Cruises
1389 S. Havana St., Aurora, CO 80012 (☎ **800/662-0090;** www.asource.com/tallship)

Windjammer Barefoot Cruises
1759 Bay Rd., Miami Beach, FL 33139 (☎ **800/327-2601;** www.windjammer.com)

World Explorer Cruises
555 Montgomery St., San Francisco, CA 94111-2544 (☎ **800/854-3835;** www.wecruise.com)

Car-Rental Agencies Contact Information

Advantage
☎ 800/777-5500
www.arac.com

Alamo
☎ 800/327-9633
www.goalamo.com

Auto Europe
☎ 800/223-5555
www.autoeurope.com

Avis
☎ 800/331-1212 in the Continental U.S.
☎ 800/TRY-AVIS in Canada
www.avis.com

Budget
☎ 800/527-0700
www.budgetrentacar.com

Dollar
☎ 800/800-4000
www.dollarcar.com

Enterprise
☎ 800/325-8007
www.pickenterprise.com

Hertz
☎ 800/654-3131
www.hertz.com

Kemwel Holiday Auto (KHA)
☎ 800/678-0678
www.kemwel.com

National
☎ 800/CAR-RENT
www.nationalcar.com

Payless
☎ 800/PAYLESS
www.paylesscar.com

Rent-A-Wreck
☎ 800/535-1391
rent-a-wreck.com

Thrifty
☎ 800/367-2277
www.thrifty.com

Value
☎ 800/327-2501
www.go-value.com

Index

A

B

D

L

M

N

S

T

U

V

W

X-Y-Z